Changes in
Working Life

Changes in Working Life

Proceedings of an International Conference on Changes in the
Nature and Quality of Working Life, sponsored by the
Human Factors Panel of the NATO Scientific Affairs
Division.

Edited by

K.D. Duncan
University of Wales Institute of Science & Technology

M.M. Gruneberg
University College Swansea

D. Wallis
University of Wales Institute of Science & Technology

JOHN WILEY & SONS
Chichester · New York · Brisbane · Toronto

Proceedings of an International Conference on Changes in the Nature and Quality of Working Life held at Thessaloniki, Greece, August 20th-24th 1979, which was sponsored by the NATO Special Program Panel on Human Factors.

Copyright (c) 1980 by John Wiley & Sons Ltd.

British Library Cataloguing in Publication Data:

International Conference on Changes in the Nature and Quality of Working Life, Thessaloniki, 1979
    Changes in working life.
    1. Industrial Psychology-Congresses
    2. Work environment-Congresses
    I. Title   II. Duncan, K.D.   III. Gruneberg, Michael M.   IV. Wallis, D.
    V. North Atlantic Treaty Organisation.
    Scientific Affairs Division
    301.5'5   HD6950.5   80-40129

ISBN 0 471 27777 0

Printed in Great Britain

List of Contributors

Harold L. Angle, Graduate School of Administration, University of California, Irvine, California, USA.

Albert van Assen, Department of Organizational Psychology, University of Nijmagen, Netherlands.

F.H.M. Blackler, Department of Behaviour in Organizations, University of Lancaster, Bailrigg, Lancaster.

Nicholas A. Bond, Jr., Psychology Department, California State University, 6000 S. Street, Sacramento, California 95819, USA.

C.A. Brown, Department of Behaviour in Organizations, University of Lancaster, Bailrigg, Lancaster.

Albert Cherns, Department of Social Sciences, University of Technology, Loughborough, Leics. LE11 3TU.

D. Cope, Department of Applied Psychology, UWIST, Llwyn-y-Grant, Penylan, Cardiff, CF3 7UX.

E.N. Corlett, Department of Engineering Production, The University of Birmingham, P.O. Box 363, Birmingham, B15 2TT.

Richard C. Crawley, Applied Psychology Department, University of Aston, College House, Gosta Green, Birmingham.

Louis E. Davis, Center for Quality of Working Life, Institute of Industrial Relations, University of California, Los Angeles, USA.

Anne T. Denny, College of Business and Management, University of Maryland, College Park, Maryland, USA.

Philip Dewe, The London School of Economics and Political Sciences, Houghton Street, London, WC2A 2AE.

Sylvia Downs, Industrial Training Research Unit, Lloyds Bank Chambers, Hobson Street, Cambridge.

K.D. Duncan, Department of Applied Psychology, UWIST, Llwyn-y-Grant, Penylan, Cardiff, CF3 7UX.

Dena B. Feren, College of Business and Management, University of Maryland, College Park, Maryland, USA.

David Guest, The London School of Economics and Political Sciences, Houghton Street, London, WC2A 2AE.

Barbara A. Gutek, Department of Psychology, University of California, 405 Hilgard Avenue, Los Angeles, California 90024, USA.

O. Richard Hackman, Yale School of Organization and Management, Box 1A, New Haven, Connecticut, USA.

Daniel R. Ilgen, Department of Psychological Sciences, Purdue University, Stanley Coulter Annex, West Lafayette, Indiana 47907, USA.

Edward E. Lawler III, Survey Research Center, Institute of Social Research, University of Michigan, Annarbor, Michigan, USA.

Edwin A. Locke, College of Business and Management, University of Maryland, College Park, Maryland, USA.

Tom Lupton, Manchester Business School, University of Manchester, Booth Street, Manchester, M15 6PB.

Vickie M. McCaleb, College of Business and Management, University of Maryland, College Park, Maryland, USA.

Roger Mansfield, Department of Business Administration and Accountancy, UWIST, Cardiff, CF1 4JB.

James C. Naylor, Department of Psychological Sciences, Purdue University, Stanley Coulter Annex, West Lafayette, Indiana 47907, USA.

Gordon E. O'Brian, School of Social Sciences, The Flinders University of South Australia, Bedford Park, South Australia 5042.

J. Patrick, Department of Applied Psychology, The University of Aston, College House, Gosta Green, Birmingham B4 7ET.

Robert Penn, Department of the Navy, Navy Personnel Research and Development Center, San Diego, California 92152, USA.

Lyman W. Porter, Graduate School of Administration, University of California, Irvine, California, USA.

Robert D. Pritchard, Department of Psychological Sciences, Purdue University, Stanley Coulter Annex, West Lafayette, Indiana 47907, USA.

Jens Rasmussen, Risø National Laboratory, Postbox 49, DK-4000 Roskilde, Denmark.

Sally J. Redfern, Department of Nursing Studies, Chelsea College, Manresa Road, London SW2 6LX.

James A. Riedel, Department of the Navy, Navy Personnel Research and Development Center, San Diego, California 92152, USA.

Karyll N. Shaw, College of Business and Management, University of Maryland, College Park, Maryland, USA.

John P. Sheposh, Department of the Navy, Navy Personnel Research and Development Center, San Diego, California 92152, USA.

A. Shepherd, Chemical and Allied Products Industry Training Board, Staines, Middlesex.

Sylvia Shimmin, Department of Behaviour in Organisations, University of Lancaster, Gillow House, Bailrigg, Lancaster.

P. Shipley, Department of Occupational Psychology, Birkbeck College, Malet Street, London WC1E 7HX.

W.T. Singleton, Applied Psychology Department,
    University of Aston, College House, Gosta Green,
    Birmingham, B4 7ET.

Peter Spurgeon, Applied Psychology Department,
    University of Aston, College House, Gosta Green,
    Birmingham, B4 7ET.

Ian Tanner, Manchester Business School, University of
    Manchester, Booth Street, Manchester M15 6PB.

Martin Walbank, Department of Management Sciences, UMIST,
    P.O. Box 88, Manchester M60 1QD.

Toby D. Wall, MRC Social and Applied Psychology Unit,
    University of Sheffield, Sheffield S10 2TN.

D. Wallis, Department of Applied Psychology, UWIST,
    Llwyn-y-Grant, Penylan, Cardiff CF3 7UX.

Philip Wester, Department of Organizational Psychology,
    University of Nijmegen, Netherlands.

G.C. White, Work Research Unit, Department of Employment,
    Steel House, 11 Tothill Street, London SW1H 9LN.

Roger Williams, The London School of Economics and
    Political Sciences, Houghton Street, London
    WC2A 2AE.

Leanne E. Young, Department of the Navy, Navy Personnel
    Research and Development Center, San Diego,
    California 92152, USA.

Contents

ix

x

Page

Preface

All highly developed industrial societies are experiencing human problems associated with rapid and apparently continuing change both in technology and social values. These problems are nowhere more acute than in the context of work. Most public and government attention has been focussed on what may broadly be called industrial relations and economic issues. The behavioural, or psychological correlates of change have received less attention. Yet the volume of research into quality of working life problems has increased dramatically in the last decade.

The general concern as to what may be happening as a result of technological and social change is well summarised by J.R. Huntley, writing in the NATO Information Service pamphlet 'Man's Environment and the Atlantic Alliance': '... there are also nagging fears in many countries that on balance technology "dehumanises" work. People fear that personal human values will be overshadowed by technical and administrative needs ... if major and concentrated attention is not given to this complicated problem - common to all advanced societies - both efficiency and work satisfaction could decline rapidly, with untold consequences for our civilisation'.

We believe it is not only timely to review progress in research but also important, now, to examine the changing relationships between the nature of work and the quality of working life. In particular we have sought to bring together protagonists of two differing viewpoints, namely, the ergonomic, which historically concerned itself with efficiency of human performance and the organizational view, which concerns itself primarily with worker satisfaction.

The ergonomic perspective has its roots in experimental psychology and production engineering, whereas the organizational perspective has grown out of social psychology and, more recently, industrial sociology. These two traditions have developed different conceptual frameworks and different research methodologies and have, consequently, developed to some extent independently, although both have a common concern with the design of work for human beings. A few human scientists have attempted to study work from both perspectives and hopefully more will do so. It is our intention in this book to put together contributions from both perspectives and to encourage recognition that, as we believe, both are necessary and neither is sufficient.

The Human Factors Panel of NATO Scientific Affairs Division made this book possible by supporting the international conference on the Nature and Quality of Working Life held in Thessaloniki in August 1979. We also wish to record our appreciation of the work of our colleague David Cope and of our colleagues in Greece, in particular, Professor Lambros Houssiadas, the Local Conference Director, Drs. Natsopoulos and Markoulis. Finally we have benefited from helpful advice from Michael Coombs of John Wiley throughout the production of this volume.

K.D. DUNCAN

M.M. GRUNEBERG

D. WALLIS

Changes in Working Life
Edited by K.D. Duncan, M.M. Gruneberg, and D. Wallis
© 1980 John Wiley & Sons Ltd

Chapter 1

The Future of Work

S. SHIMMIN

Future historians, when studying our life and times, may well find that our discussions and debate as to what lies ahead of us prove of more interest than some of the chronicles of events themselves. There is now an increasing volume of futures research, usually tending to focus on what is perceived as an ongoing process of transition from an industrial to a post-industrial society, and attempts to forecast how techno-logical, economic, social and political changes will affect work in this changing environment. This con-ference is one example of a systematic exchange of views on observed and projected changes in the nature and quality of working life between psychologists and other social scientists who have specialised in research in this area. The papers presented range from those which speculate upon the implications of current trends, such as the development of the micro-processor or the prob-lems of work organisation under conditions of techno-logical change through accounts of various empirical studies showing how problems of analysis, selection, training and effective performance in complex systems may be handled, to a critical evaluation of the concepts, measures and approaches used in traditional studies of worker motivation and job satisfaction. Although there may be common concern about the overall issues, it is also apparent that there is a diversity of opinion about the current state of knowledge and of the approaches to be followed in considering the future of work. The picture which emerges is fragmented, rather than forming a coherent whole. Much depends on the observer's own culture and background as to the position taken and it is clear that, in some areas and of some topics, we still know very little.

The purpose of this paper is to provide a general introduction to those which follow and to highlight some

of the main issues.   These may be considered under three
main headings.

    First, attention is given to the concepts of 'work'
and 'quality of working life' and the extent to which
these can be considered in isolation from other spheres
of life.

    Second, some of the possible futures predicted for
industrialised societies and their implications are
examined, again noting the association between work and
non-work.

    Third, changing attitudes and expectations are
considered as they relate to institutional and organizational policies and procedures.

CONCEPTS OF WORK

    When psychologists talk about work they are apt to
assume that its meaning and significance can be taken as
given, although the bulk of research on people's
attitudes to and behaviour at work has been conducted
in industrial settings.   It has also concentrated on
those whose work constitutes labour as a factor of production, engaged on tasks designed to achieve the
greatest output for the lowest unit costs.   The focus
of attention has been, on the one hand, the characteristics of these tasks and, on the other, the personal
attributes and responses of the workers, but with the
explicit or implicit aim of achieving a match between
the two sufficient to sustain and, preferably, to
increase the overall efficiency of the total economy.
Efforts to improve the quality of working life derive
from this desire and aim to integrate workers in the
production system, coupled with the belief that, because
it still occupies so much of their lives, experience of
work and the workplace environment is a major determinant of the quality of life itself.

    For purposes of study, work is usually identi-
fied with employment, i.e. with activities undertaken
for others on a contractual basis.   This entails an
exchange relationship whereby, for set periods of time
and within prescribed limits and policies, people put
their talents at the disposal of an employer in return
for both tangible rewards, such as pay, and less tangible rewards such as recognition and status.   It is
a view of work derived from and bound up with the
economic institutions and work organizations of advanced
industrial societies, leading to the structuring of time
in terms of work and non-work and to possession of a
paid job, i.e. employment, being regarded as quite

distinct from and socially far more desirable than the
state of unemployment.   Within this frame of reference,
to have a job confers status and self-respect.   It also
provides a standard by which to judge and be judged by
others, so that those without paid employment tend to
arouse ambivalent attitudes and to be accorded low social
esteem (Dubin, 1976).

To equate work with employment may have utility,
but it is a restricted perspective.   It conveys nothing
of the content of jobs, of the meaning and significance
of these activities to members of the workforce, nor
of whether or if to any extent these are distinguishable
from those done outside 'working hours'.   Criteria
which differentiate between work and non-work are difficult to find (Shimmin, 1966) and one writer who has
studied the subject in depth concludes that work is so
rich and complex as to defy analysis (Anthony, 1977).
Some elements of this complexity are the co-operative
aspect of work, such that in even the most coercive
forms of organization there is some kind of negotiated
accommodation between those who command and those who
obey;   the necessity of work for survival and, in the
opinion of some (Jaques, 1965), for mental health;   the
satisfying and creative elements in work;   and its moral
attributes as seen, for example, in the acceptance of
discipline and in the responsibility shown by working to
support oneself and one's family.

These characteristics underlie what Anthony
terms the 'ideology of work', used by those with legitimate authority over their subordinates to exhort them to
work willingly, to meet targets and to achieve growth.
However, he sees this ideology becoming increasingly
redundant for a number of reasons, not least because the
connection between employment work and survival is now
obscured in complex industrial societies.   As production
becomes a function of machines, rather than human effort,
as processes are controlled by computers, rather than
people, and as advanced technology supplants human
beings from many jobs, there are signs of uncertainty
and doubt about purely economic theories of work.   If
redundancy is not yet accepted as a fact of life in the
wake of technical change, it is fast acquiring this
status, and there is active concern about both the
'quality of life' and the 'quality of working life' in
this context.

What these phrases mean is not entirely clear,
although they tend to be used as if their meanings were
obvious.   Quality of life has been described as a
criterion of value taking into account imprecise but
significant factors not adequately tapped by conventional
economic and social indicators (Kumar, 1978).   These

factors are, inevitably, normative and subjective as
there is no objective measure by which to judge the
quality of experience.   However, 'quality' carries the
connotation of 'worth', so it would seem that the
expression is intended to denote experiencing life as
worth living and not as mere existence.   From such a
general interpretation, few are likely to dissent.
Some, indeed, are prepared to go further and define
quality of life as meaning having a sense of purpose,
well-being, enjoyment and fulfilment, although it is
not suggested that these attributes necessarily correlate with one another.   Life may be experienced as
both meaningful and painful, for example.   It has to
be recognised that what is seen as constituting the
'good' life differs according to personal values and
circumstances and may vary during the life-cycle of an
individual.   Nor can it be assumed, as it is by some
who seek to improve the quality of working life, that
work is always paramount in determining the value and
richness of experience.   Thus, whereas some contend
that work pervades almost all other areas of life, such
that apathy and withdrawal developed in response to
unsatisfying jobs spill over into behaviour outside the
workplace (Smith, 1965;   Meissner, 1971), others maintain that leisure and non-work activities may more
than compensate for an undesirable work environment
(Dubin, 1956).

      Increasing attention has been paid, in recent
years, to the relationship between work and leisure
and the extent to which it is possible to consider the
one without reference to the other.   It has been suggested, for example, that the notions of work and play
are not to be seen as signifying distinctly different
activities but rather as elements that contribute to all
activities (Day, 1972).   On this view, jobs are
defined as those activities which are heavily laden
with the work component, i.e. that are purposeful and
goal-directed, while games and recreation are activities that are mainly play, i.e. intrinsically
rewarding, interesting and fun.   Following this line
of argument, quality of working life will be a function
of the balance between these components in an individual's day-to-day experience and, in the sphere of
employment, the extent to which a job entails the
elements of play.

      To equate play with leisure, however, is as
problematic as to equate work with employment, task,
labour or occupation.   In other words, the terms that
are often used as synonyms for both work and leisure
have different connotations.   Likewise, as will be
noted by some other speakers, it is probably unwise to
equate quality of working life and job satisfaction.

Not only is 'satisfaction' associated in many people's
mind with retrospective evaluation, rather than active
enjoyment of an ongoing activity (Clayre, 1974), but
it is also useful to distinguish between satisfaction
with a job and satisfaction in a job (Daniel, 1969).
Most surveys show that people are satisfied with their
jobs, in the sense that they feel they have made the
best bargain in relation to their opportunities as they
see them, but this does not mean that they find fulfilment in their work. Conversely, it was found in a
study of Suffolk agricultural workers (Newby, 1977)
that nearly all of them were satisfied in the job, but
not with it, and we shall hear later of similar findings
relating to hospital sisters in the U.K.

        Given these problems of definition, the evidence
that patterns of work-leisure relationships vary
between cultures and occupations (Triandis, 1973;
Parker, 1976) and that, for many people, non-job-
related variables may be more important to a full life
than job satisfaction (London, Crandall and Seals, 1977),
it is important that we do not take too narrow a view of
work when considering changes in the nature and quality
of working life. There are several occupations which
have been little studied by psychologists (Rose, 1956)
and the publication of autobiographical accounts by a
variety of workers (Fraser, 1968; Terkel, 1975) has
shown the gap between received theories of work and how
it is actually experienced. We need to look and listen
to people talking about their work in their own words
far more than perhaps some of us are inclined to do, if
we are to avoid the danger of letting theory drive out
good practice in the work environment.

POSSIBLE FUTURES

        Scenarios for the future range from the optimistic
to the profoundly pessimistic. Whichever stance is
taken, however, there seems to be general agreement that
the importance and value of considering alternative
futures lie in our ability to change our ideas and institutions, so that we do not presume or allow the future
to be the past writ large. There is growing recognition that the advantages and achievements of advanced
industrialism seem, increasingly, to be outweighed by
the costs and negative effects (Kumar, 1978) and that
we are living in a world of global interdependence for
which the cultural heritage of the industrial revolution
has left us unprepared (Trist, 1978). Consequently,
faced with a transition from an industrial to a post-
industrial order or an emerging countereconomy (Henderson,
1978), it is essential that we re-think and re-structure
our technologies to meet this new situation. This is

seen as a matter of sheer survival (Kumar, 1978; Trist, 1978), entailing formidable problems of re-adjustment as people in the developed nations realise that their present life-style and expectations rest on outmoded premises about both the availability of material resources and the political configuration of the world.

Time and space do not permit a synopsis of the large volume of literature which now exists on this subject, some of which is written in a visionary, pro- phetic vein and some of which attempts to assess what is happening now and its implications for the future. There are those who believe that powerful economic and political forces, together with sheer social inertia, continue to push the human race toward a mechanised society, which carries within it the 'seeds of its own destruction' (Ferkiss, 1978).   Others see the possi- bility of technology as liberating people from de-humani- sing forms of work and giving more scope for the design of intrinsically attractive and more socially rewarding jobs.   Thus, it is suggested that life in the future will be lived in more individualised circumstances; that, although there will always be some work that simply has to be done, it will be much more varied and diverse in character; and that it will not be incumbent for everyone to be employed, so that people will have the choice of whether or not to enter the labour market (Bryan, 1973; Seashore, 1974).

As with all attempts at extrapolation, e.g. demo- graphic forecasting, the problem is not merely to iden- tify trends but to assess their significance.   A typical list of influences which can be discerned within industrialised countries at present is: (i) a better educated work-force; (ii) changing attitudes and aspi- rations, reflected in a lack of consensus on objectives and ways of achieving them; (iii) technological and organizational constraints and opportunities; (iv) greater demands for workers' participation; and (v) increased leisure and the growth of leisure-oriented industries (O.E.C.D., 1974).   These are closely linked with a changed emphasis in the economy from the pro- duction of capital goods to the production of consumer goods and the provision of services.   As a result, people have become more concerned with consumption than with production so that, in an affluent society, 'the appropriate and significant consumption of goods and services becomes the definition of the good citizen' (Dubin, 1976).   If Dubin is right about this then, as he suggests, the function of educational institutions could change from that of largely vocational preparation to that of socialising individuals for the new society, i.e. equipping them for a pattern of life not dominated by the need to work for a living.

There is, however, another side to consumerism which indicates caution in accepting the above arguments. Kumar points out that, in Britain, the industrial system which has led to plentiful consumer goods and profession- alised services has also undermined the competence of people to deal with many things themselves (Kumar, 1978). Whether for advice, routine servicing or repairs, we have been made dependent on experts and professionals, so that the 'de-skilling' which has occurred in the sphere of work also pervades that of non-work, as does the resulting apathy and frustration. Some reaction against this state of affairs is shown by the do-it-yourself enthusiasts, but there are many who, for reasons of health or age, are incapable of such activities.

A pre-occupation with consumer interests and acti- vities can also reinforce instrumental attitudes to work. Employment opportunities are then judged in terms of how much money and time will be available for spending it off the job. It can also lead to a conflict between the desire for more money to purchase the good things of life and the desire for more leisure in which to enjoy them.

Willingness to accept dreary jobs and to work under conditions of stress and monotony so as to main- tain or increase material standards of living and con- sume more and more is an element in the harshest of three possible scenarios of working life in Sweden in the 1990s, which emerged from a recent study (Ekvall, 1979). It is seen as a possibility which could arise if economic growth were the predominant political goal and a high standard of living the over-riding social value, but where the economy is strained and technolo- gical development is regarded as a force with a momentum of its own which people cannot control.

Of the two other scenarios presented, the first depicts an extension of current trends which seek to humanise and incorporate values and goals other than purely economic ones in working life, so that a high material standard of living is maintained but to increase it further is not the prime goal and the satisfaction of psychological needs is also given high priority. A pre-requisite for this situation is that Swedish industry and trade can produce and sell goods and services profitably on an international market.

The third picture is one of small-scale production and de-centralisation in a country which has changed its economic and political goals so that it is more self- reliant and not trying to keep up with foreign compe- tition. Industrial production is work-intensive and energy-saving, thus providing many jobs with flexible working arrangements to suit people's needs.

Associated with these changes is a decline in the material
standard of living, with fewer consumer goods, but an
easier working pace and more corporate activities outside working hours.

These contrasting possibilities are of particular
interest because of the image of Sweden as a country
which has been ahead of many others in its attempts to
improve the quality of working life. The study included
three groups of people who were felt to be competent to
give an opinion on working life in the future - staff
managers and consultants in personnel administration,
senior municipal officials, and a group of experts, com-
prising both researchers on working life and consultants
engaged in long-term planning. Although members of the
latter group were all agreed that working life in Sweden
in the future will be characterised by extensive employee
influence and a philosophy of self-realisation, they
were divided as to whether large-scale computerisation
and automation would be the dominant feature of production or whether the envisaged decentralisation into
small, labour-intensive units would occur. It is important to note, however, that, although they did not like
the prospect, a more inhuman future for work was anticipated by the municipal officials and by many of the
managers and consultants.

This raises the question, inherent in all future
studies, of whether a deterministic standpoint is taken,
especially with regard to technological developments,
or whether ideas can and do influence the future.
Social scientists who subscribe to the latter view
argue that we have to look at the psychological nature
of men and women and their aspirations and intentions
as a guide to future choices (Emery and Emery, 1976).
Hence, rather than assume that the next decade will be
much like the last, we have to look at the shift in
human values that has taken place over the last ten
years.

CHANGING EXPECTATIONS AND VALUES

Although there is a widespread belief that attitudes to work are changing, particularly in industrialised societies, the proposition is extremely difficult
to validate (Wedderburn, 1974). To whose attitudes
does it refer? Men and women equally, the young, the
middle-aged and elderly, those who are employed and
those who are not, or only to certain members of these
groups? As soon as one poses these questions and
others relating to, say, specific sectors, regions or
localities, it becomes obvious that the statement has
to be made more specific if it is to be meaningful.

Attention has also to be paid to the person(s) making
the assertion and the context(s) in which it is made.
Thus, when made by managers or government spokesmen it
may refer to worker behaviour to which they are unaccus-
tomed, such as unwillingness to respond to financial
inducements if these entail greater responsibility,
longer hours or moving to another area.   Made by older
people of the young, it may signify not so much a change
of attitude from one generation to the next as a change
in social outlook and circumstances which permits the
young to express what their elders also thought, but
were not allowed to say because they had been socialised
to accept the coercive necessity of employment.

     Some indication of changing attitudes and values
is given by the growth of legislation relating to
employment practices and conditions of work which has
occurred in Britain and elsewhere in recent years.
For example, Governments have sought wider statutory
powers to promote the health and safety of workers.
Equally significant is the legislation concerning the
employment of women, who now constitute a much higher
percentage of the total labour force than formerly.
Although the equality of treatment sought is still far
from being realised in practice, the existence of these
laws, as also those directed against racial discrimination, is an important development.

     Another way in which the state is active, in
industrialised countries, is in the commissioning and
funding of surveys and research concerned with the
design of work and the quality of working life.   The
nature of these investigations shows an awareness of
the dysfunctional aspects of many modern work systems
and of the need to restructure them to make more effective use of human resources.   This is partly a response to problems of inflation and of how to achieve
greater labour efficiency and economic growth, against
a background of social, educational and technological
changes which challenge traditional assumptions about
work.

     The evidence is conflicting, but increased edu-
cational opportunities and higher standards of living,
leading to enhanced expectations of what life should
offer, create a fundamental disparity for many people
between their aspirations and realisations.   They are
aware of what they have become, given their particular
circumstances, and what they might become in the most
favourable circumstances.   This is not confined to
those in repetitive, monotonous jobs, but occurs also
among professional groups for whom the inherent interest
of and attachment to their work do not survive in large,
bureaucratised organizations.   Under these conditions

there is a tendency to look for alternative occupations
or to seek meaning and self-expression in non-work
activities.

No discussion of changing values can ignore the
ideas (and ideal) of industrial democracy which have
come to the fore throughout the western world during the
last ten years. The pressure for workers to have more
influence on decision-making at all levels of their
organizations is part of a wider debate about the
distribution of power and authority in society as a
whole, which also underlies people's desire for an
increased say in local and community affairs. Given
full expression, industrial democracy would lead to
far more extensive and fundamental changes than are
usually envisaged by those who perceive participation
programmes at the shop-floor level or job design
exercises as contributing to this end. As a result,
for psychologists who engage in such activities 'it is
often their misfortune to meet distrust and obstruction
from the workers who often view consultation and job
design programmes as tricks on the part of management to
squeeze more from them, or to make some jobs redundant'
(van Strien, 1978).

On this cautionary note it might be wise to end,
emphasising once more the need to look beyond the immediate job environment if we are to understand more fully
the forces which will shape the future of work. Before
doing so, however, it is perhaps important to note the
relevance of two topics, neither of which form the basis
of specific papers at this conference.

The first of these is structural unemployment,
i.e. a mismatch between the demand for and the supply of
labour, which many now see as a permanent feature of
industrialised societies. What the impact will be on
the allocation and distribution of jobs and on forms of
work organization has still to be determined, as also on
the definition of work and on living without it, although
a project on this theme is being undertaken at St.
George's House, Windsor. As Jahoda (1979) emphasises,
research on this issue is urgently needed and the need
to adjust to an unprecedented situation of widespread
unemployment accompanying high growth and minimal
inflation in the wake of new technologies is argued by
Jenkins and Sherman (1979) in prophesying the future
'collapse of work'. It may be that one way forward
here is to follow the suggestion, made by Gabor, that a
transition from a situation in which employment is the
norm to one in which it may be necessary for only a
minority, requires a bridging period of unnecessary work
and waste in which people are kept artificially employed
in order that they may not feel socially useless (Gabor,

1964).   But in his view, ultimately a stage must be
reached where man is brought into equilibrium with his
new environment:- 'He must be adapted to leisure, and
his work must become <u>occupational therapy</u>.   It must not
only entertain him ... but must keep him mentally alert,
and give him the feeling that he is useful and even
creative.   We shall never reach this goal by merely
improving push-button machinery'.

        The second topic concerns developing countries.
There has been a widespread tendency on the part of
developed countries in recent years to try and overcome
some of their labour problems by employing people from
less developed nations.   This has taken two forms.   It
has involved importing foreign labour to fill some essential, but low-status jobs no longer attractive to the
nationals of the host country; and it has involved
exporting advanced technology to countries needing
labour-intensive industries rather than highly mechanised production systems.   In both these respects, we
have sought to let others do our dirty work for us and
neglected to look at the quality of their working lives.
To the extent that, as Palm (1977) observes, work in
poorer agricultural countries may, in human rather than
material terms, be better than that in advanced, industrialised societies, transition from the former to the
latter represents impoverishment rather than enrichment.

        Thus, in discussing research and experiments
focussed on the work done by members of various occupational groups in industrialised societies, we need to
look more closely than formerly at the relationship
between those who are in employment and those who are
without it, and also at the relationships between industrialised and developing countries which affect the
meaning of work in both.   As Trist points out, 'the
contemporary world environment is characterised by much
higher levels of interdependence and complexity than
hitherto existed' (Trist, 1978).   This means we have to
endure much higher levels of uncertainty and, that in
looking at possible future directions in work, or indeed
in any other sphere, we cannot afford to be complacent.

REFERENCES

Anthony, P.D. (1977).   <u>The Ideology of Work</u>, Tavistock,
        London.

Bryan, G.L. (1973).   'Introduction', in <u>Work and Non-
        Work in the Year 2001</u> (Ed. M.D. Dunnette), pp. 1-
        12, Brooks/Cole, Monteroy, California.

Clayre, A. (1974).   Work and Play, Weidenfeld and
       Nicolson, London.

Daniel, W.W. (1969).   'Industrial behaviour and orien-
       tation to work - a critique', Journal of Manage-
       ment Studies, 6, 366-75.

Day, H.I. (1972).   'Work and leisure: two sides of
       the same coin', Canadian Counsellor, 6, 251-259.

Dubin, R. (1956).   'Industrial workers' worlds; a
       study of the central life interests of industrial
       workers', Social Problems, 3, 131-142.

Dubin, R. (1976).   'Work in modern society', in Hand-
       book of Work, Organization and Society (Ed. R.
       Dubin), pp. 5-35, Rand McNally, Chicago.

Ekvall, G. (1979).   'Working life in Sweden in the
       1990's' (mimeograph).

Emery, F. and Emery, M. (1976).   A Choice of Futures,
       Martinus Nijhoff, Leiden.

Ferkiss, V. (1978).   'The pessimistic outlook', in
       Handbook of Futures Research (Ed. J. Fowles),
       pp. 479-495, Greenwood, Connecticut.

Fraser, R. (Ed.) (1968).   Work, Penguin, Harmondsworth.

Gabor, D. (1964).   Inventing the Future, Penguin,
       Harmondsworth.

Henderson, H. (1978).   'The emerging countereconomy',
       in Handbook of Futures Research (Ed. J. Fowles),
       pp. 515-531, Greenwood, Connecticut.

Jahoda, M. (1979).   'The impact of unemployment in the
       1930's and the 1970's', Bulletin of the British
       Psychological Society, 32, 309-314.

Jaques, E. (1965).   'The mental processes in work',
       in Glacier Project Papers (Eds. W. Brown and E.
       Jaques), pp. 74-84, Heinemann, London.

Jenkins, C. and Sherman, B. (1979).   The Collapse of
       Work, Eyre Methuen, London.

Kumar, K. (1978).   Prophecy and Progress, Penguin,
       Harmondsworth.

London, M., Crandall, R. and Seals, G.W. (1977).
       'The contribution of job and leisure satisfaction
       to quality of life', Journal of Applied
       Psychology, 62, 328-334.

Meissner, M. (1971). 'The long arm of the job: a study of work and leisure', Industrial Relations, 10, 239-260.

Newby, H. (1977). The Deferential Worker, Allen Lane, Harmondsworth.

O.E.C.D. (1974). Work in a Changing Industrial Society (Documents prepared for an international conference convened by the O.E.C.D.), O.E.C.D., Paris.

Palm, G. (1977). The Flight from Work, Cambridge University Press, Cambridge.

Parker, S.R. (1976). The Sociology of Leisure, Allen and Unwin, London.

Roe, A. (1956). The Psychology of Occupations, Wiley, New York.

Seashore, S. (1974). 'Work and the future: an independent view', in Work in a Changing Industrial Society, pp. 121-134, O.E.C.D., Paris.

Shimmin, S. (1966). 'Concepts of work', Occupational Psychology, 40, 195-201.

Smith, K.U. (1965). Behavior, Organization and Work: A New Approach to Industrial Science, College Printing and Typing, Madison, Wisc.

Terkel, S. (1975). Working, Wildwood House, London.

Triandis, H.C. (1973). 'Work and nonwork: intercultural perspectives', in Work and Nonwork in the Year 2001 (Ed. M.D. Dunnette), pp. 29-52, Brooks/Cole, Monteroy, California.

Trist, E.L. (1978). 'Technical, economic, social and cultural developments and their implications for people in organizations', Plenary lecture to 1st European Forum on Organization Development (mimeograph).

van Strien, P.J. (1978). 'Paradigms in organizational research and practice', Journal of Occupational Psychology, 51, 291-300.

Wedderburn, D. (1974). 'Changing attitudes to work', in Work in a Changing Industrial Society, pp. 50-63, O.E.C.D., Paris.

Problems of Work Organization and Training Under Conditions of Technological Change

Changes in Working Life
Edited by K.D. Duncan, M.M. Gruneberg, and D. Wallis
© 1980 John Wiley & Sons Ltd

Chapter 2

Problems of Work Organization Under Conditions of Technological Change

E. N. CORLETT

WHY JOBS ARE WHAT THEY ARE

If we are to consider jobs and the changing of jobs, with their subsequent impact on the experience of work, it might be useful to start by looking at how jobs have become what they are.

When James Watt was making engines in Soho at the end of the Eighteenth Century his centre-lathe turner might have been told, 'another cylinder arriving from Wilkinson's on Thursday, here's the drawing', and he would be responsible for machining the cylinder and probably the piston which fitted into it. He was technically competent and responsible for finishing the work.

His home might have been a small house in a row, amongst other rows, with little to do out of working hours except what was within walking distance. In contrast to his home life, his working life had a lot of comparative advantages; it identified him from others and demonstrated his ability with respect to others.

In those days engineers who built manufacturing machinery concentrated on making it work. It was a relatively new field and there was a lot to learn. Whitworth's pillar drill was built in 1847, the vertical turret lathe stems from 1838; work with them could involve many activities, and was usually done in a climate in which you did the job or were out on the street.

In the last 100-150 years, machines have developed technically but the relationship between the machine and

operator has not changed noticeably.   Still the controls are mainly where they traditionally have been, on
the ends of whatever spindles drive the mechanism;
there is rarely a transfer of the human controlling
device to a point remote from the driving mechanism.
It is still common to design equipment on the assumption
that people stand at work, based on a combination of
tradition, respect for the boss and the concept that
work would not be done if the worker sat.

WHAT IS NEEDED TO MAKE JOBS BETTER

For many years there has been no serious contact
between machine designer and operator, nor has there
been consideration of the operator's role by management,
except in the limited terms set by work study practice.
In the last two decades the development of ergonomics,
which looks specifically at the relationships between
people, their work, their performance and its impact on
health and well-being, has begun to provide a framework
within which the work people do can be deliberately
designed.

The design of work implies the intentional
creation of work situations from a basis of knowledge
and against performance criteria.   Performance can
mean output, long term health, even behaviour in the
larger society and if some standards are not specified,
no evaluation is possible which can lead to improvement.
Design, then, requires reliable knowledge in an appropriate form, methods and criteria.

The work design scheme of figure 1 indicates,
briefly, the areas to be covered if work design is to
be successful.   It takes no dimension of the process
as invariable and, although expressed in popular terminology, each of the three columns can be supported
by a base of scientific knowledge, some methods and
some criteria for evaluation.   Strenuous efforts are
being made to increase the extent and reliability of
this material.

The schema implies three separate routes; and
in many studies, the work which is reported implies
that the routes are separate.   Any experienced worker
in the field knows that this is not the case although,
in practical applications, the two right hand columns
have too often been followed at the expense of the
left hand side.   This may arise from a lack of appreciation of the flexibility of the technology or even
from a lack of awareness of the impact that a mis-match
between machine and operator has on the attitudes
adopted.

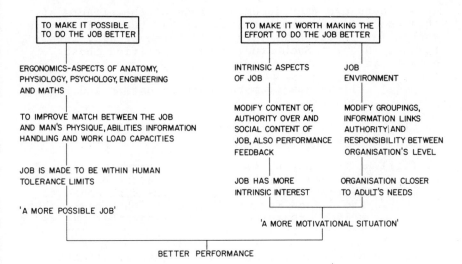

Figure 1.   An outline schema for work design

WHO MAKES JOBS WHAT THEY ARE

Conceptually it would be feasible to combine the
first two columns and argue that man-machine relationships are included as part of the content of the job.
This omits to recognise that those in industry responsible for specifying job content are usually independent
of those designing equipment and working environments.
Each has little or no influence over the others and is
engaged in a separate and diverse range of activities.
The senior production management may well have responsibility for both functions but if a scheme is to be
such that it can be used by practitioners, it must conform in some respects to the structure within which
current professional industrial tasks are done.

The factors taken into account by production
engineers when setting out job tasks have been stated
by Davis et al. (1955) and, in general, do not appear
to have changed significantly.   That the least involvement by an operator means high productivity and high
quality is a widely accepted assumption justified by
common industrial experience.   This diminution in the
role of the direct operator and a continuing concern
with advancing the technical efficiency of processes
and operations puts human considerations low in priority.
The operator's role is specified by custom and practice,
as is his range of payment, and any excursion beyond
accepted bounds is seen as an error in design requiring
rapid and appropriate correction.

There are many documentations of the effects of
this concept, and the car industry has been a favourite
source for researchers (e.g. Goldthorpe et al., 1968;
Beynon, 1973).   Such studies have specified these
effects as -

    (i)   Alienation from the work situation and from
industry.

    (ii)   Limitations of`output and cross-booking of
work (Klein, 1964).

    (iii)   A tendency by firms to buy themselves out of
problems by introducing different payment
systems or bonuses.   This is a response to
the demand for more pay which they have, themselves, fostered by emphasising that pay is
the only reward for work.

There are also other, less well recognised, effects -

    (iv)   The results of the reduced depth and range
of work activities on the short-term stress
and long-term behaviour of people in such
jobs and on their involvement in outside work
activities (Argyris, 1964).

    (v)   Mis-match between equipment and its users,
giving rise to a direct loss of output due
to the machine obstructing the operator and
an indirect loss arising from the ill-health
generated by the mis-match (Corlett and
Bishop, 1978;   van Wely, 1970).

    (vi)   The less well investigated effects of job
characteristics.   In a study of production
operators, Hill (1970) showed that the
strongest factor in a factor analysis of
several possible items relating to job variety
was the length of time to process the batch.
It had a well defined optimum.   The diagram
of Figure 2 (drawn from Kjellstrand's 1974
data) provides another illustration.   It
indicates that constrained working caused
those involved to view the physical environment as being more stressful than those in
jobs with less constraints upon them.

A CLOSER LOOK AT THE RECENT PAST AND THE NEAR FUTURE

In the second quarter of this century, it is commonly stated that the experience of work for the 'blue
collar' worker, in general, declined in quality.

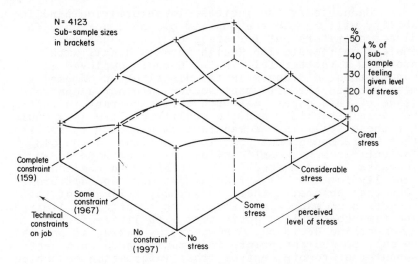

N = 4123
Sub-sample sizes
in brackets

% of sub-sample feeling given level of stress

Complete constraint (159)

Some constraint (1967)

Technical constraints on job

No constraint (1997)

No stress

Some stress

Considerable stress

Great stress

perceived level of stress

Figure 2.   Relationship between perceived job stress
             levels and amount of freedom left to the
             individual by work (from Kjellstrand, 1974).

Regardless of the potential of the technology for providing a range of experiences to each operator, the
managerial pressure was towards the withdrawal of the
worker from control over the process.   Hence, not only
were skills reduced by automation but 'horizontal' activities, i.e. the number of separate tasks making up a
job were also reduced.   People each did a small part
because they were readily replaced in an emergency, could
be more closely controlled to suit the production
schedule and the whole production process became
increasingly deterministic and predictable in output.

     The third quarter of the centry has seen the
arrival of information technology, which has rapidly
increased in sophistication as the period has progressed.
It is clear that the last part of this century will see
the handling, transmission and manipulation of mathematical and linguistic information become widespread and
increasingly simple for the man in the street to take
advantage of.   Not only, therefore, will more sophisticated equipment control become commonplace but more
information and facilities will become available at the
workplace.   Whereas an assessment of the level of
advanced technology of an industry was previously done by
estimating the horsepower available per direct worker,
more likely measures for the work force of the near
future will be the individual programmed capacity
available or a measure of the decision flexibility per
operator.

Undoubtedly the increase in information handling ability will reduce the quality of jobs, not only for direct operators but for areas of line management (unless deliberate job design work is done), with probably a further fall in the numbers employed in manufacture.   Changes in the distribution of employment between the different sectors are not a central issue of this paper, although very important in relation to social stability and the quality of life as a whole. For those still in the manufacturing sector it is clear that where management practices continue in the old 'scientific management' style, the likelihood of an increase in fragmented jobs is high, with the added capacity for them to spread across more and different jobs than before.   There is already evidence of the reduction of many clerical jobs to a series of limited and time-constrained activities with little freedom of movement and decision.   However, by making it possible to call up and manipulate information held on a central computer at remote centres, the 'information technology revolution' has markedly increased the potential for extending the involvement in, and authority over, individual jobs, as well as making it managerially easier to cope with the complexity of a wide variety of individualised jobs.   Thus, where management has the perception of the potential and the knowledge how to exploit it, the opportunities for increased work life quality are enormous.

Management here is referred to as those concerned with deciding what shall be done, how it shall be done, and so on.   Although a management hierarchy will no doubt always exist, where an improved quality of working life is one of the criteria, management functions must be widely spread amongst direct and indirect operations. There is no possibility that the application of 'scientific management' concepts and their resultant management styles can fully utilise the potential of either the work force as a whole or the technological opportunities presented by information technology.   In many situations the most effective application of management information, i.e. information which is the basis for a decision, is at the point of use and the role of management as a giver of orders must, for the sake of economic efficiency if for no other reason, change to providing the information on which decisions will be based, equipment to carry out those decisions, and updating of targets and criteria required for adequate performance of the plant.   A major point arising from the previous discussion is that the next quarter century will see an enormously increased potential for better quality jobs; but the technology will have to be exploited to achieve them.   It will be perfectly easy to continue in the traditional manner, and make jobs

even worse.   The alteration of this trend, for many
companies, will require knowledge as well as motivation.

CHOICES FOR DIRECTIONS FOR CHANGE

        If the statements made above represent the true
state of the world of industry, in so far as the specification of technology and work tasks, the perceptions
of managements regarding their role and the effects
of these factors on the people employed are concerned,
are we likely to see a better working life for industrial
workers?   Hackman (1978) is clearly pessimistic.   He
proposes two possible routes, route 1 being the optimistic, direction proving a better quality of working
life, and route 2 the direction of a further extension
of current management practices to exploit the development and use of new technologies.   He comes down,
firmly but regretfully, on the side of route 2, pointing
out that managers feel comfortable in this role,
knowing what to do and what is expected of them.   It
fits the current ethic of management as an entrepreneu-
rial, risk and decision-taking activity and is supported
by current accounting conventions, which evaluate
managerial alternatives with little concern for the
social or behavioural costs.   (As an aside, when firms
were modest in size and there were many of them, the
costs they passed on to society were infinitesimal when
returned to them in taxes.   It is interesting to speculate whether or not it is possible to evaluate the
effects on, say, General Motors' tax bill, of dis-
charging part of their work force.   As a firm's
operating budget becomes a recognisable fraction of a
nation's budget, this equation must become more possible
and make it important to evaluate a deliberate use of
people against the loss of profit sustained if they are
discharged.   The requirement for redundancy payments in
the UK is already causing some companies to manage their
human resources more positively than heretofore.)

        Undoubtedly the factors supporting the 'route 2'
direction are significant and formidable barriers to a
changed management which, after all, is the key to
improved jobs.   But Hackman is too pessimistic, there
are changes under way which are steadily removing the
support for route 2.   We may not go all the way down
route 1 but then, there are more than two routes which
can be postulated.

        A major point against Hackman's analysis is that
it refers only to the US scene and presents no influences from outside.   In the light of the interest displayed by US managers in, for example, Japanese industrial practices, it seems unlikely that they would not

be influenced by successful overseas, particularly European, developments. Other positive factors for the
current generation of managers include having to recognise, from union and government pressures, the fear of
new technologies held by those whose jobs and job control are threatened (The Times newspaper is an interesting example); the evidence of the problems created
when purely technical solutions are imposed; the effects
of laws designed to protect health; and, not least, a
disenchantment with the status quo. All these factors
will influence even more the up-and-coming generations
of managers who are always steadily replacing the current
people, bringing new training and new ideas and values
with them. The combination of these factors with the
increased potential for devising different jobs and
managing arrangements will apply a considerable pressure for change on an increasingly professionally
oriented management.

SOME PROBLEMS TO BE OVERCOME

It is now, perhaps, easier to see where some of
the problems lie, where they will be in the near future
and what needs to be done to help in overcoming them.
Earlier, the people engaged in creating jobs were identified and it was pointed out that the decisions on
jobs were preponderantly based on technological considerations mediated by a view of the human contribution
which stressed minimal involvement. Although a
greater interest in jobs as jobs will widen the areas of
management which express an interest in these matters,
the structure, content and relationships of jobs are
still likely to arise mainly from the work of production/
industrial engineers and methods technicians and, as
Klein (1978) has pointed out, production engineers are
the people who create industrial work.

With only modest influence on policy, such staff
will still have fairly clearly set objectives, involving the maximum use of resources at minimum cost.
This is the case now, has been so for the last 50 years
at least and there are no signs of change; indeed, it
is arguable whether it should change. But if the definitions of optimality alter, and the production engineer
is expected to optimise incorporating new criteria,
clearly he needs new knowledge, methods and measures.
It may be useful to give some consideration to these
new needs across the range of activities necessary to
set up and operate a manufacturing plant. It will
then become very clear that there are large gaps in
research interests which must be attacked before industry
can be said to have enough resources at its command to
make a successful foray into the unknown territory of

new work organisations.

(i) Equipment Design

The challenge of technology is still high and there are many functions which engineering cannot achieve, or achieve economically.   These will remain to be done by people but if designers are to look towards combining tasks to provide good jobs, or even to intro- ducing design features which improve operator-machine relationships (be they physical, time, or informational relationships) then the designers require clear speci- fications to this effect, methods of achieving their objectives compatible with their methods for engineering design, and ways of measuring their design's success.

From this, and all succeeding sections, the use of external consultants can be omitted.   They may (and do) play the part of 'on the job' instructors but can- not replace a company's own staff expertise in any long- run situation.   Interest must be focussed on the regular operation of a company's work force, at all levels, and on what it can do for itself.

To assess, then, the problems of the designer it is evident that, though well supported by technical material for dealing with engineering problems, he is handicapped when it comes to human ones.   Feedback from actual users (not purchasers) of equipment is minimal and most have a sketchy knowledge of ergonomics principles and methods.   Design handbooks do not usually present data in a form to suit engineers, as Easterby (1964) amongst others, has indicated, and the work described by Clark (1979) is perhaps the first attempt to structure ergonomics information for engi- neering designers across the whole field of equipment design practice.   This is a start, but will no doubt need refining.   There will also be the need to pro- vide some minimum of instruction to designers, in spite of the considerable effort that is going into the formulation of the data.

Given that methods of design exist, is it worth doing?   Furthermore, if it is done, how do we measure success?   Case studies of machine design are now more frequent than when Beevis and Slade (1970) drew atten- tion to the virtual absence of measures of the financial benefits of ergonomics.   A case study by Corlett and Bishop (1978) demonstrated a procedure for evaluating ergonomic changes which incorporates some measure of operator benefits as well as company gains.   More recent work (Corlett and Coats, 1976;   Corlett and Parsons, 1978;   Schirro and Cox, 1978) proposes a cost-benefit

model supported by techniques and micro-models to
measure and evaluate levels of concern within a company
as a result of various job and organisational factors,
as well as including measures of the ergonomic quality
of the workplace.   It is not too difficult to recognise gains in job quality and performance once new
equipment is installed; it is in the prediction of
benefits at the design stage that there is a shortage
of procedures, and hence a greater risk for designers.
The work referenced above seeks to devise cost-benefit
formulations which will have some diagnostic and predictive contributions to make to this problem.

(ii) Equipment Layout

        This is an important influencing factor on commu-
nications and the opportunities for cooperative working,
as well as on comfort and health, but present texts on
factory layout present no information to production
engineers on how to develop plants which will achieve
Quality of Life objectives.   A few case discussions
exist of how such ends have been achieved, e.g. Åberg
(1977) discusses the building of a new SKF steel mill in
Sweden.   Work now being done by Veibäck (1978) is aimed
at formalising these procedures and integrating them
with current methods for plant layout so that the technical, social, and organisational requirements are
satisfied.   Incorporated in the human requirements
area of plant layout is a methodology which positively
involves those who will work in the plant, a new depar-
ture for some engineers and managers.   However, the
provision of structure for what might otherwise be a
loose or informal activity, a structure which defines
responsibilities, relationships, target setting and
modes of operation for working groups, provides a framework for managements to evolve to new operating methods
in plant design as a whole.

(iii) Job Content and Organisation

        There is a large and growing literature on the
design of jobs which can give company engineers and
managers clear ideas on the ways jobs affect people
and some dimensions and directions for change.   What
is difficult is to know who wants change, what sorts of
jobs people want and can do and how to introduce such
changes.   From what has been said earlier, it will be
clear that the changing of jobs is seen as one part of
a total process in which the technology is also
flexed to give a better match to each individual engaged
in its manipulation.   When matching the content of jobs
and organisational arrangements to people, the main body

of the literature concurs that the people concerned
should be involved in the decisions.   Publications from
the British Work Research Unit describe case studies
where various approaches to job change in a range of
occupations have been tried, and the effects monitored.
Almost all case studies deal with projects where job
change has been the prime objective;   what the manager
needs is reliable methods to evolve job changes.   In
this area the job change case study does give considerable guidance, although only recently have a few authors
attempted to produce management texts on 'how to do it',
an early example being by Glaser (1976).

(iv) Worker Participation

        Although the context of this paper has been 'tech-
nological change', a thread throughout is the major
changes seen in the roles of managers and the mutual
relationships between workers and managers.   Technological developments in the immediate future must modify
even further the conventionally perceived roles of these
'two sides of industry' and reduce the differences and
status between their tasks.   The differences will be
stated more in terms of the extent of the range of
authority held rather than the presence or absence of
authority.   There is a long evolutionary trend, in
British society at least, towards an increase in personal authority over decisions affecting an individual's
own life (see, for instance, Williams, 1961) which
suggests a need to change the structure of industrial
management if companies are to operate with a willing
work force.   This may be seen, by some managers and
some unions, as a matter of power being given up, or
retained, and this may be one of the more intractable
problems to be faced.   Even so, there are pressures for
change which may direct the efforts into more profitable
channels, not least the development of a view of management as operating in an open system context as detailed
in the extensive research and field studies in socio-
technical systems theory and applications.   These are
areas of recent research which provide positive directions for management to modify its span of responsibility, forms of authority and general operations, to
achieve specified social/organisational targets whilst
maintaining equally clear commercial goals.

ARE THE CHANGES LIKELY TO ARISE?

        Some problems have been set out above, preceded
by indications of how the present situation has arrived
in both the social and technical areas.   The technical
and social trends are seen as a long evolutionary

process and the technical and organisational research as a continued response to this process.   There is no likelihood that the millenium will arrive, but there is no evidence to confirm a gloomy belief that current problems will not be overcome.   Solutions must wait upon events, and be implemented after the problems have arrived, because solutions are reached only after experiencing and studying problems.   The process of change must, hence, be slow and pragmatic.

What does come out of the above discussion is the need to see the problems of job change and working life quality in the context of the whole plant and its operation and in a wider social context.   Those who will actively create new jobs require tools, information and measures of effectiveness which match what they are trying to achieve.   In many cases they have not yet got some of these and to expect changes to appear without them is to expect someone else to take quite a considerable risk with his professional life.   Some people will always take the risk, particularly if backed up by outside expertise, but for the general run of industry to change, the general run of management must be competent to do it by themselves.   The other point which arises from the discussion is the need for 'technology' rather than 'science'.   People who do things in business and industry are not running experiments and adding to scientific knowledge, but using techniques for short term ends.   It is an over-simplification to make the point that changing an industrial plant needs techniques of known reliability to arrive at chosen targets, and the job of research workers interested in improving business operation is to develop such techniques.   If success in capitalising on the potentials of advancing technology and advancing social aspirations is to be achieved, there is a great need for the truly scientific activity of generalising, classifying and producing 'laws' for the design, implementation and evaluation of the structure and quality of working life in both business and industry.

REFERENCES

Argyris, C. (1964).   Integrating the individual and the organisation, J. Wiley, New York.

Åberg, U. (1977).   Personal communication.

Beevis, D. and Slade , I.M. (1970).   'Ergonomics, costs and benefits', Applied Ergonomics, 1, pp. 79-84.

Beynon, H. (1973).   Working for Ford, Penguin Books

Ltd, London.

Clark, T.S. (1979). 'Ergonomics Procedures for
    Designers', Design Engineering, January, pp. 53-
    57, Publishers: Morgan Grampian, London.

Corlett, E.N. and Bishop, R.P. (1978).   'Ergonomics
    of spot welders', Applied Ergonomics, 9, pp. 23-32.

Corlett, E.N. and Coates, J.B. (1976).   'Costs and
    benefits from human resources studies', Int.
    Jnl. Production Research, 14, pp. 135-144.

Corlett, E.N. and Parsons, A.T. (1978).   'Measurement
    of changes, what criteria do we adopt?', Omega,
    6, 5, pp. 399-406.

Davis, L.E., Canter, R.R. and Hoffman, J. (1955).
    'Current job design criteria', Jnl. Industrial
    Engineering, 6, 2, pp. 5-11.

Easterby, R. (1964).   'Anthropometric data for machine
    tool designers, Proc. 2nd Int. Ergonomics Assoc.,
    Conference, Dortmund, pp. 511-515, Taylor &
    Francis Ltd, London.

Glaser, E.M. (1976).   Productivity gains through work-
    life improvements, Harcourt, Brace, Jovanovitch,
    New York.

Goldthorpe, J.H., Lockwood, D., Bechofer, F. and Platt,
    J. (1968).   The affluent worker, Cambridge Univer-
    sity Press, Cambridge, UK.

Hackman, J.R. (1978). 'The design of work in the 1980's',
    Organisational Development, Summer, pp. 3-17.

Hill, A.B. (1970).   'The measurement of work variety',
    Int. Jnl. Production Research, 8, pp. 25-41.

Kjellstrand, L. (1974).   'Quality of life at the work-
    place', in The quality of life at the workplace,
    pp. 33-42, Regional T.V. Seminar, O.E.C.D., Paris.

Klein, L. (1964).   Multiproducts Ltd, H.M.S.O., London.

Klein, L. (1978).   'The production engineer's role in
    industrial relations', The Production Engineer, 57,
    12, pp. 27-29.

Schirro, S.G. and Cox, D.E.H. (1978).   'A New Approach
    to the Evaluation of Ergonomic Change', Proceedings
    of the Human Factors Society, H.F.S., Santa Monica.

Williams, R. (1961).   The long revolution, Penguin Books
      Ltd, London.

van Wely, P. (1970).   'Design and disease', Applied
      Ergonomics, Volume 1, No. 5, December 1970,
      pp. 262-269.

Veibäck, T. (1978).   Personal communication.

Changes in Working Life
Edited by K.D. Duncan, M.M. Gruneberg, and D. Wallis
© 1980 John Wiley & Sons Ltd

Chapter 3

Facilitating Change: Two Problem Areas and Suggestions for their Solution

S. DOWNS

The first part of this paper discusses some of the problems of how we can better select for new types of jobs. The second part considers how we can modify our training methods for new skills when there is not enough time to develop conventional instruction.

SOME PROBLEMS IN RELATION TO SELECTION AND TECHNOLOGICAL CHANGE

False Conceptions of Jobs

As the work content of new jobs is unknown to the aspiring job holder or his traditional sources of information, people may or may not offer themselves for jobs because of their own false conception of what the job entails. For example, as a visitor to the Royal Naval Air Station Culdrose to look at the training of helicopter observers, I had assumed that an observer acts as the pilot's eyes searching the sea for ships or submarines. In other words, an observer observes. In fact, the observer is the navigator. He also manipulates radar equipment in order to home in on ships, and acts as a communication link between other aircraft, ships, ground stations and the pilot. In action, he can take control and direct a number of ships and helicopters, and thus assume responsibility for tactical decisions. This is a completely different job from my original idea of it.

Variability among Job Applicants

Where different types of applicants are concerned, whether for new or existing jobs, the employer wants to know if the applicants are trainable, and the applicant

31

wants to know what the job involves and whether he or
she can learn it.   For example, if a woman wants to
take up what is traditionally a man's work, how can the
selectors validly make their decision if all their norms
are based on male trainees?

Validity of Conventional Tests with New Skills

The transfer of traditional selection methods to
new skills runs the risk that they are no longer valid
predictors;   in which case, they may result in unin-
tentional discrimination.   Very large studies of conventional tests used in the clothing industry (mainly of
the pin board and form board type) were conducted by
the Hosiery and Allied Trades Research Association
(H.A.T.R.A., 1972).   They found that none of these
tests predicted which operators would be the most
suitable.   One reason for this could be the extensive
change in the machines and processes used in this industry since the original tests were validated in the 1920s.
Long production runs have become a rarity, owing to
constant style changes and new types of material.   The
shorter production runs involved mean that operators
must be versatile and quickly retrainable.

TESTING FOR TRAINABILITY

Trainability tests go some way to satisfying these
points (Downs, 1977;   Robertson and Downs, 1979).
These tests involve giving the applicants a short,
highly-structured period of training in skills crucial
to the job, and then asking them to carry out the task
they have just been taught.   The applicants' performance on this task and the way they go about it is
used as a means of assessing ability to benefit from
training.

Trainability tests differ from other selection
devices in that their main aim is to identify training
potential for a specific job rather than to measure
innate abilities or aptitudes.   They differ from a work
sample test, because training is given and the applicant's ability to respond to this instruction is taken
into account when assessing performance.   The work
piece or task is carefully chosen, the training method
closely controlled, and the observations systematically
recorded (Warren, 1978);   there is no assumption that an
applicant has any previous experience.

It is possible to look on trainability tests as
practical and structured interviews or as condensed
probationary periods.   They have a number of advantages

over conventional selection tests.   For example, they
enable applicants to learn about the job and thus remove
any misconceptions that may have been harboured about it.
Recently we had a report from the prison service in
Northern Ireland, where the training officer was introducing a new course for plastering.   He was told by the
prison authorities that no-one would apply for this
course because of its unfavourable image.   In the
event, the training department introduced four different
trainability tests, including one for plastering.   After
experiencing each of the tests, which were used for job
sampling rather than selection, eight men asked to go
on the plastering course where they did very well.   Two
other tests, for bricklaying and carpentry, are also
being used in an Irish Borstal to help in the assessment
and allocation of trainees to vocational courses;   and
the feedback we have obtained is that they are proving
useful.   There has been a reduction in the number of
trainees submitting requests for reallocation to other
courses.

      Not only does this form of test enable applicants
to learn about the job;   it also enables them to assess
themselves and their ability to learn it.   A validation
study was done in more than fifty companies by the Knit-
wear Lace and Net Industry Training Board.   Tests were
given to 1134 applicants, all of whom had already been
selected by some other method (K.L.N.I.T.B., 1975;
Downs, Farr and Colbeck, 1978).   When the time came for
them to report for work it was noted that, although
they had all been offered jobs and no-one had been given
his trainability test result, there was a direct and
positive relationship between level of performance on
the trainability test and the proportion of people performing at a particular level who did actually report
for work (see Figure 1).

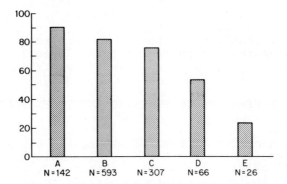

Figure 1.   Percentage of persons at each level of per-
             formance on a trainability test for sewing
             machinists who started training (All 1134
             were offered training).

The essential components of the skill to be
assessed were cloth handling and hand-eye-foot coordination.   The test took the form of machining three
seams between two pieces of cloth, to make a small open
bag.   One bag was made by the applicant, with full
instructions and help from the instructor.   The applicant had been warned that after making this bag, she
could not receive any further help: she would need to
remember all she was told, and could ask any questions
she wished during the learning period.   After this
period of learning, she was required to make three more
bags, exactly as explained.   The very practical form of
this test, and the careful instruction which went with
it, had evidently enabled many of the sewing machine
applicants to assess themselves realistically.   In
addition, the subsequent validation study showed the
test gradings to be significantly related to training
success and drop-out during training.

The self assessment aspect of this new form of
selection test has also been utilised by the British
Steel Company, where redundant men were able to experience 'suitability assessments' to help them to form
their own judgements in selecting retraining courses.
The name trainability test was changed to suitability
assessment in this context, to emphasise the guidance
rather than the selection role of the procedure.

Since trainability tests are administered in the
company's, or institution's, own training school, by
its own instructors, they are firmly rooted in the job
for which applicants are being selected.   If this job
changes, then the instructors are likely to be aware
that the test may no longer be applicable and they will
take steps to modify it and revalidate it.

Some of the ways have been described in which a
new form of selection can be of help both to individuals
as well as to industrial organisations, especially where
new jobs are concerned.   Let us now consider how
training problems engendered by technological change
can also be helped, by an unconventional training method.

A PROBLEM IN RELATION TO TRAINING AND TECHNOLOGICAL
CHANGE

STK, a member of the ITT group, had developed a
new telephone system for the Norwegian Telephone Company,
and were faced with the problem that the Telephone Company wanted their own maintenance staff to be capable of
testing the new equipment as soon as it was installed.
This meant that the maintenance staff would have to
undergo training at a time when the prototype of the

system had not yet been completed, and therefore traditional training methods could not be used.   STK had no
instructors or training manuals available for the new
system, and no previous experience of training anyone to
maintain this type of exchange.

It was decided that the best people to be responsible for the training were the engineers who had been
working on the development of the new system.   The
first priority was therefore to train these engineers as
instructors.   The engineers were obviously worried
about their lack of instructional experience, and to
give them confidence their training as instructors was
designed as a reflection of the form of training they
would themselves be giving later.   This involved problem-
solving in groups, as this also reflected the nature of
the eventual maintenance and testing work to be carried
out on the newly-installed telephone system.

The trainee instructors from STK were first given
group exercises, during which they 'discovered' that
they could make better decisions as a group than they
could individually.   Working with the help of a consultant they decided that the objectives of the course
would have to be to arrive at the test plan, stated in
specific, step-by-step, terms.   They also established
schedules for development of course material.   The
next stage was to develop a series of maintenance problems for their eventual trainees in the Telephone Company to solve, involving the available documentation
which the trainees would, in any case, be required to
use on-site.   They also prepared other written materials that might be necessary to the solution of the
problems.   Even so, the trainee instructors were still
worried about the effectiveness of any learning experience which was not founded upon a formal theoretical
background;   so it was arranged for the STK design
engineers to give lectures covering the theoretical
material.

The new instructors formed their first trainees
into small groups of four or five.   As with the
instructors' group itself, the initial period of training
was concerned with exercises which allowed the group to
discover that solutions arrived at jointly were better
than those attained individually.   Then each group was
given a series of about 100 problems which would take
them through all the test activities in the new telephone exchange.   Every problem required some new knowledge, which the group obtained either from the engineer
instructor or from a self-study aid.   An important difference from traditional training was that until the
participant discovered a need for tuition, none took
place;   and so participants learned only what was needed

to solve the problem currently under consideration.
After dealing with each training set of problems on each
part of the system, the group had to solve a special
test problem.   Documentation was available as it would
be on site; but the solution had to be found within a
time limit.   Pass or fail was based on whether the
solution, and the work done to arrive at it, would be
acceptable on site.   Groups were reformed after each
test.

A total of 60 trainees had all successfully completed the course by July 1978 and the Norwegian Telephone Company was enthusiastic about the results.   They
asked for other training conducted for them by STK to
be done in a similar way.

This unconventional training method is characterised as follows:

(i) Instructors need not be conventionally trained
     teachers: they become practitioners of the experi-
     ential method by going through the process them-
     selves.

(ii) Problem-based learning, providing the problems are
      set at the right level of complexity, provides
      good motivation, as well as making the trainee
      quickly operational.   The learning method,
      involving problem solving by groups, was a fac-
      simile of the work itself; procedures were learned
      and an understanding gained which were directly
      applicable on the job.

(iii) The method produces constant feedback for both
       trainees and instructors, allowing them to evalu-
       ate continually their own progress.   This enables
       the instructors to modify the course for subse-
       quent groups.   Problems that were too difficult
       were left out, and when instructors noticed that
       trainees were having difficulty in relating one
       part of the system to another, they introduced
       material to link the various parts of the system
       together.

(iv) The instructor is not tempted to include irre-
      levant items which could extend the training
      unnecessarily.   They taught only what the
      trainees needed to know.

(v) Trainees like the method.   Of the sixty who had
     completed the course, only one thought he might
     have preferred conventional classroom methods.

One of the pitfalls often encountered after introducing this type of training is its gradual erosion and

transformation into a conventional course.   More theory
and traditional classroom instruction is gradually
introduced, and less is left to the trainee's initiative
and self motivation.   However, if technology constantly
changes it is to be hoped that a course like the one described here will not have time to suffer this metamor-
phosis before a new course is needed to match yet another
technological advance.

SUMMARY

        Accelerating technological change will create
more new jobs, for which people have to be selected and
quickly and efficiently trained.   The selection method
described is one that helps the applicant to learn something about the job and his or her ability to master it,
as well as enabling the organisation to select more
effectively.   With fewer jobs available and restrictive employment legislation it is more important than
ever to get the right people selected into the right
jobs.

        Accelerating change may also lead to sudden
training demands without the normal training resources.
The experience of STK in Oslo showed that these demands
can be met effectively by adopting a training scheme
based on a problem-solving approach closely related to
the job to be performed.

        Both these techniques involve reconciling the
changing processes in industry with the needs and attributes of individuals.   Both give the individual the
opportunity to use his or her own judgement and capabilities, and the evidence suggests that these methods
are of value both to the organisation in dealing with
change and to the individuals concerned in adapting to
it.

REFERENCES

Downs, S. (1977).   Trainability Testing: A Practical
        Approach to Selection, TSA Publication, Training
        information Paper No. 11, London, H.M.S.O.

Downs, S., Farr, R.M. and Colbeck, L. (1978).   'Self-
        appraisal: A Convergence of selection and
        guidance', Journal of Occupational Psychology, 51,
        271-278.

H.A.T.R.A. (1972).   Research Note 9: Hosiery and Allied
        Trades Research Association, Gregory Boulevard,
        Nottingham, England.

Knitting, Lace and Net Industry Training Board (1975).
    Report on the 1973/1975 Research Project (Ref.
    1974/75 R2): Validation of Trainability Tests.

Robertson, I. and Downs, S. (1979).   'Learning and
    the Prediction of Performance: Development of
    Trainability Testing in the United Kingdom',
    Journal of Applied Psychology, Vol. 64, No. 1,
    42-50.

Warren, A. (1978).   Trainability Tests: A practi-
    tioner's guide. Research Paper SL2, Industrial
    Training Research Unit Ltd, Cambridge, England.

ACKNOWLEDGEMENT

The author would like to thank ITT Europe for permission to quote from their training experience in
Norway.

Changes in Working Life
Edited by K.D. Duncan, M.M. Gruneberg, and D. Wallis
© 1980 John Wiley & Sons Ltd

Chapter 4

Technological Change, Working Hours and Individual Well-being

P. SHIPLEY

> "Six days thou shalt do thy work, and on
> the seventh day thou shalt rest."
>
> Exodus 23.12

Technological advance has been colossal in the past 100 or so years in the developed countries, bringing with it unprecedented material prosperity.   But some critics say that these material benefits have been bought at too high a price, and hope the developing and less industrially-advanced nations achieve their newly-sought prosperity without incurring all the painful side-effects encountered in the developed world;   by learning, as it were, from some of the mistakes that have been made by those in the vanguard of industrialization.   In some respects, one could argue, the safety, health and control aspects of changing industrialized systems and societies have not kept pace with such advances.   New employment opportunities have been created, and other liberating benefits, but at the expense of the health and well-being of some individuals working in the 'riskier' jobs and living in 'riskier' environments. A general opinion also holds that the social and institutional adaptations to material and technological growth in the industrialized world have stimulated widespread alienation and loss of well-being, of which the absence rates from work and the incidence of 'psychoneuroses' and 'psychosomatic' disease, are often cited in evidence.

There are many jobs and environments where the organisation and scheduling of working hours results in unconventional or unsocial work-patterns, and to some authors (e.g. Carpentier and Cazamian, 1977) represents an important example of how technological change has had an adverse effect on the well-being of the workers

concerned and their families.   Considerable research of
variable quality has been devoted to the study of
working hours, particularly since the well-planned and
early work conducted in Britain on worker fatigue, hours
of work and accident rates, under the auspices of the
Health and Munitions Workers Committee, in armaments
factories at the time of the First World War.   Several
reviews have been compiled since, of which Harrington's
(1978) review recently commissioned by the UK Health and
Safety Executive, is perhaps the most critical.

The major interest in earlier investigations
centred on the effects on efficiency of different
working patterns and schedules, but more recently 'humanistic' concern for the individual worker's health and
well-being has become dominant.   Such interest is reflected in the growth of new sciences like 'chronobiology'
which is the scientific study of human and animal body
rhythms.   Perhaps it is time for a new science of
'chronopsychology', also.   It is, after all, more than
two decades since the United Nations proposed that the
state of an individual's health be accepted as a major
'quality of life' criterion, and many would define
health these days to include psychological as well as
physical well-being.

SHIFTWORK AND OVERTIME

Shiftwork and overtime are an accepted part of
the industrialized workscene, having increased rapidly
since the end of World War II, with at least 20% of the
work force of European countries working shifts (currently 31% of industrial workers in France).   Apart
from the service industries the majority of shift and
overtime workers are male manual workers in manufacturing;   but encroaching mechanisation and automation
of the 'factory-office' is resulting in increasing use
of shifts and overtime work among white-collar personnel.

It is often thought that working 'abnormal',
'unsocial' hours is a phenomenon unique to the industrialized era, but the practice is centuries old.
Keeping watch at night or providing services and entertainment for others has for centuries engaged some
people at work in hours when others sleep or pursue their
leisure, as in the case of ships' pilotage which is a
centuries-old 'round the clock' and 365 days a year service to the shipping industry.

The main reasons given for using overtime or shiftwork have been: to meet heavy production demands;   to
meet an essential or desired service;   technical process
requirements;   and to get a better return on capital

invested in expensive equipment, plant or machinery.
But new technologies and working practices often seem
to bring new stresses and strains to workers involved,
and in a kind of 'lead-lag' process technological change
and advance runs ahead of our ability to adapt to it in
a bio-social sense. Levels of disability are high among
a growing population of elderly people in the industrially-advanced countries, while so-called 'diseases of
affluence' are responsible for high proportions of the
total mortality rate in those countries.

          Shiftwork arrangements are varied in kind.
Broadly-speaking there are double-day and three-shift
systems; continuous and discontinuous; stabilized and
rotating. Continuous stabilized systems would win the
approval of many scientists but discontinuous, weekly
alternating shifts are more conventional in practice.
In Britain now the continental, rapidly rotating 2-2-3
pattern, is becoming popular to both sides of industry,
and represents two days each of morning and afternoons
followed by three night shifts. The growth of substantial overtime practice in work processes which may
or may not include shiftworking, seems to have been a
customary expectation of both labour and management in
this country since the last war, much of it masking
inefficient utilisation of resources, according to a
government survey (National Board for Prices and Income
Report, 1970). The report also stresses that the
economic gains of such practices must be balanced against
any identifiable human and social costs. There is a
major problem, however, in identifying and quantifying
such costs and benefits, and in finding out to whom they
accrue.

          The International Labour Office in Geneva adopted
the 40-hour week convention in 1935 though it did not
come into force until 1951. This official standard work
week for blue-collar workers did not arrive in Britain
until the early 1960s. People worked for 60 hours weekly
in this country in the mid 1800s, and the work week was
gradually reduced to 53 hours before World War I with
its pre-breakfast shifts, and then to 48 hours in 1918.
But overall hours worked through overtime practice do
not appear to have reduced very much since the turn of
the century, even though the standard 8-hour day has
replaced the 14-hour day of that period. In the late
1970s, the average hours worked in Britain by controlled
labour who 'clock-in' is still as high as in the late
1930s, at about 46 hours per week. The NBPI report
referred to one quarter million workers doing 70 hours on
average, and many self-employed and 'workaholic' professional and management groups put in long hours of demanding and responsible work. So we are not yet a leisure-
filled and affluent society.

Productivity gains presumably have been responsible for increased opportunities to reduce working hours, but leisure has been consistently bartered for more money (N.B.P.I., 1970). It is the youngish middle-aged married man with dependants and heavy financial commitments who is often to be found working overtime or doing shifts in industry, primarily because it brings in extra wages. The younger and older sections of the workforce and higher paid skilled workers seem less enthusiastic. Salaried white collar workers tend to work shorter hours here compared with other European countries, but our blue-collars work longer hours each week on average and with fewer annual and public holidays. Shiftworkers earn about 20% more than dayworkers on similar jobs. Some jobs have working hours sufficiently flexible to allow their encumbents to do 'double-jobbing' (sometimes referred to as 'moonlighting'), which means having a second paid job in effect. Opinion is mixed over the question whether this practice represents an additional strain on the worker or a beneficial change. Others would argue that it deprives those out of work of better employment opportunities; that double-jobbing is a greedy practice in antithesis to the currently developing 'work-sharing' ethic in Britain during a period of economic recession.

In a study of health and working conditions of ships' pilotage in Britain (Shipley, 1978), a variety of working arrangements at stations was found; arrangements depending on a number of factors both within or outside the control of local pilots. The tidal changes in a port cannot be altered but manning levels and work-rest schedules are subject to human control. Manning levels at various ports are determined by the authorities but stations are free to operate below their quota, thus ensuring more work per man (i.e. number of ships piloted). Pilots are technically self-employed and income relates to workload levels. Some stations were found to operate schemes which resulted in pilots taking less than their annual statutory free time. Watch systems with prolonged periods of time on duty, up to 24 hours in some cases, were also found; and there were systems which incorporated a run of several consecutive duty days (e.g. 14 at one port) before a break of a few days was taken.

There were noticeable differences between stations, therefore, in terms of time spent travelling or waiting on standby, and whereas the pace at some stations appeared leisurely, at others there were chronically fatigued pilots. The London district with its tidal port and long sea pilotages can lead to strains of fatigue and social disruption among its pilots when the finely-tuned workload system is not quite right.

Here an alphabetic roster or turn system is characteristic, and the unpredictability of shipping is reflected in the uncertainty the pilot experiences about when he is likely to be called. Sometimes the roster changes quickly, sometimes slowly, and usually fluctuates in pace. A sea pilotage is long, about six hours, and several hours elapse before the pilot finally arrives home, usually during unsocial hours. Pilots complained of long pilotages normally at night-time, long travel home at awkward times, irregular meals and disturbed sleep. Many pilots and their wives mentioned the disruptive effects of such working conditions on their family and social lives.

Local working schemes can be a subject of endless debate among pilots, because of the unpredictable factors in the system, and because of differences of opinion about exchanging leisure time for more income and working extended periods in order to qualify for a longer break at the end. There was some evidence for the older men favouring taking more leisure and more frequent rest breaks. Pilots generally enjoy a good standard of living but the 'piper is paid' in other ways, by sacrificing leisure and in some instances well-being.

In general, UK legislation sets no limits to the pattern and length of working hours of adult males, with the exception of some named occupational groups at particular risk; such as seamen, bakers, and coal-miners. Women and children have been subject to such limits since the 1833 Factory Act, but over 10% of women workers are now exempt because of the nature of their work, nurses being one obvious example. The government takes the view that work hours are a matter for individual and collective negotiation, and that legislation can be too rigid for particular and local needs. Codes of practice may guide, support and reinforce voluntary actions, though the N.B.P.I. report recommended the formal institution of joint control over hours of work to reduce the uncertainty for both sides.

HEALTH EFFECTS OF WORKING HOURS

There is little concrete medical evidence of adverse health effects from working irregular hours, with the exception of gastro-intestinal disorders (Harrington, 1978). Shiftworkers have a different, less nutritious, diet from dayworkers, consume more alcohol, and enjoy fewer catering facilities. Such factors may, quite independently of the actual hours of work, themselves contribute to the initiation and exacerbation of such disorders. Just after World War I Vernon (1921) found a high incidence of stomach disorders

among armaments workers in Britain. This type of
disease is less evident now in peace time without such
wartime compulsory shift and overtime working.

About one fifth of the workforce (which is probably an underestimate since not every case gets into
the records) fails to adapt to shiftwork and transfers
to daywork in consequence (Walker, 1978). A few
studies have checked the health of these casualties
against shiftworking and dayworking controls and have
tended to find their health status to be rather worse
(Kundi et al., 1979). This kind of finding has given
rise to the notion that people who stay on shifts are
a robust, self-selecting elite, with bio-rhythms,
personality, and social and domestic circumstances compatible with such a way of life, enjoying the rewards of
extra pay, more personal discretion and freedom and less
close supervision. Problems of adaptation, suggests
Harrington, may be as much social in origin as medical,
and pre-requisites are: a happy marriage, good
housing, and strong motives for doing shiftwork.

NIGHTWORK AND SLEEP DISTURBANCE

It has been suggested (de la Mare and Walker, 1968)
that volunteers should be permanently employed on nights,
properly compensated, while the remainder are rotated
between mornings and afternoons, although such alter-
nations and rotations can be more disruptive of family
and social life than continuous nightwork. It is also
widely-known that many workers are prepared to trade
ergonomic and scientifically balanced and designed
work-rest schedules for larger blocks of duty time,
because at the end of the block they can enjoy a long
spell of free time with their families, often taking a
holiday away from home.

Night shifts often last ten hours and are known to
work physiologists as being more strenuous and more
demanding of effort than equivalent daywork. 'Fatigue'
is a common complaint in nightworkers. Indeed, sleep
disturbance is the most frequently appearing complaint
in all shiftwork surveys (Weitzman, 1976). Day sleep
patterns of nightworkers are a series of fragmented
episodes and naps. The shiftworker in general has a
smaller amount of sleep than regular dayworkers who
have more uninterrupted blocks of sleep. There are
long periods of wakefulness in day sleep and studies
record phase disruption; for example the phase of REM
sleep (rapid eye movement) comes at an earlier stage in
the nightworker's sleep (Wedderburn, 1975). How far
these factors affect the quality of sleep, and the
implications for health, is unknown. Short-term sleep

deprivation occurs in shiftwork and nightwork, but
there is no firm evidence yet that this is harmful in
the long-term.   One leading sleep researcher has
likened the large individual differences in sleep needs
to differences in shoe sizes.   Perhaps those who adapt
better to nightwork have less need of sleep or are more
resistant to such disruption.   Although the average
sleep of the nightworker is less than the dayworker it
lies well within the normal range reported for dayworkers.

     Harrington (1978) advocates more objective field
studies of sleep, especially now that we have the technology for it in the form of small, portable EEG recor-
ders which subjects can learn to operate themselves.
Akerstedt (1976) believes that the considerable sleep
complaints found in subjective reports by workers in
transportation industries have been to some extent verified in EEG studies.   A popular view is that sleep is
essential for the restorative needs of mind and body;
but in his report to British Steel, Wedderburn (1975)
found that sleep strategies bore no relationship to
shiftwork adjustment.   Those expressing a liking for
shiftwork took no extra sleep or naps, though the
second biggest dislike reported was 'irregular sleep'
(47%), after 'social disruption' (61%).   Many studies
report that the sleep-deprived seem to find ways and
means of catching up somehow by taking naps when convenient, as Bink (1976) observed in his study of fatigue
and scheduling of Dutch ships' pilots.   Sleep
duration, it has been shown in one laboratory study,
varies with the phase position of sleep onset in the
circadian rhythm; Zulley (1979), in his study of 6
people isolated from external time cues, found that the
higher the body temperature at sleep onset, the longer
the sleep.

DIURNAL RHYTHMS AND HOURS OF WORK

     The question still remains whether sleep that is
substantially shorter or prone to more interruptions
and disturbances than the norm is of poorer quality
and deleterious to health.   Many bodily mechanisms
and processes, it has now been firmly established,
operate to a daily (diurnal or circadian) rhythm in
normal people; illustrated by 24-hour sinusoidal
variations in body temperature and chemical changes in
the body's hormonal, sodium and potassium levels.
Evidence of cyclic changes over greater periods of time,
such as the hypothesised ultradian 'biorhythms' of
intellectual and emotional functioning, is less clear-
cut; and research on infra-rhythms of shorter than 24-
hour cycles, has only just begun.

It is debatable that de-synchronisation and
uncoupling of spontaneous oscillators in the biorhythmic
process could lead through age, stress and chronically
irregular work patterns, to bodily and mental pathology.
The process may work through the mediation of hormonal
changes, such as via the amplitude of plasma cortisol
concentration, for example. Disturbance of body
chemistry, perhaps as a result of severe emotional stress,
may be expected also to upset normal sleep patterns and
rhythms.

Sleep-wakefulness is one of the most prominent
and apparent circadian cycles in human beings, governed
it is thought, by internal neuro-chemical 'clocks' as
well as external 'zeitgebers' such as social factors and
daylight.

Studies of sub-human species (Halberg, 1976) have
demonstrated morbidity and mortality as a consequence
of artificially-disturbed biological clocks or rhythms.
Synchronisers can be removed entirely from the animal
or insect, altered in phase or altered in periodicity.
Hypothetically arrhythmic hormonal secretion could
unbalance internal 'zeitgebers'. According to Halberg
(1976), hard data exist to show that shiftwork can be
good, bad or neutral in its effects depending on when in
the life of the worker the shiftwork exposure begins,
coinciding with different 'chronobiological' phases or
stages. He claims that adjustability declines with age.
The peak amplitudes of certain key hormonal excretions,
like catecholamines, have been shown to be higher, and
the rate of body temperature changes faster in 25-30
year old subjects, and it is suggested that this is the
optimal age for shiftwork adaptation. But many of
these generalisations are based on findings in animals
and laboratory studies of humans, with few studies made
of actual shiftworkers involving carefully planned and
sufficiently spaced recordings.

It is important to have control data and continuous
monitoring of 'real-life' experiences. Wedderburn's
study (1975) was based on 17 computer operators on a five
nights on and two nights off regime, and 25 nurses on a
2-2-3 pattern. These workers showed an immediate
adjustment to night work but little adaptation occurred
thereafter, and an immediate return to day rhythms
occurred on the first day off. These findings are
quite common (e.g. Wilkinson, 1978). Other researchers
have failed to find evidence from body temperature monitoring of any inversion of rhythms in shiftworkers but
instead obtained a clear-cut flattening of the curve
with a delayed minimal point. In other words the nightwork rhythms were not fundamentally different from day
curves, even for consecutive nights, which contradicts

the view that nightworkers adapt by reversing their body
rhythms.   Wedderburn also found alertness levels
lowest on nights, which one might predict from temperature curves, and he recommends that decisions should be
made locally about work-scheduling without external
interference and without reference to questions of
'adaptation'.

         People vary in their needs and in the extent to
which certain working arrangements inconvenience them.
Even Webb (1976), who believes that many problems with
sleep arise from our expectations and attitudes about
'having a good sleep', admits the existence of disturbed
sleep patterns under chronic stress in some people.
But the body has 'reserves' to call on, and we do not
yet know the extent, if any, of associated impairment.

VIGILANCE TASKS AND HOURS OF WORK

         Some tasks, such as repetitive and vigilance
tasks, are more vulnerable to the effects of circadian
change effects, than other more stimulating activities.
There is plenty of evidence in the literature to confirm a drop in alertness typically at about 0300 hours
(the low point of the temperature curve), and at 1500
hours (the 'post-lunch' dip effect).   There is a well-
documented increase in errors in both laboratory and
field studies in vigilance-type activities at these
times.   These facts are especially critical in hospitals
and in transportation work.   'Microsleeps' seem to
occur at these times and various counteractive measures
can be adopted, such as educating shiftworkers about
their effects, or injecting artificial stimuli into the
environment.   Locomotive drivers have to work irregular
hours and much of their work is of a vigilance kind, as
is the work of sea pilots, air traffic controllers and
aircraft pilots.

         In the transportation industries task-dependent
sleep loss can be critical for efficient performance,
especially where automated technology is steadily changing
the pilot's and controller's jobs in the direction of
more vigilance and low-stimulus monitoring.   Lapses in
alertness may occur more frequently in a sleep-deprived
person who has to work in a monotonous, unchanging
environment.   These effects have to be minimised,
therefore, by self-management and self-discipline on the
part of the workers themselves, and by more enlightened
organizational and systems management.   Special sleeping
and recreational facilities may have to be provided and
better crew and workload scheduling.   Such procedures
may help to combat possible individual ill-health effects,
as well as to maintain systems efficiency.

The Civil Aviation Authority (1975) has published guidelines for British airline operators on
flight-time limitations for aircrew.   The guidelines
include a clear break of at least 36 hours on at least
one occasion in any 7-day period, and crew members
should not be scheduled for more than two successive
night flights unless they have had a rest period of at
least 24 hours prior to the first of these, to allow
them to adjust their sleep patterns in preparation.
Management is advised to instruct crews how to conduct
themselves in their personal lives so as to obtain the
necessary benefit from mandatory rest periods between
flights.   No such official guidelines however, exist
for ships' pilots in Britain and only one or two local
pilotage districts have independently adjusted their
operating practices to cater for such problems.
'Natural selection' for shiftwork tolerance may be a
reality, but having the appropriate attitude to the constraints which shiftwork and irregular hours impose
may be just as important for adequate adjustment to
occur.   Folkard et al. (1978), for example, observed
that night nurses who adjusted better in the long run
had scheduled and re-arranged their personal lives to
better accommodate their 'unsocial' working hours.

INDIVIDUAL DIFFERENCES AND HOURS OF WORK

        Individual differences in shiftwork tolerability
continue to be found;   both in differences in circadian
profiles and personality types.   'Morning larks' and
'evening owls' correspond to introverts and extroverts
in personality theory, and there is some evidence for a
better tolerance of night work and a peak of alertness
later in the day in the owls.   Breithaupt et al. (1978)
maintained that owls have a constitution inherently less
susceptible to delayed sleep because of the delayed phase
characteristics of their circadian profile.   Colquhoun
and Folkard (1978) appeared to have uncovered a similar
phenomenon in their studies when they suggest that more
neurotic extroverts are evening types with an underlying
circadian periodicity greater than the usual 24 hours.
Akerstedt (1976) observed that the magnitude of circadian
phase adjustment varies between people and that those
less tolerant suffer fatigue and sleep disorders in the
first few months of shiftwork.   Whether physiological
or psycho-social in origin there appear to be threats to
the well-being if not to the objective health of susceptible individuals, which seem to be potentiated by
environmental conditions.

        Chronobiological research may well in due course
have implications for the maintenance of mental health,
and rhythmicity in mood may relate to underlying changes

changes in body rhythms. Significant differences have
also been found in the temperature rhythms of natural
long and short sleepers (Foret et al., 1979), and some
researchers would go so far as to argue a case linking
rhythm stability, performance efficiency and psychological well-being in a causal way.

This evidence of the influence of individual
factors emphasises the value of taking an approach to
work design wherever reasonably practical, which tailors
the work to meet individual needs, allowing individuals
to pace themselves and have a say in their own job
design. Human needs for stability and predictability
may conflict sometimes with the commercial goals of an
airline or shipping company for a high utilisation and
quick turn around of high capital cost equipment.
Standard designs, on the other hand, disadvantage the
minority.

Any model which emphasises individual job-person
fit in essence captures this perspective, so long as it
is dynamic enough to accommodate the interchange and
inter-active effects of changing environments and
changing people. The principle is incorporated in
ergonomic equipment and building design in which features
of the system can be adjusted by individual users to
meet their own needs, allowing for a measure of personal
control, an example of which is some means of personal
thermal and ventilation regulation in a shared office.

POST INDUSTRIAL SOCIETY?

It is fashionable to emphasise the non-human side
of industry, to draw attention to exploitation, pollution,
and suffering on the part of some individuals as the
price for higher material standards of living. In his
essay on the post-industrial society Kumar (1978) refers
to the 'tyranny of the clock'. He suggests that 'tem-
porally-phased mass work discipline' has constrained
individual freedom and undermined the family. One
speculates how much freer in their work lives people may
have been in Victorian England, as they followed the
seasons 'tramping' in search of work in the countryside.
It was in the interests of factory owners to gain control
over the whole span of a workers' year as a single unit
of worktime. Industrialization has produced its own
values, norms and institutions and coupled with the
Protestant ethic of the time generated a workforce of
thrifty, hardworking time-keepers. If such industrialized norms and practices are adopted by developing
countries, one wonders how far they will conflict with
existing traditions and attitudes deeply-entrenched in
such cultures.

In Europe there are signs that both labour unions and management are prepared to experiment with the 'time and tempo' of work. The VW company in Germany is gradually dispensing with the practice of 'clocking-in' at the beginning of shifts, seemingly without loss of productivity (Incomes Data Services, 1979). The compressed working week, flexi-time, staggered hours, and shared jobs question some traditional assumptions about working hours. The shorter working week is currently a main bargaining point with labour unions in Western Europe, but employers are more prepared to concede extra holidays as an alternative to alterations in shift arrangements. More time off is being granted in compensation to workers for exacting working conditions, such as night work, rather than on traditional grounds of status, age and length of service.

In 1975 the EEC recommended that by the end of 1978 all workers in member countries should have at least four weeks off each year. There are, however, considerable variations between countries, partly because of traditional attitudes and customs. Two-thirds of all UK manual workers still get less than 4 weeks holidays each year. There are doubts about how far 'official' views on more leisure time will be shared by individual workers at the grass-roots level, especially in an economic period of declining real income. One would predict that, left to themselves, workers will continue to barter leisure and rest time and possibly some of their health for more money. Granting more free time at one point will lead to accepting more overtime at another, and an increase in double-jobbing and moon-lighting, despite the caveats of some chronobiologists. An idealistic view would be to let individuals choose for themselves on the basis of information about the pros and cons of different working arrangements, but the opinions of scientists clash and their evidence about optimal work scheduling is not unequivocal. Moreover, in practice many individuals would be faced only with the choice between work on shifts or no work at all.

A complete answer to individual well-being at work, furthermore, involves much more than the manipulation of working hours. For many years now the job design experts have been saying that satisfaction and well-being at work depend as much on higher level needs associated with self-esteem and social worth as on lower order needs of comfort, safety, and security. Intrinsic and extrinsic factors are both relevant. The psycho-social aspects of the design and organisation of work (including the psycho-social aspects of temporal conditions) are as relevant now as ever.

There is enough evidence from the literature on

working hours, however, to warn us that we should not
let our enthusiasm for structuring work on the basis of
psychological principles lead us away from people's limitations as biological organisms. The ideal is for
enterprises to become enlightened and flexible enough to
arrange separate contracts with each individual worker
as far as working hours are concerned. Where this is
impractical one would hope for the implementation of
group schemes which put as high a premium on biological
and psycho-social considerations, as has been traditionally put on economic values. For that to happen,
scientists must work quickly to resolve their disagree-
ments in order that a set of consistent and coherent
guidelines can be made available as soon as possible to
those industrialists and Trades Unions concerned to
optimise schedules, in accordance with individual worker
health and well-being.

REFERENCES

Akerstedt, T. (1976).   'Shiftwork and Health: inter-
    disciplinary aspects', in Shiftwork and Health,
    HEW Publication No. (NIOSH) 76-203, US Government
    Printing Office, Washington D.C.

Bink, B. (1976).   Workload of Pilots.   Unpublished
    report of Netherlands Institute for Preventive
    Medicine.

Breithaupt, H., Hildebrandt, G., Döhre, D., Josch, R.,
    Sieber, U.,and Werner, M. (1978).   'Tolerance
    to Shift of Sleep, as related to the Individual's
    Circadian Phase Position', Ergonomics 21 (10).

Carpentier, J. and Cazamian, P. (1977).   Night Work:
    its effects on the health and welfare of the
    worker, International Labour Office, Geneva.

Civil Aviation Authority, Board of Trade (1975).
    Flight-time Limitations, HMSO, London.

Colquhoun, W.P. and Folkard, S. (1978).   'Personality
    Differences in Body-Temperature Rhythm, and their
    Relation to its Adjustment to Night Work',
    Ergonomics 21 (10).

Folkard, S., Monk, T.H. and Lobban, M.C. (1978).
    'Short and Long Term Adjustment of Circadian
    Rhythms in "Permanent" Night Nurses', Ergonomics
    21 (10).

Foret, J., Benoit, O., Merle, B. (1979).   'Can the
      Short-Term Adjustment of an Individual to Schedule
      Inversion be Predicted?', Abstract in Chrono-
      biologia 6 (2).

Halberg, F. (1976).   'Some aspects of Chronobiology
      relating to the optimisation of shift working',
      in Shiftwork and Health, HEW Publication No.
      (NIOSH) 76-203, US Government Printing Office,
      Washington D.C.

Harrington, J.M. (1978).   Shiftwork and Health: a
      critical review of the literature. Report Com-
      missioned by the Employment Medical Advisory
      Service of the Health and Safety Executive, HMSO,
      London.

Incomes Data Services (1979).   International Report
      No. 98, June edition, London.

Kumar, K. (1978).   Prophecy and Progress: The Sociology
      of Industrial and Post-Industrial Society, Penguin
      Books, Harmondsworth.

Kundi, M., Koller, M., Cervinka, R. and Haider, M.
      (1979).   'Consequences of Shiftwork as a function
      of age and years on shift', abstract in Chrono-
      biologia 6 (2).

De la Mare, G. and Walker, J. (1968).   'Factors
      influencing the choice of shift rotation',
      Occupational Psychology 42.

National Board for Prices and Income (1970).   Hours of
      Work, Overtime and Shift Working, Report No. 161,
      HMSO, London.

Shipley, P. (1978).   A Human Factors Study of Marine
      Pilotage, Department of Industry, London.

Vernon, H.M. (1921).   Industrial Fatigue and Efficiency,
      Routledge, London.

Walker, J. (1978).   The Human Aspects of Shiftwork,
      Institute of Personnel Management, London.

Webb, W.B. (1976).   Sleep the Gentle Tyrant, Prentice-
      Hall, Englewood Cliffs.

Wedderburn, A. (1975).   Studies of Shiftwork in the Steel
      Industry, Unpublished Report to the British Steel
      Corporation, Heriot-Watt University, Department of
      Business Organisation, Edinburgh.

Weitzman, E.D. (1976).   'Circadian Rhythms: a dis-
    cussion', in Shiftwork and Health, HEW Publication
    No. (NIOSH) 76-203, US Government Printing Office,
    Washington, D.C.

Wilkinson, R.T. (1978).   'Hours of Work and the Twenty-
    Four-Hour Cycle of Rest and Activity', Psychology
    at Work, 2nd Edition (Ed. P. Warr), Penguin Books,
    Harmondsworth.

Zulley, J. (1979).   'Relationship between the cir-
    cadian temperature cycle, sleep duration and sleep
    structure in human subjects', Abstract in Chrono-
    biologia 6 (2).

Chapter 5

Job Analysis, Training and Transferability: Some Theoretical and Practical Issues

J. PATRICK

It is apparent from the literature that considerable differences in terminology exist, and that the terms job, task and skills analysis are often used interchangeably. Singleton (1974) suggests that there might be twenty-four such terms although even this may be a conservative estimate. Job analysis is a broad term used in various branches of occupational psychology to refer to any systematic breakdown of the work situation for a particular purpose.

The term skills analysis is generally used in at least three ways. It can be a synonym for job analysis or it can refer to a particular technique devised by Seymour (1966) which records detailed movements in perceptual-motor tasks. A final usage, more commonly known as analysis of skills or a skill taxonomy approach, is based on the assumption that efficient behaviour at work is dependent upon certain underlying skills. An example of such an approach is the identification of 'generic skills' (Smith, 1973) which include mathematics, communication, reasoning, interpersonal and manipulative skills.

Fortunately the term task analysis is less varied in its usage and generally refers to the breakdown of a job into a series of tasks for the purpose of training (Annett et al., 1971). Miller (1962a) has distinguished between task description and task analysis. The former is concerned with describing the goals of behaviour whilst the latter is an attempt to specify the psychological demands experienced by the trainee whilst performing the tasks. In certain situations it is difficult to preserve this distinction (Cunningham and Duncan, 1967), and consequently most writers use the general term task analysis in the training area.

The above discussion illustrates some of the common
terms used to designate some types of analysis of the
work situation.   In the present article the general
title of job analysis will be used to encompass all such
terms.

TYPE OF DESCRIPTIVE BASE

One means of classifying the different job analysis methods is by the descriptive variables employed
(Wheaton, 1968).   Morgan (1972) usefully identifies
the variables which might be used when describing jobs
and distinguishes three general categories of variable
which describe the job in terms of context, content or
the requirements of the job incumbent.   For the present
discussion it is useful to distinguish between types of
job analysis which uses task-oriented descriptive
variables and those which use person-oriented ones.
(A similar distinction has been made by Prien and Ronan,
1971.)   Task oriented descriptions concern the goal of
performance, the equipment or conditions in the work
situation or the observable activities associated with a
task.   Person-oriented descriptors relate to the cognitive capacities used or required by the person performing the job.   For example, the description of a
task associated with the job of a production technician
in industry as 'establish the machine conditions for
operating' would be task-oriented.   On the other hand
a description of the same situation in terms of the
abilities, skills, aptitudes or capacities required by
the technician for efficient performance would be person-
oriented.   Similar observations have been made by
Fleishman (1975, 1978) and Wheaton (1968) in describing
four possible conceptual bases for the classification of
performance.   Two of these utilise descriptors which are
in my terms person-oriented (the behaviour and ability
requirements approaches) whilst the remaining two are
task oriented (the behaviour description and task characteristics approaches).   At this juncture the importance
of this dichotomy is to note that person-oriented descriptors which are ability or aptitude based are typically those used in the world of personnel selection
since they can be translated into the appropriate psychometric testing instruments.

USES OF JOB ANALYSIS

Another means of classifying the variety of job
analysis methods could be in terms of their different
purposes.   Blum and Naylor (1968) quoting a survey by
Zerga (1943) of some 401 articles distinguish approximately 20 uses of job analysis.   Some forms of job

analysis (e.g. McCormick et al.'s (1969) Position Analysis Questionnaire; Smith's (1973) Generic Skills
Questionnaire) attempt to solve a variety of personnel
problems which might include selection, job evaluation,
vocational guidance, manpower planning and training.
Some multi-purpose forms of job analysis are often
linked with various wide-ranging job classification
systems (e.g. US Department of Labor's Dictionary of
Occupational Titles and the Canadian Classification and
Dictionary of Occupations).   Fleishman (1975) is concerned with the development of a taxonomy of tasks which
would predict many aspects of human performance, and
would be particularly relevant to personnel placement
problems.   Other forms of job analysis (e.g. Annett
and Duncan, 1967; E.E. Miller, 1966; and Primoff, 1975)
are concerned with the problems in one specific area such
as training or selection although as will be shown later,
a variety of functions can be identified even within the
training system.

It is not possible to find a clear relationship
between the purpose of a job analysis method and the
type of descriptor it uses although some trends do emerge
from the literature.

The majority of forms of job analysis in the
training context (as one would expect from the widely
used term task analysis) emphasise the use of task-
oriented data which is necessary to determine accurately
the content of training.   Smith (1964) is typical in
describing how a job can be broken down into a series of
tasks and sub-tasks.   Christal (1974) finds an inventory of tasks useful in describing a job.   Flanagan's
(1954) well known Critical Incident Technique records
job behaviour which will have a significant effect on
satisfactory or unsatisfactory performance of the job.
Whilst most forms of job (or task) analysis in the
training context initially derive task-oriented data, it
is also generally true that most attempt subsequently to
derive person-oriented measures in order to prescribe an
efficient training design.   Smith (1964) describes how
one must infer the requisite knowledge and skills from
task-oriented data whilst R.B. Miller (1962b) uses certain information processing terms such as identification
of cues and long-term memory to represent the demands
placed on the human operator.   The reader is referred
to a useful review by Wheaton et al. (1976) of some
lesser-known forms of job analysis in the training context.   Most of these begin by deriving task-oriented
data and then move uneasily into problems of training
design from a consideration of a mixture of task and
person-oriented data.

Some techniques for job analysis which are typically

not solely concerned with training, collect data which is initially both task and person-oriented. Fine (1974) in his functional job analysis scheme describes a job in terms of people (co-workers), data (information and ideas) and things (machine and equipment) and develops a hierarchical ordering of complexity within each category.   Primoff (1975) does not use task-oriented data and analyses a job into a series of job elements.   The elements are equivalent to worker characteristics such as knowledge, skill, interests, etc. and are selected because they are judged useful in selecting superior workers or eliminating likely causes of trouble.

This brief overview of varieties of job analysis techniques is not intended to be exhaustive and the reader is referred to more extensive treatments by Freshwater and Townsend (1977), McCormick (1976), Prien and Ronan (1971) and Smith (1965).

FUNCTIONS OF JOB ANALYSIS IN THE TRAINING SYSTEM

In this section the changing role of job analysis in the training system as a consequence of technological change will be examined.   It will be argued that the need to consider selection for retraining makes the relationship between task-oriented and person-oriented data bases even more important than in the past.   This will be discussed with respect to the problem of determining transferability estimates when selecting between potential trainees for retraining.

We are constantly being reminded of the increasing rate of technological change, the trends to greater automation and the widespread consequences of the applications of microtechnology within industry.   The results of a variety of surveys recently commissioned by the Manpower Services Commission, detail a number of interesting predictions concerning training.   One of these concerns the increased demand for people with diagnostic and problem solving skills who can use these in a variety of situations (e.g. instrument mechanics and production technicians).   It also appears that a variety of industries will be concerned with retraining even when unemployment is high and predicted to rise. The overall significance of these factors is that there is a need for increasing transferability between jobs by more efficient training (or retraining) and selection techniques.   The issue is not so much training or selection but selection for retraining.   For example such an approach has been investigated when retraining existing company personnel to perform the job of a production technician within the Plastic Injection Moulding Industry (Patrick and Spurgeon, 1978).

Let us now consider the relationship between the
training and selection decisions of such a training
system (see Figure 1).   It is assumed that the changing
needs identified (1) require a training solution (rather
than an ergonomic one) and that a pool of potential
trainees are available for retraining from which some
must be selected (2).   Therefore how do we decide to
select trainees for retraining?   Such a decision will
depend upon estimating their transferability to the new
job.   Some of the most important indicators of transferability are concerned with extraneous factors in the
work environment and the motivation and interests of the
potential trainees.   Examples of these include union
demarcations, pay scales, status and various other job

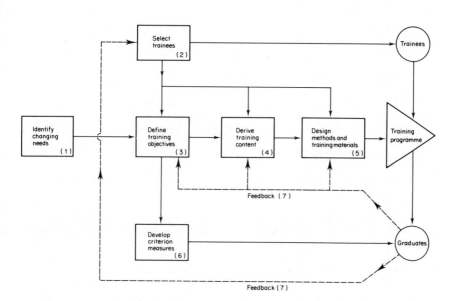

Figure 1.   Relationships between training and selection
             decisions in the training system (Adapted
             from Eckstrand, 1964).

and personal characteristics.   Given that these indicate
that transferability is possible, it is then necessary
to determine the extent to which a person's existing
repertoire of knowledge and skills affects transferability to the new job.   Transferability in this sense
can then be measured by an estimate of training costs
(in the widest sense of the word).   In order to estimate these training costs (e.g. time required to learn,
training equipment, etc.) it is necessary to envisage
the selected trainees' interaction with the training
programme.   Obviously a delicate tradeoff between
selection and training will exist which will be ultimately resolved by measures of transferability.   As
can be seen from Figure 1, the selection decision
affects both the objectives and the content of training
(1 and 2) and also the training design (4).   These
issues will now be considered.

(a) Training Content

        An example will illustrate the sort of problems
involved.   The following list of seven areas defined
the job of a production technician and they were progressively redescribed using a non-rigorous application of Annett and Duncan's (1967) hierarchical task
analysis (Patrick and Spurgeon, 1978).

1.   Prepare for an implementation of an order.

2.   Secure appropriate tool and materials for job.

3.   Check machine/tool/materials correct in trial run.

4.   Establish final product/production specifications.

5.   Remove and prepare tool for storage.

6.   Prepare machine for production.

7.   Maintain production within acceptable time and
        quality.

        Such a job analysis yields useful task-oriented
data which specifies what the trainee should be able to
accomplish after training.   However it is only possible to select between potential trainees after infer-
ring the psychological demands of the tasks and then
subjectively assessing transferability.   In this
example a detailed examination of areas three and four
of a technician's job would reveal the need for high
level decision making and problem-solving skills.   In
transferability terms it might be cost-effective to
select a person with such capacities and no such job

experience rather than a person competent in areas other
than 3 and 4 but no proven decision making capacities.
In other words the time required to master various sub-
tasks of the job will depend upon their demands and the
trainee's existing knowledge and skills.   Consequently
in order even to 'guestimate' transferability one needs job
analysis information which is both task and person-
oriented.   Various theoretical frameworks for classifying person-oriented data will be subsequently examined
for their usefulness in predicting transferability.

(b) Training Design

        The transition from training content to efficient
training design is notoriously difficult (Duncan, 1972;
Resnick, 1976; Wheaton et al., 1976).   Whilst no definite rules exist for this transition there are a number
of useful principles.   Posner and Strike (1978)
summarise seventeen principles for sequencing content of
training material.   These can be grouped into five
categories which are related to words, concepts, inquiry,
learning and utilisation.   Two of these principles
which are called logical and empirical prerequisites
characterise the well known principles of sequencing
for instruction expounded by Gagné in a variety of publications (e.g. 1970).   In the analysis of what Gagné
(1975) refers to as intellectual skill, it is possible
to identify a hierarchy of eight types of learning
ranging from simple stimulus-response to complex problem solving situations.   Simple types of learning
form the prerequisites for more complex types of
learning and consequently the instructional sequence
can be specified and directly related to the task.
Gilbert (1962) proposes the concept of retrogressive
chaining when learning a series of responses and Naylor
and Briggs (1963) are concerned with the task characteristics of organisation and complexity for determining whether whole or part training is appropriate
for a particular task.

        The above principles of training design relate to
essentially task-oriented information and the emphasis
tends to be on the ingenuity of the training specialist
to effect training.   However training design is unlikely
to be efficient unless the characteristics of the
trainees are also appreciated.   Cognitive approaches to
learning conceptualise the learner as active in attempting to restructure the information which he receives in
terms of his existing cognitive structures.   This
led Ausubel   to advocate the use of 'advance organi-
sers' to facilitate the comprehension and absorption of
new information.   Mager (1962) and Pask (1976) and
Pask and Scott (1972) emphasise that the preferences and

cognitive styles of the trainees in sequencing new
information are potentially important.   If these
styles are not matched by the instructional style of
the training system, then subsequent learning might be
suboptimal.   Snow (1978) has suggested that the
instructional method might interact with the trainee's
aptitudes.

   In conclusion it appears therefore that it is
necessary to consider the aptitudes of the trainees in
relation to the task which would require training.
This is necessary in the areas of both training content
and training design when considering the issue of
selection for training.   It is evident that at the
present state of our theoretical knowledge it is premature to attempt seriously to derive transferability
estimates which are required to resolve the selection
versus training issue.   Whilst most forms of job
analysis in the training context pay some attention to
the characteristics of the trainees, there is no univer-
sally agreed classification system of person-oriented
data which will predict transferability and which can be
systematically linked to task-oriented data.

SOME THEORETICAL FRAMEWORKS

(a) The 'Abilities' Approach

   A vast amount of literature exists concerning
traditionally named abilities and aptitudes which is
usefully summarised by Dunnette (1976).   Typically
this involves the area of differential psychology and
psychometrics.   If one believes that people can be
described as possessing relatively enduring traits and
abilities, then it is quite useful in the present discussion to conceptualise these as reflecting 'transfer
potential' (Ferguson, 1954, 1956).   Consequently a
trainee with a high score on verbal comprehension
should be better able to transfer between situations
involving such similar abilities than a trainee who had
a low score.   Notice however that any assessment or
psychological similarity necessarily depends upon extrapolating from task-oriented data.   Prien (1977) also
makes the point that for psychometric instruments to
have high content validity, it is necessary to utilise
job analysis information which is task-oriented besides
person-oriented.

   The problem with the abilities approach is that
it is difficult to specify the level of description
required and consequently the number of abilities in any
one area.   Guildford (1967) with his structure of intel-
lect model presents 120 in the area of intellectual

processing; whilst Fleishman (1962) elaborates 11 perceptual-motor abilities.   Despite the problem of level
of description, maybe the ultimate criterion for any
classification is its efficiency and utility (R.B.
Miller, 1974) which in this context is validly discri-
minating between trainees in terms of transferability.

Attempts to link empirically the ability approach
with task-oriented data have characterised the work of
Fleishman and his associates.   Fleishman (1978)
reports some studies in auditory signal identification,
problem-solving and concept formation in which characteristics of the task were manipulated and concomitant
changes in the ability requirements produced.   For
example, the task characteristics manipulated in the
auditory signal identification task were signal duration
and signal-to-noise ratio.   Subjects received a battery of reference tests which measured various perceptual and memory abilities and then performed the differing criterion tasks.   Factor analysis of these
results indicated the varying contributions of particular abilities (e.g. auditory perceptual) given changes
in the task characteristics.

The work of McCormick and his associates at Purdue
University investigates the relationship between elements of the Position Analysis Questionnaire, Form B
and ability (or attribute) requirements of a job.   This
work is summarised by Sparrow (1979).   Studies by
Marquardt (1972) and Marquardt and McCormick (1974)
develop ability profiles for each job element of the
PAQ from expert ratings of 76 attributes (which included
most of Fleishman's abilities).   Investigations have
attempted to validate the use of such ability profiles
for jobs derived from rated weightings of job elements
but have only been partially convincing due to a variety
of methodological considerations.   Marquardt and
McCormick (1974) report the correlations between only
the factored ability dimensions and General Aptitude
Test Battery scores whilst Shaw and McCormick (1976) use
a cross product methodology to estimate ability profiles
for jobs.   This assumes that ability requirement is
directly proportional to the rated importance of a job
element.

It is evident that with the abilities approach to
person-oriented data one is confronted with a dilemma.
On the one hand, it is doubtful to what extent it will
lead to fine discriminations between potential trainees
without being linked with task-oriented data.   On the
other hand, the time required and methodological complexities of making such a link is a major drawback at
present.

(b) The Information Processing Approach

The information processing model of skilled performance (e.g. Welford, 1976) describes a variety of
processes intervening between input and output which
affect performance.   R.B. Miller (1974) has adopted
this approach in his type of job analysis which uses
twenty-five categories which fall into the input-memory-
processing-output format.   The obvious advantage of
using such terminology is that it is possible to
characterise a job independent of its context.   Again
the problem arises as to the level of description and
consequently the number of categories which are useful
for predicting transferability.

Altman (1976) is one of the few writers to have
attempted to answer this problem at the vocational
level.   Transferability (defined in a slightly different
way from above) according to Altman depends upon the
similarity between and within the motivational, contextual and behavioural domains.   The behavioural
domain is of concern to us at the present and is divided
into five interacting stages of perception, memorisation,
intellectual processing, response and integration.
Each of these is subdivided into a variety of interacting
sub-stages.   For example intellectual processing is
broken down into perceptual transfer, conceptual, principle, discovery, invention, formulation and evaluation.
Altman summarises an impressive variety of theoretical
evidence to justify each category as being potentially
relevant to the notion of transferability.   Ultimate
evaluation of this framework will await its implementation in the educational or industrial contexts.
Although again it will require massive resources.

The information processing approach as outlined
above is unlikely however to provide all the answers
concerning transferability because it tends to adopt a
static view of skilled performance.   Many writers (e.g.
Adams, 1971; Fitts, 1962) have emphasised that different stages characterise skill acquisition whilst
others have suggested that skilled behaviour becomes
progressively more hierarchically organised (e.g.
Miller, Galanter and Pribram, 1960).   If one observes
the skilled behaviour of a concert pianist or a tennis
player, it is remarkable how flexibly behaviour can be
organised to achieve the desired end.   Such subtle
flexibility includes changes in timing and sequencing
of behaviours and reflects what has been called a well
developed 'plan' (Miller, Galanter and Pribram, 1960)
or 'strategy' (R.B. Miller, 1974).   Duncan (1972) makes
a similar point in the training context.   It would
appear therefore that the identification and development
of appropriate plans or strategies for organising a job

would be an important determinant of transferability.
It might be recalled that an example quoted earlier,
involved the job of a production technician in the
Plastics Industry in which some parts of the job required decision making skills.   In such a situation
when one is considering selection for retraining, the
possession of a similar plan or strategy albeit from a
different context might be a better predictor of transferability than either other information processing-
type skills or the amount of job related knowledge.   It
is likely that prediction of transferability will be
more accurate when all these sources of information are
taken into account.

CONCLUSIONS

       Two different theoretical approaches have been
discussed with respect to their possible use in predicting transferability of trainees.   The abilities
approach emphasises that transferability will be mediated
by the individual's possession of certain traits which
are relatively enduring.   The information processing
approach views the interaction of various cognitive
capacities as determining skilled performance and consequently transferability to a new job.   Both of these
approaches utilise data which is essentially person-
oriented although this must be inferred from task-
oriented information in order to be an accurate reflection of the demands of the job.   Consequently when considering the problem of selection for retraining, which
is likely to be an increasingly important issue, it is
necessary to use job analysis techniques which produce
both task and person-oriented data.   In specifying
training content and design the interaction of the
characteristics of the trainees (in person-oriented
terms) with characteristics of the task has important
consequences for transferability.   Consequently the
interface between classification systems which are task-
oriented and those which are person-oriented is vital
(Dunnette, 1976; Prien, 1977).   At the present translation between these data bases on an empirical basis is
not sufficiently developed to enable confident predictions concerning transferability between jobs to be made.

ACKNOWLEDGEMENTS

       This paper arises out of research sponsored by the
Training Services Division of the Manpower Services
Commission although this paper only reflects the author's
opinions.   Some views expressed in this paper have been
formulated by discussions with colleagues in our research
staff at the University of Aston who include Mr. P.

Spurgeon, Mr. J. Sparrow and Mr F. Barwell.

REFERENCES

Adams, J.A. (1971).   'A Closed-Loop Theory of Motor
    Learning', Journal of Motor Behaviour, 3, 111-149.

Annett, J., Duncan, K.D., Stammers, R.B. and Gray, M.J.
    (1971).   Task Analysis, Training Information,
    No. 6, London, HMSO.

Annett, J. and Duncan, K.D. (1967).   'Task Analysis
    and Training Design', Occupational Psychology, 41,
    211-221.

Altman, J.W. (1976).   Transferability of Vocational
    Skills: Review of Literature and Research Infor-
    mation Series No. 103, Center for Vocational
    Education, Ohio.

Blum, M.L. and Naylor, J.C. (1968).   Industrial
    Psychology, New York, Harper & Row.

Christal, R.E. (1974).   'The United States Air Force
    Occupational Research Project', Technical Report
    AFHRL-TR-73-75, Occupation Research Division, Air
    Force Human Resources Laboratory, Texas.

Cunningham, D.J. and Duncan, K.D. (1967).   'Describing
    Non-Repetitive Tasks for Training Purposes',
    Occupational Psychology, 41, 203-210.

Duncan, K.D. (1972).   'Strategies for Analysis of the
    Task', in Strategies for Programmed Instruction:
    An Educational Technology (Ed. J. Hartley), London,
    Butterworth.

Dunnette, M.D. (1976).   'Aptitudes, Abilities and
    Skills', in Handbook of Industrial and Organi-
    sational Psychology, Chicago, Rand McNally.

Eckstrand, G.A. (1964).   'Current Status of the Tech-
    nology of Training', Technical Report AMRL-TDR-
    64-86, Wright Patterson Aerospace.

Ferguson, G. (1954).   'On Learning and Human Ability',
    Canadian Journal of Psychology, 8, 95-112.

Ferguson, G. (1956).   'On Transfer and the Abilities of
    Men', Canadian Journal of Psychology, 10, 121-131.

Fine, S.A. (1974).   'Functional Job Analysis: How to
    Standardise Task Statements', W.E. Upjohn Institute

for Employment Research.

Fitts, P.M. (1962). 'Factors in Complex Skill Training', in Training Research and Education (Ed. R. Glaser), Reprinted 1965, New York, Wiley.

Flanagan, J.C. (1954). 'The Critical Incident Technique', Psychological Bulletin, 51, 327-358.

Fleishman, E.A. (1962). 'The Description and Prediction of Perceptual-Motor Skill Learning', in Training Research and Education, (Ed. R. Glaser), Pittsburgh, University of Pittsburgh.

Fleishman, E.A. (1975). 'Toward A Taxonomy of Performance', American Psychologist, 1127-1149.

Fleishman, E.A. (1978). 'Relating Individual Differences to the Dimensions of Human Tasks', Ergonomics, 21, 12, 1007-1019.

Freshwater, M. and Townsend, C. (1977). Analytical Techniques for Skill Comparison, Volume I. Training Services Agency of the Manpower Services Commission, London.

Gagné, R.M. (1970). The Conditions of Learning, New York, Holt, Rinehart and Winston.

Gagné, R.M. (1975). 'Taxonomic Problems of Educational Systems', in Measurement of Human Resources (Eds. W.T. Singleton and P. Spurgeon), London, Taylor & Francis.

Gilbert, T.F. (1962). 'Mathematics: The Technology of Education', Journal of Mathematics, 1, 7-73 and 2, 7-56.

Guildford, J.P. (1967). The Nature of Human Intelligence, New York, McGraw-Hill.

Mager, R.F. (1962). 'On the Sequencing of Instructional Content', in Contributions to an Educational Technology (Eds. I.K. Davies and J. Hartley), London, Butterworth.

Marquardt, L.D. (1972). 'The Rated Attribute Requirements of Job Elements in a Structured Job Analysis Questionnaire - the PAQ', M.Sc. Thesis, Purdue University.

Marquardt, L.D. and McCormick, E.J. (1974). 'The Job Dimensions Underlying the Job Elements of the Position Analysis Questionnaire (Form B)', Report

No. 4, Purdue University.

McCormick, E.J. (1976).   'Job and Task Analysis', in
    Handbook of Organisational and Industrial Psycho-
    logy (Ed. M.D. Dunnette), Chicago, Rand McNally.

McCormick, E.J., Jeanneret, P.R. and Mecham, R.C.
    (1969).   A Study of Job Characteristics and Job
    Dimensions as based on the Position Analysis
    Questionnaire, Occupational Research Center,
    Purdue University, Report No. 6.

Miller, E.E. (1966).   A Taxonomy of Response Processes,
    Study BR-8, HUMRRO, Fort Knox, Kentucky.

Miller, R.B. (1962a).   'Task Description and Analysis',
    in Psychological Principles in System Development
    (Ed. R.M. Gagne), New York, Holt, Rinehart &
    Winston.

Miller, R.B. (1962b).   'Analysis and Specification of
    Behaviour for Training', in Training Research and
    Education (Ed. R. Glaser), New York, Wiley.

Miller, R.B. (1974).   A Method for Determining Task
    Strategies, Technical Report AFHRL-TR-74-26,
    American Institute for Research.

Miller, G.A., Galanter, E. and Pribram, K.H. (1960).
    Plans and the Structure of Behaviour, New York,
    Holt, Rinehart & Winston.

Morgan, T. (1972).   Occupational Description and Classi-
    fication, Air Transport and Travel Industry
    Training Board, Report RE-D-19.

Naylor, J.C. and Briggs, G.E. (1963).   'Effects of Task
    Complexity and Task Organisation on the Relative
    Efficiency of Part and Whole Training Methods',
    Journal of Experimental Psychology, 65, 217-224.

Pask, G. (1976).   'Styles and Strategies of Learning',
    British Journal of Educational Psychology, 46,
    128-148.

Pask, G. and Scott, B.C.E. (1972).   'Learning Strate-
    gies and Individual Competence', International
    Journal of Man-Machine Studies, 4, 217-253.

Patrick, J. and Spurgeon, P. (1978).   Redeployment by
    Upgrading to Technician, Report for the Training
    Services Agency in Grouping of Skills, Sub-project
    1.

Posner, G.J. and Strike, K.A. (1978).   'Principles of
     Sequencing Content', in Contributions to an Edu-
     cational Technology, Volume 2, London, Kogan Page.

Prien, E.P. and Ronan, W.W. (1971).   'Job Analysis: A
     Review of Research Findings', Personnel Psychology,
     24, 3, 371-396.

Prien, E.P. (1977).   'The Function of Job Analysis in
     Content Validation', Personnel Psychology, 30,
     167-174.

Primoff, E.S. (1975).   How to Prepare and Conduct Job
     Element Examinations, Report TS-75-1, Research
     Section Personnel Research and Development Center,
     US Civil Service Commission, Washington.

Resnick, L.B. (1976).   'Task Analysis in Instruction',
     in Cognition and Instruction (Ed. D. Klahr), Wiley.

Seymour, W.D. (1966).   Industrial Skills, London,
     Pitman.

Shaw, J.B. and McCormick, E.J. (1976).   The Prediction
     of Job Ability Requirements Using Attribute Data
     Based upon the PAQ, Report No. 11, Purdue Univer-
     sity.

Singleton, W.T. (1974).   Man-Machine Systems, London,
     Case & Wyman.

Smith, R.G. (1964).   'The Development of Training
     Objectives', Research Bulletin II, HUMRRO, George
     Washington University.

Smith, B.J. (1965).   Task Analysis Methods compared
     for Application to Training Equipment, Technical
     Report, HAUTRADEVEEN 1218-5, US Naval Training
     Device Center, New York.

Smith, A.D.W. (1973).   General Skills in the Reasoning
     and Interpersonal Domain, Prince Albert, Saskat-
     chewan, Training Research and Development Station.

Snow, R.E. (1978).   'Individual Differences and
     Instructional Design', in Contributions to an
     Educational Technology, Volume 2 (Eds. J. Hartley
     and I.K. Davies), London, Kogan Page.

Sparrow, J. (1979).   A Theoretical Model of the Factors
     Involved in Behaviour Acquisition, Unpublished
     paper, University of Aston.

Welford, A.T. (1976).   Skilled Performance: Perceptual
    and Motor Skills, Illinois, Scott, Foresman & Co.

Wheaton, G. (1968).   Development of a Taxonomy of Human
    Performance: A Review of Classificatory Systems
    Relating to Tasks and Performance, Technical
    Report 1, American Institute for Research,
    Washington.

Wheaton, G.R., Rose, A.M., Fingbroman, P.W., Korotkin,
    A.L. and Holding, D.H. (1976).   Evaluation of
    the Effectiveness of Training Devices, Literature
    Review and Preliminary Model Research Memorandum
    76-6, US Army Research Institute for the
    Behavioral and Social Sciences.

Zerga, J.E. (1943).   'Job Analysis, A Resume and
    Bibliography', Journal of Applied Psychology, 27,
    249-267.

Comments on Section I

D. WALLIS

So far as industrialised societies are concerned, it can hardly be disputed that the nature of working life throughout the past 200 years has been regulated more by technological change and development than by anything else. Work itself, the content and environment of jobs, is determined primarily by technological factors. This is as evident of clerical and banking jobs as of piloting a ship or maintaining a telephone exchange. And even though extrinsic features such as payment for the work one does and the social satisfaction and esteem it may bring, are clearly critical to the appeal a job may have, the overall quality of working life must surely be conditional upon experience of what one's job entails in the way of tasks to be completed and skills to be achieved.

Now whether or not this experience is humanly appealing and satisfying is going to depend significantly upon the way a work-study or organization and methods practitioner, or more likely, a production engineer, has specified the tasks which have to be carried out. It is also conditional upon how effectively people have been selected and trained to perform these tasks, and on how well the relationships between various people and their respective jobs have been organized.

Speakers in this session come together as specialists, inter alia, in personnel selection, vocational training, and ergonomics. These three areas of applied human science grew up as complementary approaches to the optimisation of a 'fit', or adjustment, between people and their work. On the whole, this optimal 'fit' has been seen in terms of performance and satisfactoriness, rather than as equally a function of quality of work experience and satisfaction. Indeed, this is how

the selection, training, and ergonomic practices in modern industry are viewed by most trade unions today.
Yet a growing number of managers and designers, and certainly most applied psychologists and ergonomists, might
well argue that a satisfactory 'fit' which is also optimally satisfying to workpeople, is preferable to an
even more satisfactory one (judged purely on cost effectiveness) which is relatively low on job satisfaction or
quality of working life.

        Indeed, Nigel Corlett's exposition of the ergo-
nomic approach to optimising work shows that he holds
firmly to a radical view of what production engineers
and managers could and should be doing.   The objectives
of improved work design, in his view, are not only to
make it possible to do a job more effectively but also
to make it worthwhile for an operator to make the effort
to do the job more effectively.   There could be no
neater way of epitomising the underlying theme of the
Conference as a whole.   Somewhere along their respective lines of approach to technological change and the
human response to it, there must be common ground between ergonomists and industrial psychologists (who have
customarily emphasised the nature and demands of work)
on the one hand, and organizational psychologists and
industrial sociologists (who have concentrated more on
the quality of working life and the satisfactions it may
hold) on the other.

        As Corlett pointed out, the application of ergo-
nomic principles is a necessary complement to the
guidance which social scientists can give to engineers
and managers, for example, in order to slow down the
trend towards a lower quality of life which so often
accompanies the spread of automatic control.   Corlett
also emphasized that ergonomists and social scientists
would not have much impact upon technological issues if
they stopped short at suggesting to managers what
changes were desirable.   They must also offer sound
guidance, based on research, on how to introduce and
sustain the changes.   This prescription appears also in
later papers.   It was taken up implicitly by Sylvia
Downs and John Patrick, who focussed attention upon some
of the problems in selection and training which are
occasioned by technological change.

        Personnel selection is very largely a psycholo-
gically-based 'technology', with a respectable history
of development and application going back to the origins
of industrial psychology around the turn of the 20th century.   Yet it has lost its appeal latterly for many
applied psychologists, seeming to lack an infusion of
fresh ideas and technical innovations.   It was distinctly
heartening therefore to hear Sylvia Downs describe what

I would judge to be the most interesting, and possibly
the most fruitful, new development in industrial selection technique for several decades.   Her 'trainability
testing' approach is already backed by persuasive evidence from her own and others' research and development
studies.   It appears to offer substantial advantages
over conventional psychometric or interview-based methods,
not the least of them being an additional 'spin-off'
from the opportunity which trainability testing affords
of self-selection among applicants for training.   Trainability tests exemplify one of the effects which rapid
technological change is forcing upon selection testing
and assessment generally.   Selecting people who will
respond suitably to training or to re-training is a
more sensible strategy, when the nature of jobs is
changing frequently, than trying to select people who
happen already to have the ability to perform.

        Another consequence of rapid change is that the
details of job requirements may not be clear enough,
whilst a new system is under design and development,
for the trainable elements of required skills to be
forecast before that system is in operation.   In such
circumstances - and they are increasingly common
training for 'versatility' or 'generalisable skills' may
be the answer, at least if one can envisage what underlying and generalisable skills will be relevant and how
to train for them.   The application of 'discovery'
learning to STK's maintenance problems, which Sylvia
Downs described, is a case in point.

        Just as the assessment of each individual's dif-
ferent talents and trainability is fundamental to systematic selection and training, so too is the accurate
delineation of task demands.   The latter is also a
critical requirement of sound ergonomic work design.
John Patrick has given us an informative account of the
principal methods of 'job analysis'.   The distinction
between 'person-oriented' (skills analysis) and 'task-
oriented' (task analysis) techniques is a reflection of
our customary reliance on the former for personnel
selection and the latter for deriving training needs.
He has presented the view that continuing technological
change implies not only a growing dependence on effective selection of people for re-training, but also as
high a degree of transferability between jobs as possible.

        A consequence of this is that job analysis tech-
niques should be used which yield both task- and person-
oriented data.   As Patrick notes, analyzing jobs in
task-oriented terms is valuable for training purposes,
but doesn't directly help in picking out the trainees
who are potentially most successful.   He also argued
that it is necessary to infer the person-oriented data

from data which emerge from task analysis, in order
adequately to take account of job demands. Yet those
of us who have tried will know how difficult it is in
practice to 'translate' from one system of analysis to
another; as Patrick pointed out, the classifications
used in skills or abilities analysis do not match up in
any consistent fashion with those employed for task
analysis.

Pat Shipley's paper returns our attention to the
theme of work design and organization which Corlett
introduced. She is keen to pursue the argument that
an individual worker's health, with psychological well-
being as an essential aspect of it, should serve as a
leading criterion of quality of life. Reviewing evidence on how shiftwork and overtime in modern industry
can affect psychological and social factors in health,
she draws upon her own investigation into ships' pilots
to show how working conditions and well-being interact.
Pilots, it appears, are inclined to trade-off leisure
and rest breaks against greater income. Shipley suggested that whilst shift-working may present more health
hazards, those who choose this pattern, including night-
shift workers, seem likely to be the more healthy, hardy,
and socially-adjusted types. They not only value the
pay but the relative freedom of action which goes with
shift-working.

In her opening address, Sylvia Shimmin remarked
that future scenarios about work ranged from the optimistic to the profoundly pessimistic. Corlett was
inclined to be reasonably optimistic, given that human
factors specialists can provide the basic data which
managers and designers with a progressive and enlightened
outlook will need. Shipley's view of the 'post-
industrial' society incorporates a plea for greater
flexibility with respect to the duration and tempo of
work schedules. She wants to see more accommodation
of individual preferences and needs, on the assumption
that bargaining for more pay rather than more leisure
or better working conditions is what some individuals
will prefer. Perhaps a timely warning was contained
in her insistence that whilst psycho-social factors are
certainly important, we should not let our enthusiasm
for re-structuring work to meet 'higher-order' needs
divert us from the 'lower-order' ones i.e. that people
have limitations and needs inherent in their biological
nature.

Sylvia Shimmin refers to alternative possible
futures. How likely is it then that future trends
will look like a continuation of past ones? Or will
quite unforeseen developments intervene, to change the
directions in which the nature and quality of work seem

currently to be pointing?   Can we use scientific knowledge and insights to influence the future advisedly?
Sylvia Shimmin seems unwilling to be drawn from her
'neutral' position with respect to optimism or pessimism.
In any case, she argued that abstractions and generalisations on a 'worldwide' scale were wholly premature.
We should look closely at our own local work organizations, those we understood best, and draw what inferences we can with respect to those particular organizations;   not neglecting, of course, to make use of
relevant information from other more distant sources.

Whereas the contributors to this section do not
speculate about the future quality of working life, they
seemed during the conference discussions to view the
future availability of work with some pessimism at
least in technologically-advanced societies.   Reference
was made to the 'exporting' of assembly work from
Britain to the Far East, with the likelihood of other
kinds of work following as computer developments gathered
pace in that area.   Shipley observed that some confident
predictions were being made that within a decade we
shall see automated ships, with no resident crew aboard,
needing only an 'invigilating manager'.   However,
others felt that changes in the nature of work will be
more conspicuous than widespread elimination of the
opportunity to work at all.   Examples were cited of
companies whose policy was consistently to re-deploy
staff rather than lose them as job requirements change.
And ships' pilots, in Shipley's opinion, would still be
needed for a long time to guide automated ships through
the tricky manoeuvring phases of entering and leaving a
busy port.   No-one was openly confident, however, about
the extent to which growing unemployment in some western
industrialised societies would be checked, or indeed
should be checked on purely social and psychological (as
distinct from economic) grounds.

Reflecting on the approaches outlined in these
papers to present and imminent work design, selection,
and training, problems, one can be encouraged by the
evidence of a lively and informed interest by applied
human or social scientists in the human aspects and
implications of technological change.   Application of
known principles and reasonably well-developed techniques
continues to be uneven and concentrated in rather
special problem areas.   How far those areas reflect
the relative seriousness of probable future trends in
work demands and environments, as well as the particular
interests of the researchers, is not altogether clear.
A pragmatic insistence that we have to do what we can to
tackle the problems we do know about, rather than concentrating only on more distant and problematic futures, was
a welcome feature of the general discussion.

Work Problems in Capital-intensive and Continuous Process Industries

Changes in Working Life
Edited by K.D. Duncan, M.M. Gruneberg, and D. Wallis
© 1980 John Wiley & Sons Ltd

Chapter 6

Problems of Work in Capital-Intensive Continuous Process Industries

K. D. DUNCAN

INTRODUCTION

Put very simply, one of our purposes is to look
into the likely future of 'the real world of work' - to
use a tired phrase beloved of administrators and finan-
ciers, especially when proposing measures to deal with
unemployment, retraining, industrial unrest and, perhaps
most of all, when decrying the research of academics who
evidently neither live in the real world of work nor know
anything about it.

It seems to me that we can see something of what
the real world of work will be like, in a decade or so,
if we look at the nature of work as it now is in certain sectors of the petroleum, petro-chemical, and
other industries, where quite drastic changes have taken
place in the recent past following the adoption of
'capital-intensive' economic philosophies on the one hand,
and the production engineering technologies of continuous process control, on the other. (The volume
edited by Edwards and Lees, 1974, provides perhaps the
most adequate overview.)

Now whilst we might debate at some length the
merits of economic philosophies, or the desirability of
technologies, we should recognise that there are powerful people who believe that the capital-intensive, continuous, industrial production process is 'a good
thing'. And we should seriously consider the possibility that more and more industries will be cast into
the capital-intensive continuous process mould.

If one looks at the work of operators in a large,
modern, petro-chemical complex, physical labour is
scarcely required, if at all. Perceptual-motor skills,

(in which considerable investments of psychological
research have been made), are occasionally required, but
these disappear as increasingly accurate servo-mechanisms
are developed.   There is possibly more clerical work
than ten years ago, such as record keeping, making
calculations from production schedules and the like.
However, the most crucial and difficult components of
the job are relatively recent and involve problem solving and decision making, sometimes of a very high order.
For instance, on rare occasions the operator will be
required rapidly to interpret an array of alarms and
other indications, to distinguish which of several
failures, such as pumps, valves, steam supplies, compres-
sors, and the like, has occurred, and will shutdown the
plant, perhaps even blow up the plant, if it is not
quickly identified and remedied.

        I will return to the problems of enabling oper-
ators to perform this sort of task.   For the time
being, I would just draw your attention to two features
of these tasks which give rise to serious concern whenever they are encountered.   First of all if the operator
fails to cope, the costs of 'down time' in a capital-
intensive plant can, by definition, be massive and, of
course, the costs of the kind of disaster which might
result in some industries are immeasurable.   It is
the unacceptable costs of down time, not to speak of
hazards, which has been the driving force behind the
work on electronics trouble shooting in aerospace industries and in other agencies responsible for sophisticated control systems - the kind of work which Dr. Bond
will be speaking about.   The unacceptable hazard of an
operator failing to cope also looms large in nuclear
power stations, and is a central pre-occupation in Dr.
Rasmussen's contribution.

        The second feature of this sort of task which con-
cerns Rasmussen, me and, possibly, Bond too, is the
infrequency with which these tasks occur.   The infrequency is reassuring, in the sense that holocausts are
not daily occurrences and our long term survival on the
planet remains in principle possible.   However for the
operator who has to learn to cope with these infrequent,
improbable and sometimes, from his point of view, completely novel situations, these are formidable tasks.
Not surprisingly, people who currently tackle these
tasks tend to be the more able and intelligent members
of the work force, and may indeed only attain their jobs
after various formal and informal selection procedures.

        So my thesis is that work in the last quarter of
the 20th century will place increasing demands on intellectual capabilities and that one crucial contribution
which might be made by psychology, depends on how

successfully it can prescribe ways which enable people
of a wide range of ability to perform difficult cognitive tasks. Just how difficult these tasks may be,
compared with the mini-tasks of the psychological laboratory, is illustrated in the paper by Shepherd and
Duncan. If my thesis is correct, then it is somewhat
paradoxical that those psychologists and social scientists who are most concerned with the nature and quality
of working life now and in the future are, for the most
part, interested not in the cognitive features of tasks,
but rather, indeed almost exclusively, in the affective
domain.

Some of the prognostications which one hears about
the impact of micro-electronic technology make matters
worse rather than better. For example, how often have
we heard that the new technology will make tasks simpler?
I do not deny that in principle the new technology has
the potential to do this. But in practice I believe
that, combined with the harsh pressures of economic
reality, micro-processors will not be developed to make
tasks simpler; rather they will be developed to make
simple tasks disappear.

Political and social pressures may, in the event,
drastically alter the extent to which people are required to work. Fully recognising such possibilities,
my purpose in this paper is to establish the constraints
on change, if the trend towards difficult cognitive tasks
continues. Specifically I shall address two questions:

(i) what can psychology contribute to enable people to
     master the cognitive difficulties presented by
     advanced industrial systems;

(ii) need the difficult cognitive tasks of the future
     remain only within the reach of a more able,
     intelligent minority?

FAULT FINDING TASKS - THE ENABLING PROBLEM

Automatic Fault Location

In the first place, production engineers in any
capital-intensive continuous process plant face a
dilemma: to include or exclude the human operator? On
the one hand, human fault diagnosis can often be shown
to be inferior to an automated fault diagnostic system.
On the other hand the automaton will fail to diagnose
rare or unexpected faults if, as is usually the case,
they are not completely specified by its decision rules,
whereas a versatile human might have more success.

Versatility

It is known that long experience may enable, but
certainly does not guarantee, the acquisition of versatile fault diagnostic skill.   So the question arises
as to what sort of training might possibly enable people
to learn fault diagnosis?   This has proved to be a difficult question in several contexts.   My own research,
to which I now turn, has made progress but the task is
far from completed.   I hope the following excursion
into the applied psychology of problem solving will
serve to convey to you something of the difficulty of
the research which needs to be done and something of
the complexity of the skills involved.

Research Context

I will attempt first, to indicate briefly the
sorts of experiment on fault-finding which we undertake,
and second, to address the more general question of how
the acquisition of this problem solving skill, depends
on the nature and timing of information available to the
problem solver.

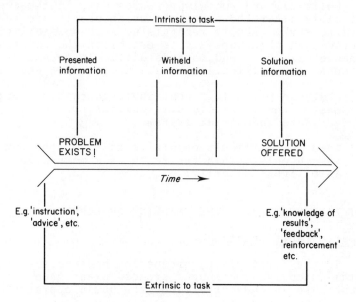

Figure 1.   The problem solving process - 1.

As to the nature of information, it is useful to
distinguish between information intrinsic and information extrinsic to the task;   and, in considering

timing, to distinguish between information provided before, after or during the problem solving process (Figure 1). We can think of information intrinsic to problem solving tasks as consisting of (i) information about the problem, and (ii) information about its solution.   Information about the problem (in the case of fault-finding, various indications of malfunction) may be either presented or withheld.

On the control room instrument panel in Figure 2, all the intrinsic problem information is presented. The panel presents, at the outset, the information necessary for the operator to identify which of several plant failures, for example, pumps, steam supplies, control valves, has produced this particular array of alarms and instrument indications.   Whether he is able successfully to do so is another matter.   For the moment, I wish only to distinguish the case of presented problem information from other tasks where information is withheld.   In such tasks as locating a leak in a pipe-network, or a short circuit in a radio receiver, information may be withheld; that is to say, the timing of this information depends on the problem solver who must engage in definite actions to obtain particular problem information.

Solution information intrinsic to fault-finding tasks is often limited to whether or not fault location was correct and sometimes to what the correct solution was.   Simply practising with only this intrinsic solution information may produce some learning.   However industrial training officers often provide other extrinsic information, e.g. about how the plant or equipment concerned works, information which they consider will facilitate fault-finding.   Note that this extrinsic information is usually provided before practice in solving fault-finding problems.

Findings when Problem Information is Presented

We have found that the provision, before problem solving practice of this, 'conventional', extrinsic information does little to improve performance on the control panel task, whereas providing information about how experienced operators construe plant functions substantially improves trainees' subsequent achievement. This latter information is more 'strategic', in the sense that it specifies to some extent which indications to seek in what sequence.   In particular this information improves the trainee's ability to solve fault-finding problems which he has not previously encountered during training, i.e. it facilitates a more general fault-finding skill - conceivably one which might enable

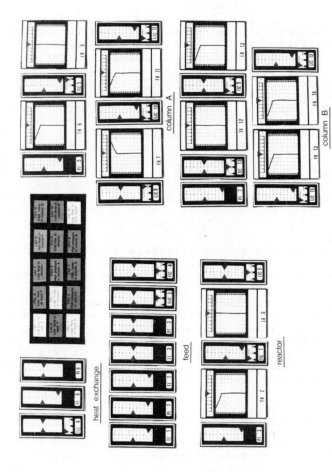

Figure 2.   A simulated instrument panel during plant failure.

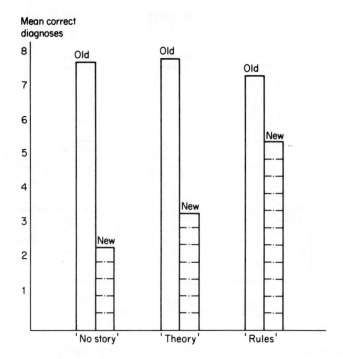

Figure 3.   Fault diagnosis following three training
             .regimes.

the human operator, confronted with an unforeseen emergency or contingency, to avert an economic or social
catastrophe (Shepherd et al., 1977).

    With hindsight, the timing of information in this
study may not have been ideal.   Because all the intrinsic problem information - the various indications - is
presented from the outset, the extent to which the
operator applies any prior instruction, about which indications to seek in what order, is uncertain when he
comes to practise problem solving;   nor can we readily
ensure thatthis instruction will not be ignored to a
greater or lesser degree.

    However, returning to the case of tasks in which
intrinsic problem information is withheld rather than
presented, it is possible to extend extrinsic information from interventions before and after problem
solving practice to interventions during the course of
the problem solving process.   Specifically we can
advise the subject about the 'efficiency' of consulting
the various indications he may wish to consult;   and,
more generally, provide information about the quality of

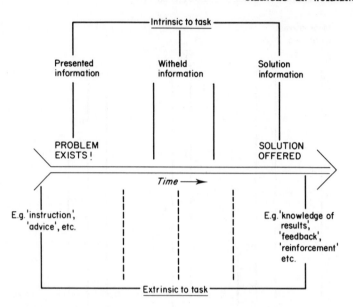

Figure 4.   The problem solving process - 2.

the questions or moves he may consider during the course
of problem solution.

In passing, it seems that this approach may also be
used, with advantage, in tasks, where all or a lot of
the problem information is presented, like the control
panel task.   We now have some evidence that, for
training purposes, presented information may be withheld
and that subjects can later transfer to problem solving
with information presented, as in the original task
(Marshall et al., 1978).

Extrinsic 'Strategic' Information

To return, then, to providing extrinsic strategic
information, when intrinsic problem information is withheld, we were interested in the effects of informing the
subject, when he asks a 'redundant question' or an 'extra
question' or makes a 'premature diagnosis' (Duncan, 1977)
- see Figure 5.

To illustrate the use of these terms, consider the
problem solving task in Figure 6.   The task is to discover which of several factories is the source of
pollution in an effluent processing plant by asking
various questions about the state of a river.   At any
stage in the solution of a problem there will always be

PREMATURE DIAGNOSIS   CFS > 1

REDUNDANT QUESTION   CFS > 1   and unchanged

EXTRA QUESTION   CFS = 1

CFS or "Consistent Fault Set" is the set of
faults consistent with information so far provided.

Figure 5.   Indices of problem solving based on consistent
            fault set.

		Indicators			
	FD	LI	AP	SO	SM	CR

FACTORIES

	FD	LI	AP	SO	SM	CR
Bedlington Factory	N	AV	FR	NO	OK	Y
Oxley Refinery	Y	AV	C	FW	OK	BR
Shipham Works	N	AV	FR	FW	OK	BR
Denton Factory	N	AV	FR	NO	BD	Y
Eltham Plant	N	AV	FR	FW	OK	CL

INDICATOR   POSSIBLE READINGS

FD = Fish dead   N = No   Y = Yes
LI = Lime   AV = Average
AP = Appearance   FR = Frothy   C = Clear
SO = Solids   NO = None   FW = Few
SM = Smell   OK = OK   BD = Bad
CO = Colour   Y = Yellow   BR = Brown
                                         CL = Colourless

Figure 6.   Fault symptom matrix for the effluent
            contamination problem

a set of faults consistent with the information which
has thus far been provided - the consistent fault set
(CFS). To what extent the subject is aware of CFS, is
of course, a matter for conjecture. Indeed, the aim is
to try to make him aware that solving the problem consists in reducing the consistent fault set to one in an
efficient way.

Suppose that in trying to decide which of these
factories has produced a polluted state in the river,
the problem solver has established that there are no
dead fish in the river and that its colour is yellow.
The consistent fault set contains two factories, DENTON
and BEDLINGTON. Now suppose that, on the strength of
'no dead fish' and 'yellow', the operator puts forward
the diagnosis that DENTON is the factory to blame.
This is a 'premature diagnosis', in terms of our definition, because the consistent fault set is greater than
one.

If at this stage of problem solving, the subject
asks about lead compounds, this is an instance of a
'redundant question'. Whichever of the two factories
is to blame, the answer will be 'yes' - consistent fault
set remains two.

If, however, the question next asked is 'smell?'
and the answer is 'OK', consistent fault set is now one.

The only solution consistent with the indications
'no dead fish', 'yellow colour' and 'smell OK' is that
BEDLINGTON factory is at fault. Consistent fault set
is now one. It is at this point that the subject may
ask an 'extra question', for example, he may ask the
question: 'are there solids?' and be told 'no'. Any
further questions will now be extra by definition since
consistent fault set is one and cannot be less.

Effects of 'Strategic' Information when Problem
Information is Withheld

To provide extrinsic information of this strategic
kind during problem solution we employ a computer
(Brooke et al., 1978). When the subject asks a redundant question the computer terminal demonstrates graphi-
cally that the consistent fault set will not be reduced,
no matter what the answer to the question might turn
out to be and, in that case, the subject has the option
to choose another question instead. If the subject
proposes a premature diagnosis, the terminal indicates
that consistent fault set is greater than one, that
there is more than one possibility! Finally, if the
trainee asks an extra question he is informed that

consistent fault set is now equal to one, and that he
has enough information to solve the problem, that is, to
locate the fault.

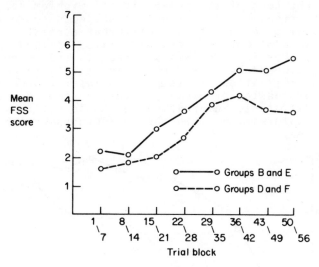

Figure 7.   Fault diagnoses (FSS: first shot success)
             during training.

        Figure 7 illustrates the effect, on the number of
correct solutions, of providing extrinsic information
of this strategic type during problem solving.   The
solid line indicates the progress of subjects who had
this extrinsic information provided by the computer,
but only during the first 30 problems - over which this
computer help was gradually 'faded out'.   The broken
line represents a comparable group of subjects who
received no such help.   Both groups received intrinsic
information about the correctness or otherwise of their
solutions - as operators would in reality.

        It seems, then, that providing extrinsic infor-
mation of this strategic kind, during problem solving,
has (i) improved the accuracy of solutions and (ii), more
importantly, continued to do so after provision of this
help ceased (that is to say after the 30th problem).

        Now the strategic information to which this effect
is attributable is general to all problems of this form.
So the interesting question is whether subjects have
learned a skill which is general, and which transfers
from one context to another.   To answer this question
we used a second task which is formally the same as
the effluent processing task.   In this task the subject
has to identify (instead of which fault) which person

the computer is 'thinking of', by asking questions about the unknown person's age, marital status and so forth.

So the test of the generality of problem solving skill, the transfer task, requires subjects to solve the same kind of problem but in a different context.   (By the way, some of our subjects were first trained on effluent processing problems and then tested on people identification problems - others were first trained on people identification problems, then later tested on effluent processing problems.)   But, no one received extrinsic strategic information on the second task, only intrinsic information as to the correctness or otherwise of solutions.

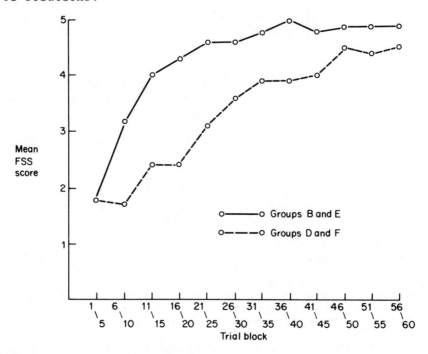

Figure 8.   Correct diagnoses (FSS: first shot success) on the transfer task.

Again the solid line in Figure 8 refers to subjects who received strategic information (during the earlier training task) and the broken line to those subjects who did not.   The important point is that strategic information was only given during the earlier training task and not during the solution of these problems.   So it seems reasonable to conclude that the effects of providing general strategic information, during the process of problem solution at the earlier training stage,

persists at this later stage when subjects learn to
solve problems in a quite different context.

DIFFERENCES IN ABILITY AND PROBLEM SOLVING

        I now turn to the second question I posed, namely
how may less able or less intelligent people be enabled
to solve difficult cognitive tasks, in particular, fault
diagnostic tasks.   The subjects or trainees in the
research I have just described have been a mixed bag
including, at the lower end of the range, apprentices
with one or two CSE passes.   In the course of our work
for the industry, we probably only encounter people in
the top 30% of the ability range in the general population.   Whether the techniques of instruction I have
described could be extended downwards, say, by providing
more practice or refining explanations, is problematic.
The results to date with abler people are in any case
far from perfect.

        I shall nevertheless be concerned in future work
with just how far we can extend the ability range of
subjects consistent with acceptable attainment.   I
fear, however, that at some point it may be necessary to
resort to rather different training procedures, procedures which are algorithmic and specific and which can
hardly be expected to favour versatility.   Any capabilities thus acquired would be of limited scope.   The
possibility which immediately comes to mind is the use
of decision trees to turn the fault diagnostic problem
into a procedure.

        Figure 9, for example, is a decision tree which
only requires trainees to learn how to read instruments.
Provided they can do this, the tree leads them to identify the failure, in this case, in a distillation-reactor
system.   But such devices as this decision tree may so
evidently 'de-skill' the task that they create other
problems, for instance persons using them may find this
demeaning and consequently take little interest in the
task, become careless, and so forth.   This may be
prevented to some extent by writing the decision tree
in more general language.   I have done this for the
tree in Figure 9 (Duncan, 1974), and M.J. Gray has developed a similarly general tree (Figure 10) which applies
to the fault finding of the crude distillation unit in
oil refineries (Duncan and Gray, 1975).

        The use of general language to extend the scope of
a decision tree seems to make it more interesting to use.
Nevertheless the scope of any such device is still restricted to the set of faults which it discriminates.
To cope adequately with the fault diagnosis problems in

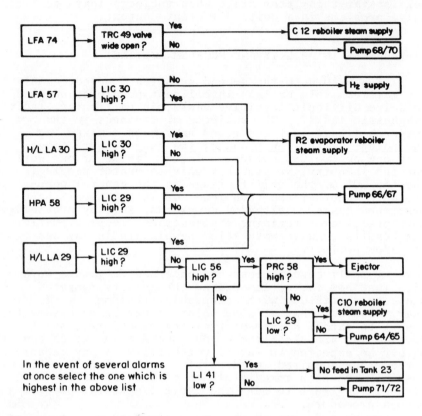

Figure 9.   Decision tree for fault diagnosis in an
             acid purification plant.

plants of the future, one can envisage diagnostic tasks
being shared between, on the one hand, people using
restricted algorithmic procedures and, on the other,
people trained to apply more general strategies along
the lines described earlier in the paper.   However
such a combination of an explicitly intellectual élite
and 'the rest' might create new human relations problems of an unhappy kind.   Moreover 'the rest' would
always be vulnerable in a way the élite would not.
The temptation would always exist to replace 'the rest'
by automata, since their capability is algorithmic and
its scope defined.   The élite, however, would face no
such threats of displacement.

CONCLUSION

        In conclusion, let me attempt to provoke you by

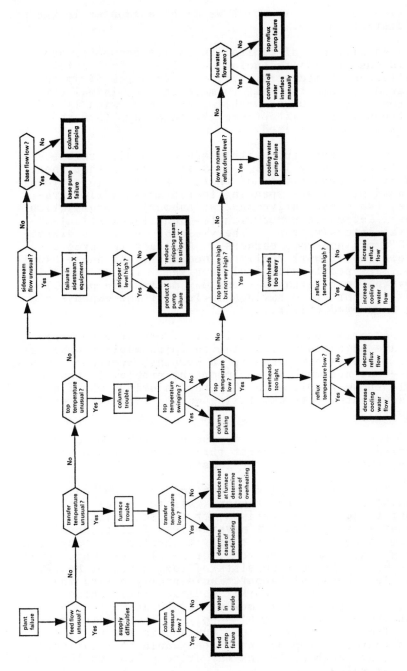

Figure 10.   Decision tree for diagnosing faults in crude distillation units.

the kinds of scenario which we might encounter in the not
too distant future.

1.   An alliance of capital-intensive economics and
continuous process technologies rules.   Only a few,
intellectual élite work, i.e. receive wages (I am not
prepared to commit myself to more than a minimal contractual definition of work).   What provision is made
for the majority without wages?   Who pays them and
how is the money raised?

2.   Governments rule with planned and discernible
effects on working life.   (I still believe that there
is a finite probability of that, despite a professional
and academic career spanning four British administra-
tions, two Conservative and two Labour).   Legislation
imposes levies in proportion to each organization's
capital-intensiveness.   The yield of levies is distributed among non-wage earners.   At least two problems
arise: (a) if work really is necessary for human happiness, many people will feel deprived;   (b) an unstable
situation, e.g. organizations may manipulate payroll
size for short term savings in levy at the expense of
long term productivity.

3.   A variation of Scenario 2.   Permitted hours of
work are adjusted by legislation (presumably downwards),
so if there is any pleasure in working, everyone can have
some - but not much.   An important problem is how to
enable those people, probably the majority, who find
the new, intellectually taxing work difficult to perform
adequately.

    Lastly, there is of course a scenario of a rather
different kind.   The first three scenarios are all
energy-hungry, to   say the least.

4.   The energy problem is not solved.   Dedicated
administrators and politicians fail to muster adequate
resources for the scientists, or the scientists are
adequately supported but nevertheless fail to develop
in time a nuclear fusion energy technology.   Many problems are avoided.   Everyone, or nearly everyone, can be
employed.   The work consists of long hours of heavy,
unskilled, physical labour, incidentally easing the
problems of defining 'work', and the prime source of
energy becomes as it formerly was, human muscle, of
which there is a plentiful supply.   The limited evidence from such communities, now and in the past, suggests that this employment system would be relatively
stable, although questions may arise as to its long term
survival value.

REFERENCES

Brooke, J.B., Duncan, K.D. and Marshall, E.C. (1978).
'Interactive instruction in solving fault-
finding problems', International Journal of Man-
Machine Studies, 10, 603-611.

Duncan, K.D. (1974). 'Analytical Techniques in Training
Design', in The Human Operator in Process Control
(Eds. E. Edwards and F.P. Lees), London, Taylor
and Francis.

Duncan, K.D. (1977). 'Plans, Human Problem Solving
and Industrial Process Control', Inaugural Lecture,
Department of Applied Psychology, University of
Wales Institute of Science and Technology.

Duncan, K.D. and Gray, M.J. (1975). 'An evaluation of
a fault-finding training course for refinery
process operators', Journal of Occupational Psychology, 48, 199-218.

Edwards, E. and Lees, F.P. (1974). The Human Operator
in Process Control, London, Taylor and Francis.

Marshall, E.C. and Duncan, K.D. (1978). 'Presented
versus withheld and static versus dynamic information in process control training', Proceedings
of NATO Conference on Visual Presentation of
Information, Het Vennenbos, Netherlands.

Shepherd, A., Marshall, E.C., Turner, Ann and Duncan,
K.D. (1977). 'Diagnosis of plant failures from
a control panel: a comparison of three training
methods', Ergonomics, 20, 347-361.

Changes in Working Life
Edited by K.D. Duncan, M.M. Gruneberg, and D. Wallis
© 1980 John Wiley & Sons Ltd

Chapter 7

What Can Be Learned From Human Error Reports?

J. RASMUSSEN

INTRODUCTION

The purpose of the present contribution is to raise a discussion on the role and responsibilities of designers and operators of large and complex industrial installations. Several lines of technological development make me uneasy since there is ample evidence that the traditional problem, with designers relying on Procrustes' beds of training and instruction rather than on a fit of the systems to natural man, is getting increasingly serious. The lines of technological developments I have in mind are well known and often discussed, but should be mentioned here briefly to set the stage for the following discussion.

First of all, the general trend in the industrial development is a rapid and steady growth in centralization and, consequently, in the size and complexity of the systems. Large installations typically imply large consequences of faults and maloperation. Furthermore, highly optimized operation means that the operating staff at times has to navigate through the narrow strait between large loss of production and serious damage to equipment and personnel. Large installations must be designed for a very low probability of the release of inherent potentials for loss, and the limits of freedom for operators are consequently tight and strictly controlled. At the same time, operators are maintained in the system because they are flexible, can learn and do adapt to the peculiarities of the installation, and thus they are expected to plug the holes in the designer's imagination. These conditions can only be met if the design is based on a systematic set of criteria derived from risk consideration as well as from consideration of inherent human properties. What bothers me is that the explanations of major

industrial incidents in terms of human errors are often
based on superficial analyses which result in ad hoc
changes of the system and, almost invariably, in recommendations for better training together with 'stricter
administrative control of the adherence to instructions'.
Needless to say, we have good evidence that this will
not solve the problem - especially when at the same time
the acceptable probability of the release of potential
accidents is steadily decreasing.

Another feature of the technological development
is the rapid increase in the level of automation made
possible by the flexibility of the process computer.
The effect is a drastic increase in the automation of
sequence control for plant start-up, optimization and
protective functions.   It is frequently argued that
automation removes the operators' feel for the process,
thus causing problems when his intervention is needed
in case of maloperation.   I am not convinced that the
skills developed during normal operation are a satisfactory basis for infrequent improvisation.   Instead,
the operator's task and work organisation should be
restructured to ensure that he has the necessary knowledge available when abnormal situations demand his
understanding of the system's physical functioning.
Another problem is connected with the fact that high
levels of automation necessitate the embedding of a
large number of control decisions taken by the designer
in the functions of the control system.   This has at
least two important consequences.   First, the functions
of the control system are much more difficult for the
operators to understand, since its behaviour cannot be
inferred from a knowledge of its physical structure but
only if the control decisions during design are known
and remembered.   Secondly, operators and designers are
in a situation involving a complex sharing of responsibility which can lead to conflicts in infrequent, complex situations.   Therefore, in a situation with
increased public concern about safety of industrial
installations and rapidly increasing but badly defined
demands on the performance of the operating staff, it
seems important to reinterpret the concepts of 'human
error' and its role in system design strategies.

HUMAN ERRORS

When compared with technical components, human
operators have some peculiar features which must be
analysed more closely to see whether the present general
attitude towards faults and errors is reasonable and
expedient.   How are faults and errors defined?   Basically they are defined as causes of unfulfilled purposes.
If the performance of a system is below standard, it is

necessary to back-track the causal chain to find the
causes. How far back to seek is a rather open question;
generally, the search will stop when one or more changes
are found which are familiar and therefore acceptable
as explanations, and to which something can be done for
correction.

In the case of a technical break-down, the failure
of a component is generally accepted at the level where
replacement is convenient. In some cases, however,
component failure will not be found to be an acceptable
cause; for example, if it occurs too frequently, or if
the fault is intermittent. In such cases, the search
will often continue to find an external cause of the component's malfunction. In summary, the characteristics
of a fault are: it is the cause of deviation from a
standard; the causal path back from this effect is
passable; it is accepted as a familiar and therefore
reasonable explanation; and a cure is known. In all
these respects, the human operator is in an unlucky
position. Due to human complexity, it is generally
very difficult to 'pass through' a person in causal
explanations, at least it takes a very careful analysis
of the work conditions in each specific case by a competent work psychologist - and they are rarely engaged in
such analysis. In addition, it is generally accepted
that 'it is human to err' and finally, you can always
ask people to 'try harder'. However, to stress the
analogy, human errors can be compared with intermittent
faults in an electronic system. For such faults, you
will often stick to the deterministic explanation and
look for external causes such as noise interference.
The remedy would be to remove the noise or make the
equipment more noise immune. In the human case, the
corresponding cure would be to rearrange the work situation to bring about a better fit to human resources
and mechanisms. This solution has since long been
advocated by Swain (see for instance Swain, 1972) in his
critique of the traditional motivational programs, but
still today we witness the problems safety authorities
have in keeping operators following the instructed procedures.

If we do not consider emotional or legal aspects
of guilt, we can relax with respect to the question as to
whether system malfunction is caused by human error or by
man-machine misfit due to inappropriate design. Instead,
we can consider the possibility of reducing the number of
misfits in any case by a proper design of work conditions
and effective use of new technology for man-machine interface design. From this point of view it is of interest
to see whether the previously reported cases of such misfits represent a haphazard collection of individual
events, or whether some general trends can be found which

are related to normal psychological mechanisms.   In
addition, it is worth while to evaluate whether reasonably general criteria for system design can be generated to decrease the potential for man-machine misfits.

FINDINGS FROM REVIEW OF CASE REPORTS

     What should one look for in such reports to get
information in a reasonable format?   Man is an extremely
flexible and adaptive behavioural system and in the
general case he will develop a skill and pattern of performance which fit the peculiarities of a system in an
effective way.   The interaction can be seen as a complex, multidimensional demand/resource fit.   To discuss
the misfits and evaluate means for improvement, it is
more important to find the nature or dimensions of the
misfits than to identify their causes.   In other words,
it is necessary to find what went wrong rather than why.
Fortunately, to identify the error modes in this way from
case reports is much more realistic than to trace the
different causal conditions, since a simpler and a more
structured pattern can be expected if the detailed
causal events or circumstances are not sought.   In
the following, there is reference to events and reports
from nuclear power plants for the simple reason that
legal requirements exist for systematic reporting.   Consequently a very valuable data base is emerging in this
area.   Furthermore, very convenient access can be made,
since reports are published and continuously updated
(Nuclear Power Experience, 1978).

     A preliminary review of a number of reports from
this source has been made, not to extract valid statistical information, but to highlight the general pattern.
The first indication from a review of cases in the
category of 'Operational Problems, Miscellaneous',which
include most of the operator errors, is that about twice
as many reports originate from work out in the plant
compared with work in the control rooms, and that the
major contributors are events originating from test and
calibration and from repair and modification.   It is
therefore reasonable to focus on events in the categories test/calibration and repair/maintenance, which
are important categories in highly automated systems,
since the safety of such installations to a large extent
depends upon the potential for latent faults in protective systems.

     The immediate impression one gets when reviewing a
large number of case reports is that they are not reporting the errors people commit, but the errors which are
not corrected because they have an effect that is either
irreversible or not immediately apparent to the person

himself.   It is in a way trivial that people do correct
the errors they can see but, on the other hand, it means
that the incident reports give a picture of human variability which is heavily biased by the potential for feedback correction in the actual work situation.   Generally
speaking, human errors are the inevitable side effect of
human adaptability.   Adaptation basically depends on
variability and selection;   unsuccessful trials manifest
themselves as errors only when selection is ineffective
due to irreversible or latent effects.

From the Nuclear Power Experience compilation, a
little over one hundred cases classed as technician's
errors during test and calibration have been reviewed.
The most significant categories of error modes found in
this task are indicated in Table 1.   A principal observation is the major contribution of omissions of steps
in the task sequence which are functionally isolated
from the substance of the task as expressed by a name
like 'test' or 'calibration'.   Typical samples are
omitted returns of switches and valves from test to
operation;   no verification of the operation of stand-by
equipment before disconnecting operating equipment for
test;   and omissions of purely administrative tasks.
The fact that the omitted steps are unrelated to the
verbal label of the task may be a condition directly
contributing to their frequency.   Analysis of industrial fires led Whorf (1956) to the conclusion that 'the
name of a situation affects behaviour'.   Two other
major categories of error are related to simple mistakes
among alternatives, such as up/down;   plus/minus;
decreasing/increasing, etc.;   and to operational
'improvement' in procedures either spontaneously or in
response to changes in work conditions.   These three
categories of human error contribute 80-90% of the 110
cases of errors during test and calibration which have
been reviewed, and the picture has been found very similar for 40 cases classed as errors during repair and
modification.   The point in the present context will be
that the increasing size of process plants with their
safety depending upon automatic protection makes it
more and more unacceptable to have work conditions for
the maintenance staff which cannot tolerate simple and
quite natural human variability.   The feed-back from
operating experience to design of work situation seems
to be quite unsatisfactory considering the available
empirical data.

To have an indication as to whether this conclusion is specific for maintenance and repair or typical
for the work situation in general, some 200 cases in
the wider category of 'Operational problems' were
reviewed and the findings are illustrated in Tables 2
and 3.

		Task Elements		
		Test circuit set-up	Adjustment calibration	Restoration of normal operation
OMISSIONS	Functionally isolated acts	12		50
	Others	1	2	1
ERRORS IN TASK	Improvization insufficient knowledge	2		
	Secondary conditions not cons.	3	3	1
	Misinterpretation	2	2	
	Mistakes among alternatives	4	13	3
	Manual variability 'clumsiness'	1	2	
EXTRANEOUS ACTS	Topographic misorientation	3		
	'Clumsiness'	1		

<u>Table 1</u>.   Human error modes in 111 cases from test and calibration in nuclear power plants.

        In this general category, repair, maintenance and test again play a major role.   Probably, these tasks have more ill-structured conditions and more potential for errors, the effect of which are less apparent to the man himself than say control tasks.   The errors of the 'Operational Problems' reports are categorized according to their mode, i.e., what was wrong, not why.   The classes were formed iteratively during the review. Omission of functionally isolated acts is again a major contribution.   To find a pattern, the distribution across tasks was tabulated (Table 2), but, apart from 'omission of functionally isolated acts in test and repair', the pattern does not present any clear structure.   However, when the errors are distributed according to their dependence on the mental operations implied in the task

Monitoring and inspection	Supervisory control	Manual operation and control	Inventory control	Test and calibration	Repair and modification	Administrative task	Management, staff planning	Various; not mentioned	TASK / ERROR MODE	Distribution across error modes
3	13	17	30	47	60	4	13	13	Distribution across tasks	200
-	-	-	-	-	1	1	-	1	Absent-mindedness	3
1	3	-	1	-	1	-	-	-	Familiar association	6
-	2	-	3	1	-	-	4	-	Alertness low	10
-	1	3	5	21	31	1	1	5	Omission of functionally isolated act	68
-	1	2	3	7	4	-	-	-	Omissions - other	17
-	1	1	4	3	-	-	1	1	Mistakes among alternatives	11
1	1	2	2	2	-	1	1	-	Expect, assume - rather than observe	10
-	1	1	4	1	7	-	1	-	Side effect not adequately considered	15
1	2	2	2	5	4	1	3	-	Latent conditions not adequately considered	20
-	-	1	1	3	4	-	-	1	Manual variability, lack of precision	10
-	-	2	2	2	3	-	-	1	Topographic, spatial orientation weak	10
-	1	3	3	2	5	-	2	4	Various; not mentioned	20

Table 2.   Distribution across task and human error mode of 200 reports of 'operational problems' in in nuclear power plants.

(Table 3), a more clear pattern emerges: In the majority of the cases the people have identified the system state correctly; they have pursued a proper goal and selected the related task; but they have failed to

Dectection of demand	Observation - communication	Identification of system state	Goal - strategic decision	Target - tactic system state	Task - determine, select	Procedure - plan, recall	Execution	Various	ERROR MODE	Distribution across error modes
11	12	17	-	5	-	117	36	2	Distribution across mental task phase	200
-	1	1	-	-	-	-	1	-	Absent-mindedness	3
-	-	5	-	1	-	-	-	-	Familiar association	6
6	2	-	-	-	-	1	1	-	Alertness low	10
1	-	-	-	-	-	65	2	-	Omission of functionally isolated act	68
1	2	-	-	1	-	12	1	-	Omissions - others	17
-	1	-	-	-	-	1	9	-	Mistakes among alternatives	11
-	4	3	-	-	-	3	-	-	Expect, assume - rather than observe	10
-	-	1	-	1	-	13	-	-	Side effect not adequately considered	15
-	-	5	-	-	-	15	-	-	Latent conditions not adequately considered	20
-	-	-	-	-	-	-	10	-	Manual variability, lack of precision	10
-	-	-	-	-	-	-	10	-	Topographic, spatial orient. weak	10
3	2	2	-	2	-	7	2	2	Various; not mentioned	20

Table 3. Distribution across mental task phase and error mode of 200 reports of 'operational problems' in nuclear power plants.

carry through a proper procedural sequence or failed in the manual operations. In other words, people typically know what to do and when, but not always how.

Besides the reccurrence of the omissions, there

is a major contribution in the erroneous procedures
from inadequate consideration of latent causes or
inappropriate side effects in selecting procedural
steps.

These two kinds of error are very probably related
to difficulty of the human mind to keep track of the
spread of events in the complex causal net of a technical system. Constructive recall of a procedure, or
modification of a procedure to fit special circumstances,
demands a simultaneous consideration of several potential
causal conditions and possible side effects of the
intended actions. This is difficult for unsupported,
linear natural language reasoning due to the limitations
of working memory.

The importance of this category reflects back on
the results of some of our previous studies (Rasmussen
and Jensen, 1974).   From an analysis of verbal proto-
cols recording the mental procedures of electronic
repair technicians we found several principles in
operation for minimising memory load: the adopted
strategies allowed the technicians to process and dis-
card observations individually. The strategy of least
resistance was used so that a familiar step or act
having only a small effect in the proper direction was
chosen without consideration of possibly more effective steps. Finally, the effect of a 'point of no
return' caused information observed after a decision to
have very little probability of initiating a reconsi-
deration of the prior decision. These heuristics of
the mental strategies would lead to precisely the difficulties in using linear thought in causal nets which
were found in the event reports.

The point to make in the present discussion is
that general training and stricter administrative control are more formal than real counter-measures against
these modes of man-machine misfits. Whatever is the
cause of the specific individual case: a change in work
conditions; a spontaneous slip of memory; high work
load; distriction, etc., etc.; then the resulting
margin to misfit between situation and man can be
increased by giving the operator better access to information about the underlying causal net so as to improve improvisation and recall. In particular, the
margin can be increased by making the effect of the
operator's activity directly observable and reversible,
that is to say, by using the feed-back design concept
which is the normal way to cope with variability in a
technical design context.

Difficulties with proper consideration of complex
causal nets are enhanced when operators are controlling

process plants from control consoles.   Information on
the actual state of affairs in the complex causal net
of the process which is invisible to the operators, is
typically presented to the operator as magnitudes of
physical variables.   Natural language reasoning is,
however, not based on nets of relations among variables,
but upon linear sequences of events in a system of interacting components or functions.   To circumvent the need
for mental effort to derive states and events from the
sets of variables and their relations, indications of
variables which are typical for the normal events and
states are generally adopted by process operators as
convenient signs for the presence of such familiar operational states in the system.   This is a very effective and mentally economic strategy during normal and
familiar periods, but leads the operator into traps
when changes in plant conditions are not adequately reflected in his system of signs.   Such mental traps often
contribute significantly to the operator's misidentifi-
cation of unfamiliar, complex plant states.   When abnormal tasks or plant states demand counter-measures from
human operators, a shift in the mental work strategies
and the nature of the underlying internal representation of plant properties is needed by the operators,
and their dependence on characteristic signs leads to
very typical effects.   The use of signs basically
means that information from the system is not really
observed, but is obtained by 'asking questions' which are
heavily biased by expectations based on a set of well-
known situations.   Examples are found in the cases of
Table 3 under errors in observation and identification,
but more illustrative cases are found in reports from
analyses of major accidents which frequently contain a
remark about operators not making simple functional
inferences from their instrument readings (for examples,
see Rasmussen, 1978).

    Again, these kinds of difficulties cannot be effec-
tively counteracted by administrative measures or by
better training.   In large installations, we also have
to consider rare events for which operators cannot be
prepared by trained procedures.   In such cases, operators have to generate proper procedures by functional
evaluation and causal reasoning based on knowledge about
system properties.   For this task he clearly needs support to prevent that he will be trained to use individual
indicators as representative signs during normal routines.   Quantitative signals representing measured
physical variables are suitable for data processing by
electronic control systems, and designers can process
sets of quantitative variables when their use of rules
and numerical relations is adequately supported by cal-
culators, graphs, tables and ample time.   To support
stressed operators during abnormal system operation, the

introduction of digital computers must be considered for
a complex and flexible transformation of the measured
physical variables into a consistent representation of
the internal state of the system which is suited for
unsupported natural language reasoning.   Representation
in terms of qualitative and relative representations of
states of components, systems and functions which interact by chains of events should be considered to counteract the misuse of convenient signs.   For the overall
functions of the plant, representations in terms of the
state of mass, energy and information flows can be very
effective for immediate perceptive identification of the
state of a causal net.   This solution is similar to
Beer's (1975) use of 'quantified flow charts' as means
of communication to workers in his cybernetic factories.
The key criterion behind this is the presentation of
information in the form of symbols which are directly
applicable in the operator's causal reasoning, not in
the form of convenient signs which have great affinity
with stored, stereotyped patterns and responses.

DESIGN FOR ERROR TOLERANCE

     To sum up the main points of this discussion and
their significance for design criteria, it may be illustrative to relate the different categories of 'human
errors' to a simple model of human performance.   In
Figure 1, three different categories of control of human
behaviour are distinguished, and their relation to the
human error categories from the previous sections is
indicated.   The modes of control of human behaviour are
important since the identification of an error depends
upon the specification of proper behaviour.   For human
actions, error can only be directly detected if an
explicit prescription for a sequence of actions is stated.
However, more often, the goal or effect of an activity
is the explicitly given norm while self-monitoring with
correction of inappropriate actions is tolerated without
classifying intermediate unsuccessful actions as being
erroneous.   It follows that a situation can invite
'errors' when the norm for judging the correctness of the
related behaviour does not also control the behaviour,
e.g., when goal controlled behaviour is judged by an
(ineffective) normative procedure.   The different modes
of control of human behaviour are therefore important
for considering criteria for a 'design for error tolerance'.   As shown in Figure 1, three levels of control
of human behaviour are relevant for the present context:
1. Sensori-motor-pattern controlled, skill-based behaviour; 2. Goal-oriented, rule-based behaviour;   3. Goal-
controlled, knowledge-based behaviour.

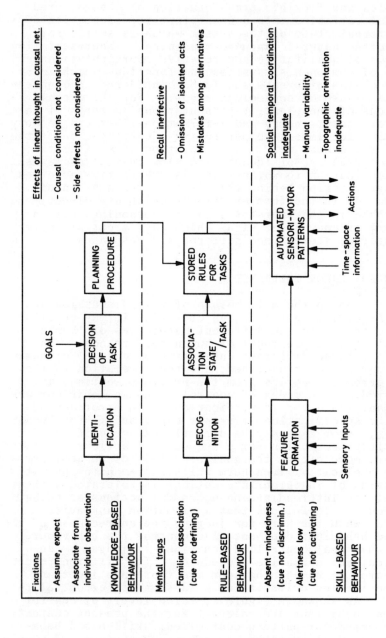

Figure 1.   Schematic illustration of categories of
human data processes and typical errors.

1. Sensori-motor Pattern Controlled and Automated Behaviour

This is controlled by the structure of the adaptive patterns stored in the nervous system. This means that behaviour is controlled by physiological laws governing the data processing structure, and the concept of error becomes meaningless. Inappropriate behaviour can only be explained by changes in the external world leading to a 'misfit' with the trained structure in the responding person. In this domain, errors cannot be counteracted by asking people to 'try harder' in adherence to instructions. If smooth, skilled performance with low probability of errors is to evolve, the work situation must be designed to facilitate good discrimination; i.e., patterns must be state defining, not convenient secondary cues or signs. This also relates to discrimination of situations which demand activation of higher level mental activities. Consequently, misfits in abnormal situations due to effective adaptation to normal system behaviour cannot reasonably be referred to as operator error.

2. Goal-oriented, Rule Controlled Behaviour

This is typical for less frequent tasks in a familiar work environment. A sequence of skilled actions or routines is controlled by stored rules associating states of the environment to familiar actions. Behaviour is not goal controlled directly, although inappropriate terminal states can lead to goal controlled feed-back corrections of errors which have observable and reversible effects. The rules underlying behaviour can be empirically derived from trial and error, they can be formed by causal reasoning, or they can be prescribed as formal work instructions. In this domain, errors will often be detected by their effect in terms of goal/terminal state discrepancies, but they will probably be judged against a normative rule or procedure.

The designer has to face two problems. One is to create work situations for the operating staff which lead to clear discrimination of (a) occurrences where goals are normative and operators are not only allowed to, but also expected to, generate and optimize efficient work procedures, and (b) occurrences where normative rules are effective on account of potential but latent risky conditions. In the latter case, the designer takes responsibility for correctness of the action sequence and he should support operators by proper cues for control of the sequence. When designers take control of a sequence of actions by instructions or by automatic sequence control, they face the other problem:

they have to arrange the work conditions of operators in
such a way as to maintain their understanding of reasons
and conditions for instructions and automatic functions
and an ability to judge their actual relevance, not only
to take over in some specific abnormal cases, but - just
as important - not to interfere because of a misinter-
pretation of the response of the automatic system.
Several cases can be referred to, when the consequences
were aggravated in an abnormal situation due to an irrelevant struggle between operator and automatic control.

3. Goal Controlled, Knowledge-based Behaviour

This is the level of intelligent problem solving
which should be the prominent reason for the presence of
human operators in an automated industrial plant.
Behaviour in this domain is activated in response to
unfamiliar demands from the system. The structure of
the activity is an evaluation of the situation and planning of a proper sequence of actions to pursue the goal,
and it depends upon fundamental knowledge on the processes, functions and anatomical structure of the system.
Apart from the problems already mentioned, i.e., supporting linear thought in a causal net and defining
responsibility (- when are the operators expected and
allowed to think and when not) there is an increasingly
important problem of keeping the operator's knowledge
base satisfactorily updated in large complex systems.
The generally proposed solution - to keep automation
level reasonably low - is probably not effective, since
this mostly implies activities for operators in level 2;
the solution must basically be to give the operating
staff technically qualifying tasks in idle periods to
prepare for their response to abnormal situations. In
many cases, this solution probably will presuppose a
change in organisational and educational structures.

In conclusion, when analysing causes of human
errors it is necessary to take into account the development of highly skilled routines during plant operation.
The control of human activity shifts from level 3 through
2 to 1 in case of self-instruction and from 2 to 1 when
an instructor or written procedures are active. This
leads to the situation that an event which will be called
a human error in early stages of training, cannot properly be so if it happens after highly skilled routines
have developed. This distinction has also been identified by Toulmin (1969): 'A man may be drilled to behave
in some required mode so effectively that he ends up by
doing so automatically, without having learned to notice
whether he is acting as required or not. Such behaviour
ceases to be rule-conforming: the concepts of a rule and
of mistakes or lapse cease to be relevant to it'.

DESIGN FOR RISK ANALYSABILITY

In addition to the need for error tolerance, the
increasing centralization and size of production units
lead to a demand for 'design for analysability'. The
potential for major losses, especially in terms of damage to persons and environment, gives rise to a design
target for safety which cannot be empirically verified
due to the extremely low acceptable probability of the
accidental chains of event.   Since direct empirical
evidence cannot be found, methods for analytical verifi-
faction of the design target are necessary.   The basic
idea in analytical risk evaluation is decomposition of
the rare chains of events for which the probability is
needed, into elements which are found frequently enough
in other contexts to make it realistic to obtain statistical information.   The technique is well developed for
reliability analysis of electronic equipment, and it is
under development for industrial risk analysis.
Presently, there is a trend towards the situation where
major industrial installations will not be accepted
unless the design targets for risk can be verified -
including the consequences of erroneous human performance.
Analytical prediction of human performance is only
feasible under certain restrictive assumptions and conditions and, consequently, the situation can be foreseen
when designers will have to accept these assumptions
and conditions as 'criteria for analysability' to be
used during plant conception.

The fundamental problem is to identify elements
of human performance which can be separated from their
context in a way so as to make collection of statistical
information on their quality and reliability meaningful.
To make transfer to other situations and contexts possible, attributes of psychologically similar work
situations must be defined to form the appropriate categories of errors and to identify the data sources to be
used for data collection schemes.   For this purpose,
the cause of human errors must be known or it will be
necessary to define 'similar situations' very narrowly.
In the current methods of human reliability analysis (for
a review, see Meister, 1971), performance elements are
generally defined with reference to their external effect
or purpose as 'task elements' which is acceptable only if
the attributes adopted to define task elements are precise enough to define also the characteristics of the
internal mode of control of operator behaviour.   This
cannot be practically realized in general reliability
data collection programs.   There is a need for a careful analysis of critical operator tasks to find adequate
design criteria and to define the attributes of performance elements for which a selective data collection
scheme can be devised.

Quite naturally, we have found (Rasmussen, 1978)
that 'criteria for design for analysability' reflect the
different modes of control of behaviour. The general
line of such criteria is based on the following considerations:

When a taks is designed to follow a normative procedure, the elements of the sequence should be cued individually to counteract systematic changes and 'optimization' and to identify separate task elements as categories for data collection.

When a task is allowed or expected to be goal-
controlled, this is presumably because adaptation and
learning are advantageous. The task sequence will
then be flexible and will depend upon the particular
circumstances. In this case, identification of task
elements for data collection is generally irrelevant
since they cannot be separated from their context in a
meaningful way. Analysis of goal controlled tasks is
more realistic if a feed-back concept is realized.
The task is designed so as to make the effect immediately observable and reversible, then the reliability
of the task can be evaluated from the frequency of opportunities for error together with an analysis of the
reliability of the error detection act.

Finally, if human mistakes and extraneous acts
are found to be significant contributors to irreversible
and unacceptable effects, the system should be made
error tolerant by introduction of interlocks or barriers,
since reliable data on the probability of such human acts
cannot be obtained in practice.

Generally, criteria for analysability will act in
unison with design for error tolerance. It will force
designers to consider more carefully the distinction
between situations where he takes control by normative
instructions and where he leaves control to the operator.
He will also have to consider in detail the conditions
for observability, reversibility and error tolerance.

CONCLUSION

The essence of this argument is that the development towards large, centralized installations has
now reached a state where the design and operation of
many systems can no longer be considered separate
activities which are effectively decoupled by a commissioning test period. Effective feed-back of operational
experience, especially concerning the co-performance of
system and staff during the entire plant life is important for acceptable systems design. Event reporting

schemes are existing/emerging in several areas and should
be used and extended more systematically.   Also transfer of information the other way should be improved.   To
cope with unplanned situations and to co-operate effectively with automatic instrumentation and control functions, operating staff needs much more systematic access
to the information base, performance criteria and decision strategies used by designers.   The use of computers
to develop a systematic data base during system design
and to give the operating staff effective access to this
data base during plant operation must be carefully considered.

REFERENCES

Beer, S. (1975).   'On Keeping our Science Together', in
        Trapple, R. and Hanika, F. de P. (Eds.), Progress
        in Cybernetics and Systems Research, Vol. 2, Hemi-
        sphere Publishing Corporation, Washington.

Nuclear Power Experience (1978).   Edited by Nuclear
        Power Experience Inc., P.O. Box 544, Encino,
        California, USA (The January 1978 state of the
        compilation was used).

Rasmussen, J. and Jensen, A. (1974).   'Mental Proce-
        dures in Real Life Tasks: A Case Study of Elec-
        tronic Trouble Shooting', Ergonomics, 1974, Vol.
        17, No. 3, 293-307.

Rasmussen, J. (1978).   'Notes on Human Error Analysis',
        in Apostolakis, G. and Volta, G. (Eds.), Pro-
        ceedings of the NATO Advanced Study Institute on
        Synthesis and Analysis Methods for Safety and
        Reliability Studies, SOGESTA, Italy, 1978, Plenum
        Press, London.

Swain, A. (1972).   'Design Techniques for Improving
        Human Performance in Production', Industrial and
        Commercial Techniques, London.

Toulmin, S. (1969).   'Concepts and the Explanation of
        Human Behaviour', in Mischel, T. (Ed.), Human
        Action. Conceptual and Empirical Issues, Academic
        Press, New York.

Whorf, B.L. (1956).   'The Relation of Habitual Thought
        and Behaviour to Language', in Carroll, J.B. (Ed.),
        Language, Thought and Reality, Selected Writings of
        Whorf, M.I.T. Press.

Changes in Working Life
Edited by K.D. Duncan, M.M. Gruneberg, and D. Wallis
© 1980 John Wiley & Sons Ltd

Chapter 8

Human Trouble Shooting in Very Complex Systems: An Application of Instructional Technology

N. A. BOND

It is nearly midnight in a data-processing center of a large bank. All during the day and evening, messengers have been delivering bags of financial paper to the center. The messengers have picked up the bags from the bank branches, from other banks, from corporate lock boxes around the city, and from government offices. Most of the items in the bags are checks of one kind or another, but there are also payroll listings, vouchers, tax forms, personnel records, and many kinds of branch-operations tab sheets.

The center is organized functionally. There is a 'check-killing' room, where checks are cancelled and charged to accounts. A 'service program room' prepares payroll and tax programs for outside firms; in this operation the bank performs computer services under subcontract. The data center also runs regular operating programs which update the financial picture of the central bank and of each branch; these are produced daily. Underlying all this is a mainframe computer and its many software packages. Manufactured in the medium-scale integrated technology of 1975, the mainframe itself is not very impressive physically; the central processor comprises only three cabinets. But there are tape and disc drives to feed the computer, along with several high-speed printers and video terminals.

At 12:18 AM, the mainframe computer suddenly announces that it is malfunctioning. It has been testing itself continually as it runs, and when it fails one of its own tests, it turns on indicator lights, and stops processing entirely. When the operators see the malfunction lights, they dump the programs running at that time onto a disc file; and they then load a set of

specific test routines to check the functional extent of
trouble in the machine.   These runs do indicate an
input-output discrepancy, the machine officially goes
down, and a technician is called at 12:35.   Some urgent
work is immediately assigned to a smaller-capacity mini-
computer, which is used for backup, and for special
programs that do not require the large-capacity machine.

The computer technician arrives about 1:30 AM.   He
has with him two large fitted cases of tools and instruments, but he does not reach for any tools or begin to
unbuckle any hardware.   Instead, he loads some fault-
locator programs and studies the printout of these, comparing them with desired results in a set of manuals.
With this particular trouble, the machine is not completely inoperative;   rather, it is failing some very
specific numerical tests.   The technician inserts a
program which 'stresses' some particular sections of the
equipment by means of voltage excursions which are
slightly outside of normal.   He also makes a few voltage readings by means of an extender board and a logic
probe.   Evenutally the technician goes to a parts
storage bin and replaces a suspected circuit board with
a new one;   the exchange takes only a short time.   On
this occasion, the replacement restores the system, the
computer passes its own tests, and soon the system is
back on the air.   The technician has been on the scene
less than an hour.

An observer might notice several things about this
troubleshooting performance.   To start with, the
search was successful, and it was efficient in both time
and materials.   The technician did not resort to wholesale parts substitution, and his routine, if perhaps
not exactly smooth and perfect, seemed to be well
focused and directed.   A second noticeable feature was
the 'clean hands' nature of the technician's work.   He
wore a white shirt and tie.   A computer is a physical
device, full of wires, little parts, and thousands of
connectors;   the technician had to make some voltage
readings and equipment alterations.   He surely knew how
to solder parts together, how to fix broken wiring, and
so forth.   But he generally does rather little of that
sort of thing - his main job is logical search for a
particular chip, can, or circuit board.   As a third
performance aspect, we would see that the technician
generally works alone.   After an initial contact with
the operators and a confirmation of their report of the
malfunction, he is mainly concerned with his manuals
and his test programs;   unless a trainee technician is
present, the troubleshooter will not describe his search
logic to anybody, and he almost certainly will not
attempt an immediate inspired guess about the seat of
the trouble - there are too many possibilities for this

sort of thing.   At the end of the technician's search,
assuming that it is successful,   there will be a few
minutes of verification;   he makes a brief entry into
the computer's trouble diary, and then he is gone.

This technician that we have been talking about
is in a rather remarkable position.   His work and his
materials would be completely unintelligible to an out-
sider.   He obviously must have good memory and
reasoning powers;   rather few people are trained to do
what he does;   yet he is not considered to be a professional.   He has an important role, and in a real sense
the computer center cannot run for very long without
him;   yet he is paid less than a carpenter or a plas-
terer, and should not expect promotion out of the maintenance department.   His output is essentially intellectual, his skills can be developed to almost any
extent, yet we have never heard of a 'champion' technician, nor have we seen one that was treated as a hero.
Few people start out early in life to become system
maintenance technicians.

This chapter addresses the work life of the high-
technology technician from three viewpoints.   First we
take up the cognitive features of the technician's work,
the types of reasoning and other behaviors required,
and how the technician must cope with these requirements.
Next we consider the training and job aids which are
applied to the technician's work.   Our third area is
that of job design;   here we look briefly at practices
and trends in the high-technology maintenance areas
which have to do with current ideas of job enlargement
and work satisfaction.   This three-phase examination,
we believe, gives a fairly consistent picture of the
technician's present work life.

It is hard to define the domain of the high-
technology maintenance man.   The illustration above
took a computer center as the setting, but of course
there are many other kinds of high-technology environments.   Some of the highest technology of all is that
involved in certain physical and aerospace laboratories.
Those beautiful pictures we get of Jupiter and Mars are
consturcted out of logical 1's and 0's which are sent
back from digital radios on space probes;   it takes a
building full of equipment and many trained people to
assemble these signals into images.   In a similar way,
neutrino counters and other laboratory devices can be
incredibly involved and delicate machines, which are
often maintained by non-professional technicians.
Perhaps less exalted, but still complex enough to be
considered high-technology are such devices as word-
processing machines, computer controlled typesetters,
and pattern recognizers.   The mechanics who work on

these often have to deal with memory registers and video
display terminals, in addition to the electro-mechanical
stuff in the typewriters and printers. At least some
maintenance jobs in petrochemical plants would qualify
as high-technology; one example here would be the people
responsible for 'adaptive' control programs which
'learn' the parameters of an input substance (say, a
crude oil) and attempt to optimize some complex plant
around those parameters. For present purposes, perhaps it is sufficient to say that the technicians we
have in mind are usually involved with specialized
sensors, an abstract realization of a physical system,
some high-speed control electronics, and advanced input-
output devices.

COGNITIVE PROCESSES IN MAINTENANCE WORK

General Trouble Shooting

     Much troubleshooting is very simple. When some-
thing goes wrong, all or most of the possible causes of
the fault are listed, and are then successively eliminated. The process is continued until only one 'cul-
prit' remains; this item is repaired or replaced and
the problem solved. Or maybe one component is known
to be likely to fail, and it is therefore summarily
replaced, without much of an attempt at fault-tracing;
only if this 'obvious' replacement fails to clear the
trouble is any further search undertaken. Such troubleshooting is applied in all practical trades and professions, and in daily life. It seems so natural that it
may not even be formulated in an explicit way. Technical difficulties can arise, of course, when the list of
possible causes is incomplete, when it is impossible to
eliminate some possible causes, or when there are a
great many related 'partial causes'. But the commonsense conception of trouble-isolation stands up very
well, and is especially effective in easily visualized
physical systems, such as a plumbing layout.

     When systems get more complex and the number of
alternatives becomes large, a simple enumerate-and-
eliminate strategy will not be practical. It was just
barely practical in the vacuum-tube TV era; during
that time, a TV set would have about twenty tubes, and
all of these could be replaced in a few minutes, so that
a TV mechanic could enter a living room, start replacing
tubes, and expect to be finished pretty soon. But a
big air-control radar may have thousands of components
in it, with many of these linked together in complex
ways. Furthermore, there is good reason to think that,
if a technician attempted simply to replace every part,
he would introduce far more troubles than he would

eliminate.   Evidently, more efficient search strategies
are needed.

        About twenty-five years ago, applied psycholo-
gists started to investigate trouble-shooting principles
and behavior.   There was some interesting work on fault
location in idealized systems.   The best known example
comes from Robert Miller and his associates (Miller et
al., 1953), who formulated the 'half-split' technique.
The half-split procedure recommends that a chain of
system elements should be checked first in the middle
of the chain, or in such a way that the two groups of
elements on both sides of the test point are equally
likely to contain the faulty element.   There is no
doubt that the half-split concept is efficient for
simple linear chains; but there is also no doubt that
most interesting systems are not simply linear chains;
and even if they were, troubleshooting would be no real
problem, because even inefficient search would be con-
clusive and rapid.   The half-split idea has been extended and generalized in various ways, to permit inclusion
of parallel paths, probability-of-failure data, and
cost figures into the analysis.   And people can learn
the half-split idea (Hannom et al., 1967).   For some
years, however, it has been evident that abstract
search strategies are not very useful to a working
technician.   An efficient scheme is meaningless if the
technician is unsure of what has been logically eliminated by his tests.

        Studies were also done which compared the trouble-
shooting sequences of real technicians with an ideal or
'optimal' search strategy.   Such strategies can be
determined for any equipment and test situation, as
long as the conditional probabilities between symptoms,
tests, and parts are known.   Bond and Rigney (1966),
for instance, computed a Bayesian search policy which
adjusted the failure probabilities of all system components as successive tests were made.   When a trouble
was inserted into a hardware setup, the Bayesian computer program ran parallel to a real person who worked
on the same defective system and had the same information.   The Bayesian program would always find the
trouble with the smallest number of steps or checks.
It would not forget anything, and it updated the failure-
likelihood estimates for each component after each test.
The psychological point of interest was how closely
the human troubleshooting attempt resembled the Bayesian
path.   Such studies always found that the human technician is not an optimal troubleshooter.   He makes many
redundant checks, forgets things he has already done,
replaces components which logically cannot be faulty, and
often seems to mill around the equipment in a near-
aimless way.   Taken together with the half-split

experience, the experimental comparison of real troubleshooting performances to an ideal search routine might
suggest that technicians are often illogical and reck-
less.   This is not so.   The situation resembles that
which is found in the psychology of logical reasoning.
If you give intelligent people syllogistic problems to
solve, there will be many errors and incorrect inferences.
On close examination, however, it turns out that these
mistakes are largely due to the artificiality of the
syllogism, and to the subject's unfamiliarity with the
way that terms like 'or' and 'some' are used in logic
(Henle, 1962).   When corrected and practiced, and
especially when syllogisms are cast in a familiar context, subjects are indeed quite logical, and tend not
to repeat their previous logical mistakes.   Without
this special correction and training, though, all sorts
of language and experience factors can cause the apparent
logical failures (Johnson, 1972; Wason, 1968).   An
analogous situation applies to the troubleshooter.   He
often appears to behave illogically because his conception of the system is too vague or too incomplete
for him to be sure of the implications of what he has
done, when he has taken a string of electrical or
mechanical measurements.   So perhaps all he can do,
given this logically fuzzy situation, is to repeat tests
and to replace parts, and to hope for some indication
that will be drastic enough to be an unequivocal clue.

Digital Systems Troubleshooting

A large digital system is an assembly of many
copies of a few standard units.   There are only about a
dozen basic logic functions such as AND, OR, NOR, and
NAND; each of these functions has a logical truth
table, and can be realized in hardware by means of various
technologies.   Usually an item such as an OR gate is
encapsulated as a small integrated circuit package.
Operating sections of a system can then be put together
by an array of the simple functions.   For instance,
information which is coded in four binary digits as 0's
and 1's can be converted to decimal form by means of 8
inverters and 8 NAND gates, and the whole converter can
be smaller than a letter, or even a dot, on this page.

Understanding a digital system seems to be a
psychological challenge for many people.   It takes
some time to get used to all the logical 0's and 1's that
are processed and transferred about.   Since transistors,
resistors, and diodes are often employed in the tiny
circuits, the student also must know enough electronics
to follow the current states in a bistable device or an
operational amplifier.   Often, there is not much
imagery to assist human memory in holding the big logic

arrays in mind.   The digital system with its abstract
design may seem to be austere and counter-intuitive.

Digital components such as counters and shift
registers are driven by special clocks, and so the
timing is extremely critical.   The clean and definite
nature of the signals, and of the flip-flop circuits,
means that a timing diagram of signals and events in a
circuit can be very precise.   A timing layout might
show free-running clock pulses running along a top line,
with real time going to the right;   below this there
could be many other event lines, which show preset,
clear, and output synchronous events.   Such diagrams
seem not to be very memorable, however;   and the
meaning of all the little time intervals can quickly be
forgotten.   Furthermore, unless every event is understood at a 'deep' level, the diagram may be useless in a
real trouble search, and the technician can get lost in
a jumble of microsecond-duration events.

There is another type of intellectual effort that
is required of any electronic technician, and particularly so of somebody working on a digital system.   A
quote from an engineering text will give the flavor:

'... When we look at the overal system ...,
we see feedback loops, DAC's, LED displays,
and digital counters ...   The troubleshooter must develop the ability to separate in his thinking the individual sub-
circuits from the complete circuit or
system.   This is a mental separation at
first for the purpose of understanding the
small circuit and large system operation.
The second step will be to apply the mental separation to the physical hardware
to accomplish the task of troubleshooting.'
(Coffron, 1979)

Again this 'mental separation' depends on a very
detailed appreciation of circuit functions and interrelations.   In fact, someone who could troubleshoot
each little subcircuit would probably not need much
further capability to do the whole thing.   There is a
'big picture', of course, but working inside the big
picture depends on many little perceptions which are
accurate.

Coping with Cognitive Difficulties in Troubleshooting

Our short summary indicates that the troubleshooter's basic cognitive difficulty is an informational
one, and that in complex systems the technician is

hampered mainly by the limitations of his knowledge,
rather than by the inefficiency of his search logic.
If this is so, then there are two fundamental approaches
to improving performance.   One of these is to provide
the requisite information by way of job aids, manuals,
and training;   a few such possibilities are discussed
in the next section.   A more psychological approach is
to improve learning capabilities in the technicians,
so that the material can be mastered and remembered
better, and the working person can direct his own
learning.

Why is it so hard to learn technical material,
such as electronics or physical chemistry?   One reason,
certainly, is that the learner may not be 'ready' for
the new material, in the sense that his prerequisite
information base is insufficient (Rothkopf, 1978).
Some years ago, we found this factor to be critical for
shipyard electronics apprentices.   These men were
taking instruction on specific Navy radios and radars.
The training school assumed that, since all apprentices
had been exposed to 'basic electronics', the main laws
of electronics were fully appreciated by the trainees.
Well, the typical student had heard of Kirchoff's law,
and knew vaguely about RC networks, voltage drops across
the screen grid of a tube, and so forth;   but he could
not really use them well enough to solve circuit problems.   Until real clarity and fluency were available
at the basic level, the new lectures and labs just continued to pile up incomplete, superficial, and insufficient knowledge.   Almost none of the technicians really
benefited from the new instruction, and none of them
could work effectively when the course was over.   The
social pressures were such that neither students nor
instructors could admit this state of affairs.

Most technical students do not know much about
their own psychology of learning.   They assume that
practice and rehearsal is the way to learning.   Actually,
it is through such features as visualization, mnemonics,
and meaningfulness that material is easily and accurately
remembered (Norman, 1978).   The technician would probably
benefit from training in 'how to learn'.   And if he
knew more about his preferred 'cognitive style', he
might select or arrange his learning materials to match
that style (Pask, 1975).   Memory is often facilitated
if the items to be learned are linked together into a
'story line'.   The story does not necessarily have to be
'true', as long as it is memorable, and if it can yield
veridical inferences in the technical domain.   Among
other techniques that might be pursued are requiring
appropriate depth of processing by the student, tutoring
by analogy and metaphor, and socratic questioning of the
student's present knowledge (Norman, 1978).

TRAINING AND AIDING THE TECHNICIAN

Troubleshooting Aids

An engineering approach to the corrective maintenance problem goes like this: since the man is so
limited, and it takes so long to train a good one, then
get the man out of the system, and have the troubleshooting done by automatic fault locator technology.
Let the human duties be the loading of automatic test
routines, reading the output, and then replacing those
items which are indicated to be defective by the program.
At its extreme, this approach implies a reactive but non-
insightful technician, hence the term 'trained-ape
maintenance', which is heard frequently in the military
services.   Supporters of automatic fault locator concepts like to observe that, for many modern systems, a
mechanized automatic routine is the only possible
method of testing anyway, because of the fantastically
fast events in the equipment, the miniaturization and
inaccessibility of the components, and so forth.

There is no doubt that automatic tests are essential for big systems.   A shipboard-based missile, for
instance, will have literally hundreds of parameters to
be checked before a launch can proceed, and there is no
way that this can be done without automation.   And
though a large computer can sometimes be slowly 'stepped
through' its operations, this is not usually a practical way to test its capabilities.

The main trouble with automatic fault locators is
that some equipment states occur which have not been
anticipated by the program.   At such times, nobody knows
what to do, and outside people such as factory engineers
have to be brought into the act.   But there are other
difficulties.   The automatic test equipment itself can
go down, and it is quite complicated.   The VAST system
is a good illustration here.   VAST (Versatile Avionics
Shop Test) was designed for fault isolation in US Navy
avionics equipment from several different aircraft.
There is a large central computer, and many plug-in outlets distributed around an aircraft carrier;   these outlets lead from the airplane to the computer.   The whole
thing is an engineering tour de force;   but consider the
following quote from Myles (1978):

'... The original concept of VAST envis-
ioned the use of an operator with minimal
training.   This concept has been shown
lacking because it anticipates a situation in which the program will be perfect.
The machine will always operate properly,
and documentation associated with the

> testing process will always be upt-to-date
> and correct.   Experience has shown that
> these factors seldom prevail in spite of
> the most stringent efforts ...   The VAST
> maintenance technician required more
> training and experience to effectively
> troubleshoot the complex VAST system.'

Recently, VAST training has been expanded once again, and
a new job designation of 'Test Program Set Analyst' has
been established (Van Hemel, 1979).

    As a result of such experiences, people who
manage real systems recognize that there always must be
some highly trained people, and that no automatic check-
out procedures will eliminate them.   The best present
practice is to provide the technician with as much automatic test support as is economically feasible, to supple-
ment this with carefully prepared manuals and guides
which are oriented to human use, and to train the man in
the use of these materials.   The human is still highly
skilled, but he no longer is expected to deduce his
troubleshooting procedures from his knowledge of electronics theory and a series of schematic diagrams.
Instead, he employs such aids as elaborate maintenance
dependency charts (MDCs) and detailed procedural guides.
If the system is digital, there will be a technical data
sheet for each basic logical function and subsection,
and all the circuit parameters will be called out there;
a few test-probe checks can often eliminate whole sections of the equipment, and these will best be done
according to some previously determined sequences.

    The present state-of-the-art in decision aids pro-
bably is represented by the LOGMOD test set (DePaul,
1979).   This portable unit is about the size of a 15-
inch TV set, and it contains its own microprocessor.   To
use it, a disc for a given prime equipment is inserted
into LOGMOD;   then, the technician can call up all sorts
of diagnostic, sequencing, and parts-cost data.   The
device can guide a technician through the stages of a
trouble-search process, and it stores the logic from
about 500 pages of written material onto one $5\frac{1}{2}$-inch
floppy disc.   Suppose that you had to troubleshoot a
modern airborne radar, and that the fault-isolation
logic for this radar had been put into the LOGMOD format.
In all probability, a LGOMOD-equipped technician would
beat any 'expert' in working on that radar, at least for
that large proportion of troubles which are locatable by
the stored data base.

Advanced Maintenance Trainers

As we indicated above, all present trends con-
verge on the idea that the maintenance technician is
primarily a highly-skilled user of complicated special
aids and test routines. He must be fluent in such
activities as selecting which fault-locator routine to
run, choosing which obtained patterns of logical 0's
and 1's should be compared with the expected patterns,
and identifying integrated-circuit parts and pins. The
logic is quite clean and definite; and, naturally,
computerized training concepts have been proposed for
teaching these procedures. One example of a computerized trainer is the AIDE system; detailed accounts of
AIDE have been published elsewhere (Towne, 1979), and
we summarize the concept here.

AIDE (Automated Instruction, Direction, and Exercise) is controlled by a general-purpose monitor program
which extracts and combines information from a data base
containing specific content. The monitor and data base
structure share generic maintenance concepts, such as
controls, indicators, malfunctions, functions, symptoms,
and so forth. Any new equipment can be implemented on
AIDE by preparing an appropriately formatted listing of
control names, settings, indicator names, possible
symptoms, functions, malfunctions and so on, plus a set
of graphic aids.

AIDE, therefore, consists of (1) hardware to
process data and interact with the maintenance technician,
(2) a large computer program, and (3) a visual and
logical representation of the target equipment. The
first two of these elements remain fixed so that only
the data base needs to be changed for the system to work
on an entirely different equipment.

The major hardware elements of AIDE are as follows:
(1) a small computer (microprocessor CPU random-access
    memory and mass disc storage);
(2) a 9-inch CRT: displays words, list, names, etc.;
(3) a micrographics unit, this displays color photographs
    under computer control (can be either 35mm random
    slide projector or color microfiche unit);
(4) a sonic touch-pen, for user inputs;
(5) a small hard-copy printer;
(6) a voice synthesizing device.
Towne (1979) gives detailed brands and specifications of
the hardware; the market is moving so fast that new
display and computational facilities are available almost
every month. At this writing, the hardware is attractive and compact, but will be improved shortly. The
present version takes up about as much space as the usual
secretarial desk.

The AIDE command menu is simply a removable card labelled with the several commands to which AIDE will respond when touched by the sonic pen.   These commands allow the user to select modes of interaction (assistance, instruction, drill), and to obtain any information about theory of operation of a section of the equipment.

AIDE can greatly assist a trainee, or a working technician, in the identification of units, controls, and displays on a prime equipment.   As an illustration, we utilize the AN/SPA-66 Radar Repeater, an operational major equipment item for the US Navy.   A technician who wishes to become familiar with this equipment would begin by entering the instruction mode, whereupon he would observe an image of the total hardware configuration. For a large system this image might be a simplified line drawing showing entire equipments as sub-units.   AIDE presents whatever text is available to explain the pur- pose, operation, and function organization of this entity. Next, each major sub-unit would be similarly shown and explained, all at the technician's pace.

Upon completing a rundown of this fixed-sequence presentation, the technician may freely explore the physical system by selecting sub-elements of particular interest (with the touch pen) and reviewing whatever associated text and graphic aids he wishes.   It is expected that some natural motivation will exist for pur- suing this self-controlled study, since the drill phase will require that the technician locate and identify these elements.

The sequence of drawings and photographs shown below provides some indication of how the technician can 'zoom-in' from the initial overall photograph or drawing, to very detailed photographs of small sub-elements. When the technician completes his exploration, study, and review of the physical system he progresses to a similar instructional phase related to functional orga- nization.   Then, instead of viewing photographs of hard- ware elements he studies functional diagrams.   As before he progresses to increasingly more detailed diagrams by use of the touch pen.

The routines for assisting troubleshooting operate in cooperation with the technician to locate a malfunc- tion.   In the fully-supported condition AIDE provides sequenced directions, which the technician carries out on his failed equipment.   In less fully-supported conditions, the technician requests particular advice.   The assis- tance which is available consists of:

    (1) recommended next test to perform (the
         computer knows which ones have been done);

Projected Image

Comment

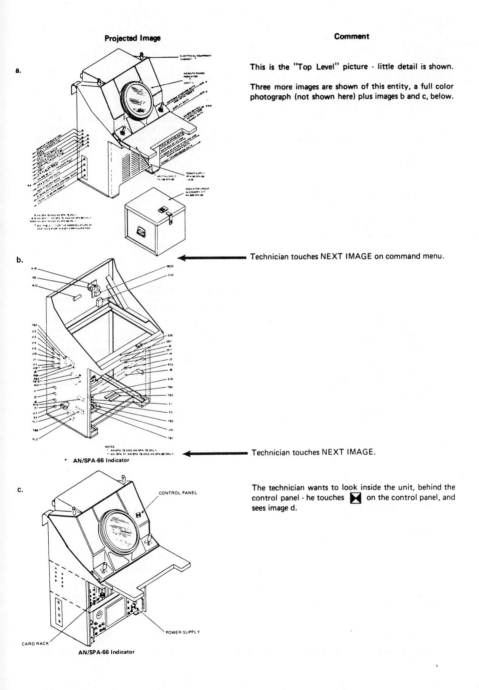

a.

This is the "Top Level" picture - little detail is shown.

Three more images are shown of this entity, a full color photograph (not shown here) plus images b and c, below.

b.

Technician touches NEXT IMAGE on command menu.

* AN/SPA-66 Indicator

Technician touches NEXT IMAGE.

c.

The technician wants to look inside the unit, behind the control panel - he touches ◪ on the control panel, and sees image d.

AN/SPA-66 Indicator

Projected Image   **Comment**

d.

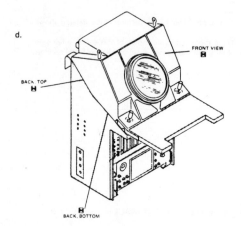

FRONT VIEW

BACK, TOP

BACK, BOTTOM

Touching Front View would produce a full-color close-up of the front panel, each section of which may be selected and 'operated' (described later).

The technician wishes to see behind the front panel - he touches BACK, BOTTOM and receives a photograph of the interior (not shown here). He touches the label, Cursor Origin Joystick, and sees image e.

e.

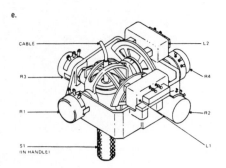

CABLE

R3

R1

S1
(IN HANDLE)

L2

R4

R2

L1

Since there are no ![] symbols on image e, the technician can go no <u>deeper</u> into the joystick mechanism[1]. He touches 'UP' on the command menu and again sees the interior view. From here he could select any of the other sub-elements or continue UP again. Suppose he wishes to look at a circuit card - he touches UP, sees image d, touches UP again, sees image c, then touches CARD RACK and sees image f.

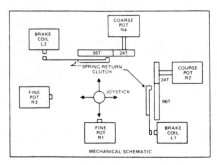

MECHANICAL SCHEMATIC

Cursor Origin Joystick, A20

[1] He can, however, request text which explains the purpose and theory of operation, as well as a functional diagram.

Projected Image   **Comment**

f.

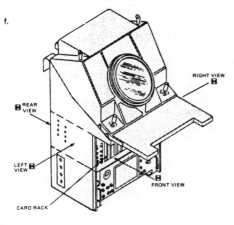

Card Rack

The technician touches Front view and sees image g.

g.

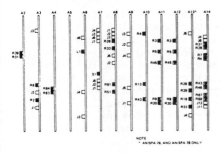

Card Rack, Front

Two additional images are shown, a color photograph and a labelled drawing. If the technician touches the over board A2 on the labelled drawing, he sees image h.

h.

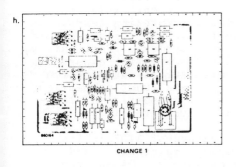

CHANGE 1

Three additional images are view; a color photograph, a part location index, and a pin number designation list. None of these contain a ▶◀ thus no further hardware detail is available of the circuit board. Touching FUNC-TIONAL APPEARANCE on the command menu, however, produces image i.

(2) displayed explanations of how to perform the
test (if available in the data base);

(3) interpretation of the implications of the
symptom, in terms of the fault areas confirmed
or suspected.

This cycle is repeated until the process termi-
nates at some fault area.   As with virtually all
troubleshooting aids, such a system will be sensitive
to entry technician errors, and to 'nasty' faults (such
as multiple failures) which are not accurately isolated
by the malfunction-symptom scheme in the data base.
The likelihood of technician errors is reduced somewhat,
however, since he 'reports' the symptom by identifying
a pictorial image which matches the observed symptom.
And, since AIDE interprets each new symptom in terms of
the elements which are suspected or have been eliminated
from suspicion, the technician can gain insights into
the hardware-symptom relationships even when the inter-
active process does not totally succeed.

The current data base, which was developed just to
test and demonstrate AIDE, covers a few areas of a large
radar repeater.   It contains just a few of the possible
setups, and it offers troubleshooting intelligence in
only a small portion of the equipment.   This reduced
data base contains 125 images, approximately 50 of which
were taken directly from existing technical manuals.
It is estimated that a complete, detailed AIDE data base
for the AN/SPA-66 would involve approximately 1000 images
with perhaps one-quarter taken directly from the technical manual, one-half taken from the actual equipment,
and one-quarter taken from specially prepared logic
diagrams, matrices, and text.   Troubleshooting training
and aiding is generated by AIDE from a troubleshooting
'tree' which specifies a detailed, conditional, fault-
isolation approach of a content 'expert', photographs of
normal and abnormal symptoms for each involved indicator
(including test equipment), and sufficient explanatory
text to assist in performing and interpreting tests.
Since the prime equipment itself is complex, an accurate
representation of it will also be complex.   Fortunately,
our experience has been that a subject-matter expert can
produce data-base information with surprising dispatch.
One reason for this is that symptom-malfunction matrices
tend to be sparse, and only a small proportion of test-
point checks are relevant to any given trouble.

Perhaps the most unique feature of AIDE is its
advanced software, which can accept maintenance and
troubleshooting data from any equipment.   Among the
other advanced training concepts which should be mentioned are SOPHIE (Brown et al., 1976) and the Hagan FIS

or Fault Identification Simulator (Brock, 1978).   SOPHIE
is an integrated collection of programs which can answer
student questions, and allow the student to change parameters in a circuit simulator.   A 'natural-language
interface' and electronic knowledge semantic net are
among the software packages included.   FIS is capable of
simulating 23 different fault conditions for a complex
boiler control system.   Though a steam boiler is less
abstract and less complex than an electronics system,
the FIS training does pursue a definite 'tree procedure'
in troubleshootings.   Students are not so much trained
to deduce fault conditions, as to apply procedures which
performed the deduction.

        None of these advanced training concepts have yet
been fully evaluated.   Preliminary trials of AIDE and
SOPHIE show very good acceptance by students, and by
instructors;   the hardware packages are attractive, and
are available now in stand-alone configurations.   Substantial time savings also can be realized;   for
instance, boiler-control technicians who took a FIS-
aided course learned about twice as fast as those in the
regular course.   There is good reason to expect more
positive evaluations as experience is gained with these
trainers and the training community appreciates their
ability to teach complex procedures.

JOB DESIGN AND THE MAINTENANCE TECHNICIAN

        About twenty-five years ago, job design was
defined as '... the organization (or structuring) of a
job to satisfy the technical-organizational requirements
of the work to be accomplished and the human requirements
of the person performing the work' (Davis and Kanter,
1955).   The second part of this definition is the key
one, as it directs attention to the fit between the work
and the needs of the worker.   Many proposals have been
offered for improving the fit.   For example, Davis
listed twenty-three techniques which might simultaneously
increase worker satisfaction and lead to more effective
output (Davis, 1957).   Many of his proposals have to
do with increasing worker autonomy, discretion,
achievement, growth, and the meaningfulness and variety
of tasks;   these ideas have been mentioned at other
places in this volume.

        Despite the absence of definitive survey data, it
may be worthwhile to speculate about the present job-
design status of the maintenance technician's work.   For
this purpose, we can consider the three job characteristics that Hackman and Lawler (1971) identify as contributing to worker need satisfaction and to organizational goals.   Their first attribute is that the

worker must feel personally responsible for his work.
On this dimension, the high-technology troubleshooter
should score fairly high. He does usually work alone,
and he seldom turns to other people for help. At the
same time, however, he certainly must know that he is
really a skilled user of materials which were originated
and validated by others, and that he is not ordinarily
free to vary the procedures very much. Technicians are
not allowed to change maintenance software, though we
have heard of some doing so. The company attitude
usually is, if the test software doesn't work, let's
fix it so that it does; and then all technicians should
apply it in a standard way. On Gulowsen's scale of
work-group autonomy, the technicians would come out about
the middle of the range (Gulowsen, 1979).

        The second Hackman-Lawler job requirement is that
a work outcome is perceived as meaningful and worthwhile
to the individual. According to Turner and Lawrence
(1965), meanginful job processes have a clear beginning
and ending of the work, they utilize skills and abilities
which the worker personally values, and they require
considerable variety. On these grounds, skilled
troubleshooters certainly should perceive their work as
meaningful.

        Feedback is a third job-design criterion. A
person who is having higher order needs satisfied wants
to know how he or she is doing. Superficially, the
troubleshooter gets almost perfect objective feedback,
because the failed machine either is restored or it is
not, and the technician always knows which state prevails.
This immediate task feedback, of course, is not necessarily identical with the performer's own perception of
his effectiveness, since he may be evaluating himself
against some other standard.

        The technician, then, should be rather highly
motivated in his work, and from nearly all indications
he is indeed quite satisfied. Personnel statistics
are difficult to find, but one large computer company
reported to us that turnover and absence rates for maintenance men are very low, lower than for design
engineers or programmers; this is especially so for
medium-size cities. A few on-site interviews with
roving computer technicians did reveal a couple of common sources of dissatisfaction. One of these was the
technician's non-professional status, which was related
to what the person does. Though the work is very
technical and demanding, experience in restoring computers results in a person's learning more and more
about one particular company's computers, manuals, and
fault-isolation procedures; it does not result in
general engineering knowledge. Thus, many technicians

feel that they are regarded as 'less than engineers', and that they can never attain engineer status, regardless of how expert they become at their work.   The companies are probably missing an opportunity to satisfy these growth needs of the technician.   A similar growth-need situation was observed in the US aerospace industry. Engineers in that industry perceived their real worth depended in their state-of-the-art capabilities.   As a result, when design work was to be done, they tended to design new items, and to reject existing and off-the-shelf hardware.   They did this to improve and keep up-to-date, but it was very costly to the company.   A solution was for the firm to consider both the engineer's perceived need to sharpen intellectual skills, and the design demands.   Management guaranteed that an individual had career-advancing assignments often, though at any one time he might be doing a routine job (Davis and Taylor, 1979).   A similar strategy could be used with high-technology maintenance people.

A more subtle negative factor which was frequently mentioned was the 'psychological distance' between the technicians, and other people in the computer centers. The roving maintenance person may have few close relationships with other workers, as he is always moving from one place to another, and the other technicians back at maintenance headquarters are also usually on the move.   Some respondents even confided that the work leads to a general sense of isolation.   Perhaps there has been some self-selection early in the technician's career; if you can't handle the isolation, then you leave the occupation, or search for a position where you service just one center.

CONCLUDING REMARKS

Our review indicates that the high-technology maintenance person is typically an expert at carrying out complex test procedures, and at doing the activities called for by the results of the test.   The work is intellectual and precise, as the test procedures are often driven by discrete logic and critically timed electronic circuits.   Trouble-isolation work is often supported by special procedural guides, manuals, and fault-locating computer software; these aids have evolved because of the economic consequences of large equipments being down, and also because of the limitations of human memory and knowledge.   Automated trainers can be effective teaching aids for the procedural and logical-inference parts of the job; these trainers are now reaching the stages of validation and wide applicability.   Though his skills can be developed almost indefinitely, the technician's on-the-job

experience usually produces fluency in working on a
particular kind of hardware, and this experience may not
generalize much to other devices.

A technician's quality of work life is apt to be
fairly high, and he probably enjoys relative good work
autonomy, variety, meaningfulness, and feedback.   With
his very technical but non-generalizable knowledge,
however, he can be locked in occupationally; and the
circumstances of his work may lead to a sense of social
isolation.   These conditions suggest that more attention should be given to extending on-the-job social
satisfactions, and to providing job experiences that go
beyond the technological imperatives of a particular
kind of hardware.   Such efforts should enhance the
social and psychic growth of the individuals who perform
this necessary work, and should also intersect with
goals of the sponsoring organization.

REFERENCES

Bond, N.A. and Rigney, J.W. (1966).   'Bayesian aspects
    of troubleshooting behavior', Human Factors, 8,
    377-383.

Brock, J.F. (1978).   'Development of a nonelectronics
    maintenance training simulator', paper presented
    at Sixth Annual Psychology D.O.D. Symposium, US
    Air Force Academy.

Brown, J.S., Rubinstein, R. and Burton, R. (1976).
    'Reactive learning environment for computer assis-
    ted electronics instruction', US Air Force Systems
    Command, Brooks Air Force Base, AFHRL-TR-76-68.

Coffron, J.S. (1979).   Getting Started in Digital
    Troubleshooting, Reston Publishing, Reston,
    Virginia.

Davis, L.E. (1957).   'Toward a theory of job design',
    J. Indust. Engng., 8, 19.

Davis, L.E. and Canter, R.R. (1955).   'Job design',
    J. Indust. Engng., 6, 3.

Davis, L.E. and Taylor, J.C. (Eds.) (1979).   Design of
    Jobs, Goodyear, Santa Monica, California.

DePaul, R.A. (1979).   'Do automated maintenance depen-
    dency charts make paper-covered JPAs obsolete?',
    in Third Biennial Maintenance Training and Aiding
    Conference, pp. 19-22, US Navy Training Equipment
    Center, Orlando, Florida.

Gulowsen, J. (1979).   'A measure of work-group autonomy',
     in Design of Jobs (Eds. L.E. Davis and J.C.
     Taylor), pp. 208-218, Goodyear, Santa Monica,
     California.

Hackman, J.R. and Lawler, E.E. (1971).   'Employee
     reactions to job characteristics', J. Appl. Psych.,
     55, 259-265.

Hannom, T.J.B., Azzari, A.J., Brooks, A.I., Hunter, J.R.
     and Steinberg, L. (1967).   'Development of a
     computer program for generating trouble-shooting
     decision trees', US Air Force Medical Research
     Laboratories, Wright-Patterson AFB, Ohio, AMRL-TR-
     67-83.

Henle, M. (1962).   'On the relation between logic and
     thinking', Psy. Rev., 69, 366-378.

Johnson, D.M. (1972).   Systematic introduction to the
     Psychology of Thinking, Harper, New York.

Miller, R.B., Foley, J.D. and Smith, P.R. (1953).
     'Systematic troubleshooting and the half-split
     technique', US Air Force Human Resources Research
     Center, Chanute AFB, Illinois, TR-53-21.

Myles, M.D. (1978).   'The VAST experience', in ATE:
     Bane or Blessing for the Technician? (Eds. W.J.
     King and J.S. Duva), US Navy Training Equipment
     Center, Orlando, Florida, IH-301.

Norman, D.A. (1978).   'Notes toward a theory of com-
     plex learning', in Cognitive Psychology and
     Instruction (Eds. A.M. Lesgold, J.W. Pellegrino,
     S.D. Fokkema and R. Glaser), pp. 39-47, Plenum,
     New York.

Pask, G. (1975).   Conversation, Cognition, and
     Learning, Elsevier, Amsterdam.

Rothkopf, E.Z. (1978).   'On the reciprocal relationship
     between previous experience and processing in
     determining learning outcomes', in Cognitive Psy-
     chology and Instruction (Eds. A.M. Lesgold, J.W.
     Pellegrino, S.D. Fokkema and R. Glaser), pp. 465-
     474, Plenum, New York.

Turner, A.N. and Lawrence, P.R. (1965).   Industrial
     Jobs and the Worker, Harvard Graduate School of
     Business Administration, Cambridge, Massachusetts.

Wason, R.C. (1968).   'Reasoning about a rule', Quart.
     J. exp. Psychol., 20, 273-281.

Van Hemel, P.E. (1979).   'Technician training and
    aiding: where the defense readiness buck stops',
    in Third Biennial Maintenance Training and
    Aiding Conference, pp. 1-4, US Navy Training
    Equipment Center, Orlando, Florida.

Chapter 9

Analysing a Complex Planning Task

A. SHEPHERD and K. D. DUNCAN

INTRODUCTION

One trend in moves to improve efficiency in
industry is to bring together several previously independent production units to produce a co-ordinated
production system. This brings with it a type of control task where an operator has to co-ordinate the
operation of production units or subsystems. His
task is to monitor information from a variety of
sources, e.g. instruments or production schedules or
interpersonal communications. Whenever a perturbation
is registered, he must decide which changes to make to
optimise system performance and instruct sub-system
operators to implement these changes.

The operator has thus forsaken the traditional
role of himself effecting changes to plant running.
Instances can be seen increasingly in petroleum, chemical and other process plants, where a control-room
operator has to co-ordinate the activities of other
operators in charge of otherwise independent units.
Similar examples can be seen in some warehouse operations
where the foreman has to co-ordinate the activities of
clerks, fork-lift truck drivers and packers in accordance with deliveries, breakages, lost items and orders.

Training for these planning tasks presents problems. The changeover to such tasks does not always
come about gradually, thereby providing useful operating
experience that can be built on. Furthermore it cannot
be assumed that an operator's experience of the various
subsystems is going to help him learn the new, overall
control, task. Prior experience of this sort may provide some useful language and, perhaps, invest the
operator with some unjustified credibility, but little

else.   Competence of operators is usually achieved
exclusively by the time-honoured and notoriously costly
method of gaining experience in the job. With only
experience to guide them, however, operators may consistently fail to recognise situations leading to optimisation.   Alternatively inefficient sequences of actions
will be reinforced simply because they eventually lead
to a successful outcome.

        An organisation relying on its operators mastering
these tasks purely through experience is unlikely to
achieve the performance which the system design would
otherwise permit.   However, analysing and designing
training for these tasks is often difficult.   This is
compounded by the fact that most approaches to analysing
jobs in industry concentrate on what an operator does
and throw no light on planning or decision making skills.

Plans in Hierarchical Task Analysis

        To overcome this common weakness in analysing
industrial tasks Annett et al. (1971) and Duncan (1974)
advocate the redescription of an operation to include
a set of subordinate operations and a plan governing
when these subordinates must be carried out.   In their
terms, a minimal plan need merely reiterate the goal
of the superordinate operation being redescribed.   For
example a plan could merely state 'perform the following
operations to establish target caustic concentration:

        - put on gloves and goggles
        - oper man-lid
        - dip for sample
        - close man-lid
        - test sample
        - estimate caustic required
        - collect required caustic from store
        - bring caustic to vessel on sack trolley
        - tip caustic into vessel
        - take off gloves and goggles.'

The practical value of this plan is questionable.
Indeed to state a plan specifying the rules for carrying
out these ten subordinate operations is difficult.
However, while the nature of this plan may elude the
analyst, an equivalent hierarchy of three simpler
plans,as in Figure 1, may be more readily understood.
Achieving this restructuring can be difficult, but is
essential for training design.

        The plan for the caustic correction task now
states the rules for carrying out subordinate operations.
This is much more useful for several reasons:

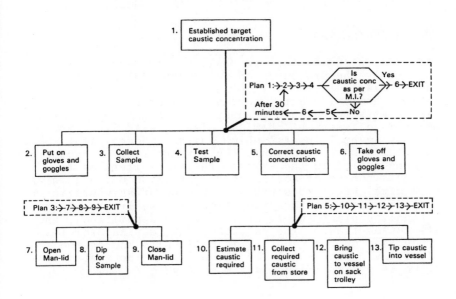

Figure 1.   The caustic correction task, illustrating
            how a hierarchy of simple plans accounts for
            complex planning.

1. It can be used rather directly to guide a trainee
    to mastery.

2. It specifies an additional criterion against
    which training can be measured, namely _how_ rather
    than _if_ the goal is achieved.

3. It may provide a rule to be taught, or a set of
    conditions which specify simulation for training.

4. If the task is too complex to be practised as a
    whole, such a plan will indicate parts to practise
    together in a part-task training regime.

5. Without a plan stating when they should be carried
    out, the subordinate operations may not exhaust
    or they may exceed those necessary for completion
    of the superordinate objective.

    This paper describes how analysing a complex plan
can be simplified by replacing it with a hierarchy of
simpler plans.   By seeking groups of subordinate
operations, such that members of each group are all
instrumental in realising a common sub-goal, plans can
be sought for each group, while a further plan is sought

to govern the sub-goals themselves.

THE BALANCING TASK

        The planning task we shall use to demonstrate
more fully the procedure of restructuring a complex
and seemingly intractable plan is carried out by a
senior chemical plant supervisor called a 'controller'.
His task is to balance production of a gas, by several
units in a system of chemical plants, with its consumption by several 'users' which further process it.   When
an event occurs to disturb the current rate of production
or consumption in the system, the controller has to
select a course of action to re-establish balance in an
economical way.   Disturbances can occur anywhere in the
system, affecting the production of gas, its treatment in
a handling plant (where it is dried and purified), and
its consumption.   The gas, chlorine, depends for its
production on the capacity in cell units and on the
electrical power supply to the units.   The system is
shown in a simplified diagram in Figure 2.

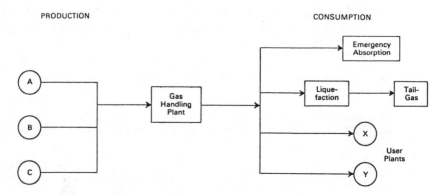

Figure 2.   Integrated production and consumption.
             Gas is produced in units A, B and C and is
             then piped via the gas handling plant to
             the liquefaction plant and the two user
             plants.   The absorption plant is only used
             in emergencies if, for example, one of the
             user plants has to shut down suddenly.

        We became involved because the plant managers felt
that other senior operators from the handling plant
should be trained to balance the system, thereby giving
controllers more time for their supervisory duties.
Previously, skill at the 'balancing' task was acquired
through experience over several months in a very

haphazard way.

THE ANALYSIS

During initial discussions with the informants,
(the two plant managers and the five controllers) fifteen operations involved in the task were listed as
follows:

    1)   Check handling plant availability
    2)   Check power availability
    3)   Check unit availability
    4)   Obtain load distribution
    5)   Check user availability
    6)   Instruct power controller
    7)   Instruct cellroom personnel
    8)   Instruct user plants
    9)   Check consumer plant conditions
   10)   Balance handling plant
   11)   Identify and locate fault
   12)   Check existing loading limitations
   13)   Sound low level alarm
   14)   Check effect of putting item ON/OFF load
   15)   Put cellroom on Class 3 level

Training each of these operations was considered to be
straightforward and, since trainees were already senior
operators on the plant, probably unnecessary.

Stating a single plan to indicate the conditions
under which these fifteen operations should be carried
out (rather than merely reiterating the superordinate
goal), seemed to be an intractable problem.   A solution
began to emerge when further discussion with our informants indicated that the various disturbances controllers
had to cope with fell into 24 categories.   These were
'warned increases', 'warned decreases', and 'sudden
decreases' in each of the following eight variables:

        Power availability;   Liquefaction capacity;
        Cell availability;   User consumption;
        Unit availability;   Emergency Hypo tower
        Compressor availability;   capacity;
        Tail gas system capacity.

By asking controllers how they would select and then
sequence operations to cope with instances of each of
the 24 types of disturbance, it became apparent that
operations tended to be clustered in sub-groups.

Closer inspection revealed that members of each
group were all instrumental in realising a common sub-
goal.   The four groupings were as follows:

a) Alert Other Operators where the controller alerts
   other personnel in the complex to stand by for a
   potential emergency (operations 13 and 15).

b) Deal with alarms - in the event of 'sudden' disturbances (operation 11).

c) Check availability of other Resources - to determine whether sufficient resources are available
   to improve productivity (operations 1, 2, 3, 5,
   12 and 14).

d) Balance the System - how the controller effects a
   change in the running of the complex (operations
   4, 6, 7, 8, 9 and 10).

Identifying these four groups suggested that the initially obscure fifteen operation plan could be
restructured by seeking sub-plans governing the members
of each group, then a further plan to govern the sub-
plans themselves.   Since none governed more than six
operations, we felt more confident that these plans
could be teased out.

INVESTIGATING THE FOUR SUB-PLANS

Alert Relevant Personnel to Operating Problems

     During examination of this sub-plan, informants
recognised that they had omitted a crucial operation,
namely alerting cellroom personnel to standby for a
potential emergency during maintenance.   The plan
governing the three operations now constituting this
sub-group was simply a statement of the circumstances
when each type of warning had to be given.   There was
no problem in identifying when one of these special
circumstances occurred so it was concluded that training
this plan was quite straightforward.

Deal with Alarms

     Discussion indicated that controllers were expec-
ted to do more than merely 'identify and locate fault'.
They were also expected to 'put standby item on load',
if it was available, in order to avert the effects of
the fault they had identified, thereby avoiding the
need to rebalance the system.   This plan also proved
straightforward and easy to train.

Check Availability of Other Resources

Fresh examination of the six operations identified within this group showed that operations 12 and 14
were covered by the other four and could, therefore, be
dropped.   Identifying the plan governing these four
operations revealed opportunities for controllers to
optimise running the system not hitherto recognised by
plant personnel and enabling the analyst to propose
training simulation and suitable part-task training.

'Check availability of other resources' is always
carried out to determine whether an offered resource
increase can lead to increased productivity.   For
example, a 'warned power increase' can increase gas
production provided there is:

1)   production unit capacity
2)   handling plant capacity
3)   user capacity.

A warned power increase offered when one or more
of the other resources is not available must be rejected.
But for some disturbances, rather less obvious patterns
of resource availability lead to improved productivity.
To investigate these fully each type of situation initiated by a 'warned resource increase' needed consideration.   To have done this at the outset of the
analysis would have been out of the question, since the
different types of situation with which the controller
was expected to cope were too numerous.   But looking
only at those situations concerned with 'warned resource
increases' was feasible.   There are only 32 different
situations to be dealt with by this plan - the product
of the four types of disturbances that could be presented
and the eight possible combinations of availability of
the three remaining resources, withheld from the controller to be examined via the telephone, tannoy or radio.

A table, an extract of which is shown in Table 1,
was prepared so that the appropriate decisions for each
situation could be considered in turn.   This examination showed that the offered resources could be either
rejected or accepted and used in one of three rebalan-
cing actions leading to improved productivity.   Furthermore, examination of some of these situations indicated
profitable course of action that controllers had never
previously realised.

The plan of 'Check availability of other resources'
was stated as follows.

'Sufficient of the four checking operations
must be carried out to enable the controller

to decide which of the following four
actions should be taken:

i)   increase production;

ii)   redistribute power to units;

iii) redistribute gas to users; or

iv)   do nothing.'

DISTURBANCE (PRESENTED)	RESOURCES (withheld until requested)				DECISION
	power	cell unit	user	handling	
1. Warned power increase	-	·	·	·	Increase production
2. Warned power increase	-	·	·		Do nothing
3. Warned power increase	-	·		·	Do nothing
4. Warned power increase	-		·	·	Do nothing

· resource available

Table 1.   First four rows of 32 row table relating
            patterns of resource availability to re-
            balancing decision.   For full table see
            Shepherd (1976).

        In itself, this plan appears unsatisfactory, since
it fails to specify the conditions under which each of
the four checking operations should be carried out.
But, in conjunction with Table 1, it enabled the analysts
to propose suitable training hypotheses.   First, since
Table 1 distinguishes between presented and withheld
information, it can be used to devise suitable training
simulation.   Secondly, cumulative part task training
can be designed according to the manner of Belbin (1964)
or Duncan and Shepherd (1975) by gradually increasing
the number of situations with which the trainee is
expected to cope.   The table can also be used as a
training criterion to examine whether the trainee has
used insufficient or excessive information in reaching
a decision.   In particular, the most efficient sequence
of checking resources for a particular disturbance will
vary on different occasions.   A controller retaining a
running memory of the state of the system can perform
more efficiently than one who does not.

Balance System for Identified Disturbance

Although only governing six operations, this plan
was difficult to state. The problem was again resolved by restructuring the plan. Achieving a satisfactory redescription required one operation 'obtain load
distribution' to be redescribed further. In addition
the vital stage of determining how gas should be distributed between 'users', overlooked in the original
listing of operations, was now stated as 'plan gas
distribution'.

Determine the Nature of the Rebalance

Analysis of the four sub-group plans had relied
on controllers responding to general classes of disturbances. Performance, therefore, required controllers to translate a specific event into its general
class. To produce an analysis enabling us to train
new controllers, it was necessary to introduce an
initial operation 'determine nature of the rebalance'.
Having stated it, to achieve a logical completeness, it
transpired that further analysis was unnecessary since
trainee controllers would be capable of making this
translation from their previous plant experience.

The Remaining Plans

To complete the analysis, two plans were proposed
to govern the five groups (a) to (e) above, as shown in
the final hierarchy in Figure 3. Corresponding plans
are recorded in Table 2.

THE EFFECTS OF ANALYSIS

The effects of analysis are reflected by the fate
of the fifteen operations originally recorded. Of
these fifteen, twelve remain as primitive operations,
i.e. operations not further redescribed, two were judged
to be redundant and the remaining operation was further
redescribed. Apart from the two subordinates of the
operation needing redescription, four further operations
had to be proposed in order to make sense of the task.
The analysis resulted in a hierarchy of nine simple
plans each governing no more than four subordinate
operations.

THE OVERALL TRAINING PROGRAMME

The restructuring procedure resulted in a

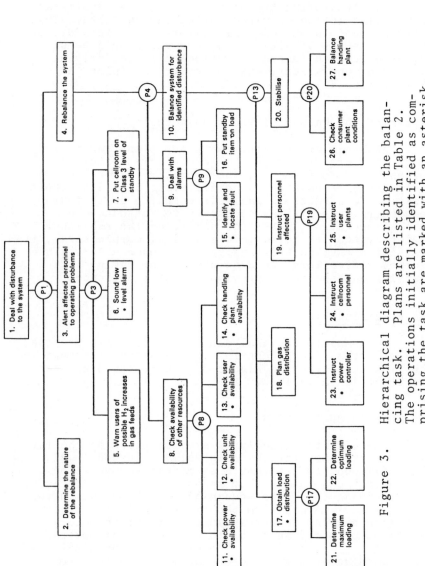

Figure 3.   Hierarchical diagram describing the balancing task. Plans are listed in Table 2.
The operations initially identified as com-
prising the task are marked with an asterisk.

Super-ordinate Operation	Plan
1. Deal with disturbance to the system	→— 2 — 3 — 4 —→
3. Alert personnel affected to operating problems	For disturbances during maintenance →— 7 —→ For sudden decreases →— 6 —→ For cell availability decreases →— 5 —→
4. Rebalance the system	For 'warned increase' →— 8 — 10 → For 'warned decrease' →— 10 —→ For 'sudden decrease' →— 9 — 10 →→
8. Check availability of other resources	See text
9. Deal with alarms	See text
10. Balance system for identified disturbance	For 'warned' or 'sudden' decrease: →— 17 — 18 — 19 — 20 —→ For 'warned increase', carry out above sequence 17 to 20, but omit operations as follows in accordance with decision reached in plan 8: to increase producton, carry out complete sequence. to redistribute gas, omit 17 to redistribute load, omit 18
17. Obtain load distribution	As specified in operating instructions 21 or 22
19. Instruct personnel affected	Give new running rates and time of change to whoever is affected in 10
20. Stabilise	If users are affected by 10 →———— 26 If handling plant is affected by 10 →———— 27

Table 2.   Plans from the balancing task in Figure 3.

hierarchy of plans for which satisfactory training had
been prescribed plus a set of operations, easy to train
or already within the trainee's repertoire.   To complete the training programme the training of the
operations and plans had to be sequenced.

Skill at the balancing task requires the controller
to link a series of decisions, which were separated
during analysis in order to state them clearly for
training purposes.   The overall planning skill would be
mastered, first by teaching plan 1, so that trainees
could indicate the order in which operations 2, 3, and
4 should be carried out in response to disturbances.
Then the trainee should be introduced to plan 3 and
practise it in the context of the whole task by indicating the order of operations 2, 5, 6, 7 and 4, i.e.
substituting operations 5, 6 and 7 and their plan for
operation 3 in the previous sequence.   Then the trainee
should be introduced to plan 4, and practise it in the
context of the whole task by indicating the order of
operations 2, 5, 6, 7, 8, 9 and 10.   This process of

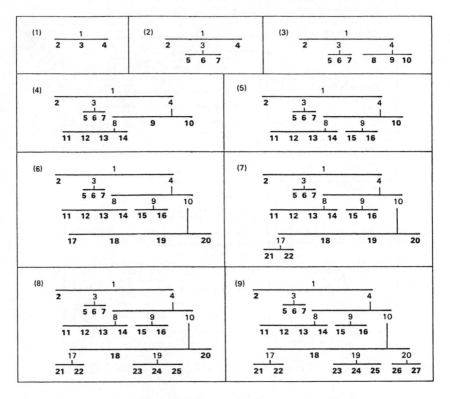

Figure 4.   The development of the training sequence.
             Through stages 1 to 9, the trainee is
             required to respond to disturbances in pro-
             gressively greater detail (the operations
             indicated by the bold print), thereby prac-
             tising increasingly complex planning.

gradually increasing the level of detail with which the
trainee is expected to respond to disturbances is continued until the whole hierarchy of plans is mastered.
Then trainees can practise the entire task by carrying
out simulated exercises on plant.   The complete sequence is shown in Figure 4.

CONCLUSION

Rules for Analysis

      At an early stage we could describe the balancing

task, in terms conforming to Annett and Duncan's minimal
rules for hierarchical task analysis, by listing the
original fifteen subordinate operations and specifying
that they must be planned in order to achieve the superordinate goal 'deal with disturbances to the system'.
But this description suggested no hypotheses for training
the plan and hence was of little value.   It was also
apparent that the original fifteen operations provided
by our informants were neither exhaustive nor distinct.
So, our first general criticism is that the supposed
set of subordinate operations of a plan which merely
reiterates its superordinate goal, may include some not
entailed in the task and exclude others which are essential.   Plans which do not explicitly state the conditions for carrying out subordinate operations, do not
guarantee an accurate task analysis, let alone enable
training hypotheses to be stated with any confidence.

        Our second criticism has to do with the method of
progressive redescription.   Little progress towards a
satisfactory description was made until it was realised
that a single complex plan can often be restructured
into a hierarchy of simpler plans.   In retrospect, it
can be said that this is what Annett and Duncan had
implied in their approach to analysis.   It may be that
a procedure progressively redescribing operations in
greater detail can be followed in some tasks.   However
in the balancing task, as initially stated, further
redescription of any of the operations was not called
for.   This underlines the point that Annett and
Duncan's rules are concerned primarily with the adequate
description of tasks, rather than the analytic process
of collecting and organising data to provide such descriptions.

Restructuring

        Restructuring was achieved by examining the set
of subordinate operations to identify groups sharing a
common superordinate goal.   Smaller groups identified
in this way are easier to examine and their plans
easier to state.   Two complementary mechanisms can be
suggested to account for this.   One is that focusing
on a smaller chunk of the task means that the plan must
cope with a narrower range of situations.   Table 1 was
a case in point.   Here the plan had to deal with only
32 different types of situation, far less than the
total range of situations confronting the controller in
the overall task (a conservative estimate exceeds 3000
types of situation).   The other mechanism is that the
analyst and his informant can more easily think through
likely ways of dealing with variable sequence plans
governing only a few subordinate operations.   Tables

such as Table 1 are rarely necessary. The mere fact
that a plan now involves fewer operations and must
cope with fewer situations is sufficient to enable the
analyst and his informant to sort it out.

Part Task Training

        For the most difficult plan stated, it was pos-
sible to prescribe part-task training exercises,
training simulation and training criteria. The
remaining plans seemed sufficiently simple to suggest
that, once outlined, trainees would soon master them
with a little guidance and practice. Had they proved
more difficult, then, again, part-task training regimes
could have been employed (e.g. Clay, 1964) or further
restructuring might have been envisaged.

        Having prescribed training for the plans, there
still remained the problem of the overall training
sequence. A number of different part-task training
regimes based on the analysis might have been chosen.
In the event, the preferred solution amounted to a type
of cumulative part training. But while cumulative part
training usually requires the trainee gradually to practise increasingly large amounts of the task, the procedure in Figure 4 requires the trainee to practise the
whole task with increasingly detailed planning. This
regime meets the need for a trained controller to integrate a number of plans in dealing with disturbances.
Hierarchical task analysis thus offers some interesting
alternatives to the 'standard' part-task training
methods, especially when dealing with complex planning
skills.

        In conclusion, a training design was achieved
for this complex planning skill, regarded for some years
by management as intractable. It is likely that other
complex tasks are assumed to be intractable and difficult to train simply because a suitable means of analysing them has never been seriously attempted.

REFERENCES

Annett, J., Duncan, K.D., Stammers, R.B. and Gray, M.J.
     (1971).   Task Analysis, D.E.P. Training Infor-
     mation Paper No. 6, H.M.S.O., London.

Belbin, E. (1964).   Training the Adult Worker, H.M.S.O.,
     London.

Clay, H.M. (1964).   Research in Relation to Operator
     Training, D.S.I.R., London.

Duncan, K.D. (1974).   'Analytical technique in
    training design', in The Human Operator in Process
    Control (eds. E. Edwards and F.P. Lees), Taylor
    and Francis, London.

Duncan, K.D. and Shepherd, A. (1975).   'A simulator
    and training technique for diagnosing plant
    failures from control panels', Ergonomics, 18,
    627-641.

Shepherd, A. (1976).   'An improved tabular format for
    task analysis', J. Occup. Psychol., 49, 93-104.

Changes in Working Life
Edited by K.D. Duncan, M.M. Gruneberg, and D. Wallis
© 1980 John Wiley & Sons Ltd

Chapter 10

Changing Job and Job Demands in Europe

W. T. SINGLETON and R. C. CRAWLEY

There are a great many factors which can influence
what research is done by psychologists on the subject of
Quality of Working Life, as indeed there are for any
type of research: the availability of finance, ease of
access into organisations, freedom to speak to employees
and to publish findings, and the scope for contributing
to the area are some that spring to mind. In cases
where these factors combine positively there is likely
to be a concentration of research effort. The emphasis
that has been placed on studying the quality of working
life of assembly workers during the past thirty years
is a good example of this process at work. It is important to keep reminding ourselves that, simply because
research is being carried out and problems have been
defined, we are not necessarily focussing our attention
on the most important or relevant problems. Changes
may be occurring of a social, political and economic
nature at the macro level which, without our realising
it, are altering the importance of our research at the
micro level.

This paper presents a combination of statistical
and case study data in an attempt to show the major
changes to jobs and job demands since 1966, focussing on
Western Europe in general and the UK in particular.
The stimulus for the paper was that we felt that the
aforementioned changes had overtaken social science
research into Quality of Working Life, with the result
that important areas of work are being under-researched,
and that our existing techniques have become less adequate.

The first section is concerned with changes in the
labour force, using statistical data of labour movements
according to industrial sectors; whilst the second

section examines the widespread impact of technological
change on job content and job demands by the integration
of findings from a number of case studies of practical
skills, with the emphasis on high technology jobs.

TRENDS IN THE DISTRIBUTION OF LABOUR

        If we examine national and international labour
statistics it is clear that, right across Western Europe,
there has been a steady increase in the number of people
working in the tertiary sector (ISIC Categories 6-8)
whilst the number of people working in the primary and
secondary sectors has declined.

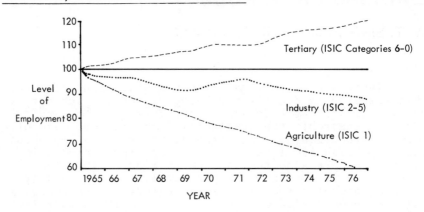

Figure 1.   Evolution of civilian employment by sector
             in Western Europe, 1965-1976.   1965 = 100.

Over the period 1965-76 in Western Europe, employment
in the tertiary sector rose by 20%, whilst in Agriculture it fell by nearly 40%, and in Industry (ISIC
Categories 2-5) by 10%.   The labour force in the tertiary sector now comprises more than half of the total
labour force in most Western European countries.   Averaging the figures for Austria, France, West Germany,
Italy, Norway, Sweden and the UK, the tertiary sector
labour force rose from 43% in 1966 to nearly 52% in
1976, whilst in Industry it fell from 42% to 39%.

        The picture in Sweden and the UK shows this trend
even more clearly.   During the same period, civilian
employment in the tertiary sector rose from just over
49% to nearly 59%, whilst in industry there was a fall
from 44% to 37% (average for the two countries).

        The major rise in employment has occurred within
public and social services.   In the UK the period
under discussion has seen manufacturing lose 1.2 million
employees, whilst ISIC Categories 8 and 9, which include
public and social services, finance and insurance, have

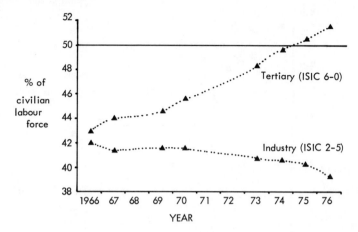

Figure 2.   % Civilian labour force in industry and
             tertiary sectors 1966-1976.   Average for
             selected Western European countries.
             (Figures not available for 1968, 1971, 1972.)

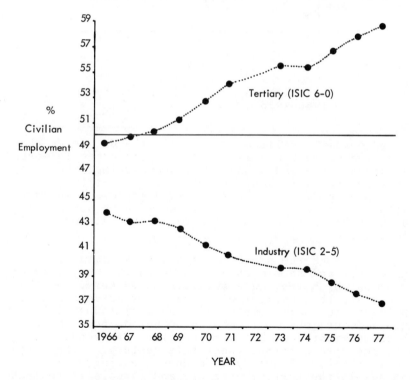

Figure 3.   % Civilian employment in industry and ter-
             tiary sectors, 1966-1977.   Average for
             Sweden and UK. (Figures not available for 1972.)

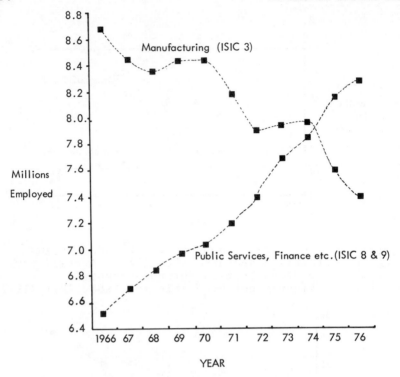

Figure 4.   Civilian employment by activity in UK,
             1966-1976.

gained nearly 2 million.   By 1976, the UK was in the
situation whereby nearly one million more people worked
in categories 8 and 9 than in manufacturing, when only
ten years earlier manufacturing had a majority of 2
million people.   Of the $7\frac{1}{2}$ million employees in manufacturing industry, over 2 million were in non-manufac-
turing jobs, i.e. administrative, technical and
clerical.

        Although the preceding statistical data are
imprecise, and should only be used in the very general
terms in which they have been discussed here, they
illustrate the movement of labour from private sector
employees to public employees, and from industrial jobs
into service jobs.   It should be noted, too, that
these movements are but continuations of trends that
have been present throughout this century.   The problem is that our knowledge and understanding of job
demands in the tertiary sector, and especially the public services, are rudimentary.   Partly this is because
there is not the demand for us to study jobs in these
areas.

Such jobs are subject, to a much greater extent than jobs in the private sector, to social, economic and political change which can affect the quality of working life of employees and be beyond the control of either supervisors or employers. The problems of the public services are discussed by Midwinter (1977) with particular respect to the employee-client relationship. This aspect of work, the interaction that takes place between employees and members of the public, is one that must influence greatly employees' satisfaction with their work, yet it is an aspect that has received little attention from either the job satisfaction or the training point of view. As Ellis (in press) notes, when the training and education of the 'interpersonal professions' such as Social Workers, Teachers, and Health Visitors are analysed through published syllabuses (McWhirter, 1976) the development of social skills is all but ignored in the curriculum. If the public professions receive little training in interpersonal interaction, it hardly seems likely that the clerical staff will do so.

If one adds to this lack of appropriate training the bureaucratic systems within which public employees so frequently have to work, is it surprising that 'the young, the sick, the poor, the homeless, all these groups of social casualties, find themselves faced by complicated and incomprehensible procedures negotiated by varying species of techno-bureaucrat' (Midwinter, 1977)? For the employee, such a situation frequently feeds back to him in the form of a discontented or aggressive client. Furthermore, what of the satisfaction of the public employee who is expected to carry out a job structured by political demands, such as the street cleaner who is expected to clean streets in a given area once a week irrespective of whether they require daily or monthly cleaning?

A very obvious question arising from the statistical trends discussed above is what sort of jobs or occupations are taking the weight of this increase in employment? The short answer is that we really do not know, because complete data is not readily available. In fact, this leads on to a wider issue altogether. As Payne (1977) states very clearly, the industrial classifications which have formed the basis of the paper so far are a poor substitute for occupational hierarchies, for the purpose of studying occupational changes, since the hierarchy of occupations contained in each industry does not enter into the ISIC system. However, there is no occupational hierarchy information more recent than the 1971 Census in the UK. This revealed that, under the Registrar-General's classification of occupations, there had been a substantial movement of

Socio-economic groups (SEGs) Registrar-General's classification	Occupations	1951	1961	1971
1 - 5	Highly skilled non-farm	12.2	16.1	20.3
6, 8, 12	Intermediate skilled non-farm	23.8	25.7	27.5
7, 9 - 11	'Manual' non-farm	56.4	51.1	46.3

Table 1.   % of all economically active employed in
            highly skilled (SEGs 1-5), intermediate
            skilled (SEGs 6, 8, 12) and low skilled
            (SEGs 7, 9-11) non-farm jobs.   England and
            Wales 1951-71.

employees into 'highly skilled' and 'intermediate
skilled' occupations, (i.e. socio-economic groups 1 - 5,
6, 8, and 12) and away from low skilled jobs (SEGs 7,
9 - 11) during the preceding ten year period.   It is a
pity that such data is not available at shorter time
intervals, and that it is not related in any way to the
ISIC classification.

     Even allowing for this occupational data, it is
apparent that we have nothing approaching a psychological
classification of occupations, in which occupations or
jobs might be classified according to, for example, the
skills they require and the degree of autonomy they allow.
According to the Registrar-General (General Register
Office, 1960) 'an occupation of a person is the kind of
work which he or she performs, due regard being paid to
the conditions under which it is performed ...'   Nevertheless, we then find that, for example, within SEG 12
(Own Account Workers) are classified certain self-
employed pilots, flight engineers, fishermen, gardeners
and chimney-sweeps.   Quite clearly, this classification
is of very little use to us as an indication of jobs
and job demands in psychological terms.   Regrettably,
the onus appears to be on psychologists themselves to
collect the sort of job data that would enable us to,
firstly, compare one job with another in psychological
terms, and secondly to specify how individual jobs have
changed over a period of time.   This is undoubtedly a
huge task, and one that Governments ought to support,
because these sorts of data are needed and not only by
psychologists.   The Department of Employment (D.E.) in

the UK sponsored a two-year research project in the
Applied Psychology Department at the University of Aston
in Birmingham between 1972-1974 to examine this problem
with respect to the D.E.'s 'Classification of Occupations
and Directory of Occupational Titles' (Lawrence, 1974).
Unfortunately, under conditions of economic pressure,
this sort of research providing source data of wide
utility is given low priority.

CHANGING JOB DEMANDS DUE TO TECHNOLOGICAL CHANGE

The following section moves from the macro to the
micro level of analysis, to examine a number of case
studies of technological change.   In the previous section, we were able to show that many more people are now
working in situations that are susceptible to influences
on the quality of working life not found generally in
the jobs studied most frequently by psychologists.
What we were not able to show was to what extent and in
what way the pattern of jobs has changed since 1966,
although it is reasonable to infer from the data that
such a change has happened.   There is another level of
change which this section will discuss, namely the impact
of technological change on individual occupations and
jobs in terms of skills and job demands.   The focus of
attention will be on high technology jobs.

There have been few systematic studies of how
technology has changed job content and structure.   There
are two very obvious reasons why this is so.   Firstly,
that social scientists are often not called in until the
change has taken place, by which time it is next to
impossible to establish precisely what change to the job
content has occurred.   Secondly, many of the techniques
that were evailable for studying the effects of such
change on either the job or the job holder have been both
imprecise and laborious, especially those involving task
and skills analysis.   Although more recently techniques
such as the Job Diagnostic Survey (Hackman and Oldham,
1975) and the Position Analysis Questionnaire (McCormick
et al., 1969) have become available to measure jobs and
job behaviour, the question of just what comprises skill
and how to measure it is far from answered satisfactorily.

The following case studies are based mainly on
examples from Singleton (1978).   Each of the studies was
carried out by a different researcher, and with low
standardisation of method and technique.   Indeed, the
objectives of the analysts were different, ranging from
productivity, through health and safety, to systems
design.   The studies selected for this paper have one
thing in common however: they all have something to say
about the effects on the jobs concerned of technological
change.

The Forest Worker and the Farm Worker

There are two main types of forest worker in Sweden, the cutter and the machine operator. The cutter is still the most common category of forest worker, but machines of various types are becoming more and more important to the industry (Pettersson, 1978).

The work of the cutter is very physically demanding, although significantly less in recent years with the introduction of lightweight power saws. During the winter, he will often be plodding through deep snow, carrying equipment of which the saw alone weights 7-8 kg. He fells, bucks (i.e. strips) and rolls away the trees, all of which demand a high level of physical exertion. There are moderate perceptual demands, especially in the activities of tree selection and stem cutting, during which assessment of sensory input from eyes, ears and proprioceptors is involved. Mental processes are involved in deciding where to buck the tree, and the best way to crosscut together with a certain amount of planning of his work.

The machine operator, of which the most common is the logging machine operator, has a much more perceptually demanding job, but much less physically demanding, since 65-70% of the work is done from the cab of the machine. The speed at which the operator works at some stages is determined by the speed of machine operation during tree processing. The activity might, for example, be feeding in previously felled trees to be limbed and bucked. The high feeding speed of the machine places high demands on the worker to process perceptual input, sometimes at too high a level, especially for the older worker.

In summary, the new 'tree processing' jobs have replaced physically active jobs with more sedentary jobs. This is having an effect on the workers' health, since their food intake has remained fairly constant at between 4000-5000 calories per day, and they have consequently become overweight. The faster tempo of the work means that they have less scope for influencing their own work performance. In particular, they have had to sacrifice some quality for quantity.

The farm worker, like the forest worker, has seen a substantial increase in productivity occur due to new technologies. New machinery has greatly decreased the old manual skills, such as hedge laying and rick thatching, with almost complete automation of some activities such as milking (Matthews, 1978). The introduction of motorised vehicles, for example the combined harvester, has greatly increased the control skills

required, and this too has become characteristic of the
machine-operating forest worker.   There are greater
demands now put on the farm worker's processing of perceptual information.   The amount of machinery has
raised the importance of service and maintenance tasks,
of setting up and adjusting.   The farm worker now also
is something of a monitor, checking that more or less
automatic processes, from milking to potato selection,
are proceeding normally.

The Pilot, the Air Traffic Controller and the Process Controller

Aircraft operation, air traffic control and
process control are all examples of high technology,
capital-intensive fields of work, although air traffic
control is unusual in combining a relatively large
capital input with labour-intensive operation.

On the flight-deck, there has been a dramatic rise
in the use of automatic devices and on-board computing
facilities, with developments in control systems and
instrument presentations (Thorne and Charles, 1978).
The role of the pilot has evolved from that of a highly
dexterous individual to a highly qualified technician
operating as computer controller, crew manager, monitor
and planner.   The use of automatic flight control
systems has reduced the need for manual dexterity and
coordination and increased the amount of monitoring,
whilst increasing complexity of air traffic control
and of aircraft systems has pushed to prominence the
pilot's need to plan - routes, crew arrangements and
workload.

The air traffic controller (ATCO) does not have
the same level of technological advancement in his job,
since at the moment none of his executive functions
are carried out by computer or automatic device.   However, there has been a similar trend away from motor
skills towards reliance on perceptual and cognitive
skills (Whitfield and Stammers, 1978).   Technological
change in the aircraft industry has, over the years,
put increasing demands on the ATCO's decision-making
skills, communication skills, perceptual processing
and vigilance, as traffic levels have rapidly increased
and the airspace become greatly structured.   Subsequent improvements to radar and communication networks
have accelerated this trend, and made even more demands
on the ATCO's perceptual and discriminatory skills.
Like the pilot, the ATCO now requires both management
and planning skills, although in the ATCO's case he is
dealing with peers rather than subordinates, and his
planning tends to be more short-term and intense.

Common to all three occupations is a high memory load, both short and long-term for the pilot and the ATCO, but mainly long-term for the process controller. There is a requirement for all three types of employee to learn to a high level and retain large quantities of knowledge: for example, of process behaviour, mechanisms, rules and geographical layouts. They can be faced with a complex choice of strategies, perhaps under severe time pressures, and a high degree of mental flexibility is required.

All these occupations can present the job-holders with a particular type of problem that is a feature of high-technology jobs. At times, automatic control or information systems can fail, leaving the operator to revert to a pattern of behaviours and skills that used to be required but now rarely are. It is increasingly true that where this sort of system failure occurs, it presents the employee with considerable problems, as use of the earlier methods of operation becomes less and less common. Under these conditions, it is well-known that skills atrophy, and recall of knowledge deteriorates. This situation not only presents problems for trainers, but also of course for the job-holders who are required to handle the usually stressful situation. It is arguable that the operator who takes over from automatic control under fault or failure conditions is faced with more complex control decisions, and therefore needs more process knowledge and high levels of skill, than the operator who is using manual control the majority of the time (Bainbridge, 1978). The high level of technology present on the flight-deck and in process control have already turned the pilot and the process controller respectively into monitors for much of the time, and the same prospect is possible for the ATCO if system concepts current in the USA are introduced there (e.g. Jenney and Lawrence, 1974). This presents obvious problems not only of vigilance and human error, but of motivation and boredom.

CONCLUSIONS

From an analysis of case studies, both of those quoted above and of others, some generalisations can be made and some issues raised. Firstly, the effect of new technology on jobs is rarely a simple case of de-skilling on the one hand or improvement on the other. A number of studies of process work have pointed to the gains in quality of working life resulting from automation, either because of reduced alienation or improved working conditions (e.g. Blauner, 1964) although there are conflicting reports (Wilson, 1973). It would be wrong, however, to generalise these findings to the

effects of automation in highly skilled non-manual occupations.   Whereas in many cases to date, automation has
been introduced into previously blue-collar occupational
areas, where the existing jobs often left much to be
desired, there is a new trend towards automation, or at
least a high degree of computer assistance, in occupational areas that are already high on Hackman and
Oldham's (1975) core job dimensions, for example, pilots
and air traffic controllers.   With these jobs, the
problems that automation might bring to the operator
seem just as likely as the benefits.

        If one includes under deskilling the atrophy of
skill and deterioration of knowledge through lack of
use, then this does seem a likely effect of new technologies.   However, in addition there is a complex
redistribution of skills, existing ones supplemented by
new skills or replaced by them.   It remains a case
for empirical verification to determine whether the
overall result in each case is deskilling or not.

        Finally, there is a need for a widespread accep-
tance of technology as a flexible, malleable input to
systems.   This is already a view shared by most social
scientists (e.g. Mumford, 1971).   The problem with
high-technology systems is that there is usually a long
period of systems research before the more concrete
stage of system building and implementation is reached.
This research period, perhaps lasting a number of years,
is usually carried out by specialist organisations who
then sell their system concepts as a ready-made package
to their clients.   Although these systems research
teams may on occasion include ergonomists, it is almost
unknown for them to include psychologists to consider
human motivation.   Consequently, system designers may
impose constraints on individual jobs which make the
adherence to social values and employee needs very difficult later on.

        The value of our contribution to such research
teams depends on our ability to develop techniques
and methods that may be used at such an early stage in
technological change.   Systems designers require an
input to their research in terms of, for example, allocation of function.   Thus our model of employee motivation needs to be more specific than existing models,
relating 'personal and work outcomes' to task and skill
in more detail than is allowed for in Hackman and
Oldham's (1975) model, although theirs is the most
detailed existing model.   Of course, it is possible
that such a level of detail of explanation is beyond
our capability, at least in the foreseeable future,
given the imprecision of existing techniques.   A preliminary investigation of the requirements of socio-

technical systems design in high-technology systems is
being carried out at the University of Aston in Birmingham, with reference to Air Traffic Control systems
(Crawley and Spurgeon, 1979; Crawley, 1979).   This
research which is sponsored by the Civil Aviation
Authority over a four year period, is examining in
greater detail the task and skill inputs to motivation
and other personal and work outcomes, by the use of task
and skills analysis.   The limitations of time and
resources have restricted the research to a small but
important aspect of the problem.   If the problem of
employee motivation in advanced technological systems
is to be dealt with effectively a much broader based
programme of research is required to examine, for
example, work group structure, training problems,
relative importance of intrinsic and extrinsic features
of the job, and in particular the effects on motivation
of different levels and types of computer assistance
and automation.

REFERENCES

Bainbridge, L. (1978).   'The process Controller', in
     The Analysis of Practical Skills (Ed. W.T.
     Singleton), pp. 236-263, MTP Press Ltd, Lancaster.

Blauner, R. (1964).   Alienation and Freedom, University
     of Chicago Press.

Crawley, R.C. (1979).   Air Traffic Controllers'
     Reactions to Computer Assistance, EDU Memo 7902,
     Applied Psychology Department, University of Aston
     in Brimingham, UK.

Crawley, R.C. and Spurgeon, P. (1979).   'Computer assis-
     tance and the air traffic controller's job satis-
     faction', in Satisfactions in Work Design (Eds.
     R.G. Sell and P. Shipley), pp. 169-178, Taylor and
     Francis, London.

Ellis, R. (in press).   'Simulated Social Skill
     Training for the Interpersonal Professions',
     Paper presented at NATO conference 'Analysis of
     Social Skills', June 5-9, 1979, Leuven, Belgium.

General Register Office (1960).   Classification of
     occupations, HMSO, London.

Hackman, J.R. and Oldham, G.R. (1975).   'Development
     of the Job Diagnostic Survey', J. App. Psychol.,
     60, (2), 159-170.

Jenney, L.L. and Lawrence, K.A. (1974).   Implications
     of automation for operating and staffing an
     Advanced Air Traffic Management System (AATMS),
     Washington, D.C., Department of Transportation,
     DOT-TSC-OST-74-32.

Lawrence, D.R. (1974).   The Department of Employment
     Codot Human Factors ("CHUF") Research Project:
     Final Report, AP Report 55, October 1974,
     Applied Psychology Department, University of Aston
     in Birmingham, UK.

McCormick, E.J., Jeanneret, P.R. and Mecham, R.C. (1969).
     The Development and Background of the Position
     Analysis Questionnaire (PAQ), Report No. 5,
     Occupational Research Center, Purdue University,
     Indiana.

McWhirter, E. (1976).   'Psychology in Professional
     Courses', Bull. BPS, 29, 211.

Matthews, J. (1978).   'The Farm Worker', in The
     Analysis of Practical Skills (Ed. W.T. Singleton),
     pp. 55-84, MTP Press Ltd, Lancaster.

Midwinter, E. (1977).   'The Professional-Lay Relation-
     ship: A Victorian Legacy', J. Child Psychol.
     Psychiat., 18, 101-113.

Mumfort, E. (1971).   Economic evaluation of computer-
     based systems, National Computing Centre Ltd,
     Manchester.

Payne, G. (1977).   'Occupational transition in advanced
     industrial societies', Soc. Rev., 25, 5-39.

Pettersson, B. (1978).   'The Forest Worker', in The
     Analysis of Practical Skills (Ed. W.T. Singleton),
     pp. 44-54, MTP Press Ltd, Lancaster.

Singleton, W.T. (1978).   The Study of Real Skills:
     Volume 1. The Analysis of Practical Skills, MTP
     Press Ltd, Lancaster.

Thorne, R.G. and Charles, G.W.F. (1978).   'The Pilot',
     in The Analysis of Practical Skills (Ed. W.T.
     Singleton), pp. 189-208, MTP Press Ltd, Lancaster.

Whitfield, D. and Stammers, R.B. (1978).   'The Air
     Traffic Controller', in The Analysis of Practical
     Skills (Ed. W.T. Singleton), pp. 209-235, MTP
     Press Ltd, Lancaster.

Wilson, N.A.B. (1973).   On the quality of working life,
    Manpower Papers No. 7, Department of Employment,
    HMSO, London.

Changes in Working Life
Edited by K.D. Duncan, M.M. Gruneberg, and D. Wallis
© 1980 John Wiley & Sons Ltd

Chapter 11

The Centrality of Skill-Utilization for Job Design

G. E. O'BRIEN

Recognition of the importance of skill utilization as a determinant of psychological 'well-being' is relatively slight within the psychological literature. This seems surprising since it is widely accepted that technological change in the last fifty years has produced systematic 'de-skilling' of the workforce. The major contribution to research on skill-utilization was made by Kornhauser (1965) in his study of United States' automobile workers where he found that skill-utilization was the major factor accounting for variations in job satisfaction and 'mental health'. In his study, skill-utilization was defined in terms of the extent to which a job used employee abilities and mental health was a composite of manifest anxiety, self-esteem, hostility, sociability, life satisfaction and personal morale. He concluded that '... workers' feelings regarding the use of their abilities is unmistakeably associated with the superior mental health of the group in higher factory jobs and the poorer mental health at low level jobs' (Kornhauser, 1965, p. 99).

This does not seem to be the most important or interesting finding. Rather it is the finding that still-utilization has a stronger association to mental health than other job attributes. Again quoting Kornhauser '... this particular set of findings appears to occupy a crucial place among the determinants of the mental health of individual groups when compared to characteristics such as job security, physical conditions, pay, repetitiveness, speed and intensity, social conditions (supervision, co-workers' company), advancement opportunities, and income-pay as means of economic "gratification"' (Kornhauser, 1965, p. 107). A restricted sample together with other methodological weaknesses should have encouraged further research but

little is available.   There is an abundance of research
on the effects of jobs on satisfaction but little that
is relevant to the evaluation of Kornhauser's main
findings.   Two main reasons for this appear to be:

(i)   Defined job attributes have not included skill-
       utilization.   Often skill level has been measured
       or the number of skills required but these are not
       the same as skill-utilization.   Skill-utilization
       is defined as the degree of match or congruence
       between an individual's skills and the opportunity
       to use these skills in that individual's work
       role.   It has some resemblance to the concept of
       mental load as it is used in ergonomics (Bainbridge,
       1974, 1976), but is much broader in that it
       includes skills other than those required for
       information processing.

(ii)   The relative importance of various job attributes
       as predictors of job outcome measures has not been
       tested.

Some job attributes measured appear to be very
similar to skill-utilization, but closer examination
shows this resemblance to be tangential and superficial.
Herzberg's job motivators (Herzberg, 1966) could generally imply skill-utilization but are interpreted in such
a broad way that there is no way to identify and separate
other job attributes which could also be involved, such
as absolute skill level, influence or autonomy and
variety.   Maslow's self-actualization job potential is
also too broad for use in testing the centrality of
skill-utilization as there is no precise and systematic
attempt to define the job attributes which contribute to
self-actualization.   Typically jobs are defined not in
terms of job attributes, but as potential need fulfillers
(Maslow, 1943, 1965).

Much research on reactions to job attributes has
been derived from Turner and Lawrence's study rather
than Kornhauser's.   Turner and Lawrence (1965) developed a Requisite Task Attribute Index which was a
weighted total of six job attributes - variety, autonomy,
required and optional interaction, responsibility, skill
and knowledge.   The weighted combination assumed that
all such attributes were important although the extra
weighting given to autonomy and variety reflected the
author's belief that they were especially important.
The attribute 'skill and knowledge' was not really
skill-utilization as it was measured with one question
where the respondent was required to estimate the amount
of time required to learn the job proficiently.   It is
thus more appropriately interpreted as a measure of skill-
level.   Strangely, Turner and Lawrence maintained the

view that autonomy and variety were the most important
attributes even though the only task attribute to correlate significantly with job satisfaction was skill/know-
ledge.   It is not surprising to find that research that
used Turner and Lawrence's method of job analysis also
fails to measure skill-utilization.

Hackman and Lawler's (1971) approach to job
design used four 'core' job dimensions derived from
Turner and Lawrence's study - variety, autonomy, task
identity and feedback.   The potential importance of
skill-utilization was recognised but not defined separately.   The questionable assumption was made that high
variety jobs tapped a number of different skills which
'may be important to the employee'.   In practice, they
assumed what Kornhauser had shown not to be the case -
that variety and skill-utilization have equally strong
effects upon job outcomes.   More emphasis was given to
skill in the job diagnostic survey (Hackman and Oldham,
1975) by inclusion of the attribute of 'skill-variety'.
However, the definition again assumed that variety and
skill were identical.   Nor did skill refer directly to
the match between job requirements and worker abilities,
but rather to the number of different skills and talents
of the employee.

The unique contribution of job attributes to
critical psychological states and work outcomes was not
investigated because a composite 'motivating potential'
score was used which combined job attributes in a multiplicative fashion.   Even if skill-variety were
replaced by a valid skill-utilization measure, the job
diagnostic theory assumes that job satisfaction could be
relatively high despite low skill-utilization if
autonomy and feedback were high.   This is untested and
appears an unlikely occurrence.   This is perhaps one
reason why some researchers (Wall, Clegg and Jackson,
1978) have not found the theory to predict job satisfaction or mental health.

Another influential approach to job design which
appears to minimize skill-utilization is the socio-
technical approach (Emery and Thorsrud, 1976;   Emery
and Phillips, 1976;   Davis and Cherns, 1975).   This
approach has provided a framework for understanding
organizational change in terms of the need to integrate
the interpersonal and technological systems.   The
structure of these two systems is generally not specified and the critical components vary across studies.
This, in itself, limits the usefulness of the approach
but some papers have tried to identify the characteristics
of jobs which will enable employees to express their personal and interpersonal needs.   Emery and Phillips

(1976) and Emery and Thorsrud (1976) defined variety, learning, elbow room, mental challenge and desirable job future as central intrinsic characteristics of a job. As these judgments were highly correlated (the actual magnitudes were not reported), the authors felt justified in pooling the judgments in order to form a single index - the 'objective quality of their work'. This measure was significantly correlated with global job satisfaction and it was concluded that good quality jobs could motivate workers and increase their social adjustment. The problems with such findings are that: (a) it is not possible to say which are the most important elements of the good quality job; and (b) job design which is aimed at constructing 'good quality' jobs may neglect to consider the most important elements or set of elements. This could be the case with the use of semi-autonomous groups which may provide autonomy, variety and learning, but neglect to consider the skill-match between tasks and employees. Multi-skilling or high skill levels is not the same as matching given skills to the job.

In an important manner, Taylor was more aware of the importance of skill-utilization than the socio-technicians. In his apparently mythical experiments with Schmidt (Wrege and Perroni, 1974) he did illustrate his concern with appropriate selection of employees so that skills were matched to the task requirement. Unfortunately, subsequent practitioners of scientific management neglected skill-match in favour of rational simplification and economic need theory. The relationship between skill-utilization and self development has been explored theoretically by a few authors (White, 1959, 1963; French and Kahn, 1969), but no explicit theory relating skill-utilization to personal and job outcomes is currently available. It may be assumed that experience of family, educational, and work structures results in an individual internalising a self identity based upon judgements about what he or she is capable of doing. It is also assumed that positive evaluation of a given social structure occurs when an individual perceives that his or her social role within the structure requires the use of abilities which are consistent with his or her self-identity. When match occurs this should also enhance or increase individual expectation that it is possible to maintain and develop self-identity through personal action. Hence, positive evaluation of a job should be directly related to the perception of match or consistency between the abilities associated with self-identity and the abilities required for job performance, i.e. skill-utilization. When the job does not require use of central abilities, then under-utilization occurs. This should lead to lowered evaluation of the job or job dissatisfaction and lower expectation of the efficacy of personal action in producing desired personal outcomes.

Prolonged experience of jobs with low skill-utilization should also lead to anxiety and mental strain (Murrell, 1978).   Initially, strain should be due to the inability to achieve consistency between identity as defined by valued abilities and identity as defined by abilities required for job performance.   If the job cannot be changed then consistency can only be achieved by changing self-identity.   Hence, further and lasting strain can occur when there is ambiguity about identity or lack of acceptance of an externally defined identity.

The associations between skill-utilization, job satisfaction, mental strain, and personal control were examined in a survey of a representative sample of Adelaide employees.

THE ADELAIDE SURVEY

Sample

The sample was a $\frac{1}{2}$% household sample drawn from metropolitan Adelaide using the technique of multi-stage cluster sampling (Kish, 1965) to obtain adequate representation of occupations and socio-economic status.   A sample frame (based on the Australian Burea of Statistics Census sampling frame) constructed by the Flinders University Centre for Applied Social and Survey Research was used.   Of a total of 1,473 households approached, 1,123 households allowed research access which resulted in a final number of 1,383 persons in current employment completing useable questionnaires.   This gave a household response rate of 76% which was considered satisfactory.   Since the sample was drawn from a metropolitan area, it is under-represented in the farm workers' category, but the occupational profile is reasonably similar to the South Australian 1971 Census distribution.   Sample characteristics and questionnaire items are given in O'Brien, Dowling and Kabanoff (1978).

Measures

(a)   Job attributes   The job attributes of influence, skill utilization, variety, pressure and interaction were measured on five-point scales with the influence scale having 10 items and the other attributes having 4 items for each scale.   These attributes were derived from an analysis of the formal job structure using concepts of structural role theory (Oeser and Harary, 1962, 1964;

Oeser and O'Brien, 1967;   O'Brien, 1967, 1968;   Trahair, 1977).

Influence was measured using more items than the other attributes as it was considered that there were a large number of job aspects which a worker could potentially have influence upon.   Items asked about the amount of say or influence that workers had over who they chatted with, design of the work place, speed of work, new skills learned, choice of supervisor, choice of co-workers, organization of work, rest periods, overtime, and the jobs done.   The categories of response were none, very little, some, a great deal, and a very great deal.

Skill-utilization items asked respondents to indicate how much they used their abilities or training on the job.   Items asked about opportunities for learning new jobs, working in the way they thought best, using abilities and using training and experience.   The categories of response were not at all, very little, some, a reasonable amount and a great deal.

Variety items asked about amount of job changes, change in location, variation of work pace, and frequency of interacting with different people.   Response categories were not at all, a little, a fair amount, quite a lot and a very large amount.

Pressure items asked about the extent to which respondents felt they were rushed by other people, received feedback on work quality, worked to deadlines, and had time to correct mistakes.   The categories of response were all the time, quite a lot, a fair amount, occasionally and never.

Interaction items asked how much respondents had to work together with others, had opportunities to chat, were required to talk to others as part of the job, and did work which depended upon the previous work of others. Response categories were all the time, quite a lot, a fair amount, occasionally, and never.   Factor analysis of all job attribute items indicated a high correspondence between theoretical scales and empirically derived factors (Table 1).

(b)   Desired job attributes or work values   The desired attribute or work value scales were similar to those used to measure actual job attributes but instead of asking respondents to describe their jobs, they were asked to describe how they would like their jobs to be. The scales were desired influence (10 items), desired skill-utilization (4 items), desired variety (4 items),

Scale	Item	Factor 1	2	3	4
Skill-utilization	1 Chance to learn new jobs	.17	.11	.42	.29
"	2 Opportunity to use own work methods	.30	-.05	.46	.13
"	3 Able to use abilities	.21	.01	.85	.11
"	4 Able to use training and experience	.17	.10	.80	.06
Influence	5 Say in being able to chat	.36	.23	.16	.15
"	6 Say in design of work place	.60	.03	.23	.15
"	7 Say in deciding speed of work	.43	-.01	.12	.20
"	8 Say in deciding on new skills to be learnt	.62	.08	.36	.27
"	9 Say in deciding on supervisor	.78	.01	.08	.10
"	10 Say in deciding on coworkers	.84	.04	.10	.11
"	11 Say in deciding on work organization	.51	-.07	.20	.18
"	12 Say in deciding on breaks	.54	-.02	.08	.23
"	13 Say in deciding on overtime	.55	-.07	.18	.09
"	14 Say in deciding on job allocation	.69	.03	.16	.17
Variety	15 Amount of change and variety in job	.24	.06	.39	.49
"	16 Amount of moving around	.13	.00	.04	.62
"	17 Amount of variation in work place	.24	.00	.09	.54
"	18 Ability to meet different people	.20	.16	.19	.67
Pressure	19 Degree to which you are rushed by others	-.07	.06	-.03	-.02
"	20 Amount of feedback	.20	.06	.23	.14
"	21 Pressure to complete deadlines	.08	.04	.04	.03
"	22 Time to correct mistakes	-.01	-.09	-.11	-.01
Interaction	23 Time spent sharing jobs	-.04	.71	-.01	.00
"	24 Dependence of job upon work of others	-.03	.44	.06	-.01
"	25 Ability to chat while doing job	.08	.61	.02	.11
"	26 Amount of interaction required by job	.09	.38	.19	.25

Table 1.   Item Factor Loading on main factors obtained from principal components factor analysis of job attribute items (Varimax Rotation).

desired pressure (4 items), and desired interaction (4
items). The categories of response were none, very
little, some, a great deal, and a very great deal.

(c)   Job satisfaction   This scale contained 18 items
covering different facets of the job including co-
workers, supervision, pay, variety, skill level, opportunities for learning, influence, pressure, feedback,
promotion, physical conditions, challenge, and opportunities for growth.   The items were designed to
include the intrinsic attributes of the job, together
with extrinsic attributes which described the job context.   Each facet was rated on one of five points
(very dissatisfied, dissatisfied, neither satisfied nor
dissatisfied, satisfied, very satisfied).   It was
decided to develop a measure of job satisfaction rather
than use a standard measure such as the Job Descriptive
Index (Smith, Kendall and Hulin, 1969).   Although
widely used in the USA, the J.D.I. has provided less
satisfactory results when used by researchers outside
the USA who have tended to use their own modified version of the scale (Cross, 1973).   Other reasons for
developing another scale were to reduce questionnaire
time and to sample a wider range of job facets.   The
relationships between the new facet satisfaction scale
and the Job Description Index was established by giving
both scales to a separate sample of pharmacists (N =
120).   The correlations between the total satisfaction
score and component scales of the J.D.I. were .71 (work
itself), .37 (pay), .28 (promotions), .19 (supervision)
and .38 (coworkers).   Factor analysis of the facet
satisfaction items identified only one factor which
accounted for more than 10% of item variance.   This
factor loaded most highly on intrinsic (cf. job context)
job facets and account for 41% of item variance.   A
one-item measure of global satisfaction was also included.
There were seven possible response categories ranging
from 'I love it' to 'I hate it'.

(d)   Demographic and personal variables   This set of
variables included area of socialization, age, sex,
income, occupation, education, national origin and job
tensure.

(e)   Health symptoms   A list of 70 symptoms and illnesses was used and respondents were asked to indicate
which of the symptoms or illnesses they had experienced
in the past year.   The list contained 30 complaints
which were considered non-organic, because it could not
be directly related to a specific physical disfunction.
Responses to these non-organic items were correlated and

items which correlated .30 or more with the total score
were retained as 'strain' items.   Twenty-one items
used in the 'strain' scale were migraines, other head-
aches, stomach pains, indigestion, heartburn, trembling
of hands, fidgety or tense, frequently irritable,
becoming tired early, nail biting, loss of weight, severe
loss of appetite, depression, anxiety, other nervous
trouble, nightmares, sleeplessness, tired on waking,
stress feelings, feeling worn out, and short tempered.

(f)   Internal-external control   The scale used was
Rotter's (1966) original scale which measured an individual generalised expectancy about the locus of control.
The scale contains 29 items (including 6 buffer items)
each with two statements.   Respondents were asked to
choose the statement that they agreed with most.   The
scale score is interpreted as a measure of the degree
to which an individual believes that important outcomes
happen because of individual effort and abilities or
because of external agents such as other people, social
forces, lack of chance.   Factor analysis of this scale
showed that there were two main factors.   These corres-
ponded to those found in previous studies and one refers
to personal control beliefs and the other to political
control beliefs.   Scores on the personal control items
highly correlated with total scores and so the total
score was used in analyses.

(g)   Life-satisfaction   This scale contained 10
7-point items which asked the respondent to describe
his/her present life.   The scale was previously used
by Quinn and Shepard (1974) and Emery and Phillips
(1976).

RESULTS

Job Satisfaction and Job Attributes

All scales had high internal reliability except
pressure (α = .33).   The correlations between scales
are shown in Table 2.   In order to establish the
association between job satisfaction and task attributes,
simple regression analyses were performed using standar-
dised scores.   All beta coefficients, except pressure,
were significant but the magnitude of the skill-utilization coefficient was much higher (Table 3).   As the
predictors were correlated the meaning of this coefficient is unclear due to problems of collinearity
(Cohen and Cohen, 1975).   One way of dealing with this
was to obtain orthogonal factors for task attributes and
use these in the regression analyses.   Using varimax

	1	2	3	4	5	6	7	8	9	10	11	12	13	14	15
1. Global job satisfaction															
2. Facet job satisfaction	.55														
3. Skill utilization	.42	.65													
4. Influence	.31	.51	.53												
5. Variety	.28	.46	.47	.53											
6. Pressure	.01	-.12	.05	.06	.07										
7. Interaction	.10	.14	.19	.14	.22	.08									
8. Desired skill utilization	.04	.02	.16	.26	.25	.16	.12								
9. Desired influence	.11	.14	.25	.58	.35	.16	.08	.44							
10. Desired variety	.05	-.07	.06	.17	.36	.14	.13	.57	.36						
11. Desired pressure	.16	.10	.13	.18	.15	.23	.11	.25	.20	.14					
12. Desired interaction	.12	.13	.14	.16	.25	.06	.41	.26	.21	.30	.19				
13. Strain	.15	-.23	-.13	-.10	-.06	.19	.05	.16	.06	.16	-.00	.03			
14. Internal/external control	.16	-.21	-.19	-.22	-.13	-.01	-.03	-.11	-.14	.01	-.18	-.03	.19		
15. Life satisfaction	.27	.37	.26	.19	.18	-.08	.05	.01	.03	-.03	.06	-.03	.06	-.30	-.21

Table 2. Intercorrelations of job attributes, desired job attributes, job satisfaction, strain, internal/external control and life satisfaction. N = 1383, r ≥ .08 for p < .001.

BETA COEFFICIENTS

Predictor	Facet Satisfaction (sum)		Global satisfaction	
	Original scale	Factor scale	Original scale	Factor scale
Skill-utilization	.47*	.47*	.34*	.35*
Influence	.18*	.26*	.09	.14*
Variety	.17*	.23*	.08	.14*
Pressure	-.12*	-.24*	-.04	-.09
Interaction	.04	.02	.00	.02
R	.69*	.72*	.44*	.46*

*p < .001

Table 3.   Simple multiple regression of job satisfaction measures with job attributes
(original and factor scales).

rotation six factors were obtained, four of them having
eigen values greater than 1. The scale item factor
loadings are shown in Table 1.   It is clear that factor
1 has 9 out of 10 influence scale items loading at
values of .4 or above and so can be labelled influence.
Similarly, factor 2 can be labelled interaction, factor
3 skill-utilization, and factor 4 variety.   Factor 5
was a mixed factor while factor 6 only loaded at .4 or
above on two pressure items.

The regression analyses were repeated using factor
scores and results are shown in Table 3.   There were
slight differences on the beta coefficients.   The beta
coefficients for influence, variety and pressure were
slightly increased, but still significant.   Interaction
is still insignificant.   The analysis is not greatly
different when adjusted scales for the job attributes
are used with items omitted with factor loadings of less
than .4.   An alternative method of checking the stability and relative strength of job attribute associations
with job satisfaction is by partial correlation.   When
this was done, the fourth order partial correlations
between job attributes and facet satisfaction (all other
attributes being partialled out) again showed that the
skill-utilization association was strongest.

When regression analyses were performed using interaction terms formed by multiplying skill-utilization

scores by other job attribute scores (Cohen and Cohen, 1975), no significant interactions were obtained.   It can be concluded that total facet satisfaction is not significantly related to any two-way interaction of skill-utilization with other job attribute scores.

It was possible that the association between skill-utilization and satisfaction was related to occupational groups.   The analyses reported in Table 3 were repeated with each occupational group, except mining and agriculture where the number of subjects was too small. There were some variations across occupations in the beta coefficients but for all occupations the beta coefficient for skill-utilization was the highest. The magnitude of this skill-utilization coefficient varied from .65 (professional) to .34 (retail).

These analyses indicated that skill-utilization was likely to be the most important task variable for differentiating satisfied from relatively unsatisfied workers. Other variables may also predict job satisfaction as well or better and so a discriminant analysis was used to distinguish between satisfied and unsatisfied workers. Besides task variables each employee had measures of age, education, income, number of physical and strain symptoms reported in last year, internal-external control, leisure attributes (skill-utilization, variety, pressure, interaction and influence), degree of home involvement and collaboration, and use of helping agencies.   These measures are described in O'Brien, Dowling and Kabanoff (1978).   Skill-utilization had the highest discriminant function coefficient of all variables (.53). The next highest was variety (.31) and influence (.29). When groups were divided on the global satisfaction score skill-utilization had the second highest discriminant coefficient (.35) with influence highest (.4).

Skill-Utilization, Health and Internal Control

The relation of skill-utilization to reported health symptoms was examined firstly, by examining the frequency with which various symptoms were reported in low, medium and high skill-utilization jobs.

The following symptoms were reported significantly more by occupants of low skill-utilization jobs than by occupants of medium or high skill-utilization - trouble hearing, blackouts, irritability, epilepsy, loss of weight, loss of appetite, depression, nervous trouble, nightmares and tired on waking.

Using the overall strain score, a simple regression analysis was performed using task attributes, age,

income, education, internal/external control, hours
worked per week, number of people worked with, size of
firm and number of people supervised, as predictors.
Significant predictors of strain were skill-utilization,
pressure, internal/external control, and age. Those
reporting most strain symptoms had jobs with low skill-
utilization and high pressure, a relatively higher
external orientation and were younger.

Employees reporting high strain also used significantly more helping agents than those of low strain.
The distinction between high and low strain was made by
splitting the sample at the median. These results
applied to each of the following agents - family,
friends, social workers, supervisors, doctors and psychologists.

Although there has been a great deal of research
on the internal/external scale, little of this has been
related to work variables. An important exception is
the study of Andrisani and Nestel (1976). Using
national samples in the United States they found that
internality was associated with greater occupational
attainment, higher earnings and higher job satisfaction.
Over a three year period increases in internal control
were associated with advancement in occupational status,
annual earnings and re-entry into the labour force.
Such a finding suggests that experience in jobs with high
opportunity for skill-utilization and influence would
tend to develop an internal orientation. The negative
correlation shown in Table 2 would support this (-.19).
Obviously, internal/external control is also related to
other factors including socialization experience.   In
this study internality was likely to be more often
shown by older, more educated, higher salary workers and
those with better physical and psychological health.

Finally, the association between skill-utilization,
internal control and life satisfaction was obtained
through simple correlation (Table 2). The correlations
show that those employees with high levels of life satisfaction also tended to possess an internal control
orientation and occupy jobs high in skill-utilization.

DISCUSSION

The results obtained show significant associations
between skill-utilization, strain, locus of control,
life satisfaction and job satisfaction. Causal relationships have not been demonstrated although the associations do suggest some causal paths are more probable than
others. Experimental and longitudinal studies of the
effect of skill-utilization are needed to provide evidence

for strong causal relationships.   A recent series of
small group experiments provides some supporting evidence that reduced opportunities for using abilities
is associated with low perceived skill-utilization, low
satisfaction and low productivity (Kabanoff, 1978;
Kabanoff and O'Brien, 1979; Kabanoff and O'Brien, in
press).   Group members creative ability was systematically varied in groups performing creative tasks.
Opportunities for using abilities were varied by impo-
sing different cooperation structures.   When groups
were required to integrate their efforts by coordination through sequencing sub-tasks then satisfaction and
productivity was higher than in groups where collaboration without coordination was used.   Collaborative
groups prevented high ability members using their skills.
It was found that the perceived skill-utilization of all
leaders and of high ability subordinates was higher in
coordinated than in collaborative structures.

The survey results have important implications for
quality of work-life programmes.   Such programmes are
unlikely to improve significantly employee job satisfaction and mental health if they are not concerned with
matching employee skills to the skills required by the
job.   Changes which are only concerned with changing
autonomy, variety, feedback and task-identity will have
very limited effects on job satisfaction.   It could be
argued that increased employee influence in decision
making could eventually lead to demands for skill-match.
This cannot be assumed as many forms of industrial democracy do not appear to have resulted in any basic job
re-structuring at all.   Consultative committees, participative management, semi-autonomous groups and worker-
directors may allow employees to express their views
but rarely have such programmes led to a major analysis
of the problems of skill-utilization.   Semi-autonomous
groups may be given training in the use of multiple
skills so that one employee can perform different jobs
but this is a secondary problem to that of establishing
whether the tasks associated with a given technology
actually are capable of allowing high skill-utilization.

Obviously it will be very difficult to design
organizations where jobs match employee skills, training
and interests.   Ideal design would not only provide
initial skill-match but also allow employees to change
their positions and jobs as they increase their skill
through experience and training.   Modern technology
has probably created too many low skill jobs which
under-utilize the available work-force.   Increased use
of automation, micro-electronics and computers seems to
be associated with a general lowering of the job skill
levels.   Unfortunately, little information is available
about the overall degree of skill-match in modern society.

The evidence that is available suggests that at least a
third of the work-force has low skill-utilization and
that this proportion is increasing.   In the United
States 1977 Quality of Employment Survey (Quinn and
Staines, 1978), 35.6% of employees reported under-utilization of skills.   Only 31.8% of employees said that
it was 'very true' that they had an opportunity to
develop their own special abilities.   This percentage
was a decrease of 25.9% from the percentage so reported
in 1973.   In the survey reported in this article, 38.7%
of the sample desired more skill-utilization than the
level currently experienced in their jobs.   What can
be done to improve person-job match?   Firstly, for existing jobs, selection could be made on the basis of an
objective analysis of the skill-requirements of various
jobs.   Those with too little or too much skill should
be rejected as their satisfaction and productivity would
be relatively low.   It appears that selection psychologists, when used, have done well in rejecting applicants
with below required skill levels but have been less
careful about rejecting applicants whose skill repertoire
exceeds the job descriptions.

A second method of improving person-job fit is
through industrial democracy or employee participation.
Giving employees more say in decisions which affect the
way in which their jobs are done might lead to job
changes towards skill match.   If changes do occur they
are likely to be gradual.   Obviously, job changes of
this kind cannot be separated from changes in pay and
power structures.   Problems of job security, work
values, wage changes in relation to job changes, and
management responsibilities will require prolonged
negotiation before a general social movement occurs.
This movement could be accelerated if there was government legislation requiring organizations to eliminate
gross discrepancies in employee-job match on skill-
utilization.   As there are government safety regulations for exercising minimal standards of physical
health, there could be regulations governing psychological health.   Results such as those reported in this
survey, show that low skill-utilization is a health
hazard - being associated with low job satisfaction,
high mental strain, low life satisfaction and high use
of government welfare agencies.   Some government
agencies have made such recommendations.   For example,
the Jackson committee of enquiry into the Australian
Manufacturing industry recommended that all employees
be recognized as having the right to jobs which promote
reasonable opportunities for expression of their skills
and training.   This report seems to have had the same
influence on Government as the H.E.W. Work in America
report for no action has been taken.   Another reason
for expected delays in introducing job reform through

industrial democracy is the lack of information about effective methods (Cummings and Salipante, 1976; Bolweg, 1976; O'Brien, 1978). The literature is rich with ideology, humanistic sentiments and values but hard evidence is scarce. A final reason for believing that job reform from within existing structures will be slow is due to the inexperience of many employees in self-determination. This powerlessness was found in the present survey and in many others. The less skill-utilization and influence people have in their jobs, the more likely it is that they see their lives as being determined by others. They expect that their own ability and effort is unlikely to produce the outcomes they desire. This expectation makes it difficult for them to respond initially to changes in jobs or power structures which provide them with more autonomy.

Job reform and job selection have been identified as two possible ways of producing improved skill-match in existing organizations. There are two other long term approaches - 'organizational' design and improving the match between educational training and organizational requirements. Organizational design has been discussed many times (Davis and Taylor, 1972; Cherns and Davis, 1975). Design of new factories and organizations should not be left to production engineers and work-study experts. Perhaps these groups should not be the victims of attacks by social scientists but those in society, who require social acceptance of principles of productivity, efficiency, and specialization. Attacking the engineers, bureaucrats and 'scientific' managers for not using skill-utilization principles is not likely to be effective without associated attempts to gain acceptance of new principles of organizational design by those who have the power to change current practices.

Even if skill-utilization was adopted as a design principle care would need to be taken to allow for individual differences. In the present survey, a significant minority (27 - 13%) wanted less skill-utilization and influence. When compared to those who wanted more they were older, less-educated and had a more external control orientation. Differences in desired levels of skill-utilization could reflect different personality needs for mastery or responsibility or possibly differences in the prescribed importance of work as a source of self-identity. Some employees may exemplify the Peter Principle in that they have been promoted to jobs which are beyond their level of competence. Others may desire a reduction in the challenge of skill-utilization as they prepare to retire. Whatever the reason, individual differences exist and need to be allowed for in organizational design.

The fourth and final approach to person-job match is to promote an educational policy which encourages students to have realistic assessments of their own abilities and the probability of obtaining jobs which match these abilities. In the Adelaide sample, the part of the work-force with the greatest job dissatisfaction and highest number of strain and physical symptoms was the group under 24 years of age. Even controlling for differences in income and type of job, it was this group that experienced the greatest amount of mismatch between what they wanted and what they experienced in their jobs. Increased match would be achieved if objective job structures were changed. However, the educational system could also help by ensuring that students had realistic estimates of their own abilities and the abilities required by various jobs. With another Adelaide survey (O'Brien and Dowling, 1978), it was found that 60 - 70% of secondary school students not only wanted, but expected, to obtain professional and highly skilled jobs. Only about 17% of the work-force occupies such jobs. Students may be realistic in trying to avoid jobs low in skill-utilization, but it seems that many are encouraged to be unrealistic because they have little knowledge of their own skill potentials or the skill requirements of jobs in different occupational categories. Hence some of the problems of low skill-match in young employees are probably compounded by unrealistic expectations and lack of job knowledge.

The results of this survey might be criticised on the grounds that it assumes that measures of job satisfaction are reasonable estimates of how employees really feel about their jobs. Some critics (Cherns and Davis, 1975) have questioned their value because respondents give the socially expected answers or because people can adapt to or tolerate intolerable situations. The implication seems to be that persons in a prison, concentration camp or other wretched situation would report satisfaction if given a five point scale. If this was true, then job satisfaction would not be a useful measure. If this adaptation effect was operative in the present study and employees responded similarly regardless of their job situation, then there should not be any relation between satisfaction and job attitudes. Actually, there are consistent relationships between job satisfaction. High levels of satisfaction are associated with high levels of skill-utilization, influence and variety. Adaptation effects do occur and probably account for the greater similarity between actual and desired job attitudes with increasing age. The criticism may refer to the danger of using absolute levels of satisfaction scores as indices of 'real' feelings. Certainly this is a dubious use of satisfaction scales as the levels obtained depend on the form of

the scale and the way it is administered.   However,
what is important is the relationship between variations
on a given satisfaction scale and differences on
variables used to predict satisfaction.

Another criticism is that the obtained relationships reflect similarities between job satisfaction
scales and job attribute scales.   The response categories for satisfaction and job attitudes are similar
and ideally they should be constructed to minimize
common method variance.   This was not practically possible in this study.   While allowing that some degree
of association is due to scale similarity, this cannot
be used to explain the strong relationships between
satisfaction and job attributes.   All job attribute
scales used the same format yet not all were strongly
related to job satisfaction.   The ideal attribute
scales also had similar formats to the job satisfaction
scale, yet these were only weakly related to satisfaction.   Also I-E and strain used quite different
formats.

Another interesting criticism of job satisfaction
research is made by Cherns and Davis (1975) when they
say that such research is committed to the status quo.
Certainly, some researchers appear to have been concerned with maximizing satisfaction by changing people
and not organizational structures.   But this study is
an example of one where satisfaction research indicates
that large structural changes are required to improve
the quality of work-life.   In this, it is not unique,
as many satisfaction studies have been used to advocate
and introduce changes in job and organizational structures (e.g. Hackman and Oldham, 1975; Emery and
Phillips, 1976; Wall and Lischeron, 1977).

In summary, the survey reported demonstrates that
skill-utilization has stronger associations with job
satisfaction than other job attributes.   Skill-utilization also has significant, but weaker associations
with mental strain, internal control, physical health
and life satisfaction.   Such results support those
found by Kornhauser (1965) and indicate that quality of
work life interventions are likely to have little impact
unless skill-utilization is a central concern.

REFERENCES

Andrisani, P. and Nestel, G. (1976).   'Internal-external
    control as a contributor to and outcome of work
    experience, Journal of Applied Psychology, 61,
    156-165.

Bainbridge, L. (1974). 'Problems in the assessment of mental load', Le Travail Humain, 37, 279-302.

Bainbridge, L. (1976). 'The Process Controller', in Singleton, W., The Study of Real Skills, Academic Press.

Bolweg, J.F. (1976). Job Design and Industrial Democracy, London, Nijhoff.

Cohen, J. and Cohen, P. (1975). Applied Multiple Regression/Correlation Analysis for the Behavioral Sciences, N.Y., Wiley.

Cherns, A. and Davis, L. (1975). 'Assessment of the State of the Art', Chapter 1 in The Quality of Working Life, Vol. I, Davis, L. and Cherns, A. (Eds.), The Free Press.

Cross, D. (1973). 'The worker opinion survey: A measure of shop-floor satisfactions', Occupational Psychology, 47, 193-208.

Cummings, T. and Salipante, P. (1976). 'Research-based strategies for improving work life', in Warr, P. (Ed.), Personal Goals and Work Designs, Wiley.

Davis, L. and Cherns, A. (Eds.) (1975). The Quality of Working Life, Vol. I and II, Free Press.

Davis, L. and Taylor, J. (Eds.) (1972). The Design of Jobs, Penguin.

Emery, F. and Thorsrud, E. (1976). Democracy at Work, London, Nijhoff.

Emery, F. and Phillips, C. (1976). Living at Work, Canberra, Australian Government Publishing House.

French, J. and Kahn, R. (1969). 'A programmatic approach to studying the industrial environment and mental health', Chapter 2 in Industrial Organizations and Health, Vol. I. (Eds. Baker, F., McEwan, P. and Sheldon, A.), Tavistock.

Hackman, R. and Lawler, E. (1971). 'Employee reaction to job characteristics', Journal of Applied Psychology, 55, 259-286.

Hackman, R. and Oldham, G. (1975). 'Development of the Job Diagnostic Survey', Journal of Applied Psychology, 60, 159-170.

Herzberg, J. (1966).   Work and the Nature of Man, World.

Kabanoff, B. (1978).   The Effects of Task Type and Group
     Structure upon Group Performance, Ph.D. Thesis,
     Flinders University, South Australia.

Kabanoff, B. and O'Brien, G.E. (1979).   'The effects
     of task type and cooperation upon group products
     and performance', Organizational Behaviour and
     Human Performance, 23, 163-182.

Kabanoff, B. and O'Brien, G.E. (in press).   'Cooper-
     ation structure and the relationship of leader
     and member ability to group performance', Journal
     of Applied Psychology.

Kish, L. (1965).   Survey Sampling, N.Y., Wiley.

Kornhauser, A. (1965).   The Mental Health of the Indus-
     trial Worker, N.Y., Wiley.

Lefcourt, H. (1976).   Locus of Control, N.Y., Wiley.

Maslow, A. (1943).   'A theory of human motivation',
     Psychological Review, 50, 370-396.

Maslow, A. (1965).   Eupsychian Management, Irwin.

Murrell, H. (1978).   Work Stress and Mental Strain,
     Work Research Unit Occasional Paper No. 6,
     London.

O'Brien, G.E. (1967).   Methods of Analyzing Group Tasks,
     Technical Report 46, Group Effectiveness Research
     Laboratory, University of Illinois.

O'Brien, G.E. (1968).   'The measurement of cooperation',
     Organizational Behaviour and Human Performance,
     3, 427-439.

O'Brien, G.E. (1978).   'The Evidence for Industrual
     Democracy', in Proceedings of the Adelaide Inter-
     national Conference on Industrial Democracy, CCH,
     Australia.

O'Brien, G.E., Dowling, P. and Kabanoff, B. (1978).
     Work, Health and Leisure, Working Paper 28,
     National Institute of Labour Studies, Flinders
     University, Adelaide.

O'Brien, G.E. and Dowling, P. (1978).   Student Work
     Values and Job Expectations, Working Paper 32,
     National Institute of Labour Studies, Flinders
     University, Adelaide.

Oeser, O.A. and Harary, F. (1962).   'A mathematical
    model for structural role theory I', Human
    Relations, 15, 89-109.

Oeser, O.A. and Harary, F. (1964).   'A mathematical
    model for structural role theory III', Human
    Relations, 17, 3-17.

Oeser, O.A. and O'Brien, G.E. (1967).   'A mathematical
    model for structural role theory III. The ana-
    lysis of group tasks', Human Relations, 20, 83-97.

Quinn, R. and Staines, G. (1978).   The 1977 Quality of
    Employment Survey, Institute of Social Research,
    Ann Arbor, Michigan.

Rotter, J.B. (1966).   'Generalised expectancies for
    internal versus external control of reinforce-
    ment', Psychological Monograph, 80, 1-28.

Smith, P., Kendall, L. and Hulin, C. (1969).   The
    Measurement of Satisfaction in Work and Retirement,
    Rand McNally.

Trahair, R. (1977).   'Miniers' Judgement of their
    Jobs', in Bordow, A. (Ed.), The Worker in
    Australia, Queensland University Press.

Turner, A. and Lawrence, P. (1965).   Industrial Jobs
    and the Worker, Harvard University Press.

Wall. T., Clegg, C. and Jackson, P. (1978).   'An evalu-
    ation of the job characteristics model', Journal
    of Occupational Psychology, 51, 183-196.

Wall, T.D. and Lischeron, J. (1977).   Worker Partici-
    pation, McGraw Hill.

White, R.W. (1959).   'Motivation reconsidered: The
    concept of competence', Psychological Review, 66,
    297-333.

White, R.W. (1963).   Ego and Reality in Psychoanalytic
    Theory, Psychological Issues Monograph 11.

Wrege, C. and Perroni, A. (1974).   'Taylor's pig-tales:
    A historical analysis of Frederick W. Taylor's
    pig-iron experiments', Work Study and Management
    Services, 564-575.

Comments on Section II

J. PATRICK

      The development of high technology jobs in capital
intensive and continuous process industries presents
both the occupational psychologist and design engineer
with a variety of problems.   Some of these problems are
well discussed in the papers by Duncan, Rasmussen, Bond
and Shepherd and Duncan.   The contents of these four
papers vary and include the petro-chemical industry,
nuclear power plants, digital computer systems and the
production and use of chlorine in a complex of chemical
factories.   Despite these variations in context, there
are a number of common themes which can be distinguished
and to some extent they contrast with the majority of
those from other papers in this volume.   Firstly, one
important and vital aspect of the changing nature and
quality of working life in such capital intensive industries is the increasing <u>cognitive</u> demands of the tasks
performed by the operator, controller or technician.
Intervention by <u>homo sapiens</u> into such highly automated
systems whilst being infrequent is likely to be highly
critical.   The consequences of inefficient performance
are great since suboptimal production or shut-down of a
plant can be extremely expensive whilst of course some
errors can lead to near catastrophes as we have recently
witnessed in the nuclear power industry.   In order to
avoid such problems either more effective selection and
training programmes are required for such personnel or
the plant system needs redesigning.   Of course the
solution is a delicate combination of both these alter-

natives although as Rasmussen suggests optimising the
balance between the operator and the technical system is
difficult.   I will return to this issue later.

     This leads me to my second common theme which can
be extracted from these four papers.   No serious
training and/or design solution can be considered in the
absence of an adequate analysis of the situation.   The
cognitive demands of the tasks described in these papers
can only be fully understood after an analysis of the
job.   What therefore constitutes an adequate analysis?
The information collected must be reliable, valid and
useful for the problem which is being tackled,   This is
often both difficult and time consuming.   Shepherd and
Duncan report a useful extension of Hierarchical Task
Analysis, originally developed by Annett and Duncan
(1967), which can be used to analyse complex planning
skills.   Such an analytic technique not only revealed
the covert strategic decisions made by the controller of
the chlorine plant but also pointed to a training
solution using a cumulative part method with increasingly
more detailed planning.   Nevertheless the refinement of
this technique together with careful data collection for
the chlorine plant spanned a period of about three years.
It is my own experience that a job analysis even using
conventional well tried techniques is likely to take
some considerable time if it is directed at producing a
training solution.   Often such time periods may be
unacceptable not only to some industrialists and company
personnel but also to some academics who feel pressured
to publish frequently.   Possibly this is one reason for
the paucity of academics involved in such areas.
Obviously Shepherd and Duncan's analytic technique needs
application to other training situations involving strategic decision making.   In such tasks when there are few
externalised behaviours to be observed by the job analyst,
it is clearly up to the ingenuity of the analyst to
elicit units of covert behaviour or 'operations' which
correspond to the 'natural language' of the expert or
skilled job incumbent.

     Rasmussen, in his paper, also underlines the impor-
tance of adequate analysis but of a different kind.   In
this case analysis of reported problems in nuclear power
plants provides a rich source of information concerning
different types of human error.   It is interesting to
note that the majority of errors are errors of omission
when testing and repairing equipment.   In these situations procedures are often inadequately performed.
Rasmussen argues that the development of taxonomies
relating different kinds of error to different types of
task (see Tables 2 and 3) can provide the basis of vital
feedback for the designers of such plants.   Presumably
the categories of such classifications should ultimately

be not only mutually exclusive and exhaustive but also
lead to unique and viable design (or training) solutions.
forward is also necessary from the design stage to Feed-
provide sufficient information from which operators can
extrapolate to cope with unforeseen situations.   Since
such large scale plants are continuously developing and
involve a number of interacting subsystems, it appears
that a systems approach at both the macro and micro level
might be a useful analytical device.   Of course the plea
that designers and psychologists should get together
during the conception and development of such systems is
a familiar one which was also echoed by a number of other
papers including that by Singleton and Crawley.

        Let me conclude consideration of the importance of
an adequate analysis with an example from Duncan's
studies concerned with training fault finding skills.
Duncan highlights in this paper (and previous publications) the importance of a fault-symptom matrix.   From
such a matrix it is possible to evaluate performance and
provide the trainee with strategic information during the
problem solving process which facilitates both learning
and transfer.   The development of such fault-symptom
matrices is dependent again upon the expertise of the
analyst to elaborate those symptoms which efficiently and
consistently can be used to reduce the 'fault set' to 1,
in Duncan's terms.   In some industries this is difficult since the analyst may be provided with 'unclean'
information concerning the relationships between faults
and symptoms: technical experts may disagree over the
association of faults and symptoms and the relationship
between them might be complex and variable due to varying production circumstances.   Again, therefore, the
application of an adequate analysis in terms of the above
criteria is a significant start to solving the problem,
which in this case, was a training one.

        I should now like to focus your attention briefly
on the person who might repair, maintain and troubleshoot
equipment and is often called the 'technician'.   Bond,
in his paper, presents an articulate picture of the different aspects of the technician's work in maintaining
computer systems.   A number of these aspects of the
technician's job are common not only to nuclear power
and petro-chemical industries but also to other production industries such as rubber, plastic, cement, etc.
The good technician is a crucial creature without whom
production would stop.   However this is not always
recognised and his position is rarely accredited with the
focus of selection and training policies which it
deserves.   If therefore technicians are important in a
variety of industrial contexts, are there common psychological elements to these jobs?   Both Bond and Duncan
describe the cognitive nature of troubleshooting making

demands on the person's intellectual skills.   It would
be useful if we could pinpoint within the intellectual
processing domain which functions were required and then
use these to differentiate fault finding situations.
Maybe such a development has already been accomplished or
maybe it is a task requiring massive resources.   Nevertheless it would have important consequences for selection and training policies when considering the diagnostic parts of a technician's job and might ultimately
facilitate mobility of people between such jobs.

Computers are well suited to providing training
for diagnostic aspects of the technician's job.   They
can provide strategic feedback (or feedforward) to the
trainee during solution of the problem, they can provide
simulations of the problem and they can display and
provide quick access to the various components of a
faulty system.   Bond describes the facilities of AIDE
which enable the technician to explore the relationships
between malfunctions and symptoms associated with some
equipment using a VDU and sonic touchpen.   The AIDE
system has a number of appealing facilities for training:
potentially it could be programmed with the data bases
for different equipment and it not only faithfully represents the cognitive demands of fault finding but also
can present visual images of part of the equipment with
associated names and test points which the trainee can
explore.   Intuitively AIDE provides a useful training
environment.   Nevertheless evaluation is critical and as
Bond reveals, this is only yet in its preliminary stages.
The facilities of such a system go beyond our present
knowledge of instructional principles and consequently
the comparison of different instructional strategies
and sequences using AIDE is likely to make an important
contribution to the theory of instruction.

A penultimate issue which the conference and my
own prejudices provoke me to raise briefly is concerned
with terminology and level of description.   For example,
most papers or conference participants at some point
mention 'skilled performance' or 'skills' and there is
often a mistaken assumption that use of the same phrase
is a guarantee of communication and understanding.   It
is probably not useful to become embroiled in arguments
that attempt to define skilled performance but rather to
acknowledge that it is a label which can be used for a
variety of purposes.   The purpose will dictate the
appropriateness of the researcher's concept of skill and
its measurement.   For example O'Brien's construct and
measurement of 'skill utilisation' using self-report,
questionnaire techniques would be unacceptable to most
psychologists involved in the areas of training, selection and design.   Nevertheless if it is possible for
O'Brien's concept of skill utilisation to reliably and

independently predict job satisfaction, then the remaining issue is whether the label adequately reflects the concept's operational definition.   Another example will hopefully clarify my point.   Singleton and Crawley in their paper detail the need for occupational classification systems which are psychologically oriented. This is undoubtedly correct although we should bear in mind the reason for requiring such data.   Even in the psychological contexts of training, selection, design and measurement of job satisfaction, different psychological classification systems might be used and it would often be difficult if not impossible, to translate between them.   Consequently the development of a multipurpose psychologically oriented occupational classification system should pay careful attention to the particular demands which it hopes to fulfil.

The final issue which I should like to discuss concerns the old but often overlooked debate of how far the social scientist or researcher should become politically involved in organisational changes which his research implicitly or explicitly suggests.   Lawler makes the important point that for effective change to take place in any one organisational subsystem, then all the other subsystems should be considered.   The psychologist implementing new training packages knows that they must be carefully interfaced with the selection and production departments of the organisation.   It is often difficult for us to admit that imbedded in our own applied occupational research are assumptions concerning the nature and amount of change that we perceive as being acceptable to an organisation.   We possibly only include solutions which we guess are likely to be viable from a number of non-academic perspectives. Consequently change tends to be slow and often conservative.   Duncan courageously concludes his discussion of the need to train for versatile faultfinding with some considerations of the possible social and political implications of this change in the nature of work. The questions which he raises are fundamental and far-reaching and yet they will probably only be answered in a haphazard way with the passage of time.

REFERENCES

Annett, J. and Duncan, K.D. (1967).   'Task Analysis and Training Design', Occupational Psychology, 41, 211-221.

SECTION III:
The Working Environment

Changes in Working Life
Edited by K.D. Duncan, M.M. Gruneberg, and D. Wallis
© 1980 John Wiley & Sons Ltd

Chapter 12

Changes in Work Environments: The Next 20 Years

L. E. DAVIS

INTRODUCTION

Changes in the nature and quality of working life over the next 20 years will be determined largely by the adequacy of the responses to the continuing changes in the physical, political, technological, demographic and social environments of employing organizations. Western societies have yet to grapple realistically with the combination of changes whose total effect is referred to as the 'post-industrial era'. Too many problems carried over from the Industrial era are unfortunately still unsolved. In Western societies in particular, where the consequences of engaging with employment have been viewed, until very recently, as a problem to be overcome by the individual, the growth of public awareness and the development of responses have been dangerously slow. A substantial number of changes in environments are already visible in varying degrees. Of concern for the future is whether critical changes in environments and the consequences or problems that flow from them are recognized as such by policy makers, employers, managers, union leaders, and staff technical specialists.

That sufficient acknowledgement and understanding of the changes in working environments have not yet taken place can be seen in the rise of a series of silent crises. Some of the crises are recognized, some

partially, some not at all, and few get attention in the
press.   When, not if, they explode, Western societies
will be altered either politically, economically or
socially depending on how appropriate were the responses
to their causes.

Changes in the physical-economic environments have
been visible for some time.   What is significant, however, is the recently emerged specific requirement that
organizations and their jobs be designed or redesigned
so that they are adaptable.   The emergence of adaptability as a central response to assure organizational
and individual survival in the face of environmental
uncertainty is not yet fully appreciated.   These environments are characterized by market, product and materials
turbulence of which the first two are stimulated in part
by technological change.   Changes in the technological
environment while also visible are insufficiently understood in terms of their effects on the workplace,
organization structure and values of society.   The technological environment is characterized by constant change,
by growth of automation and computer data processing in
production and service activities.   Waiting in the
wings is a technological innovation with major effects -
the microprocessor.

Changes in the social-demographic environments
have been most difficult to assess in terms of effects.
However three notable effects related to changes in the
values of individuals, in schooling, in living standards
and in work-related rewards and punishments provided by
society are crucial to the future of Western societies.
These are (1) the increasing transfer from the individual
to society of the consequences of engaging with employment, (2) the inability to find appropriate employment
for better and higher educated youth, and (3) the individual-organization crisis or the growing mismatch
between the expectations, aspirations and values of the
workforce, particularly its younger segments, and the
conditions and opportunities provided by employing
organizations.

EVOLVING CRISES

There are a number of societal issues challenging
the future of Western societies, their forms of economic
organization and their organizational forms as now known.
To properly understand these issues they must be seen in
ecological terms, in the scientific sense of the term
ecology, i.e., the science concerned with organisms and
their environments, their interactions and the processes
which change both organisms and their environments.   The
future survival of Western economic organizations may be

seen in terms of organizational ecology - as a question
of organization-environment interactions.

Of the many crises affecting Western economies
and their organizations, the crises of concern here are
those of the relations between people and organizations.
Western societies are very much structured for and
focused on individuals, on the options available for
individuals, on individual opportunity and yet, as
functioning societies they have to get their work done
in a variety of ways.   Organizations are the frameworks
through which most of a society's work is executed and
within which individuals seek to satisfy many of their
needs.   Organizations, as the common instrument for
meeting both societal and individual needs, are therefore sensitive to changes in the expectations and
demands from both quarters.

The Increasing Transfer of Consequences of Employment

The past 100 years have seen a gradual and continuing transfer from the individual to society of the
consequences of engaging with employment ranging from
compensation for injury to providing for burden of lack
of employment security.   The last ten years have seen
a markedly increased rate of transfer, building potential
crises in the closing period of the 20th century.   The
two most significant for potential impact on the quality
of working life are stress and the growing 'psychology
of entitlement' regarding the quality of jobs or its
obverse, compensation for lack of high quality.

Stress   Work related stress may become one of
the major evolving crises having profound implications
for the structure of work systems and of organizations.
To date this potentially explosive crisis for advanced
societies has gone unrecognized because it is thought to
be restricted to certain occupations and professions,
and compensation law is still primitive.   However,
studies now reveal that stress effects are widely distributed and the body of law dealing with the assumption
of responsibility by society for stress related consequences is also growing.   It would seem to be a matter
of time before the crisis becomes threatening.

The indications are that work related stress is
very widespread in industrially structured organizations.
Recent analysis shows that it is not only the hard
working leader who dramatically falls prey to untimely
illness because of the stresses of his job, but that very
large numbers at all levels and in all occupations suffer
stress effects in varying degrees.   Until now it was

comforting to believe that stress effects were under the
control of the individual who, if wise and not driven
by the furies of success, could limit the amount of work
he undertook.   Karasek's new studies (Karasek, 1979)
undermine that belief requiring us to see stress not
only as a problem of the individual but of the structure
of work organization and thus of society.   His studies
show that stress effects are strongest when high work
demand is accompanied by low control over the variables
and forces affecting the outcomes for which one is responsible as well as low discretion in choosing how and
when to respond.   This recognition, together with the
slowly building body of law dealing with compensation
for stress induced illness, sets the stage for two possibilities.   One is a time bomb - the addition of huge
costs stemming from compensating myriad victims, without
any change in work structure likely accompanied by rigid
governmental regulations limiting the development of
responses.   The second may be a social gain - making
work organization open to public review and the subject
of public social policy while stress consequences are
compensated.

  Entitlement to high quality jobs   In 1977 in a
newspaper comic strip in the US a father says to his son
on the day of his graduation from the university, 'I see
that you are not interested in looking for a job'.   To
this the son replies, 'I am looking for a job'.   Father
then asks, 'What kind of job are you looking for?'
Son answers, 'I am looking for a job I will enjoy'.
Father: 'Aha, I knew you were not interested in finding
a job'.

     There is a widespread growth in the perception,
that it is not the individual who is at fault if and
when expectations are not met; it is the institution's
and/or society's fault.   This is not simply a matter of
placing blame but signifies a very important shift in
what was called the 'Protestant' or 'work' ethic.
Success was attributed to individual endeavors and each
individual had obligations to meet.   'If I am not
successful, something must be wrong with me.'   Among
younger people, this value is strongly declining.   Now
it's 'Something is wrong, and it is not necessarily wrong
with me.   In fact, it might not have anything to do
with me, but with the situation in which I find myself.'
In terms of organizations, this means that employees
were formerly socialized to the Protestant Ethic as the
basis of their value system and accepted a mismatch
between their own needs and organizational rewards as an
individual burden.   Today, people have thrust this mismatch back at society, and in particular, at organizations doing society's work.

Extended education in Western societies has brought with it rising expectations that personal needs will be met and that one is entitled to have his expectations met in the workplace, referred to as 'the psychology of entitlement'. What were once seen as privileges to be earned are now seen as entitlements which are slowly becoming rights due one as a matter of course. Young people are beginning to claim the right to an interesting, self-fulfilling, self-developing, individually, centered job. This is expressed through the extraordinarily high value being placed on individuals as individuals rather than as members of organizations. The obverse is revealed in very recent US social survey data (Yankelovitch, 1979) indicating that there are millions of people holding paying jobs who find the contents and present incentives or rewards provided by their engagement with work to be so unappealing that they are no longer motivated to work very hard. Coupled with this is a curious, totally counter-intuitive, phenomenon which has interfered with understanding of what is going on. It has been observed that while people are withdrawing their involvement with their jobs, they insist on steadily rising increases in pay and fringe benefits. Some have inferred that compensation is all that is of interest to workers. A more appropriate inference may be that this is compensation for the lack of appeal of the work that people are required to do. A good way to state this phenomenon is the less employees are committed to do, the more they want. This gives us a perspective very different from the conventional wisdom about the decline in productivity levels in the US (perhaps applicable to other Western societies). The withdrawal of organizations' members from involvement in unrewarding jobs may be a key contributing factor to productivity decline.

Youth Employment

The inability of advanced Western societies to find employment for its youth and appropriate employment for its highly educated youth is a tragedy of growing consequences. Three aspects of youth employment contribute to the emerging crisis: (1) first employment of youth, (2) employment of youth at jobs beneath their educational and intellectual levels, and (3) inability of organizations to utilize the talents brought to the workplace by youth whose better and higher education is increasingly being provided by advanced societies.

There are two difficulties impeding transition from school to employment. The first is the classic labor market problem related to general employment levels implicating technology, particularly advanced technology,

which reduces man-hours needed and contributes to a high
rate of obsolescence of skills.   That young people are
disproportionately represented (2 - 5 times) among the
unemployed makes this aspect crucial for the survival
of Western societies in their present forms.   The
second is the precipitous break with the social values
of the school society on engaging with employing organizations.   After 10 - 12 years of living in a school
society whose values center on individuals, needs and
aspirations, entering employment in organizations with
very different values can be very disruptive.   As an
example, recent US data show that first-time jobs are
held for only 7 months on average.

Employment of highly educated youth at lower level
jobs is a social waste of both educational resources and
a blunting of the hopes of young people.   Further, it
tends to result in the introduction of falsely high job-
entry criteria whose effect is to exclude unnecessarily
those with lesser but adequate educational preparation.
The gratuitous advice of many leaders of Western
societies to young people to desist from higher education will continue to go unheeded given the changing
environments of advanced societies and the more realistic understanding held by students and their parents
that more education provides more options for facing the
future.

Similarly the inability to utilize the talents of
young people whose advanced education is not specific
to business or industry constitutes a waste of human
resources made available by society and a denial of
aspirations of a crucial segment of a nation's population.   Additionally, the crisis between individual
and organization is intensified with spill-over effects
for other institutions of society.   Other aspects of
the individual-organization crisis are reviewed later.
Responding to various aspects of this crisis will require
employing organizations to add an additional social goal,
that of maximally utilizing the valuable human resources
made available to them.   This will require re-exami-
nation of values, organization and work structures and
goals of employing organizations.

Individual-Organization Crisis

One reason for the lack of acknowledgement of the
individual-organization crisis is that people are seen
as employees, and, as such, as members of organizations
while it is forgotten that, perhaps more importantly,
they are members of the social environment.   They are
affected by the organizations in which they work and by
the social environment in which they reside.   They bring

aspects of that environment with them into their organizations and <u>vice versa</u>.

The ecology of any organization is very much affected by what its members bring with them from their other environments. The present crisis between people and their organizations is closely related to that process. Changes in Western societies and, in particular, the changes in the values of their workforces have seriously undermined the traditional relationship between organizations and their members. This crisis for organizations is likely to be resolved only by the evolution of new organizational forms. At the base of the crisis is the mismatch between values, needs and expectations of employees and the responses, opportunities and rewards provided by their employing organizations. The consequences of the mismatch have many manifestations including declining productivity levels in some instances, minimum control by managers permitted by employees over their life space on or off the job, high absenteeism, in some countries high turnover, early retirement, refusal to perform difficult or unpleasant work and specific compensation for each task performed.

CHANGES IN ENVIRONMENTS

Each advanced society, responding partially to its history and geography and partially to worldwide changes and forces, has environments with unique characteristics. However, there are changing environmental characteristics common to advanced Western societies that will impact the quality of working life over the next 20 years.

Technological Environment

Changes in the technological environment have had major impacts on organizations and their workplaces. The effects of advances in technology generally are not sufficiently understood. They are perceived as a factor in eliminating jobs; this may not be the primary effect. Technological advances have so increased the material producing capability of Western societies, that scarcity as a concern has almost disappeared. The transfer payments to large segments of their populations for welfare, health and retirement purposes are not simply money payments, but claims to goods and services. They are only possible because of the tremendous productivity that technology has helped achieve. Therefore, the changes in the values and expectations of the workforce and the social policy of reducing the cost to the individual of not working, are both, to a considerable extent, results of advances in technology.

The increasing rate of technological development is causing turbulence in the economic and marketing environments of most large organizations. In a state of turbulence, environments are no longer passive, but interactive such that the actions of an organization and others may lead to unanticipated outcomes. In Western societies, particularly in the United States, the rate of change is so great, individual organizations find it very hard to reduce the relative uncertainty with which they have to exist, no matter what kind of long-range planning they undertake. Indeed, long-range planning may become a trap. Ackoff has focussed on the crux of the problem of the turbulent environment for organizations when he indicated that under turbulent conditions, experience is not the best teacher. It may even be the worst teacher preparing one only to deal with situations that have ceased to exist. The best teacher may be experiment (Ackoff, 1975). But how can organizations be designed to learn from experiments?

The widely taught and applied theories of bureaucratic organization are based on environmental stability and control as the means of achieving success. Usually, lip service is paid to the need for change, and seldom is there concern with designing adaptive capabilities into organizations. In addition to the effects of turbulent environment on organizations, there has been rapid increase in the capital investment required to use new sophisticated technical systems. The increase has come from the application of advanced technology and frequently, in addition, pollution control requirements. Even a simple product such as mayonnaise which was only recently made in large-sized batches by mixing measured ingredients is now made continuously using computer-monitored pulsating valves. A recent new petro-chemical plant (Davis, 1979) with an organization design to suit the new values has an investment of $2.1 million per worker. A new energy project is on the drawing boards that will cost $4 billion and take seven years to develop. The precondition for such enormous capital investment was stability and the ability to effectively plan for, at least, the useful life of the project. That is exactly what turbulent environments have denied modern organizations who must now address themselves to the complex question of adaptability.

The rapidly increasing capital requirements for sophisticated technical systems have not helped managers understand the impact of such systems on the workplace. Based on the unrealistic promise by engineers of automated people-proof production systems spewing out products with virtually no one in attendance, the public has come to believe that automation decreases, if not completely eliminates, the dependence of organizations on their workers. This simply is not the case. True, the number of employees per unit of product output is reduced by automation; however, the dependence of the organization on the remaining members increases with the sophistication of the technical system. Why? The answer is counter-intuitive. The necessary insight comes from hard experience and deep analysis gained from working with organizations having sophisticated technical systems. Consider the petrochemical plant which cost over $2 million per worker. At that level of investment most programmable or controllable tasks have been built into the system, i.e., taken over by machines. What remains in addition to a number of operating tasks are the unprogrammable tasks such as monitoring, diagnosing, adjusting (fine-tuning), overcoming disturbances and maintaining the system. These are skilled tasks on which the organization is critically dependent if output is to be maintained. Not only are extremely large investments in sophisticated technical systems required, but the organization has high vulnerability as a consequence of its increased dependence on the commitment of the relatively few remaining workers to act when and how needed.

Additionally, advancements in technology have altered the nature of work itself. Since 1900 when F.W. Taylor introduced 'scientific management', many millions of jobs have been fragmented into measured and programmable single elements. The environment was stable then and technology was simple. Efficiency was easily measured in output-per-unit of time, and anything that could distract workers from the purely mechanical execution of their tasks was eliminated. Modern sophisticated technical systems largely absorb these fragmented tasks. The easily programmable and measurable tasks are automated. What remains for people to do is radically different. People working in high technology settings, live in a work world consisting of abstractions, not concrete objects, which is very similar to that of professionals. Whether producing piece parts or continuous liquids, they increasingly work by reading dials, meters, and computer printouts, and remotely operate valves, pumps, gates and other devices by pressing buttons in control rooms far from the objects or machines being manipulated. These activities would have absolutely no meaning to workers unless they had developed cognitive (mental) maps of the interacting processes which frequently cannot be seen or touched.

There is no way to fit this kind of work into the principles of scientific management and bureaucracy. Skills come to have different meanings; efficiency and productivity take on different meanings as do the notions of management direction and control.   To managers, control has meant being able to tell employees what, when, and how to do their tasks, and measuring employees' performance against the manager's expectations.   In advanced technical systems, the most a manager can do is ask the employee to use his best judgment in situations which he is likely to understand better than does the manager.   Thus, advances in technology have resulted in new kinds of work relationships which present new challenges to management and confound the principles on which organizations have been traditionally designed.

Lastly, the spread of the microprocessor raises a series of issues for organizations and jobs and thus for working environments.   Microprocessors permit decentralization of the production of goods and the provision of services.   Will the microprocessors signal the beginning of new small decentralized forms of industrial and service organizations and jobs?   Will the evolving alternative forms of centralized organizations now slowly becoming visible (Davis, 1977) be useful paradigms?   In either event there is likely to be a further shift in the definition of skills away from how-to skills toward diagnostic adjusting, maintaining skills.   Such emphasis can be expected to continue changes in organization and jobs away from scientific management and bureaucracy (Davis, 1980).

Social Environments

The discussion of the changes in the social environment is undertaken in terms of what affects values, expectations and aspirations of workers.   At present there is wide agreement and support for the conventional wisdom about work and workers.   Most frequently workers are seen as economic beings motivated by increases in pay and fringe benefits;   what they must do to earn these rewards is largely irrelevant as long as there are no dangers to life and limb.   Some have said that the durability of the conventional wisdom about work and workers derives from the fact that the workplace is perhaps the most conservative of social institutions.   This may be the consequence of the enormous number of issues that are entangled in the workplace.   Included are management issues of authority and control, and worker issues of identity, rewards, compensation, and equity.   The meaning of work and jobs as part of the lives of members of organizations should make the workplace a central concern for society.   One may well understand the fears that underlie the reluctance to examine the workplace, but such conservatism will not serve society well in meeting the challenges of the future.   Unfortunately not

many organizations are preparing for these challenges.
Given present trends, one may predict that by the 1980s
the human side of organizations will be very unsafely
left to low-level personnel specialists.   Instead,
given the evolving values of the workforce, intimate
knowledge of values and of people and their needs will
become an essential part of a top manager's training if
he is to effectively direct large-scale institutions.

The workplace continues to be the locus of the
individual's strongest connections with advanced society.
There are millions of people who want jobs and compete
for available jobs.   Millions of young people cannot
find a connection with society for lack of a workplace
while others are under-utilized.   While the trend is to
retire at younger ages among many who would, presumably,
enjoy doing something else, the retirement age has been
extended in the US, presumably, for the very few who do
enjoy their work.   Finally, there are millions of jobs
that are either unfilled because no one is willing to
suffer them or filled by imported workers.   For many it
appears to be more desirable to live on welfare payments
or on unemployment compensation, with all the associated
undesirable side effects, rather than take some kinds of
jobs.

A central change affecting the values and expectations of those who are employed comes from rising
levels of education.   Rising educational levels are
phenomena of all advanced Western societies.   The United
States may be used as an illustration in this instance.
According to the United States Office of Education, 1978
was the year in which the average length of schooling of
the workforce of approximately 97 million people had
reached 12 years.   Most US organizations are designed
on the basis of principles developed by Frederick W.
Taylor in 1900-1910 when only three years was the average
length of schooling of the workforce.   The issue here
is not how much students learn in 12 years.   Rather,
the issue for organizations is that students have been
socialized, during the formative years of their lives,
into a particular kind of society, a school society.
Organizations, overlook this socialization process at
their own peril.   In the school socialization process
the individual is paramount, which is as it should be.
Twelve years of such socialization may be expected to
have an enormous impact on these future members of organizations who now ask 'Who am I?', 'What am I here for?',
'What is my engagement with work all about?', and 'What
are you (the organization) doing to and for me?'.

Traditional work incentive and reward systems are
being challenged to a growing degree.   There is a mismatch between the carrot and stick incentives - the

carrot of more pay and the stick of withdrawing security
- and new motivations arising among the workforce.
While carrot and stick incentives appear to have worked
well enough in the past, the values of advanced societies
have changed dramatically with regard to how and why
people associate themselves with the work organizations
of society.   An important source of the mismatch arises
from the uniformity of the system of rewards and incentives provided by employing organizations.   As all
else, it is a poor assumption that says that everybody
wants the same thing, i.e., that money motivates everyone equally.   The systems of rewards do not reflect the
diversity of expectations and goals held by different
people.   For some, money may be the main consideration;
for others leisure, status, challenge of the work, the
well-being of the organization or future rewards may be
very important incentives.   Different segments of the
workforce assign greater or lesser importance to each of
these goals of work, and therefore, a variety of rewards
should be available to fit the variety of goals.   Stated
otherwise, the workplace should afford opportunities for
meeting various personal goals.   At present, organizations are inflexible in their pervasive and singular
reliance on economic incentives.   The exclusive reliance
on economic incentives has another drawback - organizations must continuously prove their ability to meet the
demands for money and security.   During the 25 years of
growth since World War II, this ability was amply demonstrated.   But in the 1970s, there has been a loss of
confidence in many Western countries in the employer's
ability to meet the needs of money and security.   The
'stick' of withdrawal of security, once an instrument of
control by the employer, is now turned into a measure of
the employer's inability to meet worker's needs.

       An important value change in the workplace in many
countries is the growing refusal on the part of individuals to subordinate their own personalities to the work
roles that they have to carry out.   Contrast this with
the recent past when men defined their identities through
their work roles.   Today that is looked upon by younger
people as depersonalization.   Almost all Western organizations fundamentally are built on the principle of
depersonalization - a central criterion of bureaucratic
organization.   All bureaucracies start with the proposition and 'scientific management' makes a religion out
of depersonalization, but younger people are strongly
opposed to depersonalization.   Another way of looking
at this refusal by younger people to accept subordi-
nation of their own personalities is that there is a
strong aversion to becoming an object in the work role,
i.e., a cog in the machine.   This is producing new
challenges to managerial concepts of efficiency and
control.   This value change has generated a strong

movement toward participation and worker control of the
workplace.   One area where considerable conflict may be
expected is the growing concern with occupational health
as well as safety.   This largely applies to those
industries using newer materials and fuels.   The occupational health issue of stress has been discussed elsewhere (e.g. in this volume by Shipley).

     In countries where unemployment has been low,
older workers who remember the great depression of
1929-39, and experienced the effects of unemployment,
are moving out of the workforce.   For the depression
generation, economic success and security were survival
issues;   today's workforce take these more for granted
and few contemplate hunger.   As with all else in life,
the past cannot be recreated.   'A good dose of unemployment' will not bring back old work values.   Meeting
the challenges of the future, therefore, requires that
organizations and jobs be designed on the basis of the
new and emerging values.   There is a growing mismatch
between the educated 'new breed of workers', who are
becoming the majority of the workforce, and existing
design of organizations (Gyllenhammer, 1977).   Organizations, both public and private, have been designed
according to the principles of rational bureaucracy and
scientific management, complete with fragmented,
routinized jobs.   There is a very long way to go in
making the necessary changes in organization design,
incentives, reward systems, and performance measures,
that will enable organizations to cope with the requirements of the 1980s.

     The economic and organizational systems that have
been remarkably successful until now have come to the
point where significantly new directions must be found
both at the level of society and at the level of organizations.   Most societies are still bemused by past
successes thus failing to recognize that they are
passing a watershed in individual-organization relationships.   This is the silent crisis.   It is clear that
in the 1980s it will be perilous, if not wilfully negli-
gent, to examine the functioning of organizations, to
create new ones, to modify existing ones and the jobs
of employees without taking into account in open meaningful ways quality of working life considerations.

NEW DIRECTIONS

     To indicate that there is a growing crisis between
individuals and organizations does not need mean that it
cannot be contained.   There are prospective solutions
and more can be developed.   Significant and rewarding
new directions are being developed in some leading firms

largely through new forms of organization which constitute effective and efficient alternatives to bureaucracy
and scientific management.   These forms provide very
flexible and adaptive organizations designed to meet the
challenges of the changing economic and political
environments, the demands of complex technologies, as
well as the expressed needs of their members for
enhanced quality of their working lives.   An examination of the characteristics of these organizations
reveals the potentials of the new designs.

Most of the alternative forms of organization are
not invented following practices usual in the past.
They are the product of deliberate organizational
design or renewal (redesign) activities undertaken in
response to openly developed organizational social
policy or philosophy stating the desired societal,
organizational and personal (individual) objectives to
be embodied in the design.   The charter or guide for
design states the values on which the organization is to
be built or rebuilt.   Since the design process is
itself participative, the design team doing the actual
work of design has representatives from all levels and
functions of the organization contributing to the process
of inventing the organization structure, its jobs, reward
systems, etc.   Frequently, particularly when designing
new organizations, all who can contribute are not available, therefore, as little as possible of the structure
is usually specified leaving to those who come to work
in the organization the maximum amount of input to
design the specifics of their working situations (see
Cherns, 1976).

Contemplate the shift in values exhibited in the
structure of these evolving alternative organizations.
The central design issue is no longer how to maintain
authority and achieve control by management as in scientific management and bureaucracy.   Instead, individual
and societal values are included and the structure of
the organization is taken to be evolutionary with the
specifics to be worked out as needed by members of the
organization.   The design of a highly automated new
paper mill serves as a case illustration.   The operating
functions of workers in this kind of setting also include
monitoring, adjusting, controlling, and maintaining the
equipment, anticipating breakdowns, and acting to minimize down time.   People are primarily there to exercise
discretion and act upon their own decisions in decentralized locations;   in conventional organizations these
are management functions.   In this regard the designers
of the organization perceived that in settings where responses to randomly occurring events cannot be specified
as to time and place, workers must be given the authority
to do what must be done (Davis, 1971).   Heretofore,

authority to act when, where, and how needed (work authority) had never been extended to workers (except to craftsmen) who in actuality have the responsibility for achieving the outcomes.

A second characteristic of the new forms of organization resides in the choice of self-maintaining groups as the building blocks of the organization. Set aside is one of the fundamental principles of scientific management and bureaucracy, namely that it must be possible for a supervisor or manager to hold each of his subordinates directly responsible as an individual for his or her performance. This requirement has led to the one person-one task organizational building block basic to scientific management. The new or alternative forms of organization utilizing self-maintaining organizational units as the basic components of the larger organization have internal boundaries selected on very different principles. The internal boundaries separating such organizational units are located so that the units or teams can develop and maintain themselves as mini-societies capable of achieving multiple goals coming from the needs of the larger organization and from its members. Boundaries are located so that the units, or teams can operate as small systems, within a larger system internally coordinating their activities and leaving to management the boundary control functions plus integration of the units. Each organizational unit or team is associated with identifiable product or process outcomes for which it can take responsibility. The outcomes are measurable so that feedback and accountability can operate. The work activities of each team or group consist of a systemically bounded set of transforming operations and related inspection and planning tasks plus the activities needed to maintain the organizational unit as a functioning social system. Frequently, equipment maintenance tasks are also part of the team's work activities. To be self-maintaining the organizational unit must possess the requisite response capability, i.e., skills and knowledge needed to respond to the demands placed upon it and to the exigencies in its environment. Therefore, the members of such units or teams possess individually or collectively all the requisite skills and knowledge necessary to operate and achieve its product or service goals. These include operating skills, maintenance skills, planning and evaluation skills and the social skills needed to maintain the team or unit as a social system.

An illustration of such an organizational unit is to be found in the Shipping and Receiving Team of a new food products manufacturing organization structured on alternative concepts. Among other activities, this team receives incoming materials which subsequently are

transformed into products by processing teams and ware-
houses, and ships finished products.   Usually, receiving
departments are designed as necessary but not quite
acceptable appendages to a production organization.
They carry out the drudgery of bringing in and storing
materials, and later withdrawing them for delivery to
processing units.   The activities of such departments
usually consist of low skill level, routine, and sometimes physically demanding movement of materials.
People performing this work are usually classified as
materials handlers or forklift drivers performing routine
activities under the direction of supervisors who plan
and control.   Any leavening of this situation by record
keeping, inventory control, etc., is minimized by
specializing such tasks and assigning them to clerks.

In the design of this new food manufacturing organization and its Shipping and Receiving Team, the application of the concept of the self-maintaining organizational units (mini-societies) led to the structure and
roles of the team such that it came to see its responsibility to be the 'buying' of incoming materials and the
'selling' of usable raw materials to the processing
teams.   The members of the Shipping and Receiving Team
while doing the routine work of unloading, transporting
and warehousing, also test incoming materials to determine whether they meet specifications, decide on their
acceptance and receive them by placing them in storage,
or reject them by returning them to suppliers.   Each
team member performs various combinations of all these
activities and associated record keeping.   The members
of the team see themselves as being in the 'wholesale
business' of 'buying' raw materials and supplies, keeping
them in inventory and 'selling' on a timely basis usable
raw materials and supplies to the processing organizational units.   The team is measured and held responsible for these activities, and sees its reputation built
on how dependable it is as a 'wholesaler'.   How and
when team members carry out their activities is left to
them; there is no supervisor.   It is the members'
responsibility to organize and reorganize themselves to
do all the work required.   Since the team is measured on
outcomes achieved, it sees itself and functions as a
self-maintaining mini-organization performing the needed
work tasks and the activities needed to maintain the team
as a mini-society nested within a larger one.   Team
members are evaluated on the basis of their contributions
to the team.   The requisite response capability of the
team, not only includes the necessary work and decision
skills but also the social skills for maintaining an
organizational unit and its members.

A third aspect of the new designs is that they are
the outcome of the effort to optimize jointly the

technical systems and the social systems of organizations since both are totally interrelated in the process of achieving desired outcomes.   Traditionally,
engineers design technical systems and their machine and
tool components by optimizing on the basis of economic
criteria.   Optimizing on the basis of social criteria
is seen most often to be satisfied by designing the
technical system so that it is people-proof.   People
(the social system) are then expected to adapt themselves
to the technical system which usually has been designed
to minimize the feedback of needed information and the
possibilities of human intervention.   In contrast,
joint optimization seeks to combine the complementary
advantages of the technical system and the social system
and, in particular, to integrate the very great adaptive
(problem solving) capacity of people with the great
productive capacity of complex technical systems.   Joint
optimization reflects the reality that in the short run
technical systems are rigid or nonadaptive in the face of
various deviations or changes.

     A newly designed chemical plant illustrates this
very well.   The plant is operated by 6 teams, each with
17 workers and a team coordinator who have operating,
laboratory, mechanical, electrical and social maintenance
skills.   Each team assigns its members to their daily
tasks as limited by available skills.   Flexibility and
adaptability will better be served as the skill-mix of
each member increases.   Therefore, training opportunities are built into the work programme so that members
may accumulate knowledge, skills, and experience.
Workers are not paid according to tasks performed or job
titles but on the basis of the levels of knowledge and
skills each has achieved. The technical and social
needs are so complex that several years will be required
to master all of the operating and maintenance skills
needed by team members, contrasted with the few hours
under scientific management.   The working life of team
members is not preprogrammed.   Indeed, given the great
variety of tasks available to the team, the team 're-
invents' the working lives of its members weekly and
sometimes daily.   The team is responsible for its output and quality as well as for the utilization of its
resources - the efforts of its members, raw materials
and plant.   Thus, not only is there no such thing as
one man-one job, neither is there direct control of an
individual's performance by a supervisor.

     The technical system was designed to be integrated
with the social system; control rooms were consolidated
to permit team operation, quality control procedures are
built into the team's tasks, and monitoring information
or feedback belongs to the teams.   A critical decision
in the design of the technical system was to operate the

costly computer system off-line, permitting substantial
operator decision making rather than computer control.
Thus, learning will take place because the computer
cannot learn while people can.   Learning how to effectively operate the complex process is central to economically successful performance.   By means of this design
which provides needed work authority, stimulates and
rewards learning and relies on self-management of individuals and teams, the quality of working life of individuals is strongly enhanced while the technical and economic success of the organization is assured.   Importantly, this organization design, undertaken with cooperation and participation of the union, led to a unique
union-management collective agreement emphasizing quality
of working life factors (Davis, 1979).

The efficient and effective performance of these
alternative organizational forms, which provide high
levels of satisfaction of most criteria of quality of
working life, represent a beginning.   The challenge in
the immediate future is to devote sufficient learning,
ingenuity and effort to organizational architecture to
develop a variety of organizational forms that are
alternatives to scientific management and bureaucracy.
If successfully done, Western societies may be able to
avert the coming crises or successfully overcome them.

REFERENCES

Ackoff, Russell (1975).   'The   Second Industrial
       Revolution', Mimeo.

Cherns, Albert (1976).   'The Principles of Sociotech-
       nical Design', Human Relations, 29, 8, 783-792.

Davis, Louis E. (1971).   'The Coming Crisis for Produc-
       tion Management: Technology and Organization',
       Int'l Journal of Production Research, 9, 1, 65-82.

Davis, Louis E. (1977).   'Evolving Alternative Organi-
       zation Designs: Their Sociotechnical Bases',
       Human Relations, 30, 3, 261-273.

Davis, Louis E. (1979).   'A Labor-Management Contract
       and the Quality of Working Life', Journal of Occu-
       pational Behavior, 1, 1.

Davis, Louis E. (1980).   'The Process of Organization-
       Plant Design', Organizational Dynamics, Winter, 1980.

Gyllenhammer, Per (1977).   People at Work, Addison-
       Wesley.

Karasek, Robert A. Jr. (1979).   'Job Demands, Job
    Decision Latitude and Mental Strain: Impli-
    cations for Job Redesign', Admin. Sci. Quarterly,
    24, 2, 285-308.

Yankelovitch, Daniel (1979).   'Work, Value, and the
    New Breed' in Work in America: The Decade Ahead
    (Eds. C. Kerr and J.M. Rosow), Van Nostrand-
    Reinhold, New York.

Changes in Working Life
Edited by K.D. Duncan, M.M. Gruneberg, and D. Wallis
© 1980 John Wiley & Sons Ltd

Chapter 13

Work Design in Europe

T. LUPTON and I. TANNER

During the last decade a considerable number of articles has appeared in the academic and popular press describing the 'experiments' in work design which have been carried out in Europe.   These have been collectively discussed in some circles as the job design 'movement'.   This paper reports some findings of a research programme which has examined some of the main recent experiments in manufacturing system design in European heavy engineering;   especially vehicles and consumer durables.   One of the main aims of this research is to discover the reasons for the European experiments. We were, and are, also interested in the models of manufacturing systems which their designers work with. These models are, we think, significant influences on the engineer designer as he creates the environment in which the operative lives and works.

All of the data presented here have been collected at first hand.   Factories have been visited in each of six European countries.   The manufacturing systems have been discussed with their designers in situ.   This is not a comprehensive survey;   there are, for example, few British cases, and some notable innovators in this field have yet to be included, e.g. Philips in the Netherlands. The research continues and we intend to include light engineering and process plants in our future enquiries. This paper presents some results of only the first stage of a lengthy project.

1. VALUES AND THE LOGIC OF WORK-SYSTEM DESIGN

The designer of a manufacturing system is likely to be confronted with the problem of reconciling conflicting aims and values, especially if he is charged with the task of providing a high quality of work life for those who will man the system. Although it is conceivable that in a given case all the aims are consistent, logic and the experience of practitioners combine to show that there is no necessary connection of cause and effect between efficiency and the quality of working life. Our purpose here is to display the reasoning in support of this proposition and to examine its implications for the design of manufacturing systems.

Efficiency means pursuing successfully the means to a particular set of valued ends. Goodness and rightness are attributed to activities that bring together resources - labour, energy, raw materials, for example - in ways that minimise the money cost of producing a good or a service. The term 'added value' expresses the idea well. If one is rightly striving successfully to maximise the difference in money value of inputs used and outputs disposed of in the market place, then one is being efficient - and good. In Western Europe and North America this value is all pervading.

To ignore the efficiency values is a little more difficult than to set aside the humane values which relate to the quality of working life. The humane values impose a duty on those who design and manage work systems not to cause unnecessary physical pain and suffering to those who work in them. More significantly and positively, they call for action to promote human wellbeing and satisfaction, and also to afford one's fellow humans, so far as it is within one's power to do so, every opportunity to realise all the potential skill, intelligence, adaptability, that is within them to achieve. Not enough is known of the means to reach these ends, nor of the consequences for efficiency of making the attempt to encourage the apparently risky enterprise of designing directly to maximise the humane values.

Despite that, it is easy to see how the idea that to pursue the humane values would, or could, promote efficiency. If, as the argument goes, conditions are created which allow full rein to all the talents of every individual person, how much waste of resources would/could thereby be avoided. The motivation to work, which it is argued is eroded by the constraints placed on people by, e.g. repetitive tasks in cramped, noisy and dirty conditions, is released when these constraints are removed. Therefore, the designers of manufacturing systems should strive mightily to eliminate those constraints

from their designs, in the interests not only of
improving the quality of work life but also of improving efficiency.

The opposite proposition, namely that manufacturing systems designed with only efficiency values in
mind, would necessarily maximise quality of work life
values is very much more difficult to find support for.
Examples abound where efficieny is high and where little
or nothing has been included in the design to promote
positive humane values.   It is not obvious either that
any change in such systems with that end in view would
further raise efficiency;   nor that any change designed
to raise efficiency would improve the quality of work
life.

To see why this is so, it is useful to widen the
set of interconnections referred to.   Figure 1 shows
the logic of a manufacturing design.   The design of a
set of production arrangements need not be affected by
considerations of the needs, aspirations and potentialities of any of the persons who will be set those job
requirements.   However, if we look at the labour supply
position on the diagram, we see that it would be mistaken
to assume that any set of job requirements generated by a
product market logic would attract people to the job and
keep them there.   The pursuit of efficiency might then
be undermined by shortage of labour, and the designer
would have to look for alternative designs of manufacturing system which would generate more acceptable job
requirements.   Quality of work life considerations now

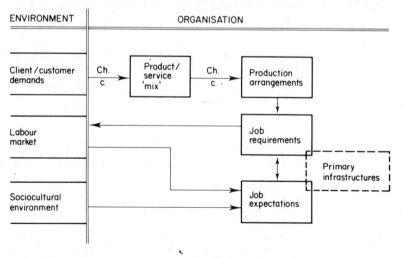

Figure 1.

enter, but only as a reaction to actual or anticipated
job expectations.   These may or may not include all the
humane values.   As we shall see later, many of the new
designs of manufacturing systems in Europe have arisen
for that reason.   Also, educated and articulate people
have been publicly pressing for improvements in the
quality of work life.   This demand has found its way
into the present (or anticipated) expectations of blue
and white-collar workers - and has thus influenced
designers.

This simple diagram, if it represents reality,
and we believe it does, underlines the absence of a
necessary connection between efficiency and quality of
work life.   It is possible that a design made to meet a
set of known expectations, which included quality-of-
work-life values, would satisfy the efficiency values
also.   There are some who cite the Volvo Kalmar plant as
an example, but some say that it would cease to be possible to achieve that correspondence between the two
sets of values if product volumes were to be higher, or
if the product became less price-competitive in that
sector of the market.

It is also possible that a designer responding only
to product market changes might by chance produce a
design that would meet a set of job expectations which
included the whole set of human values.   We cannot
think of an empirical example of this, but we shall show
later many examples where a response to a product market
for adaptable, flexible manufacturing capacity has produced manufacturing designs with enriched jobs, semi-
autonomous work groups, and such like.   The more common
case is where a balance has to be achieved by trading off
one set of values against another in the domains of
choice provided by the environment and by the process of
reaching decisions in adapting to the environment.   The
double-headed arrow in Figure 1 shows where the problem
arises, the Cs and Chs indicate the areas of choice and
constraint.

2. ANALYSIS OF THE LOGIC OF THE PROCESS OF MANUFACTURING
   SYSTEM DESIGN

In Table 1 the components of manufacturing systems
are listed and used as a starting point for analysis of
the process of reasoning-out a design from a set of
values.   In Column A the elements are characterised by
reference to a set of attributes, e.g. a job can exhibit
variety of different kinds.   Column B assigns a value to
these attributes, e.g. to provide a lot of variety may
add to the cost of production, and therefore be bad according to an economic value that considers low cost to be

good in itself.   Conversely, variety may be thought to
offer challenges to the skills, ingenuity, etc. of the
worker, and be seen as good in terms of a value which
stresses the full development of human potential.

        For simplicity's sake, the stark contrast between
the efficiency value and the humane value is emphasised
by placing them side by side in columns - (Bi) and (Bii).
In Column C there is a measure of the various elements
that go to make up the job attribute, so that it is possible in a particular case to establish the extent that
a particular job does or does not provide, e.g. variety.
The column headed 'Design parameters' shows how a job
might be designed if it were to conform to a particular
set of values, e.g. a job designed to provide the degree
of variety needed to conform to efficiency values would
probably be low on the measures in Column C, and the
design parameters would be as in (Dii).   From these
parameters it is possible to derive logically the physical features that must be built into the actual design.
Again, to use variety as the example, a job designed for
high variety according to a set of humane values would
have the attributes described in (Ei) and one designed
according to efficiency values would be as described in
(Eii).   It will readily be appreciated that in a particular case a design for efficiency values could produce
design features that also enhance all or some of the
humane values.   More likely, there will be conflict
between the two which may be resolved by ignoring one or
other set of values, or by finding some way of trading-
off as between the conflicting criteria.   This need to
make trade-offs has been explicitly recognised by some
European designers, and in the concluding section of this
article we shall make brief reference to the methods they
have evolved.

        We can conceive of a set of observable manufacturing
system characteristics which would result from the application of efficiency values to given design problems.
Those mentioned in Column (Eii) would form part of this
set.   Equally, we can conceive of such a set of observable characteristics which would result from application
of humane values as in (Ei).   This can be represented
diagrammatically.   Figure 2 shows three of the possible
relationships between these sets (where a circle represents a consistent set of observable characteristics
derived from either efficiency or humane values).

        The content of these sets is not constant even if
we assume that the values do not change.   Different
product-market problems will require different solutions
for either efficiency or humane values to be attained.
It is therefore possible that changes in the product market could increase or decrease the overlap between the

Table 1.

	(A)	(Bi)	(Bii)	(C)
	JOB ATTRIBUTE	HUMANE VALUE	EFFICIENCY VALUE	MEASURE
T H E J O B	VARIETY a) of tools, parts	Variety offers challenge to skill, ingenuity, memory, intelligence, capacity for judgement, endurance.	Variety is costly, difficult to control and predict. Wasteful, disorderly, risky.	Quantity
	b) of work-place			% of work done at own pace
	c) of physical location			% of time spent in one place
	d) of operations			% of time spent on same operation
	LEARNING TIME	The longer the training, the more skilled, responsible, demanding = the more pride, satisfaction.	Training is costly, is at risk by labour turnover.	Elapsed time

(Di)	(Dii)	(Ei)	(Eii)
HUMANE DESIGN PARAMETERS	EFFICIENCY DESIGN PARAMETERS	DESIGN (HUMANE VALUES)	DESIGN (EFFICIENCY VALUES)
Complex jobs, long cycles			Buffers only for economic reasons. Layout confines worker to own space and task. Work groups structured by technical design.
Built-in requirement to vary pace in same job, rotate through jobs paced differently, provision of opportunities to choose	Simple, short cycle jobs, restricted choice and opportunity, repetitive routine work. Single location.	Buffers between jobs, allowing choice of pace change, layouts permitting or demanding rotation - training for rotation.	
Built-in requirement to change location during same job, rotate, or provision of opportunities to do		Buffers between jobs allowing time to shift location within work-station. Planned shifts of location - as part of agreed or emergent rotation pattern.	
Built-in requirement to complete sequence of operations each distinguishable and demanding of different motor skills, or opportunities to do so.		Work groups structured by differentiated operations. Formally planned or informal rotation - boundary conditions allow changing, e.g. 'chariots', to carry assemblies.	
Jobs with long cycle times; numerous complex sequences, demands for precision, quality, high probability of error by untrained.	Simple jobs without much responsibility. Managers detect errors.	Complex work-station, many tools components, materials, services.	Minimum of tools components. Simple sequences. Job closely defined.

Table 1 continued

	(A)	(Bi)	(Bii)	(C)
W O R K E R	**TASK IDENTITY** a) Clarity of closure	If job has clear beginning and end, 'ownership', which = satisfaction is easier to claim.	Psychological 'ownership' of job inhibits high control/coordination.	Sharpness of job definition
	b) Visibility	Output is visibly and meaningfully different from inputs = sense of achievement = satisfaction.	Worker creativity creates risks in product market.	Sharpness of job definition.
	c) Magnitude	The costliness of one's creations are a source of pride.		Value added by operation.
	AUTONOMY a) Choice of method, · tools. b) Choice of sequence c) Choice of pace. d) Choice of inputs. e) Choice of services.	Freedom of choice is main basis of job satisfaction. To be one's own boss; to decide: 1. What to do. 2. How to do it. 3. When to do it. and to be responsible for inputs, and the outcomes is to have a job worth doing well.	Freedom of worker choice raises risk of disorder in absence of worker responsibility for outcomes like volume, quality.	% of job-elements as defined, that are specified by and checked by the operator.

(Di)	(Dii)	(Ei)	(Eii)
A job designed in such a way that the operator knows the source of the inputs and is in control of them, knows the boundaries of the job and the nature and distinction of the outputs, and knows that they are valuable enough and complex enough to engender pride.	Management controls work in and out of work stations, also job methods.	Well-bounded work station. Access to and control of materials, components, services, etc., necessary. Clearly bounded position where outputs of satisfactory standard are handed over as inputs to another job, and are acknowledged at that point to be satisfactory.	Materials and components handling designed for ease of managerial control. Flow of work through stations similarly.
Complex, long-cycle jobs, which allow scope for choice. Availability of range of tools components, services, which allow scope for choice. Job designed to offer scope for changes of sequence, or pace, as the operator decides.	Restrict choices to level of acceptance of responsibility by worker.	Stocks before and after operation to create time and opportunity for choice. Work station designed to store and display tools, parts, etc. Operator as own supervisor, quality controller - to be specified in job description. Services at call of operator as and when required. Job elements combined to make possible alternative sequences of operations, alternative methods, alternative tools etc. No machine pacing.	Job elements designed and combined by system designer. Layout, material, and component handling gear, and between-station stocks will optimise share of discretion between management and work force.

Table 1 continued

		(A)	(Bi)	(Bii)	(C)
C O N T R O L		**RESPONSIBILITY** a) Problem- solving	Determining outcomes by personal choice is satisfying.	When a complex product has to be machined, assembled, processed in quantity, responsibility and authority must lie where standard-setting and coordination has to be formally done. Planning and coordination by workers raises high risk of disorder and uneconomic cost.	Complexity/ ambiguity of causes for errors and remedies
		b) Time-span of discretion	Choosing to commit resources when checks are not immediate is satisfying.		How long before sub-standard work is detected?
		c) Probability of error.	Challenge to succeed in minimising error in conditions of high risk is satisfying.		How probable the error? How costly the error?
		REQUIRED INTERACTION	The more inter-personal contact the doing of the job demands, the more satisfied the person doing the job.	Attention to externally-determined standards is at risk if work is designed with satisfactory social interaction in mind.	Number of interactions. Amount of time spent interacting.

(Di)	(Dii)	(Ei)	(Eii)
"	Design of system should be consistent with planning and control by specialists in that function, in pursuit of clear system objectives.	Complex work situation as above + low supervision (much that is expansion is in charge of the operator).	Simple work-stations. Clear distinctions in design between operator work and manager/technical work.
Absence of close and continuous checking (either intrinsic to job design or deliberate policy).		Quality requirements high and are the responsibility of operator.	Quality/quantity check point designed to allow management to control, at frequent intervals.
All the above + expensive tools, materials, equipment components fine tolerances.			Minimise probability of error by jobs designed to minimise worker choice.
Pattern of layout not 0-0-0 but Sequences of task and allocation of sequences of tasks gives opportunities to interact.	Interactions between workers to be governed by task-definitions and manufacturing sequences consistent with economic operation.	Quietness, visibility of others, low requirement for continuous mental concentration, physical proximity - functional interdependence (high) = job satisfaction.	Position of work stations in layout (and thus required interaction) governed by need to economise space, work-in-progress, materials and components. The degree of functional interdependence of workers is logical consequence of design.

Table 1 continued.

WORKER PARTICIPATION	**POSSIBILITY OF LEARNING** a) Improvement of functional skills b) Improvement of innovative skills.	Continuous challenge to tackle changing problems and tasks is satisfying.	To optimise control and predictability, learning and doing are best kept separate.	Degree of workers' involvement in continuous adoption and improvement of job design.
WORKING CONDITIONS	**ENVIRONMENTAL CONDITIONS** a) Safety	Freedom from health hazards and physical injury is good.		No. of accidents /1,000,000 working hours.
	b) Working posture.			Ergonomics.
	c) Atmosphere			Temperature, composition of air.
	d) Noise			dB
	e) Light			Lux, degree of reflection.

two sets.   The greater the overlap the more easy it is
to satisfy both sets of values - the less conflict exists
between them.   Where there is some significant overlap
in these sets it is likely that a manufacturing system
designer whose attention is directed solely to the
achievement of efficiency values will nonetheless find
that his designs are welcomed by those who believe that
there should be more emphasis on the humanity of work.

Our research reveals that amongst those designers
studied, the dominant values and rationality in the production of the new work designs have been technical,
efficiency values.   Table 2 shows the ten factors from a
mixed list of technical and human elements in manufacturing system design which the design engineers thought to
be most important.

Allowing workers to change job design as they think it is appropriate (in cooperation with technical and administrative departments).	Changes in job design should be done by technical experts.	Space and time available allowing workers to work on job-design problems off-job.	Design of system should assume fully-trained workers, employed full-time on their job.
Non-dangerous working places, compatible with natural movements. Temperature, noise and light conditions adequate for human characteristics.			Working places made as safe and as pleasant as is consistent with minimising cost and ensuring implementation of production plans.

The results of Table 2 were underlined by the answers to a set of detailed questions as to the criteria the engineer-designers adopted when choosing between methods of performing operations in a manufacturing system. The results of this analysis are shown in Table 3. By comparison with American engineers studied by Davis et al. (1955), the emphasis in our sample was slightly more towards the social and psychological variables. We have not a big enough sample to determine with any accuracy whether there are any differences between countries and companies in Europe. That must await the next stage of our work, when we shall cover a much larger number of companies.

It will be no surprise to many people that a group of industrial engineers faced with the task of designing manufacturing systems happen to emphasise those aspects

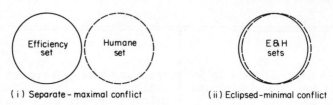

(i) Separate - maximal conflict   (ii) Eclipsed - minimal conflict

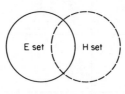

(iii) Partial eclipse

Figure 2.   Relationships between 'efficiency' and
             'humane' sets of manufacturing system
             characteristics.

Table 2.   Top Ten Factors in Designers' Perspective of
            Manufacturing System Design

Rank	Factor Number		Importance of Factor: weighted score
1	(21)	The volume of production	100
2	(32)	The quality requirements of the product	99
3	(3)	The amalgamation of tasks into jobs	93
4	(33)	The position of quality controls in the work flow	92
5	(8)	The size of buffer stocks between operations	90
6	(18)	The possibility of automating the process	89
7	(24)	The limits on capital expenditure	89
8	(40)	The system for materials handling - components	89
9	(5)	The system for materials handling - main products	89
10	(2)	The position of work stations in the layout	88

Table 3.   Major Considerations in the Choice of
            Particular Methods for Performing Operations

		Importance: Weighted Score
Rank		
1	To obtain the highest quality possible	94
2	To provide maximum safety	94
3	To provide maximum production flexibility	91
4	To minimise tool costs	91
5	To minimise the time required	87
6	To minimise materials handling costs	86

Davis' (1955) ranking

1. Minimise time required

2. Obtain highest quality

3. Minimise skill required

4. Utilise tools and equipment on hand

5. Minimise floor-space required

6. Achieve specialisation of skills

of the task concerned with efficiency and technical merit.
The surprising thing is that each of the designs when
completed has attracted, or been given, attention as an
innovation in the improvement of work life.   The reason
for this, we believe, lies in the changing product markets of the companies involved.   There has been a
requirement, in motor cars especially, for increased
variety of products to satisfy differences in demand and
safety legislation in the various markets where the
products are sold.   The dominant system of production,
the assembly line, is not suited to products with high
component variety and short batch requirements.   As a
result, engineers have sought ways of assembling their
products which relieve the strains of 'balancing the
line' and scheduling.   Semi-autonomous work groups
happen to be a feasible solution in some cases.   In
terms of our sets (Figure 2) we have witnessed the
increasing eclipse of the humane set by the efficiency
set - but this eclipse is by no means total.

3. THE 'MODELS' OF DESIGNERS AND SOME METHODS OF
   TRADE-OFF

       Starting with the abstract idea of a manufacturing
system as an open system in which commercial, technical,
organisational, physical and psychological variables
interconnect in complex ways, we drew up a mixed list of
forty variables to characterise the system, as reproduced
in Appendix 1.   The engineers-designers we interviewed
were first asked to 'score' each variable on a scale
ranging from 'no importance' to 'high importance'.   We
then asked them to say - taking each pair of variables -
whether in their view the connection between them was
strong or weak, or whether they saw no connection.   From
the replies it was possible, as we will show presently,
to represent each engineer's 'model' as a matrix of
interconnections.

       The forty variables can be divided into three broad
groups - social and ergonomic factors, product and process factors, and environment and control factors.   More
succinctly, people, technology and context groupings.
A matrix is said to be connected to the extent that the
responses it contains show causal linkages between these
groupings.   A disconnected matrix is one in which, while
there may be responses within each of the groups referred
to, there are no linkages between the groups.   Density
refers to the degree to which the respondent sees connections between each variable and every other.   A dense
matrix has many interconnections and a thin matrix few.
Any matrix, as well as showing degrees of connectedness
and density, may also exhibit bias.   Bias can be of two
kinds, either social or technical, and this is indicated
by a predominance of connections between social or technical variables respectively and the absence of connections in the other one.   Table 4 shows the types of
matrix which can result from these definitions.   Dense
connected matrices (types A, B, C), indicate that the
engineers whose responses are exhibited by them, work
mentally with an open socio-technical system model of a
complex kind.   Thin connected matrices (types D, E, F),
show their authors as working mentally with a simple
system model of the same kind.

       A hypothesis suggests itself to us when we compare
the conclusions reached from our logical design table
(Table 1) with the results of the analysis of the matrices;   it is that engineers who work mentally with a
matrix of type A, and to a lesser extent type B, will be
confronted by the need to find trade-offs between tech-
nical/economic and humane considerations much more than
will the engineers who exhibit matrices of types C and
D, the inference being that these latter choose to ignore
just those connections which raise the trade-off problem.

Table 4.

1. Connected Matrices

	Technically Biased	Unbiased	Socially Biased
Dense	A possible but difficult to discover	B	C possible but difficult to discover
Thin	D	E	F

2. Disconnected matrices

	Technically Biased	Unbiased	Socially Biased
Dense	These are excluded by definition		
Thin	G	H	I

There is already a little evidence that this might be so. During our researches we have found three examples of methods for arriving at trade-offs in the design process, each arrived at independently but logically very similar. In two of the cases we know that the 'models' that led to their development are represented by highly connected matrices, and the other we are confident from published work is also so represented (Lucas, 1976; Lupton, 1975; Metzger et al., 1975).

To examine the three methods in detail is beyond the scope of this paper. Suffice to say that each of them tackles the problem revealed by our Table 1, namely, to embody in a design the optimum pattern of trade-offs between the design features predicated by humane values and/or worker expectations on the one hand, and cost/ efficiency values on the other. They all follow roughly the same pattern which is:

1. To generate a set of alternative design solutions from the design problem (e.g. to assemble a product at given volume, variety, quality).

2. To evolve criteria for making a choice between the alternatives.

3. To choose the best design in the light of the criteria.

4. CONCLUSION

As we said at the beginning, this chapter reports work in progress. There is much yet to be done both descriptively and analytically before a comprehensive picture can be drawn of what is happening in Europe.

We propose to extend our sample to cover companies in the engineering sector who have not adopted novel designs, and to companies in process industry.

Although the general depression of the Western economies has reduced the incentive to remodel manufacturing systems and has stunted investment in experimental systems, there is bound to be a renewal of interest. The economic, social and political influences that gave rise to the work-design movement will intensify with prosperity; and ideas about changing the inhuman face of technology have been around a very long time and are gaining in strength.

We have seen our task as one of accurate reportage so that knowledge of current best practice is more widely known. More importantly, however, we wish to draw upon, and add to, the methods that are being evolved to identify the nature and extent of the conflict between humane values and economic efficiency, to embody a reconciliation of them in practical system design procedures, and in consequence create the optimal set of conditions under which people can gain material and non-material satisfactions from productive work.

REFERENCES

Davis, L.E., Canter, R.R., Hoffman, J. (1955). 'Current job design criteria', Journal of Industrial Engineering, Vol. 6, No. 2, 5-11.

den Hertog, J. Friso (1977). 'The search for new leads in job design: the Philips case', Journal of Contemporary Business, Spring.

Lucas, André (1976). R.N.U.R., Les Profils de Postes, Sirtes et Masson, Paris.

Lupton, T. (1975). 'Efficiency and the quality of work life - the technology of reconciliation', Organisational Dynamics, Autumn.

Metzger, H., Schafer and Zippe, H. (1975). 'Methode zur Bewertung von Arbeitssystemen' in Arbeitsstrukturierung in Der Deutschen Metallindustrie, (2), Institut fur Angewandte Arbeitswissenschaft, EV Koln.

APPENDIX 1

Factors in System Design	Of little importance Extremely important	Strength of relationship		
		Strong	Weak	None
1 The layout of machines in workshop	1....2....3....4....5	___		
2 The positions of work stations in the layout	1....2....3....4....5	___		
3 The amalgamation of tasks into jobs	1....2....3....4....5	___		
4 The length of the job-cycle	1....2....3....4....5	___		
5 The system for handling materials - main products	1....2....3....4....5	___		
6 The requirements for storage of parts & products	1....2....3....4....5	___		
7 The level of work in progress	1....2....3....4....5	___		
8 The size of buffer stocks between operations	1....2....3....4....5	___		
9 The maintenance requirements of machinery	1....2....3....4....5	___		
10 The physical (comfort) needs of workers	1....2....3....4....5	___		
11 The system of production planning/control	1....2....3....4....5	___		
12 The degree of autonomy of the worker	1....2....3....4....5	___		
13 The system of payment for workers	1....2....3....4....5	___		
14 The cost control system	1....2....3....4....5			___
15 The make-up of unit costs	1....2....3....4....5			___
16 The attitudes of management	1....2....3....4....5	___		
17 The availability of automated machinery	1....2....3....4....5	___		
18 The possibility of automating the process	1....2....3....4....5	___		
19 The skills required of the workers	1....2....3....4....5	___		
20 The physical space available/required	1....2....3....4....5	___		___
21 The volume of production	1....2....3....4....5	___		

Factors in System Design	Of little importance Extremely important	Strength of relationship		
		Strong	Weak	None
22 The average batch size	1....2....3....4....5	_____		
23 The variability in batch size	1....2....3....4....5	_____		
24 The limits on capital expenditure	1....2....3....4....5	_____		
25 The technological demands of tasks	1....2....3....4....5	_____		
26 The physical attributes of the product	1....2....3....4....5	_____		
27 The availability of working capital	1....2....3....4....5	_____		
28 The variability in product variety	1....2....3....4....5	_____		
29 The availability of labour	1....2....3....4....5	_____		
30 The supply of materials/ components	1....2....3....4....5	_____		
31 The fragility of components	1....2....3....4....5	_____		
32 The quality requirements of the product	1....2....3....4....5	_____		
33 The need for and position of quality controls in work flow	1....2....3....4....5	_____		
34 The mental skills of workers	1....2....3....4....5	_____		
35 The size/shape of workers	1....2....3....4....5	_____		
36 The physical attributes of workers	1....2....3....4....5	_____		
37 The physiology of workers (needs, etc.)	1....2....3....4....5	_____		
38 The attitudes of workers	1....2....3....4....5	_____		
39 The need for supervision	1....2....3....4....5	_____		
40 The system for handling materials - components/ materials	1....2....3....4....5	_____		_____

Changes in Working Life
Edited by K.D. Duncan, M.M. Gruneberg, and D. Wallis
© 1980 John Wiley & Sons Ltd

Chapter 14

Designing Meaningful Jobs: A Comparative Analysis of Organizational Design Practices

A. VAN ASSEN and P. WESTER

INTRODUCTION

The first attempts at improving the quality of working life (Q.W.L.) in organizations were undertaken in the fifties by Herzberg and Davis in the USA, and by members of the London Tavistock Institute. Since then, this topic has become increasingly popular among researchers as well as practitioners throughout the industrialized western countries. The Netherlands had its share of involvement in the big boom of publications on job redesign, work structuring, job consultation, worker participation and the like.

However, if one takes a closer look at the results and the impact of this 20-year history of Q.W.L. projects, the picture is rather dismal. A lot of these projects, though reported to be successful, never seemed to have outgrown their particular status of experiments, and little or nothing of them sparked off to their organizational surroundings. In their apparent isolation from the objectives and circumstances of the surrounding organization, they are like exotic gardens in a desert, requiring a disproportional amount of care, attention and energy for their survival.

There are several reasons for this disappointing state of affairs. First, many managers do not perceive the relevance of improvements in working conditions for

the solution of the problems of organizations as they see
them.   Perhaps little effort has been taken to make
such a connection clear to them.   Moreover, even in
cases of massive absenteeism or turnover, it is often far
easier for management to draw upon minorities or immi-
grants who may consider themselves lucky to become
employed, instead of embarking upon hazardous adventures
like Organisation Development (O.D.).   Second, the way
social scientists handle Q.W.L. projects is often a
clearcut example of the 'piecemeal syndrome' described by
Skinner (1971).   Often they seem to confine themselves
to processes and relations on a micro level, often
accepting technology and organizational structures as
natural phenomena not to be touched upon.   The resulting case studies tend to be mere descriptions of the
course of events and processes, with less systematisation
in their conclusions and recommendations, like cooking
recipes or lists of do's and dont's.

The third reason, consequently, lies in the fact
that Q.W.L. projects offer little or no systematic knowledge about how to proceed with work design and worker
participation programmes (see also Hackman, 1978), which
is also partly due to the lack of a general theory of
organizations.   An exclusive social stamp and the lack
of an integrative approach seem to be common characteristics of Q.W.L. projects.   In more than one case we
observed that both an organizational change project and
work structuring/job consultation project were carried
out at the same time in one and the same factory, but
completely isolated from each other in almost every
aspect.   In these instances, the organizational change
projects carried an economic label and the Q.W.L. projects went under a humanistic or social banner.   It was
this observation that triggered our attempts to elucidate
the connection between organizational design and opportunities for work structuring and job consultation/worker
participation.

APPROACH

We started with an inventory (Wester, 1977)
obtained from a number of internal consultants in order
to get acquainted with organizational change projects in
manufacturing plants which were being carried out at
that time.   This inventory indicated that many of the
organizational change activities had the same goal and
were directed at the same design characteristics.   The
goal can be broadly characterized in two words : greater
flexibility.   The organization design variables and the
related direction of change appeared to be:

(a) Functional versus product orientation of

transformation processes;   direction of change:
towards a product orientation.

(b) Degree of integration of staff and other, non-
production activities;   direction of change: a
stronger integration.

(c) Degree of delegation of authority down the line of
hierarchy;   direction of change: stronger delegation down the line, towards small-scale, autonomous groups.

These variables seemed to determine to a large extent
the basic differences in design of the various manufacturing organizations.   At first sight they also
appeared of major importance for job design and the
opportunity for worker participation.

These notions were worked out more systematically
into a theoretical model based on a number of case
studies on Q.W.L.

We then started an empirical research programme to
investigate further the connections between the three
organization design variables and the possibilities for
work structuring and worker participation.   Our activities constituted a special blend of research and consultation.   The research was aimed at validation and
further development of our model in practical situations.
The consulting activities were intended to further a
state of 'self redesign' of the organizations involved.
The theoretical model and our activities, as well as
their results so far, will be the subject of this paper.

THE THEORY

Twenty years of experience in more than 50 job redesign projects at Philips' factories reveals (Den
Hertog, 1978) that job content is determined by a number
of factors: product design, technology and in particular the manufacturing process, and the structure or
design of the organization, being the most important ones.
In designing work systems, job content is the last link
in a chain of decisions.   Each one is further curtailing
the elbow-room of the job designer (see Figure 1).

Traditional job enrichment and job redesign practices, trying to alter already existing jobs, are often
limited in range, because the consequences of the other
choices cannot be easily undone.   Therefore to be effective, job design should be preventive: at each link in
the chain of choices the consequences for the job design
resulting from it should be made clear and, if necessary,

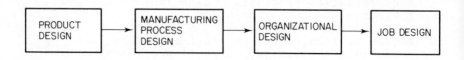

Figure 1.   Hierarchy of choices in work system design.
             This study deals especially with organi-
             zational design in relation to job design.

alternative ways of reaching a desirable job content
should be explored.

        Often there are alternative ways in the choice of
manufacturing processes as well as organization structure and even product design may show alternatives.   In
a study (Dekkers, 1977) concerning the relation between
technology and tasks, it was established that at least
nine different manufacturing processes were in use to
produce a certain category of products, in this case
small consumer products assembled manually, like shavers,
hair stylers, electrical percolators, etc.   Also, there
appeared to be a connection between a particular manufacturing process and the characteristics of the tasks
associated with it, as measured by means of the Job
Diagnostic Survey (Hackman, 1978).   The importance of
this pilot study is two-fold: it shows that there are
often alternative technologies which can be used, and
also that some manufacturing processes are socially more
desirable than others.

        As can be seen in Figure 1, the structure of the
organization or the organizational design also has its
impact on the content of jobs.   In this area it appears
too that choices can be made which are of particular
relevance to Q.W.L. in the organization;   this paper will
be focused entirely on the design of organizations in
relation to job design and worker participation.

        In our model it is reasoned that the design of a
particular organization - that is the relative position
of that organization on the three dimensions mentioned -
entails both an information and task structure, which are
characteristic for that particular position on these
three dimensions.   The information/decision control pattern, in its turn, determines at large the opportunities
for job consultation/worker participation, i.e. its topics,
its participants and its role in organizational decision
making.   On the other hand, the task structure which also
results from the design, determines at large the different
opportunities for job redesign.

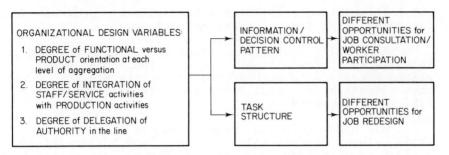

Figure 2.   Interdependencies between the organizational
             design variables and job consultation/worker
             participation and job redesign.

        For a schematic representation of the interdepen-
dencies described above, see Figure 2.

        An extensive discussion of this theory is beyond
the scope of this paper.   Therefore as an illustration,
some organizational forms will be discussed which will
show striking differences in their internal organization
and hence in their opportunities for Q.W.L., resulting
from differences in the design variables mentioned.

        At one of the extremes of the model the true
Tayloristic organization can be located.   This type of
organization has a strictly functional orientation in all
departments and at all levels, even those of the individual jobs.   Its staff and service departments are often
strictly separated, each department also representing an
independent discipline due to the functional orientation.
The number of supervisory levels in this kind of organization is rather high with a centralized decision structure.

        The result of these design choices for the infor-
mation flow is that the complete information concerning
the product and its course through the organization is
available only at the highest levels of the organization,
and these levels also are necessary to involve activities
from staff departments.   This location of product information accounts for the centralized decision structure.
At lower levels this information is rather fragmented or
even lacking on the shop floor.   Due to this lack of
information and because of the large distance of the shop
floor from these decision organs, there are few opportunities for worker participation/job consultation on the
level of the shop floor.   The task structure in this
organization is characterized by a strict separation of
operational activities (at the shop floor level), managerial tasks and service and staff activities.   Within

these three categories further specialization can be
found resulting from a functional orientation.

Especially at the shop floor level, this results
in tasks which contain only one or a few of the operations necessary to manufacture the entire product.   In
this situation job rotation is the only available alternative for improvement in Q.W.L.

All other solutions make a removal of the separation between operational, managerial and service/staff
activities necessary, and hence a change in organizational
design.   In this way, job enlargement becomes possible
if the production departments become product-oriented.
Further redesign of jobs, like job enrichment, is possible only as a result of delegation of authority down
the line or of transfer of staff activities to production
departments or both.

At one of the other extremes of the model, organizations which employ autonomous groups can be localized.
The autonomous group produces a complete product or a
sub-assembly, and so has a product orientation.   The
members of these working parties not only perform operational activities but also staff and service activities
(maintenance, quality control, methods engineering), and
they have the authority to plan and mutually divide work.
Job consultation is a must with respect to the progress of
work.

Other organizational forms can be distinguished
which lie in between.   For instance matrix organizations
are characterized by the formalization of lateral
relations between staff and production departments in
order to decentralize the decision structure of the formal
organization.   As another example, so called 'operational
groups' consisting of staff and service employees of
various disciplines, are temporarily or permanently
placed under the authority of a production manager in
order to solve manufacturing problems.

These instances not only show the relevance of the
actual design of the organization with respect to opportunities for improvement in Q.W.L., but also show that in
order to design new tasks, alternative organizational
forms must emerge.   These new organizations differ from
traditional Tayloristic concepts and also from one another
in various ways, e.g. in their ability to cope with
changes, in power to attract and hold employees, in sus-
ceptibility to disturbance, in flexibility and adaptability.
It is this link between characteristics of the organization at the macro-level, which is of special interest
for management, and, at the micro level, task characteristics and worker autonomy, often so troublesome for the

core of employees, which seem to open new perspectives
for Q.W.L.

SIX CASE STUDIES

        The main focus of our paper is a description of
the actual changes in the three design variables of our
model and their impact on organizational performance as
well as on improvements in Q.W.L.   From the factories
which responded to our inventory, six plants indicating
recent changes in the design variables mentioned, were
selected for a case study.   The plants show large differences with respect to size, manufacturing technology,
products and types of tasks to be performed at the lowest
levels (from machine-tending to craftsmen's jobs).

        The reasons for change also vary.   Most plants
suffered from economic problems and it was felt that
internal reorganizations might point a way out;   in two
cases, however, changes were necessary in order to adapt
the plant to alterations in flow of products or raw
material within the multi-national organization of which
they are a part.

        A systematic description of each case now is given.
Special attention is paid to the former organization and
its problems, to the changes which occurred in the design
variables of our model, and to the outcomes for both
Q.W.L. and organizational performance.   In the subsequent section, a number of conclusions concerning the
assumed relations between organizational design and
opportunities for improvement in Q.W.L. will be discussed.

DISCUSSION

        The descriptions in Table I show a difference in
main points of change between the cases.   All change
projects started with alterations either towards a product orientation, or more integration of staff with line,
or both;   these changes were eventually followed by a
further delegation of authority to the lowest levels of
the organization.   In the first two cases, the plants
changed their functional orientation toward a product
orientation;   further integration of staff with line
will be the next step in the factory for electronic
components, but is virtually impossible in the Diamond
Drawing Die Factory, because this kind of manufacturing
process hardly calls for staff activities.

        In cases 3 (thermoplastics department) and 4 (molyb-
dene and wolfram processing factory) changes towards a
product orientation are not really possible because both

TABLE I

Case	Brief outline of manufacturing processes	Formal organization	Problems	Changes toward a product orientation
1. Diamond drawing die factory. ± 135 employees	-Diamond drawing dies are made through a succession of different drilling and polishing operations (electrolytical, ultrasonic, laser, powder and needle, etc.). -Each craftsman masters only one technique. -Tolerance of each operation is low (3 μ). -Issue of specifications before and checking after each operation by management.	-Functional orientation (low controllability of processes dependence on craftsmen's skills) -Long line, in charge of planning, coordination and checking.	-Maintaining high quality standards. -Planning and product flow are complicated and disorderly. -Problems concerning pay and individual bonuses. -Little or no consultation between craftsmen and management, or between craftsmen processing the same stones. -Problem solving ad hoc.	-Set up of autonomous work groups of craftsmen with different skills. Each group now manufactures complete dies.
2. Factory for electronic components. ± 2500 employees	-Mass fabrication of a variety of electronic components (capacitors, TV deflection units); large series.	-Functional orientation of production departments. -Functional orientation of staff departments (16 different departments each with its own specialism). -Long managerial line. -Extensive task specialisation and division of labour.	-Growing inability to compete due to high production costs, serious quality problems. -Problems with meeting deserted product volume and delivery times. -Low responsibility of the internal organization for products or processes. -Low problem solving ability of the organization. -Communication problems.	-Reorganization of factory into 4 large product groups (± 600 employees in each group), according to product type. Each group is supervised by a product manager who has product responsibility.

3. Thermoplastics department. ±100 employees.	-Manufacture of plastic components by means of an injection moulding process. -800 different products in series of mixed length. -8 different types of injection moulding machines.	-Machines are supervised by machine-tenders (unskilled). -Setters and mechanics from auxiliary depts. are making machine adjustments and mould exchanges resp. doing maintenance and repair tasks. -Three shift system; each shift (10-15 workers) is supervised by a charge-hand. -Dept. lead is assisted by a planner and a supervisor; the latter directing the chargehands.	-Amount of planning and coordination needed. -Frequent exchange of moulds and frequent adjustments to be made. -Relatively low controllability of production process. -Large fluctuation in product quality. -Relatively high production costs. -Chronic employee shortage and high turnover rate due to unattractive job.	-After reducing the number of machine types from 8 to 2, and the number of series from 800 to 200; three clusters of injection moulding machines have been formed according to differences in product; each cluster is supervised by a senior operator.
4. Molybdene and wolfram processing factory. ±425 employees.	-The factory consists of two departments: *dept. PS: wolfram and molybdene ore is made into ingots. *dept. HT: ingots are rolled, lammered and drawn into wires, ready to be processed into filament. -Products and processes are very critical.	-Functional orien.tation of departments. -Traditional long line. -Extensive task specialisation and division of labour. -Both departments share the same quality engineering assistant; other contacts with staff and auxiliary departments only on the level of production manager.	-Quality problems, resulting in frictions between the two departments. -Built-in conflicts in job of quality engineering assistant are steadily increasing. -Complaints from production departments about lack of cooperation from staff depts.	-Product responsibility is transferred from production manager to each dept.

TABLE I CONTINUED

Case	Brief outline of manufacturing processes	Formal organization	Problems	Changes toward a product orientation
5. Central Tool Shop + 300 employees.	-The central Tool-shop is a production centre for tools, moulds and press tools, which are used in mass production. It employs + 240 craftsmen with various metal working skills and + 60 employees in other functions.	-The Toolshop consists of four production units with a functional orientation. -Staff and auxiliary functions in separate depts. -Managerial line relatively long: plant manager, dept. heads, senior foreman, foreman, craftsmen.	-Difficulties in meeting delivery times. -High turnover rate and absenteeism of craftsmen.	-The four functional oriented units are replaced by four product groups each with their own product range supervised by dept. heads now called product group leaders, directly linked to plantmanager. -Product group is made directly responsible for price, quality and delivery times and becomes customer-oriented. -Further customer-orientation of work groups within some product groups.
6. Electric bulb and filament factory. + 2000 employees	-Manufacture of several types of electric bulbs and filaments, both in large and small series. -Highly mechanized processes with much short-cycle manual work (machine tending).	-Functional orientation of production depts. -Traditional long line.	-Organization needs more flexibility in order to cope with frequent changes in processes and products and for reasons of expansion. -Bureaucratic tendencies due to long line. -Difficulties in communication and co-operation.	-Functional units are reorganized into three product groups.

Case	Integration of staff with line	Delegation of authority	Improvements in organizational performance	Improvements in Q.W.L.
1. Diamond drawing die factory. + 135 employees.	No changes.	-Autonomous groups now arrange: *(the number of) operations required to complete a die. *product flow *planning of work *quality control of own work.	-Considerable improvement in product quality. -Product flow less complicated. -Management capacity required for planning and coordination is greatly reduced; results: *line shortening *more attention to long-term problems and development *more consultation/communication.	-Higher individual wages. -Additional group bonuses. -Higher responsibility and more opportunities for craftsmen to make decisions concerning their own work. -Mutual consultation and problem solving by group members.
2. Factory for electronic components. + 2500 employees.	A first step combination of staff departments to a few large ones. Future goal: Matrix organisation or cooperational groups (decentralization of staff departments toward each product group).	Only on the higher levels of the organization, especially from plantmanager to the four product managers.	-No fall in production costs yet. -Higher costs of the organization; due to an addition of positions. -Higher product responsibility. -Higher problem solving ability of the organization. -Opportunities for each product group to pursue a specific price policy. -Communication problems are greatly reduced. -General feeling that the organization will again be able to compete in the future.	-No improvements, maybe except for the highest levels of staff and line.

TABLE I CONTINUED

Case	Integration of staff with line	Delegation of authority	Improvements in organizational performance	Improvements in Q.W.L.
3. Thermoplastics department. ± 100 employees.	-The tasks of machine tender, setter and mechanic are combined into a newly created job: machine operator. -Operational integration of auxiliary technical functions (industrial engineers) with line functions (dept. head and senior operators).	-Managerial line is heavily shortened: *the job of the planner, more or less operating in the line, is removed. Planning is now done by the senior operator. *the chargehand function is also removed; responsibility for each shift now rests with each working party.	-Considerable lowering of production costs, partly resulting from lower costs of the organization due to line shortenings (see next column). -Less quality problems. -Higher controllability of production process.	-Considerable upgrading of the lower jobs: *from unskilled to semiskilled *amount of pay raised accordingly. -More responsibility and room for own decisions. -Opportunities for learning to know intricacies of production process and application of experience (e.g. adjustments of process parameters. -Scheduled meetings for job consultation.
4. Molybdene and wolfram processing factory. ± 425 employees.	-Breakthrough of functional orientation of staff depts. by set up of operational group. This group consists of: *two process engineers *a quality engineer *two trouble-shooters *an organ. efficiency engineer *a planner. This operational staff group is directly linked to the production manager.	Only at higher levels of the organization, from plantmanager to product manager and from the latter to the department heads.	-Improvements not clear yet, for the reason that production is at this moment hampered by severe quality fluctuations in raw materials. There is a general feeling, however, that only this new organization is able to overcome problems.	-No improvements, maybe except for the highest levels of the organization.

5. Central Tool Shop. + 300 employees.	-Methods engineers quality officers and planning/scheduling officers were transferred from staff depts. and integrated into each product group. -Cooperation with other offices by means of a matrix structure.	-Shortening of managerial lines: *product group leader directly linked to plant manager *some craftsmen are made responsible for certain projects *more direct responsibility of craftsmen in various ways.	-Organization is more able to meet delivery times. -Responsibilities have been cleared with respect to price, quality and delivery times of products.	-More direct responsibility of craftsmen. -Various forms of enrichment of craftsmen's jobs in relation to project and customer orientation.
6. Electric bulb and filament factory. + 2000 employees.	-Functional orientation of staff and auxiliary depts.. is replaced by matrix structure and operational groups: Technical Management Teams (focus on processes) and Product Group Teams, both groups assisting product group leaders. -Matrix structure is also created for lower auxiliary functions (mechanics, fitters).	-Line shortening: *removal of function of production assistant and foreman. *More responsibility on the level of production manager.	-Shorter lines of communication. -More cooperation in matrix structures. -More (group) responsibility for products. -Changes can more easily be met.	-Improvements on the higher levels of the organization. -Job enrichment of the lower production functions is often hampered by: *technology and mechanization *criticism on wage system.

plants act as subcontractors.   For ease of comparison
the main points of change in each case and their results
are tabulated in Figure 3.

As can be seen from Figure 3, changes in the first
two organizational design variables (that is, towards a
product orientation, further integration of staff with
line, or both) generally resulted in considerable improvements in economic performance of the plants.   Only in
case 4 is this connection not clear, due to quality
problems with raw materials.

It also appears that the first two organizational
design variables also determine to a large extent the
opportunities for improvement in Q.W.L.   The direction
in which their influence goes also confirms our assumptions: there are more opportunities for improvement in
product organizations and/or in organizations in which
staff activities are integrated within the line, as compared to organizations with a more functional orientation of both production and staff departments.   However, actual improvements in job content at the lowest
levels appear to be conditional upon the presence of
delegation of authority towards these levels, as is shown
in cases 1, 3 and 5.   From these cases it appears too
that delegation of authority not only serves to improve
Q.W.L., but that it also contributes to a further enlargement of organizational performance.

These observations may offer a way out from the
rather dismal state of affairs with respect to work structuring.   Organizational changes with economic goals and
those with social objectives need not be antagonistic.
On the contrary, they are often in direct line with each
other, and then there is an opportunity to use change
projects with economic goals as carriers for changes in
Q.W.L., as is shown in cases 1, 3 and 5.

Therefore, instead of isolated attempts to improve
job content afterwards, we should concentrate our efforts
on helping to redesign whole organizations from both an
economic as well as a social point of view.

REFERENCES

Alink, J.B. and Wester, Ph. (1978).   'Organisatieveran-
        dering in een gereedschapmakerij', Internal Report,
        Social Research Dept. Philips N.V., Eindhoven.

Assen, A. van (1978).   'Organisatie-ontwerp en de speel-
        ruimte voor werkoverleg en werkstrukturering',
        Internal Report, Social Research Dept. Philips N.V.,
        Eindhoven.

Case	MAIN POINTS OF CHANGE			IMPROVEMENTS	
	towards a product orientation	further integration of staff with line	delegation of authority to lowest levels	in organisational performance	in Q.W.L. for lowest levels
1. Diamond drawing die factory	*		*	+ +	+
2. Factory for electronic components	*			+	0
3. Thermoplastics department		*	*	+ +	+ +
4. Molybdene and Wolfram processing factory		*		±	0
5. Central tool shop	*	*	*	+ +	+
6. Electric bulbs and filament factory	*	*		+	±

Dekkers, J. (1977). 'Produktiesysteem en taakstruktuur',
    Internal Report, Social Research Dept. Philips N.V.,
    Eindhoven.

Hackman, J.R. (1978). 'The design of work in the 1980s',
    Technical Report 15, School of Organization and
    Management, Yale University.

Hayes, R.H. and Schmennes, R.W. (1978). 'How should you
    organise manufacturing?', Harvard Business Review,
    January/February, 105-118.

Hertog, J.F. den (1978).   Arbeitsstrukturierung;
    experimente aus Holland, Verlag Hans Huber, Schrif-
    ten zur Arbeitspsychologie, nr. 21, Berlin.

Skinner, W. (1971). 'The anachronistic factory',
    Harvard Business Review, January/February, 62-70.

Wester, Ph. (1977).   'Inventarisatie organisatieverand-
    eringsprojekten in produktiebedrijven', Internal
    Report, Social Research Dept. Philips N.V.,
    Eindhoven.

Changes in Working Life
Edited by K.D. Duncan, M.M. Gruneberg, and D. Wallis
© 1980 John Wiley & Sons Ltd

Chapter 15

Work and Work Organizations in the Age of the Microprocessor

A. CHERNS

The physical and social separation of work to which we are accustomed is among the many revolutionary effects of industrialization. Separated physically by the building of mills and factories to house the new machines, work became socially segregated by place and by time. The lives of urban industrial people were split into working time and personal time, between workplace and personal space. The physical and social boundaries around work are now strong and sharply defined; they are among the most salient boundaries we encounter early in life and accept as natural phenomena. The physical and social separation of school and school 'work' prepare us from childhood, but even before that we have learned the daily routine of departures for work and returns, the pattern of weekends and holidays. 'Going to the office' may carry different nuances even to children from 'going to work', but the boundaries of separation are still sharp; although we should not forget that the small child who can speak on the 'phone to Daddy in his office has a different experience of the degree of separation from his counterpart whose Dad 'goes to work'.

When we speak, then, of the work environment we incorporate in our thinking all the consequences of the segregation of work. We make implicitly a distinction between the environment of work and the environment of other aspects of our lives. This is certainly realistic but it may limit our thinking about future possibilities.

We need to take as broad a view of the environment as
possible so that we provide ourselves the opportunity to
perceive possible impacts of environmental change on the
boundaries of work itself.

I shall be following the example of many, including
myself (1977a), by dividing the environment into physical,
economic, political, technological, social and cultural
aspects.   My aim is to explore the changes taking
place, and to be anticipated, in these environments, to
show how they are interconnected.   I shall then discuss
their impacts on work organizations and the nature of work
and, in particular, the effect on the organization and
experience of work of the choices of technology which
will become available.   I shall then consider the dynamics of the internal work environment in that context.

THE PHYSICAL ENVIRONMENT

It may be useful to point out that what we take as
our physical environment is partly a function of our
interests, capacities and understanding.   Far more concern and attention is given today to the physical environment of the workplace than at any time in the past,
finding its most notable expression in attempts to huma-
nize and to harmonize.   Humanizing implies a corrective
to the monumental aspirations of organization builders of
a generation ago, a feeling for a human scale which allows
the individual to have significance in contrast to the
grandeur which inspires both awe and a sense of personal
insignificance.   Harmonizing implies a relationship between the buildings and their surroundings, between their
appearance and the activities they house.   The former
constrains the latter;   stark functionalism is often in
strident disharmony with its neighbours, however internally consistent and satisfying.   Functionalism tends
also to emphasize specialization, the separation of
function and thus the distinction between work and life.
In this it is aided by the green field syndrome.   Land
is invariably cheaper away from the town and city centres
which formerly housed industry.   The mobility of workers,
more and more of whom own cars or motorcycles, make
sub-urban or ex-urban sites accessible, the freedom from
the constraints of urban building regulations and of
neighbouring buildings all make green field sites and
industrial parks or estates attractive to firms.   Most
of us find their spacious, clean, open and green environment pleasant.   In the same way and for the same reasons
campus universities and schools are attractive.   But the
consequence is greater segregation of the functions of
schools, universities and industry from one another and
from other aspects of life.

The humanizing impulse urges the provision of facilities for which the campus setting offers opportunity and increases the need. Catering, shopping, sport, entertainment, banking, insurance and other services compensate for geographical remoteness, can be subsidized by or provided by the firm and enhance its attractiveness as an employer. And the tangible benefits of paternalism readily compensate for the philosophical objections. Physical environment and internal culture are by no means unconnected. The humanizing impulse which selects a human scale prefers buildings which are small, unpretentious but with some individual character - a campus rather than a blockbuster. The campus tends to isolation and paternalism. The city blockbuster, if truly large enough, becomes equally encompassing, housing the same range of facilities exclusive of outdoor sports; the dehumanizing scale of a Shell Centre is compensated by an immense range of internal facilities. But this was the choice of a management already deeply paternalistic.

Insofar, then, as the physical environment of the workplace reflects increasingly a humanizing and harmonizing current, work-life becomes increasingly separated physically and its associated facilities are enlarged. Humanizing and harmonizing trends will not necessarily continue; they are social choices and reflect social beliefs and values. The expressive forms that they take are influenced by technological developments and by resource constraints and these in turn influence values. A technological development which renders abundant a good which was formerly scarce may have a profound effect on social attitudes and values.

The technological environment affects an organization in two ways. Technology is concerned with the transformation of inputs into outputs. Alternative technologies offer alternative modes of transformation. They may achieve the same output through the use of more readily available, abundant or cheaper units. Finally new processes, and the products of new technologies, make new outputs possible. The characteristic of late twentieth century technology is the development of information processing and its progressive availability and cheapness. We can be reasonably confident that entirely new industries generating entirely new products will emerge. So far the anticipated benefits appear marginal, as did the effects of electricity, the internal combustion engine and telecommunications in their infancy.

However, new technologies can reverse trends rather than accelerate or facilitate them. The trend towards concentration of industry and centralization of control may already have moved into reverse; the

microprocessor makes dispersion and dcentralization
more technically feasible.   One way in which such rever-
sals occur is by reducing the costs of a valued social
good.   One form of concentration is a consequence of the
greater strength of the widespread desire for access to
valued goods and services rather than the desire for
peace and quiet.   Technological change which provides
dispersed access to these goods and services permits the
reassertion of the values of peace and quiet;   it does
not create a new value so much as to remove the constraints preventing its realization.   It may result in
the appearance of a new value because its possible realization permits the articulation of what was formerly
unexpressed because unattainable.

        Underlying the choices of technology are more fun-
damental social values.   Value and technology will differ from collectivist to individualistic society.   In
the latter we would expect, for example, the production
of small home operated washing machines, in the former
improved communal laundries.   We need to enquire into
the underlying 'pattern variables' governing a society's
social choices, if we wish to anticipate the way technological potentialities will be exploited.   This approach
contradicts technological determinism which sets technology outside and against society as an exogenous force.
The demand for more social control over technology is
growing but is misconceived if it rests on the assumption
that technology has been an external force.   The nature
of technology is largely determined by the nature of
society and by the ownership of the power to command it,
which in our societies means anyone who could raise the
capital;   only complex and expensive technology required
early sponsorship by large organizations or by the state.
Developments which threatened existing large investments
could be bought up for suppression rather than exploitation.   Thus the economic organization of society strongly
influences the nature of its technology.   New technology may call into existence new forms of economic
organization but their shape derives from the basic pattern variables.

        The term 'pattern variables' was coined by Talcott
Parsons to designate the 'choices' all society makes as
to the basis on which its members shall relate to one
another.   The five he designated were: Ascription -
Achievement;   Affectivity - Affective Neutrality;   Col-
lectivism - Individualism;   Universalism - Particularism;
and Role Specificity - Diffuseness.

THE   ECONOMIC ENVIRONMENT

        Economics concerns the allocation of scarce

resources.   The economic environment is then the current degree of scarcity or abundance of valued resources.
In one meaning 'valued' is virtually synonymous with
'evaluated';   has been or can be measured or assessed.
When economists have found a way, what they can measure
becomes an economic good or resource.   Cost benefit
analysis rendered accessible to treatment as economic
goods such intangibles as quiet, time, and aesthetic
aspects of the environment.   Thus pressures from the
economic environment include the market forces which
register scarcity and availability.

The economic environment of an organization is
affected by the choices of consumers, the abundance or
scarcity of capital and labour and their costs which
include the monopoly pressure which the latter can
exert, the costs of its inputs which government can vary
through taxation or subsidy, and the value of its outputs which should register the choices of consumers but
which again government can vary.   Furthermore, the
economic environment can be changed very significantly
by legislative or other action which forces internal
accounting for former 'externalities'.   Goods previously 'free' may have to be paid for as, for example,
the consequence of legislation to restrict pollution.
The economic environment mediates the impact of the
political environment.

The political environment of an organization
includes acts of governments and the unlegislated pressures they bring to bear, the pressures exerted by
trades unions, employers' associations, professional
bodies, and pressure groups.   They may seek action
through legislation, through the direct action of consumers or through persuasion.   Pressure group action
has been growing and seeks legislative control whenever
and wherever that seems attainable.   We have simultaneously pressure for more legislation and for more
direct action.   However, the range of activity in which
government intervention is now treated as legitimate
entitles us to conclude that our societies' preferred mode
of bringing social pressure to bear is through legislation.   Thus the political environment mediates the
impact of the social environment.

The social environment of an organization includes
the social valuation of its products and its methods.
The economic value of products reflects their social
valuation and clearly a product or service cannot be sold
unless there are willing buyers.   But there may be significant minorities or even thumping majorities who dis-
approve or who grant them and those associated with them
low esteem.   The esteem given certain kinds of work is
significant in the social environment of many organizations,

and all are affected by their societies' valuation of
work itself, their preferences for leisure as against
income, and the place allotted to work in their culture.
The decline of the work ethic concerns many organizations.

The impact of the social environment is also
mediated through the technological environment. Some
technologies are disallowed through social pressure;
examples range from certain methods of killing animals to
the development of nuclear power. Social criticism of
technology has acquired new overtones. On the one hand,
the choices of technologies have come to be seen as
overtly political; on the other hand, their significance
for the individual has been stressed. And whereas
technology was dangerous, science was pure and benefi-
cent. When misused it was technology. Attacks on
science itself assail technology from a new quarter.

The cultural environment is to the social as
means are to ends. The social environment defines per-
missible goals, the cultural environment constrains the
means by which they may be obtained. Organizations have
their own internal culture, the informal understandings
of the ways in which things are done. Culture is not
only what differentiates one organization from another
in the same country in different lines of business, it
is also what differentiates organizations in the same
line of business in different countries. That an
organization's culture is partly a function of technology was shown by Woodward (1965), but the influence of
national culture is pervasive. Cultural norms specify
how people are to be treated, what kind of relationships
they will have with one another at work, what will be
the attitudes of supervisor, manager, worker, to one
another, what can be expressed openly and what only by
indirection, and so on. The ill-starred visit of
American autoworkers to Saab Scania (Goldmann, 1975)
illustrates the cultural differences between similar organization in different countries. The differences
were those between American and Swedish cultures, not
those peculiar to automobile plants. The impact of
cultural influences on the organization is direct.

INTERACTION WITH THE ENVIRONMENT

The influence of the environment on the organization is not one way. Organizations are active. Technology does not just happen out there, organizations seek
out technological developments and create them through
their own R. and D. activities. They exercise pressure
on governments to adopt favourable economic and fiscal
policies, they support parties or candidates who advocate

policies favourable to private enterprise in general and
to their own industry or firm in particular.   Publicly
owned industries are even more active, obliged as they
are to pursue political means for the attainment of
their objectives and to engage in negotiation with their
political masters over more and more of their commercial
operations.

The economic environment is partly the product of
the activities of industrial and commercial organizations.
The market registers and regulates the economic interaction of organizations.   As a feature of the economic
environment of one organization, it is also a collective
expression of all those whose interactions it mediates'.

The organization's impact on the social and cultural environments is both direct and indirect.   'The
product of work is people' (Herbst, 1975).   The skills
and social skills which people utilize or develop in
their work are exported by the organization to the
social environment for employment there.   If the work
develops in its members no skills of social interaction
and participation in decision making, the social environment lacks these skills.   Karasek (1976) demonstrates
the extent to which work life affects life outside work;
those who had more opportunities in their work for
sharing in decision making, some autonomy, some opportunity for the exercise of social skills, were more
active politically and in leisure and voluntary pursuits.
In a more general sense, the form of the modern organization, the assumptions underlying its modes of action
and its structure, its typical response to environmental
pressures has transformed our modes of feeling and
understanding, our consciousness.   Our sense of what is
private and what is public has changed as organization
has invaded the bastions of the former.   The response to
human needs is no longer the demand for personal action
but for organizational provision.   Here the organization affects society, promoting a culture of public and
organizational provision for human and social needs,
rather than a culture of private and personal provision.

So pervasive has the organization become that
critics have predicted our transformation into a corporate state, in which citizenship is mediated by organizational memberships (Marris, 1974).

The recent report to the Netherlands Council of
Ministers from their Scientific Council (1977) has placed
unusually strong emphasis on the centrality of job content to life chances.   The argument is too complex to
be treated adequately here.   One quotation may serve:

        'The job plays a central part in the

distribution processes with regard to knowledge, material and immaterial income from
work, wealth and power ... causal relations
operating through the job always carry more
weight than relations effected outside the
job.' (p. 7).

Thus the organization's influence on its environment is partly mediated by its members. Their experience within the organization affects their lives outside; their lives outside and those of their dependants
are part of the organization's environment. Stratified
and segmented jobs and a stratified and segmented society
reinforce one another.

The way the organizational environment will develop,
then, depends upon the ways in which the organizations
will evolve. Let me offer two opposite scenarios.

Scenario A

Organizations seek to manage turbulence in their
environment by bringing under control its principal
sources - suppliers or outlets or competitors. Vertical
and horizontal integration, and consequential size lead
to greater stratification and segmentation within the
organization which at the same time seeks to obtain its
members' greater identification by improved and extended
benefits. The process is both applauded as rationali-
zation and harried as monopolist by government.

The extended organization is more vulnerable to
union action although less often the victim of struggle
between union and supplier or outlet. But to bring con-
certed action to bear, the unions have themselves become
more centralized. The organization relates to its
environment in the negotiating mode, but negotiation is
between powerful heavy-weights. The awkward, the
unusual, the unauthorized, the unsponsored are, at best,
disregarded and discouraged; at worst, squeezed or
suppressed. Innovation becomes a governmental responsibility either because the big organization is powerful
enough to resist innovative competition or because the
potential disturbance of accommodation with the unions
is too costly.

Scenario B

Organizations respond to turbulence by seeking a
distinctive competence and by decentralizing decision
making, giving greater freedom to their members to deal
with local developments. A small unit within its own

special competence can take advantage more easily and
quickly of opportunities than large integrated organizations which rely on centralized decision making.   But
it is more vulnerable; the large organization can, by
spreading the risk, survive blows which would eliminate
the small.   Jobs are both more flexible and more at risk.
Unions negotiate the payment of a percentage of takings
into a trust fund to guarantee substantial payment for
redundancy through business failure or cut-back, thus
acquiring a further stake in the organization.   Trained
for participation in decision making within the organization, its members are better equipped to participate
actively in local affairs, especially those which concern their own organization.

        How scenario B continues is a matter of choice;
we have shown that the future environment of organizations is partly a function of the way organizations
shape it as they shape the physical environment.
Would scenario A organizations prefer the campus and the
monumental?   Would scenario B organizations prefer the
small, central location, redevelopment of centres and
inner suburbs?

        While there will be momentously significant
choices facing organizations, their centrality in modern
societies ensures that they will be made under intense
social and political as well as economic pressure.
Organizations are already theatres of conflict.   As
the Dutch study reminds us, because the job is so much
the determiner of life chances, it is the most attractive
point of leverage.   And when other inequalities have
been greatly reduced, those remaining in work become
more salient.   The Dutch report stressed job content
while most conflict is over the retention of jobs, demar-
cation, and the effort-reward bargain, rarely over
content.   Pressure to upgrade content has generally come
from employers.

        In a society where employment is the principal
means for distributing its resources, values opposed to
traditional forms of work have to be strongly and widely
held before they can effect change.   While new values
are favourable to more participative modes of organization, organizations become even more battlegrounds for
social conflict.   Organizations distribute power and
status which are as transferable across the organizational boundary as more tangible rewards.   Nor am I
referring only to the status which goes with high office
in a major company, but also to that which goes with
having a job at all.   Organizations and the employment
they provide will occupy the centre of the political
arena; political parties and pressure groups will pay
them increasing attention until some other acceptable way

of distributing resources is found, when the post-
industrial values promote citizenship above employment as
the individual's claim on society's resources.   Since
the expression of these values will appear as distrac-
tions from struggle for power in and over organizations,
they will lack serious political expression and will
dramatise themselves in strange and unaccountable ways,
exasperating and incomprehensible to politicians, industrialists and unionists alike.

The political environment of organizations can be
expected to be increasingly active;   their areas of
unfettered action will shrink and what remains will be
under scrutiny.   Nor can organizations do much except
prepare themselves to anticipate and respond to political
pressure.   And where governments as well as unions are
ready to enforce their will, local government and pressure groups can follow.   The accommodation between
industry and community, between organizations and other
social institutions is changing.   At present the forces
for change are expressing themselves through political
channels.

The technological environment is affected by the
actions of industrial firms themselves.   By their own R.
and D. they seek to create a favourable environment for
themselves and thereby influence that of many others.
But government is increasingly active, anxious that
national wealth be created and desperately concerned
about levels of employment.   These concerns, particularly the latter, are shared by unions.   Organizations
face an excruciating dilemma: invest in new technology
and risk union non-cooperation or government restraint
on obtaining its benefits, or eschew investment and risk
obsolescence and the pillory for failing to modernize?
Once again the initiative slips to government.   The
technological environment is increasingly under political
influence.   Industry will become more inclined to wait
to see whether government is going to sponsor a new
technology before hazarding its own resources, thus progressively relinquishing the initiative in technological
development to government, forcing technology into the
political arena.   Governments are attracted by technologies which appear likely to increase employment;   not
labour intensive technologies but technologies which can
create new industries, new processes, new products which
can stimulate new needs and provide their satisfaction.
Hence the especial interest in the microprocessor.

The microprocessor has potential for decentralization.   Rapidly processing information at small cost
and without large power sources or installations they
could sponsor a new generation of cottage industries.
And if production of goods can be decentralized, so can

the provision of services. What need for bank and
insurance staffs to congregate if they can exchange all
necessary information by microcomputer?   But technology does not dictate the form of its use.   The microprocessor could also promote centralization, making
vast amounts of information available to the centre and
even more giant enterprises possible.   We recall that
the factory system which destroyed earlier cottage
industry was not an inevitable outcome of the new technology.   Indeed the choice of technology partly reflected the seizure of the opportunity to eliminate the
independence of the craftsman and sub-contractor.
Questions about technology are questions about politics.
Will pressure groups and governments urge centralization
or decentralization?   Governments find big organizations easier to regulate, inspect and extort tax from.
Compare the simplicity of collecting tax by deductions
at source from the thousands of people employed by a
large firm, with the problems of assessing and collecting
the tax from the same number of self-employed or small
partnerships. And more indirect pressures are easier to
bring upon large centralized than scattered decentralized
units.

Unions find large organizations much easier re-
cruiting grounds; small units are harder to recruit and
to serve if recruited.   Both government and union, for
example, were hostile to the 'lump', labour only sub-
contracting in the construction industry;   the former
because of tax evasion, the latter because of recruitment
difficulties among the 'self employed'.   The 'lump'
certainly gave rise to abuse.   But in considering the
impact of technological change upon organizations we
need to take into account the political, social and cultural pressures as well as the economic.

What would be the social consequences of using the
microprocessor for decentralization?   A new industrial
peasantry with stronger economic family units?   A new
version of the village school with the difference that
one teacher, instead of providing the knowledge for a
wide range of pupils, would monitor the programmes of
pupils each equipped with a computer?   Imagination
easily takes wing.   And many social scientists have a
romantic yearning for the small scale having experienced
only large scale organizations.   Much depends upon
whether social preferences move towards greater integration or greater separation of work from life.   The
former is made more possible by decentralization.   But
unless facilitated by government, large organizations
and unions, it will make only sporadic appearance.   And
at present the trend is probably towards even greater
separation of work from life as the prospect grows of

fewer hours spent at the workplace.   And much will
depend on the developments within organizations.   As
Karasek (1976) shows, greater autonomy and participation
at work lead to greater activity and participation outside work.   If organizations evolve in this direction,
we can expect more people with a taste for autonomy and
for participation in communal affairs to seize the opportunities for both.   If the microprocessor had been
available at the start of the industrial revolution we
should certainly have evolved a different industry, a
different civilization;   just as if the internal combustion engine had been available at the start of the
agrarian revolution we should never have had the towns
and cities we have.   The change that will be brought
about by the microprocessor is a function not of its
potential so much as of the accumulated weight of the
past.

New technological possibilities are sure to affect
profoundly the internal environment of the traditional
organization.   The capacity they offer for pre-program-
ming extensive areas of work, and for storing immense
libraries of repertoires will tend to shift the judgmental skills away from deciding how to act in this situation towards deciding what kind of situation this is.
As in modern medicine, treatment becomes routine, diagnosis becomes the key.   The thrust of technology will
move towards the facilitation of diagnosis.

Technological sophistication is likely to grow in
those sectors of organizations where technology is now
promitive - in personnel and industrial relations functions in particular.   This happens now;   mechanization
and computerization of banking and insurance and 'office-
of-the-future' scenarios bear witness.   They will also
affect organizations' relationships with one another.
If organization A's operations require computer compatible
inputs as outputs of organization B, A will have to persuade B to change, possibly offering B specialist advice.
The alternative to advice and assistance may be vertical
integration.   The choice will be influenced by political
pressures (fiscal, regulative or both) and also by an
assessment of the vulnerability of integrated as against
separate units to external forces including trade unions.
In the case of personnel and industrial relations operations, will firms offer advice and assistance to unions
to make their inputs and outputs technologically compatible?   And what would be the consequences?   Unions
whose own organizations are at present under-powered will
undergo very considerable change which will inevitably
affect their policy-making machinery and hence their
policies.

But what will be the internal effect on organizations

of advancing technology in its specialist and support
functions?   Technology offers a set of options including
both more and less bureaucracy.   Early applications of
computers to white collar work tended to centralize
control, bureaucratize management and de-skill operations.
Many managements learned from the uncovenanted consequences;   systems are now more often designed in co-operation with their operators.   Instead of using computer
systems for information-gathering and processing to centralize all decisions, we see exploitation of its possibilities for providing the essential information at
the lowest point in the organization at which decisions
can be taken.   Information can be used for control or
for autonomy;   the choice is political, not technological.
Those who have advanced work group autonomy as a means
of enhancing the quality of working life have urged the
devolutionary use of information systems (Cherns, 1976,
1977b).   We have encouraging case studies, embracing a
wide range of organizations and revealing increasingly
revolutionary organizational designs.

The economic environment increasingly channels
political and social pressure.   Organizations increasingly rely on governments' handling of the national
economy;   governments increasingly use organizations as
vehicles for their social as well as economic policies.
The more that the organization is seen by government and
by political pressure groups as the distributor of resources and status, the more the economic environment
will be the instrument of government policy.   In response, organizations can be expected to seek to influence
governments directly, to build countervailing strength
and to exert indirect influence through public opinion.
Large organizations employ political lobbyists and 'public affairs' consultants, form alliances with firms in
other jurisdictions and reinforce their 'public relations'.
These efforts may have diversionary effect and register
limited local success, but will not stem the tide.   The
battleground is the division between that area where
firms have economic autonomy and that where economic
decisions have to be shared with government.   Line
management will have to learn how to utilize political
information in their economic decisions, an agenda for
the business schools.   They cannot afford to leave politics to the specialists.

The social environment in Western Europe is of
growing dissensus or, perhaps, of lost consensus.   The
disappointment of hopes for an ever rising standard of
living and for an ever improving quality of life have put
increasing strain on the accommodation reached across the
lines of cleavage in society.   Rapid social change has
widened the cleavage between young and old, male and

female, new regions and old, centre and periphery, consumer and producer, indigene and immigrant.   In Britain,
it is claimed, class division has widened, though it is
not easy to distinguish between a widening of a gap and
its exposure due to increased strain upon it.   One
casualty is a shared sense of 'social' justice.   As
Goldthorpe (1978) has described it, the notion of 'generalized social worth' breaks down, the legitimacy of
status as justifying differential reward is lost and
'once the normative ordering of status is removed, there
is no obvious reason why the pay claims of different
groups of workers should not expand and lead to the pursuit of relativities that are highly intransitive;   nor,
moreover, why in pursuing their claims such groups should
not raise new challenges ... to the authority of employers
and managers ... or to the power which the latter have in
the past derived from the status order over and above
their authority as functionally and legally grounded'.

        Our own analysis pointed to the decline in genera-
lity of authority.   Authority is not so much rejected as
confined - restricted to what is required to get the work
done.   The corollary to this is that if I have the
necessary expertise or if the group of which I am a
member possesses it, we should be granted the resources
and necessary authority to get the work done.   Only in a
few new style organizations is this logic followed
through, but it appears to be the most constructive way
of accommodating, and indeed benefiting from, this social
trend.

        With the confinement of authority to what is func-
tionally necessary comes a denial of the organization's
right over non-work life and beyond what is expressly
within the work contract.   Since contracts of employment
are both new and imprecise there is abundant room for
disagreement.   Where contracts are between union and
management there is a residual area of what is left
unspecified, consisting mainly of 'management's right to
manage';   this 'right' is by no means secure.   Possession of the residual area can pass and with it the balance
of power.   Already much that was formerly taken for
granted by management has to be bargained for including
rights over the allocation and control of overtime working.

        But organizations still dispense the highly valued
commodity of work.   A job is still the passport to full
membership of society.   Will this continue?   And if it
does, will organizations retain control over its dispen-
sation?   Both are very real questions.   The organization's right to hire and fire is hedged continually
about;   in Britain, equal opportunities for women and

minorities are established by law - in the USA 'affirmative action' does not stop at equality of opportunity
- many forms of dismissal are 'unfair' in law, redundancy
is expensive and may be made prohibitively so by union
action.   And the appearance of claimants' unions marks
the assertion that full social rights should not depend
upon the accident of employment.   It is possible to
imagine some other means of distributing both financial
and status resources without the intermediacy of job.
That this is neither easy to achieve nor a necessary consequence of a non-capitalist system is apparent from the
fact that it is communist societies that place most
emphasis on the universal obligation to be employed.

The cultural environment has changed towards less
deference in relationships between subordinates and
superiors, less formality, less constraint.   And as
work is less physically arduous and as more women have
entered employment, so has work become less of a man's
world with its masculine values.   Enclaves remain: coal
face, steel works, combat units.   One characteristic of
masculine cultures is the harsh initiation, another is
the solidarity among initiates.   It is too soon to dis-
cern the effect of feminine infiltration, although women
are traditionally less ready than men to strike, and
industries which are male preserves have the reputation
of being more strike prone.   Solidarity is not only
demonstrated by striking;   it is manifested in the support given to a weaker or unfortunate or sick colleague.
Absence or lateness which increases the burdens of others
conflicts with solidarity.   Nor is solidarity to be
measured by union membership when that has become essentially instrumental.

Moralists have deplored a growing concern with
rights rather than duties.   The more that is enshrined
in legal obligation, the less becomes the moral obligation.   The calculative orientation to work appears
where moral involvement was the norm: hospitals, schools,
universities, police forces are new scenes for industrial
action.   As a legalistic spirit grows in the schools,
so will their pupils become accustomed to an instrumental
orientation to learning, identified as schoolwork, and to
employment.   How deeply the Quality of Working Life
approach can penetrate is an open question: it cannot
make great headway while confined to the world of employment.

Training

What are the consequences for training?   Recyclage,
continuing training are predicated on continuous, rapid
technological change.   The concept of career is being

revised.   But what concept of work are people to be
trained for or train themselves?   Even vocational
training is more than the acquisition of skills;   the
context in which they are to be used is implicit if not
explicit.   Is education and training explicit about the
nature of work, its role in society, the boundary between work and non-work?   Is management education explicit
about the boundaries between management and politics?
We have a long agenda.

REFERENCES

Cherns, A.B. (1976).   'The principles of sociotechnical
    design', Human Relations, 28, 8, 783-792.

Cherns, A.B. (1977a).   'Social change and social
    values', Journal of Social and Economic Studies,
    V, 1, 83-100.

Cherns, A.B. (1977b).   'Can behavioral science help
    design organizations?', Organizational Dynamics,
    Spring, 44-64.

Goldmann, Robert B (1975).   'Work values: six
    Americans in a Swedish plant', mimeo.

Goldthorpe, J.H. (1978).   The Political Economy of
    Inflation (Eds. F. Hirsch and J.H. Goldthorpe),
    pp. 199-201, Martin Robertson, Oxford.

Herbst, P.G. (1975).   'The product of work is people',
    in The Quality of Working Life (Eds. L.E. Davis and
    A.B. Cherns), vol. I, pp. 439-442, The Free Press,
    New York.

Karasek, R. (1976).   'The impact of the work environ-
    ment on life outside the job: a longitudinal study
    of the Swedish labour force 1968-74', Ph.D. thesis,
    MIT.

Marris, Robin (Ed.) (1974).   The Corporate Society,
    Macmillan, London and Basingstoke.

Netherlands Scientific Council for Government Policy
    (1977).   On Social Inequality: Report to the
    Council of Ministers.

Woodward, J. (1965).   Industrial Organization: Theory
    and Practice, Oxford University Press, London.

Changes in Working Life
Edited by K.D. Duncan, M.M. Gruneberg, and D. Wallis
© 1980 John Wiley & Sons Ltd

Chapter 16

Manager-Organization Linkages: The Impact of Changing Work Environments

L. .W. PORTER and H. L. ANGLE

Today, we live in an organizational society. Most of us, in industrialized nations, spend the bulk of our active lives in organizations. The individual entering a work organization soon establishes a quasi-stable relationship with the larger system, in which individual and organization agree, tacitly or explicitly, to exchange something of value with one another, as part and parcel of a continuing association. Each makes demands on the other and offers resources in response to the other's demands (Porter, Lawler and Hackman, 1975). The psychological contract (Levinson, Price, Munden, Mandl and Soley, 1962) 'drawn up' between the parties includes appropriate economic 'clauses' - as the ostensible basis for work-organization membership is economic - but (as the term implies) there are psychological aspects to the exchange, as well.

A central psychological issue in the 'contract' is that of member attachment to the organization. This bond has been studied under a number of frameworks such as loyalty, identification, ego-involvement, and organizational commitment. At this point, rather than splitting hairs over nuances of meaning, let us speak, more generically, about 'individual-organizational linkages'. (Later on, the focus will narrow to 'manager-organization linkages'.)

The bond between an employee and the work organization can be thought of as involving two broad categories, from the perspective of the individual: (1) joining and retaining membership in the organization; and (2) becoming psychologically attached to the organization (Porter and Dubin, 1975). The former aspect implies security for the individual and stability for the organization; the latter has perhaps more significant implications, both for the individual and for the organization.

Early socialization processes teach children group identifications that go beyond the immediate family (Katz and Kahn, 1978). Children are taught the social value of loyal participation in whatever social institutions and organizations are valued by parents and other socializing agencies. This early training '... furnishes some of the bedrock of later organizational identification ... The reference to the company as a family, for example, has become a management cliche' (Katz and Kahn, 1978, p. 377). The implications of the organization as a surrogate family are not trivial. One's membership in a work organization may provide the basis for the same sort of psychological need fulfilment provided by earlier membership in such primary social groups as the parental family - fulfilment of needs related to such basic aspects of psychological structure as the self-concept. A number of scholars (e.g. Levinson, 1965; Selznick, 1957) have portrayed organizations as becoming invested with this sort of psychological meaning for their members.

The concept of deep psychological self-investment on the part of members has equally important implications from the organization's perspective. While some personnel turnover is no doubt healthy for nearly any organization (i.e., turnover is a necessary component of renewal), the organization has to avoid unnecessary personnel turbulence. Members must, in general, be induced to join and remain.

Once in the organization, some motivational basis must exist for the performance of necessary behaviours. These include not only the behaviours that meet explicit role prescriptions, but also (at least for some organizational members) spontaneous and innovative behaviours that transcend role prescriptions (Katz, 1964). At least ideally, routine work behaviours are part and parcel of the economic exchange that takes place between organizations and their members. Spontaneity and innovation, however, may be another matter. While it is certainly possible to establish contingent reward systems that reinforce innovation, this presents even greater difficulties than does the contingent reinforcement of routine task performance. Some alternative motivational basis would be useful.   One such alternative might lie in the psychological attachment of the individual to the organization.

Whether this attachment is viewed in terms of organization commitment as defined by Porter and his colleagues (Porter, Steers, Mowday and Boulian, 1974) or Buchanan (1974), or in terms of identification as conceived by Hall and Schneider (1972), Ingham (1970) or Patchen (1970), at least one aspect of attachment seems to be an internalization of the organization's (perceived) goals.   Thus, the individual need not be goaded or cajoled to perform discretionary behaviours on behalf of the organization.   Such behaviours are, in a way, their own reward.   In acting in the organization's interests, the individual is automatically pursuing his/her self-interests, as well.   To the extent that one's linkage to the organization becomes an expression of the ego or its central values, organizational activity can become self-rewarding (Katz and Kahn, 1978).

The foregoing is not intended as a preamble to an assertion that high levels of attachment are necessary (or even desirable) for all organizational members.   On the contrary, organizations are, by their nature, systems of role differentiation.   In most utilitarian organizations (Etzioni, 1975), there are many roles for which adequate role behaviour need not involve deep self-investment.   Such roles are found, for the most part, however, at relatively low organizational levels.

It is in the managerial ranks that Katz's (1964) requirement for spontaneity and innovation can become critical for the organization.   Effective management (especially at the higher levels) is proactive - at least part of the manager's role involves the search for new problems and for opportunities to exploit (Thompson, 1962), as well as the performance of 'nonprogrammed' activities (March and Simon, 1958).   Hence, we propose that the issue of attachment to the organization is particularly salient at managerial levels.

Allowing, for the moment, the assertion that strong attachment to the organization is most necessary at the managerial level, it may also be the case that development of such linkages may also be more likely at managerial, rather than lower, levels.   Mayntz (1970) held that the vertical differentiation in organizations makes it '... rather difficult at least for lower participants to develop full identification on the basis of normative commitment to the organizational goal' (p. 374).   It is, by contrast the higher organization levels where 'inclusion' (i.e., movement toward the inner circle or core of the organization) (Schein, 1978) becomes more likely,

which provides at least a basis for the process of identification.   Buchanan (1974) found 'personal significance reinforcement' to be a key ingredient in the
organizational commitment of managers in both business
and government settings.   In effect, those who are 'in
the know', and in a position to influence organizational
outcomes by virtue of their position in the organization
(to wit: the managers), are the ones most likely to
become ego-involved in that organization.

Thus far, we have attempted to make a case for
organizational attachment as a sufficient condition for
motivating organizationally-beneficial discretionary
behaviours on the part of managers.   We are less sanguine
with respect to attachment as a necessary condition for
such motivation.   It is not difficult to name other
possible routes to high performance levels, including:
intrinsic motivation or job involvement;   personal normative beliefs akin to the Protestant work ethic;   internalization of the values of a craft or profession;   or
commitment to an occupation or career.   Some of these
alternatives will be considered further, later on.   For
the present, however, the discussion will focus on manager-organization linkages, per se, and the influence of
work environments (and changes in work environments) on
these linkages.   Our review of the literature dealing
with attachment, organizational commitment and similar
concepts, suggests the existence of three rather distinct
kinds of linkages:

Link 1:   Membership Continuance: the desire to retain
                                   organizational mem-
                                   bership

Link 2:   Ego-Identification: self-perception in
                                   terms of organiza-
                                   tional membership

Link 3:   Loyalty: Allegiance;   placing
                                   organization above
                                   all competing inter-
                                   ests (including self
                                   interests)

For the purposes of this paper, we will be considering
environmental impacts on those three manager-organization
links.   This discussion begins with an exposition of the
multiple environments inhabited by today's manager, and
an extrapolation of some current trends in order to project
how those environments might change over the next quarter-
century.

CHANGING WORK ENVIRONMENTS

Work environments are generally acknowledged to exert a powerful influence on the behaviour of organizational members - managers being no exception. The interactionist perspective in psychology gives the environment co-equal billing with the individual in the determination of behaviour (cf. Lewin, 1935). 'The' environment, however, would imply a gross oversimplification of reality. Work environments can be, and have been, conceptualized as consisting of any number of more-or-less independent dimensions, including the physical, structural, procedural, technological, interpersonal and task characteristics of the work situation. Elsewhere in this volume, Cherns characterizes the work environment as divisible into its physical, economic, political, social, and cultural aspects. In a very similar vein, Davis talks of the social, economic, technological, political and demographic environments of organizations.

Our discussion of work environments will take a similar tack, by differentiating 'the' work environment, rather arbitrarily, into three dimensions: the socio-normative, economic, and technological environments. While this three-way taxonomy may be at a somewhat higher level of abstraction than many of the more elaborated breakdowns, we believe that parsimony and space limitations dictate such an approach for our present purpose, which is not an analysis of work environments, per se, but an attempt to assess the impact of the environment on manager-organization linkages.

An attempt will be made, however, to subsume the important categories that might comprise a more differentiated listing under one or another of our three 'environments' (although it may soon become apparent that certain such categories may not fit neatly - or exclusively - into one of the three).

In the remainder of this section, several prevalent societal trends will be discussed under each of the three major headings (viz. socio-normative, economic, technological). The discussion will be focused specifically on those apparent trends which, we believe (at least in the United States) have the most relevance for the shape of organizational life in the immediate future, and hence for the nature of the linkages between managers and their organizations.

In so doing , however, we remain aware that 'futurism' is an inexact science, and that, as Davis has put it elsewhere in this volume, the lessons of the outgoing era may be less than helpful - even misleading - in attempting to cope with the future.   Therefore, we shall try to limit the discussion to a few of the ongoing changes in work environments that appear to be leading toward the most predictable trends in manager-organization relationships.

The Socio-Normative Environment

Perhaps the most influential facet of the work environment on managers' organizational attachment is that related to the social cues regarding which behaviours are 'correct'.   Organizational socialization is largely a process of peer influence (VanMaanen, 1975), and all members (managers included) undergo a developmental process, over the lifespan, in which early-acquired cultural and subcultural norms are fused with later experiences (in such settings as work organizations) to result in an organized system of normative beliefs.   Accordingly, societal norms will influence the manager in two ways: directly, in terms of the normative beliefs brought to the organization as a result of primary socialization; and indirectly, through exposure to the normative beliefs that others bring to the organization.   The latter is a particularly salient aspect of the manager's immediate work environment.   The ambiguities in organizational life quite frequently force the manager to depend on collective others, in order to answer 'ought to' questions (cf. Festinger, 1954).

Of all aspects of the socio-normative work environment, few have received more attention, of late, than what is commonly referred to as the 'changing work ethic'. While some would assert that the existence of such an ehtic has always been illusory, i.e., more a matter of 'received doctrine' (Barrett, 1972, p. 9) than one of evidence, few would dispute that the decade of the 1960s saw a strong movement away from whatever the 'base rate' Protestant Ethic might have been.   Wholesale rejection, on the part of youth, of their elders' assumed preoccupation with status, achievement, acquisition of material wealth and consumption, precipitated a revolutionary reversion toward pre-industrial lifestyles.   The theme 'tune in, turn on and drop out' characterized a vocal segment of the youth subculture, engaged in seeking noninvolvement with work as their parents and grandparents had known it.

Ironically, a case can be made that a prime antecedent of the 'flight from achievement' might have been the unprecedented level of affluence that had been the fruit of the labors of earlier generations.   Clark Kerr has alluded to a paradoxical chain of events whereby hard

work leads to affluence, but affluence, in turn, leads
to erosion of the work ethic.

Closely related to the unprecedented affluence
experienced during the past several years has been an
explosion in formal education (although some would hold
that quality has not always kept pace with quantity).
The implications for organizations are considerable.
In the mid-sixties Bennis (1966) prophesied that the gap
in formal education between the top and bottom echelons
in organizations would shrink.   This has been borne out,
at least in the United States, by data from the periodic
Quality of Employment Survey (Quinn and Staines, 1979),
which has shown a steady increase in worker education
levels during the period 1969 to 1977.

Increased education levels can be expected to
impact the managerial ranks, as well as the lower strata
of organizations.   While this might result in fledgling
managers' arrival at their first organization better
equipped technically to manage, as well as more firmly
grounded in world knowledge than were their predecessors
of a generation or so, these neophytes can also be expected to have higher levels of aspiration.   Education
brings with it, not only an elevated perspective on what's
acceptable in terms of one's inputs and outcomes (cf.
Adams, 1965) in the employment exchange, but a fuller
awareness of alternatives, as well - in effect, a raised
'comparison level for alternatives' (Thibaut and Kelley,
1959).

Also concomitant with generally rising education
levels appears to be increasing societal mistrust of
authority and of large authoritative institutions, such
as big business or big government.   Large corporations,
in turn, have responded to the public mood by expanding
the organizational goal structure to include a new major
category: 'corporate social responsibility' (Walters,
1977).   Abstract notions of duty to society are, in
turn, more difficult to operationalize than some of the
more concrete indicators of organizational performance
such as market share, or return on investment.   Hence,
inclusion of social-responsibility objectives in corporate goal structures might have the unintended consequence
of increasing goal ambiguity for organizations.   This,
in turn, would make it more difficult for the individual
manager to identify his/her personal contribution toward
accomplishment of significant (and specific) organizational outcomes.

Some corporate actions aimed at fulfilling societal
duties may be as much the result of legal constraints as
they are a voluntary response to the public mood.   At
least in the United States, organizations of all types are

coming under increasing pressure to redress past inequities in which certain racial or ethnic groups (and women) ostensibly had been denied equal employment opportunity. Under the rubric of 'affirmative action', organizations have seen an infusion of these formerly disadvantaged groups - and, since the largest imbalances originally existed at the managerial level, it can be expected that the greatest affirmative action impact will eventually be in the management ranks.

While the underlying social motives behind the affirmative action movement seem unimpeachable, here too may lie a serious unanticipated consequence. Buchanan (1974) contrasted business and government organizations, by citing the ethnocentric nature of the former in contrast to the more pluralist governmental organization. Buchanan alleged that 'In industry, discrimination and favoritism are employed as team-building devices. Management groups as a result have similar characteristics, which fosters unanimity on policy and general harmony in organizational operations' (p. 345). This aspect of government-business contrast that Buchanan saw in 1974 may be a vanishing phenomenon.

One major feature of the 'new corporate pluralism' (at least, in the United States) has been a dramatic rise in the number of women in the workforce - and again this trend has been particularly strong at the managerial level. If not a contributing factor, this has been at least consistent with a larger societal trend away from sex-role differentiation. Thus, traditional norms whereby males' locus of identification was related to occupation while females' primary status anchor was the home, may increasingly be subject to question.

Another outcome of the infusion of women into management seems, inevitably, to be an increase in the number of dual-career families (Hall and Hall, 1978; Schein, 1978). This, in turn, has economic ramifications. Discussion of these implications, however, will be held in abeyance until the ensuing section on the economic environment.

As a final point, an apparent societal trend, which seems to have several potential impacts on the nature of managers' linkages to their organizations, revolves around attitudes towards permanency and change, per se. We live in what has been termed a 'temporary society' (Bennis and Slater, 1968). In some quarters, change itself appears to have positive value. Social contracts (from marriage to employment), that might once have been imbued with a sense of permanency, seem increasingly to be subject to continual re-evaluation.

In some industries, executive 'headhunters' recurringly approach organizational managers, making salient the idea that one's skills may be both transferable and highly marketable.   At least one popular guide to management careers advises that the sensible manager should always be planning for the next job change (Bolles, 1972).

In some occupations there has been an expansion, into the managerial ranks, of temporary-hire or 'contracted' employment.   This mode of employment appears to range from the provision of ad hoc accounting teams to the temporary assignment of top management, per se. The latter phenomenon was encountered recently, in a study of mass transit organizations in the Western United States (Perry, Angle and Pittel, 1979).   Thus, some managers never 'join' the organization in the traditional sense.

Another aspect of temporariness seems to reside in the currently popular notion of the 'midcareer crisis' (Schein, 1978).   Executives appear, in increasing numbers, to be facing existential dilemmas once thought to be the exclusive property of youth.   It has even been suggested that mid-career sabbaticals might be offered, in which the employing organization may subsidize some type of formal education (Beckhard, 1977).

Other trends appear to militate towards partial- rather than full-inclusion (Allport, 1933) in the work-role.   One such trend is that toward more part-time employment.   A more radical evolution is the concept of job sharing.   At least one employer, the State of California, had adopted a hiring plan whereby pairs of employees are hired for a single job.   For each prescribed work period, one of the two job incumbents is to report for work.   This system is reputed to be finding wide appeal among married couples who share child-rearing duties - further indication of a changing socio-normative environment.

The Economic Environment

The preceding section noted a trend toward dual careers, i.e. husband and wife both immersed in full-time employment.   The economic impact of this trend may be considerable.   In the first place, the diffusion of breadwinner responsibility between the two marital partners reduces economic dependence, in the sense that neither job is as essential to economic security as it would be if it were the only job.   With neither partner totally dependent on his or her employing organization, the economic linkages of both to their respective organizations might be weakened considerably.

On the other hand, once the family has accommo-
dated to a double income, there may be some reluctance
to give up either source of earnings.   Hence, the 'zone
of indifference' (Barnard, 1938) may be narrowed with
respect to which orders of the organization will be
obeyed.   If, for instance, the organization wants one
marital partner to re-locate to another city, the move
might be resisted or refused, on the basis that the
other partner's job would have to be forfeited.

Increasing levels of affluence are only partly, of
course, the result of multiple sources of income within
families.   Personal income is higher currently than ever
before in history for sole breadwinners as well as for
dual-income family units.   In combination with the
graduated income tax, which seems to be a fact of life in
most if not all Western nations, the marginal utility of
money may be severely diminished.   Accordingly, the
organization may find the use of economic inducements to
be less and less effective.

At the same time that economic growth has had the
paradoxical effect of loosening the economic ties of
manager-to-organization, increases in discretionary
income have enabled managers to become more involved than
ever before in leisure activity.   Additionally, projected innovations in time scheduling of work such as flexi-
time, the 4-day, 40-hour workweek, and even the 25-to-32-
hour workweek advocated by some labor interests, could
eventually spill over into management work schedules, as
well.   With the workrole occupying a decreasing proportion of the manager's life space, there could be some
decrement in the extent to which his/her relationship to
work organization assumes personal importance.

The Technological Environment

The most salient feature of the technological work
environment is rapid change.   The evolution of some
technological systems, such as computers, has been
occurring at a near-exponential rate.   This fantastic
rate of advance renders all but the most circumspect
prediction a very hazardous undertaking.   (The field is
littered with the remains of bold forecasts of twenty
years ago, or so, regarding the nature of management in
the 1980s time frame.)   Nonetheless, there are a few
recent trends, for which there is no apparent reason to
foresee a reversal, and which appear to have strong
implications for manager-organization linkages.

One rather obvious aspect is the rapidity, _per se_,

of technological change.   The furious pace of innovation presages an ever shortening cycle of knowledge
obsolescence (Hall, 1976).   In contrast to an earlier
age, in which a trade or craft could be handed down for
generations, it is not inconceivable that occupations can
now come into existence, flourish and become obsolete,
all within the career span of a single person.   Thus,
an individual's usefulness to a particular organization
might be transitory, unless the organization were to
develop an affirmative policy of re-cycling members by
retraining.

     Aggravating the problem of technological obsoles-
cence has been an information explosion.   A comparison
of the number of published pages in one's own area of
expertise during the past year, with a like publication
period say twenty years ago, is an eye-opening experience.
Our ability to transmit, process, print and store information is rapidly outstripping the capabilities of the
human information processor.   In organizations, the outcome of all this is a powerful force toward increasing
differentiation.   The general-purpose manager may be a
dying breed, because no single person can assimilate
enough knowledg to 'do it all' (Schein, 1978).

     The decline of the generalist, and the attendant
rise of the specialist, should exert a considerable force
toward professionalization.   A segmentation of management
knowledge, necessitated by human limitations, might be
the critical antecedent to creation of the rest of the
occupational characteristics that have come to be associated with the professions (cf. Ritzer, 1977).   One of
the more agreed-upon attributes of the professions, of
course, is a 'cosmopolitan' rather than a 'local' orientation (Gouldner, 1957).

     While cosmopolitanism is fostered by a profes-
sional work orientation, it is also facilitated by technical systems that permit easy exchange of information
with distant peers.   Attendance at a conference in
Europe would have been a major undertaking in an earlier
age, for a participant from the United States (or
Australia).   The relative ease of air travel, along with
the near-instantaneous electronic communication that is at
least technically possible between almost any two persons
on Earth, facilitates peer interaction with persons far
removed from one's own organization.   In combination
with current media programming, such electronic aids provide today's manager with an unprecedented array of information on alternatives - both with respect to viewpoints
on issues and with respect to his/her occupational options.

     These considerations, in the aggregate, carry

implications both for the likelihood that managers will
develop strong attachments to their organizations, and
for the consequences - for managers, organizations, and
society at large - should such attachments fail to occur.
These will now be discussed.

IMPACT OF CHANGING WORK ENVIRONMENTS ON MANAGER-ORGANIZATION LINKAGES

Combined Impact: Weakened Linkages

As strongly implied in our discussion of environmental trends, there seems to be one clear conclusion
regarding the collective effect of those trends on the
linkages of managers to their respective organizations:
the linkages will be significantly weakened or reduced.
This is not to say that each environmental trend will
have an equivalent impact, or that any given trend will
affect all types of linkages. Rather, our fundamental
thesis is simply that there is an unmistakable and probably irreversible effect: weakened linkages.

We see membership continuance being affected by
trends in each of the three environmental areas (socio-
normative, economic, and technological). To the extent
that: (1) individuals are less convinced than before
that work is 'good' in its own right; (2) societal norms
look more positively on temporary or transient relationships; and (3) increasing educational levels predispose
managers to re-evaluate their career lives, then it would
seem to follow that the strength of their desire to
remain with a particular organization will be weakened.
Likewise, increasing economic affluence makes it more
possible for the manager to consider leaving an organization without suffering undue financial disadvantage.
And, if managers are more prone to consider the possibility
of leaving their present organization because of some of
the reasons listed above, then technological advances in
communication and transportation tremendously facilitate
the ability to learn more about other organizational
alternatives, which in turn makes it easier to think about
leaving (following through on 'the other organization's
grass is greener' syndrome).

Ego-identification, in which the manager tends to
see the expression of his/her talents and capabilities in
terms of his/her organizational membership, will likely
be weakened by such trends as: the tendency of more
people in society to re-evaluate their careers; the tendency toward a more relaxed view of temporary relationships; and the more pluralistic nature of the managerial
workforce ('there are not a lot of people here I closely
identify with'). In the economic sphere, the increased

emphasis on leisure provides other, often very appealing, areas of life with which the manager can identify. In contrast with the past, there are many more non-work opportunities for the person to say 'that role is also me'. Technological trends, especially the possibility of early obsolescence of whatever skills or knowledge the manager had at the time he/she started with the organization and the necessity to become increasingly specialized because of the knowledge explosion, also make it harder and harder for the manager to maintain an ego-identification with any given organization.

Multiple trends also serve to reduce the tendency toward loyalty and placing the value of serving the organization above all else. The manager will be less likely to feel that 'my organization is the best of all possible organizations' or that 'I owe my organization (as opposed to family, profession and the like) a special obligation', to the extent that: (1) ready opportunities exist for the manager to serve in other organizations; (2) economic factors such as general affluence allow the luxury of considering other employment options; (3) the existence of dual-career families permit (or encourage) a focus on more than one organization; and (4) technological advances confront the manager with considerable information about other organizations, or facilitate contact with professional peers from other organizations.

To reiterate: Each of the three major types of linkages - membership, ego-identification, and loyalty - are and will continue to be affected by a number of the trends we have been discussing. We have highlighted what we think are some of the particular areas where the impacts will be strongest in the direction of weakening the links. We have not pointed to any areas where the environmental trends will be likely to strengthen links because we view the trends as having an almost totally one-way effect. If this analysis is correct, then there will be a number of implications for managers, organizations, and society.

Implications for Managers

At first glance, it might appear that reduced linkages would only help managers and harm organizations. That is not necessarily the case, for either managers or organizations. With respect to managers as employees of organizations, reduced linkages will provide a kind of 'freedom' that will make it easier both physically and psychologically to 'leave' organizations. As the preceding discussion indicated, a number of trends combine to increase the ease with which a person can change actual membership in organizations, and also ease any feelings of 'guilt' about transferring loyalties from one organization to another.   After all, if one considers oneself as a true 'professional', then the work is valuable regardless of location.   The environmental trends, then, would seem broadly to favor the manager at the expense of a particular organization.

However, there is another side to the manager's coin that ought not to be overlooked.   First, it is not obviously clear that high performance capabilities can be transferred easily from one organization to another. Just because an individual was highly successful in a particular organizational setting - thereby being sought after by other organizations - does not guarantee similar success in the next organization.   (See the example of American professional baseball or football players.) Even if the manager acts and thinks like a professional and thus is more bound to a specialized area of competence than to an employing organization, it is likely that particular organizational environments may have considerable effects on the tangible enactment of the professional performance.   Therefore, while the transfer possibilities are greatly aided and abetted by environmental trends, the transplant may not take hold in the new surroundings.   Second, quite aside from how successfully managers can move their performances from one organization to another or reduce their investment in an organization even without moving to a new one, there is the question of how easy it will be to cope with the potentially reduced sense of identification with an organization and a concomitantly reduced sense of continuity and stability.   For those who transfer their specialized skills to another organization, this potential problem may not be too great if they are able to retain a focus on the professional skill rather than on their organizational 'homes'.   For those who stay with a given organization but decide to invest less of themselves in it, the problems may be greater.   As Levinson (1965) has stressed, individuals have a need to have an attachment to something.   It may not always be easy for some managers to substitute other 'somethings' for the work organization, and thus reduced organizational linkages could have some degree of adverse impact on their psychological well being.   (We would expect, of course, considerable individual differences in this regard.)

Implications for Organizations

Reduced manager linkages to organizations would seem to have especially critical implications for organizations.   To examine briefly some of the more important ones, we might ask a series of questions:

(1)   Is it necessary for a minimum number of key managers to be strongly linked to the organization? Earlier we stated the assumption that from the organization's perspective it is not necessary that all or even most employees be strongly linked to the organization.   Regardless, a crucial issue is whether some sort of 'critical mass' of strongly linked managers must exist in any organization.   If the trends are in the direction of reducing linkages, and if it is necessary for some minimum percentage of managers in any organization to be linked with strong bonds, then what steps does the organization take to insure that enough managers will be so linked?

(2)   Where are the strongest managerial linkages needed in the organization?   Following on the previous question, if it is assumed that it is necessary that at least some portion of the managerial workforce be strongly linked to the particular organization, then the organization will need to determine where these locations are that require this kind of organizational involvement of specific managers.   This, in effect, raises the notion of the differentiated organization: strong linkages are not needed throughout, but they are needed at certain places.   An obvious answer to the question of 'where?', is to say 'at the top', since it is here that key policy decisions that have the broadest impact are made.   If it is agreed that 'the top' is one place, are there any other places that require strong linkages, or is it enough that only those at the very highest levels are, and feel themselves to be, firmly attached?   We would suggest that for many organizations the top level is probably not the only location where strong linkages are needed, and that therefore if an organization lets all other linkages decrease or attenuate, serious repercussions may result for organizational effectiveness and survival.   This leads to the next basic question:

(3)   Is it possible to have a highly productive organization with only a moderate to low average level of managerial linkages?   One answer may be that technology can largely substitute for high levels of organizational commitment or loyalty.   While this seems clearly to be the case in many 'shop floor' production situations, it may not be so clear that technology is an equivalent substitute for such commitment at managerial levels. Another type of answer could evolve around the extensive and effective use of extrinsic incentives (combined with the manager's intrinsic motivation in the work itself and a commitment to professional standards).   Application of extrinsic incentives in such a way as to substitute for the type of performance and continuance behaviour that is generated by strong linkages is certainly possible in

theory (and being demonstrated in many specific organizational circumstances today), but is not always easy in
practice. It requires constant attention to the type,
amount, and scheduling of such incentives and is prone to
severe miscalculations on the part of those who devise
and administer extrinsic incentive programs. How usefully extrinsic incentives can replace strong organizational linkages raises a related issue:

(4) Where will extra-role behaviour (e.g., innovations that help the organization; proactive behaviour
that protects or advances the organization) come from, if
linkages are weak? The trend for managers to be more
'professional' may be part of the answer, as a devotion
to professional standards may bring about certain types of
behaviour that serve the organization as well as the
profession. However, such cosmopolitanism by its very
nature does not guarantee extra-role behaviours on behalf
of the specific organization. Indeed, attention is
often diverted to the needs of satisfying the profession,
and especially one's peers in the profession, rather than
the needs of the organization (which, while not necessarily opposed to those of the profession, may often be
quite independent of it). In any event, while it seems
likely that reduced linkages would not greatly affect the
bulk of routine managerial work, those acts and behaviours
that involve unique service to the organization may well
become a casualty unless other measures can be substituted.
It would appear that such substitution is not an easy task
for the organization.

(5) What is the impact on non-management employees
if managers do not appear to be strongly linked to the
organization? Since behaviour by example appears to
have such pronounced impacts on the behaviour of individuals generally, and especially on lower-level employees
in organizations, any tendency for the linkages of higher-
level managers to appear weak could negatively affect
those working at the operative levels. This would be
the 'If the boss doesn't care about the organization, why
should I care?' type of phenomenon. The issue, then, is
that reduced managerial linkages may have direct effects
on the performance of managers and also wider indirect,
but important, contagion effects on other employees.

The above issues do not constitute an exhaustive
list, but they suggest some of the kinds of implications
that reduced managerial linkages may have for the organization. In toto, the implications would appear to be
a matter of concern if looked at strictly from the organization's vantage point.

Implications for Society

If managers in the future tend to become less
strongly linked to whatever organizations they happen to
be working for at a particular time, the most important
implication for society will arise if the basic fabric
of society is changed in any non-trivial way.   Does
society need or require a certain level of commitment to
work organizations on the part of those who lead and
manage them?   Or, is society better served by having
its members enjoy multiple commitments to a wide variety
of institutions?   On the one hand, society may well gain
by a reduction in the amount of over-zealous behaviour (a
decline in 'true believers') on the part of those who
lead any type of organization, whether a work organization, a religious organization, or a political party.
On the other hand, multiple, diverse, but shallow, linkages to organizations may present some collective problems.   Since one major area of society is composed of
work organizations, the probable impact for society of
reduced managerial linkages to those organizations would
depend on whether such reductions affect, or do not
affect, organizational productivity.   If the answer is
negative - that there is little or no effect on the productivity of work organizations - then society can
largely ignore the issue.   If the answer is affirmative,
then there may be some cause for concern.

REDUCED MANAGER-ORGANIZATIONAL LINKAGES: SOME BEHAVIORAL CONSEQUENCES

Thus far, it has been argued that the prevalent
trends in managers' work environments will have the net
effect of reducing the strength of manager-organization
linkages, and that this will, in turn, have impacts on
the managers themselves, on their organizations, and on
society as a whole.   In the present section, the discussion will narrow somewhat, to consider in detail the
ultimate effects on organizations of this generalized
weakening of manager-organization bonds.   Figure 1 presents a simple model which depicts trends in work environments (i.e., a combination of socio-normative, economic,
and technological aspects) as an exogenous influence,
attenuating manager-organization linkages.

Proposition 1:

In the last quarter of the twentieth century,
trends in work environments will reduce the strength of
manager-organizational linkages.

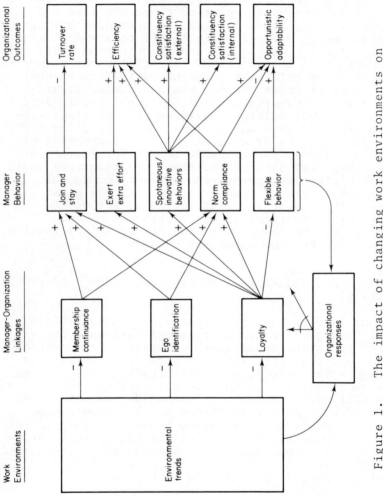

Figure 1.   The impact of changing work environments on
             manager behaviour and organizational outcomes
             through attentuation of manager-organization
             links.

Proposition 1.1:

Managers' membership continuance linkage to their organizations will be reduced. This will result in search behaviour to locate alternatives to their organizational membership, and an increased amount of time devoted to comparison of alternatives.

Proposition 1.2:

Managers' ego-identification in work-related matters (including the organization) will decrease, relative to increased identification with non-work entities (leisure time roles, etc.).

Proposition 1.3:

Managers will begin, increasingly, to specialize. This will result in professionalization of management, along with a concomitant cosmopolitan orientation, which will serve to attenuate loyalty to a given organization, per se.

The weakening of manager-organizational linkages will have impacts, in turn, on certain manager behaviours. The polarized arrows in Figure 1 show only the most significant expected impacts. These generalizations are not offered, of course, as universal hypotheses, of the type 'if A then B'. Rather, they are presumed to be statistical relationships ('the more A, the more probable B') (cf. Blau, 1970). In addition, the predictions are all formulated on a ceteris paribus basis.

Proposition 2:

Attenuation of manager-organization linkages will have consequences for managers' behavioural propensities.

Proposition 2.1:

Managers will change organizations relatively more frequently than they have, historically.

Proposition 2.2:

Managers will tend to exert less effort toward accomplishment of their work role prescriptions, and will engage in fewer innovative and spontaneous behaviours on behalf of a particular organization.

Proposition 2.3:

    Managers will tend to comply less fully with the norms of the organization. Organizational norms will have force primarily to the extent that they correspond to internalized societal/professional norms.

Proposition 2.4:

    Fewer cases of extreme (i.e., dysfunctional) loyalty to organizations will exist. This will facilitate divergent thinking and enhance managerial flexibility (except to the extent that substitute loci of loyalty, such as the profession, encourages 'one best way' thinking).

    In addition to responding to direct environmental pressures, organizations can be expected to react to the indirect effects of work environment changes that are manifest through managers' behaviours. Organizational efforts toward adaptation to the consequences of reduced manager-organization linkages might take two general forms: (1) attempts to shore up the linkages themselves; and/or (2) attempts to minimize the organizational impacts of linkage attenuation.

Proposition 3:

    Trends in work environments will have a dual impact on organizations: (1) via their impacts on relevant manager behaviours; and (2) directly. These impacts will engender organizational attempts to adapt.

    One possible mode of adaptation would be to try to provide a broader spectrum of professional opportunities for the manager, within the organizational framework. Recent growth trends and the prevalence of diversification and organizational mergers, may have increased this tactic's feasibility for many organizations.

Proposition 3.1:

    The more that organizations provide in-house opportunity for variety in experiences, career progression, and professional growth for managers, the less managers will search for alternatives to organizational membership. Consequently, manager turnover will be reduced.

    Organizations might attempt to take into account the rising education level and concomitant level of aspiration of the new generation of managers.   Accordingly, they may be able to provide a more realistic match between manager and job, by means including, but not limited to, realistic recruiting and placement.

Proposition 3.2:

The more that organizations match managers' jobs to their aspirations and expectations, the stronger the manager's membership continuance link to the organization.

Another way the organization might attempt to bolster manager-organization linkages could be to increase the amount of the manager's life space occupied by the organization, thus crowding out competing loci of attachment.   This is typical, for instance, of Japanese industry, which tends to become involved in all aspects of employees' lives.   Recent efforts to export Japanese neo-paternalism to the United States have appeared relatively successful (Johnson and Ouchi, 1974).

Proposition 3.3:

The more that organizations occupy non-work aspects of managers' life space, the less the opportunity for the managers to become ego-involved with, or develop loyalties to, competing institutions;   hence, the stronger the manager-organization linkages.

The dual-loyalty literature is relatively consistent in the view that loyalty to both profession and organization is facilitated when the organization avoids placing the member in a role-conflict situation (i.e. between organizational and professional roles) (e.g., Thornton, 1970).

Proposition 3.4:

The more that organizations align their norms and expectations regarding managerial behaviour with professional norms, the less will be the role conflict. Assuming that such professional norms encourage high levels of performance, managers will tend to exert high levels of effort and to emit extra-role behaviours toward organizational purposes.

Finally, it may be possible for organizations to lessen the impact of higher manager-turnover rates by planning and organizing for relatively limited-term managerial tenure.

Proposition 3.5:

The more that organizations adapt to high manager turnover by such means as explicit, limited-term contract arrangements with managers, the lower the negative organizational impact of manager turnover.

The final proposition is the only one not formulated at a micro level. However, there are a number of other macro or organizational ramifications of the micro-behavioural outcomes in Figure 1. Rather than listing another set of propositions, we simply provide a set of polarized arrows that indicate where the most pronounced organizational effects should occur.

CONCLUDING OBSERVATIONS

Throughout this paper we have emphasized one basic point. A combination of trends occurring in most of industrialized society is resulting in a reduced bond or linkage between managers and their work organizations. We have further stated that, if our basic premise is true, then there is likely to be a set of important repercussions for organizations, for managers, and for society at large. While we have attempted to spell out what some of these impacts might be, we want to make it clear that we have not passed judgment on whether the consequences for these three societal elements are 'good' or 'bad'. That is the kind of normative assessment best left to each organization, each manager, and to society's institutions.

Regardless of how positively or negatively any particular group or individual views the likelihood of weakening linkages between managers and their organizations, there are probably responses available to organizations that would be likely to lessen the decline. Furthermore, there may be other responses that would assist the organization in adapting to declining linkages. In the preceding section, we noted what some of these organizational responses might be, and what effects these might have. What we did not do is recommend whether organizations should make any of these responses. That depends on the extent to which organizations see a decline in manager-orientation linkages as a problem and, of course, where such 'problems' fit into organizational priorities, as the year 2000 approaches.

REFERENCES

Adams, J.S. (1965). 'Inequity in social exchange', in Advances in Experimental Social Psychology, Volume 2

(E.L. Berkowitz), pp. 267-299, Academic Press, New York.

Allport, F.H. (1933).   Theories of Perception and the Concept of Structure, Wiley, New York.

Barnard, C.I. (1938).   The Functions of the Executive, Harvard University Press, Cambridge, MA.

Barrett, G.V. (1972).   'Symposium. Research models of the future for industrial and organizational psychology. 1. Introduction', Personnel Psychology, 25, 1-17.

Beckhard, R. (1977).   'Managerial careers in transition: Dilemmas and directions', in Organizational Careers: Some New Perspectives (Ed. J. VanMaanen), pp. 149-160, Wiley, New York.

Bennis, W.G. (1966).   Changing Organizations, McGraw-Hill, New York.

Bennis, W.G. and Slater, P.E. (1968).   The Temporary Society, Harper and Row, New York.

Blau, P.M. (1970).   'A formal theory of differentiation in organizations', American Sociological Review, 35, 201-218.

Bolles, R.N. (1972).   What Color is Your Parachute?, Revised, Ten Speed Press, Berkeley, CA.

Buchanan, B., II (1974).   'Government managers, business executives and organizational commitment', Public Administration Review, July-August, 339-347.

Etzioni, A. (1975).   A Comparative Analysis of Complex Organizations (Revised), Free Press, New York.

Festinger, L. (1954).   'A theory of social comparison processes', Human Relations, 7, 117-140.

Gouldner, A.W. (1957).   'Cosmopolitans and locals: Toward an analysis of latent social roles - I', Administrative Science Quarterly, 2, 281-306.

Hall, D.T. (1976).   Careers in Organizations, Goodyear, Santa Monica, CA.

Hall, F.S. and Hall, D.T. (1978).   'Dual careers - How do couples and companies cope with the problems?', Organizational Dynamics, Spring, 57-77.

Hall, D.T. and Schneider, B. (1972).   'Correlates of
    organizational identification as a function of
    career and organizational type', Administrative
    Science Quarterly, 17, 340-350.

Ingham, G.K. (1970).   Size of Industrial Organization
    and Worker Behaviour, Cambridge University Press,
    London.

Johnson, R.T. and Ouchi, W.G. (1974).   'Made in
    America (under Japanese management)', Harvard
    Business Review, September-October, 61-69.

Katz, D. (1964).   'The motivational basis of organi-
    zational behavior', Behavioral Science, 9, 131-146.

Katz, D. and Kahn, R.L. (1978).   The Social Psychology
    of Organizations, Second Edition, Wiley, New York.

Levinson, H. (1965).   'Reciprocation: The relationship
    between man and organization', Administrative
    Science Quarterly, 9, 370-390.

Levinson, H., Price, C.R., Munden, K.J., Mandl, H.J. and
    Solley, C.M. (1962).   Men, Management, and Mental
    Health, Harvard University Press, Cambridge, MA.

Lewin, K. (1935).   'Environmental forces in child
    behavior and development', in K. Lewin, A Dynamic
    Theory of Personality: Selected Papers (Translated
    by D.K. Adams and E.K. Zener) McGraw-Hill, New York.

March, J.G. and Simon, H.A. (1958).   Organizations,
    Wiley, New York.

Mayntz, R. (1970).   'Role distance, role identification,
    and amoral behavior', Archives Europeenes de
    Sociologie, 11, 368-378.

Patchen, M. (1970).   Participation, Achievement and
    Involvement on the Job, Prentice-Hall, Englewood
    Cliffs, N.J.

Perry, J.L., Angle, H.L. and Pittel, M.E. (1979).   The
    Impact of Labor-Management Relations on Productivity
    and Efficiency in Urban Mass Transit, Final Report,
    US Department of Transportation, Research and
    Special Programs Administration, Washington, D.C.

Porter, L.W. and Dubin, R. (1975).   The Organization and
    the Person, Final Project Report, (NR 151-315), US
    Office of Naval Research, Arlington, VA.

Porter, L.W., Lawler, E.E., III and Hackman, J.R. (1975).
    Behavior in Organizations, McGraw-Hill, New York.

Porter, L.W., Steers, R.M., Mowday, R.T. and Boulian, P.V.
    (1974).   'Organizational commitment, job satis-
    faction, and turnover among psychiatric technicians',
    Journal of Applied Psychology, 59, 603-609.

Quinn, R.P. and Staines, G.L. (1979).   The 1977 Quality
    of Employment Survey, Institute for Social Research,
    Ann Arbor, MI.

Ritzer, G. (1977).   Working: Conflict and Change, Second
    Edition, Prentice-Hall, Englewood Cliffs, NJ.

Schein, E.H. (1978).   Career Dynamics: Matching Indivi-
    dual and Organizational Needs, Addison-Wesley,
    Reading, MA.

Selznick, P. (1957).   Leadership in Administration, Row,
    Peterson, New York.

Thibaut, J.W. and Kelley, H.H. (1959).   The Social
    Psychology of Groups, Wiley, New York.

Thompson, J.D. (1962).   'Common and uncommon elements
    in administration', Social Welfare Forum, pp. 181-
    201.

Thornton, R. (1970).   'Organizational involvement and
    commitment to organization and profession',
    Administrative Science Quarterly, 15, 417-426.

VanMaanen, J. (1975).   'Police socialization: A longi-
    tudinal examination of job attitudes in an urban
    police department', Administrative Science Quar-
    terly, 20, 207-228.

Walters, K.D. (1977).   'Corporate social responsibility
    and political ideology', California Management
    Review, 19 (Spring), 40-51.

Changes in Working Life
Edited by K.D. Duncan, M.M. Gruneberg, and D. Wallis
© 1980 John Wiley & Sons Ltd

Chapter 17

Organizational Climate: Can it be Controlled?— An Exploration of Possibilites for Improving the Quality of Working Life

R. MANSFIELD

The quality of working life experienced by an individual depends in part upon the nature of the particular job he is doing and partly on the environment in which this job is carried out. This environment is made up of many components, such as the physical environment, relationships with other employees, relationships with supervisors and the general psychological environment in the employing organization. The concept of organizational climate has been widely used to characterise this latter component of the individual's overall environment. There is clear evidence that some aspects of climate are closely related to individual feelings of job satisfaction (e.g. Friedlander and Margulies, 1969; Pritchard and Karasick, 1973) to demonstrate its importance as a factor influencing the quality of working life.

Considerable attention has been paid to this concept of organizational climate by researchers in recent years. In addition to its importance in attempts to examine and improve the psychological experience of work for the individual, it has also been considered an important variable in the search for a theoretical understanding of organizational behaviour. Payne and Pheysey (1971) have described climate as 'a molar concept reflecting the content and strength of the prevalent values, norms, attitudes, behaviour and feelings of the members of a social system'. As such Payne and Mansfield (1973) suggest that 'the concept of organizational climate would

appear to be a possible conceptual linkage between analysis at the organizational level and analysis at the
individual level'.   Despite the apparent reasonableness
of this approach and a considerable amount of empirical
research relating dimensions of climate to both organizational and individual variables, our understanding of
the linkages between system parameters and individual
behaviour and experience is still very limited.   In
particular little is known of the underlying processes
which create the relationships discovered in empirical
research.   [In the present context one cannot claim to
understand the dynamics by which organizational climates
are created and maintained or modified.   This being the
case it is difficult to say to what extent aspects of
climate and hence the quality of working life for
employees can be controlled.]   Even in a situation where
management and other employees wished to cooperate in an
effort to change the organizational climate there is
little clear evidence to guide their actions.

However, the above should not be construed to
suggest that there has been no progress.   At the purely
empirical level there has been a considerable increase
in our knowledge of the relationships which are likely to
be observed between aspects of climate and a range of
other variables.   Relationships between different aspects
of the organizational environment and internal climate
were demonstrated by Dieterly and Schneider (1974).
Payne and Mansfield (1973) showed relationships between
organizational size, technology employed, and a number of
aspects of organizational structure and different dimensions of climate.   However, the influence of structure
has been shown to vary somewhat, as comparison of their
results with those of Payne and Pheysey (1971) and George
and Bishop (1971) reveals.   Climate has also been shown
to be influenced by leadership style (Litwin and Stringer,
1968) and by human relations training (Hand et al., 1973).

[In examining the implications of this research it
is necessary to distinguish between those correlates of
climate which are largely or entirely beyond management's
direct power to control and those correlates of climate
which are to a considerable extent manipulable by
management, at least with the cooperation of other
employees.]   [If an attempt is to be made to change the
quality of working life then the former set of variables
must be largely considered as constraints, whilst the
latter variables may be levers by which change can be
accomplished.]

Of the variables shown to relate to climate mentioned above the one which has most clearly been used as
a lever is human relations training.   This has been used

both to ameliorate the situation of employees and to improve organizational performance.   In the case of many of the other variables shown to relate to climate it is less clear to what extent management can exercise control, at least in the short term.   For example, organizational structures are usually to some extent under management's control but they are also likely to be heavily constrained by other factors.   However, if elements of structure can be changed and these do modify the organization's climate then it would seem likely that this would be of a more permanent nature than changes brought about by training programmes, particularly where these are of very short duration.   With this in mind the remainder of this paper considers evidence from two studies of relatively small companies, one examining relationships between parameters of company payment systems and climate, and the other examining relationships between decentralization of decision-making and climate. In addition the influence of a number of constraining variables upon climate is examined in each study.   The parameters of payment systems and the extent of decentralization were chosen for examination, as they are likely to be manipulable by management with the consent of the workforce and they are both widely believed to affect the psychological experience of work for the individual (e.g. Shimmin, 1959; Litwin and Stringer, 1968).

THE EMPIRICAL STUDIES

The two studies were carried out using postal questionnaires addressed to the chief executive of the company concerned.   The first study involved companies based in South Wales manufacturing products in four industrial classifications, namely: rubber and plastics, basic metal, electrical and electronic, and machinery and equipment.   The survey was carried out in Summer 1977 and useable responses were obtained from 59 companies. The large majority of these were independent companies although a few ere subsidiaries of larger companies located elsewhere.   These companies varied in size from fifty to nearly six hundred employees.   The second study also involved companies based in South Wales.   In this case companies in the construction, food and beverage, and metal products industries were approached.   This second survey was carried out in the Autumn of 1978 and useable responses were obtained from 52 companies, varying in size from fifty to just over fourteen hundred employees.

Study 1 - The Measures Used

In the first study the climate questionnaire used

consisted of twenty statements taken partly from the
Business Organization Climate Index developed by Payne
and Pheysey (1971) and partly from the climate measure
developed by Hall and Lawler (1969).   In the case of
each statement respondents were asked to rate their
degree of agreement with it as a description of their own
organization, on a seven point scale going from 'strongly
agree' to 'strongly disagree'.   The data from the questionnaire were factor analysed using a varimax rotation
which provided eight factors accounting for over seventy
per cent of the variance.   These factors were conceptualized as career orientation, planning orientation,
industriousness, social support, leaders' psychological
distance, laissez-faire orientation, orientation to
rewards and control, and innovativeness.   The number of
items loaded significantly on each factor ranged from
two to four.   Factor scores were obtained by simple
addition of those items loaded on each factor.

The measurement of organizational climate solely
in terms of the perceptions of the chief executive is
clearly likely to lead to a rather biased estimate
being obtained.   There is considerable evidence that
climate is in general perceived more favourably at higher
levels in the hierarchy (e.g. Payne and Mansfield, 1973).
However, Payne and Mansfield (1978) report significant
correlations between the climate perceptions of managers
and those of their subordinates even though the managers
in general had a more favourable view.   Moreover, if any
such bias is approximately constant across organizations
it should not have a serious effect on the differences
between organizations and hence not invalidate any analysis
based on analysis of variance or correlational techniques,
although the results may be less reliable than those which
could be obtained with a larger sample of organizational
employees.

The second part of the questionnaire investigated
two broad aspects of company payment systems.   The
first aspect considered was the methodology by which jobs
are allocated to positions in the overall hierarchical
system within an organization and differentials established between positions.   In other words it investigated the extent and nature of the utilization of techniques such as job evaluation.   The second aspect of
payment systems considered was the extent and method of
relating pay to employee effort of achievement;   that is,
whether incentive schemes, merit payments or performance
appraisals were used to provide a basis for rewarding
individuals or groups.   In nearly all cases respondents
were asked to answer each question twice, first referring
to the practice in their company with regard to manual
employees and second referring to the practice with regard

to clerical employees.   Respondents were also asked the
extent of unionization amongst manual and clerical employees in their company.   In addition the size of each
company in terms of number of employees, its status as an
independent or subsidiary company, and the nature of its
products were all ascertained from public records.

Study 1 - The Results

     The relationships between variables were explored
using both analysis of variance and correlational techniques.   However, for simplicity of presentation all the
results are presented in terms of correlation coefficients
using dummy variables where necessary to represent points
on nominal scales.   This allows a more obvious comparison between the strengths of different relationships.

     First the relationships between climate and the
constraining variables of company size, company status
and extent of unionization were examined.   Company size
was not found to be as pervasive a correlate of organizational climate as in some previous studies (e.g. Payne
and Mansfield, 1973).   It was only significantly related
to two of the eight climate factors - positively to career
orientation ($r = 0.25$) and negatively to orientation to
rewards and control ($r = -0.32$).   This latter climate
factor was the only one related to company status ($r = 0.33$, with positive scores on this climate factor being
directly related to whether the company was an indepen-
dent company rather than a subsidiary) and to the extent
of unionization ($r = -0.29$ with unionization of manual
employees).   Taking these results together, a picture
emerges that the orientation to rewards and control is
seen to be greatest in small independent companies with
low rates of unionization.

     Attention was then turned to those variables which
might provide a means for the control of climate.   The
relationships found between climate and the various parameters of payment systems were then examined;   all those
which were significantly different from zero at the five
per cent level are shown in Table 1.   Examination of
this table shows that the relationships between these two
sets of variables are pervasive, with at least two payment system parameters being related to all the eight
dimensions of climate being examined.   However, although
significant, most of the relationships are not particularly strong;   which suggests that the ability to control
aspects of climate by operating on the nature of payment
system used, may be limited if these variables are
changed in isolation.

Table 1.   Parameters of Payment Systems Significantly
            organizational climate (N = 59).   Variables

Career orientation	Planning orientation	Industrious-ness	Social support
Importance of skill as a factor in pay determination for manual workers (r = 0.41)	Payment of a bonus to manual workers based on time saved compared to standard time (r = 0.24)	Use of consul-tation in pay determination process (r = 0.38)	Importance of working con-ditions as a factor in pay determination for manual workers (r = 0.38)
Payment of cash allowances to manual workers for uncontrollable stoppages (r = 0.30)	Use of consul-tation in pay determination process (r = 0.23)	Importance of working con-ditions as a factor in pay determination for manual workers (r = 0.25)	Importance of accountability as a factor in pay determi-nation for clerical employees (r = 0.25)
Payment of a bonus to manual workers based on time saved com-pared to standard time (r = 0.27)			Use of a single company-wide payment struc-ture for manual workers (r = 0.24)
Importance of supervision as a factor in pay deter-mination of clerical employees (r = 0.27)			Importance of skill as a factor in pay determination for manual employees (r = -0.23)

(at five per cent level) related to dimensions of
listed in order of strength of relationships.

Leaders' psychological distance	Laissez-faire orientation	Orientation to rewards and control	Innovativeness
Payment of a bonus to manual workers based on time saved compared to standard time (r = 0.33)	Payment of cash allowances to manual workers for unavoidable stoppages (r = 0.29)	Use of a merit rating scheme (r = 0.34)	Importance of skill as a factor in pay determination for clerical employees (r = 0.30)
Fixed rates of pay for manual workers (r = -0.29)	Use of a single company-wide payment structure for manual workers (r = 0.23)	Importance of accountability as a factor in pay determination for manual workers (r = 0.31)	Use of consultation in pay determination process (r = 0.23)
Use of consultation in pay determination process (r = 0.26)		Importance of supervision as a factor in pay determination for manual workers (r = 0.24)	
Importance of working conditions as a factor in pay determination for manual workers (r = 0.24)			

Career orientation is the climate factor found to
be most closely related to payment system parameters.
It is positively related to the importance of skill for
manual workers and supervision for clerical workers in
the pay determination process.   This probably indicates
that these factors play roles in the career development
of the two different types of worker.   Less predictably,
this aspect of climate is also related to the types of
bonuses and allowances paid to manual workers.

The climate dimension of social support is also
related to four parameters of payment systems.   It is
positively related to the importance of working conditions
in pay determination for manual workers but negatively
related to the importance of skill in that process.   It
is also positively related to the use of a single company-
wide payment structure for manual employees.   This dimension of climate is also related to the importance of
accountability as a factor in pay determination for
clerical workers.   For manual workers social support
is seen as relating to treating workers similarly, emphasising conditions and de-emphasising skill differentials;
in the case of clerical workers social support is associated with an emphasis on accountability.

The climate dimension of leaders' psychological
distance is also significantly related to four parameters
of payment systems, being positively related to the payment of bonuses to manual workers based on time saved
compared to standard time, use of consultation in pay
determination processes and the importance of working conditions as a factor in pay determination for manual
workers, and negatively related to fixed rates of pay
for manual workers.   The reasons for these relationships
do not seem obvious.

Perhaps surprisingly, orientation to rewards and
control is only related to three aspects of payment
systems as this would seem the climate factor with the
clearest conceptual linkage.   It is positively related to
the use of a merit rating system and to the importance of
accountability and supervision as factors in pay determination for manual workers.   Clearly then, this climate
dimension is related to aspects of payment systems
emphasising relationships with a managerial ethos.

The other four climate factors are each related to
two parameters of payment systems.   Planning orientation
is linked to the payment of a bonus to manual workers
based on time saved compared to standard time and to
the use of consultation in the pay determination process.
These results are not surprising as both these elements
are often related to planning in modern management thinking.

Industriousness is related to the importance of working
conditions in the pay determination processes for manual
workers and the use of consultation in the pay determination process.   This latter relationship may be another
indication of positive outcomes stemming from greater
consultation or participation.

Laissez-faire orientation is related to the payment
of cash allowances for unavoidable stoppages and the use
of a single company-wide payment structure for manual
workers.   Innovativeness is related to the importance of
skill as a factor in manual pay determination and to the
use of consultation in pay determination processes.   In
the industries studied, the former may be an essential
precondition and the latter the mechanism of innovativeness.

It seems unlikely that the patterns of relationships
reported here can be explained by any simple model in
which changes in the parameters of company payment systems
bring about changes in organizational climate.   This
conclusion, taken in conjunction with the relatively low
correlations reported in most cases, suggests that modi-
fying payment systems will only provide limited leverage
for the control of organizational climate;   although
changing those factors which are most important in the
pay determination process may be likely to have a significant effect, particularly if taken in conjunction with
other variables within management's control.

Study 2 - The Measures Used

In the second study the climate questionnaire used
consisted of thirty-two items forming four scales taken
from the Business Organization Climate Index (Payne and
Pheysey, 1971).   The scales chosen were those measuring
leaders' psychological distance, management concern for
employee involvement, task orientation and readiness to
innovate, thus obtaining a mixture between climate dimensions relating to internal maintenance of the organization and to external goal achievement.   As in the
first study, respondents were asked to rate their agreement with each item as a description of their organization on a seven point scale running from 'strongly
agree' to 'strongly disagree', in contrast to the true/
false assessments required in the original version of
the questionnaire.   The mean correlations between items
on each scale ranged from r = 0.50 to r = 0.67.

The measure of decentralization used was that
developed by Mansfield et al. (1978).   This measure
assessed the lowest level in the organizational hierarchy
at which particular decisions could legitimately be made.

Hierarchical level was indicated on an eight point scale
from operative through various management levels to the
board of directors, and where appropriate to positions
of control in parent companies.   The operational measure
was an average score over eight decisions such as those
to develop a new product or to fix the price of a product.

It has been shown that the extent of competition
faced by a company in its product market can influence
internal behaviour (e.g. Negandhi and Reimann, 1972;
Boseman and Jones, 1974).   This was assessed in the
present study using the scale developed by Negandhi and
Reimann (1972) which assesses the degree of price competition among manufacturers of similar products, the back-
log of orders for products, and the number of alternative
suppliers or competing brands available to the consumer.

In addition measures of size in terms of the number
of employees, the ratio of profit to turnover, the ratio
of profit to capital employed and growth in turnover
over the last five years, were obtained from company
annual returns.   Due to the delays in companies making
these statutory returns there was some missing financial
data reducing the effective sample size for some analyses.

Study 2 - The Results

Table 2 shows the correlations between the extent
of decentralization, organizational size, market competition and the different measures of financial performance
and the various climate scales.   It will be noted that
the only statistically significant relationships are
between decentralization of decision-making and three of
the four climate scales.   These relationships indicating
impact of decentralization upon the climate dimensions of
management concern for employee involvement, task orientation and readiness to innovate, are surprisingly in a
negative direction.   The negative relationship between
decentralization and management concern for employee
involvement is particularly unexpected, as the former
might seem to be the natural structural embodiment of
the latter.   This result raises once again the question
of the relationship between the concepts and empirical
indicators in the areas of participation and control.
Many employees might feel more involved in a decision made
by their bosses about which they were consulted than in
one they made themselves according to closely defined
rules.   Generally, in interpreting the results presented
here, it should be remembered that all the companies in
the sample were relatively small.

In small companies centralized decision-making tends

Table 2.   Correlations between dimensions of organi-
            zational climate and other variables.
            (N = 52 except for the performance variables
            where N = 33).

Climate Dimensions

	Leaders' Psycho- logical distance	Manage- ment concern for employee involve- ment	Task orien- tation	Readiness to innovate
Decentralization of decision-making	-0.07	-0.39**	-0.45**	-0.28*
Organizational size	-0.03	0.03	0.06	0.02
Extent of market competition	-0.03	0.03	0.06	0.02
Growth of revenue in last five years	-0.30	0.02	0.20	0.27
Profit to turnover ratio	-0.19	0.22	-0.04	-0.11
Profit to capital employed ratio	-0.08	0.15	-0.03	-0.09

* signifies $p < 0.05$

** signifies $p < 0.01$

to be part of a personal style of management, and may be
expected to have rather different implications for climate than would be expected in larger companies.   However when the present sample was divided into two halves
in terms of organizational size no noticeable differences
were found in this relationship.

Among the other variables considered, the extent of
market competition is seen to have no direct impact upon
the dimensions of climate considered here.   Contrary to
results reported elsewhere (e.g. Payne and Mansfield,
1973), organizational size is also not significantly related to any aspect of climate.   This lack of relationship may possibly be due to the limited range of sizes in
the present sample of companies.   Although none of the

relationships between the financial performance measures
and the different dimensions of climate are statistically
significant, it is perhaps worth noting that growth in
particular is to some extent associated with high task
orientation and readiness to innovate and low leaders'
psychological distance.

It has been suggested that the relationship between
decentralization and a variety of variables indicating
internal organizational processes may be contingent upon
the extent of market competition (Negandhi and Reimann,
1972; Boseman and Jones, 1974). In order to see if
this affected the relationships with the different aspects
of organizational climate, the sample was divided into
two groups using the same criteria used by Negandhi and
Reimann (1972, 143). The first group included companies
facing severe market competition. The second group
included companies facing relatively low market competition. The relationships between decentralization and
climate for these two sub-samples are shown in Table 3.

Table 3.   Correlations between the extent of decentrali-
            zation of decision-making and dimensions of
            organizational climate under different condi-
            tions of market competition (N = 52).

<table>
<tr><td></td><td colspan="4">Climate Dimensions</td></tr>
<tr><td></td><td>Leaders' psycho- logical distance</td><td>Manage- ment concern for employee involve- ment</td><td>Task orien- tation</td><td>Readiness to innovate</td></tr>
<tr><td>Decentralization under conditions of high market competition (N = 26)</td><td>0.16</td><td>-0.52</td><td>-0.57</td><td>-0.27</td></tr>
<tr><td>Decentralization under conditions of relatively low market competition (N = 26)</td><td>-0.21</td><td>-0.11</td><td>-0.32</td><td>-0.38</td></tr>
</table>

Examination of the correlations reported there shows
that decentralization has rather different implications
for climate under conditions of high and low market
competition, particularly in the case of the two dimensions indicating leaders' psychological distance and
management concern for employee involvement.   Under conditions of high market competition these relationships
are both in surprising directions, with the dimension of
management concern for employee involvement being strongly
negatively related to decentralization.   Although the
results are in unexpected directions, they still make
clear that the effect of structural parameters upon climate is highly dependent upon the conditions under which
the organization is operating.

DISCUSSION

        The results of the two studies reported here
clearly suggest the complexity of the processes by which
organizational climates are created and maintained.
Such complexity obviously renders the control of climate
difficult.   The size of the relationships found between
the various parameters of payment systems and the extent
of decentralization on the one hand and the various
dimensions of climate on the other, shows that there can
be little hope of controlling climate solely by operating
on a single variable.   However the second study does
suggest that the judicious manipulation of variables
with particular relevance to the situation in which the
organization is placed may offer more scope than general
remedies.   Clearly there is scope for an extension of
contingency theory in this direction.

        The results of the second study raise very serious
questions about the implications of decentralization.
They clearly cast serious doubts upon the likely outcome
of such a structural strategy, at least in the case of
small companies operating under competitive conditions.
It would appear that a great deal more study is required
of the reality of decision-making processes and the
implications of decentralization and participation for
the quality of working life of those affected.   The
present study suggests the need for a more complex understanding but hints that such an understanding might have
enormous practical benefits for management and worker
alike.

ACKNOWLEDGEMENT

        I would like to express my gratitude to Mahnaz Azma
and Ali Dastmalchian for permission to use some results
from their research.

REFERENCES

Boseman, F.G. and Jones, R.E. (1974). 'Market con-
     ditions, decentralization, and organizational
     effectiveness', Human Relations, 27, 665-676.

Dieterly, D. and Schneider, B. (1974). 'The Effect of
     organizational environment on perceived power and
     climate: A laboratory study', Organizational
     Behavior and Human Performance, 2, 316-337.

Friedlander, F. and Margulies, N. (1969). 'Multiple
     inputs of organizational climate and individual
     value systems upon job satisfaction', Personnel
     Psychology, 22, 171-183.

George, J. and Bishop, L. (1971). 'Relationship of
     organizational structure and teacher personality
     characteristics to organizational climate',
     Administrative Science Quarterly, 16, 467-476.

Hall, D.T. and Lawler, E.E. (1969). 'Unused potential
     in research and development organizations',
     Research Management, 12, 339-354.

Hand, H., Richards, M. and Slocum, J.W. (1973). 'Organi-
     zational climate and the effectiveness of a human
     relations training program', Academy of Management
     Journal, 16, 185-195.

Litwin, G. and Stringer, R. (1968). Motivation and
     Organizational Climate, Cambridge, Mass., Harvard
     University Press.

Mansfield, R., Todd, D. and Wheeler, J. (1978). 'Com-
     pany structure and market strategy', Omega, The
     International Journal of Management Science, 6,
     133-138.

Negandhi, A.R. and Reimann, B. (1972). 'A contingency
     theory of organization re-examined in the context
     of a developing country', Academy of Management
     Journal, 15, 137-146.

Payne, R.L. and Mansfield, R. (1973). 'Relationships
     of perceptions of organizational climate to organi-
     zational structure, context and hierarchical
     position', Administrative Science Quarterly, 18,
     515-526.

Payne, R.L. and Mansfield, R. (1978). 'Correlates of
     individual perceptions of organizational climate',
     Journal of Occupational Psychology, 51, 209-218.

Payne, R.L. and Pheysey, D.C. (1971).   'G.G. Stern's
     organization climate index: a reconceptualization
     and application to business organization', Organi-
     zational Behavior and Human Performance, 6, 77-98.

Pritchard, R. and Karasick, B. (1973).   'The Effects of
     organizational climate on managerial job perfor-
     mance and job satisfaction', Organizational Behavior
     and Human Performance, 9, 110-119.

Shimmin, S. (1959).   Payment by results, London, Staples
     Press.

Changes in Working Life
Edited by K.D. Duncan, M.M. Gruneberg, and D. Wallis
© 1980 John Wiley & Sons Ltd

Chapter 18

Job Redesign and Social Change: Case Studies at Volvo

F. H. M .BLACKLER and C. A. BROWN

In recent years there has been increasing interest
shown by social scientists in the field of job design,
and an increasing confidence on the part of many that work
in this area is of some general social significance.   In
the past ten years or so one can see how socio-technical
systems theory has assumed a predominance in the field
over the more simplistic job enrichment approach, and how
much detailed work (of which many of the papers in this
volume bear witness) has been carried out into the
circumstances under which jobs satisfy people.   Indeed
the use of such approaches to improve the quality of
working life has found acceptance beyond the immediate
confines of social science itself.   Discussion and support of socio-technical ideas has been shown by other
professional groups (e.g. industrial engineers: see
Edward, 1971 or Burbidge, 1975), by policy makers within
multi-national companies (e.g. Philips, Shell UK, Volvo,
I.C.I.) and by national governments (by means of legislation on industrial democracy and the establishment of
research institutes).   So impressive has the interest
of such external groups been for social scientists that,
for some at least, it has appeared that social science
has 'come of age'.   Many of the papers delivered at the
first international conference on the Quality of Working
Life in 1972, for example (see Davis and Cherns, 1975),
appear to reflect a belief that social science has a lot
that is important to say about job design and that a
basic problem now is how a rapid diffusion and acceptance

311

of such ideas throughout the modern world may be encouraged.

Nevertheless, despite the achievements and the
optimism of this period, it would be a mistake to
assume that work in this area has passed without informed
criticism.   Elsewhere (Blackler and Brown, 1978) we
have summarised points made by sociologists and political
scientists critical of the job redesign 'movement',
laying these alongside the more detailed reviews of particular case studies and experiments with job redesign
undertaken by psychologists. The major themes we identified in this survey are summarised here on Figure 1.

One basic concern expressed at a general level by
several commentators (e.g. Braverman, 1974; Fox, 1976;
Hughes and Gregory, 1974; Nichols, 1976) has been the
suggestion that attempts to improve the quality of
working life by job redesign alone are likely to amount
to little more than a modern version of 'human relations'
management.   On this view, notwithstanding the language
of self fulfilment and personal development characteristic of job redesign writings, the use of such ideas
may serve as little more than an unobtrusive device to
control others' behaviour.   The allegation is that,
whilst fundamental changes in the quality of work experience appear to be offered, in practice the changes which
do result involve only peripheral issues.   As Child
(1973, p. 243) has put it, a possible effect of job
redesign programmes could be 'to divert attention away
from a recognition of more fundamental sources of inequality, through the effect which they may have of
increasing the employess' normative acceptance of managerial definitions of the industrial situation'.   Or,
in the words of Alan Fox: 'Discussion may be about marginal adjustments in hierarchical rewards but not about
the principle of hierarchical rewards; ... about financial rewards for greater efficiency, but not about the
possibility of other types of (intrinsic) reward with
some sacrifice of efficiency; ... about how participants'
interests can protect and advance themselves within the
structure operated by management to pursue its basic
objectives, but not about the nature of those basic
objectives' (Fox, 1973, p. 219).

Evaluations of job redesign such as these have, it
would seem, influenced the attitude of certain trade
unionists in the UK at least (see for example, Hughes and
Gregory, 1974, p. 387), although it should be said that
some leading socio-technical theorists have argued a
contradictory thesis. Herbst, for example, writing about
the progress of the Norwegian Industrial Democracy Project, which depended so much on job redesign theory,
recalled that 'our basic initial hypothesis was that

1   Job redesign may be regarded as a modern variant of
    'human relations' management. As such, despite its
    language of 'self fulfilment' and 'personal develop-
    ment', it may more correctly be described as a manage-
    ment control device.

2   This 'control' is made possible for, whilst appearing
    to promise fundamental change, in practice job redesign
    changes may involve only marginal issues. The basic
    legitimacy and appropriateness of present organisa-
    tional arrangements is assumed. At the same time,
    critics point out, the authority of an 'impartial
    science' is claimed in support of redesign ideas.

3   This need not imply that job redesigners are manipu-
    lative in their intents. It seems more likely that,
    assuming the inevitability of current business frame-
    works and the legitimacy of prevailing power struc-
    tures, the conceptual frameworks people use themselves
    limit their appreciations of alternative actions.

4   On the other hand it has been suggested that once,
    through job redesign, people have experienced the plea-
    sures of increased self-determination they will come
    to demand it in other matters also. On this view,
    rather than being a control device, job redesign is
    inherently 'subversive' of some existing organisational
    arrangements.

5   A major evaluative study of job redesign studies sug-
    gests missionary zeal, the publication of positive
    results only; and the employment of poor research
    designs are characteristic of the job redesign liter-
    ature.

6   Further analysis of such work suggests that a certain
    lack of respect for precise evaluation is common, as
    is a profusion of imprecise though fine-sounding terms.

7   The criteria used in evaluation studies are usually
    managerially rather than 'psychologically' oriented.
    Their emphasis on organisational efficiency contrasts
    with that of 'psychological growth' characteristic of
    key theories inspiring work in the field.

8   Because of this bias in published studies it is not
    presently possible to explore the value of suggestions
    that good job redesign practice may tend to far-reach-
    ing personal, organisational and social changes.
    Claims for the 'radicality' of job redesign are impor-
    tant but, especially in the light of research into the
    meaning of work, they are by no means self evidently
    true.

Figure 1.   Criticism of job redesign studies (based on
            Blackler and Brown, 1978).

industrial work organisations constitute the central
region in Western societies so that changes introduced
there should spread out and diffuse to other sectors of
society' (Herbst, 1976, p. 53).   But despite the disparity of view between those who see job design on its
own as merely a cosmetic activity and those who see it
as a leading edge of personal and social reform, there
has been little direct dialogue between proponents of
these various views.   Just as in the 1960s Baritz's
criticism of industrial social scientists was largely
ignored by them, so in the 1970s apparently fundamental
criticisms of job redesign activities have not drawn
much response from job redesigners themselves.

Despite the seriousness of these and other points
summarised in Figure 1 it remains true that there is
little empirical work which throws much light on the
appropriateness or otherwise of allegations that job
redesign is little more than a cosmetic activity effectively, if not intentionally, serving only to maintain
or restore the legitimacy of managements' call to collective endeavour.   Given a concern with this allegation,
two immediately obvious ways exist to examine it further.
One would be to trace the effects of redesigned jobs on
workers over a period to see the extent to which people's
life styles are modified.   The other would be to trace
the decision-making in an organisation aware of the
possibilities associated with job redesign, and to
analyse the reasons why work was continued or curtailed
on given projects.   This would be a particularly instructive exercise if, in psychological terms, the redesign
projects studied were significant and if they offered
potential for continuing opportunities for self development.

At intervals over the past six years the authors
have been fortunate enough to be able to carry out
research of the latter type in the Truck Division of
Volvo, comparing experiences there to those in a truck
assembly factory in the British Leyland group.   In terms
of finding a research site sympathetic to job redesign
theory, arguably Volvo provides opportunities second to
none.   Amongst managers, Volvo's reputation as an inno-
vator in this field is well known, with the President
of Volvo's book (Gyllenhammer, 1977) recording an impressive list of job design achievements in the company.
Amongst academics too the praise for this work has been
high (e.g., see Dowling, 1973 or Tichy, 1976) with Walton
(1977) commenting that 'there can be no question that
Volvo's achievements are extraordinary'.

In this review of our work we report on three
studies.   The preliminary study was conducted in 1973,
and was of little comfort to job redesign theorists,

confirming as it does the possibility that job redesign
may be used as a control device.   The second, conducted
in 1976, points to rather different options, and records how a job redesign study well done offered the
possibility of wide reaching organisational reforms.
The third, conducted in 1979, reviews the way this very
promising project was treated, and documents reasons why
the full potentials of the innovation are unlikely ever
to be realised.   In presenting this story we include
reference to parallel studies made in British Leyland in
1973 and 1976.   Our presentation of these studies must
necessarily be brief and more details may be found in
Blackler and Brown (1978).

FIRST FIELD STUDY: TRUCK ASSEMBLY IN BRITISH LEYLAND
AND VOLVO

        In 1973, we sought to compare a Volvo assembly
plant in which socio-technical redesign had taken place
with a British Leyland plant which was broadly comparable
in terms of products, organization and history and in
which assembly work was traditionally organised.   (Under
the Volvo redesigned system 3 - 9 men selected their own
leader and were given some opportunity to decide how
work on a larger part of the chassis should be done.)
The plants selected for comparison were the Volvo truck
assembly plant in Gothenburg and the British Leyland
A.E.C. plant in West London.   In each plant we employed
three main methods of data collection.   Firstly, assembly
line jobs were rated using the Turner and Lawrence (1965)
R.T.A. scales.   Thus we could compare (in terms of
variety, autonomy, interaction opportunity, responsibility,
cycle time and other factors) traditional assembly line
jobs in Leyland with assembly line jobs organised on the
autonomous team leader system that we studied in Volvo.
Secondly we collected existing documentary evidence on
turnover, absence, wastage levels, as well as data on
productivity and profitability, to investigate the claims
made by Volvo for the effectiveness of their programme.
Thirdly we conducted an interview programme with representatives of management, supervision and trade unions in
order to investigate the organisational contexts.

        We can summarise the results of our findings as
follows:

1. There were no significant differences in psycho-
   social terms between the redesigned jobs in Volvo and
   the traditional jobs in Leyland, with the exception
   of the team leader's job which was of a significantly
   different type.   Thus in spite of the many expansive
   claims made for the advantages of the team leader
   system we concluded that benefits stemming from

substantial job design change here, of necessity, needed to be conservatively estimated.

2. It was not possible to demonstrate any causal links between the redesign programme and levels of absence, turnover, quality or profitability. This failure was due to one of two reasons. Either improvements in any particular index in the Volvo plant was matched in the Leyland plant (e.g. turnover), or there was alternative competing or confounding variables to be taken into account (such as re-organisation of management functions or doubling of productive capacity in Volvo). In any case, given the previous finding that most of the redesigned jobs in the Volvo plant were still very conventional, there seemed no good reason (other than perhaps the 'Hawthorne effect') to expect that what changes had been introduced would result in a markedly improved organisational performance.

3. There is a paradox entailed by these findings. Volvo had committed considerable resources to the redesign of jobs over a decade and had stated the criteria by which their efforts were to be judged. All the available evidence suggested to us that their criteria were either non-operational or unfulfilled. Why then had they continued with this work? Further analyses led us to speculate that two other factors were relevant; firstly the marked improvement of the company's image as an innovative and humane organisation and secondly, the emergence within the organisational hierarchy of the company of career structures based upon ability in this new area.

This research was on a small scale and should not be taken to mean that all job redesign work being undertaken in Volvo at this time was necessarily of such restricted value. Nonetheless in terms of the criticisms of job redesign mentioned before this study is of interest. It appeared to provide us with a case example of where, despite the undoubted good intentions of the job redesigners, a job redesign effort had amounted to little more than a cosmetic activity, maintaining or restoring the workability of existing organisational arrangements yet involving only trivial changes. In this case there seemed to have been more talk than action, with the talk itself apparently providing the company with a sufficient return for its efforts.

SECOND FIELD STUDY: THE ARENDAL PROJECT

The focus for our second study was a small experimental redesign project begun in Volvo Truck Division in 1974, and a comparable project begun in Leyland in the

same year.   The most important feature of both projects
was that they involved the building of a truck with no
movement of the chassis along an assembly line.   As a
method of manufacture this represents a return to 1913,
that is before Henry Ford developed the moving assembly
line concept for motor vehicles.   In those days static
assembly (or dock assembly as it is now called within
Volvo) was conclusively demonstrated to be much less
efficient for the assembly of motor vehicles than the
moving assembly line.   This demonstration, of course,
has been repeated many times since and has resulted in
static, or dock, assembly being viewed by industrial
engineers as suitable only for specialised and complex
vehicles produced in very small numbers.   Yet, production considerations apart, if one considered how one
could possibly organise the work of assembling a complex technical product such as a truck so as to maximise
the variety, learning opportunities and opportunities
for interesting work for the people involved, then static
assembly, with a small group of men deciding amongst
themselves how to allocate tasks, would be one solution.
And not only does such a method result in the minimum
fragmentation of tasks, but it allows for greater contact
between operators and industrial engineers, and can allow
the operator to take over many of the traditional tasks
of the engineer (such as local material supply, product
modification or quality control).   Static, or dock,
assembly therefore entails making certain alterations
in conventional patterns of management and control, and
raises the possibility that some of those alterations
could be of a fundamental type.   And when production considerations are taken into account, as Rosengren (1979)
has demonstrated mathematically (and early work at
Arendal confirmed empirically), a maximum of 30% man hours
per truck built can be saved under dock assembly methods
compared to conventional lines; given certain technical
innovations and a motivated, skilled and co-operative
work group.

     In our research in Volvo we conducted a semi-
structured interview programme with ten people who had
either been closely involved in the execution of the
dock assembly project or who through their roles had been
able to watch its development carefully.   We talked to a
member of central H.Q., union leaders, a social scientist,
the manager of the project since its instigation, and
other production engineers and line managers.

     In Leyland, on the other hand, there was no cloak
of secrecy but in this case we found ourselves piecing
together the story of a project that had terminated some
three years previously.   Key personnel had left the company or moved within it, some had forgotten details of
the incident.   In the end we were able to reconstruct

the affair from the point of view of those most intimately involved in the project, most especially the works
manager and section supervisor.

The experiences of the two companies with dock
assembly of trucks is summarised on Charts 2 and 3.   In
both cases a shortfall of productive capacity and an
inability to increase conventional assembly truck capacity provided the initial impetus for the projects.
Later there are similarities in the way each project was
organised.   The size of teams used, the balance between
'novices' and skilled operators within them, the long
initial training and induction period, and subsequent
realization that production performance was in excess of
expectations, in all these ways experiences in Volvo and
Leyland were largely the same.   Further, while neither
company employed directly the services of consultant
social scientists on these particular projects, it seemed
that the technical problems of dock assembly on a small
scale, at least, were not found acute by either Volvo
or Leyland.

Yet these similarities should not distract attention from the differences evident in the two cases.
The facts are that Volvo personnel became aware of and
explored further a potential in dock assembly techniques not appreciated in Leyland.   Despite evidence
of the potential that dock assembly in Leyland offered,
the project was soon abandoned here; while in Volvo
the possibilities for this assembly method were studi-
ously explored in a research programme continuing for a
number of years.

In analysing the reasons for this difference three
factors emerged as important.   First was the differences
between the companies in outlook regarding the inevita-
bility of conventional production engineering wisdom.
Volvo's energetic approach to job redesign, which by now
had been demonstrated so clearly in the Kalmar plant, set
a climate where experiments could take place and where
apparently unusual ideas were not dismissed out of hand.
A second difference concerned the purposes, skills and
organisation of the people involved in managing the two
products.   In Volvo changes in modern industrial
engineering techniques, the development of new handling
and control technologies, and a realisation that more
effective use could be made of human abilities, were all
understood or discovered by members of the project
management team.   Thirdly there were very different
opportunities for each of the companies that were offered
by the general trading and industrial relations conditions in each company.   Volvo needed to consider
designs for a new truck plant, while Leyland faced a
period of uncertainty, a threat of redundancies and a

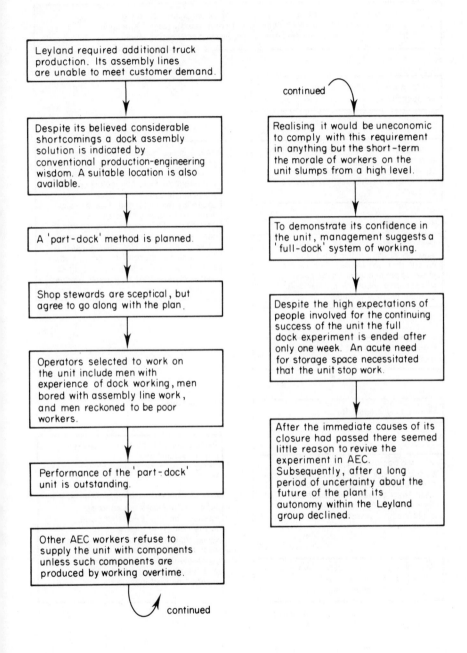

Figure 2.   A summary of AEC/Leyland's experience with dock assembly of trucks.

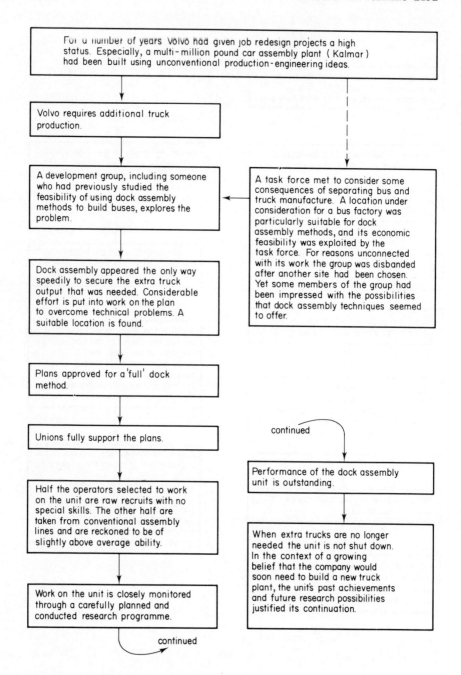

Figure 3.   A summary of Volvo's experience with dock
             assembly of trucks.

difficult industrial relations climate.

POTENTIAL FOR DEVELOPING THE ARENDAL INNOVATIONS

Apart from the intrinsic interest, however, in comparing Leyland's and Volvo's experiences with dock assembly, the Arendal project assumed a special significance within the context of certain actual and proposed legislation in Sweden. There are three pieces of such legislation primarily involved. The Act of Codetermination at Work and the Working Environment Act prescribe frameworks within which companies should be managed. Primarily these acts serve to revoke the primacy of what were previously regarded as 'management prerogatives', including exclusive rights to hold certain company information, to have priority in cases of disagreement on interpretation of collective agreements, and to design jobs without necessarily taking account of employees' psychological and safety needs as primary considerations. The third piece of legislation, to which we now primarily refer, is the Meidner proposals on employee influence on capital formation. According to these proposals a proportion of the profits of companies in the private sector of the Swedish economy would contribute to a wage-earners' investment fund in the form of 'compulsory directed stock issues'. On a time scale, dependent upon the percentage of profits set aside for the fund and on the amount of profits themselves, company ownership would gradually shift towards employees. Furthermore as Forseback (1976) has noted 'the proposal is characterised by a desire to achieve decentralisation of ownership ...'

This last point is of particular importance because dock assembly methods are well suited to, and depending upon the product may require, decentralised units of production. This is in stark contrast, of course, to conventional methods of vehicle assembly, requiring as they do such high investment in a centralised and tightly controlled production plant. On the other hand, at their most basic, all dock assembly techniques require are a warehouse, a supply of materials, relatively simple technological equipment, and some people.

Here there is a technological development in truck assembly that could make decentralised production units economic, and a legislative proposal that would encourage decentralised patterns of company ownership. It is this congruence which may lead to possibilities of significant changes in the social organisation of work. To speculate, perhaps now smaller size communities could provide perfectly adequate locations for several geographically dispersed dock assembly plants. New product designs

could be developed which were more suitable to dock
assembly, less suited to an assembly technology based
upon fast movement through a tightly controlled line
system.   With localised production centres it may be
possible for the owner of a vehicle assembled in a certain dock assembly unit to return it there for service
and spares.   Such a development would fundamentally
change the relationship of the assembly worker to his job,
through such changes in patterns of product consumption.
New opportunities for patterns of management and control
would emerge.   Local assembly plants could be organised
in various ways, as cost centres, with contractual
relationships with a central company, or as part of a
loosely knit federation of companies enjoying relative
autonomy within a framework of shared central services.
On Figures 4 and 5 these points are summarised.

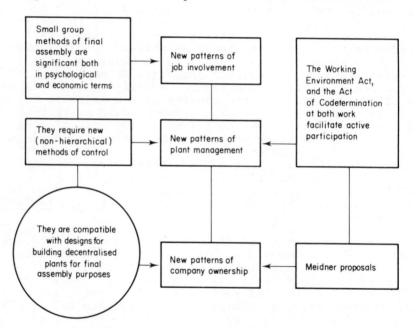

Figure 4.   Dock assembly methods in the context of
             Swedish legislation on industrial democracy.

THIRD FIELD STUDY: ARENDAL THREE YEARS LATER

        Whereas the Arendal project illuminated previously
unclear scenarios of possibilities, the question of
whether or not they are ever likely to become reality
next arises.   Given the fact that the Meidner proposals
had not (and may never be) made law and that pressures on

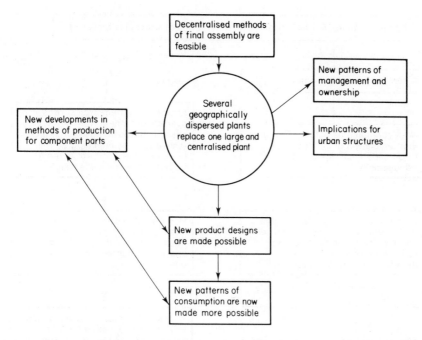

Figure 5.   Factors potentially affected by major changes
            in production methods.

companies to decentralise ownership or production in
Sweden were not strong, we doubted that any work promoting
the idea of small dispersed units of production would
have got very far since 1976.   Nonetheless we were hope-
ful that, given the success of Volvo Truck Division and
the opportunity for a major new factory, plans for a new
plant (albeit a centralised plant) based on dock assembly
methods might be far advanced.   It was somewhat disappointing to find, therefore, that at the time of our
third visit in June 1979, plans for the new factory
involved cycle times for the truck assemblers of only 45
minutes (though the opportunities for increasing these
were intentionally built into the plans) compared with
the cycle times of between 5 and 6 hours that had been
operational at Arendal some three years previously.

     On Figure 6 we very briefly summarise the main
events relevant to this project of the three years from
1976-79.   The story was reconstructed by interviewing,
as before, a sample of interested parties to the events.
It tells of the failure of the Arendal project to convince
senior managers of the suitability of full dock methods
for the new plant.   It is interesting to note that each
of the factors which we previously observed had

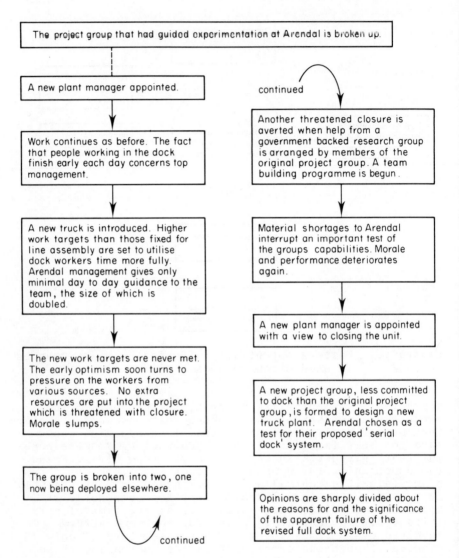

The project group that had guided experimentation at Arendal is broken up.

A new plant manager appointed.

Work continues as before. The fact that people working in the dock finish early each day concerns top management.

A new truck is introduced. Higher work targets than those fixed for line assembly are set to utilise dock workers time more fully. Arendal management gives only minimal day to day guidance to the team, the size of which is doubled.

The new work targets are never met. The early optimism soon turns to pressure on the workers from various sources. No extra resources are put into the project which is threatened with closure. Morale slumps.

The group is broken into two, one now being deployed elsewhere.

continued

continued

Another threatened closure is averted when help from a government backed research group is arranged by members of the original project group. A team building programme is begun.

Material shortages to Arendal interrupt an important test of the groups capabilities. Morale and performance deteriorates again.

A new plant manager is appointed with a view to closing the unit.

A new project group, less committed to dock than the original project group, is formed to design a new truck plant. Arendal chosen as a test for their proposed 'serial dock' system.

Opinions are sharply divided about the reasons for and the significance of the apparent failure of the revised full dock system.

Figure 6.   The course of the Arendal Project 1976-1979.

distinguished Volvo's experiences with dock from Leyland's, were changed in this episode of the story. Thus, attitudes towards conventional production engineering wisdom in the company, the skills and organisation of the managers concerned in job design experimentation, and the climate for change set by management/union relations had all taken a turn for the worse.

It is probably the first factor which is most
crucial for an understanding of the demise of full dock
in the Truck Division.   Our 1976 study had involved a
study of the attitudes of top management in the Division
towards dock methods and we had discovered then a lot of
suspicion regarding them.   While the content of particular reasons offered by them to account for their suspicion then were of interest (e.g. that the results of
one favourable small study could not be expected to
generalise, that technical drawbacks were associated with
dock methods, and that the assumptions that people could
cope and were trustworthy implied by the method were
mistaken), we concluded in 1976 that their main objections
were more emotional than rational.   Dock methods involve
a loss of immediate control by management;   this factor
we felt weighed more strongly with some individuals than
did the potential commercial advantages available from
the system.

Some three years later it was clear that opinions
had hardened along just these very lines.   Senior
managers told us they were convinced significant production savings could be achieved by dock assembly.   Yet
they felt that such methods were less reliable than conventional line assembly.   They acknowledged too that
important mistakes had been made at Arendal since 1976,
but concluded from this that the consequences only went
to show that dock methods were not as robust and reliable
as more conventional ones.   Perhaps above all they were
largely suspicious of a production method that allowed
workers to complete their quota before the end of the
working day and they wished this 'slack' to be controlled.

The consequences of these views were evident enough.
Since 1976 serious experimentation at Arendal had ceased
with the disbanding of the project team.   Since then
the system had been on trial, with a minimum of resources
put into the work, with men expected to work harder than
previously, and with the threat of closure replacing the
promise of time off at the end of the day as a motivating
factor.   The decline in morale and commitment which followed confirmed management's view that the assembly
method itself was at fault.   Thus when the time came to
select a design team for the new factory a team more
sympathetic to conventional line assembly than to dock
methods was chosen, with the inevitable consequence that
the designs produced were only moderately innovative.

Other developments relevant to the demise of the
dock assembly at Arendal had also taken place.   In contrast to their earlier reputation as innovators (see, for
example, The Guardian, 3.5.1977), the unions in Sweden
have become more militant in recent years with a world
economic recession, the passing of the socialist government

in Sweden, and problems with the Act of Codetermination
mentioned earlier. In this changed situation the
unions were much more suspicious about new methods that
might reduce jobs or upset pay agreements, and management much less prepared to open controversial debates
that might in some way be turned against them. Although
not active in curtailing the broader application of dock
methods, therefore the union seemed content with a
dilution of them.

DISCUSSION AND CONCLUSIONS

While our first study demonstrated that job redesign could be used in manipulative ways, early work at
the Arendal site showed job redesign need not necessarily be a trivial matter. This episode demonstrated
that models of personal growth applied in ways people
can recognise as practicable, in a questioning way, and
with an appreciation of the importance of context, can
assume a new significance. The early work at Arendal
illustrates, we believe, how new social possibilities
can emerge from an application of a richer understanding
of human nature than is normal.

Yet promise apart, it would seem there is little
chance these will be taken up by Volvo, even in a limited
way, and this despite the potential commercial advantages of dock assembly of trucks and the otherwise sympathetic climate towards job redesign in the company. The
last episode of this case suggests just how fragile
social inventions of the Arendal type are. It was not
the vision of decentralised assembly units that was not
given a fighting chance of succeeding, but the more
modest suggestion that Volvo's new centralised truck
plant be designed according to dock assembly principles.
These possible new methods of assembly offended some
managers' views of what worker freedoms were appropriate
and could be trusted. Their doubts meant that any set-
back to experimentation in dock assembly techniques,
even ones occurring under the most unfavourable conditions, would be understood to confirm such fears.

Theo Nichols (1976) has offered a sympathetic interpretation of why managers generally may have a limited
perspective on the use of job redesign ideas, which well
describes what we observed in Volvo:

'Management have a definite interest in
recognising that men are not simply com-
modities but thinking, social beings, with
potential to work together more productively - they also have an interest in
limiting the development of these human

potentials. And this is because, though
it would suit managements for workers to
act as if there really were socialism
inside work, managers themselves have to
operate in a world in which market forces
impede the development of the very
unstinted cooperation they wish to bring
about ... what others call ideology
managers call "commonsense". And commonsense tells them that they must not
forfeit control; that the business of
business is profit; and that whatever
ideas they might have in their heads and
whatever enriching or participatory ven-
tures they may institute, there are limits
- not of their making - to what they can
"sensibly" do. This is why it is not sufficient to dismiss their espousal of the
new human relations as a "con" ...'
(pp. 22 and 23).

Perhaps the decline of the Arendal project should
not come as a surprise. Social systems, of a political,
economic or organisational nature are all based on
assumptions about what is possible, desirable and appropriate in human affairs. The fact that the new principles demonstrated in the Arendal project threatened
some conventional ones meant, naturally, that their
chances of success were correspondingly limited. This
may indicate that in line with some of the criticisms of
job design we received earlier, conventional usage of
job redesign ideas will in practice tend to be somewhat
limited. Should this be the case, one conclusion might
be that job redesigners should be alert to the tension
and hostility their ideas may promote and, in their
efforts to promote changes in the nature and quality of
working life, should be prepared to adopt a more self-
consciously political role.

REFERENCES

Blackler, F.H.M. and Brown, C.A. (1978).   Job Redesign
    and Management Control, Saxon House, London.

Braverman, H. (1974).   Labor and Monopoly Capital,
    Monthly Review Press, New York.

Burbidge, J.L. (1975).   The Introduction of Group Tech-
    nology, Heinemann, London.

Child, J. (1973).   'Organisation: a choice for man',
    in Man and Organisation (Ed. J. Child), Allen and
    Unwin, London.

Davis, L.E. and Cherns, A.B. (1975). The Quality of Working Life Vols. I and II, Free Press, New York.

Dowling, W.F. (1973). 'Job redesign on the assembly line: farewell to blue-collar blues?', Organisational Dynamics, II, 51-67.

Edwards, G.A.B. (1971). Readings in Group Technology, Machinery Publishing Co., London.

Forseback, L. (1976). Industrial Relations and Employment in Sweden, The Swedish Institute, Stockholm.

Fox, A. (1973). 'Industrial relations: a social critique of pluralist ideology', in Man and Organisation (Ed. J. Child), Allen and Unwin, London.

Fox, A. (1976). 'The meaning of work', in People and Work, Block 3, Unit 6, The Open University Press, Milton Keynes.

Herbst, P.G. (1976). Alternatives to Hierarchies, Martinus Nijhoff, Leiden.

Hughes, J. and Gregory, D. (1974). 'Richer jobs for workers?', New Society, 14th February, 386-7.

Nichols, T. (1976). 'Management, ideology and practice', in People at Work, Block 4, Unit 15, The Open University Press, Milton Keynes.

Rosengren, L.G. (1979). 'The Potential Performance of Dock versus Line Assembly', (Paper presented at the Fifth International Conference on Production Research, Amsterdam, Netherlands, August, 1979).

Tichy, N. (1976). 'When does work restructuring work', Organisational Dynamics, V, 63-80.

Turner, A.N. and Lawrence, P.R. (1965). Industrial Jobs and the Worker, Harvard University, Graduate School of Business Administration, Boston.

Walton, R.E. (1977). 'Successful strategies for diffusing work innovations', Journal of Contemporary Business, Spring, 1-22.

Changes in Working Life
Edited by K.D. Duncan, M.M. Gruneberg, and D. Wallis
© 1980 John Wiley & Sons Ltd

Chapter 19

Group Work Redesign in Context: A Two-Phase Model

T. D. WALL

INTRODUCTION

This paper describes a model of group work redesign which has been developed as an integral part of an
action research project. The two distinctive features
of the model are that it specifies a limited set of elements which refer to both the content and context of
jobs; and that it groups these elements according to
phases reflecting the time bases of their causal impacts.
The model draws upon the existing literature, especially
on the more widely supported propositions relating work
characteristics to motivation, performance and well-
being. At the same time, the way in which the model is
structured, and its selection of work context factors,
reflects the experience gained in a field study, and in
particular participants' attributions of causality and
observed change in their attitudes and behaviour over
time.

The immediate stimulus to formalise the model
resides in the fact that the project is currently at the
cross-roads. An initial group work redesign exercise
has been successfully completed in one department of an
organisation and ways are now being sought to apply the
lessons learned company-wide. The exercise began with
the intention of using existing theory as a basis for
diagnosis, redesign and evaluation. As the study developed, however, it was found necessary to deviate from

this starting point.   The decision to extend the programme has now created the need to make explicit the
additions and modifications introduced.   In short a
'new' model of work redesign is required as a vehicle of
communication appropriate to employees ranging from
senior managers and engineers, through supervisors, to
shop-floor workers.   To be plausible to these people,
it needs to be compatible with evidence in the literature describing similar developments elsewhere,
account for the initial exercise conducted in their
midst, and relate to their own experience more generally.
To achieve these goals the model should exhibit three
main characteristics.   First it should specify the
minimum number of elements which together encompass the
variables involved in effecting and understanding group
work redesign.   Second, it should identify the causal
relationships amongst the elements.   And finally, it
should offer guidance on the time horizons within which
change is expected to occur.   Without the 'what', 'why'
and 'when' of group work redesign being clearly marked
out, one cannot expect to obtain the commitment and support of the many individuals whose co-operation is
required to put it into practice on a relatively large
scale.

Space precludes a detailed exposition of the difficulties experienced in attempting to apply existing
theory, but a few general observations are in order and
help to place this study in its theoretical context.
Two approaches initially commended themselves as of potential relevance.   One was the Job Characteristics
Model (Hackman and Oldham, 1976) modified to apply to
group work redesign (Hackman, 1977).   The other was
the socio-technical systems approach as illustrated in
the work of Davis (1957), Emery (1959), and Trist et al.
(1963).   Both focus on the same work characteristics as
being causally implicated in employee well-being and performance;   namely variety, work identity, work significance, feedback and above all, autonomy.   Indeed, the
extent of overlap between the two approaches on these
and other grounds is much greater than usually recognised
(Kelly, 1979).

An approach based on the modified Job Characteristics Model offered commendable specificity with respect
to job content variables and the causal relationships
of these with job attitudes and behaviour.   Its main
deficiency in practice was that it left out of account a
range of contextual variables of evident significance -
in particular those concerned with technology, supervisory roles, and managerial practices.   From the point
of view of the participants this restriction in scope
meant the model mapped neither convincingly nor compre-
hensively onto their own experience.   Problems are also

evident from a theoretical standpoint.   To implement
model-specified change requires manipulation of 'extraneous' factors, and any findings are thereby inter-
pretable in terms of these rather than the variable
included in the model itself.   This of course is not a
difficulty unique to this model.   Reports of theoreti-
cally-based change studies show how authors, or their
critics, so often have recourse to new variables to
explain their findings (e.g. Lawler et al., 1973;   Locke
et al., 1976).

        The sociotechnical systems approach, in contrast,
is capable of accommodating a broader range of variables
and causal relationships.   But this complexity is
achieved at a cost to specifity.   In spreading its net
so wide this approach leaves undefined the factors to be
included (or excluded) and the nature of the relationships amongst them.   Yet such specificity was necessary
in order to communicate effectively with those involved.
Specificity is also required for theoretical reasons.
Where an approach is too open-ended it leads to what
Cherns and Davis (1975, p. 50) have identified as an
existing impediment to the accumulation of systematic
knowledge in the area of job redesign, the 'incompara-
bility of case reports of innovation each written to
suit what the author believed was significant'.   That
systems theory approaches encourage such development is
recognised by Payne (1976, p. 218) who argues that 'fully
accepting a systems point of view means accepting that
every system is almost certainly unique'.

        In short, whilst both approaches have much to
offer, neither was sufficient in itself.   The modified
Job Characteristics Model proved too narrow to cope with
the problem area, and the socio-technical systems approach
was unable to provide sufficient structure.   The
difference between the two reflects that between the
nomothetic and idiographic orientations within psychology
as a whole.   What was required in this instance, and
seems desirable more generally (see den Hertog and Wester,
1979), was development in the middle-ground, of a model
providing breadth of coverage without sacrificing specificity with respect to the salient elements and the
relationships amongst them.   With the current state of
knowledge on work design the development of such a model
could not be achieved solely through deductive processes.
It required inductive reasoning, and a willingness to
conceptualise ahead of available data.

        What follows is the account of one attempt to
build a middle-range model to meet the needs of a long-
term action research project.   It is presented here for
two reasons.   First because it provides the framework for
describing the particular innovation to which it gives

structure and from which it draws support; and
secondly, because the model offers insights into the
direction in which theoretical work might usefully
develop.

BACKGROUND TO THE STUDY

Subjects and Setting

     Before describing the model, the context from
which it developed will be characterized. The focus of
the redesign exercise was on one department of a medium-
sized, partly-unionised, confectionery company in the
North of England. Thirty four individuals were
employed full-time in the department in non-supervisory
positions. Before the introduction of change the
management structure comprised a departmental manager,
two supervisors, and one working supervisor. The work
consisted of making and packing forty types of high
quality specialised sweets by batch process. This
required cooperation among some sixteen individuals
through whose hands the raw materials passed in their
various stages of development. Each person's performance intimately affected the ease with which the next
person contributed to the standard of the end-product
and to the performance of the group as a whole. In
Meissner's terms (1969) it was a situation of 'technically required cooperation'.

Presenting Symptoms

     From the point of view of the company the reason
for engaging in a collaborative exercise lay in enduring
problems in the department which six changes of manager
in the previous eight years and increases in the number
of supervisory positions had failed to resolve. Line
management and shop floor alike characterised the problem
in terms of 'poor work attitudes', 'low morale', 'low
work motivation' and 'work apathy'. The more objective
symptoms were very high labour turnover, and production
consistently falling below targets based on work study
standards.

Research Strategy

     In undertaking the study three decisions were made
concerning the approach to be adopted. The first was to
adopt as participative and open a style of investigation
as possible. To this end the study was undertaken
only once full agreement of all parties involved had been
achieved, and it was a requirement that any findings or

recommendations would be made freely available to all.
The research contract also specified that should any
changes be introduced, these would be designed by a project group involving representatives of all levels and
the change-agents.   (Greater detail of the strategy
adopted is provided by Clegg, 1979.)

The second decision concerned the period of study.
It was decided to heed Weis and Rein's (1970) plea to
take an historical perspective concentrating on the
unfolding of events over time. The study was therefore
initiated as an intensive exercise spanning years rather
than weeks, with the objective of seeing whether effects
produced as a result of change would survive the test of
time and, if so, what consequences they had for the
organisation as a whole.

The final decision on research strategy concerned
the methods and measures to deploy.   The decision was
made to use as wide a range of techniques as possible
for obtaining both quantitative and qualitative data.
The cornerstone of this, particularly during the diagnostic stage, was close observation of work supported
by regular interviews.   To this were added self-report
measures of perceived work characteristics and individual
attitudes, as well as the collection of performance data.

A TWO-PHASE MODEL

To identify precisely the various influences which
shape the model is a difficult task and one outside the
scope of this contribution.   As will become apparent,
however, the model is eclectic, owing much to the existing
empirical and theoretical literature.   The more immediate stimuli, however, came from the diagnostic phase
of the initial change exercise.   This consisted of
several months of observations and repeated unstructured
interviews, the latter being directed towards respondents' own attributions of causality.   It is from this
perspective, therefore, that the model will be described.

The model is depicted diagrammatically in Figure 1.
Its central feature is a recurring sequence of events
involving group performance, supervisory behaviour, work
characteristics and individual work motivation.   These
comprise Phase 1.   On a short-term basis the most significant events occurring in the department may be characterised as follows.   Departmental performance was the
overriding concern of management and supervision, being
recognised as the lowest in the organisation.   Improvement was sought by pushing hard for production.   Since
shop-floor employees were the only resources over which
supervisors had direct control, this was where their

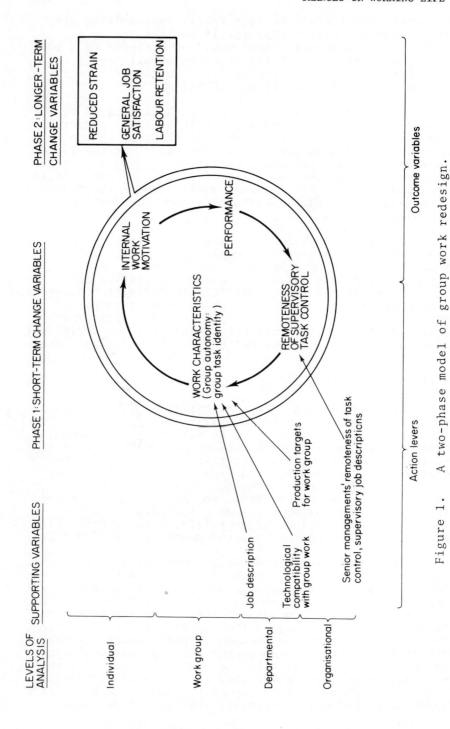

Figure 1.   A two-phase model of group work redesign.

attention focussed.   The supervisors, striving for
higher performance, adopted very close task control by
allocating key positions to those subordinates seen as
most able and co-operative, setting machine speeds,
organising breaks, starting and stopping times, and in
all other respects determining the minutiae of work.
On average supervisors spent eightyfive per cent of
their time on these tasks.   The lower the levels of
performance, the greater was the felt pressure for production, and the closer the supervisors' task control.
This action greatly restricted shop-floor employees'
opportunity for individually or collectively exercising discretion and self-regulation over their activities, which they openly resented.   In particular this
was shown in low levels of perceived autonomy and work
identity.   Feeling that their skills and knowledge
were neither catered for nor recognised, shop-floor
employees took a certain pride in finding ways to neut-
ralise the pressure.   They kept to the letter rather
than the spirit of supervisory instructions, expressing
little motivation to raise performance.   Turning full
circle this negatively affected their performance, and
so the cycle continued.

        The next feature of the model is a second phase
involving job satisfaction, strain, labour turnover and
performance.   The long-term persistence of the cycle
depicted in the first phase was seen by individuals as
the main cause of their low general job satisfaction,
feelings of strain, and the department's poor labour
retention record.   In effect they perceived the continuation of the pattern of events surrounding their day-
to-day activities as the main cause of their more general
orientation towards work.

        Three further factors served to cement the inter-
relationships among the variables described above, and
were perceived to be particularly important in the context of change (see Figure 1).   The first concerned the
pressure for production emanating from senior management.
Senior managers' own marked emphasis on task control
reinforced commensurate behaviour on the part of supervision.   For reasons of self-preservation supervisors
were unwilling to change in this respect on their own
initiative.   The second factor was relevant to group
autonomy.   The production and packing functions in the
department were physically separate, for technological
reasons.   In practice this limited the extent to which
people engaged in either function could identify with
the end-product and thus sensibly attempt to influence
the production planning requirements.   Information on
production targets was provided only for the department
as a whole and not for the two natural work groups.   This
meant that shop floor employees had little specific

guidance as to their progress relative to external
expectations.   This lack of information denied them the
opportunity to organise themselves effectively towards
required levels of production even if supervisory practices had allowed them so to do.

Thus taking individuals' attributions of causality
in conjunction with observations and analysis of behaviour
relating to existing work practices led inductively to
the two-phase model depicted in Figure 1.   This has two
characteristics distinguishing it from existing concep-
tualisations.   First it identifies a limited set of
variables involving abstraction of different levels of
analysis, from the individual, through work group and
department, to the organisational level.   Secondly, it
groups these according to phases with differing time bases
relating to their hypothesized causal impacts.   Concern
with the time bases of change is notably absent in existing approaches but central to both the practice and
evaluation of work redesign exercises.

FROM ANALYSIS TO CHANGE

The above model was found to be generally consistent with the diagnostic data obtained from observation,
interview, self-report measures and departmental records,
thus providing it with rudimentary support.   However, as
corroborative evidence this is manifestly insufficient,
since the model was in practice generated in the light of
known levels of the variables which it encompasses and
inferred causality amongst them.   More illuminating is
to show how the model was used in the context of introducing and accounting for the effects of group work
redesign.

Changes Introduced

The particular work characteristics perceived as
most deficient within the department were group autonomy
and task identity.   Being both within the first phase of
the model and directly manipulable these provided the
initial focus for change.   In order to increase substantially group autonomy a fundemntal shift in responsibilities from supervisory roles was implemented.   Two permanent leaderless teams were instituted, each being given
control over setting the pace of production, the distribution of tasks among team members, the organization of
breaks and changeovers, and the allocation of overtime.
To increase task identity as an aid to the exercise of
autonomy, the physical and symbolic barrier between production and packing was removed, both functions being
amalgamated within each team.   This involved no

improvements to nor rationalisations of the work process
which would of themselves reduce the time to complete
the task.

Supervisory job descriptions and roles were modified to reflect the changes described above.   Day-to-
day control over production was excluded from the descriptions and emphasis placed on liaison with support
services, the co-ordination of resources and forward
planning.   Because of exclusion of day-to-day control
over production the role of working supervisor was dis-
continued and full supervisory positions reduced from
two to one.   These changes were achieved without personal cost.   The working supervisor's role was not
attractive to its incumbent since it limited his overtime earnings and created interpersonal frictions.   One
supervisor resigned during the diagnostic phase of the
study in order to take up a position elsewhere in the
company and was not permanently replaced.   This resig-
nation was not attributable to the impending re-organisation.

These changes to the Phase 1 variables of the model
were supported by change to the salient variables in the
wider organisation.   The modification to technology has
already been described.   In addition, new production
targets were agreed, these being identical to those in
operation before the change except that they were converted pro rata to apply to teams separately.   This particular modification, however, was not finalized until
three months after the others.   Finally, senior management guaranteed support for the changes in supervisory
roles, suspending evaluation in terms of performance and
focusing instead on the achievement and maintenance of
high levels of group autonomy.

In short, immediate control over production was
transferred to work groups and management concentrated
on providing a service and on overseeing production.

MEASURING THE VARIABLES

In order to evaluate the effects of the group work
redesign, self-report measures taken during the diagnostic
phase of the study were readministered six and eighteen
months after the changes were introduced.   Performance
data was recorded throughout.   Observations and informal
interviews continued from the outset to eight months
after the change, at which point the investigators dis-
engaged.   These and the other events in the project are
set in their chronological sequence in Figure 2 which
also presents monthly performance figures in order to
avoid duplication of information more properly considered

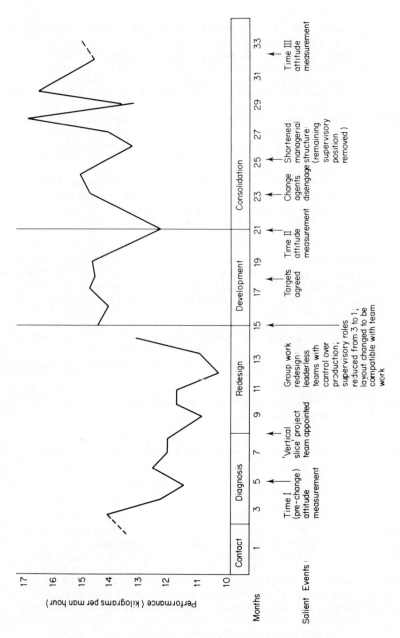

Figure 2.   A chronological account of salient events in
            the work redesign project and associated
            levels of performance.

in the Findings section.

The emphasis in the remainder of this paper will
be on the self-report, performance and labour retention
data since these provide the most readily quantifiable
and public records of the study.   It should be noted,
however, that the effects these reveal and interpretations placed upon them are entirely compatible with
the observational and interview data collected at more
regular intervals.

Measures Employed

Individual perceptions of group autonomy and group
task identity were measured using a modified version of
the Job Diagnostic Survey (Hackman and Oldham, 1975).
The modification involved translating the individual
items to the group level (see Hackman, 1977).   An item
in the autonomy scale, for example, originally read 'How
much autonomy is there in your job?   That is, to what
extent does your job permit you to decide on your own how
to go about doing the work?'.   In its revised version
it read 'How much autonomy is there in the job done by
your work group?   That is, to what extent do you decide
among yourselves how to go about doing the work?'   The
scales thus obtained showed acceptable levels of internal
reliability at each of the three measurement occasions,
closely mirroring those reported elsewhere for the original versions.

Measures of internal work motivation and general job
satisfaction were taken directly from the full version of
the Job Diagnostic Survey.   Strain was measured using
the 20 item version of General Health Questionnaire (Goldberg, 1972).   Based upon an axis running from severe
(non-psychotic) disturbance to hypothetical normality,
this scale has been well validated against clinical
assessments.

Performance was recorded on a weekly basis for the
duration of the study.   To control for variations in the
number of employees and overtime worked it was defined
as total output divided by the number of hours worked.
Labour retention was indexed, at each of the three
measurement occasions, as the percentage of employees
having more than 1 year of service in the department.
This threshold was adopted since in practice it took on
average 12 months to acquire the skills necessary to play
a full part in the production process.

The level of control exercised by supervisors was
monitored by observation.   Estimates were made of the
amount of time each spent on the shop floor managing the

production process.

FINDINGS

        The main prediction from the model concerns dif-
ferential change rates associated with Phase 1 and Phase
2 variables.   The variables which comprise Phase 1 may,
in this instance, be classified as of two types.   The
'independent variables', namely group work characteristics (autonomy and task identity) and remoteness of
supervisory task control.   The 'dependent variables'
become internal work motivation and performance.
Observable increase in the independent variables are required to signify the success of the changes introduced
and increases in the dependent variables to support the
model's causal structure.   In each case the increase
should be evident in the short-term, and the new levels
maintained in the longer-term.   Phase 2 variables, however, are predicted to exhibit slower change, with change
being revealed mainly in the longer-term.

        Statistical analyses relating to these predictions
are presented in Table 1.   Considering first the Phase 1
variables subject to deliberate change it is clear that
intended effects were achieved.   Respondents' perceptions of group autonomy and task identity show substantial
and statistically significant increases in the short term.
(Lack of change in other measured work characteristics
which were not subject to deliberate change, namely
variety, feedback and task significance, support the
validity of these findings.   These are not reported in
detail for the sake of clarity - for further details see
Wall and Clegg, 1979.)   The concomitant decrease in
supervisory task control follows inevitably from changes
in the supervisory structure described earlier.   Observational records however provide some quantification of
this, showing that the time spent on the shop-floor by
supervisory personnel declined from over 100 to less than
fifteen hours per week.   Equivalent increases are evident with respect to recorded levels in the dependent
variables of internal work motivation and performance.
For all the measured variables the data reveal a monotonic
increase in scores over time (shown by the linear trend
component) though the greatest change occurred in the
short-term (between measurement times 1 and 2).   For
the self-report and performance measures this differential
change rate is illustrated by the statistically significant F-ratios associated with the quadratic trend analyses.   The one exception in this respect relates to
internal work motivation, which nevertheless exhibits the
same general pattern of change.   (In all cases t-tests
showed statistically significant differences (p < .01)
between mean scores at times 1 and 2 (and between times 1

and 3), but not between times 2 and 3).

The next set of predictions from the model concerns
Phase 2 variables of general job satisfaction, perceived
strain and labour retention.   In the light of the Phase
1 changes, these should show increases which are most
marked in the longer term.   As Table 2 shows, such is
the case, with data from the general job satisfaction and
perceived strain measures showing exclusively linear
trends and the labour retention index exhibiting similar
characteristics.   Since equivalent improvement in labour
retention was absent elsewhere in the organisation it is
plausible to attribute this change to the work redesign
itself rather than to factors in the organisation more
generally, or to effects in the local labour market.

Qualitative Data

Other events directly attributable to the work
redesign occurred before the end of the investigation and
deserve mention.   Once the new system had settled down
it became clear that there was insufficient work to
occupy the time of both supervisor and manager.   These
roles were therefore amalgamated, and the new position
acquired by the previous supervisor.   The manager,
though transferred to a post of equivalent status, nevertheless perceived himself to be a victim of the change.
However, shop floor interest in the work broadened considerably.   Whereas before the change individuals'
attention was focused on interpersonal and immediately
work-related problems, afterwards their interest was
directed towards obtaining improvements in the service
departments, and in particular towards encouraging marketing to make greater efforts to promote their products.
This latter change was not unrelated to the fact that the
increase in production which now consistently met targets
meant that any decrement in market demand might affect
the amount of work available.

Perhaps the most fundamental development, however,
was seen in senior management.   Plans are currently
underway to re-organise existing staff into a flatter
management structure which contains no purely supervisory
positions.   Part of the definition for the new managerial roles is to promote group autonomy and group task
identity.   The model offered here is in fact being used
as the basis for introducing and evaluating the change.
In other words, the success of the exercise has fed back
into the policy-making activities of the organisation.

Table 1.   Findings Relating to Primary Cycle Variables

Measures	Time 1 Pre-change Scores	Time 2 Post-change Scores (short-term)
Group Autonomy	$\bar{X}$ = 3.29, SD = 1,38, n = 34	$\bar{X}$ = 4.35, SD = 1.43, n = 33
Group work identity	$\bar{X}$ = 4.66, SD = 1.49, n = 34	$\bar{X}$ = 5.78, SD = 1.26, n = 33
Internal work motivation	$\bar{X}$ = 4.78, SD = 0.85, n = 34	$\bar{X}$ = 5.18, SD = 0.71, n = 33
Performance (kilograms per man hours)	$\bar{X}$ = 11.76, SD = 2.00, n = 48 (weeks)	$\bar{X}$ = 14.06, SD = 1.61, n = 24 (weeks)
Supervisory task control[3]	3 persons, 85% of time on task 102 hours per week	1 person, 35 % of time on task control - 14 hours per week

Notes: 1. For Group Autonomy, Group Work Identity and
           time were tested by one-way analysis of
           (Winer, 1971; Genstat, 1977).   For perfor-
           groups was used.

        2. Numbers and degrees of freedom vary slightly
           administration, missing responses, and labour
           is solely due to weather induced absence and
           2 had twenty seven subjects in common, times
           common.

        3. See pages   and   of text for description

as Measured at Three Points in Time.

Time 3 Post-change Scores (longer-term)	Statistical Analysis of Difference[1]				
$\bar{X}$ = 4.38, SD = 1.70, n = 292	Overall F = 14.82; df, 2,50; p < .01 F linear = 27.77; df, 2,50; p < .01 F quadratic = 4.87; df, 2,50; p < .05				
$\bar{X}$ = 5.85, SD = 0.91, n = 29	Overall F = 11.74; df, 2,49; p < .01 F linear = 15.54; df, 1,49; p < .01 F quadratic = 7.95; df, 1,49; p < .01				
$\bar{X}$ = 5.28, SD = 0.83, n = 29	Overall F = 7.24; df, 2,51; p < .01 F linear = 13.98; df, 1,51; p < .01 F quadratic = 0.50; df, 1,51; ns				
$\bar{X}$ = 14.33, SD = 2.09, n = 48 (weeks)	Overall F = 23.53; df, 2,117;p < .01 F linear = 35.41; df, 1.117;p < .01 F quadratic = 11.65; df, 1,117;p < .01				

1 then 0 person,
20% of time on
task control -
8 hours per
week

Internal Work Motivation differences in scores across
variance for repeated measures with missing values
mance a one-way analysis of variance for independent

because of absence at the time of questionnaire
turnover.   The smaller number of respondents at time 3
not in reduction in establishment levels.   Times 1 and
2 and 3 twenty six and time 1 and 3 twenty subjects in

of changes in supervisory task control.

Table 2.   Findings Relating to Secondary Cycle Variables

Measures	Time 1 Pre-change Scores	Time 2 Post-change Scores (short-term)	Time 3 Post-change Scores (longer-term)
General Job Satisfaction	$\bar{X} = 4.34$, SD = 1.25, n = 34	$\bar{X} = 4.68$, SD = 1.09 n = 33	$\bar{X} = 4.99$, SD = 1.04 n = 29[2]
Strain	$\bar{X} = 3.09$, SD = 4.28 n = 34	$\bar{X} = 1.67$, SD = 2.91, n = 33	$\bar{X} = 0.50$, SD = 1.51, n = 29
Labour Retention[3]	65%	85%	97%

Notes: 1. For General Job Satisfaction and Strain,
            way analysis of variance for repeated measures

         2. See Table 1 note 2.

         3. Chi-squared is calculated on the null-
            recruits at each time period.   The figure for
            the one year time perspective used to define
            between the introduction of work redesign and
            In practice, of the 5 new recruits, two were
            introduced and three in the six months
            measurement.

as Measured at Three Points in Time.

Statistical Analysis of Differences[1]

Overall F   =   5.52;   df, 2,51;   p < .01
F linear   = 10.92;   df, 1,41;   p < .01
F quadratic = 0.14;   df, 1,51;   ns

Overall F   = 10.91;   df, 2,49;   p < .01
F linear   = 21.71;   df, 1,49;   p < .01
F quadratic = 0.10;   df, 1,49;   ns

x^2 = 10.33;   df, 2,   p < .01

differences across time were tested by one-
with missing values (see Table 1 note 1).

hypothesis of equal numbers of recent
Time 2 must be regarded as approximate since
new recruits extends beyond the period
the (short term) post-change measurement.
employed in the 6 months before the change was
between the redesign and the Time 2

Some Loose Ends

In studies such as this an issue which should be raised concerns the extent to which findings might be attributable to extraneous factors.   Three such variables are particularly salient in the present investigation, being wages, targets and the presence of change-agents. With respect to wages, the changes implemented resulted in slightly less than half the shop floor employees receiving pay increases of between 6 and 10 per cent. Sub-analysis revealed no reliable differences between these subjects and those not receiving pay increases with respect to any of the individually measured variables. It seems unlikely, therefore, that change in pay is an important determinant of the findings obtained - though it was an outcome of the change itself.   Similarly, no evidence could be found to suggest a significant causal impact due solely to the introduction of targets and the withdrawal of the investigators.   As Figure 2 shows the performance increases obtained occurred directly after the implementation of group work, and were not noticeably affected by either the subsequent introduction of targets or at the disengagement of the change-agents.   This interpretation is also consistent with the self-report attitudinal data, observation and repeated interviews.

THE TWO-PHASE MODEL IN PERSPECTIVE

The model offered here is consistent with the evidence obtained in this particular study.   It is also acceptable from the point of view of the actors whose reactions and behaviour it seeks to explain.   This is not to say, however, that the model is the only or necessarily the best framework for interpreting the findings. Moreover, had the investigation been initiated with this model in mind, even with the constraints necessarily encountered in field work, a more adequate research design would have been achieved.   In particular more frequent measurements would offer a stronger basis for examining differential change rates among the variables. All that may reasonably be claimed is that the model was fruitful as a heuristic device to guide change and interpret its effects in a particular instance, and that its predictions were borne out.

At a general level the model has many of the features associated with a systems approach, and spans 'data at different levels of abstraction - individual, group and organisation' (Kahn et al., 1964, p. 137) which many hold to be important if knowledge is to be advanced (Pugh, 1966).   Its Phase 1 structure has the characteristics of 'dynamic homeostasis' (Katz and Kahn, 1978) and matches in nature the operation of a 'regressive spiral' as observed

in other work contexts (e.g. Legge, 1970).   The model is
also consistent with the greater proportion of relevant
cross-sectional and descriptive research.   Positive
associations have long been observed between task characteristics measured at an individual or group level and
work motivation, performance, job satisfaction and strain
(e.g. Fraser, 1947; Hackman and Lawler, 1971; Hackman
and Oldham, 1976; Kornhauser, 1965; Rice, 1958; Trist
et al., 1963).   Similarly, task control has featured as
a major element of leadership style related empirically
and theoretically to motivation, performance and job
satisfaction (e.g. Likert, 1961; McGregor, 1960; Stogdill, 1974).

        More specifically, however, theoretical and empi-
rical work provides support for several of the model's
more detailed causal propositions.   Thus performance has
been identified as a cause of supervisory style (e.g.
Crowe et al., 1972; Farris and Lim, 1969; Greene,
1975; Lowin and Craig, 1968; Mitchell et al., 1977),
and similarly as a partial determinant rather than an
effect of job satisfaction (e.g. Greene, 1973; Porter et
al., 1975).   Moreover, the fact that field studies of
job redesign have more reliably revealed improvements in
performance than in job satisfaction (Cummings and Molloy,
1977), coupled with the fact that the majority of investigations have only used a short-term basis for evaluation, is compatible with the model's predictions concerning the differential change rates of these two variables.   If change in performance is more rapid than that
in job satisfaction, then short term studies are biased
in favour of recording the former effects.

        These observations are made to illustrate the
potential relevance of the two-phase model in a wider
context from that which it emerged, though it should be
reiterated that at this stage the model is necessarily
highly speculative and requires development in close
association with empirical work.   Perhaps the most
important message from this exposition, however, is that
theoretical work concerned with the psychological bases
of job redesign should begin to take explicit account of
a wider range of variables and causal relationships than
it has traditionally encompassed.   It needs also to
offer guidance on the time-span underlying change.   Without such development and the focus on longitudinal investigations which this implies, theory and practice will
continue to be pursued along largely independent paths to
the detriment of both.

REFERENCES

Cherns, A.B. and Davis, L.E. (1975).   'Assessment of
    the state of the art', in The Quality of Working
    Life, Volume One (Eds. L.E. Davis and A.B. Cherns),
    pp. 12-54, Free Press, New York.

Clegg, C.W. (1979).   'The process of job redesign:
    signposts from a theoretical orphanage?', Human
    Relations (in press).

Crowe, B.J., Bochner, S. and Clarke, A.W. (1972).   'The
    effects of subordinates' behaviour on managerial
    style', Human Relations, 25, 215-237.

Cummings, T.G. and Molloy, E.S. (1977).   Improving Pro-
    ductivity and the Quality of Working Life, Praeger,
    New York.

Davis, L.E. (1957).   'Towards a theory of job design',
    Industrial Engineering, 8, 305-309.

Emery, F.E. (1959).   Characteristics of Socio-Technical
    Systems, Tavistock Institute of Human Relations
    (Document 527), London.

Farris, G.F. and Lim, F.G. (1969).   'Effects of perfor-
    mance on leadership, cohesiveness, influence,
    satisfaction and subsequent performance', Journal
    of Applied Psychology, 53, 490-497.

Fraser, R. (1947).   The Incidence of Neurosis Among
    Factory Workers, Report No. 90, Industrial Health
    Research Board, H.M.S.O., London.

Genstat, (1977).   A General Statistical Program, The
    Statistics Department, Rothamstead Experimental
    Station.

Goldberg, D.P. (1972).   The Detection of Psychiatric
    Illness by Questionnaire, Oxford University Press,
    Oxford.

Greene, C.N. (1973).   'Causal connections among managers'
    merit pay, job satisfaction, and performance',
    Journal of Applied Psychology, 58, 95-100.

Greene, C.N. (1975).   'The reciprocal nature of influence
    between leader and subordinate', Journal of Applied
    Psychology, 60, 187-193.

Hackman, J.R. (1977).   'Work design', in Improving Life
    at Work (Eds. J.R. Hackman and J.L. Suttle), pp. 96-
    162, Goodyear, Santa Monica.

Hackman, J.R. and Lawler, E.E. (1971). 'Employee reactions to job characteristics', Journal of Applied
Psychology, 55, 259-286.

Hackman, J.R. and Oldham, G.R. (1975). 'Development of
the Job Diagnostic Survey', Journal of Applied
Psychology, 60, 159-170.

Hackman, J.R. and Oldham, G.R. (1976). 'Motivation
through the design of work: test of a theory',
Organizational Behavior and Human Performance, 15,
250-279.

Hertog, J.F. den and Wester, Ph., (1979). 'Organizational renewal in engineering works: a comparative analysis', in The Quality of Working Life in
Western and Eastern Europe (Eds. C.L. Cooper and
E. Mumford), Associated Business Press, London.

Kahn, R.L., Wolfe, D., Quinn, R., Snoek, J.D. and
Rosenthal, R.A. (1964). Organizational Stress,
Wiley, New York.

Katz, D. and Kahn, R.L. (1978). The Social Psychology
of Organizations, Wiley, New York (2nd edition).

Kelly, J.E. (1979). 'A reappraisal of socio-technical
systems theory', Human Relations, (in press).

Kornhauser, A.W. (1965). Mental Health of the Industrial
Worker, Wiley, New York.

Lawler, E.E., Hackman, J.R. and Kaufman, S. (1973).
'Effects of job redesign: a field experiment',
Journal of Applied Social Psychology, 3, 49-62.

Legge, K. (1970). 'The operation of the "regressive
spiral" in the labour market', Journal of Management
Studies, 7, 1-22.

Likert, R. (1961). New Patterns of Management, McGraw-
Hill, New York.

Locke, E.A., Sirota, D. and Wolfson, A.D. (1976). 'An
experimental case study of the successes and failures
of job enrichment in a government agency', Journal
of Applied Psychology, 61, 701-711.

Lowin, A. and Craig, J.R. (1968). 'The influence of
levels of performance on managerial style', Organizational Behavior and Human Performance, 3, 440-
458.

McGregor, D. (1960).   The Human Side of Enterprise,
    McGraw-Hill, New York.

Meissner, M. (1969).   Technology and the Worker,
    Chandler, San Francisco.

Mitchell, T.R., Larson, J.R. and Green, S.G. (1977).
    'Leader behavior, situational moderators and
    group performance: and attributional analysis',
    Organizational Behavior and Human Performance, 18,
    254-268.

Payne, R.L. (1976).   'Truisms in organisational be-
    haviour', Interpersonal Development, 6, 203-220.

Porter, L.W., Lawler, E.E. and Hackman, J.R. (1975).
    Behavior in Organizations, McGraw-Hill, New York.

Pugh, D. (1966).   'Modern organizational theory: a
    psychological and sociological study', Psycholo-
    gical Bulletin, 66, 235-251.

Rice, A.K. (1958).   Productivity and Social Organi-
    sation, Tavistock, London.

Stogdill, R.M. (1974).   The Handbook of Leadership: A
    Survey of Theory and Research, Free Press, New York.

Trist, E.L., Higgins, G., Murray, H. and Pollock, A.B.
    (1963).   Organisational Choice, Tavistock, London.

Weis, R.E. and Rein, M. (1970).   'The evaluation of
    broad-aim program: experimental design, its dif-
    ficulties and an alternative?', Administrative
    Science Quarterly, 15, 97-109.

Winer, B.J. (1971).   Statistical Principles in Experi-
    mental Design, McGraw-Hill, New York (2nd edition).

Wall, T.D. and Clegg, C.W. (1979).   'Group work
    redesign: A case study' (in preparation).

Comments on Section III

D. E. GUEST

The theme for the third day of the conference was the quality of working life in the last 20 years of this century. With its focus on rather more speculative and general· issues, this theme represents something of a dividing point, contrasting as it does with the earlier, rather more specific issues.

Despite the focus on the future, there was a marked reluctance to make forecasts. In the two more general overviews, Davis focused on emerging trends, while Cherns outlined what he considered to be the salient developments which would influence work organisations and more particularly, their choice of technology and job design. Both argued, from rather different perspectives, that concern for the quality of working life was likely to increase in the next decade. The central theme in Davis' argument, which was limited to the context of the USA, was that economic and legal pressures would make the quality of working life an issue for the boardroom. He felt that these pressures arose from the growing tendency to shift the blame from the individual to the organisation for such things as failure to meet expectations or even for stress-related illnesses; and from the high costs of technological investment, which to obtain an adequate return, required highly motivated workers exercising considerable discretion. A key requirement for organisational survival, and, for Davis, the major contribution that behavioural scientists can

351

make, is the ability to design flexible, non-bureacratic
organizations.

Cherns argued that micro-processors provided more
choice and that the choices were increasingly political.
In particular, the continuing sharp division between work
and non-work was so strongly embedded that the issue of
employment became all important. Taking this a step
further, he used the findings of a report to the Dutch
government to illustrate the crucial role of the jobs, in
determining the well-being of the job holder and his
dependents. The job, therefore, provides the major
point of leverage: improve the job and you improve all
aspects of quality of life. Given the centrality and
influence of the job, choices of direction in future
would be influenced by government desire, first to maintain employment then secondly and increasingly, to
improve the quality of working life by improving the job.

The importance and centrality of job content to
quality of working life was reflected in several of the
other papers. Rather than speculating on the future,
their aim was to demonstrate the lessons to be learned for
the future from current examples of good practice. The
results generally make depressing reading for those who
believe the behavioural scientist can be an effective
change agent.

The papers by Lupton and Tanner, van Assen and
Wester and Blackler and Brown, all had one theme in common; namely that changes which appear to improve the
quality of working life are seldom carried out with this
as the primary aim. Each draws rather different implications for the future.

Tanner, presenting his joint paper, showed convincingly that, even in the best known European quality of
working life programmes, the changes were carried out
mainly by engineers in response to market demands for
product change or modification. Behavioural scientists
usually had no role in initiating changes. The quality
of working life label attached to the studies was therefore largely fortuitous; the logic of the situation led
the engineers to design systems which resulted in
various forms of job enrichment or autonomous work group.
Although many of the engineers were aware of human factors in the design of systems, they generally viewed
them in an instrumental way. Given the dominating role
of the engineer and of managerial concerns for production
and marketing, Tanner suggested that quality of working
life changes were only likely to occur when these over-
lapped with the managerial concern for efficiency.
Whether this overlap could be created through pressure from
unions, government or even personnel managers was not

discussed.   Instead, more emphasis was placed on
influencing the engineer by providing him with guidelines for 'good' design.   In this sense, the approach
would appear to represent a contingency model based on
socio-technical criteria.

Blackler and Brown provided an enlightening and
more detailed case to substantiate many of Tanner's
points.   They were able to show that in one of the
acclaimed and well-publicised Volvo studies, the job
content of all but one type of worker (the team leader)
was not significantly different from that of their
counterparts in a conventional British Leyland plant.
At another Volvo plant, there was convincing evidence
that changes had led to significant improvements in job
content.   However, the changes were again initiated
by engineers on the rationale that, given a fully motivated workforce, static assembly had major advantages
over a moving assembly line.   A more recent follow-up
revealed how fragile such changes can be.   Movement of
key personnel, a hardening of trade union attitudes and
the deep suspicion among most engineers and managers of
the discretion given to workers, and particularly the
discretion to finish work early if the daily quota was
achieved, had resulted in retrenchment and a new plant
had been built along more conventional lines.   For
Blackler and Brown, the lesson of this type of experience
is that even in the most favourable contexts, management views quality of working life as instrumental and
is deeply suspicious of the workforce.   To be effective
therefore, behavioural scientists must become more
political and more sensitive to power mechanisms at the
plant, company and national level.   In Sweden there is
already a legislative context for such a role, yet the
attitude of trade unions, currently lukewarm towards job
redesign, appears to be crucial.

Wester, presenting his joint paper with van Assen,
described developments in Philips where, despite extensive publicity, quality of working life activity has been
very limited.   The major reason offered for this was
that it was too isolated from the policy and major objectives of the organisation.   It had not proved possible
to launch it fully as an end in itself, particularly from
an isolated position in the personnel department.   Therefore, reinforcing the findings of Lupton and Tanner, where
changes in job design had occurred, such changes had been
incidental and of secondary importance.   The aim for
the future should be to play down quality of working life
as a goal and to integrate it into economic, marketing
and production activity.   On this basis they argued,
again echoing Lupton and Tanner, situations should be
sought where the goals of efficiency and improved quality
of working life overlap.   Wester and van Assen believe

that this is most likely where greater flexibility of production is a major goal.   They identified six cases within Philips and concluded that production and quality of working life goals are best met through delegation to small autonomous work groups.

Wall, adopting a rather different perspective, but again using a contemporary case as the basis for his argument, suggested that if progress is to be made in redesigning jobs and understanding the effects of such changes, we need to use different models to those which currently dominate organisational psychology.   As explanatory models, they do not work and in communi- cating the change process to participants, they do not make sense.   In their place, he presents an alternative which, he claims, made sense to those in the organi- sation for which it was developed.   The implication of developing a model which can be used by members of an organisation is that the way ahead lies in a partici- pative approach to change;   the role of the behavioural scientist then becomes more that of a process consultant, presenting alternative models and approaches and helping to create opportunities for change.

The other papers in this section do not fit easily into the theme of the quality of working life in the next 20 years.   Mansfield presents some correlational studies highlighting the complexity of factors associated with organisational climate.   The most interesting conclusion is that, more particularly for smaller organisations, decentralisation may not have a positive impact on climate. More provocatively, Porter argues that in future, managers would become less attached or committed to organisations.   In emphasising this issue, he seemed to be reflecting a theme which Davis also highlighted, namely the 'emerging crisis' in the USA in the relationship between the individual and his employing organisation. The difficulty with Porter's argument lies in the choice of premises;   the challenge lies in selecting alternatives which support the counter argument.   In a European con- text, rather than the explicitly North American situation to which Porter referred, this could begin with an ana- lysis of trends in employee participation, unemployment and, following Cherns, the continuing centrality of work. However, one of the possible implications of a reduced attachment to organisational goals, if this can be equated with organisational attachment and Porter admitted that he was rather unclear about this distinction, is that managers may become more willing to take risks and to initiate changes to improve quality of working life. Presumably, much will depend on the alternative attach- ments and values of these managers.

ISSUES EMERGING IN DISCUSSION

At least three important underlying issues emerged. The first, which should come as no surprise, is the dominance of managerial concerns for marketing and production. Where improvements in quality of working life have been reported, they have seldom been an end in themselves; if they do become the main goal, then their chances of successful implementation are considerably diminished. In short, management cannot be relied on to promote improvements in quality of working life except as a contributory element to, or incidental factor in greater efficiency.

Hidden in the concern for managerial goals is the second issue, the question of values. However, the varying degrees of concern about the extent to which productivity, efficiency and increased effort were major goals of quality of working life programmes, become clearer. At first, it appeared that there may have been a cultural divide between North America and Europe, but later contributions showed this view to be too simplistic. It might be more accurate to distinguish those primarily interested in organisational goals from those whose main concern was the well-being of the worker. This second perspective should have raised questions of power, of the economic environment, of unemployment and of the inequality and lack of participation which allows managerial goals to dominate. Sadly, these issues, which are as central to the quality of working life as job redesign, were largely absent from the discussion.

Of course, it would be naive to deny the importance and legitimacy of managerial goals; but questions must be raised about programmes masquerading under the banner of quality of working life, whose major aim, and only reason for management support, is improved efficiency. It is this sort of programme which justifies union and worker scepticism of both job design as a means of improving quality of working life and of those behavioural scientists who implement it. There is obviously a legitimate role for the behavioural scientist who clearly and explicitly states his values and aligns himself with management; a problem arises, however if he claims to be acting in the interests of the employees, when they themselves are doubtful of the benefits of what he proposes. The critical question then becomes one of where to draw the line - should he, for example, advocate improvements in the quality of life of some at the expense of unemployment for others? It is when there is potential conflict of interest, rather than congruence that the question of values becomes critical. As an issue, it was too easily glossed over by several of the speakers. Clearly, it is also linked to the process of change and so the question of who participates in the crucial decisions; yet despite some probing questions from participants at the conference, this also received too little attention, except from Toby Wall.

The third issue, which also emerges elsewhere, is the role of the behavioural scientist. Certainly, there was concern about his lack of success in promoting and implementing improvements in quality of working life. In this applied field, the roles of researcher, analyst, commentator and change agent frequently overlap. The problem lies partly in the question of who is the client (although Davis emphasized the distinction between the financial sponsor and interested parties). All too often, the behavioural scientist is working for management in areas like selection, training, ergonomics or the design of payment systems and organisational structures. He should not be surprised at the lack of allies when he attempts to improve the quality of working life through changes in job content. The problem is increased by the fact that workers often appear to be satisficers, who show a high degree of tolerance for, and fatalism towards their jobs; only occasionally are they roused out of this, often by some kind of crisis. The unions show mixed motives and priorities; therefore in Sweden the concern for inflation compensation, unemployment and participation in policy development have pushed shop-floor changes in job design down the priority list.

All this raises difficult questions for the behavioural scientist committed to improvements in quality of working life. In particular, he has to ask on whose behalf he is working. If managers are selectively interested when it suits their own objectives, workers are relatively apathetic and quite prepared to tolerate the status quo and unions have other priorities, a heavy responsibility rests on the behaviour scientist's professional expertise. He advocates improved quality of working life, on behalf of the worker, because he 'knows', despite the lack of enthusiasm from the workers, that it will result in improvements. To adopt this viewpoint, requires considerable confidence - a confidence which the state of development of organisational behavioural sciences does little to justify.

From the various arguments put forward it is possible to begin to draw out the various roles for the behavioural scientist seeking to improve the quality of working life through changes in organisation and more particularly job design. These roles, which are not mutually exclusive, can be outlined as follows:

(1) Management Consultant

The aim here is aid in the achievement of managerial goals, while at the same time, looking for opportunities to improve job content. This is the approach which seemed to be advocated by van Assen and Wester and in practice, it might mean that the behavioural scientist becomes part of a multi-disciplinary team. Its major problems are the very secondary role of quality of working life, the limited contexts in which action might be possible, and the focus on what is feasible at the expense of situations where improvement is most needed.

(2) Educator

The primary aim of this approach is to communicate to managers, trades unions and workers, the potential benefit and feasibility of introducing improvements in quality of working life. A typical approach would involve extensive use of case studies which serve as demonstration examples of alternative design possibilities. This would appear to be central part of the strategy advocated by Davis and adopted by Davis, Cherns and others in the programmes offered mainly to managers at the Center for Quality of Working Life at UCLA. Such an approach is implicitly normative and can become more explicitly so, as in the general and company based seminars utilised by Thorsrud which constitute a form of consciousness raising. The problem here is the nature of the normative values which lie at the basis of this activity.

(3) The Academic

This role, adopted most explicitly during the day by Porter, involved research as well as description, analysis and evaluation of specific contexts or more general trends. Whether the result is positive or negative, welcome or unwelcome, is left for others to decide. While there are attractions in this apparently dispassionate scientific position, it obscures the values involved in identification of issues for study and analysis and evades the question of the way in which the information may be used or abused.

(4) The Political Action-Researcher

This approach, which appeared to be advocated, from slightly different perspectives, by Cherns and by Blackler and Brown, starts from a recognition of the importance of power and of differences of interest and therefore urges

the need to understand the political processes and form
political alliances if the behavioural sciences are to
have any influence in improving the quality of working
life.   Such a role will inevitably be somewhat opportu-
nist and rests upon the identification of reasonably clear
goals.   In practice, exertion of influence may become an
end in itself, more particularly since the behavioural
sciences appear to have exerted little or no influence on
changes to date.   The associated problem, raised earlier,
is the question of for whom the behavioural scientist is
acting.

(5) The Technical Guide

Davis, Lisl Klein and others, have for some time
been arguing that the behavioural scientist should recognise the key role of the design and production engineers
and try to influence them.   Lupton and Tanner embraced
this view, and it is also strongly advocated by Corlett.
Tanner cited guidebooks for engineers developed by Renault
and Bosch and it was clear that the research by Lupton
and Tanner was leading towards another.   The difficulty
of this approach, as with any contingency approach, is its
tendency to assume that there is only one optimal solution;   furthermore, it implies a mechanistic model of
the worker and a state of knowledge about worker motivation and individual differences which is very hard to
justify.   However, the very fact that it is a rather
mechanistic approach may represent an attraction to the
engineer and, coupled with the need to influence the
values embraced during the training and development of
engineers, may provide one way of making progress.

(6) The Process Action-Researcher

Wall adopts this approach in advocating that the
role of the behavioural scientist should be to present
alternatives and ensure participation of all interested
parties in planning change.   This is a popular role
which provides the change agent with the opportunity to
act as researcher by monitoring and checking events as
they occur.   However, the insistence of a participative
change strategy must inevitably limit the amount of
change that takes place, and it will take considerable
skill on the part of the process consultant concerned
with shop-floor change to handle the political issues.
The changes may therefore be relatively marginal in
importance.   However, if he or she can learn to work
effectively within the political situation, then this
would appear to be a sensible strategy to adopt.

This attempt to list the various role advocated for

the behavioural scientist seeking to improve the quality
of working life in the future, highlights the diversity
of perspectives and possibilities that emerged.   In
practice, of course, some of the roles outlined above
can be combined and the difference between them will
often be one of emphasis or values, or will be determined by whether the individual is based in an industrial organisation, a consultancy or an academic institution.   However, in extrapolating from current practice and current trends, it is important that the mistakes should not be ignored.   In particular, the possibility that behavioural scientists, sometimes know-
ingly, sometimes unwillingly have been used to market a
false managerial concern for quality of working life
must be confronted.   Change agents may have become too
committed to the changes with which they are associated
to carry out a dispassionate analysis.   Those adopting
the academic role, and psychologists in particular,
have often adopted too narrow a frame of reference and
too short a time perspective.   Davis and a number of
others emphasised the point that the academic rewards
associated with swift publication run counter to effective longitudinal case study research.

The papers in this volume, and in this section in
particular, should finally destroy any of the lingering
optimism of the early 1970s about the prospects of the
behavioural sciences bringing about a dramatic improvement in the quality of working life.   Yet, as Sylvia
Shimmin observed in her opening address, citing a recent
Swedish study, behavioural scientists remain more optimistic about the future of work than most other interest
groups.   This is either more foolish optimism or advance
notice of a better quality, more influential applied
behavioural science.   Given the relative conservatism of
workers, this suggests that to bring about marked improvements in the quality of working life, behavioural scientists will have to become the irritants, the subversives,
indeed the revolutionaries who seek to change both the
goals and priorities of organisations and the means by
which these goals are established and attained.   It is a
role which, by and large, they are unwilling and unable to
accept.

SECTION IV:
Job Satisfaction and Motivation

Changes in Working Life
Edited by K.D. Duncan, M.M. Gruneberg, and D. Wallis
© 1980 John Wiley & Sons Ltd

Chapter 20

The Relative Effectiveness of Four Methods of Motivating Employee Performance

E. A. LOCKE, D. B. FEREN, V. M. McCALEB, K. N. SHAW
and A. T. DENNY

INTRODUCTION

In the history of industrial-organizational psychology only four methods of motivating employee performance have received systematic attention by researchers. These are: Money, goal setting, participation and job enrichment. A more recent technique, behavior modification, has been widely touted but in practice involves little more than a relabeling of one or more of the above techniques, especially money and goal setting (Locke, 1977).

The use of money as a motivator probably traces back to the origins of money itself. In the field of industrial-organizational psychology, however, its most systematic use was by Frederick Winslow Taylor (1911/1967), the founder of Scientific Management, who believed that money was what the worker wanted most from the job. Taylor was a pioneer in the development of scientifically designed incentive plans. Since Taylor, the importance and efficacy of money has been consistently downgraded by most social scientists, including the Hawthorne researchers (Roethlisberger and Dickson, 1939/1956; for criticisms of their attack on money as a motivator, see Carey, 1967, and Sykes, 1965), industrial sociologists (Whyte, 1955), and advocates of human relations (Likert, 1961, 1967) and of job enrichment (Herzberg, 1966). Its major defenders today are Lawler (1971) and Mitchell Fein

(1976a, b, c;   1977), an industrial engineer.

⁎Historical credit for the popularity of goal setting
must also go, at least in part, to Taylor, whose concept
of the task, an assigned amount of work to be done by
the workman each day based on time and motion study, was
a key technique of Scientific Management. Taylor's
system was designed for repetitive manual work, but the
task concept was found to be applicable to managerial
work as well.   Originally developed (by extending
Taylor's ideas) at General Motors in the 1920s, the
idea of targets and performance standards for managers
and executives came to be called Management by Objectives
by Alfred P. Sloan and Peter Drucker (for an excellent
review of the history of MBO, see Odiorne, 1978).   Currently, goal setting is seen as an effective motivational
technique in its own right (Ivancevich, 1976, 1977;
Latham and Yukl, 1975a; Locke, 1968, 1978).

Participation in decision making (PDM) was popu-
larized by the classic experiments with school boys conducted by Lewin, Lippitt and White (reported in White and
Lippitt, 1953), and by the highly successful industrial
field study by Coch and French (1948). Participation
has been the subject of scores of additional experiments
over the past 30 - 40 years, although its current popularity can be attributed more to its congruence with
the ideological biases of intellectuals (both in the USA
and abroad) than to its proven effectiveness as a motivational technique (see Locke and Schweiger, 1979, for
a thorough review and discussion of the PDM literature).

Job enrichment is a more recent development.   While
job enlargement experiments had been conducted as early
as 1950 (see Lawler, 1969, for a review of the early
studies), job enrichment did not really become popular
until the 1960s as a result of the research of Herzberg
and his colleagues (Herzberg, Mausner and Snyderman, 1959;
Herzberg, 1966).   Despite the seeming lack of validity of
Herzberg's theory of motivation as a whole (e.g., see
Locke, 1976), his work has been widely influential and
job enrichment is now practised in organizations all over
the world (e.g., see Hackman, 1977; Walters, 1975).

It should be noted that there are other methods that
have been and are used to motivate employees besides the
four noted above.   These include: praise and recognition
(credit); placement (e.g., matching the individual with
the job based on values and interests); group pressure,
which is related to a social psychological phenomenon
called 'social facilitation' which has been widely studied
in the laboratory; threats and discipline; counselling
and psychotherapy.   Unfortunately none of these has been

sufficiently researched in genuine or even simulated
organizational or work settings to allow any conclusions
to be drawn as to their relative effectiveness.   (All
motivation, of course, depends on employee values - a
topic which is beyond the scope of this paper.)

In contrast, there have been a sufficient number of
studies of the four methods noted earlier to suggest the
possibility of comparing the results for the purpose of
determining their relative effectiveness or potency for
motivating employee performance.   However, before such
comparisons can be accepted as meaningful, certain assumptions must be made about the studies which used each
method.

First, it must be assumed that the pre-incentive
situations for the studies using each technique were
roughly equivalent.   If this were not the case, the
comparisons could be biased.   For example, if productivity were extremely low before a given study, there would
be more room for improvement than if it had been high.
Or if employees were very receptive to change in one situation and not in another, this would give an advantage to
whatever technique was used in the former case.

Second, it must be assumed that each technique, on
the whole, was implemented with equal skill.   Even the
best technique may not work if introduced by inexperienced
or inept consultants.

Third, we must assume that the range or degrees of
the phenomena manipulated are equivalent from technique to
technique.   For example, it is assumed that the degree of
change from hourly to piece-rate payment is comparable to
that from no specific goals to specific challenging goals,
that these are comparable to the change from authoritarian
to participative decision making, and that these are
equivalent to going from unenriched to enriched jobs.

Fourth, it is assumed that the designs of the studies
are equally good.

Fifth, we assume all relevant contingency factors
were equally present when each technique was used, e.g.,
upper management support, type of task, climate, etc.

Sixth, we assume no differential publication bias
across the different techniques.

Obviously, there is no way to determine the degree to
which most of the above assumptions were met, with the
exception of the experimental designs used which we were
able to classify.   We assumed that if a particular type
of bias occurred in one study, it was cancelled out by

another study using that same technique and/or that the biasing or contingency factors would be approximately equal across groups of studies.

Our study falls in the general category of meta-outcome studies which have been used recently to compare the effectiveness of different types of psychotherapy (Smith and Glass, 1977) and different methods of college instruction (Kulik, Kulik and Cohen, 1979). This method is not foolproof, since it depends on the quality of the individual studies and on their comparability, as noted above, but the method does have the advantage of integrating large amounts of information in a manner that would be impossible simply by reading each study separately.

METHOD

Since our interest was in the practical utility of the various methods of motivating employees, only field studies or simulated field studies were included in our analysis. Since we wanted to be able to make causal interpretations of the results, only experimental studies were analyzed (including case and survey reports if they seemed to have been based on a before-after design). Studies which entailed a clear confounding of independent variables (e.g., by changing more than one major element of the job situation) were excluded from consideration, with the exception of Scanlon Plan studies which combined two of our techniques, money and participation, and individual task and bonus plans which combined money and goal setting. The above types of studies were included in separate tables in order to carry out certain consistency checks which are discussed in the final section of the paper.

The method used to calculate percentage improvement in performance depended on the design of the study. The classification of the various experimental designs used in the individual studies and the corresponding methods of calculating performance improvement are shown in Table 1. If a study reported no actual performance means but only percentage changes, then these percentages were used. If a study reported only changes in performance means, no percentages could be calculated and therefore, the study was omitted from consideration. However, if a study reported no actual means but stated that there was no performance change, then a 0 was entered as the percentage improvement figure.

If multiple criteria were used, an improvement percentage was calculated separately for each, and the median percent improvement for all criteria used was taken as the overall outcome measure. If, for a given

Table 1.   Classification of Designs Used in Calculating
            Performance Improvement[1]

Design	Performance Improvement Calculation Formula	Description[2]
0		Survey report; only percentage change data reported
1	$\dfrac{A_e - B_e}{B_e}$	Before-After, No Control: Used one experimental (e) group and no comparison or control (c) group. Measured performance before (B) and after (A) treatment.
2	$\dfrac{A_e - A_c}{A_c}$	After Only: 2a) Used an experimental and a control group; groups were not randomized or matched on pre-measures. Only post-treatment data presented.
		2b) Used an experimental and a control group; groups were randomized or matched on pre-measures or differences in pre-measures controlled by co-variate analysis or equivalent. Only post-treatment data obtained or presented.
3	$\left(\dfrac{A_e - B_e}{B_e}\right)$ $- \left(\dfrac{A_c - B_c}{B_c}\right)$	Before-After, With Control: 3a) Used one experimental and one control group; groups were not randomized or matched on pre-measures. Both pre- and post-treatment data presented for each group.
		3b) Used one experimental and one control group; groups were randomized or matched on pre-measures or differences in pre-measures controlled by covariate analysis or equivalent. Both pre- and post-treatment scores presented for each group.

1. The above designs were based on how performance improvements were calculated from the available published data,
   not on how the researcher designed the study.   For
   example, if the author notes that baseline measures
   were obtained on two groups but does not present pre-
   treatment data in the body of the article, Design 2
   would be used to calculate performance improvement for
   the purposes of this paper.

2. Data from multiple experimental groups were collapsed
   to test for main effects of predictor of interest.

criterion, measures were taken at more than one time
interval following treatment, then the average of all
post measures was taken as the after measure, except that
only the longest significant time interval was included
(e.g., if there was a 1 month and a one year follow up
with only the one month measure significant, then the one
year data were omitted).

In cases where more than one experimental group was
used (e.g., participative and assigned goal groups being
compared with a control or 'do best' goal group), the
means of the experimental groups were combined (unweigh-
ted) whenever possible before calculating improvement
percentages, providing both experimental groups received
the treatment of interest.   Otherwise, the median for all
experimental groups was taken after calculating the individual percentages.   Different samples within the same
study which received essentially the same treatment were
considered to be part of a single study and the median of
all samples was used.   Similarly a survey of 400 companies was treated as one study - a highly conservative
procedure.

Finally, only studies with hard performance criteria
were used.   Soft criteria like satisfaction or performance ratings and non-performance measures like absenteeism were not considered.   Cost criteria, however, were
not used since costs are determined by many uncontrolled
factors.

In all tables which summarize studies, the studies
are listed first by type of design (as described in Table
1) and then chronologically within each design.

RESULTS

Money

The studies of incentive pay proved difficult to
classify due to the diversity of incentive plans used.
Studies which involved changes in money plus an additional
variable such as timed performance standards (goals) and
participation were classified separately for later use
in consistency checks.   Many studies involved case
and survey reports (especially those described in Marriott,
1968).   Studies which clearly seemed to involve confounding factors such as changes in technology were discarded.
Unfortunately virtually none of the incentive studies
employed the most advanced experimental designs (i.e.,
designs 2 and 3 in Table 1).

Table 2 summarizes experiments which compared the
effects of hourly pay with individual piece rate pay or

Table 2.   Individual Piecework Plans

Reference	Design	Performance Improvement
Jacques (in Marriott, 1968, p.223)	O	+18% (reversed)
Burnett (in Marriott, 1968, p.164)	O	+11%
Marriott (1968, p.154)	O	+35%
Marriott (1968, p.160)	O	+41%
Wyatt et al. (1934)	1 and 2a	+25%
Yukl, Wexley and Seymore (1972)	1	+38%
Berger, Cummings and Heneman (1975)	1	+49%
Yukl and Latham (1975)	1	+13%
Yukl, Latham and Pursell (1976)	1	+3%
Latham and Dossett (1978)	1	+43%

Table 3.   Unspecified Incentive Plans

Reference	Design	Performance Improvement
Viteles (1953, p.27-28)	O	+39%
Marriott (1968, p.145)	O	+75% (midpoint of range)
Marriott (1968, p.145)	O	+31% (midpoint of range)
Dale (1959)	O	+64% (mean)
Rothe (1970)	1	+25% (reversed)

hourly pay plus piece rate pay.   (More detailed versions
of this and subsequent tables may be obtained from the
senior author upon request.)   These 10 studies show a
median performance improvement of 30% with a range of 3%
to 49%.   All ten studies showed a positive gain from the
introduction of piece rate payment.

The 7 studies in Table 3 are grouped separately
because they failed to specify the type of incentive plan
used.   Thus, some may be straight piece rates plans
whereas others may involve task and bonus systems.   The
median productivity improvement in these studies was 39%,
with a range of 25% to 75%.

Goal Setting

Virtually all the field studies of goal setting
compared the performance of groups of employees assigned
specific and/or challenging goals with employees assigned
'do your best' goals or no specific goals.   We included
two studies which were reported as behavior modification
experiments since the actual techniques used in them consisted of goal setting plus feedback (see Locke, 1977,
1978, for a discussion of this issue).

It should be noted that for goals to regulate performance effectively, feedback or knowledge of results in
relation to one's goal seems necessary.   Goal effects
are consistently significant in cases where individuals
have some means of keeping track of their progress, even
when knowledge of their actual score is withheld (e.g.,
see Locke, 1967;   and Locke and Bryan, 1969).   However,
when feedback is totally eliminated to the extent that
individuals have no way of knowing their progress or performance in relation to their goal or desired work pace,
goals show no relationship to performance (Erez, 1977).
Recent studies show that only subjects who have both high
goals and some type of feedback outperform subjects with
low or no goals, with or without feedback (Becker, 1978;
Strang, Lawrence and Fowler, 1978).

Thus, in the case of two studies in Table 4 (Becker,
1978;   and Kim and Hamner, 1976), groups with goals but
no feedback were omitted in calculating the performance
improvement scores.

The overall median percentage improvement in performance for the 17 studies described in Table 4 is 16.0%,
with a range of 2% to 57.5%.   All of the studies showed
a positive increase as a result of goal setting.

Table 4.   Studies Comparing Specific Challenging Goals
            with Do Best or No Goals

Reference	Design	Performance Improvement
At Emery Air Freight (1973)	O	+54%
Latham and Baldes (1975)	1	+26%
Kim and Hamner (1976)	1	+13%
Latham and Yukl (1976)	1	+11%
Migliore (Chapter 5, 1977)	1	+16%
Migliore (Chapter 7, 1977)	1	+57.5%
Komaki, Barwick and Scott (1978)	1	+24%
Blumenfeld and Leidy (1969)	2a	+27%
Latham and Locke (1975)	2a	+2%
Latham and Yukl (1975b)	2b	+18%
Ivancevich (1977)	2b	+15%
Becker (1978)	2b	+13%
Dossett, Latham and Mitchell (1979)	2b	+12%
Ivancevich (1972)	3a	+11%
Dockstader (1977)	3a	+27%
Ivancevich (1976)	3b	+24%
Umstot, Bell and Mitchell (1976)	3b	+16%

Participation

In choosing participation in decision making (PDM)
studies we used the definition provided and defended in
Locke and Schweiger's (1979) extensive review article
which defined PDM as joint decision making.   This definition excludes delegation, which is more properly cate-
gorized as job enrichment.   We also excluded many of
what are considered to be the classic studies of PDM
such as the Hawthorne, Harwood-Weldon and System 4
studies, since they confounded the effects of PDM with
those of numerous other factors such as incentives and

technology.   This confounding is documented in Locke
and Schweiger's Table 3 (1979, p. 304).   Similarly, we
eliminated organizational development studies since they
are typically quite heterogeneous in the scope and type
of changes they introduce.

The studies used in our analysis consist of the 14
field experiments in Locke and Schweiger's Table 4 (1979,
p. 313) which included hard performance measures plus
two additional studies discovered or completed since
their review, making a total of 16 studies.   These experiments are summarized in Table 5.

Table 5.   Participation in Decision Making Studies

Reference	Design	Performance Improvement
Powell and Schlacter (1971)	O	O
Lewin, Lippitt and White (White and Lippitt, 1953)	2a	+1%
French, Israel and As (1960)	2a (figures not given)	O
French, Kay and Meyer (1966)	2a	+6%
Litwin and Stringer (1968)	2b	-7%
Latham and Yukl (1975b)	2b	+11.5%
Ivancevich (1977)	2b	-8%
Seeborg (1978)	2b	-24%
Dossett, Latham and Mitchell (1979)	2b	-2%
Bragg and Andrews (1973)	3a	+47%
Coch and French (1948)	3b	+35%
Morse and Reimer (1956)	3b	-4%
Fleishman (1965)	3b (figures not given)	O
Veen (1972)	3b	+20%
Ivancevich (1976)	3b	+5%
Latham and Yukl (1976)	3b	+3%

The median percentage performance improvement for these 16 studies was 0.5%.   The range was -24% to +47%. Only half the studies showed positive performance gains as a result of participation.

Job Enrichment

Of the four types of studies included in our analysis, those involving job enrichment were the most consistently confounded with other variables.   This is perhaps not surprising in that job enrichment frequently involves structural changes, e.g., modifications of tools, authority relationships, technology, etc., unlike the three motivational techniques to which it is being compared.   However, this suggests the possibility that the effects of job enrichment on productivity may be the result of one or more of these other factors rather than of increased motivation.   Furthermore, one of the key elements of job enrichment, feedback, is itself a technique that is typically associated with goal setting (Locke, 1978).   In fact, the only study in our survey that explicitly controlled for goal setting (Umstot, Bell and Mitchell, 1976) found no effect of job enrichment on performance.

In selecting studies for inclusion in our analysis, we deleted all studies which involved changes in any aspect of the job other than increases in: variety, autonomy/responsibility, modularization (even though it often involves group work - another possible confounding variable), feedback, task significance, and recognition. Typical confounding variables in so-called job enrichment studies included, in addition to modifications of tools and technology, changes in: incentives, selection, training, manpower allocation, and goal setting.   Confounding factors led to the rejection of 24 studies with hard performance measures alleged to be examples of job enrichment.   Even those left in were in many cases questionable in that the job changes, while seemingly in conformity with job enrichment principles, were described so briefly that confounding factors could easily have been present and yet not mentioned.   This is especially true of the Herzberg (1966) and Walters (1975) reports which were extremely brief.   The Locke, Sirota and Wolfson (1976) study was probably confounded based on the interpretation of the authors (p. 708), but it was included anyway.

The 13 studies we ultimately included are shown in Table 6.   The median percentage improvement in performance was 17%, the range being -1% to 63%.   Positive increases in performance were obtained in 92% of the studies.

Table 6.   Job Enrichment Studies

Reference	Design	Performance Improvement
Segal and Weinberger (1977)	O	+5.5%
Davis (1957)	1	+30%
Hackman, Oldham, Janson and Purdy (1975)	1	+1%
Walters (1975),pp. 244-245)	1	+50%
Herzberg and Rafalko (1976), Avionics Dept. and Magnetic Tape Library	1	+63%
Ford (1969) Long Lines Framemen Project	1 and 2a	+12%
Maher (1971) Experiments 1 - 3	2a	+61%
Orpen (1979)	2b	+1%
White and Mitchell (1979)	2b	O
Ford (1969) Treasury Dept. AT&T	3a	+17%
Hackman, Oldham, Janson and Purdy (1975) (different design and criterion than above)	3a	+32%
Locke, Sirota and Wolfson (1976) Groups A and B	3b	+21.5%
Umstot, Bell and Mitchell (1976)	3b	-1%

If the most questionable studies are deleted from the above calculations, namely, the Herzberg and Rafalko (1976), Locke, Sirota and Wolfson (1976) and Walters (1975) experiments, the median improvement reduces to 8.75%. It is striking that some of the best controlled studies of job enrichment obtained the poorest results (e.g., Umstot, Bell and Mitchell, 1976; White and Mitchell, 1979) although some studies with seemingly good designs obtained substantial performance effects (Maher, 1971).

DISCUSSION

The results shown in Table 2, 4, 5 and 6 are summarized in Table 7. Clearly, money emerges as the most

Table 7.   Summary of Studies Comparing 4 Motivational
            Techniques

Technique	No. of Studies	Median Improvement	% showing some improvement	% showing 10% or more improvement	Range
Money (Table 2)	10[a]	+30%	100%	90%	+3% to +49%
Goal setting (Table 4)	17	+16%	100%	94%	+2% to +57.5%
Participation (Table 5)	16	+0.5%	50%	25%	-24% to +47%
Job Enrichment (Table 6)	13 (10)[b]	+17% (8.75%)[b]	92% (90%)[b]	61% (50%)[b]	-1% to +63% (-1% to +61%)

[a]Individual piece rate studies only

[b]Excluding questionable studies.

effective motivator, followed by goal setting and job
enrichment, with participation being clearly the least
effective.

   Further evidence for our conclusions can be obtained
by various consistency checks, the results of which are
shown in Table 11.   These are based on the results of
our earlier analyses plus some additional data (Tables 8
- 10).   The first line of Table 11 shows the expected
result of combining individual incentives (piece rate
plans) with goal setting.   This total of 46% agrees
quite well with the median figure in Table 8 of 40% which
represents the median productivity gain obtained from 13
studies of incentive plans which included work standards
or measured day work.

   The second line of Table 11 compares the effect of
money alone (from Table 2) with the effect of adding
incentives to measured day work (under hourly pay) based
on Fein's (1973) analysis.   The latter figure of 42.9%
is larger than the figure of 30% for money alone, but

both figures show a greater benefit for money than for
any other incentive.

The third line of the table compares goal setting
alone (from Table 4) to the effect of adding measured
day work (standards) to hourly pay, again based on
Fein's (1973) analysis.   The percentages figures of
16.0% and 14.6%, respectively, agree very closely.

The bottom part of Table 11 compares the results
for Scanlon Plans (summarized in Table 9) and Fein's
(1976b) Improshare Plan (personal communication from M.
Fein), which is similar to the Scanlon Plan, with various
combined measures.   The first comparison totals the
effects of individual incentives and participation,
yielding a figure of 30.5% which is considerably higher
than the Scanlon and Improshare Plan medians.   However,
another way to estimate these effects is to sum the
medians for non-Scanlon group plans shown in Table 10
with those of money and to subtract the effects of goal
setting (since all the group plans in Table 10 involved
standards, whereas it is not clear that the Scanlon and
Improshare Plans necessarily utilize work standards).
This revised figure of 12% is lower than the Scanlon
and Improshare Plan figures.   However, the mid-point
of the two estimates is 21.2% which is not far from the
Scanlon Plan figure of 16%, and very close to Fein's
figure of 20% for Improshare.   These data would seem to
give added credence to our original results.

A note is in order about the relation between the
percentage improvement scores and the experimental
designs.   If the studies are divided into two categories:
designs 0, 1 and 2a versus 2b, 3a and 3b, the studies of
goal setting, PDM and job enrichment (10 best studies
only) with better designs yielded about 5% lower mean
improvement scores than those with poorer designs.   However, this mean may be misleading because the difference
was greater than this for the goal setting and enrichment
studies whereas the difference for PDM was in the opposite direction, with the better designs yielding superior
results.   And no trend could be determined for the pay
studies since none of them used the better designs.
Furthermore, the small number of studies involved in these
comparisons makes any firm conclusions regarding the
effects of experimental design impossible.

We performed some parametric (and non-parametric)
statistical tests on our data and found significant differences among the means for the different motivation
techniques (p's < .05).   Multiple comparisons tests
showed that the task and bonus systems were consistently
superior to the other methods, except for money alone,
and that money was consistently superior to participation.

Table 8.   Individual Bonus Plans (Goals or Standards
            plus Bonus)

Reference	Design	Performance Improvement
Murray Steel (1943)	O	+16%
Dartnell (1946)	O	+45%
Whyte (1955)	O	+40%
Davison et al. (in Marriott, 1968, p. 161)	O	+59.5% (midpoint of middle range)
Marriott (1968, p. 154)	O	+52% (mean)
Reiners and Broughton (in Marriott, 1968, p. 157)	O	+15% (mean)
Wooton (in Marriott, 1968, p. 156)	O	+10%
Illeg and Jehring (1964)	O and 1	+34.5%
Fein (1973)	O	+64% (mean)
Devlin (1976)	O	+37%
Butler (in Marriott, 1968, p. 155)	1	+63%
Wyatt (in Marriott, 1968, p. 170)	1	+38%
Dooley et al. (1964, pp. 81, 138)	1	+65.3%

Table 9.   Scanlon Plans

Reference	Design	Performance Improvement
Whyte (1955) (Acme: Metropolis)	O	+68%
Whyte (1955) (Acme: Valley)	O	0
Whyte (1955) (La Pointe)	O	+26%
Gilson and Lefcowitz (1957)	O	0
Puckett (10 cases reviewed in Frost et al., 1974)	O	+17.5%
Moore (1976)	O	+6%
Sherman (1977)	O	+16%

Table 10.   Group Bonus Plans (Standard Plus Bonus)

Reference	Design	Performance Improvement
Torbert (1959)	O	+50%
Dooley et al. (1964, pp. 51-52)	O	+11.2%
Koop (1977)	O	+15%
Henderson (1974)	1	+40%

Table 11.   Consistency Checks for Effects of Motivation Techniques

Individual Techniques	Total (expected value)	Actual Value	Obtained from:
money (Table 2) + goal setting (Table 4)	30 + 16 = 46% ◄─►	40%	individual bonus plans (Table 8)
money (Table 2)	30% ◄─►	42.9%	adding incentives to measured day work (Fein, 1973)
goal setting (Table 4)	16% ◄─►	14.6%	adding measured day work to hourly pay (Fein, 1973)
money (Table 2) + participation (Table 5)	30 + 0.5 = 30.5%	16%	Scanlon Plans (Table 9)
group bonus (Table 10 - goals (Table 4) + participation (Table 5)	27.5 - 16 + 0.5 = 12%	20%	Improshare Plans[a]

21.5%

[a]from M. Fein (personal communication)

Our findings may surprise or even shock many social scientists.   For the last several decades ideological bias (Locke and Schweiger, 1979) has led many of them to deny the efficacy of money as a motivator and to emphasize the potency of participation.   The results of research to date indicate that the opposite viewpoint would have been more accurate.

But we do not have to rely just on experimental findings to confirm the importance of money.   We can use the evidence of logic.   Former I.B.M. executive Clair F. Vough identifies the crucial mental experiment that any manager can perform: '... go down the list of the status-and-satisfaction factors at your company, and for each factor ask yourself what would happen if it were removed' (Vough, 1975, p. 14).   Obviously if pay were totally removed as an incentive, people would not show up for work at all.   But the same cannot be said for removing goals, participation or enriched work.

Money is the crucial incentive because, as a medium of exchange, it is the most instrumental;   it can be used to purchase numerous other values.   It should be noted that these other values, contrary to popular academic opinion, are not simply objects which fulfil physical needs.   Money is directly or indirectly relevant to all of man's needs.   For example, money can be used to buy tickets to plays and concerts (artistic and aesthetic needs), to take out your spouse (romantic celebration), to go on vacations (leisure needs), to travel to see your friends (friendship needs), to finance your favourite organization (self actualization needs?). Money can serve as a reward for using your mind productively and as evidence that you are capable of earning a living and thus is related to (though not a cause of) self-esteem.   No other incentive or motivational technique comes even close to money with respect to its instrumental value.   It is not surprising, then, that people will work harder when given a chance to earn more of it.

The mediocre results for participation do not prove that it cannot motivate performance, but rather that its effects are probably less robust and less direct than those of the other three incentives.   Locke and Schweiger (1979) argue that there are two ways that participation can improve productivity.   The first, and perhaps most important mechanism, is cognitive in nature.   Consulting with subordinates may help managers to acquire more knowledge than they would have otherwise and therefore lead to higher quality decisions.   The effectiveness of participation would depend, therefore, on the relative competence of supervisors and their subordinates.   The most successful participation study in Table 5 (Bragg and

and Andrews, 1973) was apparently the result of the many
ideas for work improvement originated by the employees.
The motivational effects of participation appear primarily to involve reduced resistance to change.   However, change is not always resisted and overcoming resistance can be achieved in more than one way.

     In contrast to participation, the current emphasis
on goal setting seems well placed based on the results
of our analysis.   Goals serve to guide or direct attention and action, to mobilize energy in accordance with
the demands of the task, and to encourage persistence.
All of these mechanisms affect performance relatively
directly.

     The results for job enrichment were superficially
favourable, although it is still not clear whether all
confounding (non-motivational) factors were ruled out of
the studies we included.   An obvious non-motivational
benefit that could result from job enrichment is a more
efficient use of manpower.   It has been documented in at
least three different studies that assembly lines typically involve 'balance-delay' times due to non-uniform
rates of work between and within operators (Conant and
Kilbridge, 1965;   Cox and Sharp, 1951;   van Beek, 1964).
The effect of the delays in the above studies was to
reduce productivity by around 19 to 21%.   One way to
reduce such delays, of course, is to modularize the work
so that each individual is completing a whole unit or
product.   It is conceivable that the elimination of
unnecessary delays alone could account for much of the
median 17% increase in productivity obtained in the
enrichment studies we reviewed.   A second way to reduce
delay time, without modularization, is to use 'buffer
stocks' at strategic places along an assembly line.
Future studies which involve the conversion of linear to
modular assembly might consider using an 'assembly-line-
with-buffer-stocks' control group in order to separate
the effects of technological improvements from those of
increased motivation.

     Feedback, a key element of job enrichment, is clearly
relevant to motivation since knowledge of one's performance can be used, and often is used, to set goals.   However, if this were the major motivational mechanism, it
would reduce job enrichment effects to goal setting
effects.   On the other hand, if the feedback provided
the employees with better information which was used by
them to improve their work methods, then the effects
would be cognitive rather than motivational.

     We are now conducting a detailed meta-outcome study
of job enrichment experiments.   Preliminary findings
indicate that if we separate quantity and quality outcomes,

the non-confounded studies yield only a 5% median increase in quantity but an 89% median increase in quality (in line with the conclusions of Lawler's, 1969, review). This may point to a feedback explanation of job enrichment since most enrichment studies provide quality feedback.

It remains to explain the effects of increased responsibility and autonomy. While such job changes may be very satisfying, it is not clear how they get translated into improved performance. Possibly they lead to greater job involvement or commitment to organizational goals (see Locke, Sirota and Wolfson, 1976, p. 702). Perhaps increasing responsibility is equivalent giving the individual a more complex goal. This issue is clearly in need of further research. Thus far attempts to measure commitment and involvement in ways that relate to actual performance have met with very little success.

A final note about the relevance of our findings to the issue of the quality of work life. Generally this rather amorphous concept has been treated as roughly equivalent to job satisfaction. Job satisfaction, however, as psychologists and organizational researchers well know, is not necessarily associated with and is certainly not a cause of high productivity (Locke, 1976). Since non-public organizations must be profitable to survive and since profitability depends to a considerable extent on productivity, we must consider money as an important determinant of the quality of work life, in that, without money, there would be no work life. Furthermore, since most people value money, merit pay should be an important source of satisfaction at least for capable employees.

We make no claim that money is the only motivator. But if we look at the results of using money and goal setting combined, we would have to acknowledge that F.W. Taylor, who called his method the 'task and bonus' system, identified the most successful techniques (to date) for motivating employees.

REFERENCES

'At Emery Air Freight: Positive reinforcement boosts performance' (1973). Organizational Dynamics, 1, 841-850.

Becker, L.J. (1978). 'The joint effect of feedback and goal setting on performance: A field study of residential energy conservation', Journal of Applied Psychology, 63, 428-433.

Berger, C.J., Cummings, L.L. and Henemen, H.G. (1975).
    'Expectancy theory and operant conditioning pre-
    dictions of performance under variable ratio and
    continuous schedules of reinforcement', Organi-
    zational Behavior and Human Performance, 14, 227-243.

Blumenfeld, W.S. and Leidy, T.R. (1969).   'Effectiveness
    of goal setting as a management device: Research
    note', Psychological Reports, 24, 752.

Bragg, J.E. and Andrews, I.R. (1973).   'Participative
    decision-making: An experimental study in a
    hospital', The Journal of Applied Behavioral Science,
    9, 727-735.

Carey, A. (1967).   'The Hawthorne studies: A radical
    criticism', American Sociological Review, 32, 403-
    416.

Coch, L. and French, J.R.P. (1948).   'Overcoming resis-
    tance to change', Human Relations, 1, 512-532.

Conant, E.H. and Kilbridge, M.D. (1965).   'An inter-
    disciplinary analysis of job enlargement: Tech-
    nology, costs and behavioral implications',
    Industrial and Labor Relations, 18, 377-395.

Cox, D. and Sharp, K.M.D. (1951).   'Research on the
    unit of work', Occupational Psychology, 25, 90-108.

Dale, R.T. (1959).   'Wage incentives and productivity',
    Personnel, 36, 4-5.

Dartnell Corporation (1946).   'Report on 123 companies
    which have tried wage incentives', (unpublished).

Davis, L.E. (1957).   'Job design and productivity: A
    new approach', Personnel, 33, 418-430.

Devlin, J.S. (1976).   'Improved productivity: One
    company's wage incentive program', Supervisory
    Management, 21, 7-16.

Dockstader, L. (1977).   'Performance standards and
    implicit goal setting: Field testing Locke's
    assumption', Paper presented at the American Psycho-
    logical Association meeting.

Dooley, A.R., McGarrah, R.E., McKenny, J.L., Rosenbloom,
    R.S., Skinner, C.W. and Thurston, P.H. (1964).
    Wage Administration and Worker Productivity, Wiley,
    New York.

Dossett, D.L., Latham, G.P. and Mitchell, T.R. (1979). 'Effects of assigned versus participatively set goals, knowledge of results, and individual differences on employee behavior when goal difficulty is held constant', Journal of Applied Psychology, 64, 291-298.

Erez, M. (1977). 'Feedback: A necessary condition for the goal setting-performance relationship', Journal of Applied Psychology, 62, 624-627.

Fein, M. (1973). 'Work measurement and wage incentives', Industrial Engineering, 5, 49-51.

Fein, M. (1976a). 'Improving productivity by improved productivity sharing', The Conference Board Record, 13, 44-49.

Fein, M. (1976b). 'Designing and operating an Improshare plan', Hillsdale, New Jersey (unpublished).

Fein, M. (1976c). 'Motivation for work', in Handbook of Work, Organization, and Society (Ed. R. Dubin), Rand McNally, Chicago.

Fein, M. (1977). 'An alternative to traditional managing', Hillsdale, New Jersey (unpublished).

Fleishman, E.A. (1965). 'Attitude versus skill factors in work group productivity', Personnel Psychology, 18, 253-266.

Ford, Robert N. (1969). Motivation Through the Work Itself, American Management Association, Inc., New York.

French, J.R.P., Israel, J. and As, D. (1960). 'An experiment in a Norwegian factory: Interpersonal dimensions in decision-making', Human Relations, 13, 3-19.

French, J.R.P., Kay, E. and Meyer, H.H. (1966). 'Participation and the appraisal system', Human Relations, 19, 3-20.

Gilson, T.O. and Lefcowitz, M.J. (1957). 'A plant-wide bonus in a small factory - study of an unsuccessful case', Industrial and Labor Relations Review, 10, 284-296.

Hackman, J.R. (1977). 'Work design', in Improving Life at Work (Eds. J.R. Hackman and J.L. Suttle), Goodyear, Santa Monica, California.

Hackman, J.R., Oldham, G., Janson, R. and Purdy, K.
    (1975). 'New strategy for job enrichment',
    California Management Review, 17, 57-71.

Henderson, R.I. (1974). 'Money is, too, an incentive:
    One company's experience', Supervisory Management,
    19, 20-25.

Herzberg, F. (1966). Work and the Nature of Man, World,
    Cleveland.

Herzberg, F. and Rafalko, E.A. (1976). 'Efficiency in
    the military: The Hill Air Force Base project',
    in The Managerial Choice (Ed. F. Herzberg), Dow
    Jones-Irwin, Homewood, Illinois.

Herzberg, F., Mausner, B. and Snyderman, B. (1959).
    The Motivation to Work, Wiley, New York.

Illeg, D.D. and Jehring, J.J. (1964). 'How clerical
    incentive plans work', Administrative Management,
    25, 59-61.

Ivancevich, J.M. (1972). 'Changes in performance in a
    management by objectives program', Administrative
    Science Quarterly, 17, 563-574.

Ivancevich, J.M. (1976). 'Effects of goal setting on
    performance and job satisfaction', Journal of
    Applied Psychology, 61, 605-612.

Ivancevich, J.M. (1977). 'Different goal setting
    treatments and their effects on performance and job
    satisfaction', Academy of Management Journal, 20,
    406-419.

Kim, J.S. and Hamner, W.C. (1976). 'Effect of perfor-
    mance feedback and goal setting on productivity
    and satisfaction in an organizational setting',
    Journal of Applied Psychology, 61, 48-57.

Komaki, J., Barwick, K.D. and Scott, L.R. (1978). 'A
    behavioral approach to occupational safety: Pin-
    pointing and reinforcing safe performance in a food
    manufacturing plant', Journal of Applied Psychology,
    63, 434-445.

Koop, J.E. (1977). 'Indirect labor incentives pay off',
    Industrial Engineering, 9, 26-30.

Kulik, J.A., Kulik, C.C. and Cohen, P.A. (1979). 'Meta-
    analysis of outcome studies of Keller's personali-
    zed system of instruction', American Psychologist,
    34, 307-318.

Latham, G.P. and Baldes, J.J. (1975). 'The "practical significance" of Locke's theory of goal setting', Journal of Applied Psychology, 60, 122-124.

Latham, G.P. and Dossett, D.L. (1978). 'Designing incentive plans for unionized employees: A comparison of continuous and variable ratio reinforcement schedules', Personnel Psychology, 31, 47-61.

Latham, G.P. and Locke, E.A. (1975). 'Increasing productivity with decreasing time limits: A field replication of Parkinson's law', Journal of Applied Psychology, 60, 524-526.

Latham, G.P. and Yukl, G.A. (1975a). 'A review of research on the application of goal setting in organizations', Academy of Management Journal, 18, 824-845.

Latham, G.P. and Yukl, G.A. (1975b). 'Assigned versus participative goal setting with educated and uneducated woods workers', Journal of Applied Psychology, 60, 299-302.

Latham, G.P. and Yukl, G.A. (1976). 'Effects of assigned and participative goal setting on performance and job satisfaction', Journal of Applied Psychology, 61, 166-171.

Lawler, E.E. (1969). 'Job design and employee motivation', Personnel Psychology, 22, 426-435.

Lawler, E.E. (1971). Pay and Organizational Effectiveness: A Psychological View, McGraw-Hill, New York.

Likert, R. (1961). New Patterns of Management, McGraw-Hill, New York.

Likert, R. (1967). The Human Organization, McGraw-Hill, New York.

Litwin, G.H. and Stringer, R.A. (1968). Motivation and Organizational Climate, Division of Research, Graduate School of Business Administration, Harvard University, Boston.

Locke, E.A. (1967). 'The motivational effects of knowledge of results: Knowledge or goal setting?', Journal of Applied Psychology, 51, 324-329.

Locke, E.A. (1968). 'Toward a theory of task motivation and incentives', Organizational Behavior and Human Performance, 3, 157-189.

Locke, E.A. (1976).   'The nature and causes of job
    satisfaction', in Handbook of Industrial and Orga-
    nizational Psychology (Ed. M.D. Dunnette), Rand
    McNally, Chicago.

Locke, E.A. (1977).   'The myths of behavior mod in
    organizations', Academy of Management Review, 2,
    543-553.

Locke, E.A. (1978).   'The ubiquity of the technique of
    goal setting in theories of and approaches to
    employee motivation', Academy of Management Review,
    3, 594-601.

Locke, E.A. and Bryan, J.F. (1969).   'Knowledge of
    score and goal level as determinants of work rate',
    Journal of Applied Psychology, 53, 59-65.

Locke, E.A. and Schweiger, D.M. (1979).   'Participation
    in decision-making: One more look', in Research in
    Organizational Behavior (Ed. B.M. Staw), JAI Press,
    Greenwich, Ct.

Locke, E.A., Sirota, D. and Wolfson, A.D. (1976).   'An
    experimental case study of the successes and
    failures of job enrichment in a government agency',
    Journal of Applied Psychology, 61, 701-711.

Maher, J.R. (1971).   'Job enrichment, performance and
    morale in a simulated factory', in New Perspec-
    tives in Job Enrichment (Ed. J.R. Maher), pp. 35-53,
    New York.

Marriott, R. (1968).   Incentive Payment Systems, Staples
    Press, London.

Migliore, R. Henry (1977).   MBO: Blue Collar to Top
    Executive, Chapters 5 and 7, The Bureau of National
    Affairs, Inc., Washington, D.C.

Moore, B. (1976).   'A Scanlon plant-wide incentive
    plan - A case study', Training and Development
    Journal, 30(2), 50-53.

Morse, N.C. and Reimer, E. (1956).   'The experimental
    change of a major organizational variable', Journal
    of Abnormal and Social Psychology, 52, 120-129.

Murray Steel (1943).   'More pay - more production',
    Fortune, September, 138.

Odiorne, G.S. (1978).   'MBO: A backward glance',
    Business Horizons, October, 14-24.

Orpen, C. (1979). 'The effects of job enrichment on employee satisfaction, motivation, involvement, and performance: A field experiment', Human Relations, 32, 189-217.

Powell, R.M. and Schlacter, J.L. (1971). 'Participative management: A panacea?', Academy of Management Journal, 14, 165-173.

Puckett, E. (1974). 'Survey of 10 companies', in The Scanlon Plan for Organizational Development (Eds. C. Frost, J. Wakely and R. Ruh), Mich. State U. Press, East Lansing, Michigan.

Roethlisberger, F.J. and Dickson, W.J. (1956). Management and the Worker, Harvard University Press, Cambridge Mass. (originally published in 1939).

Rothe, H.F. (1970). 'Output rates among welders', Journal of Applied Psychology, 54, 549-551.

Seeborg, I.S. (1978). 'The influence of employee participation in job redesign', Journal of Applied Behavioral Science, 14, 87-98.

Segal, M. and Weinberger, D.B. (1977). 'Turfing', Operations Research, 25, 367-386.

Sherman, G. (1977). 'The Scanlon Plan reaps productivity bonus for labor and for management', Management Review, 66, 31-32.

Smith, M.L. and Glass, G.V. (1977). 'Meta-analysis of psychotherapy outcome studies', American Psychologist, 32, 752-760.

Strang, H.R., Lawrence, E.C. and Fowler, P.C. (1978). 'Effects of assigned goal level and knowledge of resultson arithmetic computation: A laboratory study', Journal of Applied Psychology, 63, 446-450.

Sykes, A.J.M. (1965). 'Economic interest and the Hawthorne researches', Human Relations, 18, 253-263.

Taylor, F.W. (1967). The Principles of Scientific Management, W.W. Norton, New York (originally published in 1911).

Torbert, F. (1959). 'Making incentives work', Harvard Business Review, 37, 81-92.

Umstot, D.D., Bell, H.B., Jr. and Mitchell, T.R. (1976). 'Effects of job enrichment and task goals on satisfaction and productivity: Implications for job

design',   Journal of Applied Psychology, 61,
379-394.

van Beek, H.G. (1964).   'The influence of assembly
line organization on output, quality and morale',
Occupational Psychology, 38, 161-172.

Veen, P. (1972).   'Effects of participative decision-
making in field hockey training: A field experiment', Organizational Behavior and Human Performance, 7, 288-307.

Viteles, M.S. (1953).   Motivation and Morale in Industry,
Norton, New York.

Vough, C.F. (1975).   Tapping the Human Resource,
Amacom, New York.

Walters, R.W. (1975).   Job Enrichment for Results,
Addison-Wesley, Reading Mass.

White, R.K. and Lippitt, R. (1953).   'Leader behavior
and member reaction in three "social climates"',
in Group Dynamics (Eds. D. Cartwright and A. Zander),
Harper and Row, New York.

White, S.E. and Mitchell, T.R. (1979).   'Job enrichment
versus social cues: A comparison and competitive
test', Journal of Applied Psychology, 64, 1-9.

Whyte, W.F. (1955).   Money and Motivation, Harper and
Bros., New York.

Wyatt, S., Frost, L. and Stock, F.G.L. (1934).   'Incentives in repetitive work', Industrial Health
Research Board, Report No. 69, London.

Yukl, G.A. and Latham, G.P. (1975).   'Consequences of
reinforcement schedules and incentive magnitudes
for employee performance', Journal of Applied
Psychology, 60, 294-298.

Yukl, G.A., Latham, G.P. and Pursell, E.D. (1976).
'The effectiveness of performance incentives under
continuous and variable ratio schedules of reinforcement', Personnel Psychology, 29, 221-231.

Yukl, G., Wexley, K.N. and Seymore, J.D. (1972).
'Effectiveness of pay incentives under variable
ratio and continuous reinforcement schedules',
Journal of Applied Psychology, 56, 19-23.

Changes in Working Life
Edited by K.D. Duncan, M.M. Gruneberg, and D. Wallis
© 1980 John Wiley & Sons Ltd

Chapter 21

Changing Views of Motivation in Work Groups

J. R. HACKMAN

It is hard to think of an organization without thinking of all the different kinds of groups that exist there. Groups in organizations come in a great variety of different sizes and shapes, and they serve a diversity of functions for their members and for the organization as a social system. They affect the quality of members' organizational experiences, the productivity of the organization itself, and how the organization changes and evolves over time. There is little question about the importance of understanding groups if we are to understand organizations.

Yet groups are hard to understand, as the history of the last few decades of research on the topic makes abundantly clear. Although academicians know quite a bit about training groups and about temporary groups created in controlled contexts for research purposes, we have not made great progress in understanding work groups that operate in organizational settings. It is a small consolation for those of us in the academy, I suppose, that managers who are responsible for such groups in work organizations also have shown limited insight into the beast, and have not demonstrated great talent in using groups for organizational purposes.

Things do seem to be changing both on the academic and practical sides of the house, however, and I believe they are changing for the better. In this paper, I will discuss four of these changes that strike me as particularly important and interesting. Some of them have already taken place. Others are happening now, or seem likely to in the near future. And some of the changes may not happen at all - but I have included them because I think they <u>ought</u> to.

CHANGE No. 1

<u>Awareness is increasing that coacting groups and work teams are different entities that operate quite differently.</u>

It just does not do any more to talk about 'work groups' in organizations. We must be clearer than we have been about what kind of groups we are discussing. One of the most important distinctions that must be made, I believe, is between 'coacting groups' and 'work teams'.

A coacting group is a set of people who have face-to-face contact and plenty of opportunities for informal interaction, but who do not work together on a common group task. Members are not interdependent in getting the work done, but instead perform their own, individual tasks - albeit in the context of the group of coactors. A number of telephone operators, each of whom operates his or her own console in proximity to the other operators would be an example of a coacting group.

A work team, on the other hand, is itself an intact performing unit, as suggested by the following defining attributes (Hackman and Oldham, 1980, Chapter 7). First, the group is an identifiable (if small) social system in which members have interdependent relations with one another, in which differentiated roles develop over time, and which is perceived as a group both by members and non-members (Alderfer, 1977). Second, the group has a defined piece of work to do that results in an identifiable product, service or decision for which the group can be held accountable. And third, the group has the authority to manage its own internal processes to generate the group product, with members planning and labouring collectively to get the group task accomplished. An 'autonomous work group' of the type described by Walton (1972, 1977) would be an example of a work team, as would be a management committee formed to make a set of decisions about which subordinate managers to recommend for promotion. [While other types of work groups also exist in organizations (such as a team that meets the first two criteria specified above, but does not have autonomous responsibility for its internal processes), I will focus in this paper only on coacting groups and work teams as relatively 'pure' types of work groups.]

It turns out that the major influences on work motivation are rather different for coacting groups and for work teams.   For this reason, the requirements for the effective design and management of these two types of groups differ substantially as well.

Consider first coacting groups.   They are far more prevalent in work organizations than are actual work teams.   And while inter-member relationships are not critical to getting the work itself accomplished in such groups (as they are for work teams), coacting groups nonetheless can have strong effects on both the quality of the work experiences of organization members and on member productivity.

Merely having the opportunity for informal social interaction with one's workmates, for example, which Robert Shrank calls 'schmoozing', can in itself make one's work experiences more pleasant.   Such interaction not only helps satisfy the social needs that most of us bring with us to the workplace, but also helps keep our level of psychological arousal or activation at tolerable levels.   As Scott (1966) and others have shown, low levels of on-the-job stimulation result in sub-optimal levels of activation, which usually are accompanied by noxious feelings of boredom and dissatisfaction with one's work experiences.

When bored, employees often seek out activation-enhancing activities, many of which involve taking time away from the work itself and some of which are quite dysfunctional for work productivity.   Membership in a stimulating coacting group can lessen the need for such activities.   Yet the impact of coacting groups on member productivity is more complex than that.   For one thing, socially-induced increases in a person's level of activation are not always beneficial for performance. As Zajonc (1965) and others have shown, activation-enhancing social interactions appear to yield improvements in productivity for 'performance' tasks (in which the dominant responses of the performer are likely to be correct or task-appropriate), but impair work effectiveness for 'learning' tasks (in which the dominant responses of the performer are likely to be incorrect).   So the stimulation provided by a coacting group is not task-effective in all circumstances.

Moreover, coacting groups often develop social norms that enhance or depress the productivity of group members - a phenomenon well-documented in the research literature (see Hackman, 1976 for a review).   What determines how powerful such normative effects are, and

whether they are pro- or anti- productivity?   While
there are substantial data to show that the cohesiveness
of coacting groups is significant in determining the
potency of group productivity norms, there is a paucity
of research on theory on factors that affect their
direction.

     There is, nonetheless, reason to believe that the
following three factors may be important in affecting
the direction of coacting group norms about member productivity: (a) the motivational structure of the jobs
members perform, (b) the equity and munificence of the
reward system through which members are recognized and
compensated for their work, and (c) the quality of the
relationships between group members and their formal
supervisors.   Thus, when the work itself is repetitive
and boring, when rewards for the work are few and
inequitably distributed, and when relationships with
supervisors are characterized by mutual distrust and
distorted communication, then we would not be surprised
to observe productivity-restricting norms develop
among group members;   when, on the other hand, the task
is engaging, when ample rewards are available to good
performers and are distributed fairly, and when there is
trust and respect between employees and managers, then
the chances are excellent that pro-productivity norms
will develop.   Aside from a few studies that explicitly
compare well- versus poorly-performing groups in organizations (e.g., Lawler and Cammann, 1972), however,
there are few data in the research literature that can
be used to test these ideas.

     In sum, it appears that motivation and productivity
in coacting groups depends substantially on the interaction between what happens within the group itself and
the character of the work context in which the group
functions.   As will be seen below, internal-external
interactions also are critical for understanding the
quality of member experiences and the productivity of
intact work teams - although the specific factors that
are of greatest importance, and the ways they operate,
are rather different.   So let us now leave coacting
groups, and turn to some changing views about motivation
and behavior in teams whose members work together inter-
dependently to accomplish a shared group task.

CHANGE No. 2

There is increasing skepticism about the assumption that
'The team will work things out' in accomplishing its task,
and increasing attention to how such teams are designed in
the first place.

     Work teams are increasingly being used as the

basic performing units for accomplishing work in organizations, and a number of commentators have spoken
enthusiastically about their potential benefits (e.g.,
Leavitt, 1975).   Indeed, some advocates of work teams
seem to hold the view that, once formed and given a
meaningful piece of work, members of such groups will
somehow 'work things out' among themselves in a way
that results both in high team effectiveness and in high
member satisfaction.   It is almost as if an 'invisible
social hand' is assumed to operate to ensure that things
turn out well when groups perform work.

As one who has spent too much of his life in work
teams with decision-making tasks (specifically, university committees), I can only suggest that if there is
indeed an invisible social hand it certainly is not as
sure-fingered as Adam Smith's invisible economic hand
is said to be in guiding the operation of markets.   And
my experience is supported by numerous researchers who
have documented the more-than-occasional tendency of
task groups to perform less well than would be predicted
on the basis of the prior task-relevant knowledge and
skill of their group members (see, for example, Davis,
1969;   Janis, 1972;   Steiner, 1972).

What now seems to be emerging is a healthy recognition that, for all their potential advantages, groups
are not always the organizational device of choice for
performing work.   Often it is better for an individual
to be given responsibility for the entire task, or for
the work to be distributed among members of a coacting
group.   Deciding whether individuals or a team is the
more appropriate performing unit for a piece of work
is a matter as complex as it is important, and I will
not go into the matter in detail in this paper (see
Hackman and Oldham, 1980, Chapters 7 and 9 for a more
extended treatment).   Yet one important (and often
overlooked) factor that bears on that decision is the
degree to which it is possible to design the work team
well when it is created.   If the group cannot be set up
right in the first place, then it may be better to forego
the potential advantages of a team for the very good
reason that those advantages are unlikely to appear: as
noted above, poorly-designed teams generally do not
'work things out' satisfactorily.

What, then, are the components of a good design for
a work team?   What features should be built in to
foster high work motivation and effective collaboration
among members in accomplishing the team task?   While
systematic knowledge about this matter is only beginning
to accumulate (see, for example, Cummings, 1978), my own
research on the topic suggests that the following three

design features may be of special importance.

First is the motivational structure of the group task.   When the group task is motivationally engaging, then collective motivation to perform effectively is heightened;   when it is not, then the team as a whole may exhibit the same pattern of withdrawal from work and low commitment to effective performance that has been shown to characterize the behaviour of individuals on routine and repetitive jobs (Hackman, 1977;   Herzberg, 1976;   Walker and Guest, 1952).

Second is the composition of the work team.   Of greatest importance, of course, is the level of task-relevant knowledge and skill of team members: good people are more likely to do good work.   Also significant, however, is the size of the group and the degree of heterogeneity of member knowledge and skill.   When the group is just (barely) large enough to carry out the work and when members are neither too similar nor too different from one another for effective performance, then chances are improved that members will be able to bring their task-relevant knowledge and skill effectively to bear on the task.   But when the group is too large (excessively small work teams are almost never formed in work organizations), or when members are too similar (or too different) from one another to collaborate well in carrying out the work, then the energies of team members may be spent more on coordination and 'process problems' than in getting the work itself done.

Third are the group norms that are created early in life of the group about how members will arrive at (and enforce adherence to) the performance strategies they will use to accomplish the task.   If up-front norms are created that support open exploration and invention of alternative ways of proceeding with work on the task, then chances are improved that groups' members will develop ways of working together that are particularly appropriate for the task being performed.   But if group norms specify instead that matters of performance process are not to be dealt with openly (usually in the interest of keeping members' anxieties low and avoiding the onset of potentially-sticky 'process problems'), then performance strategies may emerge as much by accident or by habit as by choice, and these strategies may turn out to be inappropriate for the task being performed (Hackman and Morris, 1975).

In many instances, those who are responsible for the creation of work teams will be in a position to affect the three design features mentioned - task, composition, and norms about performance strategies - and in such cases the organizational cards can be stacked in favour of effective team process and performance. But sometimes existing organizational systems or managerial practices so constrain how the group can be designed that it is impossible to develop a design that fosters team effectiveness (Oldham and Hackman, 1979). In such circumstances group members will have to spend at least some of their time and energy (and often much of it) trying to overcome these design flaws - and even so may fail.

So designing work for groups is not always a good idea. Creating effective work teams always requires careful thought and often requires a good deal of organizational clout as well. And sometimes it just cannot be done well. Given that a poorly designed work team may well perform worse, not better, than individuals on the same task, it strikes me as a very bad idea indeed to casually form organization members into a work team, give them the team task, and hope that they will somehow 'work things out' so that they perform well.

CHANGE No. 3

The organizational context in which work teams function is increasingly being recognized as important to team performance.

When studies of small group behavior and performance were in vogue in social psychology, in the 1950s and early 1960s, little attention was paid to the organizational context in which the groups operated. The dominant research setting was the experimental laboratory, and great care was taken to make sure that 'extraneous' contextual factors were controlled (usually by holding them at constant levels). The idea was that relatively subtle intra-group phenomena could be teased out and examined if external sources of variation were ruled out by the methodology employed.

That view was correct, of course, but it also is one of the reasons why that round of research on task-oriented groups was so barren of substantively interesting findings about group performance effectiveness. Even when design features such as those discussed above were manipulated or measured (which sometimes they were, especially variables having to do with group composition), the role of the social system in which the group did its work was generally not viewed as of substantive interest. Now it has become clear that the organizational context of a work group can powerfully affect what happens within the group, and how well the group performs. The context is no longer seen as something to be ignored or set at constant levels if one wishes to understand group

performance effectiveness or to learn how to create
groups in organizations that perform well.

The problem, of course, is that there is a multitude of contextual factors that potentially can affect
the process and the performance of groups in organizations. My reading of the literature (and my observations of work teams in organizations) suggests that
four aspects of the context warrant special attention
in the study of motivation and performance in work teams
(for a more extended discussion of the first three of
these factors, see Hackman and Oldham, 1980, Chapter 8).

First are the rewards and objectives for team performance. While (as noted above) the design of the
group task itself can have strong effects on member
motivation to perform the task well, this motivation can
be reinforced (or undermined) by the rewards that good
performance brings (Lawler, 1977), and by the performance objectives that are set by the group (Zander,
1971). To have a motivationally engaging group task
without the support of the reward system and/or without
challenging performance objectives will result in only
short-term motivational gains; to have rewards contingent on excellent group performance or to set high performance objectives for a relatively meaningless, de-
motivating group task is to invite all manner of process
problems within the group and conflict between the group
and organizational management. The group task and
organizational supports for group task accomplishment
must be congruent.

Second is the availability of training and technical
consultation available to the group for its work. While
the composition of the group (discussed above) powerfully determines the level of talent in the group,
members often need access to outside expertise as well -
especially for thorny performance problems on complex
and challenging group tasks. Once again the view that
'the group can handle it' can cause problems. Unless
outside assistance is readily available (and unless
seeking such help is encouraged by organizational management), group members may feel that they must handle
things on their own - even if the knowledge and skill
required for excellent performance is not available
within the group itself. Once again, solving the
design problem (in this case, composing the group well)
is only half the story: even well-composed groups often
need expertise that exists outside the group's boundaries, and the availability of such help (and the ease
with which it can be obtained) sometimes makes the difference between excellent and poor group performance.

Third is the clarity of the objective requirements

of the group task.   As noted above, a well-designed
work team has norms that foster active consideration of
alternative strategies for carrying out the work.   The
success a team has in exploring and choosing among possible strategies depends in part on how well group
members understand just what are (and what are not) firm,
immutable task requirements and what the constraints
are on how members can work together.   Unfortunately,
these matters often are obscure, either because nobody
has taken the trouble to analyze them or because organizational managers have neglected to share the information with group members.   Unless such information is
clear and available to the group, there is a real risk
that group members will develop ways of working together
that are based on incorrect (or incomplete) perceptions
of what the task actually requires, or what the constraints are under which the group must operate.

     Last is the pattern of relationships between the
group and other groups in the organization.   It is
widely recognized that the character of the relations
between groups in an organization has a great deal to do
with what happens within the respective groups (Alderfer,
1977).   On the one hand, if groups are too differentiated from one another inter-group coordination can
become a problem and (depending in part of the nature of
the reward system in the organization) dysfunctional
group conflict can develop between groups.   While such
conflict usually increases the internal cohesiveness of
the constituent groups, heightened cohesiveness in itself is not necessarily associated with either good
group performance or healthy inter-member relationships
(Hackman, 1976; Janis, 1972; Seashore, 1954).   On
the other hand, too much integration among separate groups
can obscure the boundaries of those groups, and compromise their identity and their capability to take con-
certed action in carrying out their work.   So managing
the relationships among work teams is something of a
balancing act between the risks of excessive differentiation and excessive integration, both of which can
compromise the task effectiveness and the quality of the
social relationships that take place within the groups.

     In sum, any discussion of the motivation, produc-
tivity and internal cohesiveness of work teams that
fails to address the organizational context in which
those groups function is seriously incomplete.   Poor
contextual arrangements can compromise the effectiveness
of even well-designed work teams, and can further worsen
the performance of poorly-designed teams.   And a supportive organizational context, while unlikely to compensate for serious flaws in the basic design of a work
team, can help well-designed groups more fully exploit
their built-in opportunities for excellent performance.

CHANGE No. 4

<u>Less attention is being paid to juicy interpersonal
process issues in work teams.</u>

When we observe a work group in trouble, we
usually see all manner of problems in the interpersonal
process of the group. Members may have fallen into a
pattern of interpersonal conflict and competition, or
they may provide insufficient support to one another as
they go about their work, or they may even have become
so oriented toward sharing warmth, support and good
feelings that the task itself is all but forgotten about.

Because such process problems are so obvious, and
so obviously dysfunctional for task performance, the
temptation is to go to work on them directly, with the
expectation that improvements in motivation and/or work
effectiveness will materialize when the process difficulties have been cleared up. And, indeed, a number of
approaches to group consultation seem to be based on this
view (e.g., Argyris, 1962; Blake and Mouton, 1975; Dyer,
1977; Merry and Allerhand, 1977). Such approaches
often involve experiential sensitivity training and/or
team building, and they tend to focus more on the
relationships among members than on the interface between the group and the task or the group and the organization. Ideally, these process-oriented approaches
help group members develop their interpersonal skills,
and foster the development of group norms that favour
interpersonal openness about ideas and feelings and
social risk-taking in the interest of improved performance.

In general, research findings show that such interventions do affect what actually happens in the group
while it is undergoing training, and that member beliefs
and attitudes about appropriate and desirable behavior
in groups are altered as well. Unfortunately, it
appears that the lessons learned do <u>not</u> transfer readily
from the training setting to on-line work settings. Nor
do newly-learned behaviors or revised group norms persist for long in the absence of on-going support and
reinforcement. Worse, the actual task effectiveness
of groups whose members have received training in group
process skills is rarely improved - and sometimes is
impaired (see, for example, reviews by Campbell and
Dunnette, 1968 and by Hackman and Morris, 1975).

How are we to understand this? Obviously group
process is important not only to member beliefs and
attitudes but to group performance as well. Why are
process-oriented interventions so inconsistent in their
effects?

The explanation, I suspect, has to do with the reason for the observed process problems.   If the problems develop because the group is poorly designed for the work it has to do, or because of insufficient support (or contradictory messages) from the organizational system within which the group operates, then the observed process difficulties are better construed as signs of problems than as problems in themselves.   To try to improve group functioning and task effectiveness by working directly on members' interpersonal relationships, when those relationships are merely manifestations of more basic flaws in the design of the group or its environment, is to swim upstream against a very strong current.   A temporary fix may be obtained - but it is likely to be only temporary.

A better approach to problems of interpersonal process, in my view, is to make sure first that the group is well-designed for its work and that the organizational context provides the support that members need to carry out their work effectively.   Then, when the organizational cards have been stacked in favour of effective collaboration by group members on their task, attention can turn to the interpersonal issues that may be impeding group effectiveness, or that may represent unexploited opportunities for 'synergistic' interaction among members.

Issues of interpersonal process, in this view, assume a less central role than is advocated by many who are invested in team-building, sensitivity training, and related devices for improving group effectiveness: process is viewed as an important thing, but not as the only thing, and not as the first thing to be addressed when a group is having problems in its work.   To the extent that this view continues to gain credence on the part of those charged with the design and management of work teams in organizations, I suspect that we will see less time and money spent on 'group development' activities - but that we also will see more substantial and more enduring improvements in team functioning in those instances when process consultation is appropriate and appropriately used.   And I suspect that we will see research on the role of group process in understanding the effectiveness of work teams that is rather more helpful and informative than was the case when we sought 'yes' or 'no' answers to questions such as 'Does sensitivity training improve group performance effectiveness?'.

CONCLUSION

Views of work groups in organizations are changing.

We are seeing increasing recognition of the fact that different types of groups in organizations operate quite differently, more attention is being paid to the design of work teams and to the features of the organizational context in which teams function, and we are gradually arriving at a more differentiated view of interpersonal process as one factor that affects team performance.

If these changes in perspective persist and evolve, I predict that we will soon have a rebirth of research interest in task-oriented groups. And, I hope, we will find that decision-making about when to use groups to accomplish work will be based less on ideological preference - and more on a firm understanding of the circumstances under which such groups are and are not an appropriate design device. While this will require more knowledge than we now have about the design imperatives of various kinds of group tasks, about the people who compose the groups and perform the tasks, and about the organizational context in which the work will be done, I believe that the time for informative research on such questions has now arrived.

REFERENCES

Alderfer, C.P. (1977). 'Group and intergroup relations', in J.R. Hackman and J.L. Suttle (Eds.), Improving life at work: Behavioral science approaches to organizational change, Santa Monica, CA, Goodyear.

Argyris, C. (1962). Interpersonal competence and organizational effectiveness, Homewood, Il, Irwin-Dorsey.

Blake, R.R. and Mouton, J.S. (1975). 'Group organizational team building: A theoretical model for intervening', in C.L. Cooper (Ed.), Theories of group processes, London, Wiley.

Campbell, J. and Dunnette, M.D. (1968). 'Effectiveness of T-group experiences in managerial training and development', Psychological Bulletin, 70, 73-103.

Davis, L.E. (1969). Group performance, Reading, MA, Addison-Wesley.

Dyer, W.G. (1977). Team building: Issues and alternatives, Reading, MA, Addison, Wesley.

Hackman, J.R. (1976). 'Group influences on individuals in organizations', in M.D. Dunnette (Ed.), Handbook of industrial and organizational psychology, Chicago, Rand-McNally.

Hackman, J.R. (1977).   'Work design', in J.R. Hackman
    and J.L. Suttle (Eds.), Improving life at work:
    Behavioral science approaches to organizational
    change, Santa Monica, CA, Goodyear.

Hackman, J.R. and Morris, C.G. (1975).   'Group tasks,
    group interaction process, and group performance
    effectiveness: A review and proposed integration',
    in L. Berkowitz (Ed.), Advances in experimental
    social psychology, Vol. 8, New York, Academic Press.

Hackman, J.R. and Oldham, G.R. (1980).   Work redesign,
    Reading, MA, Addison-Wesley.

Herzberg, F. (1976).   The managerial choice, Homewood,
    IL, Dow-Jones-Irwin.

Janis, I.L. (1972).   Victims of groupthink: A psycho-
    logical study of foreign-policy decisions and
    fiascos, New York, Houghton-Mifflin.

Lawler, E.E., III (1977).   'Reward systems', in J.R.
    Hackman and J.L. Suttle (Eds.), Improving life at
    work: Behavioral science approaches to organi-
    zational change, Santa Monica, CA, Goodyear.

Lawler, E.E. III and Cammann, C. (1972).   'What makes
    a work group successful?', in A.J. Marrow (Ed.),
    The failure of success, New York, Amacom.

Leavitt,H.J. (1975).   'Suppose we took groups
    seriously ...', in E.L. Cass and F.G. Zimmer (Eds.),
    Man and work in society, New York, Van Nostrand
    Reinhold.

Merry, U. and Allerhand, M.E. (1977).   Developing teams
    and organizations, Reading, MA, Addison-Wesley.

Oldham, G.R. and Hackman, J.R. (1979).   'Work design in
    organizational context', in B.M. Staw and L.L.
    Cummings (Eds.), Research in organizational behavior
    (Vol. 2), Greenwich, CT, JAI Press.

Scott, W.E. (1966).   'Activation theory and task
    design', Organizational Behavior and Human Perfor-
    mance, 1, 3-30.

Seashore, S. (1954).   Group cohesiveness in the indus-
    trial work group, Ann Arbor, Institute for Social
    Research, University of Michigan,

Steiner, I.D. (1972).   Group process and productivity,
    New York, Academic Press.

Walker, C.R. and Guest, R.H. (1952).   The man on the
    assembly line, Cambridge, MA, Harvard University
    Press.

Walton, R. (1972).   'How to counter alienation in the
    plant', Harvard Business Review, November-December,
    50, 70-81.

Walton, R.E. (1977).   'Work innovations at Topeka:
    After six years', Journal of Applied Behavioral
    Science, 13, 422-433.

Zajonc, R.B. (1965).   'Social facilitation', Science,
    149, 269-274.

Zander, A. (1971).   Motives and goals in groups, New
    York, Academic Press.

Changes in Working Life
Edited by K.D. Duncan, M.M. Gruneberg, and D. Wallis
© 1980 John Wiley & Sons Ltd

Chapter 22

Effort in Motivated Work Behaviour

M. WALLBANK

Some of the issues involved in matching people, their physical and mental capacities, skills and abilities, to industrial and organizational tasks have been examined by studies in the disciplines of Ergonomics and Industrial Engineering. Jobs can be designed which minimise unnecessary task demands and maximise the use of people's unique human abilities. The design of 'more possible jobs' (Corlett, 1979) however, does not guarantee that individuals or groups of workers will put in the 'effort' to achieve a satisfactory level of performance, or that they will gain an adequate level of satisfaction from their working activities. The study of work performance and work related satisfactions is still of great conceptual and practical importance in the design and management of work and working organisations.

The search for an understanding of people's reactions to work and for the determinants of performance and satisfaction has formed one of the major research areas in psychology for many years. To date, this research has led to some limited success in explaining the affective responses of satisfaction with work. Although significant relationships between motivational factors and performance have been demonstrated in many individual and laboratory studies, the general level of predictive success in establishing the determinants of performance in manufacturing jobs has been very limited (e.g. Mitchell, 1974; Steers and Porter, 1975; Campbell

and Pritchard, 1976).   Measures of inter-worker and
intra-worker variability over time often exceed changes
in levels of performance following experimental manipulation, by an order of magnitude (Khaleque, 1979;
Muchinsky, 1977; Muramatsu and Miyazaki, 1976).

This 'failure' to reach the levels required for
effective prescriptive application has important consequences for the development and diffusion of work structure and work design change programmes.   Many practising managers are aware of the limited success and of
the transience of earlier theories and panaceas.   As
they are normally held accountable for results, they are
naturally reluctant to accept the risks involved in
changes of work organisation and management unless they
can see very clear evidence that the potential benefits,
judged by their success criteria, are going to outweigh
the risks inherent in the changes.   Most organisations
judge their managers by traditional performance measures.
There is a strong inclination to play it safe and not to
experiment if the currently negotiated situation is
running smoothly.   Workers and workers' organisations
still concentrate their bargaining on the tangible and
readily quantifiable aspects - pay, job gradings, working
hours and employment levels, and have shown little general
interest yet in negotiating on quality of working life
and workers' satisfaction (Giles and Holley, 1978).

As Wild and Birchall (1975) point out, the 'right'
things, i.e. job re-structuring, are initiated in very
many organisations for the 'wrong' i.e. traditional technical organisation, reasons: of absenteeism, labour turnover, skill shortages, or high costs.   Moves towards
widespread adoption of work design programmes depend on
being able to demonstrate clear and significant results,
based on conceptually sound theories with clearly defined
factors or action levers, both to the workers and to
the managers working in organisations.

There are many recent and current studies aimed at
improving the conceptual precision and predictive accuracy of theories of work motivation.   The construct
'effort' enters into many theories, as a measure of
motivational force, as an intervening variable between
motivation and performance, as a first level response
outcome, as an individual perception of a current construct, or as an integrated long term outcome.   At
present, effort is interpreted in many ways which are
neither conceptually satisfactory nor amenable to satisfactory experimental measurement.

> 'It is in the measurement of effort in situ
> where we are really hurting and it would be
> well worth our while to start an in-depth

look at the meaning and measurement of
just this variable' (Campbell and Pritchard, 1976).

The role and key aspects of 'effort' in work motivation theories can be examined in the context of:

(a) use of the construct 'effort' in models of moti-
     vated behaviour;

(b) conceptual and operational definitions of effort;

(c) measurement of effort and its relationship with
     performance;

(d) application in continuing work situations.

EFFORT IN MOTIVATIONAL THEORY

The dominant paradigms in work motivation research
are currently variations of the valency - instrumentality
- expectancy (V.I.E.) theories. These have developed
from the basic cognitive approach of Tolman and Lewin.
Hull's earlier drive theory postulated that the impetus
to respond, $_sE_R$, was the product of habit strength, $_sH_R$,
and drive strength, D.

$$_sE_R = f_h(_sH_R) \times f_d(D)$$

Later modifications by Hull include an anticipating goal
reaction (incentive), K.

$$_sE_R = f(D \times K \times {}_sH_R)$$

In the cognitive theories (Vroom, 1964) the formulation is superficially similar. Impulse to action, F,
is a function of the expectancy of a given outcome, E,
and the valence, the anticipated value of the outcome, V.

$$F = E \times V$$

As more than one outcome may be sought by selection
of one action from a set of alternative, the outcomes may
be determined by the instrumentality in achieving outcomes.
The Vroom (1964) model of motivation can be expressed as:

$$F = \sum_{j=1} E_{ij} \cdot V_j \qquad$$ F is force to perform
                                                  (Job effort)

V_j valence of outcome j

$$V_j = \sum_{k=1}^{n} I_{jk} \cdot V_k \qquad V_k \text{ valence of outcome k}$$

I_{jk} instrumentality of outcome j for attainment of outcome k

Consideration of differing valencies of intrinsic (felt by the worker) and extrinsic (delivered by outside agencies) forms of outcomes led to modifications of the basic model.   One model (House, Shapiro and Wahba, 1974) is:

$$M = IV_b + E_1 [IV_a \sum (E_2 \cdot V)]$$

where M is work motivation,

V the valency of second level outcomes

IV_b - the intrinsic valence of behaving on a task

IV_a - the intrinsic valence of task accomplishment

E_1 - Expectancy 1 - perceptions that effort will lead to first level outcomes or task accomplishment

E_2 - Expectancy 2 - perceptions that first level outcomes will lead to second level outcomes - extrinsic rewards.

Such models postulate rules for the combination of measurements or scaled perceptions of factors into a force, or performance vector, which a rational subject can compare with the forces for other currently available actions to select the particular action which is most attractive.   Workers may appear to be inconsistent in their rationality if relevant factors are omitted in the calculation.   Such models provide little insight into how the current perceptions of expectations, instrumentalities, and valencies are established, or how they change over time in response to continuing work experience.

A number of recent studies present approaches to clarifying the concepts and processes underlying valency-expectancy theories: Behling and Stark (1973), Brief and Aldag (1977), Broedling (1977), Connolly (1976), Herold and Greller (1977), Lindell and Solomon (1977), Reinharth and Wahba (1975) and Wahba and House (1974).

The basic form of the V.I.E. theories is essentially of within person behavioural choice models.   As
pointed out very clearly in a major survey by Mitchell
(1974), this distinction appears to have been overlooked
by nearly all researchers when designing tests of the
theory.   Almost all investigations have been in the form
of between-person tests.   (Dyer and Parker, 1976 and
Matsui et al., 1977, present two of the few within-person
experimental designs.)   In the Vroom model, factors combine into a force which induces the subject to select a
particular course of action, activity A, instead of other
currently available activities, B, C, etc., or to select
a particular level of effort from within the subject's
range of effort levels.   In the basic form of V.I.E.
theories, this selection tends to imply that having made
the choice, the worker will persist for some time with a
stable course of behaviour until there is a major change
in the situation.   This may apply in some highly motivated conditions, in sport and some laboratory studies,
but it will be argued later that such conditions rarely
apply to normal workers in typical working situations.

Development of systems models of the motivational
process (Porter and Lawler, 1968;   Lawler, 1971;
Wernimont, 1971;   Dachler, 1973) presents a more satisfying conceptual framework for analysis.

These systems models offer two main advances over
the earlier 'formula' based theories.

Firstly, they are dynamic, recognising that the work
related constructs may change as outcomes are experienced
or delivered during the work.   The response to feedback
of information inherent in all working situations can
continually modify the worker's perceptions, and thus his
evaluation of combinations of factors used in determining his behaviour can be expected to change over time.

The second advance is representation of a logical
structure of the decision making process in the form of
perceptions of sets of Effort-Performance, Performance-
Outcome, and Valencies of outcomes (and the information
flows linking these constructs to the particular characteristics: self-esteem, achievement and affiliation
needs, problem solving and other abilities which distinguish one worker's 'personality' from another).

Effort enters into the Porter-Lawler (1968) model
at two stages:

-      in the set of perceptions held by the worker,
       representing his current beliefs of the relation-
       ships between his input of levels of effort and
       his subsequent levels of performance;

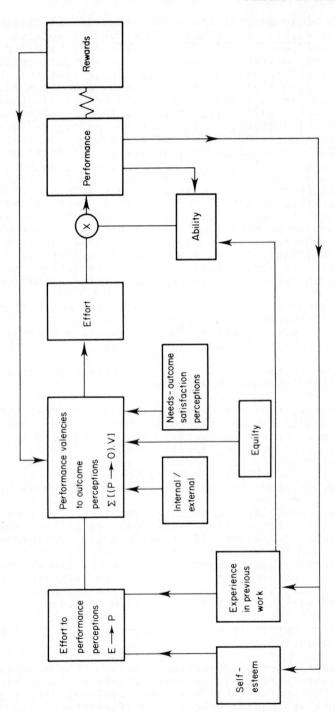

Figure 1.   Porter-Lawler (1968) model.

- as an intervening variable between the motivational process and performance.

The first aspect raises the problem of partitioning
levels of effort equivalent to specific levels of performance of values of $\sum (E_{ij} \cdot V_j)$'s.   This point is discussed as Postulate 7   by Behling and Stark
(1973).   Simple binary partitioning into work or non-
work, or rest, poses few problems.   Multi-level partitioning as a within-person scaling process introduces the
problems of the information processing characteristics of
the brain: thresholds, levels of discrimination,
averaging variable data over time, and setting stable
reference levels.   Slow, comfortable, fast, maximum
effort are typical verbal descriptions.   Anchoring such
descriptions to stable reference levels for measurement
is more difficult.   Effort is a multi-dimensional construct.   Individual reference and scaling can be based
on individually weighted combinations of pace, or speed
of motions, forces to be overcome, degree of concentration, attention, duration and continuity of working,
felt physical fatigue, felt mental fatigue.   Under the
social interactions inherent in most forms of industrial
and organisational jobs, comparisons with the perception
of others' efforts is a convenient and widely used
reference, but one which is situation dependent and
varies over time (Rothe, 1978).

A similar range of problems is encountered in
measuring effort as an intervening variable.

Force expended while working, rate of working, degree
of attention required, are typical dimensions as a basis
for measuring and scaling effort during the work activity.
An alternative approach is to measure the integrated
effects over a period, expenditure of energy from limited
resources;   a low level of effort does not result in
fatigue, high levels of effort are ones which result in
physical or mental fatigue.   This has shades of the
work study approach: 'At the end of the day the worker
shall go home healthily tired'.   Rates of working and
expenditure of energy on tasks including physical activities can be measured quite accurately by physiological
techniques of respiratory analysis.   Variations of
physique and methods of working introduce considerable
variations in the energy expended by different workers
carrying out identical tasks (Aquilano, 1968).   A given
rate of energy expenditure also represents differing
fractions of individuals' capacity (Drury and Pfeil, 1975).

Once an individual has been 'calibrated' by measures
of oxygen consumption on a standard task, effort and work
performance can be estimated from pulse rate changes,
respiratory rate and body temperature changes during

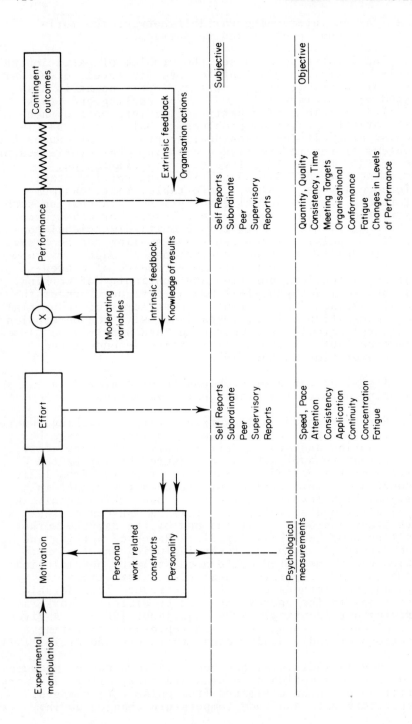

Figure 2.   Measuring effort as an intervening variable.

activity, and recovery during rest periods.

Most industrial jobs and administrative jobs are,
however, essentially mental in nature: controlling,
monitoring, problem solving.   Nevertheless such activities are often linked to physiological changes, alpha
rhythm suppression, cardiac costs, which can be measured
by E.E.G. and E.C.G. techniques (Hartmann, Manigault and
Tarriere, 1969) or by biochemical changes in saliva,
blood and urine (Cox, 1979).   In such studies it is possible to demonstrate progressive changes over working
periods.   Linking such changes to within-person perceptions of effort introduces high levels of inter- and
intra-personal variability, and there seems to be little
immediate prospect of using these techniques for anchoring or partitioning scales.

A further feature of nearly all jobs is that over
time they involve the repetition of a sequence of different forms of activity, observations, decision making
or analysis, exert force or physical action, test outcome for completion.   The averaging of such series of
differing activities, of peak and low level steady
levels, is difficult for the human brain which tends to
suppress stable information and to overestimate fre-
quencies and intensities of intermittent or peak signals
(Slovick and Lichentein, 1971).   Thus both within-person
perceptions of E → P relationships, and both self and
others' reports of effort as a motivational or level 1
outcome, are subject to many sources of instability in
reference levels and variability between subjects.
Avoidance of halo effects and development of behaviourally anchored multi-dimensioned scales has been discussed by Landy and Guion (1970) and Williams and Seiler
(1973), who report that effort ratings made by independent observers showed only small correlations (0.24,
0.33) and that effort ratings showed no discriminant
validity.

DIMENSIONS AND SCALING OF EFFORT

Assuming that the weighting, anchoring and scaling
problems can be solved for multi-factor constructs, the
next conceptual problem is that of arithmetic combination within the models.   In the physical sciences,
dimensional consistency is a necessary condition in any
mathematical expression or equation setting out the
relationship between variables.   In an expression -

$$M = \sum E_{ij} \sum (I_{jk} \cdot V_k)$$

the dimensions of M would have to be identical with the
dimensions of the summative terms and each of the $I_{jk} \cdot V_k$

terms would have to have the same dimensions. In the
House, Shapiro, Wahba (1974) model, the motivation M
would have to be the same dimensions as the intrinsic
valence IV_b and also as the whole expectancy summation:
$E_1(IV_a \sum(E_2^b.V))$.

Similarly for a relationship

$$M \rightarrow E \rightarrow X \rightarrow P$$
$$\uparrow$$

Moderating
factors

the motivation, effort, performance and moderating factors should be of the same dimensions if any causal
mathematical relationship is to be implied.

Whilst dimensional consistency may not be a necessary condition in behavioural research, it is such an
important principle in other branches of science that
adherence to the principle might be expected to lead to
increased conceptual clarity and predictive efficiency of
behavioural models.

The underlying ideas of some of the definitions of
effort can be listed with their physical dimensions to
show the range of implied dimensions:

Frequency	T^{-1}	Rate of working-power	$M L^2 T^{-2}$
Force	$M L T^{-2}$	Pressure	$M L^{-1} T^{-2}$
Speed	$L T^{-1}$	Integrated force - work done	$M L^2 T^{-2}$

Ratio of effort to subject's capacity -
Dimensionless (ratios are dimensionless)

One pragmatic view (Hackman and Porter, 1968) is
that arithmetic combination is not a strictly mathematical process which demands strict adherence to rules such
as transitivity (Behling and Stark, 1973), but that the
multiplicative summation of $\sum I.V$'s leads to a score which
can be distinguished from other scores and thus used to
make decisions. An alternative, following Graen (1969),
is to consider changes or increments. As ratios are
dimensionless, the expression of factors in ratio form
offers the most attractive route to avoiding any dimensional qualms.   At the within-person level, construct
relationships can be as ratios. This however, leads to
problems as the anchor levels and partitioning of such
ratios are unique to each individual. Comparison of
scores in between-person studies may prove interesting
but devoid of mathematical precision and of doubtful

validity as a measure of causal relationships.   Schmidt
(1973) points out that, in the absence of rational zero
points and true ratio scales, it is unreasonable to
expect any valid or reliable relationships between
measures of motivating force, effort, and subsequent performance.

> 'Vroom's original model was meant to predict
> the force on an individual to engage in a
> specific act;   most researchers have applied
> it to predict a poorly specified criteria.
> Clarification in this area is sorely needed.'
> (Mitchell, 1974).

WORKER BEHAVIOUR AND EFFORT

When attempting to overcome problems during the
development of theories, a very useful question to ask is
'What answer do we want?'   A survey of many of the
studies of work motivation can soon induce a sense of
doubt.   ('Yes, I can imagine such a creature behaving
that way ... but I don't remember ever actually meeting
one in the plant.')   Is the limited success of current
theories a consequence of asking the wrong questions and
solving the wrong problems?   What do we know about how
workers behave during continuing real-life work?

Detailed study of worker behaviour in real-life
situations appeares to have fallen out of fashion.   In
the 1920s many studies were made aimed at establishing
'work curves', optimum rest schedules, and the relationships between performance and fatigue.   Wyatt and his
colleagues in the Industrial Fatigue Research Board
carried out extensive and detailed studies of individual
workers in factory situations.   Many of their results,
and those of subsequent workers, are enshrined in basic
texts on psychology;   related to warm-up, fatigue,
learning curves and ideas on relationships between boredom and fatigue.   Typical theoretical curves such as
those of Katzell (1950) and Murrell (1971) are reproduced widely.   In analysing the earlier experiments,
major problems arose from the variability of worker
performance over short periods and the sensitivity of
performance to environmental changes in the conditions
of working.   The series of studies reported by Rothe
(1978) shows that both intra- and inter-worker performance recorded weekly in company production records is
highly variable.   An interesting hypothesis, that control of effort by 'effective incentivisation' can be
detected by the ratio of intra- and inter-worker correlations of performance, has not yet been conclusively
demonstrated.   (When using records relating to incentive
situations there is always the risk of distortion by

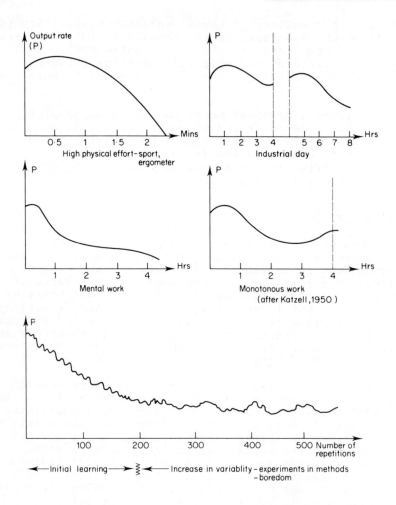

Figure 3.   Theoretical and practical performance curves.

cross booking and other forms of manipulation.)

A feature of detailed study of worker performance in real-life work is that the idealised performance curves prove very resistant to replication.   One reason proposed by Murrell to account for the divergence between theory, laboratory studies and real life experience, is that standards of performance have changed.   General attitudes to work technology, changing nature of jobs and technology, have changed the detailed mix of activities carried out by people in working systems.   Workers are allowed rest periods within a generally shorter working period.   Observations of individual cycle times (Murrell,

1971; Bevis, 1973) have shown characteristic forms of
cycle time or short term performance distributions.

Figure 4.   Basic Sequential Action Choice Model

     The response to motivational stimuli in working
situations is determined by a three level process.
Each level is characterised by the type of information
process involved and the stability of the information
stored or processed over time.

ACTION CHOICE DECISIONS

  (a)   Motivated behaviour in working situations is a
        continuing series of discrete consecutive action
        choices.

  (b)   The subject's immediate actions are determined by
        a continuing series of short term evaluations of
        his perception of the situation.

  (c)   The information used in this evaluation process
        is processed in short term memory which is of
        limited capacity.

  (d)   The memory span for decision is short.

INFORMATION USED IN DECISION PROCESS

  (a)   The information employed in the continuing evalu-
        ation process is selected from a set of learned
        constructs held in long term memory.

  (b)   The set of Learned Constructs is much larger than
        the set used in any single or short term series
        of evaluations.

  (c)   The Learned Constructs are relatively stable.

  (d)   The constructs are modified by feedback from
        experienced outcomes.

  (e)   The learning process will be limited by signal
        detection thresholds and interference from
        other perceived information.

  (f)   The learning process may follow the exponential
        form or may be of a dichotomous, switching, form.

  (g)   In the absence of feedback the information held
        in the set of Learned Constructs will decay by
        forgetting.   The forgetting may be progressive
        for exponentially learned constructs; dichotomous
        constructs may switch back to the initial state.

Figure 4 continued.

CHARACTERISTICS OF INDIVIDUALS

    (a)   Each individual subject has a characteristic set
         of highly stable constructs, needs or drives,
         his 'personality', traits.

    (b)   These personality factors are highly stable and,
         under normal working conditions, changes as the
         result of learning are very small. High stress
         or traumatic experiences may induce significant
         changes.

    (c)   The Set of Stable Constructs will determine ini-
         tial values of the Learned Constructs.

    (d)   They exercise a strong influence on the learning,
         forgetting and selective perception of the set of
         Learned Constructs.

Intrinsic motivation occurs when the subject modifies his
set of learned constructs, expectations, instrumentalities, valencies, by direct comparison between expected
outcomes and experienced outcomes in a single evaluation
cycle.

Extrinsic motivation occurs when the subject updates his
set of learned constructs by re-evaluation of the state
that led to the motivated action choice.

    Cycle times or performance rates for trainee workers
have low mean performances and are generally both widespread and skewed. As the worker becomes fully trained
the performance improves and the distributions tend to
become nearly normal with low dispersion. Where both
manufacturing and administrative tasks are either highly
repetitive, in totality or in many individual job or
task elements, the experienced worker continues learning
on such elements. This learning may be slow, but over
long periods the progressive development of skills leads
to a characteristic distribution showing a high performance peak with a long tail of slow or low performance
cycles. The worker's potential performance increases
but, for many reasons, the improvement is not declared.

    Murrell (1971) presents a set of data based on out-
put measured every minute over a working day. The output varies from 0 to 11 units per minute. The mode for
this distribution was 0, even allowing for breaks:

Mean Rate/min.	Standard Distribution	
3.84	3.37	Whole work period
6.07	2.27	Production minutes only

Using 90% of the maximum performance (9/minute) as a work standard, this data shows a worker performance of 44% of the potential.   Visual inspection of the data plot, and averaging over different periods, both fail to show any systematic pattern in the series of events making up the overall performance which can reasonably be attributed to fatigue or increased variability resulting from boredom.

DOES EFFORT APPLY TO REAL WORK?

When studies show that workers typically work at less than half their potential performance, that during the work period the times for repetition of job elements varies widely, and that systematic patterns of performance over the work periods are very elusive, a natural reaction is to question the application of the concept of effort.   The interpretation of motivation theories in many studies implies a 'pressure' concept of effort. That is, a combination of motivating factors determines a level of effort which, subject to moderating factors such as ability, and in the absence of constraints such as machine pacing or shortage of work input, leads to a stable level of effort and performance which can be correlated with measures or manipulations of the relevant motivating factors.

Such 'static' approaches may describe the behaviour of workers declaring their maximum performance in laboratory or sporting situations.   They do not offer an adequate explanation of the observed behaviour of experienced workers in continuing jobs.   Unless theories are dynamic in structure, there is little likelihood of their exhibiting significant predictive success when applied to real life situations.   The current use of effort in the systems models is unsatisfactory.   Its use can be avoided while yet retaining the conceptually-attractive structure of these approaches to work motivation theory (Walbank, 1979).

The core concept is to consider the within-person decision making aspects inherent in performance of a job or series of tasks.   Having selected a course of action and initiated its execution, the worker is presented with a continuing sequence of behavioural choices.   He can continue with the action or he can terminate it and

do something else. On completion of an action he can
immediately proceed to the next work-related activity or
action, and exhibit a high level of work performance;
or he can select some other action from the set available
to him at that instant, which he perceives as being more
currently attractive than the other alternatives.

This may be a minor change to a different set of
movements or mental activities, introducing variety and
allowing him to experience a sense of control within a
repetitive situation; or it may be non-working, rest,
temporary withdrawal, or social interaction with others
at or away from the work station.

It must be recognised that although such models
may appear complex, they are still a gross simplification of the complexities of behavioural response in
human beings. Even such simple models can be used to
demonstrate a very wide dynamic range of 'behaviours';
simulation studies of very simple creatures with limited
construct and action sets demonstrate complex patterns
of construct levels varying over time, and indicate some
of the problems of attempting to study motivation by
cross-section and between-person studies.

The valency-expectancy concept fits in well as a
building block in the action choice area of such models.
By using Action-Performance perceptions in the sequential
decision making process, and Action-Choice as the first
level outcome of the process, it is possible to avoid
many of the problems associated with the construct of
effort. This represents a return to theories of predicting the force on an individual to perform a specific
act; Vroom's concept of relative forces leading to
selection from alternatives. For the time being we
should abandon the use of effort in work motivation
studies and consider work motivation as a process where,
extending Galbraith and Cummings' (1967) comment - the
worker has a choice among many alternative levels of
task-related and non task-related activities and is able
to act out his choice.

REFERENCES

Aquiland, N.J. (1968). 'A physiological investigation
     of time standards for strenuous work as set by
     stopwatch time study and two pre-determined motion
     time data systems', Journal of Industrial Engineering,
     19, 425-432.

Behling, D. and Stark, G.A. (1973). 'The postulates of
     an expectancy theory', Academy of Management Journal,
     16-3, 373-388.

Bevis, F.W. (1971).   U.W.I.S.T. Research Conference.

Bevis, F.W. and Towell,D.R. (1972).   'Managerial systems
    based on learning curve models', Int. Jnl. Prod.
    Res., 11-2, 217-238.

Brief, A.P. and Aldag, R.J. (1977).   'The intrinsic-
    extrinsic dichotomy toward intellectual clarity',
    Academy of Management Review, 496-500.

Broedling, L.A. (1977).   'The use of the intrinsic
    extrinsic distinction in exploring motivation and
    organisational behaviour', Academy of Management
    Review, 2-2, 267-276.

Campbell, J.P., Dunette, M.D., Arvey, R.D. and Mellervick,
    L.W. (1973).   'The development and evaluation of
    behaviourally based rating scales', J. App. Psych.,
    57, 15-22.

Campbell, J.P. and Pritchard, R.D. (1976).   'Motivation
    theory in industrial and organisational psychology',
    in M.D. Dunette, Handbook of Industrial and Organi-
    sation Psychology, Rand McNally, N.Y.

Connolly, T. (1976).   'Some conceptual and methodological
    issues in expectancy models of work performance
    motivation', Academy of Management Review, 1-3,
    37-47.

Corlett, E.N. (1979).   'Isolation and curiosity as
    sources of work attitudes', Satisfactions in Work
    Design (Eds. R.G. Sell and P. Shipley), pp. 51-56,
    Taylor and Francis, London.

Cox, T. (1979).   'Repetitive work', Current Issues in
    Occupational Stress (Eds. C.L. Cooper and R. Payne),
    In Press, Wiley, London.

Dachler, H.P. (1973).   'Construct validation of an
    instrumentality-expectancy-task-goal model of
    work motivation', J. App. Psych., 58, 397-418.

Dunnette, M.D. (Ed.) (1976).   Handbook of Industrial
    and Organisational Psychology, Rand McNally, New York.

Dyer, L. and Parker, D.F. (1976).   'Expectancy theory
    as a within-person behavioural choice model: An
    empirical test of some conceptual and methodological
    refinements', J. Organisational Behaviour and Human
    Performance, 17, 97-117.

Galbraith, J. and Cummings, L.L. (1967).   'An empirical
    investigation of the motivational determinants of
    task performance: Interactive effects between
    instrumentality - valence and motivation ability',
    Org. Beh. and Hum. Perf., 2, 237-257.

Giles, W.T. and Holley, W.H. (1978).   'Job enrichment
    versus traditional issues at the bargaining table:
    What the unions want', Academy of Management Journal,
    21-4, 725-730.

Graen, G. (1969).   'Instrumentality theory of work moti-
    vation: Some experimental results and suggested
    modifications', Journal Applied Psychology Monograph,
    53, 1-25.

Hackman, J.R. and Porter, L.W. (1968).   'Expectancy
    theory predictions of work effectiveness', Organi-
    sational Behaviour and Human Performance, 3, 417-426.

Hartmann, F., Manigault, P. and Tarriere, C. (1969).
    'An endeavour to evaluate the nervous load at work
    stations in link production', Int. J. Production
    Research, 7, 3-10.

Herold, D.M. and Greller, M.M. (1977).   'Feedback: The
    definition of a construct', Academy of Management
    Journal, 20-1, 142-147.

House, R.J., Shapiro, H.J. and Wahba, M. (1974).
    'Expectancy theory as a prediction of work behaviour
    behaviour and attitude: A re-evaluation of experi-
    mental evidence', Decision Sciences, 5, 481-506.

Katzell, R.A. (1950).   Handbook of Applied Psychology
    (Eds. D.H. Friar and E.R. Henry), pp. 74-84, Holt,
    Rinehard and Winston, NY.

Khaleque, A. (1979).   'Performance and job satisfaction
    in short-cycled repetitive work', Satisfactions in
    Work Design (Eds. R.G. Sell and P. Shipley), pp. 95-
    100, Taylor and Francis, London.

Landy, J.L. and Guion, R.M. (1970).   'Development of
    scales for the measurement of work motivation',
    Organisational Behaviour and Human Performance, 5,
    93-103.

Lawler, E.E. (1971).   Pay and Organisational Effective-
    ness, McGraw-Hill.

Lindell, W.W. and Solomon, R.J. (1977).   'A total and
    stochastic test of the transitivity postulate under-
    lying expectancy theory', Organisational Behaviour

and Human Performance, 19, 311-324.

Matsui, T., Kagawa, M., Nagamatsu, J. and Ohtsuka, Y.
    (1977).   'Validity of expectancy theory as a within-
    person behavioural choice model for sales acti-
    vities', J. Applied Psychology, 62-6, 764-767.

Mitchell, T.R. (1974).   'Expectancy models of job
    satisfaction, preference and effort', Psych. Bull.,
    6, 1053-1077.

Muchinsky, D.M. (1977).   'A comparison of with and
    access subjects analysis of the expectancy, valency
    model for predicting effort', Academy of Management
    Journal, 20, 354-158.

Muramatsu, R. and Miyazaki, H. (1976).   'A new approach
    to production systems through developing human
    factors in Japan', Int. J. Prod. Research, 14,
    311-326.

Murrell, K.F.H. (1971).   'Industrial work rhythms', in
    Biological Rhythms and Human Performance (Ed. W.P.
    Colquhoun), Academic Press, London.

Porter, S. and Lawler, E.E. (1968).   Managerial Atti-
    tudes and Performance, Dorsey, Homewood III.

Pritchard, R.D. and Sanders, D.S. (1973).   'The
    influences of valence, instrumentality and expec-
    tancy on effort and performance', J. Applied
    Psychology, 57, 55-60.

Reinharth, C. and Wahba, M.A. (1975).   'Expectancy
    theory as a predictor of work motivation, effort
    expenditure and job performance', Academy of
    Management Journal, 18-3, 520-537.

Rothe, H.F. (1978).   'Output rates among industrial
    employees', J. Applied Psychology, 63-1, 40-46.

Schmidt, F.L. (1973).   'Implications of a measurement
    problem for expectancy theory research', Organi-
    sational Behaviour and Human Performance, 10,
    243-251.

Slovick, P. and Lichenstein, S. (1971).   'Comparison
    of Baysian and regression approaches to the study
    of information processing in judgement', Organi-
    sational Behaviour and Human Performance, 6,
    649-746.

Steers, R.M. and Porter, L.W. (1975).   Motivation and
    Work Behaviour, McGraw-Hill, NY.

Vroom, V. (1964).   Work and Motivation, Wiley, NY.

Wahba, M.A. and House, R.J. (1974).   'Expectancy theory
    in work and motivation - some logical and methodo-
    logical issues', Human Relations, 27-2, 121-146.

Walbank, W.M. (1979).   An Integrating Model of Moti-
    vated Work Behaviour, Omega (in press).

Wernimont, P.F. (1971).   'A systems view of job satis-
    faction', J. Applied Psychology, 57, 49-54.

Wild, R. and Birchall, D.W. (1975).   'Job structuring
    and work organisation', J. Occupational Psychology,
    48-3, 169-178.

Williams, W.E. and Seiler, D.A. (1973).   'Relationship
    between measures of effort and job performance',
    J. Applied Psychology, 57, 49-54.

Changes in Working Life
Edited by K.D. Duncan, M.M. Gruneberg, and D. Wallis
© 1980 John Wiley & Sons Ltd

Chapter 23

Job and Organization Characteristics as they pertain to Job Satisfaction and Work Motivation

R. PENN, J. P.SHEPOSH, J. A. RIEDEL and L. E. YOUNG

Increasing attention has been given to the quality of the work experience of individuals in organizations. In particular, attention has been directed at how quality of worklife affects the well-being of the worker, the effectiveness of the organization and how it can be improved to the benefit of both. There is also increasing awareness that there are no monistic or universal strategies for improving quality of worklife. The impact of any specific strategy is contingent on the characteristics of the setting in which it is used and the composition of the organizational members to whom it is applied. Suttle (1977) maintains that probably the most important set of facets that dictates whether a strategy is viable for the improvement of quality of worklife involves people's needs. Individuals differ with respect to their job experiences, educational level and cultural background. These differences will influence the relative importance of various needs and the manner in which they are satisfied. In the interest of improving quality of worklife, one must take into consideration organizational properties and job characteristics as well as individual differences.

* The views in this paper are those of the authors and do not necessarily reflect those of the Navy Department.

The present study is an attempt to investigate the
pattern of relationships between various individual,
organizational, and task variables and their relative
influence upon employee perceptions of job satisfaction.
While recent research has focused on determining the
individual, task, and organizational properties influencing satisfaction (Ford and Jackofsky, 1977; Lawler
and Hall, 1970), an attempt to examine the relative
importance of these variables requires further elabor-
ation.

This study focuses on the interrelationships of
these variables within the public sector. Historically,
the focus of organizational research has been on private
industry.   Although no explicit comparisons between
public and private organizations are presently proposed,
this study should provide information concerning organizational functioning in the public sector as well as
clues concerning the generalizability to the public
sector of those principles of organizational functioning
derived from the private sector.

Until recent years, little research has been directed
toward the relations among ethnic groups in organizations.
As discussed by Alderfer (1977), studies of organizational
life have for the most part been slow to recognize that
ethnic differences may influence perceptions of the
quality of life within organizations.   The three organizations under study employ sizeable numbers of both
Blacks and Whites.   The present study attempted to
determine the extent to which Blacks and Whites are satisfied with their job, and the individual, task, and organizational variables influencing their reported satisfaction.

Also included in the individual variables of
interest was motivation.   By means of open-ended questions, an attempt was made to identify those things
which occur at work that make employees feel good about
working, as well as those that frustrate them on the
job.   Once identified, these factors were then related
to satisfaction to elucidate further the components of a
good quality of worklife.

Satisfaction was conceptualized as a general index
of one's perceived quality of worklife.   In this regard,
it was believed that an investigation into the individual, organizational, and job variables related to
satisfaction would suggest components related to one's
perceived quality of worklife.

A subject of much research has centered on perceived
sources of job satisfaction.   In this context the issue
of the intrinsic/extrinsic distinction deserves mention.

There is no widely accepted definition of intrinsic or
extrinsic satisfaction.   Some researchers see these two
types of satisfaction differing in terms of the kinds of
rewards an employee receives, whether they are intrinsic
or extrinsic to the job itself (Pritchard and Peters,
1974).   Others draw the distinction in the basis of the
levels of needs satisfied (Maslow, 1970).   Still others
have called into question the appropriateness of distinguishing intrinsic and extrinsic satisfaction as they
seem to be overlapping concepts in terms of both rewards
and need levels (Guzzo, 1979).   The present study
attempted to address the relationships of variables and
sources of satisfaction while not defining a priori the
source of satisfaction as intrinsic or extrinsic.

To recapitulate, several major issues relevant to
the quality of worklife are addressed in this paper:
(1) the relative influence of individual, organizational,
and job characteristics upon employee perceptions of
satisfaction, (2) the differing patterns of relationships
between individual, organizational, and job characteristics as a function of sources of satisfaction, (3) the
degree of similarity between the interrelationships of
these various factors and satisfaction as a function of
ethnic identification, and (4) the differential relationships of motivational aspects and satisfaction as a
function of ethnicity.

METHOD

Description of the Organization Studied

The Navy Public Works Centers (PWCs) are service
organizations providing engineering, maintenance (including rehabilitation construction), utilities, transportation, and housing for the US Navy shore establishments.
Worldwide there are nine sites.   Three sites located in
the continental United States were included in this study.
Each organization is responsible for serving customers in
their distinct geographical area.   The annual operating
budgets for the three organizations under study range
from $60 million to $125 million per year.   The number of
members within each organization ranges from 675 to
2,200 people.

One unique aspect of these different centers is that
they are quite similar in terms of their tasks, technology, organizational structure, and cultural/ethnic background of management.   Since the centers service one
large organization, the nature of the services provided
and the means of work accomplishment are consistent across
sites.   Structurally, each organization consists of four
major levels: (1) top management, the officers from the

Navy's Civil Engineering Corps; (2) middle management, civilian department heads; (3) several civilian supervisory levels; and (4) the civilian labor force. The large majority of top and middle management consists of individuals who are Caucasian and male. The lower levels of the organizations, however, are comprised of individuals possessing cultural characteristics reflecting the community in which the PWC is located.

Sample

The sample consisted of 524 employees from the workforce level of three Navy Public Works Centers. Questionnaires were administered to small groups of approximately 5 to 25.

Research Instrument

The research instrument consisted of items assessing demographic characteristics (e.g., education, ethnicity), areas of organizational functioning, motivation, and satisfaction. Items were based on two sources: research literature on organizations and information distilled from interviews conducted with PWC personnel.

The majority of the items in the questionnaire measuring dimensions of organizational functioning were responded to on a 5, 6, or 7-point scale, anchored with a positive response and a negative response. The items assessing motivation were open-ended. The measures selected as pertinent to the issue of job satisfaction are described in detail below:

1. Demographic Characteristics.   These items surveyed education level, length of time working for the PWC, and ethnicity.

2. Commitment.   These items assessed employees' feelings of personal responsibility and commitment regarding the success of their jobs.

3. Value Agreement.   This item assessed the degree to which workers felt management had values similar to their own with respect to the way people are viewed.

4. Organizational Climate.   Measures of

perceptions of organizational climate (Campbell and Beaty, 1971) were factor analyzed. All factors presented in this study attained eigenvalues of 1.0 or greater and interpretation of the factors was based on items with loadings of .35 and above. The factors which emerged represented: (a) Perceptions of Military Management, (b) Openness of the Organization, (c) Esprit de Corps, and (d) Ethnic and Theft Problems.

5. Perceptions of Supervisor. Workers were asked to respond to questions assessing various aspects of supervision. These responses were factor analyzed and three factors emerged representing (a) Supervisory Support, (b) Supervisory Competence, and (c) Supervisory Bias.

6. Role Stress. Items taken from a scale developed by Rizzo, House and Lirtzman (1970) were included to measure perceptions of role stress. Two clear factors, very similar to those obtained by Rizzo et al., emerged, one measuring Role Ambiguity, the other Role Conflict.

7. Job Characteristics. Questions designed to assess characteristics of the job itself were included. Responses to these items were factor analyzed. Factors representing perceptions of (a) Pay and Fringe Benefits, (b) Job Challenge, (c) Reward Contingencies, (d) Job Importance, and (e) Time Constraints were obtained.

8. Intention to Leave. Items were included that measured employees' intentions to look for a new job both within and outside the organization.

9. Satisfaction. Nine items assessed the degree of satisfaction with specific aspects of the job such as chances to accomplish something, pay, security, and recognition. The responses to these items were factor analyzed, yielding two discrete factors, one measuring satisfaction with job facets and the other measuring satisfaction with pay and security.

10. Motivation. Employees were asked to provide up to five responses to each of two open-ended questions assessing what motivates them to accomplish something on the job and what demotivates them, or keeps them from accomplishing their work. Responses to these two questions were classified following the procedure outlined in

Barthol and de Mille (1969).   This procedure entailed
randomly dividing all of the responses to be classified
among three classifiers.   Each classifier independently
classified responses into as many categories as he thought
appropriate.   Responses that each classifier felt did
not fit into his classification scheme were placed in a
'Miscellaneous' category.

Since one classifier's 'Miscellaneous' responses
might fit into a different category for another classifier, each classifier's 'Miscellaneous' responses were
passed to the other two in an attempt to minimize the
size of each one's 'Miscellaneous' category.   The
classifiers then pooled their separate category schemes
to produce a joint category scheme.   Last, they sorted
the responses into this new category scheme.   This procedure was employed to classify responses to both questions; however, responses to each question were classified separately.

RESULTS

As stated in the introduction the purpose of this
study was to examine the pattern of relationships between
perceived job and organizational characteristics and
satisfaction.   Since zero-order correlations can only
determine relationships between two variables, they would
not optimally capture the structure of the interrelationships of all of the variables under study.   Additionally,
multivariate techniques such as factor analysis or multiple regression are bound by such data requirements as
interval scales and homoscedasticity, and therefore,
would not be appropriate for the analyses of responses
to the semi-structured questions dealing with motivation.
An approach that does not require metric data and that
indicates all the interdistances for the variables of
interest and explicates the discernable patterns of association was required in the present study.   Therefore,
smallest space analysis (SSA) was considered an appropriate multivariate technique for this study.   SSA is
tantamount to a nonmetric factor analysis in the sense
that it determines the minimum number of dimensions in
which the data can adequately be represented.   It can
also be viewed as the nonmetric equivalent of multiple-
regression analysis, since it provides a graphic portrayal
of the analyzed data matrices in a format that enables
users to view the space in toto and to examine the pattern of relationships within and between variables.

A brief discussion of the essential characteristics
of SSA may be helpful to those who are unfamiliar with
this technique.   SSA requires as input a correlation
matrix of all variables under study.   The output is in

the form of a space diagram illustrating the location of
all the variables with respect to each other. Very
short distances between variables spatially represented
indicate positive correlations, while very long distances represent negative correlations. The SSA program places all variables in N-dimensional space in
which interpoint distances are stretched out from one
another as far as possible. A one-dimensional solution
stretches all variables along a straight line. If sufficient tautness is not obtained a distribution of the
variables in a two-dimensional space is then required.
This process is repeated until the distances are sufficiently taut (i.e., the best fit is obtained). The
measure indicating the degree of tautness is the coefficient of alienation, which ranges from 1.00 (distances
are completely slack) to 0.00 (completely taut). A discussion of the mathematical and statistical properties
of SSA can be found in Guttman (1968) and Lingoes (1973).

The first analysis describes the interrelationships
of 20 individual, organizational, and task variables.
Seventeen of the variables represented PWC workers' perceptions of their job and organization, two represented
demographic characteristics, and one was a measure of
satisfaction with various facets of their job. The
second analysis of interest differed only in that the
satisfaction measure was an indication of workers' satisfaction with pay and job security.

Representations of these two analyses are presented
in the form of space diagrams (Figures 1 and 2). The
scale on the two coordinates is arbitrary and interpretations of the space diagrams are made in terms of the
distances among variables or clusters of variables,
without reference to the meaning of the underlying dimensions (coordinates). The coefficients of alienation
obtained from the two-dimensional solutions (coefficient
of alienation = .166, .167, respectively) are adequate
and in line with those obtained in other studies (Shirom,
Eden, Silberwasser and Kellerman, 1973; Elizur, 1970).
Since this study was concerned primarily with understanding the relationships of the job and organizational
variables to satisfaction and not in identifying specific
clusters of variables, no attempt was made to partition
the space into identifiable regions based on clusters.

In Figure 1 it can be seen that the variables most
closely associated with the index of satisfaction with
job facets, are perceived openness of the organization,
supervisory support, job challenge, low role ambiguity,
job importance, and reward contingencies; while role conflict is negatively related. Figure 2 is a representation of the SSA performed on the identical variables
used in the first analysis, with one difference: the

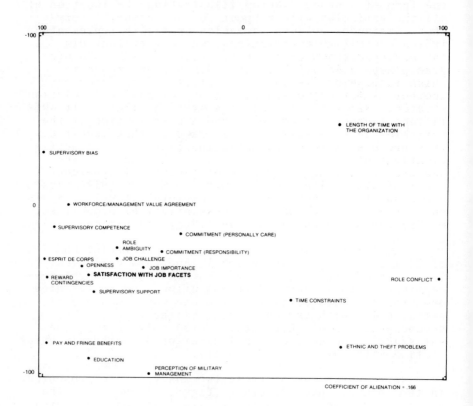

Figure 1.   Space diagram representing the interrelation-
             ships of demographic characteristics, organi-
             zational and job variables and satisfaction
             with job facets for the three PWCs.

index of satisfaction in this analysis was linked to pay
and security.   The pattern of relationships between the
19 variables and satisfaction obtained in this analysis is
strikingly similar to that presented in Figure 1.   Overall the distance between the job and organizational
variables and satisfaction in this analysis are not as
closely associated as those shown in Figure 1.   Supervisory support is closest, followed by reward contingencies, openness, pay and fringe benefits, esprit de corps,
supervisory competence, and low role ambiguity;   while
role conflict is negatively related.

     The correlations for those variables showing the
closest relationship with the two satisfaction indices
were assessed.   In general, the correlations were

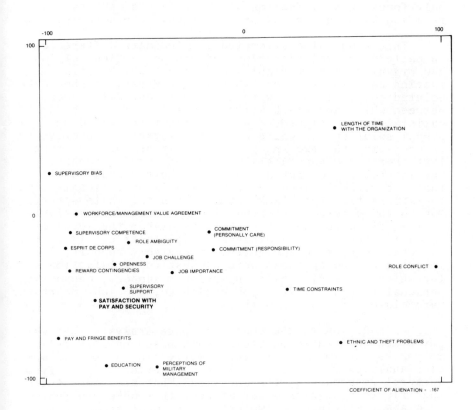

Figure 2. Space diagram representing the interrelation-ships of demographic characteristics, organizational and job variables and satisfaction with pay and security for the three PWCs.

stronger for satisfaction with job facets than for satisfaction with pay.   Not unexpectedly the workers' beliefs
concerning fairness of pay were correlated more strongly
with satisfaction with pay than with the other index of
satisfaction.   Since the two space diagrams revealed a
high degree of similarity the remaining analyses will
only focus on satisfaction with job facets and its
relationships to job and organizational characteristics.

This study also attempted to elucidate differences
in patterns of relationships between perceptions of job
and organizational variables and reported job satisfaction as a function of ethnicity.   First, it should be
pointed out that there were no significant differences
between white and black workers in terms of expressed
satisfaction.   Figures 3 and 4 project the two-dimensional solution for white and black workers respectively.
In comparing the two space diagrams it becomes apparent
that there is a substantial degree of correspondence.
One interesting difference between the two analyses is
that the worker's level of education is more closely tied
to satisfaction for black workers than for white workers.
Due to the nature of scoring of the educational variable,
a small distance indicates that the higher the level of
education the less the expressed satisfaction.   Briefly,
job challenge, role ambiguity, supervisory support, job
importance, and openness were closest to satisfaction
for white workers;   while supervisory support, openness,
personal responsibility, job challenge, and job importance
were closest for black workers.

In addition to the smallest space analyses that were
performed on structured items, data based on workers'
responses to two semistructured motivation questions were
also analyzed.   There were five categories derived from
workers' responses to the question 'What are some of the
specific things which occur at work that make you feel
good about working?'   Two categories most frequently
cited on motivators were cooperative and supportive co-
workers and a sense of accomplishment.   The remaining
three categories: supervisory support, pay and adequate
time and material to perform one's job were cited less
frequently.   Proportionally a larger number of white
workers (55.1%) relative to black workers (42.2%) reported
that sense of accomplishment contributed to positive
feelings toward their work, while the reverse held true
for adequacy of time and material (10.2% and 28.1% for
white and black workers respectively).

Six categories were derived from the workers' responses to the question 'What specific kinds of things
occur at work that turn you off, frustrate you or make
you angry?'   The three most important demotivators were
problems with material/equipment, supervisors' handling

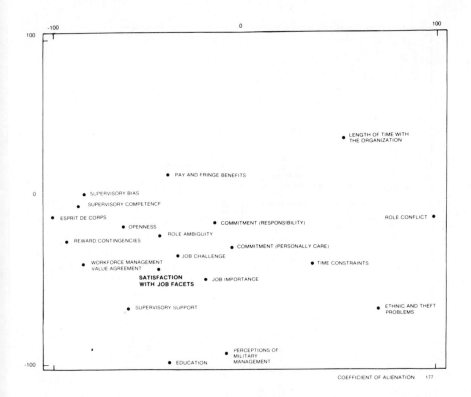

Figure 3.   Space diagram representing the interrelation-
            ships of demographic characteristics, organi-
            zational and job variables and satisfaction
            with job facets for White workers across
            centres.

of personnel matters, and co-workers.   The remaining
three categories concerning problems with planning and
estimating, supervisory handling of task-related matters,
and organizational practices were cited less frequently.
Proportionally, a larger number of white workers relative
to black workers reported that co-workers, material/equip-
ment, and organizational problems contributed to negative
feelings toward their work (32.2% versus 21.9%, 44.0%
versus 20.3% and 21.9% versus 10.9%, respectively).

     The smallest space analyses that were performed on
the 11 categories investigated workers' level of satisfaction with job facets along with two additional items:
desire to take a different job within the organization

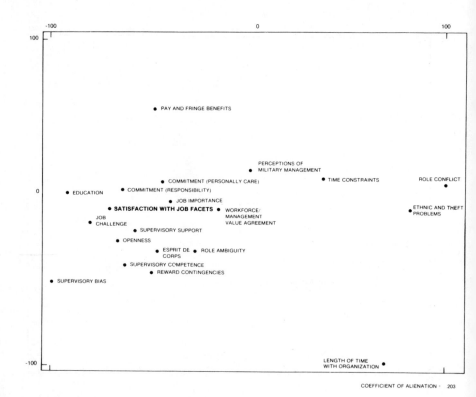

Figure 4.   Space diagram representing the interrelation-
             ships of demographic characteristics, orga-
             nizational and job variables and satisfaction
             with job facets for Black workers across
             centres.

and desire to look for a new job outside the organization.
Separate analyses were performed on white and black
worker samples and the space diagrams are shown in
Figures 5 and 6.   Turning first to Figure 5 it can be
seen that for white workers, satisfaction is negatively
correlated with intention to seek a different job
within the organization and intention to seek a new job
outside the organization.   Satisfaction is also negatively correlated with organizational problems (e.g., too
much paperwork) and supervisory problems (task and personnel).   The category found to be most closely associated with satisfaction is concern over material and
equipment problems.   The category closest to 'desire to
leave' items is supervisory problems (task).   Thus,

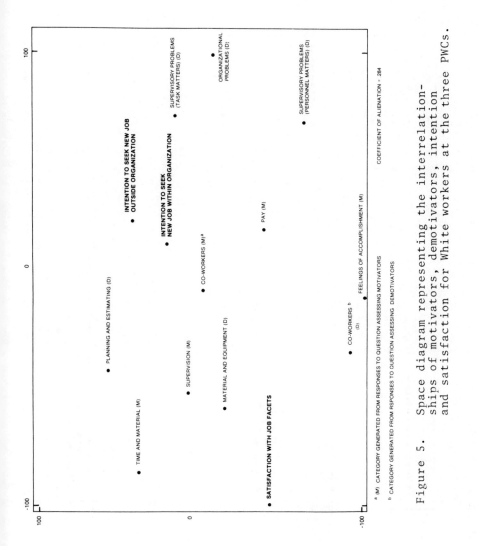

Figure 5. Space diagram representing the interrelationships of motivators, demotivators, intention and satisfaction for White workers at the three PWCs.

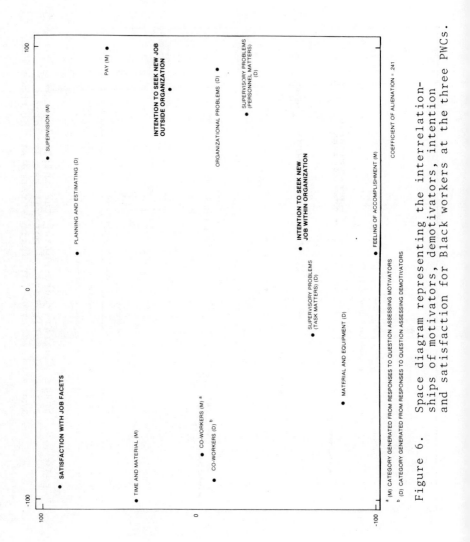

Figure 6. Space diagram representing the interrelationships of motivators, demotivators, intention
and satisfaction for Black workers at the three PWCs.

workers who are dissatisfied with various facets of their
job cite as frustrating features of their job, (1) organizational problems and (2) problems with supervision,
such as the lack of interpersonal skills and job incom-
petence.

Figure 6 presents the space diagram for the black
worker sample.   The configuration of interrelationships
as portrayed in the space diagram differs from that
obtained for the white sample.   For this group, workers
who express dissatisfaction also cite organizational
problems and supervisory problems (personnel matters)
as frustrations;   however, they are also more likely to
list pay as a major motivator.   In addition they are
less likely to view adequate time and material to do the
job as an important motivator.   Of particular interest
is the separation that is evident between the two
'desire to leave' items.   Poor interpersonal skills on
the part of supervision was closely linked to a desire
to find a new job within the organization.   Those people
who were more likely to desire to find a new job outside
the organization were more likely to report pay as a
salient motivator.

DISCUSSION

Regardless of the focus, whether it is directed at
the interests of the workers (quality of worklife) or at
the goals of the organization (organizational effectiveness), the theoretical and empirical literature paints
an extremely complex picture of organizational functioning
where a multitude of factors (e.g., organization members'
attitudes and values, organizational structure and
climate, job characteristics and processes of interaction) are seen as affecting organizational life
(Alderfer, 1976).   The focus of the present investigation has been on the identification of the factors, as
analyzed from a multidimensional perspective, that contribute to workers' satisfaction with their work.   The
results of the present study provide some insights and
raise some questions with respect to the nature of the
interrelationships of various individual, organizational,
and task variables and job satisfaction.

First, with respect to the findings based on perceived job and organizational characteristics, as
measured by the structured questionnaire, it was found
that the majority of dimensions examined were significantly correlated with workers' satisfaction with various
facets of their job.   The SSA technique employed in this
study enabled an examination of the overall structure of
the intercorrelations.   Relative distances portrayed in
the space diagram (Figure 1) indicate that workers who
characterized the organization as open, who reported low

role ambiguity, low role conflict, high supervisory support, accurate reward contingencies and viewed their job as important and challenging expressed the highest levels of satisfaction. It would appear then that the foremost consideration of workers with respect to felt job satisfaction centered on the adequacy of information, guidelines, and supervisory support required to do their job.

Correlations for climate, job characteristics, and role perceptions with the satisfaction measure were of comparable magnitude. These results are at variance with those of Schneider and Hall (1973), for example, who found that measures which focused on an individual's immediate job showed stronger correlations with satisfaction than did organizational climate measures. The results of this study suggest that a number of aspects of the organization impinge on the individual worker's sense of satisfaction in varying degrees and that partialling out one group of factors as prepotent without reference to other factors operating in the situation results in a limited and, at times, incorrect reading of the problem under study.

The role ambiguity and role conflict dimensions are also of interest. Ford and Jackofsky (1977) note that relatively little research has examined the relationships between role perceptions and climate variables. In the present study both role ambiguity and role conflict were found to be related to the various job and climate measures.

One of the purposes of the study was to determine the extent to which the pattern of interrelations of job and organization variables obtained for workers' satisfaction with pay and security differed from that obtained for satisfaction with job facets. A comparison of the smallest space analyses (Figures 1 and 2) indicates high agreement. These results are supportive of Guzzo's contention that a neat dichotomization of work rewards into intrinsic and extrinsic categories based on the function they serve, is of questionable value (Guzzo, 1979). This functional differentiation is not unequivocal since more than one level of need can be served simultaneously by a particular reward. Germane to this particular finding is Staw's commentary on the implications of viewing intrinsic and extrinsic motivation as separate independent factors. 'Whether or not intrinsic and extrinsic sources of motivation are independent or do in fact have an effect upon each other is a question of considerable practical as well as theoretical significance ... if they are positively interrelated, then we might expect that extrinsic rewards will increase a person's interest in a task' (Staw, 1977, pp. 71-72).

The extent to which ethnic identification has an
impact on an individual's evaluations of the organization and one's job was also of major interest.   Separate smallest space analyses of white and black workers'
perceptions of the organization revealed similar patterns of associations.   With one or two exceptions the
same dimensions were related in a similar fashion to
the satisfaction measure.   The differences that are
evident between the two samples merit attention.   While
the correlations were significant for both white and
black workers, educational level (negative relationships),
sense of personal responsibility for one's job, supervisory competence and support (all positive relationships), were more closely associated with expressed
satisfaction for black workers than for white workers;
whereas the relationship for role ambiguity and the
measure tapping value agreement between workers and
management were more closely associated for white workers.

The space diagram based on the information supplied
by the workers as to what aspects of work motivate or
frustrate them provide a fuller understanding of the
concerns of white and black workers (Figures 5 and 6).
Workers who mentioned organizational problems and poor
personnel practices on the part of supervisors tended to
express less job satisfaction.   This held for both white
and black workers.   The clearest differences between
white and black workers revolve around the two items
dealing with desire for a new job.   For white workers it
was found that those who regarded supervisory incompe-
tence with respect to job matters as a salient demotivator were more eager to find a new job within the organization or outside the organization.   A different pattern emerged for black workers.   Lack of understanding
and inconsiderate treatment by supervisors was the category most closely related to finding a new job within
the organization, whereas organizational problems as a
demotivator and pay as a motivator were most closely
related to finding a new job outside the organization.
Although many of the correlations in the two correlation
matrices, with the exclusion of those discussed above,
were insignificant the difference in the general patterns
of associations revealed by the two space diagrams is
apparent and provides insight with respect to the job
related concerns of the black and white workers.

The technique employed in this study of asking
workers to indicate the salient work-related motivators
and demotivators, and the procedure used to classify
them (Barthol and de Mille, 1969), holds promise as a
diagnostic tool for several reasons.   First, relative
to structured items this technique is less open to the
vagaries of such effects as the pressure to respond in a
socially desirable manner, and other forms of response

sets.   Second, the focus of these categories is job related and highly specific.   Third, this procedure enables the investigator to ascertain those areas that are most salient to the respondents themselves, which in turn enables the investigator to circumvent the imposition of personal biases and possible gaps in knowledge about the subject under study.

Thus, it is evident that this technique may be a potentially fruitful strategy in the diagnostic phase of an investigation.   It is felt that this is particularly so when this technique is combined with and analyzed from a multidimensional perspective such as the SSA employed in this study.   Further, the present methodological approach and findings have practical as well as theoretical significance.   This approach serves an especially useful function toward obtaining an understanding of an organization for planning of interventions, in that it permits an idiographic assessment (Allport, 1937) of individual, job and organizational variables specific to one organization which should have implications for enhancing functioning.

ACKNOWLEDGEMENT

The authors would like to express their gratitude to Dr. Linda M. Doherty for her comments and suggestions on this manuscript.

REFERENCES

Alderfer, C.P. (1976).   'Change processes in organizations', in M.D. Dunnette (Ed.), Handbook of Industrial and Organizational Psychology, Chicago, IL Rand-McNally.

Alderfer, C.P. (1977).   'Group and intergroup relations', in L.R. Hackman and J.L. Suttle (Eds.), Improving life at work: Behavioral science approaches to organization change, Santa Monica, CA, Goodyear Publishing.

Allport, G. (1937).   Personality: A psychological interpretation, New York, Holt, Rinehart & Winston.

Barthol, R.P. and de Mille, R. (1969).   Project ECHO (CR-0018-2), Santa Barbara, CA, General Research Corporation (NTIS No. AD 702-740).

Campbell, J.P. and Beaty, E.E. (1971).   'Organizational climate: Its measurement and relationship to work group performance', Paper presented at the meeting of the American Psychological Association, Washington, D.C.

Elizur, D. (1970). Adapting to innovation, Academic Press, Jerusalem.

Ford, D.L. and Jackofsky, E.F. (1977). 'Role perceptions, organizational climate, and satisfaction in newly created organization subunits', Paper presented at the meeting of the American Psychological Association, San Francisco.

Guttman, L. (1968). 'A general nonmetric technique for finding the smallest coordinate space for a configuration of points', Psychometrika, 33, 469.

Guzzo, R.A. (1979). 'Types of rewards, cognitions, and work motivation', Academy of Management Review, 4, 75-86.

Lawler, E.E., III and Hall, D. (1970). 'The relationships of job characteristics to job involvement, satisfaction and intrinsic motivation', Journal of Applied Psychology, 54, 305-312.

Lingoes, J. (1973). The Guttman-Lingoes nonmetric program series, Ann Arbor, Michigan, Mathesis Press.

Maslow, A.H. (1970). Motivation and personality, Second Ed., New York, Harper.

Pritchard, R.D. and Peters, L.H. (1974). 'Job duties and job interests as predictors of intrinsic and extrinsic satisfaction', Organizational Behavior and Human Performance, 12, 315-330.

Rizzo, J.R., House, R.J. and Lirtzman, S.I. (1970). 'Role conflict and ambiguity in complex organizations', Administrative Science Quarterly, 15, 150-163.

Schneider, B. and Hall, D.T. (1973). 'Towards specifying the concept of work climate: A study of Roman Catholic Diocesan priest', Journal of Applied Psychology, 56, 447-455.

Shirom, A., Eden, D., Silberwasser, S. and Kellermann, J.J. (1973). 'Job stresses and risk factors in coronary heart disease among five occupational categories in Kibbutzim', Social Science and Medicine, 7, 875-892.

Staw, B.M. (1977). 'Motivation in organizations: toward synthesis and redirection', in B. Staw and J.R.

Salencik (Eds.), New Directions in Organizational Behavior, Chicago, IL, St. Clair Press.

Suttle, J.L. (1977).   'Improving life at work - problems and prospects', in J.R. Hackman and J.L. Suttle (Eds.), Improving life at work: Behavioral Science Approaches to Organization Change, Santa Monica, CA, Goodyear Publishing Co., Inc.

Changes in Working Life
Edited by K.D. Duncan, M.M. Gruneberg, and D. Wallis
© 1980 John Wiley & Sons Ltd

Chapter 24

Job Satisfaction and Motivation— The Development of Practical Strategies for their Enhancement

G. C. WHITE

This is an account of the way in which some of the
recommendations made by Wilson (1973) in his report 'On
the Quality of Working Life' have been worked out in practice. ·The account cannot pretend to be entirely objective since the author has been closely involved with most,
and personally responsible for some, of the developments
stemming from that report in the United Kingdom. The
views expressed result in part from discussions with colleagues, but they are not necessarily shared by them or
by the Department of Employment.

There are several interesting strands which might be
explored. First, there is the development of a unit set
up to explore what could be done to enhance the quality
of working life in the UK. Units with a similar purpose,
with which it can be compared, have been established in
other countries. Secondly, it can be seen in terms of an
attempt to translate the results of an increasing volume
of empirical and theoretical studies on the topics of
satisfaction and motivation at work, into sound principles
for dealing with some of the problems faced by people at
work. A third strand in the story concerns the dissemination of concepts and ideas in this field and the uncertain and unpredictable ways in which new ideas reach the
level of common sense and 'received' thinking; sometimes
demonstrating the truth of Keynes's dictum that practical
men who believe themselves to be quite exempt from any
intellectual influences are usually the slaves of some

defunct theorist.   A fourth is the changes in ideas and
concepts themselves as a result of their exposure to the
tempering fires of practical problems, particularly in a
political and economic environment in which security of
employment and preservation of living standards in face
of inflation have been high on the list of most wage
earners' priorities.

During 1970-71 Wilson (1973) undertook for the UK
Government, at the request of the NATO Committee on the
Challenges of Modern Society, to enquire into problems
of work motivation and satisfaction (and their opposites).
From a review of what he called 'the state of the art' he
suggested two practical steps for the Department of Employment, the relevant government department in UK, to undertake or sponsor.   The first was to be a co-ordinated programme of development in real industrial and commercial
settings which, suitably researched and monitored, would
provide valuable documented demonstrations of what ideas
might be tried out under defined conditions and with what
identifiable results.   There was, at the time, some dissatisfaction with the way in which British industry and
commerce failed to use ideas about how work might satisfactorily be structured.   It was thought that providing
more 'success stories' would lead to the dissemination
and extensive adoption of the principles and practices
which had demonstrably succeeded in improving individual
satisfaction and, at one and the same time increasing
or at least holding constant organisational
efficiency.

The second practical project was to be a periodic
sample survey of workers' occupational experiences,
expectations and attitudes, on the lines of the then
experimental survey carried out in the USA by the Survey
Research Centre of the University of Michigan (1971).
The purpose of this was to create systematic information
on a national scale about people's attitudes to and
experiences of work, including significant changes over
time.

In order to co-ordinate and manage the collection
and use of information about the satisfactory design of
work systems and individual jobs, Wilson suggested a
small unit within the Department of Employment which,
working with relevant university departments and research
institutes, would carry out the programme.   He added,
almost as an afterthought, that measures for involving
representatives of trade unions, employers and other
organisations in the planning and monitoring of these
activities are vitally important.

Although this account is only concerned with how
Wilson's recommendations to the Department of Employment
have worked out in the UK, it is relevant on this occasion

to note the recommendations made to NATO.   These were
that:

(i)   the NATO Committee on the Challenges of Modern
       Society should organise an international confer-
       ence of experts to study the implications of
       existing work and to consider how progress might
       be achieved;

(ii)   each member country should be invited to consider
       introducing programmes of new-type work systems;

(iii) there should be an increase in research and
       development related to specific occupational
       topics;

(iv)   special separate attention should be paid to the
       future of work.

     Accounts of the development of the UK programme as a
whole (White and Jessup, 1979), and of the job satisfaction research programme (White, 1978) have been published elsewhere.   The research programme began in 1974.
It included a number of action research projects in work
organisations as well as some concerned with more
general problems which people experience at work, including stress and the effects that work and other aspects
of life have on each other.   Two of these are reported
in this volume (Wallis and Cope;   Guest, Williams and
Dewe).   The programme has been managed by a Work Research
Unit, set up the previous year under Professor Don Wallis,
then Chief Psychologist in the Department.   In that year
also, a Tripartite Steering Group on Job Satisfaction was
set up with a Minister as chairman and on which there are
representatives of government departments, trade unions,
and employers' organisations.   Originally seen as
having a limited life, this steering group has continued
as an advisory body, its secretariat being provided by
the Work Research Unit.

     The staff of the Work Research Unit, which by 1976
had grown to a total of 28 and included professional staff
with a range of social scientific and technical experience, have been engaged not only in the management,
monitoring, and stimulation of research in the field of
quality of working life but also in direct intervention,
by invitation, in private and public enterprises;   in
providing information in response to direct inquiries;
and in promoting discussion of issues and action aimed at
improving people's experience of working life.   This is
done by arranging regional conferences for managers and
union officers and by contributing to professional and
industrial journals.

DEVELOPMENTS IN THE EMPHASIS OF ACTIVITIES

At the basis of these activities are two tenets. First, jobs can and ought to be designed with human, as well as technical and commercial criteria in mind. These objectives are not entirely contradictory and incompatible. Secondly, people should participate directly and through representatives in the process of design of work as well as in decisions about the nature of the changes. The words 'ought' and 'should' are to be interpreted as stating conditional imperatives: that is to say, if these principles are applied, then the objective of enhancing people's experience of work will be approached.

In applying these principles to the problems of job design presented by companies to the Unit or to its associates in Universities, we have found that the Unit's activities have needed modification in a number of ways during the five years since it began. First, although still focusing on the content and arrangement of jobs, aspects of the organisational context of work are also considered. (For example, the payments system and managerial structure). Secondly, although improving individual experience of work is still a primary objective, an important corollary is increasing the effectiveness with which organisations function, this being a somewhat broader concept than technical efficiency or commercial profitability. There are some potential immediate advantages to be gained by enterprises through reductions in labour turnover and absence, and through improved output or quality of goods or services. These are readily understood by managers, are reflected in their objectives, and occasionally included in accounting procedures. Less tangible, less readily quantified, advantages can also accrue, such as the capacity of the enterprise to manage changes in technology, materials or product satisfactorily, to deal with and perhaps anticipate new pressures from both external and internal environments, and to benefit from the consequences of fuller development of human potential available within the enterprise.

The third way in which the emphasis of the work of the Unit has changed since 1974 is that greater attention is given to developing within client organisations appropriate systems for managing the process of change, using current problems relating to the design of jobs as the focus. This implies helping to develop resources within the company for handling problems of similar kinds as well as improving the jobs that exist. In almost no case has the Unit felt able to regard a change process as finished. There is always some other way in which the same or other jobs in the company can be improved.

	1974	1979
Consultancy objectives	Improving job satisfaction	Improving quality of working life
		Increasing effectiveness of enterprise
Focus	Content of individual jobs	Content of jobs and their organisational environmental
Emphasis of strategy	Diagnosis of areas of job dissatisfaction and redesign of jobs	Developing process of change and resources in companies
Orientation of consultant	Data collection Diagnosis of problem	Minimum intervention to facilitate change and maintain momentum
Point of entry	Shop floor, desk or counter	Department (all levels) rather than single level
Presenting problems	Morale, absenteeism, turnover	Managing organisational change satisfactorily in face of technical innovation
	Poor quality output	
		Increasing involvement and 'motivation'

Figure 1.   Developments in work research unit consultancy activities.

These changes in orientation and objectives are summarised in Figure 1.

The lessons learned from the attempts so far to apply these principles to the problems brought to the Unit from managers and trade unions in a wide range of enterprises during its first five years, will now be described and discussed.

FEATURES OF THE GENERAL STRATEGY

Preliminary contacts and discussions between the management and unions in the enterprise and the staff of the Unit, may reach a stage where it seems worthwhile to proceed with a project. This stage is not easily or quickly reached and the preliminary discussions are of crucial importance to the development of trust, of

understanding of the differing objectives of groups and
individuals (including those of the consultant) and to
reaching agreement to go ahead with what becomes identified as a project, using a stage-by-stage strategy including some or all of the features described below.
Failure to deal with important issues at this early stage
can lead to continuing misperceptions and conflicting
objectives.

In one case, help was given in a company employing
some 7000 people on complex construction.   Men in a
skilled trade were subject to high turnover and, according to the management, low morale.   Data from interviews and written questionnaires indicated high satisfaction with the tasks, problem-solving, and variety of
the work itself but high dissatisfaction with the organisation of work, with the amount of discretion with job
security, and inadequate scheduling of work and materials.
Attention was also drawn to the frequent movement of individuals from one work group and task to another, with
consequent lack of feedback on performance and, more
seriously, effects on output, safety, and the important
informal contacts and relationship which provide the
essential network for social learning of attitudes and
behaviour to which Karl-Olof Faxén has drawn attention
(Faxén, 1979).   In this project the problems seemed to
stem from difficulties elsewhere than the jobs of the
skilled tradesmen.   This was not fully accepted by the
senior management whose interpretation of the problem
was being questioned.   A further survey with other skilled craftsmen and labourers carried out by staff of the
company trained to use a schedule developed with the help
of a joint management steering group, confirmed the data.
The change agent/consultant saw the interviews as a means
of collecting data about people's perceptions of the
least satisfactory aspects of their jobs, from their own
viewpoint as well as from the viewpoint of getting the
job done;   expecting that this data would be used by
work groups and their managers to start discussing ways in
which the work might be reorganised.   In retrospect, the
management saw the intervention as an application of a
'human relations' approach to solving problems, an alternative to methods study.   Data was avidly searched for
recommendations.   The subsequent disillusionment and
discussion of the difference in viewpoint and expectations
were never satisfactorily resolved.   Other differences
came to light at this stage.   The range of solutions
acceptable to management did not include changes in the
way work was organised or managed.   The prevailing view
was that, if systems did not work, it was because people
did not obey the rules;   that more and better controls
were needed to ensure that they did, and that it was of
doubtful value to involve people in making decisions,
except to canvass their views.

NATURE OF THE CONSULTANT/CLIENT CONTRACT

This suggests that the contract between people in the organisation and the change agent/consultant must be reviewed and re-drawn at suitable stages in the course of the project.   A major feature of the contract is that it is with people at shopfloor level as well as with managers, with individuals as clients as well as the company.

Assuming a satisfactory agreement to proceed at least to the first stage, the Unit consultant is concerned to see that the responsibility for the project remains within the enterprise, which also provides the resources of time and specialist knowledge.   The consultant intervenes only as minimally necessary to maintain progress, providing assistance as necessary in two main ways.

The first of these is helping to set up or identify appropriate bodies within the enterprise to deal with the data collected, to plan and implement changes.   In a few companies consultative machinery already exists, though even here it is unusual for job content to be a subject of discussion.   Where this does occur, it normally relates to management proposals for action on an issue which management had identified.

The second way consists of exploring areas where changes are contemplated, for example where alternative technical changes are possible, and especially how issues and problems are seen by different groups in the enterprise.   Using individual interviews, group discussions and, in some cases, written questionnaires, the focus is on critical incidents, the difficulties and distastes of the job content and context.   This throws up typically a wealth of material whose implications can then be discussed with work groups and ideas for action explored and examined.   This has turned out to be more productive than administering a standard questionnaire and comparing mean scores on satisfaction scales.   With a group of supervisors in a light engineering company, for example, individual interviews identified four areas for attention:

(a) planning the flow of work, variations in manning levels, and in the supply of materials;

(b) modification of product during production to suit customer requirements;

(c) span of responsibility, and other man-management problems;

(d) changing role of the supervisor, with growth of the company and standardisation of products.

Dsicussion of these areas of concern threw up suggestions
for training supervisors, re-grouping of production,
differentiation of tasks currently carried out by all
supervisors (regardless of individual differences in preference or skill) into managerial/organisational tasks
and those related to technical aspects of production.

MACHINERY FOR MANAGING ORGANISATIONAL CHANGE

    A steering group with the appropriate interests
represented, including staff associations and unions, is
a crucial step; but a number of important issues are
raised by doing so.   How does it fit into the existing
negotiating and consultative arrangements?   What powers
does it have or can it be given?   How do members represent the views of constituents?   Whether such a body is
set up or not, there is need for a small project team of
about 3 or 4 people who can be given training and time
to manage the process of change and keep up the momentum.
The consultant works with these two groups, helping to
anticipate problems, collecting data, drawing attention
to alternatives, and giving support.   In the course of
these activities, he exemplifies openly the strategy
which is being developed; and part of his attention is
on helping people in the enterprise to learn how to
change the organisation of work effectively.

    This preparatory, educational exploration is an
essential part of the change process, establishing a
framework for discussion, planning and implementing
changes which can be used as a basis for extending the
learning to other parts of the organisation and for
dealing with other issues that may not yet be apparent.
It is also an opportunity to test the likelihood that
this participative strategy will both be acceptable to
people in the organisation and be appropriate for the
problem that is identified.   Experience has also shown
that the first of these is more important than the second
and must be achieved first if ownership of the problem
is to remain within the organisation.   Experience has
also demonstrated that these preliminary stages take
much longer than is usually anticipated and that there
are often problems of maintaining impetus and continuity.

    As has been already suggested, it is essential to
clarify the nature of the process of organisational
change, the help that can be expected, the approach and
values of the various participants, to ensure that there
is enough common ground to make further association
worthwhile.   The process is usually much longer and more
difficult than is anticipated and has repercussions
throughout the organisation.   It is nevertheless more
likely to produce sensible and practical ideas for improvement based on current problem ideas that have been thought

through and tested, than applying a recipe for improving satisfaction or motivation that has been tried
elsewhere.   Each change project is in a real sense an
experiment, an exploration in which the experimenters
are also the subjects of the experiment, whose objective
is to improve the capacity of an organisation to learn
to adapt, cope with and influence its environment, and
of individuals within the organisation to design for
themselves a more satisfactory working experience.

CONDITIONS FAVOURING A PARTICIPATIVE STRATEGY

Some of the features which are shared by organisations where the approach described has been satisfactorily adopted are as follows:

(a) the enterprise is financially and commercially
    viable;

(b) there is agreement to consider the distribution
    of any financial benefits from the changes,
    including provision for manning levels and job
    security for people already employed;

(c) there is a degree of trust and openness in
    relations between management and the employees
    in the company, and the systems for negotiation
    and consultation are reasonably sound;

(d) there are no serious deficiencies in the physical
    working environment or in the conditions of
    employment calling for urgent attention;

(e) there is considerable awareness of the value of,
    and support for,a participative approach to tackling
    organisational problems, particularly among
    senior managers and trades union officials;

(f) there is room for significant changes to be made
    to the content of jobs and organisation of work.
    This is more likely to be the case when new
    investments in machinery or plant are contemplated.

TASK CHARACTERISTICS, SATISFACTION AND MOTIVATION

Organisational and job characteristics which have a
bearing on satisfaction and performance have been described by Hackman and Oldham (1976), Umstott, Bell and
Mitchell (1976), Cherns (1976), Davis (1977), and others.
The conditions under which they are likely to affect
either performance, absence, turnover and/or satisfaction
have been identified.   They are listed in Figure 2(A-C)
and are used as a check list for investigation and

2A   TASK CHARACTERISTICS

Tasks should:

.   Combine to form a coherent job either alone or
    with related jobs whose performance makes a
    significant and visible contribution

.   Provide some variety of pace, method, location,
    skill

.   Provide feedback on performance both directly
    and through others

.   Provide some degree of discretion in carrying
    out tasks, responsibility for outcomes and, in
    particular, control over the pace of work.

Figure 2A.   Task characteristics

2B   JOB AND WORK ORGANISATION CHARACTERISTICS

These should:

.   Provide opportunity for learning

.   Lead to some sort of desirable future

.   Enable people to contribute to decisions
    affecting their job and its goals

.   Ensure that the goals and other people's
    expectations are clear and provide some degree
    of challenge

.   Provide adequate support, and contact with
    others

.   Provide adequate resources (training, infor-
    mation, equipment).

Figure 2B.   Job and work organisation characteristics

2C   WORK CONTEXT CHARACTERISTICS

As a background to these task and job requirements:

. Industrial relations procedures and practices
  should be jointly agreed and understood, and
  industrial relations issues handled in accordance with these arrangements

. The payment systems and the way it operates
  should be seen as fair and should reflect the
  contribution of individual and groups of
  employees

. Other personnel policies should be seen as
  fair and adequate

. Physical surroundings should be seen as reasonably satisfactory

Figure 2C.   Work context characteristics

diagnostic exploration.

     It is rarely possible for an observer to judge
satisfactorily whether and to what extent a job has
these desired characteristics and how people are likely
to respond to changes.   This is another reason for
involving people in the process of change.   Their perception and interpretation of their present tasks, their
difficulties and satisfactions, are essential data to be
taken into account.   Variety, for example, should be
defined in terms of the worker's experience and views
rather than the observation and values of the observer.
Jobs that provide interest and variety for some may be
seen by others as a rag-bag of unconnected and perhaps
conflicting tasks.   Moreover, increases in the variety
of tasks, in autonomy, or other characteristics may not
always be desirable.   Work that is too stimulating can
be experienced as stressful.

     It is also apparent from research in this field that
the relationship of these variables to each other can be
of several kinds.   This is important when contemplating
changes in work design.   Some characteristics relate to
needs that are satiable, at least temporarily, in particular those identified by Wherry and South (1977) as
related to extrinsic motivation.   Others have to do with
intrinsic characteristics, and relate to people's expectations not from work but about work.   Characteristics
of this kind are more likely to relate to needs that are
insatiable, and may grow even stronger with experience.
Many people and certainly their managers will say that all

they want from work comes from high wages, social contact
and the least amount of physical effort, and will have
few suggestions about how the work might be changed to
satisfy other needs.   Nevertheless when asked for ideas
about how existing difficulties might be overcome and
when involved in the process or review and development,
there is seldom any scarcity of proposals to work on.
The responsibility, discretion and involvement in
planning the change is welcomed and can generate further
changes in the same direction.

    There are other concepts which have been explored by
researchers in this field and which have relevance to
the practice of job design and work re-organisation.
Among these are:

    (a) The concept of 'trade-off'.   This seems to be
         applicable to reward systems, where time and money
         are regarded as alternative rewards from work.
         It can also apply to job characteristics like
         variety - of task, pace, place, methods of work.
         In this case, what seems to be important is the
         control which the worker has and his freedom to
         manoeuvre.   Lack of variety of task can to some
         degree be compensated by variety of method, pace
         or location.

    (b) Other characteristics seem to be quite independent
         of each other in terms of their contribution
         towards overall satisfaction, so that however good
         the job is in most respects, people will express
         overall dissatisfaction with it if pay or other
         rewards are less than satisfactory.

    (c) The concept of 'optimum' also applies.   Although
         in most projects jobs seem to offer too little
         opportunity, there may be an individual threshold
         beyond which too much variety, too high responsi-
         bility and the like, may be experienced as stress-
         ful and dissatisfying.   Too much variety may be
         experienced as a collection of unconnected and
         conflicting tasks.   Too much challenge can be
         stressful, particularly if not accompanied by ade-
         quate information or training.

    (d) For some characteristics, it seems sensible to
         talk of a discrepancy between what the job offers
         and what is desired.   For other characteristics,
         this model does not apply since desire can be
         increased by opportunity and experience.

DISCUSSION

    The complexity described, and attempts to measure

experience and expectations of satisfactions with and
from work in the context of helping people in work organisations to improve the quality of working life, has led
the Work Research Unit to adopt two main guiding principles:

(i) The first has to do with the organisation of work,
     the hierarchy of authority, and the locus of
     control in the enterprise.   Changes are encouraged
     which put the control and authority for action
     where the problems are.   By and large, given ade-
     quate support and training, access to information
     and services, it is found that authority can with
     advantage be devolved; but slowly and with help.
     The advantages include shortening lines of commu-
     nication, both vertically and horizontally.   It
     includes, for example, persuading managers that
     cleaning teams can satisfactorily organise their
     own rota system, order materials and discuss prob-
     lems with customers directly rather than doing
     this through a district manager.

(ii) The second main principle concerns the content of
     jobs.   While it is important to involve people
     in the process of reviewing the way jobs are,
     nevertheless it is necessary to resist pressure
     for a universal and timelessly correct solution.
     Recognising the range of individual differences of
     perception, experience and motivation to be accom-
     modated, Cherns's (1976) principle of minimum
     specification is worthwhile as an aim.   It is
     also important for managers to plan their systems
     with a model of human motivation that is indivi-
     dualistic rather than pluralistic.   Building into
     jobs a bit more elbow-room for individuals to
     organise their own work is not without limit, but
     pays off in terms of satisfaction for the indivi-
     dual and in developing an organisation that is
     responsive to, and fits into, its social and eco-
     nomic environment.

     The experiences I have outlined in this paper have
taken the Unit a considerable distance from the original
recommendations made by Wilson (1973) to the Department of
Employment and from the ideas that were current about
what a unit might do and how it might do it.   We have
found, both in the projects we have sponsored and in the
assignments the staff of the Unit have undertaken, that
the process of organisational change has become more
important as well as more time-consuming in relation to
changes in job tasks.   We have also, as was to be expected in action research, found great difficulty in setting
up experimental conditions which do not, at the same
time, distort too radically the actual situation.   We can
only hope to understand and describe more systematically

what is happening, using techniques which have a dual
function of providing reliable and valid data for those
interested in learning about what has happened and, at
the same time, immediate information for those in the
organisation to use in interpreting problems and deciding
on changes.

In the context of this necessary compromise, Wilson's
hope of seeing well-defined results from demonstration
projects and his belief that these would persuade people
in other organisations to copy their experience seem not
only less easily realised, but even somewhat naive. The
changes in one work organisation and the arrangement of
tasks in jobs seem less important as models for others
to copy than the process by which decisions were reached,
the attitudes, beliefs and assumptions which people hold
about others, and how these have been modified, if at
all, in the course of the process.

With the benefit of hindsight it almost seems as if
we, the social scientists and change agents, have concentrated too much on the effects of changes in the content
of jobs on motivation, productivity and satisfaction,
when we ought really to have been seeking to describe
attitudes, beliefs, and assumptions, helping people in
work organisations to question them, and defining and
developing strategies for enabling people to release
themselves from their constraining influence, and for
learning effectively to manage their work environment.

REFERENCES

Cherns, A.B. (1976).   'Principles of socio-technical
    design', Human Relations, 29, 783-792.

Cooper, R. (1973).   'Taks characteristics and intrinsic
    motivation', Human Relations, 26, 287-413.

Davis, L.E. (1977).   'Evolving alternative organisational
    designs: their socio-technical bases', Human
    Relations, 30, 261-273.

Faxén, K-O. (1979).   Organisational Change, Learning and
    Productivity, Development Council, Stockholm.

Hackman, J.R. and Oldham, G.R. (1976).   'Motivation
    through the design of work: Test of a theory',
    Organisational Behaviour and Human Performance, 16,
    250-279.

Survey Research Centre, University of Michigan (1971).
    Survey of Working Conditions, US Department of Labor.

Umstott, D.D., Bell, C.H. and Mitchell, T.R. (1976).
    'Effects of job enrichment and task goals on satis-
    faction and productivity: implications for job
    design?', Journal of Applied Psychology, 61, 379-394.

Wherry, R.J. and South, J.C. (1977).   'A worker moti-
    vation scale', Personnel Psychology, 30, 613-636.

White, G.C. (1978).   'Improving jobs and work organi-
    sation', Department of Employment Gazette, 86,
    303-304, H.M.S.O., London.

White, G.C. and Jessup, G. (1979).   Quality of Working
    Life: The Development of the United Kingdom Prog-
    ramme - Occasional Paper No. 14, Work Research Unit,
    London.

Wilson, N.A.B. (1973).   On the Quality of Working Life,
    H.M.S.O., London.

Changes in Working Life
Edited by K.D. Duncan, M.M. Gruneberg, and D. Wallis
© 1980 John Wiley & Sons Ltd

Chapter 25

Pay—Off Conditions for Organizational Change in the Hospital Service

D. WALLIS and D. COPE

Since 1975 we have been engaged in an action research programme located in several Welsh hospitals. Our aims have been to identify sources of dissatisfaction among nurses and ancillary hospital staff, to advise and assist with trials of job and organizational changes which might improve matters, and to consider what such changes may imply for organizational effectiveness. Field work started in 1976 and is nearing completion.

The initial proposal came from us, but there was an enthusiastic response at the time from the Area Health Authority which had been concerned about high turnover rates and what it regarded as 'low morale' among nursing staff. Perhaps they were encouraged too because the research was to be financed by a grant from the UK government's Work Research Unit (White, in this volume). Hospital staff and trade union representatives were also very willing to cooperate.

Here we shall refer to projects in two psychiatric hospitals. In the second one we have been applying lessons learned from experience in the first. Hospital A is urban with 500 beds. Hospital B is rural, with 400. In the former we have concentrated on the psychogeriatric unit of 4 wards. Staffing levels here are comparatively generous, providing a daytime service from some 80 nursing and ancillary staff. Hospital B is organized on a geographical rather than functional basis. Here we have

been studying a unit of 5 wards, two of which are for
psychogeriatric patients.   Allowances for this unit are
below the national average, yielding about 40 daytime
staff.

Our emphasis today will be upon the problems and
process of organizational change towards higher job
satisfaction (JS) and quality of working life (QWL), as
we have experienced them and particularly as they have
influenced our understanding of QWL in psychiatric hospitals.   We shall try to develop our argument to the
stage of suggesting what the minimal requirements are
for successfully embarking upon programmes of change
directed towards gains in quality.

We would argue that the quality of working life in
a hospital is central to the overall theme of this volume
for the following reasons:

  (i) First, the trend at least in more developed
       countries is to increase that proportion of the
       labour force which is engaged in non-industrial,
       non-profit-making, and non-production-centred
       work.   The 'tertiary' sector, which includes the
       'caring' services for sick and infirm people,
       provides work of this kind.

 (ii) Secondly, we cannot be sure that prescriptions
       for securing high levels of JS and QWL will
       generalise to jobs in the 'caring' and 'service'
       occupations.   These prescriptions and job
       design principles (e.g. Davis and Taylor, 1972;
       Turner and Lawrence, 1965;   Emery, 1967) have
       after all emerged mainly from studies of work
       in industry, particularly where mass-production
       methods and relatively low levels of skill and
       personal responsibility are common.   As it
       happens, most jobs in the 'tertiary' sector of
       employment already score quite heavily on charac-
       teristics usually associated with high JS and QWL.
       Nurses, for example, certainly appear to have
       plenty of opportunities for 'psychological growth'
       (Herzberg, 1972), responsibility, variety of
       tasks, promotion prospects, and esteem within the
       community.   But this does not necessarily imply
       that job holders will actually perceive such
       characteristics (let alone value them highly) to
       be descriptive of their working lives.   Our own
       data certainly show that nurses can feel very dis-
       satisfied even though their jobs may be 'enriched'
       compared with many industrial ones.

(iii) Thirdly, even assuming that constituents of the
       'good (working) life' can in fact be identified

for professional workers like nurses, how can these be emphasised or enhanced in practice? To rephrase this very practical question, what inducements are there for management, trade unions and staff, to press for changes incorporating more constituents of a high QWL? The situation is complicated since we already know (e.g. from Goldthorpe et al., 1970) that not everyone, even in 'low-grade' work, wants his job to be enriched or to be upgraded to a 'higher-grade' job.

(iv) Fourthly, it has to be remembered that in service organizations like a hospital, the principal objective is likely to be the maintenance and extension of the service rather than 'efficiency' in simple cost-effectiveness terms. Now, if the pay-offs from an organizational change towards higher QWL are not translatable into higher productivity for the organization, nor into higher earnings and other tangible benefits for staff, are there any other pay-offs sufficiently appealing to generate and sustain the change at all?

INITIAL CONCEPTUAL FRAMEWORK

Psycho-Socio-Technical System

We were not aware in 1975 of studies other than Revans (1964) directly bearing upon satisfaction among nurses in the UK and psychiatric nurses in particular. Detailed enquiries about pay had been expressly excluded from the scope of our enquiries. Moreover staff associations (... though not, as it happened, the nursing management) had distinct reservations about how far we should look into satisfaction with professional supervision. We were in any case more interested at the time in job content and the assignment of roles and responsibilities at ward level. Ergonomic aspects were not excluded insofar as they related to JS and QWL, but were accorded relatively low priority.

Because of this task and role orientation, particularly as it related to different categories of staff, a 'socio-technical' conception of the system of psychiatric care provided a foundation for our own conceptual framework. It implied that a fair balance between ways of meeting social and technical requirements would be necessary, though perhaps not sufficient, for there to be high JS and QWL for staff. However, we also envisaged the need for a more distinctly psychological analysis of the system: one in which the work attitudes, expectations, and job satisfaction, of individuals were also revealed.

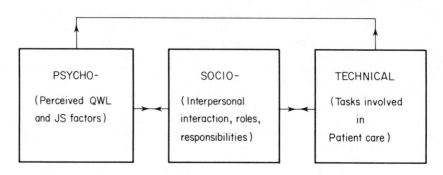

Initial conceptual framework for study of
psychogeriatric unit

Figure 1.   Psycho-socio-technical system of patient
             care.

     Our working model of patient care in the psycho-
geriatric unit was therefore a 'psycho-socio-technical'
one, as represented in Figure 1.   This had implications
for data-collection.   Whereas the 'social' and 'technical' features might be inferred directly from observation
of behaviour and conditions, it would be critical for our
understanding to know just how these features were actually perceived in QWL terms by the staff themselves.   A
complete psychological analysis of the system was not
feasible, since we were not permitted to obtain or make
evaluative assessments of individual ability and performance.

Action Research Orientation

     The other major influence on our research strategy
was an explicit commitment to the 'action-research' mode
of enquiry.   Even among <u>applied</u> psychologists there is a
good deal of anguish and controversy about this approach.
Here it is sufficient for us to point out that action
research entails two distinct roles for the investigators.
First is the customary research role of independent data
collection, analysis, and interpretation.   But equally
prominent is the consultant's role of helping to initiate,
implement, and evaluate organizational change and development.   A corollary of this was that we had to spend a
lot of time, for example in participant observation on
the wards, establishing reasonable credibility in the eyes
of the professional nursing community for our standing as
reliable observers.

Data-Collection Methods

Taken together, our systems approach and action research strategy led us to employ a number of different data collection methods, designed to encourage greater reliability than was likely from one data source, like JS questionnaires, alone.   Listed below, they were employed in both hospitals:

(a)   participant observation

(b)   interviews

(c)   questionnaires

(d)   collection of critical incidents

(e)   activity sampling

(f)   documentary evidence

(g)   experimental introduction of special patient-care programmes.

Feedback of Data for Action

An essential feature of any action research programme is to feed back information about the state of the system to those who have provided it.   We had to devise settings in which the nurses themselves could discuss, comment, and formulate their own ideas for job and organizational changes to enhance their own JS and QWL.   They could have guidance from ourselves as researchers, and advice or information from senior management, trade unions, and other specialists like consultant psychiatrists who worked in the unit.   Our feedback of questionnaire, interview, and directly-observed data took place initially through Working Groups of staff at ward and unit level.   We also offered interpretations drawn from the potentially more sensitive sources, i.e. critical incidents, participant observation, and activity sampling. Later on a Steering Group was set up, under the chairmanship of the Area Nursing Officer, with representatives from all wards and other professional groups as well as nurses, management, and trade unions.   This Group considered not only our own written reports and recommendations but also the comments and suggestions from Working Groups.

We hoped that these feedback mechanisms would provide a forum as well as the impetus for drawing up policies and plans for action in the psychogeriatric unit, and indeed elsewhere in Hospital A, to tackle the declared sources of dissatisfaction.

RESULTS FROM HOSPITAL A

We shall concentrate here on the data and subsequent outcomes in Hospital A which have significantly influenced our present views of problems and processes attending organizational change, hopefully towards higher levels of JS and QWL.

The Quality of Working Life in the Unit

It is clear that nursing staff saw themselves as trying to deal with an intractable problem. They were charged with caring for as many as 30 elderly persons in a ward, patients whose diagnoses included dementia, psychosis and senility. Prognoses were poor for such patients. Few will leave the hospital before they die. Many have been there for more than a decade. Strange and sometimes violent behaviour, or virtual withdrawal, is commonly experienced. Incontinence is endemic.

On the face of it these are hardly the conditions one might wish to offer as a recipe for high QWL, especially when hours of work can be long and the physical surroundings often drab and sparsely equipped by comparison with many working environments. From the nurses' viewpoint, their situation is inherently anxiety-provoking. It is small wonder that the rigidity of hospital regimes tends to foster institutionalised patterns of behaviour, among staff as well as patients. Moreover both psychiatric and geriatric services have been perceived as being last in the queue for National Health Service resources; in the psychogeriatric service this is felt to apply doubly so.

In the unit where we worked there seemed to be few means of coping with these problems, so far as therapeutic and psychological measures were concerned. We encountered few signs of formal treatment in use in the unit: treatment, that is, of a strictly psychiatric or psychological kind, rather than just the physical and medical care which appeared wholly adequate. Nurses felt a deep scepticism towards the possibility of any change in their regime; either in terms of what they regarded as sufficient resources on the wards, or of treatments which might moderate the psychological condition of their patients even to the point of just stabilising their afflictions.

It is not surprising that nurses' responses both in interviews and to questionnaires displayed elements of confusion as well as anxiety. They were 'unsure where they were going', uncertain what the goals of a psychogeriatric unit could or should be. Sisters complained of 'being in a vacuum'. Behaviourally, nurses tended to display extremely well-established and stereotyped patterns

of activity vis-à-vis patients and other staff.   Perhaps this was a natural reaction to their underlying
uncertainties.   Certainly the way nurses saw their role
in practice was as agents of physical care, which meant
casting patients into a very dependent role where the
nurses did everything for them from dawn till dusk.
('You've got to treat them like children' was a characteristic remark.)

The psychogeriatric regime, therefore, amounted to
a system of 'custodial' care rather than to any clearly
perceptible form of therapeutic treatment and rehabilitation.   As nurses saw it, this was an inevitable consequence of having to look after patients whose loss of
most physical as well as mental functioning was irre-
parable.

Job Satisfaction in the Unit

Yet, despite all this, and despite protestations of
frustration and complaint regarding many key features
of their work (especially during interviews and informal
discussion), nursing staff expressed a high degree of
overall satisfaction with their job.   We obtained completed questionnaires from 36 staff in psychogeriatric
wards.   92% of the sample, when asked: 'In general,
how satisfied are you with the basic task of looking after
old people?' responded that they were 'satisfied' or
'very satisfied'.   Only 3% were 'dissatisfied'.   When
asked if they were satisfied with their 'job as a whole',
81% replied that they were 'satisfied' or 'very satisfied';
only 6% were 'dissatisfied'.   Figure 2 provides an
example of job satisfaction data obtained from one portion
of a specially designed questionnaire.

A number of particular work facets were identified
as 'good', not only during interviews but also through
discussion of critical incidents and in questionnaire
responses.   They included: keeping busy, the appeal of
doing things for other people, social relationships with
other staff, having good supervisors, doing work which
was on the whole interesting, having a fair amount of
variety, and getting at least an occasional feeling of
achievement.   On the rare occasions when they 'got through'
to patients or even saw them discharged to the community,
this was regarded as particularly good.   It is significant, we feel, that so far as 'variety' and 'sense of
achievement' were concerned, the former must have been
perceived in terms of within-day activities, since the
daily routine did not noticeably vary.   And 'achieved'
must have been perceived in relation to maintenance of
physical care and cleanliness, rather than to experience
of progress and restoration regarding either psychiatric
or geriatric symptoms.

This is how satisfied I feel with:

	Very satisfied	Satisfied	Neither satisfied nor dissatisfied	Dissatisfied	Very dissatisfied
The variety in my word		69	25	6	
The amount of recognition given for doing a good job	3	53	29	15	
The general status given to psychiatric nursing by the community	3	29	47	15	6
The freedom to usually work without too much supervision	24	67	9		
The extent to which my skills and abilities are used	6	52	21	21	
Doing work that is of direct benefit to other people	29	62	6	3	
Having the chance sometimes to do different parts of my job in my own way	12	70	18		
The general interest of the work itself	26	50	15	6	3
The help I get for my job from people working elsewhere in the hospital	3	41	26	26	3
The general physical conditions and appearance of the ward		15	15	29	41
The responsibility attached to my job	12	61	24	3	
The clinical facilities and equipment in the ward		9	24	32	35
The non-clinical facilities and equipment in the ward			19	41	41
The way my hours of work are arranged	38	56	6		
The way my work is generally organised	18	67	9	6	
The sense of achievement I get from my job	21	51	18	6	3
The adequacy of the in-service training I have received	12	36	21	21	9
The amount of consultation we get before decisions are made which affect us	6	26	24	32	12
The feeling I have that patients really need me	42	39	15	3	
The help I generally get for my work from other staff on the ward	51	45	3		
The pay compared to other works in the hospital	6	30	30	30	3
The pay compared to other workers outside the hospital	3	12	29	41	15

Note Figures in the columns are the percentages of the 36 staff members who responded accordingly.

Figure 2.   Extract from Questionnaire (Psychogeriatric Nursing Staff: Hospital A)

Dissatisfactions in the Unit

Aspects which were frequently mentioned as 'bad' clustered around working conditions and amenities, particularly alleged staff shortages and consequent lack of time to exercise optimal care for patients; inadequate consultation and communication within wards and with management; and non-involvement in decisions about how to spend money allocated to the hospital. Besides lack of resources and participation, other sources of particular dissatisfaction were relationships with other departments in the hospital and various inadequacies, as nurses saw them, in their training at all levels.

OUTCOMES OF ATTEMPTED CHANGE IN HOSPITAL A

Any generalisations about a very rich and diverse data bank such as from Hospital A are naturally subject to error. But if we were asked to sum up the whole range of information, we would associate it above all with a lack of clearly perceived, far less of agreed, objectives for the system of patient care in the psychogeriatric unit. In the absence of these objectives, and therefore of felt pressures towards achieving them, the behaviour of staff (as distinct from their expressions of dissatisfaction with many features of their work situation and an expressed wish to modify them) exhibited more characterstics of a 'resistance to change' syndrome than of any enthusiastic drive for a different QWL.

This latter interpretation, however, came later. We need first to say what happened to the many recommendations for action which evolved in the Working Groups, in some cases with our assistance. A number of these were approved by the Steering Group representing all parties concerned including senior nursing management. Each recommended action was specifically identified and acknowledged as a step towards reducing dissatisfaction, removing a frustration, or enhancing a positive job-related source of satisfaction, as suggested by our study and the subsequent feedback sessions.

However, neither the Working Groups nor the higher level Steering Group had any executive power vested in them. Effective action would only follow if individuals, whether nursing managers, ward sisters, nursing assistants, or whatever, actually introduced those aspects of recommended change which they personally supported and had the authority to implement.

So what happened? After a year or so, several changes which were contingent upon management initiation and pressure had in fact been implemented. They included tighter administrative procedures for the

requisitioning and supply of equipment on the wards,
which had been a principal source of expressed frustration.   Some ward amenities, including decorative 'upgrading', had certainly improved.   And the notion of
'team management' at hospital level, involving participation by all professional groups including nurses, has
been introduced more recently.   (A main function of
'team management' is to set organisational objectives
and decide how to implement them at appropriate levels of
responsibility.)   We cannot know whether any or all of
these changes might have occurred without our intervention anyway;   but without it we doubt if they could have
happened when they did.

On the other hand, the proposition that collaborative, participative, management might be introduced
down to ward level, after the fashion of autonomous
working groups, has not been implemented despite enthusiastic discussion and adoption of it in principle by
the Steering Group.   This was one instance of what we
now regard as the more interesting and instructive outcomes in Hospital A.   For in other cases also there
was a notable failure either to get action off the ground
at all, or to sustain it after our own direct involvement
was gradually withdrawn.   In all these cases, an apparent keenness for 'someone' to bring about the proposed
changes was not enough.   To implement them actually
required personal initiatives and a sustained commitment
to action from the particular staff who were themselves
expected to benefit in QWL terms.

Three examples will serve to illustrate the point:
   (i)   First, the Working and Steering Groups themselves ceased to operate after six months or so of active
life.   By that time there was dwindling enthusiasm from
representative members, either to identify appropriate
changes or to press for action regarding changes already
adopted in principle.   A sharply diminished enthusiasm
was evident at senior levels of nursing management.   For
example, chairmanship of the Steering Group was immediately relinquished by a newly-appointed Area Nursing
Officer, who evinced no further interest in the project.

   (ii)   An attempt was made to meet the desire
expressed by nurses, especially ward sisters and charge
nurses, for a say in the way National Health Service funds
were actually expended on wards.   The idea of drawing up
budgets at ward level and allowing control of them within
approved limits of the expenditure, was seriously discussed.   Just when it seemed likely that it might be
given a trial, enthusiasm died away and the idea was
dropped.   The professed desire for more control over
resources did not go hand in hand with a desire to shoul-
der a fresh responsibility.

(iii)   The third example was in a particularly sensitive area, clearly central to the attitudes and behaviour
of all nursing staff.   They consistently expressed a
wish to introduce any changes which would improve standards and outcomes of patient care, and thereby at the
same time enhance a principal source of their own JS.
One proposed change was to adopt 'total patient care'.
This involves re-definition of a nurse's responsibilities,
so that each nurse in a ward takes care of the complete
nursing needs of a small group of patients.   This practice was indeed started on one ward, but swiftly dropped
again and at once rejected on all the other wards too,
on the grounds that 'it was not in patients' best
interests to pursue it'.   We were unable to elicit clear
statements of why this was judged to be so; but the
added personal responsibility entailed by 'total patient
care' was in our opinion one factor in the outcome.

Another proposed change, in which we became involved directly, required a trial in two wards of the
psychiatric treatment known as 'reality orientation'.
Its purpose was to produce a heightened awareness among
selected patients of their own identity and circumstances,
and the possibility of greater psychological contact at a
reality level between nurses and these patients.   Initial
results after 3 weeks suggested that the patients' condition was certainly changing, though not always in ways
which nurses regarded as wholly beneficial.   However, at
that point the programme had to be stopped because nursing
staff on one of the wards objected to the increased
stress appearing, as they saw it, on patients and themselves;   and because the procedures added to their workload.

CONCLUSIONS ABOUT HOSPITAL A

Taken as a whole, these results are not in line with
what JS and QWL theory would have led us to expect.
The assumption that certain kinds of change in job content and work organisation are not only beneficial in
themselves (high on QWL factors) but will also be experienced as more satisfying, surely implies that staff will
actively welcome them.   Our data does not support that
theory, however.   Even where nurses in Hospital A first
requested such changes themselves, they seemed disinclined
to take any initiative upon themselves to activate
changes, and they soon rejected some recommended changes
which actually did get under way.

A number of explanations are possible.   It could be
that the desire to remove dissatisfying features of work
and accentuate those claimed to be satisfying, was for
most individuals less compelling than a desire not to be
bothered by, or to risk, anxiety from changes in customary

work routines.   This might account for the failure of
those recommended changes which depended upon personal
initiatives to get them going.   On the other hand, perhaps the 'techniques' of intervention, or our own personal characteristics and competence as action researchers, were at fault.

PROJECT IN HOSPITAL B

During the past year we have been able to use some
of the previous experience and ideas to good effect in
the second, rural, location.   The approach has again
been to seek ways to improve the JS and QWL of staff
which they could reveal and implement themselves.   But
this time the QWL objective has been firmly linked with
organizational objectives to raise the standards of
patient care.

It is early yet for a definitive assessment of outcomes.   But this time our intervention, using basically
the same data-collection methods and action research
approach, has produced and is continuing to produce a
number of significant changes in patient care and hospital management procedures.   Comparing the situations
in Hospitals A and B reveals some differences which we
believe, and which our model of organizational change
(presented subsequently) implies, are crucial to success.
Broadly speaking, these relate to the perception of pay-
offs to management and staff as being tied to a compatible
organizational objective;   so that pressures from outside as well as within the organizational unit concerned,
are sufficient to generate a movement away from the previously stable level of performance.

Three differences can be discerned with respect to
pay-offs.   First, we were invited into the study of
Hospital B by senior management at Area Health Authority
level.   They were anxious to 'do something about' problems in the hospital which were not clearly defined but
were perceived as being somehow related to managerial
difficulties and staff apathy.   A willingness to under-
write expenses of the project was an indication of their
strong and continuing support.   Secondly, the senior
nursing officers responsible for management in the hospital itself, including the individual in charge of the
5-ward unit in which we have been working, were totally
committed to the research programme.   They envisaged a
number of outcomes advantageous to themselves as managers
as well as for their nursing colleagues and patients.

Thirdly, having taken steps to secure staff agreement to the various data-collection procedures, we
invited them to join with us in planning the scope of,
and drawing up items for, the questionnaire survey.

During subsequent feed-back sessions (and despite
the fact that data from this survey proved to be far
from flattering to groups at management and ward level
alike) there was evidently a much greater commitment to
and 'ownership' of the information than we encountered
in Hospital A.   The principal feedback mechanism used
was what some Organizational Development practitioners
would call a 'confrontation meeting' (after Beckhard,
1967).   Here the results of our observational, interview, questionnaire, and other sources of data, were
argued out in a 'public' but unminuted forum of all
parties from senior management down.

     Although the status and operation of this gathering
was analogous in some respects to the Steering Group of
Hospital A, it differed in that the ward staff and
nursing managers felt themselves to have been the origi-
nators and therefore 'sponsors' of the data.   Recommendations for action to remedy weaknesses in patient care
and to remove sources of staff dissatisfaction were
evolved within the ward and management groups first, and
carried through at the 'confrontation meeting' to
decisions for which there were strong and evident peer
pressures (as well as senior managerial support) to implement.   Pay-offs envisaged by staff were, we suspect,
initially as much to do with the relief of anxiety
resulting from these pressures to improve performance, as
with the anticipation of positive benefits in the form of
better QWL.

     The identification of specific directions which
organizational change might take was also different in
Hospital B.   Here the idea was to operationalise the
rather vague general objective of 'improving patient
care' by revealing just how far short of the 'ideal' the
present standards appeared to be, to staff themselves.
We therefore included with the JS questionnaire a section
designed to compare salient features of patient care, as
nurses perceived them currently to be, with how these
nurses thought they should be.   Perceived discrepancies
between actual and ideal performance in the unit provided
the limits within which specific and feasible organizational objectives could be defined and openly accepted
as being compatible to staff and management alike.
These discrepancies were also a powerful trigger to the
'unfreezing' (Lewin, 1947) or 'perturbing' action necessary to jolt the hitherto stable organizational performance towards a change.

INDIVIDUAL AND ORGANIZATIONAL PERSPECTIVES ON CHANGE

     Our involvement in Hospitals A and B was first of
all directed to improving JS and QWL.   It inevitably
became caught up with organizational effectiveness too.

The results point to inadequacies in our understanding
of what constitutes high JS or QWL.   They suggest too
that expressions of dissatisfaction and desire for
change are no guarantee at all that people will actually
press for or welcome the changes.   It is evident that
defining criteria for 'satisfying' and 'high quality'
jobs and organizational characteristics is one thing;
but moving an organization from its current state to the
new 'improved' situation is quite another.

Individual Perspectives

As psychologists we were naturally disposed first
to examine the problem from the standpoint of individuals
in the organisation.   We drew up a model of job satisfaction and motivation, adapted in the first place from
a representation by Schwab and Cummings (1970) of ideas
drawn from Porter and Lawler (1968).   A simplified version of our model is shown as Figure 3 (also see: Cope,
1979).   It clearly owes much to expectancy theory;
whilst the notions of 'discrepancy' (Locke, 1969) and
'tension' (Morse, 1953) are featured in earlier models of
job satisfaction and performance.   We would envisage our
'job-related wants' as operating rather like Locke's
'values' with respect to work, these being much more
potent in this context than basic psychological needs.

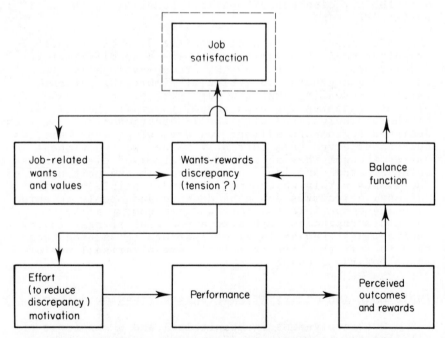

Figure 3.   Simplified model of individual job satis-
              faction.

The model accepts the usual view that JS is a consequence (albeit indirect) and not a cause, of performance and achievement at work.   But whereas JS in the customary expectancy theory formulation is a function of perceived equity of rewards in relation to actual ones, in our case JS is an epi-phenomenal correlate of the discrepancy between job-related wants or values, and perception of all outcomes including rewards.   In addition we have postulated a mechanism (we have labelled it the 'balance function') which moderates the nature and level of acquired 'wants'.   It operates to balance these wants against actual experience (perception) of the outcomes and rewards which actually follow from a a person's work (performance).   The balance function acts not only as a social comparison device, as in equity theory;   but it also ensures that an individual's job-related wants - which he values and which he reckons to be capable in principle of being met in his work situation - do in fact represent realistic expectations.   It is as though the individual says to himself: 'I will set my expectations as to what I want out of this job to the realistic level of what I believe I can achieve' (Cope, 1979).

In consequence, for most individuals and at most times, we should expect the discrepancy between job-related wants and rewards to be quite small, and job satisfaction quite high.   The model can therefore account for findings such as Taylor (1977) reported, that many if not most workers actually declare a consistently higher level of JS than an observer wearing QWL lenses would expect!   Our results in Hospital A are also consistent with it.   JS was generally high where the jobs as a whole were concerned;   and the disinclination of many individuals, including managers, to change their ways of performing is understandable in terms of low discrepancy or tension levels when 'wants' are already balanced against realistic expectations of outcomes and rewards.

Organisation Perspectives

However, this model of individual JS and motivation offers little enlightenment about organizational change and how it occurs.   It does suggest that changes are unlikely to arise from an appeal to personal initiatives unless the individual concerned can perceive clearly that rewards or pay-offs are likely.   But if our 'balance function' is operating, discrepancies will normally be small and it is by no means certain that job-related wants are present which are not adequately matched by rewards already perceived to be available. (The model does, perhaps, explain the retreat from enthusiasm and follow-up action by senior nursing managers

which we encountered in Hospital A.   There may well have
been a marked change during the course of our study in
their perception of likely pay-offs from improvements in
JS and QWL.   Two circumstances support this interpretation.   Recruitment and wastage among nurses became
markedly less of a problem for management between 1974
and 1977.   Moreover, a substantial pay settlement during
the period dampened down the emergence of widespread
signs of uncharacteristic industrial militancy among
nurses.)

       Our evidence accords with the common observation
that individuals and organizations seem to settle down to
a state of equilibrium in which the status quo is seen as
satisfactory.   To move an organization from one state of
equilibrium to another is therefore bound to be difficult.   How indeed can it be brought about smoothly, by
evolutionary development rather than disruptive 'revolutionary' means?

       Let us take the example of change in the hospital
service, and suppose that pressures from a management
level superordinate to a hospital unit were to be articulated as an organizational objective to raise the level
of patient care.   Let us further suppose that this
objective is to be achieved through changes in nursing
procedures and performance rather than just adding more
resources.   And suppose too that nursing staff have
declared high standards of patient care to be a critical
source of their QWL.   Our experience suggests that
bringing about change in this case would be difficult.
To appreciate the dynamics of this situation we need a
model of organizational stability as well as change.

       At a simple descriptive level we can conceive that,
just as the individual worker is usually in a state of
dynamic equilibrium with respect to his own performance
and JS levels, so too is there normally a state of equilibrium between the organization and each individual.
The organization makes demands upon individuals, and upon
groups of individuals, which are met in terms of job performance.   Arising from this performance (though not
necessarily contingent upon it), the organization provides rewards which individuals perceive more or less to
match their job-related wants.   A representation of
these relationships is shown as Figure 4.

       Let us assume a period of organizational stability,
defined as a satisfactory ratio between organizational
inputs and outputs.   At such times the pay-offs received
by individual members of staff are balanced by the organization's pay-off - in the form of aggregate job performance - received from them.   From the points of view of
individual staff, the demands imposed upon them are
balanced by the rewards, including pay and any other

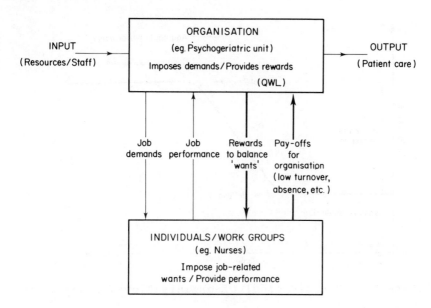

Figure 4.   Model of organisational balance.

perceived rewards, which they obtain by working within
that organization.   There is an implicit 'psychological
contract' (Schein, 1965) here between individual and
organization.   (On this view, a high QWL could be
operationally defined by the sort of job design and
organizational features which an individual perceives as
contributing optimally to the satisfaction of his job-
related wants.)

        This model implies that during a period of organi-
zational stability, performance is normally in a state of
dynamic equilibrium about a level regulated by the balance between pay-offs perceived by members of staff as
individuals and by the organization as a unit.   However,
like the model of individual JS, it still leaves open
the question of how to inject and sustain a desired
change: whether this is engineered by management in
order to raise output, or by staff pressures in order to
raise their QWL through increased rewards.

DYNAMIC MODEL OF ORGANIZATIONAL CHANGE

        In Figure 5 we have tried to represent a more
dynamic model of how the process of organizational change
can occur i.e. to shift a stable and persistent level of
performance to a new desired one.   In an organization
like the psychogeriatric unit, we may suppose that pay-
offs for individuals are the constituents, including pay,

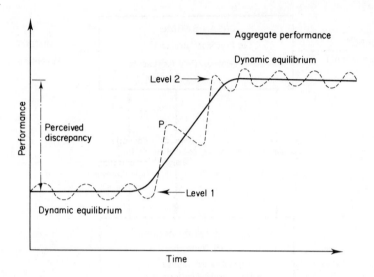

Figure 5.   Dynamic model of organisational change.

of a fair QWL.   For the organization, the pay-off is
aggregated performance leading to an acceptable output in
terms of patient care.   The delicate balance between
them is shown by the oscillating line around aggregate
performance at 'level 1'.   Positive phases of these
minor fluctuations reflect initially positive responses
(more effort and higher performance) to slight, but temporary increases in organizational demand.   If these
demands quickly subside, or if the positive responses to
them are not followed by corresponding increases in perceived rewards, then performance drops away again.   If
it falls below 'level 1', organizational sanctions may
be taken to withhold some expected rewards which individuals value enough to prevent their temporary lapse of
performance from continuing.

        Suppose now that a new performance 'level 2' is
advocated, to be achieved by redesigning tasks and organizational improvements, but without just pumping in more
resources or offering more pay.   How can the stability
be broken, a change induced, and a new stability reached
at the higher level of performance?

        Our model requires that a strong perturbation up-
wards must occur to disturb the self-regulating equilibrium of 'level 1'.   A downward shift, of course, would
occur if organizational rewards were sharply curtailed
below the return perceived by staff as equitable for
performance at this level.   If organizational demands
increased sharply without commensurate increments of perceived pay-off for staff, sustained change would not

follow: certainly not upwards.   Only if the initial
impetus were directly associated with added perceptible
benefits to staff would performance take off upwards
towards 'level 2'.

We believe that such initial 'beneficial' pertur-
bations will be substantially more likely to occur when
both staff and management in the organizational unit
have themselves identified and accepted the undesirable
nature of a discrepancy between 'level 1' and 'level 2'.
This can be regarded as part of Lewin's (1947) 'unfreezing' process.   Both parties have also to perceive progress towards 'level 2' as feasible.   If staff do
accept reduction of the discrepancy as a desirable objective, it can only be because they also anticipate
greater net rewards or QWL (which may include the avoidance of undesirable outcomes) from a higher performance
output.   In these circumstances, a rise in performance
may be swift and large enough to break the previous
dynamic equilibrium (Point 'P' on Figure 5).

We suspect that further oscillations will occur,
though declining in amplitude, until the position is
reached on the 'level 2' where performance is appropriate
to the new set of balanced pay-offs for staff and the
organization.

CONCLUSIONS

The two case studies reported here were both concerned with improving JS, QWL, and motivation of nursing
staff.   They took place in working environments which
have many more points of similarity than dissimilarity.
In both cases the same senior research staff were
involved, using much the same data-collection and feedback techniques.   Yet in one hospital a number of significant organizational changes have started;   whilst
in the other there were equally significant recommendations which either failed altogether to get off the
ground, or which were actively resisted once they had
started to take effect.

The very nature of action research' means that
generalization and causal inferences from the data are
more than usually dangerous. We have not even tried to
forecast what the nature and changes in QWL for people
in the 'caring' services are likely to be.   However, we
do think our findings point to weaknesses in theories
about JS and QWL. For example:

(i) We cannot rely only upon supposed 'objective'
     job design criteria for establishing 'better'
     jobs that will provide greater satisfaction.

(ii)   The identification of relevant facets of working
        life for people like nurses is a matter for
        empirical enquiry rather than inference from
        other occupational groups and work environments.

(iii)   Certain characteristics of the working environ-
        ment, and individual differences in values and
        expectations, may equally be important.

(iv)   A crucial omission is that even if a desirable
        change to a new organizational performance or
        output can be mutually agreed, the theories do
        not tell us how to initiate and sustain movement
        in the right direction.

We would wish to emphasize our conclusion that the
introduction and sustaining of effective organizational
change, in service-oriented organizations, is difficult
because of the internal dynamics encouraging stability.
If change is to occur, it must follow the acceptance by
staff and management alike (the latter in their organizational, not individual, persona) of objectives the
achievement of which will (i) reduce discrepancies perceived by staff, as well as managers, to exist between
actual and feasible, desirable, standards of performance,
(ii) produce adequate pay-offs to both staff and the
organization, which are perceived as such from the outset, and (iii) provide a fresh 'balance' between organizational and individual pay-offs, so that the situation
stabilises around the new level of performance.

At present the development of techniques for organizational change and development have outstripped their
theoretical underpinning. As a result, a number of workers in the area have produced sets of 'rules of thumb'
or guidelines for optimising attempts at organizational
development. These guidelines cover such things as:

(i)   avoiding the use of 'punishment' wherever pos-
        sible, and using positive reinforcement frequently
        (Jablonsky and DeVries, 1972);

(ii)   specification of desired behaviour in 'explicitly
        operational terms' (Jablonsky and DeVries, 1972);

(iii)   establishing new relationships to provide new
        patterns of reward (Dalton, 1973);

(iv)   recognising the necessity for initial tension to
        promote change (Dalton, 1973);

(v)   obtaining the support of top management within
        the system (Margulies and Wallace, 1973).

Whilst from our own experience we would agree with

all of these empirically produced guidelines (though not necessarily with all the concepts they employ), and indeed our projects have adopted similar suggestions, nevertheless we do not think there has been a theoretical framework or model into which they could be fitted and thus understood in a broader context. The model we have proposed in Figure 5 will undoubtedly require further refinement; but we believe it at least helps us to understand something about the changes, and equally important the occasional lack of changes, with which we have been involved.

REFERENCES

Beckhard, R. (1967). 'The confrontation meeting', Harvard Business Review, 54, 149-154.

Cope, D. (1979). 'Understanding the concept of job satisfaction', in Satisfactions in Work Design (Eds. R.G. Sell and Pat Shipley), Taylor and Francis.

Dalton, G.W. (1973). 'Influence and organizational change', in Changing Organizational Behaviour (Eds. A.C. Bartlett and T.A. Kayser), Prentice Hall.

Davis, Louis E. and Taylor, James C. (1972). Design of Jobs: selected readings, Penguin Books, Harmondsworth.

Emery, F.E. (1967). 'The democratisation of the workplace', Manpower and Applied Psychology, 1, 118-129.

Goldthorpe, J.H., Lockwood, D., Bechhofer, F. and Platt, T. (1970). The affluent worker: industrial attitudes and behaviour, Cambridge University Press.

Herzberg, F. (1972). Work and the nature of man, Staples Press.

Jablonsky, J.F. and DeVries, D.G. (1972). 'Operant conditioning principles extrapolated to the theory of management', Organisational Behaviour and Human Performance, 7, 340-358.

Lewin, K. (1947). 'Frontiers in group dynamics', Human Relations, 1, 5-41.

Locke, E.A. (1969). 'What is job satisfaction?', Organizational Behaviour and Human Performance, 4, 309-336.

Margulies, N. and Wallace, J. (1973). Organizational change: techniques and applications, Scott, Foreman.

Morse, N.C. (1953).   Satisfactions in the white-collar job, Ann Arbor: Survey Research Center, University of Michigan.

Porter, L.W. and Lawler, E.E. (1968).   Managerial Attitudes and Performance, Irwin-Dorsey, Illinois.

Revans, R.W. (1964).   Standards for Morale: Cause and Effect in Hospitals, Oxford University Press.

Schein, E.H. (1965).   Organisational Psychology, Englewood Cliffs, N.J., Prentice Hall.

Schwab, D.P. and Cummings, L.L. (1970).   'Theories of Performance and Satisfaction: A review', Industrial Relations, 9, 408-430.

Taylor, J.C. (1977).   'Job satisfaction and quality of working life: a re-assessment', J. Occupational Psychology, 50, 243-252.

Turner, A.N. and Lawrence, P.R. (1965).   Industrial Jobs and the Worker, Harvard University Press.

Changes in Working Life
Edited by K.D. Duncan, M.M. Gruneberg, and D. Wallis
© 1980 John Wiley & Sons Ltd

Chapter 26

Job Satisfaction and Withdrawal of Hospital Sisters in the U.K.

S. J. REDFERN and P. SPURGEON

THE PROBLEM

The initial problem, in 1974, was defined by nursing administrators as an unacceptably high turnover rate amongst hospital sisters. Although this rate has fallen since 1975, perhaps as a consequence of economic conditions, concern is still being expressed about the current state of nursing (Royal College of Nursing, 1978). The concern has focused upon alleged declining standards of patient care and low morale amongst nurses. The reasons put forward for this low morale are that standards of care have declined, there are too few nurses to meet health service needs, workloads have increased, career development facilities are inadequate, and nurses' pay is too low.

Is this gloomy picture true for sisters (and male charge nurses) who work in general hospitals? The aim of this study was to investigate this, to try to understand the perceptions and attitudes that sisters have towards the job of nursing, the organizations they work in, and the conditions they work under; and whether these relate to absence and turnover both potential and actual. Thus, the aim was to develop a model of organizational behaviour in which work attitudes and perceptions of hospital sisters could be related to their occupational stability.

Very little research on work attitudes in British professional nurses has been published (compared with overseas research) and so these claims of low morale have been unsubstantiated. Revans' (1964) early work centred on student nurses and he concluded that the hospital generates a self-perpetuating process of anxiety, uncertainty and communication blockage. There is some evidence, however, that as with many occupational groups, professional nurses say they are happy with their work and are committed to nursing. Moving from job to job is just as, if not more, likely to result from career aspirations as from dissatisfaction (Mercer and Mould, 1976).

APPROACH ADOPTED

The theoretical basis of the study has its origins in the person-environment fit model of the Minnesota Theory of Work Adjustment (Lofquist and Dawis, 1969), and the role stress theory of Kahn and his associates (1964). A conceptual model was formulated from factors which emerged as relevant from pilot work, and these have been summarised in Figure 1.

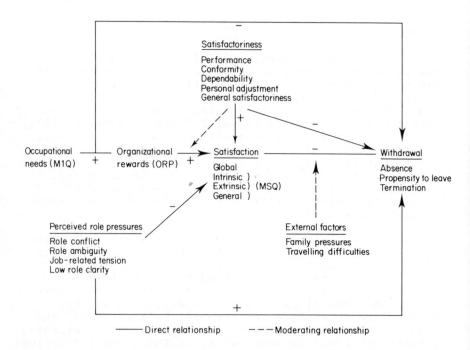

Figure 1.   Diagram of the principal variables and their hypothesised relationships.

The Theory of Work Adjustment states that satisfaction with the job can be predicted from a close relationship between an individual's 'work personality' (his occupational needs and abilities) and the characteristics of the work environment (the ability requirements of the job and organizational rewards);   and, other things being equal, this will lead to substantial tenure.   If the person-environment correspondence is low, then the outcome predicted is dissatisfaction and short tenure.   The focus of this paper concerns the occupational needs - rewards correspondence, and the individual ability dimension is not discussed here.

In the present study the withdrawal variables of absence, propensity to leave, and termination were used in preference to tenure because unacceptable leaving rates in professional nurses provided the initial impetus for the research, and the relationship between tenure and termination in qualified ward-based nurses is not a simple linear one (Mercer and Mould, 1976).   A sister who has been in the job for six months, for example, is not necessarily more likely to leave than one with two years' service.   Propensity to leave the job was included as a justifiable indicator of pending termination because the declining turnover rates in sisters suggested that the sample of leavers would be small, and expressed intention to leave has been established as the most important predictor of termination both in professional nurses (Mercer and Mould, 1976) and other occupational groups (Porter and Steers, 1973;   Kraut, 1975).

The number of absence spells was included to see if the rate was increasing during this period of low job mobility.   It may be that sisters were withdrawing from their jobs temporarily through absence rather than permanently, because they could not find alternative employment.   Short term absence has been established as a widespread and increasing problem in nurses (Blenkinsop, 1974; Clark, 1975) as well as in industrial workers (Froggatt, 1970;   Jones, 1971).

This paper forms part of a research project in which work attitudes, perceptions and behaviour of hospital sisters were examined.   For details of the work which have been excluded from this paper, the reader is referred to Redfern (1979).

HYPOTHESES

The hypotheses examined in this paper were as follows:

1. Perceived role pressure, propensity to leave and biographical variables are significantly related

to (a) intrinsic, (b) extrinsic satisfaction.

2.   Satisfaction, perceived role pressure, and bio-
      graphical variables are significantly related to
      propensity to leave.

3.   External factors (number of children and travel-
      ling distance to work) influence the withdrawal
      decision.

4.   Discrepancy between the sisters' occupational
      needs and the organizational rewards are signifi-
      cantly related to propensity to leave.   The
      direction of the relationship would depend on the
      direction of the discrepancy.

5.   The leavers have significantly lower satisfaction
      scores and higher perceived role pressure scores,
      absence and propensity to leave scores than the
      stayers.

THE MEASURES

      Questionnaires, interviews and biographical records
were used to collect the information, and the scales used
for the purposes of this paper were as follows:

1.   Occupational needs were measured with the Minne-
      sota Importance Questionnaire (MIQ) multiple rank
      order form (Gay et al., 1971).   This measure
      consists of 21 vocational needs and the respondent
      indicates to what extent each item is important to
      him/her in his/her ideal job.   The items are
      presented in 21 blocks of 5 items each and the
      items in each block are ranked according to their
      importance to the respondent.   Examples of the
      items include the opportunity to make use of one's
      abilities, gaining a sense of achievement from
      the job, and being able to try out one's own
      ideas.   The MIQ is scored by computer at the
      University of Minnesota which provides individual
      need socre profiles.

2.   The Minnesota Occupational Reinforcer Pattern
      (ORP) for the Professional Nurse (Borgen et al.,
      1972) was used to indicate the extent to which
      certain rewards exist in the working environment.
      The ORP is based on the combined ratings of the
      nurses' supervisors and includes the same items
      as in the MIQ.   Close correspondence between the
      MIQ profile and the ORP indicates satisfaction,
      and poor correspondence, dissatisfaction.

      A modified British version of the ORP was

developed in which nursing officers (the nurses immediately senior to sisters) indicated the extent to which each item was descriptive of the sister's job. Comparison with the ORP revealed no significant difference between the profiles, which justified using the ORP with British sisters.

3. Job satisfaction was measured with a unitary index and a faceted measure. The unitary index was Lyons' (1971) two-item global measure ('Considering your job as a whole, how well do you like it?' 'On the whole, what do you think of this hospital as a place to work?'). The faceted scale was the Minnesota Satisfaction Questionnaire (MSQ) short form (Weiss et al., 1967). This contains 20 items which are similar to those in the MIQ, and the individual responds to each on a weighted 5-point scale, very dissatisfied through neither to very satisfied. The MSQ is reduced to three scales by summing scores on the relevant items:

   a) intrinsic satisfaction: 12 items labelled ability utilization, activity, achievement, authority, creativity, security, social service, variety, etc.

   b) extrinsic satisfaction: 6 items labelled advancement, company policies and practices, compensation, recognition, supervision.

   c) general satisfaction: all 18 items and also co-workers and working conditions.

   Further details of the scales used in the Theory of Work Adjustment can be found in the references cited, together with evidence for their reliability and validity.

   Perceived role pressures were measured with four scales:

4. The Job-Related Tension Index (JRT) modified by Lyons (1971) from Kahn et al.'s (1964) original, consists of 9 items to which the respondent indicates on a 5-point scale how much he/she feels bothered by items which could be perceived as evoking role ambiguity or conflict. The items refer to, for example, the heaviness of the workload, having to satisfy conflicting demands, feedback about one's performance and opportunities for advancement. Lyons (1971) reported a split-half reliability coefficient of .70 with American registered staff nurses but the inter-item

correlation coefficients were sufficiently
varied to suggest a relatively heterogeneous
scale.

5.   Rizzo et al. (1970) found role conflict and
     ambiguity to be independent dimensions and their
     scales were used here.   The Role Conflict Scale
     consists of 8 items and the Role Ambiguity
     Scale has 6, and the individual responds to
     each item on a 7-point 'how true' rating scale.
     Examples of conflict items relate to insuffi-
     cient manpower and resources, having to bend
     the rules, and receiving incompatible requests.
     The role ambiguity items include having clear,
     planned goals to do the job, knowing what was
     expected, having clear explanations, etc.
     Evidence for these scales' reliability and vali-
     dity are documented in Rizzo et al. (1970).

6.   The Role Clarity Index used by Lyons (1971) con-
     sists of five items concerned with perceived
     existing clarity on limits of authority, how and
     what to do on the job, and the policies, rules
     and regulations of the hospital.   Individuals
     respond on a 5-point scale, and Lyons reported a
     split-half reliability coefficient of .70.

     Although role clarity is the obverse of role
     ambiguity, the clarity scale was included as well
     as the ambiguity scale because both included
     items appropriate to hospital sisters.

7.   The Propensity to Leave Index consisted of
     Lyons' (1971) three-item scale which refers to
     the respondent's intention to stay in or leave
     the organization, and one more item, 'How likely
     are you to leave your job in the next 12 months?'
     The responses were scored on 5-point scales with
     high scores indicating high leaving intent.
     Lyons' inter-item and item-index correlation
     coefficients were sufficiently high (r > .53) to
     indicate internal consistency of the scale
     (Lyons, 1968, 1971).

SAMPLES AND SITES

The sample consisted of all the sisters employed in
the general nursing division of two hospitals.   One hospital was small with 42 sisters, and the other large with
110.   Biographical comparisons were made between the two
samples, and, since there was very little difference between them, they were combined for the purposes of this
study.   Response rates were 88% in each hospital.

RESULTS

Zero-order correlation coefficients between satisfactions, role pressures, propensity to leave and absence are shown in Tables 1 and 2. Relatively high coefficients emerged between the satisfactions and perceived role pressures and all were in the expected direction. None of the coefficients between satisfactions and absence was significant but high negative coefficients (p < .001) emerged with propensity to leave. Likewise, none of the pressure-absence correlations reached significance, but all the pressure-propensity to leave coefficients did so; although only one was over .30.

Table 1.   Correlation coefficients (Pearson's) between perceived role pressures and job satisfactions (N = 120-131)

perceived role pressure	global satis-faction	intrinsic satis-faction	extrinsic satis-faction	general satis-faction
job-related tension	-.45***	-.46***	-.52***	-.55***
role conflict	-.32***	-.20*	-.28**	-.27**
role ambiguity	-.47***	-.49***	-.44***	-.52***
role clarity	.54***	.48***	.55***	.58***

*p ≤ .05   **p ≤ .01   ***p ≤ .001

Multiple regression analysis was used to test hypotheses 1 and 2. With intrinsic and extrinsic satisfaction as the criteria (hypothesis 1), the independent variables included in the analysis were job-related tension, role clarity, role conflict and ambiguity, absence (spells), age, tenure in present job and year qualified as a State Registered Nurse. The results are shown in Tables 3 and 4.

In the case of intrinsic satisfaction, the multiple correlation was .61, the variance in the criterion explained was 37% and the F-ratio was significant (7.07, p < .001). Only three variables emerged as significant predictors, however: role ambiguity, clarity and propensity to leave. The direction of each contribution was as expected.

Table 2.   Correlation coefficients (Pearson's) between
            job satisfactions and perceived role pres-
            sures and absence and propensity to leave
            (N = 120-129)

satisfaction/role pressure variable	absence[+] (spells)	propensity to leave
global satisfaction	ns	-.58***
intrinsic satisfaction	ns	-.36***
extrinsic satisfaction	ns	-.52***
general satisfaction	ns	-.48***
job-related tension	ns	.31***
role conflict	ns	.27**
role ambiguity	ns	.24**
role clarity	ns	-.23**

ns = not significant   **$p \leq .01$ ***$p \leq .001$

[+]absence = number of spells in 2 years corrected for
            tenure less than 2 years.

Table 3.   Summary of multiple regression analysis used
            to explore the relationship between intrinsic
            satisfaction and propensity to leave, role
            pressure and biographical variables (N = 118)

variable	simple correlation	F	p	beta coefficient
role ambiguity	-.48	7.10	<.10	-.26
propensity to leave	-.36	7.07	<.01	-.22
role clarity	.48	5.32	<.05	.26
year qualified	-.04	2.44	ns	.32
age	.10	1.89	ns	.28
role conflict	-.20	1.25	ns	.10
job-related tension	-.43	.76	ns	-.10
absence (spells)	.03	.73	ns	.07
job tenure	.12	.03	ns	-.01
constant				17.33

multiple R = .61 R^2 = .37   F = 7.07 $p < .001$

Table 4.   Summary of multiple regression analysis used
            to explore the relationship between extrinsic
            satisfaction and propensity to leave, role
            pressure and biographical variables (N = 118)

variable	simple correlation	F	p	beta coefficient
propensity to leave	-.50	23.54	<.001	-.36
role clarity	.58	19.03	<.001	.43
job tenure	.06	5.55	<.05	-.19
age	.17	1.86	ns	.25
job-related tension	-.50	1.04	ns	-.11
role ambiguity	-.44	.70	ns	-.07
year qualified	-.11	.69	ns	.15
role conflict	-.28	.32	ns	.04
absence (spells)	-.04	.08	ns	.02
constant				8.19

multiple R = .72 R^2 = .51   F = 12.57   p < .001

Table 5.   Summary of multiple regression analysis used
            to explore the relationship between propensity
            to leave and satisfaction, role pressure and
            biographical variables (n = 118)

variable	simple correlation	F	p	beta coefficient
global satisfaction	-.61	39.45	<.001	-.59
role clarity	-.25	7.59	<.01	.30
job tenure	-.20	2.55	ns	-.13
age	-.24	2.38	ns	-.29
role ambiguity	.24	1.43	ns	.11
role conflict	.27	1.08	ns	.08
year qualified	.18	.74	ns	-.16
job-related tension	.30	.58	ns	.08
extrinsic satisfaction	-.50	.26	ns	-.14
general satisfaction	-.48	.18	ns	-.22
absence (spells)	.06	.14	ns	.03
intrinsic satisfaction	-.36	.09	ns	.10
constant				25.78

multiple R = .71 R^2 = .51   F = 9.10   p < .001

With extrinsic satisfaction as the criterion (Table 4), the multiple R was .72, R^2 = .51, and the F-ratio was 12.57, p < .001.   In this case, low propensity to leave, high role clarity and <u>short</u> tenure emerged as significant predictors.

When propensity to leave was the criterion (hypothesis 2), the independent variables were as before except that satisfactions were included and propensity to leave omitted. Table 5 shows these results.   The multiple R was .71, R^2 = .51 and the F-ratio was 9.10, p < .001.   Of the 12 predictors included, however, only two had sufficiently high (p ≤ .05) individual F-ratios to contribute substantially to the prediction equation. These were global satisfaction and role clarity.   Global satisfaction was by far the more powerful predictor and contributed negatively to propensity to leave.   The simple correlation between role clarity and propensity to leave was also negative but when combined with global satisfaction, its contribution became positive.   An explanation for this interaction is suggested below.

In hypothesis 3 it was suggested that the number of children and the distance to work might be sufficiently powerful variables to influence the sisters' withdrawal decision.   The correlations between job satisfaction and absence and propensity to leave were recalculated with these two external variables separately partialled out.   As can be seen from Table 6, very little change occurred to the original coefficients.

Table 6.   Correlation coefficients between satisfactions and absence and propensity to leave after partialling out distance from hospital and number of children

satisfaction variable	correlation coefficients with			
	absence when		propensity to leave when	
	distance removed	children removed	distance removed	children removed
global	ns	ns	-.57	-.59
intrinsic	ns	ns	-.37	-.35
extrinsic	ns	ns	-.52	-.49
general	ns	ns	-.49	-.46

ns = not significant   all other coefficients, p < .001.

The 21 needs-rewards discrepancy variables were submitted to multiple regression analysis to establish the extent to which they predicted propensity to leave. The initial run revealed a multiple correlation coefficient of .48 which accounted for 23% of the variance in the criterion.   Subsequent analysis of variance revealed an insignificant F-ratio (1.31), however, and so the analysis was re-run with only those 10 discrepancy variables which had the highest individual F-ratios. Table 7 shows that three discrepancy items emerged as significant predictors, activity, achievement, and ability utilization, and a fourth, hospital policies and practices, approached significance.   The overall F-ratio was also significant.

Table 7.   Summary of multiple regression analysis used to explore the relationship between propensity to leave and the 10 'best' needs-rewards discrepancy variables (N = 112)

Needs-rewards discrepancy item	Simple correlation	F	p	Beta coefficient
3. Activity	-.15	8.05	<.01	-.33
2. Achievement	-.05	5.86	<.05	-.30
1. Ability utilization	.16	5.15	<.05	.28
6. Hospital policies and practices	.18	3.59	ns	.21
19. Variety	.04	1.89	ns	.16
7. Compensation	.11	1.38	ns	.14
9. Creativity	.18	1.31	ns	.12
10. Independence	.07	1.17	ns	.11
14. Security	-.03	1.09	ns	-.12
16. Social status	-.09	.98	ns	-.10
Constant				7.35

Multiple R = .46 R^2 = .21   F = 2.67   p < .01

The contribution of ability utilization and hospital policies and practices was positive, indicating that the more the rewards were perceived as falling short of the sisters' requirements, the greater was the likelihood that the sisters would leave.   The contribution of achievement was negative, which suggested that the more the rewards were perceived as falling short of requirements, the less likely were the sisters to leave.   The activity variable (being busy all the time) was the only one of these four variables with a negative mean discrepancy score (rewards exceeded needs), and so the greater the discrepancy, the less was the likelihood of leaving.

Hypothesis 5 was tested by comparing the scale scores of those sisters who left their jobs voluntarily during the 18 months following data collection with those from a 'matched' sample of sisters who stayed. Omitted from this analysis were those who retired or were asked to leave, and those who were transferred or promoted within the general nursing division of the same hospital.   The two groups were matched on marital status, hours worked, age, tenure, and where possible, sex, and type of ward.   Table 8 shows the significance levels which emerged from Mann Whitney U tests.   The leavers scored significantly lower than the stayers on global and extrinsic satisfaction, but not on intrinsic satisfaction.   The leavers scored significantly higher (greater role pressure) on the job-related tension and role conflict scales, and had a higher propensity to leave the job.

Table 8.   Comparison between leavers and 'matched' stayers, total sample (Mann Whitney U tests)

Global satisfaction	< .05
Intrinsic satisfaction	ns
Extrinsic satisfaction	< .05
General satisfaction	ns
'Past' absence[1]	ns
'Current' absence[2]	ns
Propensity to leave	< .01
Job-related tension	< .05
Role clarity	ns
Role conflict	.01
Role ambiguity	ns
Sample size: leavers	30-34
stayers	37-40

All 1 - tail tests   ns = not significant

1 = number of absence spells during the 2 years before data collection corrected for tenure less than 2 years.

2 = number of absence spells during the 6 months before and the 6 months after data collection corrected for tenure less than 12 months.

DISCUSSION AND CONCLUSIONS

The negative contribution of the achievement needs-rewards discrepancy variable to the prediction of propensity to leave was perplexing particularly when the contribution of ability utilization was positive.   A tentative explanation in terms of locus of control and attribution theory is suggested.   Gaining a sense of achievement from the job may be seen as an internal condition within the sister's control, and so she is perhaps more likely to persist at the job in order to achieve this goal.   On the other hand, the extent to which she is given the opportunity to use her skills and abilities may be seen as under the control of the organization and the experience of underutilization may encourage her to leave for a more challenging job.

There was no significant difference between the leavers' and stayers' scores on intrinsic satisfaction but the leavers were significantly less satisfied with those contextual features of the job which comprised the extrinsic satisfaction scale.   This suggests that the sisters were committed to nursing, but some left because they were disenchanted with their working environment and advancement opportunities.

The unexpected finding that role clarity made a positive contribution to both the satisfaction and the propensity to leave predictions is tentatively explained in terms of challenge and tenure.   It may be that in the first few years in the job, role clarity is a necessary requirement for job satisfaction because the job is unfamiliar and challenging, but not without some anxiety for the sister.   After a few years, however, the challenge and anxiety have decreased and a high degree of role clarity has become counter-productive, the job provides insufficient challenge and the propensity is to leave for more stimulating work.   The negative contribution of tenure to the extrinsic satisfaction prediction and subsequent discussion of these findings with sisters, suggest that this may be a realistic explanation.

If this is the case, the nursing management must be differentially sensitive to the needs of the sisters according to their job tenure.   To begin with, the sister requires clear guidelines about the policies of the hospital which affect her, about what to do and how to do it, and to know how well she is doing.   But, after a time, such role clarity becomes a negative influence, and the sister needs fresh challenges.   The conclusion drawn from this is that although turnover from the hospitals was probably not excessive and may have been too low in some years, some of the sisters who did leave may have done so because the organization failed to give them sufficient opportunity for personal career growth.   It

may be that pursuing a course, taking on a teaching
commitment, or carrying out a research project related
to her work would give the sister the challenge she
seeks.   Enlarging the job in ways such as these should
be within the scope of the nursing officer's role.   Such
sensitivity to the needs of the sister may increase her
respect for her senior colleagues and may encourage
those sisters to stay who are most valuable to the nursing management and to the patient.

SUPPORT FOR THE MODEL

The relationships suggested in the model based on
bivariate correlations were confirmed, except for those
involving absence (and satisfactoriness, which has not
been discussed here).   Absence did not emerge as an
important variable for this group of sisters, although
that is not to say that the rate was not unacceptably
high in certain individuals and units.   More detailed
work is required to establish the extent of sisters'
absence.

Multivariate analyses demonstrated that not all
the variables which appeared from the simple correlations
to make a significant contribution did so when the effect
of other predictors was simultaneously taken into account.
The significant correlates of job satisfaction were role
clarity, tenure and propensity to leave, and in the case
of propensity to leave, only global satisfaction and role
clarity were significant predictors.

The power of the needs-rewards mismatch to predict
propensity to leave (hypothesis 4) was really quite
weak since only three of the 21 predictors made a significant contribution.   More support may have emerged
if those discrepancy variables which demonstrated that
the needs exceeded the rewards had been treated separately from those where the rewards exceeded the needs,
since the former were likely to be associated with dissatisfaction and propensity to leave, and the latter
with satisfaction and propensity to stay.   Weiss (1969)
emphasised the importance of identifying the direction
of the needs-rewards discrepancy in predicting satisfaction, and reported a correlation between the total
discrepancy score and satisfaction of only .02.   When
only those discrepancy scores were included in which the
reinforcer fell short of the need, the correlation was
-.26, and when the analysis was made on the remainder,
where rewards existed in excess, the correlation with
satisfaction was .44.

LIMITATIONS OF THE STUDY AND SUGGESTIONS FOR FURTHER RESEARCH

The results which emerged from the multiple regression analysis raised interesting issues, but the conclusions drawn are tentative and should not be generalized from these findings. The lack of opportunity to validate the results against a 'hold-out' sample, or to use a longitudinal research design, means that the results were entirely sample-specific.

Other limitations are that the sample was small (134 maximum) and it was not selected in a way which ensured representativeness. Also, the study focused on one type of individual in a complex organization and no attempt was made to compare the sister's attitudes and perceptions with those of others in her role set, nor to validate her responses with observation.

More positively, however, a start has been made to describe the work attitudes and behaviours of an occupational group which has received very little research attention in Britain. Further research could follow Kasl's (1978) recommendation. He argued in favour of longitudinal studies which relate to the occurrence of actual events or changes likely to influence individual health and well-being. Such 'natural experiments' would enable limited descriptive cross-sectional correlational research designs to be replaced by methods which make explanation possible.

REFERENCES

Blenkinsop, D. (1974). The Problem of Nursing Staff Absence in the NHS, Paper presented at the Seminar on the Management of Staff Absence, edited by Nelson and Blenkinsop, Northern Regional Health Authority, Newcastle-upon-Tyne, UK.

Borgen, F.H., Weiss, D.J., Tinsley, H.E.A., Dawis, R.V. and Lofquist, L.H. (1972). Occupational Reinforcer Patterns (First Volume), Minnesota Studies in Vocational Rehabilitation, xxiv, Bulletin 48, Industrial Relations Center, University of Minnesota, USA.

Clark, J. (1975). Time Out? A Study of Absenteeism Amongst Nurses, Royal College of Nursing, London.

Froggatt, P. (1970). 'Short-term absence from industry: 1. Literature, definitions, data and the effect of age and length of service', British Journal of Industrial Medicine, 27, 297-312.

Gay, E.G., Weiss, D.J., Hendel, D.D., Dawis, R.V. and
    Lofquist, L.H. (1971). Manual for the Minnesota
    Importance Questionnaire, Minnesota Studies in
    Vocational Rehabilitation, xxviii, Bulletin 54,
    Industrial Relations Center, University of
    Minnesota, USA.

Jones, R.M. (1971). Absenteeism, Department of Employ-
    ment Manpower Papers No. 4, London, HMSO.

Kahn, R.L., Wolfe, D.M., Quinn, R.P., Snoek, J.D. with
    Rosenthal, R.A. (1964). Organizational Stress:
    Studies in role conflict and ambiguity, New York,
    Wiley & Sons.

Kasl, S.V. (1978). 'Epidemiological contributions to
    the study of work stress', in Cooper, C.L. and
    Payne, R. (eds.), Stress at Work, New York, Wiley
    & Sons.

Kraut, A.I. (1975). 'Predicting turnover of employees
    from measured job attitudes', Organizational
    Behavior and Human Performance, 13 (2), 233-243.

Lofquist, L.H. and Dawis, R.V. (1969). Adjustment to
    Work, New Jersey, Appleton-Century-Crofts.

Lyons, T.F. (1968). Nursing Attitudes and Turnover,
    Unpublished Report, Industrial Relations Center,
    Iowa State University, USA.

Lyons, T.F. (1971). 'Role clarity, need for clarity,
    satisfaction, tension and withdrawal', Organiza-
    tional Behavior and Human Performance, 6, 99-110.

Mercer, G. and Mould, C. (1976). An Investigation into
    the Level and Character of Labour Turnover amongst
    Trained Nurses, Final Report to the Department of
    Health and Social Security, London, Volume 1 and 2,
    Nursing Research Department, Department of Socio-
    logy, Leeds University, UK.

Porter, L.W. and Steers, R.M. (1973). 'Organizational,
    work and personal factors in employee turnover
    and absenteeism', Psychological Bulletin, 80 (2),
    151-176.

Redfern, S.J. (1979). The Charge Nurse: job attitudes
    and occupational stability, Ph.D. Thesis, Univer-
    sity of Aston in Birmingham, UK.

Revans, R.W. (1964). Standards for Morale: cause and
    effect in hospitals, National Provincial Hospitals
    Trust, London, Oxford University Press.

Rizzo, J.R., House, R.J. and Lirtzmann, S.I. (1970).
    'Role conflict and ambiguity in complex organi-
    zations', Administrative Science Quarterly, 15,
    150-163.

Royal College of Nursing (1978). An Assessment of the
    State of Nursing in the National Health Service,
    1978, RCN submission to the Secretary of State
    for Social Services, Royal College of Nursing,
    London.

Weiss, D.J. (1969). Occupational Reinforcers, Voca-
    tional Needs, and Job Satisfaction, Research
    Report No. 28, Work Adjustment Project, University
    of Minnesota, USA.

Weiss, D.J., Dawis, R.V., England, G.W. and Lofquist, L.H.
    (1967). Manual for the Minnesota Satisfaction
    Questionnaire, Minnesota Studies in Vocational
    Rehabilitation, xxii, Bulletin 45, Industrial
    Relations Center, University of Minnesota, USA.

Changes in Working Life
Edited by K.D. Duncan, M.M. Gruneberg, and D. Wallis
© 1980 John Wiley & Sons Ltd

Chapter 27

Workers' Perceptions of Changes Affecting the Quality of Working Life

D. GUEST, R. WILLIAMS and P. DEWE

INTRODUCTION

It is possible for almost everyone, whatever their position in industry or their political viewpoint, to support aspirations to improve the quality of working life. It is therefore a little surprising to find that in the United Kingdom, despite fairly extensive discussion of the topic, relatively little of the talk and the avowed enthusiasm has been translated into action. Nor does the problem seem to be limited to the United Kingdom. Commentators in the USA (Fein, 1974; Luthans and Reif, 1974; Hackman, 1975), Norway (Herbst, 1976; Bolweg, 1976), and West Germany (Bartölke and Gohl, 1976), have noted the same problem in their own country.

Since we would include ourselves among the advocates of an improved quality of working life, we believe it is necessary to understand why so little progress has been made. The first part of this paper therefore identifies six issues which we believe hinder understanding and progress. The second part reports some findings from a study which explores some of these issues in the hope of developing this understanding.

---

* The views expressed in this paper are those of the authors and do not necessarily represent those of the Work Research Unit.

ISSUES LIMITING PROGRESS IN THE QUALITY OF WORKING LIFE

The first problematic issue is [the nature of the concept of the quality of working life.] This has been widely debated elsewhere (Walton, 1973; Wilson, 1973; Davis and Cherns, 1975) so there is no need to discuss it at length here. [The problem arises because the concept covers such disparate issues as job design, safety, stress, remuneration, worker participation and even the right to employment. Therefore it is possible for both those who identify with the mainstream of the trade union movement, and those who have strong affiliations with managers of multi-national organizations, to be advocating improvements in the quality of working life while meaning something quite different and even potentially incompatible.]

The differences of interest, which become apparent when specific types of action, under the umbrella of the quality of working life, are considered, help to explain the lack of progress. This is illustrated in the following comment by Hughes and Gregory:

> 'British unions should not allow themselves
> to be trapped by their recognition that
> attempts to improve the quality of working
> life are of great importance. Neither
> should they tolerate job enrichment being
> advanced separately, either as a bar-
> gaining subject or as an innovatory mana-
> gerial practice. [Unions should insist
> that the quality of working life can only
> be improved by a comprehensive and coordi-
> nated concern with improvements in the
> total work situation, and in the total
> remuneration package] (Hughes and Gregory,
>   1974).

[This view suggests that the quality of working life should be a topic for bargaining, as opposed to the more integrative form of participation/advocated by writers such as Thorsrud (1979), and that it can be seen both as something which workers can demand and for which they can demand compensation.

In an attempt to circumvent the definitional problem, Thorsrud has suggested that

> 'QWL is not primarily concerned with defi-
> ning its area of activity but rather with
> basic values underlying and concrete forms
> of participation with people in work
> places' (Thorsrud, 1979).

While this may be highly desirable, it evades the

issue of the content and aims of the participation.
For those with sectional interests, this may serve to
heighten suspicion of the motives of those advocating
change.   Given competing and even conflicting priorities,
there is a danger, in the UK at least, of the quality of
working life becoming an empty slogan, devoid of practical meaning.   In an attempt to be all-embracing it
disguises differing and sometimes competing underlying
concerns for efficiency, control and satisfaction.
These differences in real and perceived objectives must
be recognised and made explicit if progress is to be
made.

The second issue, an extension of the definitional
problem, is the potential confusion between objective
and subjective indicators of quality of working life.
Objective indicators may include working conditions and
cycle times or measures of labour turnover and absenteeism, while subjective indicators are essentially concerned with workers' perceptions of, and reactions to,
various aspects of their employment.   Seashore (1975),
in advocating the use of both types of indicator, argues
that subjective indicators fail to take account of managerial and community criteria and in any case

> 'the individual ... is in important res-
> pects incapable of optimum judgement of
> his own life situation' (Seashore, 1975,
> p. 107).

While there is undoubtedly some truth in this, it raises
a number of questions.   Firstly, for whom are we concerned in debates on the quality of working life?
Secondly, who decides which is the more appropriate when
there is conflict between objective and subjective indicators?   Thirdly, which indicators should be chosen and
by whom?   And finally, how much trust can we put in
'objective' indicators?

The use of 'objective' indicators implies a standard type of worker, and, in effect, fails to take
account of individual differences.   Many studies of
the link between, for example, repetitive work and boredom (Guest, Williams and Dewe, 1978) or work role and
stress (Cooper, 1978) highlight the importance of differences in subjective perceptions.   We are sympathetic
to the desire to obtain 'hard' data and recognise its
potential value, but at the same time we are suspicious
of the motives of those who, in their concern for such
data, disregard the subjective perceptions of the workers.
Indeed we believe that quality can best be conceived of
as existing in the relationship between the individual
and his environment (Pirsig, 1974) and as such it must be
subjectively perceived.

The third issue inhibiting progress towards an improved quality of working life is the lack of real interest among many of those in positions of power, who, while they may not express active opposition are nevertheless unwilling personally to pursue appropriate policies with vigour. This is of particular importance in the UK where senior management is generally unwilling to initiate what may be perceived as potentially risky changes in job design, to design new manufacturing or office units along other than conventional lines or to risk cutting out shiftwork or reducing the working week when the financial costs may seem considerable. Trade unions have been reluctant to move away from the familiar and well trodden ground of bargaining over terms and conditions of employment. Elsewhere unions have sometimes taken a more positive view and sought to negotiate improvements in the quality of working life; indeed in West Germany and Italy the unions have successfully negotiated minimum cycle times.

There are a number of topics sometimes linked to the quality of working life, including equal opportunity for women, racial equality and safety, that everyone supports but few in positions of power are prepared to do much about. As a result, in the UK legislation has been deemed necessary to persuade them to take action. In an area such as job design, which is fairly central to most views of quality of working life, legislation in the UK seems a long way off and the unions are certainly not pressing for it. Yet it has been advocated by some writers (see, for example, Lawler, 1976) and is already reflected in Article 12 of the Norwegian law on the work environment which seeks to avoid repetitive work and to provide variety, social interaction and worker autonomy (Jenkins, 1978).

The lack of active support among management and unions for central quality of working life concerns such as job design must be partly attributed to the behavioural scientists and their failure to communicate a sufficiently persuasive message. In the UK in particular, it can also be partly explained in terms of the role of personnel managers who, in claiming professional status, cite their concern for human resources and their grounding in the behavioural sciences. They would therefore seem to be the natural channel through which outsiders, acting as behavioural science consultants or action researchers, might wish to initiate change. Yet on the basis of the available evidence, it appears that in a desire to protect their role, they are both extremely reluctant and often uncertain as to how to initiate change in this field (Thurley and Guest, 1979).

Action to improve the quality of working life depends not only on those in power within management and

the trade unions, but also on those on the shop floor.
Workers in the UK have been ready to act on their own
initiative with respect to pay; could they not do the
same to improve the quality of working life? This
leads into the fourth issue, for, if the major theories
in this field are to be believed, then most workers are
motivated to improve the quality of their working life
and in particular their job content and therefore ought
to be pursuing job redesign as a goal. The fact that
they are not may be attributed to irrationality or to
other priorities; or the theories may be wrong. This
last possibility seems to offer at least a partial
explanation.

The strengths and weaknesses of the various theories
of job design have been reviewed elsewhere (see, for
example, Steers and Mowday, 1977). Herzberg's two factor theory (Herzberg, 1966) is still one of the most popular among managers. Unfortunately it rests on very
shaky ground and has been widely criticised on several
counts. Our own research has failed to support it for
UK populations (Guest and Fatchett, 1974).

In Europe equal attention has been focused on
socio-technical systems theory (Emery and Thorsrud, 1976).
Yet its theoretical basis for suggesting that workers
prefer certain types of job design is extremely weak.
It rests in some poorly articulated assumptions about
worker motivation (Thorsrud, 1972; Emery and Thorsrud,
1976) and evidence from a number of case studies which
could be open to alternative explanations (Bolweg, 1976;
Kelly, 1978; Guest, 1979).

The third major theoretical approach, the Job
Characteristics Model (Hackman and Oldham, 1975) is
attractive to many psychologists because of its integrative nature, its clear theoretical roots and its carefully articulated and testable propositions. Despite
these attractions there have, until recently, been few
full field tests of the theory and in the UK it has not
yet found its way into the management literature.
Indeed the complexity of the theory may make it unattrac-
tive to both management and unions. Two recently
reported field tests (Wall, Clegg and Jackson, 1978;
Orpen, 1979) fail for a variety of reasons to lend clear
support to the model. Indeed Wall, Clegg and Jackson
conclude:

> 'The Job Characteristics Model as cur-
> rently formulated is not fully consis-
> tent with either the findings upon
> which it was developed or those of the
> present study. It cannot therefore
> be regarded as valid' (Wall, Clegg and
> Jackson, 1978, p. 194).

Some of the problems with the model might lie in its
somewhat arbitrary selection of task characteristics; in
its failure to take account of the organizational context; and its use of higher order need strength as the
major moderating variable. Another rather different
kind of problem in the context of the present discussion
is its failure to point towards any process of job redesign. Despite these factors, the model has many
attractions and probably provides the best path towards
further theoretical developments.

The fifth issue leads on directly from the last
point. The three theories listed above assume that
job redesign is central to the working lives of individuals. In fact the theories may be right to the extent
that many people would prefer an improved quality of job;
but, for the UK at least, they are wrong if they assume
that this is always a high priority. This possible
delusion is fostered by the nature of much of the
research that has been reported and which, understandably,
has focused on the nature of, or changes in job content
to the exclusion of other factors. Therefore a change
programme may be acclaimed a success if a worker, on
being asked 'Are you now more or less satisfied with
the degree of autonomy in your job?' answers that he is
more satisfied. This tells us nothing about how significant this change is for him; indeed an associated
rise in pay may have meant far more to him. Furthermore there is an inbuilt, perhaps faulty but seldom
tested assumption, that he is aware that a change has
taken place. In short, our conventional methodology for
evaluating reactions to changes in the quality of working
life, and job design in particular, rests on certain
assumptions, which may sometimes be valid, but which, at
other times, must be tested.

The final issue, again closely linked to the previous one, concerns the process of change. Many of the
studies of job redesign, in reporting positive worker
responses, may in fact be commenting on the way in which
the change was introduced. Where sophisticated education or participation programmes secured worker involvement, a form of consciousness raising and commitment may
have resulted. The critical question then becomes one
of whether the change process rather than the nature of
the changes in job content had the major impact on the
reaction. This is perhaps more likely in the approach
adopted by socio-technical theorists (Emery and Thorsrud,
1976) than in the explicitly non-participative approach
of Herzberg (Paul and Robertson, 1970). In the interesting studies of job design failures (see, for example,
Frank and Hackman, 1975; Locke, Sirota and Wolfson, 1976)
it is usually the change process, and the resultant insignificance of the changes to the workers or their antago-
nism to the changes, that is called into question. This

discussion raises a linked question which is often
overlooked, namely the considerable difficulties involved in introducing changes of this type and our relative weakness, in the United Kingdom, in managing change
of any sort.

To summarise the argument so far, we have suggested
that attempts to improve the quality of working life,
in particular through job-redesign, have not as yet
been very successful and are unlikely to become more
successful in the future unless we can recognise and
overcome six issues or constraints. These are the diffuse nature of the concept of the quality of working life;
the confusion between subjective and objective indicators; the tendency of those in power to pay lip service to the idea but not to be sufficiently concerned to
take action; the weakness of the underlying theoretical
basis for job redesign supported by the relative dis-
interest of many workers; the tendency to assume, perhaps falsely, that job design is central to workers compared with other changes; and the danger that confusion
occurs between the nature of changes and the process of
change.

THE FOCUS OF THE RESEARCH

Some of the issues outlined above are conceptual
and theoretical, others are concerned with values while
others raise questions which can be explored through
research. We believe that a central issue influencing
the direction of theory and research relates to the distinction between objective and subjective indicators of
quality of working life. Its significance is determined partly by our own values, which assume that the
individual should be the major focus of concern to organizational psychologists. Therefore his perceptions and
definitions of his work and of changes in it are of central importance.

The concern for individual, subjective perceptions
raises three questions which provide the focus for the
research reported here. The first question is concerned
with whether jobs, which are objectively the same insofar
as this is possible, are perceived as such by different
workers. It is particularly concerned with the cognitive rather than the evaluative dimension, although the
two will be related. Hackman and Lawler (1971) recognised the role of individual differences in perception
when they wrote that:

> 'individual needs, values and goals
> (would) be expected to interact with the
> objective task or job in influencing
> task redefinition'.

They go on to suggest that

> 'there are often substantial differ-
> ences between objective job charac-
> teristics and how they are perceived
> by employees, and it is dangerous to
> assume that simply because the objec-
> tive characteristics have been mea-
> sured (or changed) that the way that
> job is experienced by employees has
> been dealt with as well' (p. 265).

The problem with most studies, including the majority of those using the Job Descriptive Index is that
they present averaged group responses to changes in perceptions of the core task dimensions and in practice
ignore individual differences at this point in the
model.   We therefore need to know more about the ways
in which perceptions of job characteristics differ and
the dynamics underlying these differences.

The second question concerns the nature of individual differences.   There has always been some debate
about how many people want redesigned jobs;   and in a
number of case studies (see, for example, Conant and
Kilbridge, 1975;   Daniel, 1970;   Gyllenhammar, 1977)
there has been a sizeable but, in the euphoria of a
successful exercise, often ignored minority who have not
responded positively.   In the context of expectancy
theory and the Job Characteristics Model, individual differences in higher order need strength have received
most attention.   However, as Steers and Spencer (1977)
have observed, it is a rather diffuse concept and a more
carefully formulated alternative such as need for achievement may be equally valid.   At a more general level, if
higher order needs are considered, a fuller explanation
of differences and in particular of negative reactions
might be obtained by using Alderfer's (1972) three concepts of existence, relatedness and growth.   From differing theoretical, perspectives, it is possible to
identify studies which seek to explain differences in
reactions to job content in terms of biographical variables (Schwab and Heneman, 1977;   Birchall and Wild,
1977), sociological variables (Turner and Lawrence, 1965;
Hulin, 1971), work values (Hackman and Oldham, 1976;
Stone, 1976), and personality factors (Stinson and
Johnson, 1977;   Vroom, 1960;   Sheppard and Herrick, 1972).
The rather limited available data is far from consistent
and there are considerable problems of measurement of
some of the variables.   Furthermore there is a lack of
comprehensive theory within which the range of variables
can be located.   In studying a relatively unexplored
area such as differences in perceptions of objectively
similar job characteristics, it is tempting to introduce
established measures of certain individual differences;

but an alternative may be to start from the patterns of definitions and explanations offered by individuals and use these to develop hypotheses.

The third research question concerns the significance of changes in job content.   Levitan and Johnston (1973) have argued that changes in job design and other attempts to improve the quality of working life may be insignificant in relation to other 'conventional' changes in the work environment. To overcome the tendency of researchers to assume the centrality of the change which is the focus of their study, there is a need to test for awareness of specific changes, since this cannot always be taken for granted, and to locate it in the context of other changes.   Most studies of specific changes in quality of working life, and indeed change of most types, fail to do this.

The research reported here is concerned more particularly with the second and third of these questions, and it focuses on changes in job design, which is widely recognised as an important feature of the quality of working life.   It is part of a larger research project into individual reactions to changes in the quality of working life which also explores areas such as boredom, stress and the link between home and work.

THE RESEARCH CONTEXT, SAMPLE AND METHOD

The study involved two organizations.   Organization I is in the public service sector.   It is a stable, bureaucratic environment and has offices throughout the country where workers perform the same kind of clerical duties.   However, there are two variations on the way in which these duties are performed resulting firstly from the introduction of a centralised computer system and secondly from a form of job enrichment.

The centralised computer system changes the job in three main ways. Firstly it means that information has to be processed by a specific time each day to meet computer schedules. Secondly information has to be recorded in a precise way to conform to the pre-determined system of computer codings. Thirdly, because much of the information is now held centrally, queries which arise locally cannot easily be checked since there is limited scope to interrogate the computer.   By general consent, observers of this situation agree that the computer has reduced worker autonomy and feedback and by this 'objective' analysis should have reduced the quality of working life.

The job enrichment programme adopted the now fairly conventional approach of allocating to each member of

staff a number of clients who became 'their' clients and
for whom they were fully responsible. This was known as
the 'unit system'. 'Objective' analysis would indicate
that the unit system should enhance the quality of working life by providing more responsibility, autonomy and
feedback.

The sample consisted of 121 employees taken from 4
locations. Each individual had volunteered to be interviewed and the resulting sample comprised 45% of the
total workforce but a rather higher proportion of those
engaged in the particular type of activity under investigation. 35% were male and 65% female. 66% were under
30 years, 23% were between 30 and 50 and 11% were over
50. 17% had less than a year's experience, 34% between
one and three years', and 49% more than 3 years' experience. The workforces at Locations A and B, where the
changes occurred, were the most stable.

The locations can be distinguished as follows:

Location A. n = 44.   9 months prior to the survey the
                      unit system had been introduced.   2 years
                      earlier the computer system had also been
                      introduced.

Location B. n = 15.   In this small office, the computer
                      system had been introduced 2 months before
                      the survey.   It did not operate the unit
                      system.

Location C. n = 32.   This office had neither the com-
                      puter system nor the unit system.   Therefore
                      no 'significant' changes of any sort had
                      occurred.

Location D. n = 30.   This office had been one of the
                      first to introduce the computer system - as
                      long ago as 1969.   It had not introduced the
                      unit system.

Organization II is a successful company in the
Financial Services sector of industry. The company has
a record of consistent and rapid growth and its employees
have experienced constant internal change. Not only
are systems and procedures frequently altered as new products are marketed, but staff tend to move around and
the organizational structure is seldom stable for long.
The sample consisted of 36 staff in what is currently the
most successful department; it has grown particularly
rapidly and at times rather chaotically, making it an
exciting if frustrating place in which to work. To
overcome some of the problems of success, a new computer
based information storage and processing system was introduced. Its essential aim is to provide an effective

control system.   As a result it removes a certain
degree of autonomy from the worker and reduces the
level of responsibility and skill utilisation and could
be viewed as reducing the quality of working life.

The sample in Organisation II consisted of equal
numbers of male and female workers.   Almost 90% were
under 30 years old.   All had been with the organisation
for at least a year but 80% had been employed for less
than 3 years.

In many respects the two types of organisation differ dramatically.   Nevertheless staff interviewed in
both organizations were engaged in essentially similar
activities and in particular in processing information
and dealing with queries.   Another similarity is that in
both cases the changes were introduced with little or no
local consultation or involvement.   Indeed the changes
could best be viewed as a fairly normal part of continuing management activity.

The research design for Organization I was to carry
out a static comparative analysis across locations and
within each location.   In Organization II interviews
were conducted both before and after the introduction of
the new computer system.   However the data reported
here relates almost exclusively to the second set of
interviews.

Data was collected through the use of predominantly
open-ended interview schedules, the responses to which
were then content analysed.   This approach reflected
our desire to examine workers' own definitions and perceptions of their jobs and of the changes and to identify
the kind of issues they judged to be important and the
kind of criteria they used in making evaluative judgements.
In this way it was possible to avoid some of the obtru-
siveness of questionnaires with their risk of evoking
rather artificial responses.   At the same time, it must
be recognised that rigorous statistical analysis is rendered far more difficult.   Nevertheless the need for a
greater emphasis on the open-ended interview, as one
method of data collection in this field, has been recognised (Locke, 1976).

THE RESULTS

An 'objective' analysis, based on conventional
views about the quality of working life, would predict
the following outcomes.   Workers were asked whether their
job had changed in any way since they had first started
to do it or, in the case of Organization II, during the
previous 12 months.   Almost all the staff at Locations A
and B had been doing the same job prior to the introduction

Table 1.   'Conventional' predictions about awareness
            of and reactions to changes

		Will staff recollect that changes have occurred?	Will the changes be viewed as positive or negative?
Organization I	Location A	Yes	Positive
	Location B	Yes	Negative
	Location C	No	-
	Location D	No	-
Organization II		Yes	Negative

Table 2.   Number who reported changes

		Change Reported	
		Yes	No
Organization I	Location A	35	9
	Location B	13	2
	Location C	20	12
	Location D	10	20
Organization II		36	0

of the computer system.   The responses are shown in
Table 2.

These results do not conform to expectations in two
ways.   Firstly several staff at Locations A and B
reported no changes.   The group of 9 at Location A included the 3 staff in the sample who had joined the organization since the unit system was introduced.   This still
leaves 6 out of 41 who could not recall any changes.
Secondly at Location D and more particularly Location C,
where no 'significant' changes were supposed to have
occurred, a large proportion of staff reported changes of
some sort.

Each individual was next asked to describe the
changes that had occurred and to mention as many changes
as he liked.   The results are shown in Table 3.   The
boxed numbers show the predicted changes.   These results
indicate that the range of types of change reported is
broader than the 'objective' analysis would suggest.

Table 3.   Type of change reported

Type of change	Organization I				Organization II
	Location A	Location B	Location C	Location D	
Computer system introduced	12	11	0	2	27
Unit system introduced	15	0	0	0	0
Work broadened	10	2	2	2	3
Personal change of duty/ promotion	2	2	0	2	26
Personal development	4	0	6	4	0
Legislation	2	1	6	1	0
Other	2	0	7	1	4
No change reported	9	2	12	20	0

At Location A only 12 out of a possible 38 cited the introduction of the computer system and only 15 out of a possible 41 explicitly mentioned the unit system although those who referred to the fact that their work had broadened could have been referring to it.   Similarly in Organization II, only 27 out of 36 mentioned the recently introduced computer system.

The next question assessed whether the changes were positively or negatively evaluated.   The model outlined in Table 1 suggests that the unit system would be positively evaluated and the computer system negatively evaluated.   The results are shown in Table 4 and indicate that almost a third, comprised mainly of those reacting to the computer systems, did not evaluate the changes in the expected way.

In summary, a significant minority were not responding along the lines of conventional expectations.   25% either failed to recall changes where they had occurred or reported changes where no 'significant' organizational

Table 4.   Evaluations of the reported changes

Type of change*		Organization I				Organization II
		Location A	Location B	Location C	Location D	
Computer system	+**	6	3	0	0	4
	0	1	1	0	0	3
	−	5	7	0	2	20
Unit system	+	9	0	0	0	0
	0	4	0	0	0	0
	−	2	0	0	0	0
Work broadened	+	7	1	1	0	2
	0	1	1	0	1	0
	−	2	0	1	1	1
Personal development promotion	+	3	2	6	3	17
	0	2	0	0	3	1
	−	1	0	0	0	8
Other	+	0	0	5	1	1
	0	2	1	3	0	0
	−	2	0	5	1	3

*   some people mentioned more than one type of change.

** + = positive evaluation; 0 = neutral evaluation;
   − = negative evaluation.

change had taken place.   At the locations where 'significant' changes had occurred, only 72% cited the expected
changes.   Of those who did cite them, 68% evaluated them
in the expected way.   This means that at the 3 locations
(A and B and Organization II) where these changes occurred, only 48% of those affected by them responded in line
with conventional predictions, that is, by recalling them
and evaluating them positively.

An attempt was made to explain these differences in
response at each of the three stages outlined above.
This was done mainly by examining the different frames of
reference used in making judgements about aspects of the
job content and the changes.   An attempt was made to
relate these to the more conventional types of individual
difference.   In this we were hampered by the lack of

suitable measures, since our pilot studies had indicated that many manual and clerical workers did not find the conventional questionnaires meaningful or sensible.

To examine frames of reference, the criteria used to judge whether changes were evaluated as positive or negative were identified. At Locations A and B in Organization I, where the new computer system had been introduced, 12 evaluated it negatively as expected but 9 were positive. Those who evaluated the change negatively did so because it reduced the interest, scope and challenge of the job or, through lack of immediate information, made them less able to deal with queries and therefore do their job as well as they would like. In contrast, those who evaluated the changes positively did so because the computer had simplified their job and made it easier. The distinguishing dimension, which emerges rather clearly from the explanations offered, would appear to be close to the concept of job involvement.

At Location A, 15 had explicitly mentioned the unit system. 9 of them evaluated it positively, 5 citing greater autonomy and control, 2 citing the added responsibility and 2 citing the increased variety. In contrast 4 felt that the unit system had made no difference and 2 complained about the difficulties it caused in times of crisis. Again the main dimension for evaluation appears to be job involvement, and it is interesting to note the variety of positive responses which could be construed as falling within the general factor of higher order need strength. Clearly some people are judging changes along an easy - difficult/ demanding dimension; others use an interesting - boring dimension. Both might fall within the concept of job involvement. These results were checked against some more explicit job involvement items. These showed that although those high on involvement were rather more likely to mention the changes in the unit system, neither this nor any other results reached significance.

Turning to Organisation II, 27 mentioned the computer system and 4 evaluated it positively, one because it made the job easier and the others because they felt it made their job more interesting. The 20 who evaluated it negatively were only marginally concerned with core job characteristics. Instead 9 complained that it produced more problems than it solved, created more work and hindered task performance. A further 9 complained about the chaotic and ill-prepared way in which the change was introduced. One person cited the negative feedback provided by the computer in highlighting mistakes and one person complained that the loss of autonomy made the job more boring.

The important point to emerge from this analysis
is that the frame of reference within which evaluative
judgements are made is very different from that used by
most staff in Organization I.   The main concerns are
the impact on job performance and the process of change.
Therefore although the job characteristics have changed,
they in themselves do not seem to have affected perceptions of quality of working life.

In Organization II personal changes were almost as
frequently mentioned as the computer system.   People
who cited these fell into two categories.   First there
were those who were promoted or moved sideways into more
responsible, more challenging jobs.   Secondly there
were 8 who were moved sideways and who complained less
about the job content than about the lack of proper planning and consultation.   Several of the changes falling
in both categories were a direct result of the computer
system but it was not mentioned as the basis for the
change.

DISCUSSION AND CONCLUSIONS

This relatively straightforward descriptive data
has been extracted from a larger study to illustrate
the importance of certain issues which, while implicitly
recognised by a number of writers, are in danger of
being ignored in the debate on the future of the quality
of working life.

First the results confirm the dangers of assuming
that workers attach great significance to, or even recall,
certain types of change.   Admittedly the job redesign
and the computer changes may not have been dramatic;
but neither are many of those reported in the literature
and for which considerable claims are made.

Secondly it seems that the personalised changes,
affecting one individual rather than the section as a
whole, often take on a particular significance for that
individual.   These changes include development programmes, promotion and upgrading or a change of duties
and most can be located within one of Walton's (1973)
eight categories of quality of working life, namely
future opportunity for continued growth and security.
Continuing events of this sort, not significant to the
organization but crucial for the individual, are often
ignored in the evaluation of change programmes.   Therefore, using the analogy with signal detection theory, and
supporting the arguments of Levitan and Johnston (1973),
it may be that the impact of changes in quality of working
life gets lost in the 'noise' of everyday changes of the
type reported here.   Participation in the changes, or
perhaps education, may be necessary before some workers

come to value changes in the quality of working life.

Thirdly, the poor link between the objective changes and the subjective perception of them, plus the varying evaluations of the perceived changes, reinforces the importance of using subjective perceptions. The data further suggests that if the primary aim of quality of working life programmes is to bring about improvements recognizable to the individuals affected, then objective criteria are not very useful. The importance of subjective perceptions also highlights the role of individual differences, although our analysis of the different frames of reference used to evaluate the changes suggests that there may be dangers in using some of the conventional variables in isolation.

Finally, and perhaps not surprisingly, the process and the content of the change do appear to become contaminated in the minds of individuals when they make judgements about the changes. However this was only found in Organization II and is therefore not inevitable. However it points to the need for care in evaluating changes in the quality of working life, since judgements which might superficially relate to the content of the changes may in fact relate primarily to the process. To take account of this and to accommodate individual differences, considerable thought must be given to the design of an appropriate change strategy if real steps are to be taken to improve the quality of working life.

REFERENCES

Alderfer, C.P. (1972).   Existence, Relatedness and
    Growth: Human Needs in Organizational Settings,
    The Free Press, New York.

Bartölke, K. and Gohl, J. (1976).   A Critical Perspec-
    tive on Humanization Activities and On-going Experi-
    ments in Germany, Paper presented at the workshop
    'Humanization of work" of the European Institute
    for Advanced Studies in Management, Brussels,
    September 21-23.

Birchall, D. and Wild, R. (1977).   'Job characteristics
    and the attitude of female manual workers: A
    research note', Human Relations, 30, 335-342.

Bolweg, J.F. (1976).   Job Design and Industrial Democracy,
    Martinus Nijhoff, Leiden.

Conant, E.H. and Kilbridge, M.D. (1975).   'An interdis-
    ciplinary analysis of job enlargement: Technology,
    costs, and behavioural implications', Industrial and
    Labour Relations Review, April 1975, 377-395.

Cooper, C.L. (1978).   'Work stress', in Psychology at
    Work (Ed. P.B. Warr), 2nd Ed., Penguin, Harmonds-
    worth, Middx.

Daniel, W.W. (1970).   Beyond the Wage-work Bargain,
    P.E.P., London.

Davis, L.E. and Cherns, A.B. (1975).   The Quality of
    Working Life, Vol. 1, The Free Press, London.

Emery, F. and Thorsrud, E. (1976).   Democracy at Work,
    Martinus Nijhoff, Leiden.

Fein, M. (1974).   'Job enrichment: A re-evaluation',
    Sloan Management Review, 15, 69-88.

Frank, L.L. and Hackman, J.R. (1975).   'A failure of
    job enrichment: The case of the change that
    wasn't', Journal of Applied Behavioural Science,
    11, 413-436.

Guest, D. (1979).   'Job design, industrial democracy
    and the quality of working life', British Journal
    of Industrial Relations, 17, 119-122.

Guest, D. and Fatchett, D. (1974).   Worker Participation:
    Individual Control and Performance, Institute of
    Personnel Management, London.

Guest, D., Williams, R. and Dewe, P. (1978).   Job Design
    and the Psychology of Boredom, Occasional Paper
    No. 13, Work Research Unit, London.

Gyllenhammar, P.G. (1977).   People at Work, Addison-
    Wesley, Mass.

Hackman, J.R. (1975).   'On the coming demise of job
    enrichment', in (Eds. E.L. Cass and F.G. Zimmer),
    Man and Work in Society, Van Nostrand-Reinhold,
    New York.

Hackman, J.R. and Lawler, E.E. (1971).   'Employee
    reactions to job characteristics', Journal of
    Applied Psychology Monograph, 55, 259-285.

Hackman, J.R. and Oldham, G.R. (1975).   'Development of
    the job diagnostic survey', Journal of Applied
    Psychology, 60, 159-170.

Hackman, J.R. and Oldham, G.R. (1976).   'Motivation
    through the design of work: Test of a theory',
    Organizational Behavior and Human Performance, 16,
    250-279.

Herbst, Ph.G. (1976).   Alternatives to Hierarchies,
     Martinus Nijhoff, Leiden.

Herzberg, F. (1966).   Work and the Nature of Man,
     Staples Press, London.

Hughes, J. and Gregory, D. (1974).   'Richer jobs for
     workers', New Society, 14, 386-387.

Hulin, C.L. (1971).   'Individual differences and job
     enrichment - The case against general treatments',
     in New Perspectives in Job Enrichment (ed. J.R.
     Maher), Van Nostrand, New York.

Jenkins, D.J. (1978).   'Scandinavians pioneer work
     environment laws', Jenkins Work Report, No. 5,
     36-38.

Kelly, J.E. (1978).   'A reappraisal of socio-technical
     systems theory', Human Relations, 31, 1069-1099.

Lawler, E.E. (1976).   'Should the quality of working
     life be legislated?', Personnel Administrator,
     January, 17-21.

Levitan, S.A. and Johnston, W.B. (1973).   'Changes in
     work: More evolution than revolution', Manpower,
     September, 3-7.

Locke, E.A. (1976).   'The nature and causes of job
     satisfaction', in Handbook of Industrial and Organi-
     sational Psychology (Ed. M.D. Dunnette), Rand
     McNally, Chicago.

Locke, E.A., Sirota, D. and Wolfson, A.D. (1976).   'An
     experimental case study of the successes and
     failures of job enrichment: Implications for work
     motivation, performance, and attitudes', Journal of
     Applied Psychology, 61, 701-711.

Luthans, E. and Reif, W.E. (1974).   'Job enrichment:
     Long on theory short on practice', Organisational
     Dynamics, Winter, 30-38.

Orpen, C. (1979).   'The effects of job enrichment on
     employee satisfaction, motivation, involvement and
     performance: A field experiment', Human Relations,
     32, 189-217.

Paul, W.J. and Robertson, D.B. (1970).   Job Enrichment
     and Employee Motivation, Gower Press, Epping, Essex.

Prisig, R.M. (1974).   Zen and the Art of Motorcycle
     Maintenance, Corgi Books.

Schwab, D.P. and Heneman, H.G. (1977).   'Age and satis-
    faction with dimensions of work', Journal of
    Vocational Behaviour, 10, 212-220.

Seashore, S.E. (1975).   'Defining and measuring the
    quality of working life', in The Quality of
    Working Life, Vol. 1 (Eds. L.E. Davis and A.B.
    Cherns), Free Press, London.

Sheppard, J.L. and Herrick, N.Q. (1972).   Where Have All
    the Robots Gone?, Free Press, New York.

Steers, R.M. and Mowday, R.T. (1977).   'The motivational
    properties of tasks', Academy of Management Review,
    2, 645-658.

Steers, R.M. and Spencer, D.G. (1977).   'The role of
    achievement motivation in job design', Journal of
    Applied Psychology, 62, 472-479.

Stinson, J.E. and Johnson, T.W. (1977).   'Tasks, indivi-
    dual differences and job satisfaction', Industrial
    Relations, 16, 315-322.

Stone, E.F. (1976).   'The moderating effect of work
    related values on the job scope - job satisfaction
    relationship', Organisational Behaviour and Human
    Performance, 15, 147-167.

Thorsrud, E. (1972).   'Job design in the wider context',
    in Design of Jobs (Eds. L.E. Davis and J.C. Taylor),
    Penguin, Harmondsworth, Middx.

Thorsrud, E. (1979).   Quality of Working Life as Part of
    a Cultural Shift, Work Research Institute, Oslo
    (unpublished paper).

Thurley, K. and Guest, D. (1979).   Personnel Management:
    Choice of Strategies for the Enterprise, A paper
    presented to the 5th World Congress of the Inter-
    national Industrial Relations Association, Paris,
    September 2-7.

Turner, A.N. and Lawrence, P.R. (1965).   Industrial Jobs
    and the Worker, Harvard, Mass.

Vroom, V.H. (1960).   Some Personality Determinants of
    the Effects of Participation, Prentice-Hall, New
    Jersey.

Wall, T.D., Clegg, C.W. and Jackson, P.R. (1978).   'An
    evaluation of the job characteristics model',
    Journal of Occupational Psychology, 51, 183-196.

Walton, R.E. (1973).   'Quality of working life: What
     is it?', Sloan Management Review, 15, 11-21.

Wilson, N.A.B. (1973).   On the Quality of Working Life,
     Manpower Papers No. 7, Department of Employment,
     HMSO, London.

Changes in Working Life
Edited by K.D. Duncan, M.M. Gruneberg, and D. Wallis
© 1980 John Wiley & Sons Ltd

Chapter 28

The Relative Importance of Intrapsychic Determinants of Job Satisfaction

B. GUTEK

Researchers of job satisfaction have tended to view individuals' satisfaction with various aspects of their job as a function of objective features of the job, i.e. they have assumed that variations in subjective satisfaction are linked to variations in objective charac- teristics. The assumption is that people will be satis- fied with their jobs, for example, to the extent they have a good salary and good supervisors (e.g. Quinn and Shepard, 1974). However, although not all workers have a good salary, high job security, and a good supervisor, most American workers report that they are satisfied with their jobs. For example, Quinn and Shepard (1974) found that 90% of their national sample of working people were satisfied with their work and of that number, 52% reported that they were very satisfied. In a review of job satisfaction studies, Taylor (1977) cited several other studies which reported very high levels of job satisfaction. For example, Imberman (in Taylor, 1977) found that 79% to 85% of workers in his samples reported satisfaction with assembly line work. Another study using 576 members of the United Auto Workers who were interviewed in 1968 found that 95% were satisfied with their factory jobs (Siassi, Crocetti and Spiro, 1974). Research done by the Center for the Utilization of Scien- tific Knowledge at the University of Michigan also showed high levels of satisfaction. For example, 95% of employees of an insurance company and 76% of paper mill employees reported no dissatisfaction with their jobs

(Taylor and Bowers, 1972).   In summary, objective conditions of the work place do not seem to be reflected in
measures of satisfaction.

One's approach to this dilemma involves abandoning
the concept of satisfaction.   In fact, behavioral
indicators of dissatisfaction such as absenteeism and
turnover are only weakly related to job satisfaction
(Taylor, 1977).   On a broader level, many researchers
have tried unsuccessfully to establish a consistent,
positive link between satisfaction and productivity.

The many studies of job satisfaction - over 3,000
according to Locke (1976) - suggest that job satisfaction
is a worthy subject of study in its own right.   People
live in a subjective world as well as an objective
world and therefore job satisfaction should be an important part of work behavior research.   Satisfaction may
not be a substitute for research on absenteeism and turnover, but neither are these behavioral measures a substitute for the subjective measure of satisfaction (Gutek,
1978).

APPROACHES TO JOB SATISFACTION

The model which appears to underlie much research
on the determinants of job satisfaction suggests that
job satisfaction is a combination of the goodness or bad-
ness of aspects of the job, i.e. global satisfaction with
the job is a result of some additive or multiplicative
combination of facets of the job (e.g. salary, supervisory behavior).   Most often, instead of measuring overt
behavior, respondents are asked to report their reaction
to or satisfaction with, an aspect of the job.   Rather
than report salary level, respondents may be asked how
satisfied they are with their salary.   Likewise, instead
of using a behavioral measure of supervisory behavior,
researchers ask respondents to report how satisfied they
are with their supervisors.   No doubt one reason for
using self-reports instead of overt behavior is the
difficulty of adequately assessing behaviorally what is
good supervisory behavior, good coworkers, or adequate
resources.

Although the results of this approach may account
for 35% to 45% of the variance in job satisfaction (e.g.
Kalleberg, 1977; Nilson, 1977), there appears to be a
limit to the amount of variance which can be accounted
for by these subjective assessments of aspects of the job.
Adding up to forty variables or adding interaction terms
does not increase the amount of variance accounted for in
job satisfaction (Barnowe, Mangione and Quinn, 1972).

Using psychological theory, one would expect that

this approach to understanding satisfaction is incomplete. Social psychologists have theorized that subjective satisfaction is not only responsive to objective features of an individual's environment; it is also a function of intrapsychic mechanisms aroused in that environment. The purpose of this study is to test the hypothesis that intrapsychic determinants make an important independent contribution to feelings of satisfaction. Three types of intrapsychic factors are the focus of this study: perceptions of control, comparison level, and level of aspiration.

PERCEIVED CONTROL

Various psychologists have theorized that individuals want and need to feel personal control over outcomes in their lives (DeCharms, 1968; Kelley, 1971; Kelly, 1955; White, 1959). This desire to feel control has been predicted to lead to distortions in the perception of causality for events (Lerner, 1970; Walster, 1966) and to behavior designed to restore perceived freedom (Brehm, 1966).

Research has supported the prediction that desire to maintain control leads to distortions in attributions of causality (Langer, 1975; Wortman, 1976) and to behaviors designed to maintain perceived freedom (Wortman and Brehm, 1975). In addition, it has suggested that prolonged exposure to situations lacking in perceived freedom leads to a variety of negative states, such as depression, schizophrenia, and physical illness (Seligman, 1975; Wortman and Brehm, 1975), while experiencing control has been found to have a number of beneficial effects (Averill, 1973; Glass and Singer, 1972).

COMPARISON LEVEL

Judgements about an object depend upon the past and present context in which the judgement is made (Parducci, 1968; Eiser and Stroebe, 1972); and satisfaction with an outcome depends upon its relationship to past outcomes seen or experienced by the individual (Thibault and Kelley, 1959; Homans, 1961).

The role of past experience in evaluations of outcomes has been particularly salient within the literature upon dissatisfaction or alienation. Stouffer (1949) coined the term 'relative deprivation' to refer to his finding that feelings of dissatisfaction were linked to comparisons between personal outcomes and the outcomes of others, rather than to the objective level of personal outcomes per se. This concept has expanded into a

VARIETY OF THEORIES (e.g. Davis, 1959; Gurr, 1970;
Pettigrew, 1974; Runciman, 1966; Stokels, 1975). For
example, Brickman and his colleagues (Brickman and
Campbell, 1971; Brickman, 1975; Brickman, Coates and
Bulman, 1978) have shown that level of happiness is
influenced by a comparison of present level of rewards
with past level of rewards. There is now a large
volume of research (reviewed by Crosby, 1976), all of
which suggests that feelings of dissatisfaction and
alienation and the behaviors which flow from them
(rioting, etc.) are linked not to objective outcomes but
to comparisons of these outcomes to that which others are
receiving and/or to what one has received in the past.

LEVEL OF ASPIRATION

        Finally, an individual's satisfaction with some
aspects of his life may be responsive to the discrepancy
between what he/she has and what he/she aspires to. In
other words, individuals may differ in what they hope to
achieve as well as in what they have experienced. Hoppe
(1976) viewed level of aspiration as 'the totality of
aspirations for future achievement', and found that
aspiration level changes with success and failure experiences. (It generally goes up following success and
down following failure.) Furthermore, where there are
no clear criteria of success or failure, where feedback
regarding success and failure is poor or non-existent,
there is a greater likelihood that level of aspiration
will fluctuate. Early work on level of aspiration developed within the context of achievement (e.g. Frank,
1935a, b, c; Lewin, Dembo, Festinger and Sears, 1944;
Escalona, 1948; Rotter, 1942, 1954).

        In general, these three concepts of feelings of
control, comparison level, and level of aspiration have
developed within a laboratory setting. They have not
been used extensively in survey research. Survey
researchers, as noted above, tend to focus on objective
features in the environment, and respondents' perceptions
of these objective features as determinants of satisfaction. One exception is the recent work of Campbell,
Converse and Rodgers (1976). Those researchers looked at
aspiration level, comparison level and expectation level
with regard to satisfaction, not with job, but with two
other domains of life: housing satisfaction and neigh-
bourhood satisfaction. They measured level of aspiration by asking respondents about 'the best (housing/
neighborhood) they could hope for' and level of expectation by asking them about their housing or neighborhood
five years hence. Comparison level was measured in three
ways. Respondents were asked to compare themselves with
'the typical American', 'most close relatives' and 'most
close friends'. Level of aspiration turned out to be

the most important predictor of satisfaction. The correlation between current satisfaction and aspiration level is .39 for housing and .32 for neighborhood. When aspiration level, comparison level and expectation level are measured by a difference score (e.g. aspiration level minus current satisfaction) or a ratio score (e.g. current satisfaction divided by expectation level), the correlations are considerably higher. They range from a high of .89, the correlation between neighborhood satisfaction and a 100-point aspiration ratio scale, to a low of .28, the correlation between housing satisfaction and a 7-point ratio scale indicating comparison level with 'most close relatives'. The authors concluded that the single most important factor influencing satisfaction is level of aspiration in that area. Perhaps since they only measured these psychological variables of aspiration, expectation, and comparison within two domains of life, they focus most of their book on perceptions of objective determinants of satisfaction in their study of domains of life, and they do not analyze these psychological variables together with objective factors in the environment.

In summary, three psychological concepts: feelings of control, expectation level, and aspiration level, have been selected as possible determinants of level of satisfaction in several domains of life. In general, these three psychological concepts have been overlooked by researchers interested in the determinants of job satisfaction. These three particular concepts were selected for the present study because: (1) objective determinants leave unaccounted a large portion of the variance in satisfaction with domains of life, and (2) they have been shown to be useful concepts in laboratory studies and in some field and survey studies. Furthermore, these psychological determinants should apply to assessments of satisfaction in other domains of life. In general these three psychological concepts, along with perceptions of objective factors, will be examined as possible determinants of job satisfaction. In addition, a group of standard demographic variables will be included in the analyses. Furthermore, in order to test the generalizability of intrapsychic mechanisms as a class of variables, they will be used to predict the other domains of life: neighborhood, family, and government.

METHOD

A random sample telephone survey was conducted in Los Angeles, California in the Winter of 1978; 65 undergraduate and graduate student interviewers completed approximately six 25-minute phone interviews each, for a total of 417 interviews. Telephone numbers were chosen randomly from the central and western Los Angeles

telephone directories.   A random digit was added to
each number selected, so that individuals with unlisted
phone numbers could be included in the sample (the
method of added digit dialing).   Respondents 18 years
or older living in private residences were asked for
interviews.

The interview itself involved questions on satisfaction with four areas of life: jobs, neighborhoods,
families, and interactions with government agencies.
Besides their overall satisfaction with these areas of
life, respondents were asked about various objective
characteristics which should be related to satisfaction
in these areas, as well as subjective perceptions of
objective characteristics, and the three intrapsychic
mechanisms of control, comparison level, and aspiration
level in each area.

In order to maximize the N for the analysis of job
satisfaction, respondents who were not employed were
asked to consider their primary daily activity as their
'job'.   65% of the respondents were employed, 16% were
housewives, 10% were retired, and 9% were students.

VARIABLES

Four classes of independent variables, objective
data, subjective assessments of objective characteristics,
intrapsychic mechanisms, and demographic variables, were
assessed.   The objective features and subjective assessments varied across the four domains.   The demographic
variables - race, education, income, age and sex - were
measured by standard single-item questions.   In order
to include race as a variable in the regression equation,
two two-category variables were created: Hispanic or
not, and black or not.

The intrapsychic variables measuring control, comparison level, and level of aspiration were each measured
by a single question in each of the four areas.   The
question assessing control was worded: 'How much control
do you feel over what happens to you on your job (over
what your neighborhood is like, etc.)?   Do you feel that
you have a great deal of control, some control, a little
control, or not much control at all?'   In the case of
comparison level, the question was worded: 'Compared to
other jobs which you have had or know of (families you
know, etc.), is your current job better, about the same,
or worse?'   If respondents answered either 'better' or
'worse', they were asked if it was 'much better' or 'a
little better', or much or a little worse, yielding a
five-category variable.   Aspiration level was assessed by
asking respondents if they agreed or disagreed with the
statement that 'My experience with my job (government

agencies, etc.) is everything I want it to be'.   If
respondents agreed, they were asked if they strongly or
somewhat agreed; if they disagreed, they were asked if
they strongly or somewhat disagreed.   Thus, aspiration
level was measured by a four-category variable.

The dependent variables, the satisfaction items,
were measured with a four response category item: 'Are
you satisfied or dissatisfied with your present job
(family life, etc.)?'.   Again, respondents were probed
for degree of satisfaction or dissatisfaction.   (Because
respondents were interviewed by telephone, questions
were worded in such a way that only two or three response
options were presented at a time.)

RESULTS

Analyses of the data collected are designed to
answer two questions: whether the intrapsychic mechanisms
have a role in the determination of job satisfaction and,
if they do, whether this role is independent of the other
three clusters of predictors.   The results of the regression predicting job satisfaction is presented in Table 1.
Each of the predictor and dependent variables are measured by a single item from the questionnaire.

The one objective characteristic which was measured,
being currently employed, was not a predictor of job
satisfaction.   Moreover, three subjective assessment
dummy variables, regarding the extent to which the respondents' last day at work was either not typical, somewhat
typical, or very typical, failed to produce a significant
contribution and the total amount of variance they alone
explained was 10%.   In addition, the demographics were
poor predictors.   The three intrapsychic determinants, on
the other hand, were each significant at the .001 level
and together explained 27% of the variance.

Because we used a rather unusual way of assessing
'job', i.e. calling whatever one's primary daily activity
is 'one's job', we ran a second analysis, using only
employed respondents, in an effort to make our results
more comparable to other studies of job satisfaction.
This treatment (N = 230) yielded little change in the pattern of the beta weights associated with the first analysis.   However, the amount of variance explained by our
full model predicting job satisfaction did increase
moderately to a final 42%.

Instead of asking more questions about jobs, the
choice in this survey was to ask questions about other
domains of life in order to try to generalize the importance of these intrapsychic determinants.

Table 1.   Determinants of job satisfaction*

		Employed now
OBJECTIVE DETERMINANTS		
Currently employed	.01	--
$R^2=.00$		
SUBJECTIVE ASSESSMENT DETERMINANT		
Evaluation of last day at work when that day was not typical	.09	.10
Evaluation of last day at work when that day was somewhat typical	.11	.11
Evaluation of last day at work when that day was very typical	.11	.15
$R^2=.11$		
INTRAPSYCHIC DETERMINANTS		
Comparison level	.34***	.31***
Aspirations	.28***	.25***
Feelings of Control	.21***	.22***
$R^2=.37$		
DEMOGRAPHICS		
Black	.03	.00
Hispanic	.01	.08
Education	-.02	.04
Income	.02	-.03
Age	.05	.12
Sex (Male Hi)	.00	-.02
$R^2=.02$		
R^2	.39	.42
N	370	230

Table entries are standardized regression coefficients
     *** p < .001   ** p < .01

*If respondents were not employed, they were told to con-
sider their primary daily activity as their 'job'.   65%
of the respondents were employed, 16% were housewives,
10% were retired, and 9% were students.

    The analysis of family satisfaction has the largest
set of objective indicators: currently married, married
in the past but not currently married, having children,
living with one's family.   Of the various objective data,
being currently married was significantly related to

overall satisfaction with one's family (p < .01).   The
overall amount of variance explained by these objective
data was 9%.   No subjective assessments were measured
in this domain.   In contrast, the contributions of two
intrapsychic determinants, comparison level (beta = .11)
and, especially, aspiration level (beta = .44), were quite
substantial and the amount of variance accounted for by
the complete set alone was 29%.   None of the demographics
was significant.

The regression was re-run, treating separately
those who were married and those who were living with
their families, in an effort to increase the amount of
variance accounted for.   However, the total R^2 remained
a low .28 and .30 respectively.

The total model predicting government agency satisfaction, which explained the 42% of the variance, included one objective indicator (voluntary self-report of an
experience with an agency), the standard set of demographics, our three intrapsychic determinants, as well as
six subjective assessments of agencies: satisfaction
with outcome of specific experience, efficiency of agency,
treatment received, speed of service, amount of paperwork, and availability of information.   Assessment of
the outcome of the experience (that is, whether you got
what you came for) and the perceived efficiency of the
agency, were significant predictors (beta = .18 for each).
Indeed, the total set captured 36% of the variance when
the government satisfaction item was regressed on it
alone.   Nonetheless, the intrapsychic dimension yielded
two significant items at the p < .05 level, aspiration
level and feelings of control, and, R^2 of .21 when considered alone in the equation.   The fourth regression,
the analysis of neighborhood satisfaction, contained subjective evaluations of eight neighborhood characteristics,
including air quality, safety, quality of schools, and
the like, as well as the three intrapsychic determinants,
two objective determinants, and the demographic items.

Five of the eight subjective assessments, most
notably neighborhood safety and quality of schools, were
significant predictors.   But more important than any of
these was the comparison the respondent made between his
current neighborhood and others he had lived in or knew of
(beta = .24).   In addition, another intrapsychic determinant, the type of neighborhood one aspired to live in,
was also quite important (beta = .17).   The amount of
variance in neighborhood satisfaction these two sets
alone explained, were quite substantial: .51 and .40
respectively, while the R^2 associated with the demographics and the objective data were low (R^2 = .02 and .07
respectively).   The full model, consisting of all four
classes of predictors, explained nearly 60% of the variance, a result which is quite good considering the

heterogeneity of neighborhoods encompassed in the sample.

Thus a picture begins to emerge in which the intrapsychic determinants connoting more idiosyncratic personal concerns, make a contribution independent of subjective assessments directed toward objective characteristics in determining not only job satisfaction, but satisfaction with other domains as well. Objective indicators and demographics contribute comparatively very little to self-reports of satisfaction.

However, the procedure by which each class is considered alone in a regression tends to aggregate the portion of the variance one class shares with others. To given a more accurate depiction of the 'unique contributions', usefulness values need to be calculated. Usefulness values give the increment in R^2 for each class of variables when the other classes of variables have already been considered.

Table 2.   Usefulness values of the four classes of determinants in each of the four domains.

	Family	Jobs	Government experiences	Neighborhood
OBJECTIVE INDICATORS				
after other 3	.03	.00	.00	.00
SUBJECTIVE ASSESSMENTS				
after other 3	--	.02	.17	.17
INTRAPSYCHIC DETERMINANTS				
after other 3	.22	.27	.04	.08
DEMOGRAPHIC				
after other 3	.01	.00	.02	.01
TOTAL R^2	.33	.39	.42	.59

Note: The family satisfaction regression had no subjective assessments in the equation.

Table 2 presents a summary of the usefulness values of each of the four classes across the four domains. With the minor exception of the family domain, the unique contributions of the objective indicators are negligible while the demographics persistently tend to account for some 1 to 2 per cent of the variance across domains. In contrast, the total proportion of variance in the family and job domain that can be uniquely attributed to the intrapsychic determinants is quite high. Subjective

Table 3.   Factor loadings of intrapsychic variables and satisfaction in the four domains

	Factor 1	Factor 2	Factor 3	Factor 4	h^2
Satisfaction with job	.79	--	--	--	.71
Comparison level - job	.58	--	--	--	.31
Control over job	.50	--	--	--	.26
Satisfaction with neighborhood	--	.70	--	--	.52
Comparison level-neighborhood	--	.66	--	--	.43
Neighborhood aspirations	--	.58	--	--	.40
Control over neighborhood	--	.33	--	.20	.17
Family aspirations	--	--	.83	--	.60
Satisfaction with family	--	--	.63	--	.35
Comparison level - family	--	--	.38	--	.21
Control over family	--	--	.33	--	.16
Comparison level - experience with government agencies	--	--	--	.58	.33
Aspirations - experience with government agencies	--	--	--	.57	.38
Satisfaction with government agencies	--	--	--	.56	.33
Control over experiences with government agencies	--	--	--	.50	.26
Aspirations - job	.21	--	.27	--	.15

assessments on the other hand perform well in the government and neighborhood domains relative to the intrapsychic determinants. However, the total proportion of variance in these domains that can be uniquely attributed to subjective assessments is only moderate. This suggests the possibility of substantial overlap in our measures of the intrapsychic and subjective dimensions for the neighborhood and government domains.

The evidence then clearly supports the inclusion of intrapsychic mechanisms plus subjective assessment

indicators as determinants of job satisfaction. The
question remains, though, do the intrapsychic mechanisms
reflect broad underlying personality constructs, formed
through experiences across domains, or are they a function of experiences specific to each domain?   For
example, do people have a general sense of control over
all or many domains or are feelings of control specific
to each area of life?

These data do not permit a comprehensive answer;
however, an exploratory factor analysis of the three
intrapsychic determinants and the overall satisfaction
measure for all four domains was performed. As seen in
Table 3, the results are clear. Four distinct factors,
which can be easily labelled job, neighborhood, family
and experience with government agencies, respectively,
emerged in a manner theoretically consonant with the
situation-specific explanation. In other words, the
various intrapsychic predictors were much more highly
related to other intrapsychic predictors within domains,
than they were to each other across domains. Thus, for
example, the various measures of control seem less an
indicator of some locus of control or generalized expectancy that transcends situations. Rather they appear
more situation-specific, in that they are more highly
associated with aspiration level and comparison level
within each domain than with each other across domains.

DISCUSSION

The individual's satisfaction with his/her job is
clearly a personal experience which the traditional
objective approach, that stresses impersonal objective
indicators, only begins to unravel. These results
parallel those of others who document the limited
relationships between objective data and satisfaction
(e.g. Schneider, 1975).

These data support the rapidly accumulating
research which underscores the fruitfulness of including
subjective assessments as predictors of job satisfaction,
which has dominated the research on models of job satisfaction (e.g. Barnowe, Mangione and Quinn, 1972; Nilson,
1977; Kallegerg, 1977).   In contrast to the 'objective'
indices, as the number and presumably the comprehensive-
ness of the relvant subjective assessment items was
expanded, the predictive power of this class of determinants markedly increased. They accounted for little
variance in job satisfaction in this study because the
measures used were fewer and less comprehensive than
assessments measured by other research. However, at best,
this class of variables leaves about half of the variance
unexplained. Alone they do not explain job satisfaction.

These data suggest that the experience of job satisfaction seems to incorporate more inwardly focused, or intrapsychic mechanisms, not entirely bound by the referrent object, as well. Researchers need to explore further individual idiosyncratic self-related concerns, that are not found in outwardly directed subjective assessments alone. Furthermore, intrapsychic mechanisms appear primarily to be a result of the individual's experiences within domains and not global personality traits that transcend experiences across domains. A sense of control in one's job does not necessarily mean one has a sense of control in family life. And one's aspirations may be attained with respect to one's neighborhood but not in one's job.

A final point has to do with the general usefulness of this research. Locke (1976) deplores the fact that the many studies of job satisfaction - estimated at over 3,300 in number - have failed to shed much light on the concept, and not much theory of job satisfaction has developed. The data reported here, however, provide a theoretical perspective for job satisfaction researchers. Furthermore the approach is general and can be used by researchers interested in housing satisfaction (Burisch, 1977), life satisfaction (Andrews and Withey, 1976), and the like. Thus job satisfaction research can be linked to research on other areas of satisfaction.

ACKNOWLEDGEMENTS

Several graduate students - Harris Allen, Richard Lau, Ann Majchrzak and Tom Tyler - contributed to the theoretical perspective as well as data collection and data analysis.

REFERENCES

Andrews, F.M. and Withey, S.B. (1976). Social indicators of well-being, New York, Plenum Press.

Averill, J. (1973). 'Personal control over aversive stimuli add its relationship to stress', Psychological Bulletin, 80, 286-303.

Barnowe, T., Mangione, T. and Quinn, R.P. (1972). 'Quality of employment indicators occupational classification and demographic characteristics as predictors of job satisfaction', Paper presented at Annual American Psychological Association Convention, Honolulu, Hawaii, August.

Brehm, J.W. (1966).   A theory of psychological reactance,
    New York, Academic Press.

Brickman, P. and Campbell, D.T. (1971).   'Hedonic rela-
    tivism and planning the good society', in M.H.
    Appley (ed.), Adaptation-Level Theory. A Symposium,
    New York, Academic Press.

Brickman, P. (1975).   'Adaptation level determinants of
    satisfaction with equal and unequal outcome distri-
    butions in skill and chance situations', Journal
    of Personality and Social Psychology, 32, 191-198.

Brickman, P., Coates, D. and Bulman, P.J. (1978).
    'Lottery winners and accident victims: Is happiness
    relative?', Journal of Personality and Social
    Psychology, 36, 117-927.

Burisch, M. (1977).   'Some thoughts on a discussion con-
    cerning consumer (dis-) satisfaction', Zeitschrift
    fur Verbraucherpolitic/Journal of Consumer Policy,
    1, 293-296.

Campbell, A., Converse, P.E. and Rogers, W. (1976).
    Quality of American Life: Perceptions, Evaluations
    and Satisfactions, New York, Russell Sage.

Davis, J.A. (1959).   'A formal interpretation of the
    theory of relative deprivation', Sociometry, 22,
    280-296.

DeCharms, R. (1968).   Personal causation: The internal
    affective determinants of behavior, New York,
    Academic Press.

Eiser, J.R. and Stroebe, W. (1972).   Categorization and
    Social Judgement, New York, Academic Press.

Escalona, S.K. (1948).   An application of the level of
    aspiration experiment to the study of personality,
    New York, Columbia University.

Frank, J.D. (1935).   'Individual differences in certain
    aspects of the level of aspiration', American
    Journal of Psychology, 47, 119-128, (a).

Frank, J.D. (1935).   'Some psychological determinants of
    the level of aspiration', Journal of Psychology, 47,
    285-293, (b).

Frank, J.D. (1935).   'The influence of the level of per-
    formance in one task on the level of aspiration in
    another', Journal of Experimental Psychology, 18,
    159-171, (c).

Glass, D.G. and Singer, J.E. (1972). Urban stress: Experiments on noise and social stressors, New York, Academic Press.

Gurr, T.R. (1970). Why Men Rebel, Princeton, New Jersey, Princeton University Press.

Gutek, B.A. (1978). 'Satisfaction guaranteed: What does it mean?', Social Policy, 56-61.

Homans, G. (1961). Social behavior: Its elementary forms, New York, Harcourt, Brace and Jevanovich Inc.

Hoppe, F. (1976). 'Success and failure', in J. de Riviera (ed.), Field theory as human science, New York, Gardner Press. (Original: Hoppe, F., 'Erfolgund Misserfolg', Psychologische Forschung, 1930, 14, 1-62.)

Kalleberg, A. (1977). 'Work values and job rewards: A theory of job satisfaction', American Sociological Review, 42, 124-143.

Kelley, H.H. (1971). Attribution in social interaction, Morristown, New Jersey, General Learning Press.

Kelly, G.A. (1955). The psychology of personal constructs, New York, Morton.

Langer, E.J. (1975). 'The illusion of control', Journal of Personality and Social Psychology, 32, 311-328.

Lerner, M.J. (1970). 'The desire for justice and reaction to victims', in J.R. McCauley and L. Berkowitz (eds.), Altruism and helping behavior, New York, Academic Press.

Lewin, K., Dembo, T., Festinger, L. and Sears, P. (1944). 'Level of aspiration', in J.V. Hunt (ed.), Personality and the behavior disorders, New York, The Ronald Press, pp. 333-378.

Locke, E. (1976). 'The nature and causes of job satisfaction', in M. Dunnette (ed.), Handbook of industrial and organizational psychology, Chicago, Rand-McNally, 1976.

Nilson, L. (1977). 'An integrative model of job satisfaction', Colloquium presented at the Institute of Industrial Relations, U.C.L.A., Los Angeles, California, November.

Parducci, A. (1968). 'The relativism of absolute judgements', Scientific American, 219, 84-90.

Pettigrew, T.F. (1974).   Racially separate or together,
    New York, McGraw-Hill.

Pfaff, M. (1977).   'Who decides what is good for whom?
    A comment on the paper by F. Olander', Zeitschrift
    fur Verbraucherpolitic/Journal of Consumer Policy,
    1, 138-142.

Quinn, R. and Shepard, L. (1974).   The 1972-1973 Quality
    of Employment Survey, Ann Arbor, Institute for
    Social Research.

Rotter, J.B. (1942).   'Level of aspiration as a method
    of studying personality II. Development and
    evaluation of a controlled method', Journal of
    Experimental Psychology, 31, 410-422.

Rotter, J.B. (1954).   Social Learning and Clinical
    Psychology, New York, Prentice-Hall.

Runciman, W.G. (1966).   Relative deprivation and social
    justice, Berkeley, University of California Press.

Schneider,   (1975).   'The quality of life in large
    American cities: Objective and subjective social
    indicators', Social Indicators Research, 1, 495-509.

Seligman, M.E.P. (1975).   Helplessness, San Francisco,
    California, Freeman Press.

Siassi, I., Crocetti, G. and Spiro, H.R. (1974).
    'Loneliness and dissatisfaction in a blue collar
    population', Archives of General Psychiatry, 30,
    261-265.

Stouffer, S.A., Suchman, E.A., DeVinney, L.C., Star, S.A.
    and Williams, R.M. (1949).   The American soldier
    adjustment during army life (Vol. 1), Princeton,
    New Jersey, Princeton University Press.

Stokels, D. (1975).   'Toward a psychological theory of
    adjustment', Psychological Review, 82, 26-44.

Taylor, J. (1977).   'Job satisfaction and quality of
    working life: A reassessment', Occupational
    Psychology, 50, 243-252.

Taylor, J. and Bowers, D.G. (1972).   Survey of organi-
    zations: A machine-scored standardized question-
    naire instrument, Ann Arbor, Institute for Social
    Research.

Thibault, J. and Kelley, H.H. (1959).   The social psycho-
    logy of groups, New York, John Wiley and Sons.

Walster, E. (1966). 'Assignment of responsibility for an accident', Journal of Personality and Social Psychology, 3, 73-79.

White, R.W. (1959). 'Motivation reconsidered: The concept of competence', Psychological Review, 66, 297-333.

Wortman, C.B. (1976). 'Causal attributions and personal control', in J.H. Harvey, W.J. Ickes, R.F. Kidd (eds.), New Directions in Attribution Research (Vol. 1), New York, Lawrence Erlbaum Associates.

Wortman, D.B. and Brehm, J.W. (1975). 'Responses to uncontrollable outcomes: An integration of reactance theory and the learned helplessness model', in L. Berkowitz (ed.), Advances in Experimental Social Psychology, 8, New York, Academic Press.

Changes in Working Life
Edited by K.D. Duncan, M.M. Gruneberg, and D. Wallis
© 1980 John Wiley & Sons Ltd

Chapter 29

Motivation: Closing the Gap Between Theory and Practice

E. E. LAWLER III

Need theory, expectancy theory, reinforcement theory, intrinsic motivation theory, and last but by no means least, two-factor theory - the literature on motivation in organizations is full of different names, concepts and theories. At first glance these theories seem to be saying very different things. They use different terms, different concepts and have stressed different kinds of programmes and practices that organizations should use to improve motivation. Some have talked about the importance of extrinsic rewards, others have stressed job enrichment, and still others have talked about the importance of participation. Some research studies purport to show that two-factor theory is correct, while others purport to show that expectancy theory is correct. Given this diversity, is it any wonder that practitioners talk about being confused by apparently conflicting recommendations? Is it any wonder that the proponents of different theories seemed to be more obsessed with distinguishing their theory from the others than with showing how an organization can develop a motivating and satisfying total work system. I think not.

*Partial support for this paper was provided by the Office for Naval Research Contract N00014-77-C-0127.

Indeed, I think that the significant gap between what is known about motivation and the practices that most organizations engage in, has been caused in part by the way in which motivation theory is described, presented, and tested.   The gap between what is known about motivation and the practices in most organizations will, of course, never be completely closed.   The dissemination of knowledge always moves slowly, and practice inevitably must lag behind theory and research.   However, in the area of motivation theory, if two fundamental changes were made in the way motivation theory is described, implemented, and researched, the gap could be much smaller than it presently is.   What is needed is (1) a more explicit recognition of the large areas of agreement among the different approaches to work motivation, and (2) strategies for improving motivation that are more comprehensive and inclusive of the complexities of organizational life.   If these two changes were accomplished, I feel that our motivation theories would be better and our organizations would be more effective. A look at these two points in more detail will help to show what needs to be done and what can be gained.

MOTIVATION THEORY: AREAS OF AGREEMENT

In looking at different motivation theories, it is very easy to lose sight of the commonalities because of the many differences which are constantly raised and emphasized.   It is hardly surprising that theorists stress how their theory differs from all the others and how it can correctly predict, that it can explain behavior in some situations, no matter how unlikely to actually occur, that some other theory cannot.   In the world of research the rewards go to individuals who develop new theories, not those who look for common threads among existing theories.   Despite their efforts to be different, there is a fundamental set of common points that are characteristic of almost all motivation theories, a necessity which is brought on by the necessity of dealing with a large mass of convergent research findings.   Let me briefly review some common points to give the reader a sense of what to me seems to be generally accepted wisdom in the area of motivation.

1.   Motivation is determined by a combination of forces in the individual and forces in the environment. Neither the individual nor the environment alone determines motivation.   Individuals come into organizations with certain psychological characteristics.   Their past experiences and history influence how they look at the world and how they respond to what the organization does. On the other hand, the work environment provides structures and situations which influence behavior of people. Different environments tend to produce different behavior

in similar people just as dissimilar people tend to
behave differently in similar environments.

·2.   People make decisions about their behavior.
While there are many constraints on the behavior of individuals in organizations, most of the behaviors observed
are the result of individuals making decisions to do one
thing rather than another.   Individuals make decisions
about coming to work, staying at work, and they make
decisions about the amount of effort they will direct
toward performing their jobs.

3.   People have goals and rewards that they try to
achieve and punishments that they try to avoid.   Individuals seek certain things in the environment.   Although there are differences among individuals in what
they seek, there is a consistent pattern of people
trying to achieve those goals or rewards in the environment which are important to them.   The implication of
this is that if motivation is to be understood, it is
critical that an accurate picture of the goals and needs
of individuals be developed.   In other words, it is
critical to know what is important to people.

4.   Behavior is determined by the connection
between the outcomes that people value and their behavior.
In simple terms, people tend to do those things which
lead to rewards or goals that they desire; and they
avoid doing those things that they see as leading to
outcomes they do not desire.   Thus, motivation to engage
in a particular behavior is likely to be high when
there is a clear connection between engaging in the
behavior and the reception of valued rewards or the
attainment of a valued goal.

5.   The rewards that people receive can be both
internal and external to the person.   Much of the original thinking on motivation stressed the importance of
such external rewards as pay, promotion, and status
symbols.   More recently it has become clearly established that feelings such as a sense of accomplishment
and doing meaningful work and achieving something
meaningful can be important rewards themselves.

6.   People sometimes misperceive the situation.
There is nothing to guarantee that people will accurately
perceive the connection between performance and the
rewards they value.   Because of their past history and
individual differences, in fact, different people often
see the same situations in different terms.   Thus, an
effective motivation strategy must make very clear the
connection between behavior and rewards.

Overall, the points made so far suggest that an
individual will be motivated to perform effectively in an

organizational setting when effective performance leads
to rewards that the individual values. The challenge,
then, is to create a work environment in which this condition will exist. At one level, it does not sound
like a difficult task; but years of experience with
programmes which are designed to accomplish just this,
suggests that it is. Let us therefore turn to a consideration of the problems involved in implementing motivation theory.

MOTIVATION THEORY AND THE DESIGN OF ORGANIZATIONS

There is a multitude of reasons why it is difficult
to tie rewards to performance in complex organizations.
Most motivation theories, however, have little to say on
the point and as a result are of little value to the
person who wants to 'change something' in order to
increase motivation. The practitioner who wants to use
theory as a guide to practice is faced with long, eso-
teric and sometimes irrelevant debates about how one
theory differs from another. The situation is further
worsened by the fact that different theorists seem to
have developed their own pet micro theories about what
aspect of the organizational environment should be
focused upon in order to increase motivation. Some,
for example, have stressed job design; others, pay
systems; others, leadership; and still others, the work
group.

The focus on such things as job enrichment and
merit pay plans has served a useful purpose in emphasizing
that all of these can and do have a significant impact on
motivation. However, it has served a negative effect in
the sense that it has suggested to many that any one of
these can and should be dealt with in isolation. It
has contributed to what might be called the single
system approach to thinking about motivation in work organizations. Single system approaches, regardless of
whether their focus is on design, pay, groups or leadership, are in some cases quite misleading while in others,
they are just plain destructive and suicidal when it
comes to changing organizations. For one thing, people
differ in what is important to them; and as a result, a
system which emphasizes just job design may ignore rewards
and goals that are important to a large percentage of the
people. In addition, organizations are complex interdependent systems that are made up of a multitude of
complex subsystems. A change in any subsystem is likely
to have profound implications for and effects on other
subsystems. For example, a job enrichment programme can
lead to demands for increased pay which, if not met, can
worsen rather than improve a situation.

The clear implication of the systems nature of

organizations is that if motivation is going to be dealt
with effectively in an organization, it is important
that a total systems point of view be adopted. That is,
consideration of motivation must take into account all
the important goals and rewards that are available in
the organization and all of them must be assessed and
properly dealt with in terms of their relationship to
each other and to performance. This means focusing not
just on the pay system, the promotion system or the job
design system, but focusing on all of these to see that
they are integrated in a coherent, systematic and mutually reinforcing manner. Admittedly, this is a large
challenge, but failure to deal with the total system
virtually assures problems.

Unfortunately, there are few motivation theories
to guide the practitioner in how all the aspects of an
organization can be coordinated so that motivation will
be maximized. Motivation theorists have tended to
stress the effectiveness of such things as job enrichment,
bonus pay plans, and different leadership styles. What
they have not stressed is how all of these can be brought
together, and integrated so that a meaningful overall
motivational system can be put in place in an organization. The result is that a lot is known about how to
enrich jobs, but very little is known about how to
coordinate the enrichment of jobs with the creation of a
motivating pay system and the training of supervisors to
help their subordinates effectively set goals and reinforce subordinates for effective behavior.

RESEARCH AND THE DESIGN OF ORGANIZATIONS

Much of the research on motivation in work organizations suffers from the same problem as does the
theory - it is single system bounded. Unfortunately,
most studies which have been done in organizational
settings have focused rather narrowly on one topic. For
example, if their focus has been on job enrichment, they
typically have not focused on how job design changes
affect such things as leadership and pay systems.

Those studies which do focus on multiple systems
and variables typically suffer from another flaw as far
as their practical usefulness is concerned. They tend
to be basic research studies that are correlational in
nature rather than evaluations of organizational changes
which are driven by the theory. We have, for example,
hundreds of studies which have tried to test the validity
of two-factor theory and expectancy theory, but very few
studies which have looked at such things as how different
approaches to job design fit with such pay incentive
plans as the Scanlon plan. Basic correlational studies
may accomplish the goal of testing one theory or another,

although even here they often fail, but they are of
little help to the practitioner who must change an organization.

What is needed are studies which consider multiple
systems as broad-based, and which fall somewhere between
basic research and highly applied engineering studies.
Mason Haire once called them development research studies.
There is a tradition of this kind of research in other
fields.   It is seen as an important intermediate step
between the basic research which discovers the phenomena
and a production phase in which the research idea is
utilized in a product or treatment.   In this scheme,
developmental research plays a key role in polishing up
the idea finding how, when, and where it can be applied
and in determining its ramifications when it is applied
in different ways.   This kind of broad-based assessment
or developmental research is precisely what is missing
in the area of motivation theory.   As a result, little
is known about how best to implement such things as job
enrichment and even less is known about the side effects
it produces.   Overall, then, in order for research to
have a practical pay off, it needs to become more action
oriented and more total systems oriented: in short,
more developmental in nature.

THE MINI ENTERPRISE

Despite the failure of theory and research to
point the way to an integrated total systems approach to
motivation, there are some clues available as to what
combination of conditions is likely to lead to high
levels of motivation.   In most organizations the most
motivated employees are those at the very top of the
organization.   A good guess as to why this is so can be
found in the unusual degree to which their rewards are
tied directly to their performance.   They often are on
bonus plans which tie their pay to organizational performance;   their status and esteem gets tied into the
results of the organization;   and their jobs are ones in
which they have a great deal of control, receive feedback about how well they and the organization is performing, and they do relatively meaningful tasks.

At the top of an organization, many of the conditions exist which are stressed by people who argue the
advantages of such things as job enrichment and Scanlon
plans.   The resulting high levels of motivation should
not, therefore, be surprising.   The challenge is to
create similar conditions at different levels in the
organization.

It is not easy to translate the conditions at the
top of an organization to other parts because there is

one advantage at the top of an organization that often is
not present at lower levels: because of the way most
organizations are structured, people at the top have a
sense of the enterprise that is not shared by the rest of
the organization.   They have a unique sense of the whole
endeavour and how it is doing because they receive feedback about how effectively it is functioning.   Once one
moves down into an organization, the sense of the enterprise often rapidly deteriorates;   but does it have to?
Maybe not - there is reason to believe that by putting
together what is known about job enrichment, pay systems,
leadership, the design of information and control systems,
it is possible to create, lower down in the organization,
many of the same conditions which lead to people at the
top having a sense of the enterprise.   What is needed is
the willingness and ability within larger organizations
to develop mini-enterprises within themselves.   How
this can be done, of course, needs to be adapted to the
conditions that face particular organizations.   There
are, however, some interesting models developing in large
organizations - models that suggest the possibility that
many of the motivational advantages of small enterprises
can be realized by large ones, if an effort is made to
create businesses within the larger organizations.

For example, some large organizations are now
creating highly autonomous plants.   In order to provide
these plants with a sense of their being an independent
enterprise, they are treating them as profit centres
and tieing the pay of people in those plants to the
overall performance of that plant.   When these plants
are relatively small, e.g. less than 500, this can create
a positive feeling in the plant about the relationship
between pay and performance.   In addition, this has been
combined with a heavy emphasis in the plants upon
enriched jobs, either individually or on a group basis;
so that within the plant people have a strong sense of
doing an overall meaningful job, and they receive a considerable amount of feedback both about how well they are
performing in their area and how well the plant as a
whole is performing.   The effect is to create a strong
sense of how the overall enterprise is doing, and what
their contribution to the enterprise is.   In essence,
the assumption is that business is an exciting, engaging,
challenging activity, and that conditions need to be
created such that as many people as possible in the organization can have a real sense of participation in the
enterprise.   When this is done, responsibility for the
enterprise is spread, and as a result, motivation is
spread.

Another example of how the sense of the enterprise
can be communicated to a large number of people in the
organization is the work that is being done on autonomous
work groups.   These groups are often given charge of a

particular area of production or operation in an organization, and they are charged with total management of
this area.   This means that to make production, staffing,
and pay decisions within a large plant, a number of these
groups are developed so that people in the plant do not
feel that they are part of a large impersonal operation.
When these groups are established, they can be given not
only responsibility for production, but their pay can be
tied into performance of their activities and they can be
given extensive feedback about how well their particular
part of the plant is functioning.   To a significant
degree, the same sense of enterprise which is present
among the top people in the organization can be present
for them.

An additional source of clues about how to fit subsystems together in order to create a motivating total
system, can be found in how some very interesting new
plants have been designed and managed.   At the present
time there exist in the United States at least 50 new
plants which have been designed from the ground up to
create a highly involving and motivating work setting.
The designers of these new plants have had to design
total plants and as a result, they have not had the
luxury of single focus on job design, pay or any other
feature;   they have had to deal with them all, and they
have had to come up with systems in which the parts 'fit'
together.   Perhaps because they had had to come up
with 'practical' total systems, the designers of the new
systems seem to have relied on the common core of what is
known about motivation and to have selectively drawn from
the 'practical recommendations' of motivation theorists
in designing their systems.   What seems to have emerged
is some very effective 'melting pot' approaches to motivation that represent a creative synthesis and at times
extension of what is known.

A detailed consideration of the approaches which
have been taken in the new plants goes beyond the scope
of the present paper, since it would require a discussion
of issues ranging from job design to pay (Lawler, 1978).
A brief description of some of the design features, however, may help to clarify how these plants are designed.
The plants are organized around teams which make most
operating decisions.   Individuals are expected to learn
all or most of the production jobs in the plant, and are
given pay increases when they learn new jobs.   All distinctions between exempt and non-exempt employees are
eliminated, everyone is on salary, has the same benefits,
and uses the same physical facilities.   Plant operating
results and prospects are shared with all employees, and
in some plants, bonuses are paid to everyone based upon
these.

Perhaps the most striking point about these plants

is the degree to which the subsystems seem to fit
together to produce a coherent whole. The pay systems
seem to reinforce the approach to job design which fits
the selection system, and so on. All are designed to
encourage intrinsic motivation, the development of skills
and abilities, and an involvement in the overall enterprise. Any one of these design features is unlikely to
work in a traditional system; it is only in the context
of these other features that they work. This need for
fit and the synergistic effects of fit has been sadly
lacking in the literature on motivation. Rather than
focusing on an individual's motivation to do his or her job
well, it focuses on what it is that influences how motivated individuals are to contribute to the performance of
their organization. This distinction is important,
because the latter can produce the former (job motivation) but the former does not necessarily lead to the
latter. Thus, in situations where having individuals
perform their individual jobs as well as possible is not
optional as far as organizational performance is concerned, we would expect different behaviors on the part
of individuals who are motivated to perform their jobs
and those who are motivated to see the organization perform effectively.

Figure 1 shows that certain design features produce
psychological states which in turn influence motivation.
The following design features are included:

1. Participative gain sharing plan: plans like the
    Scanlon and Rucker plans which tie pay to the
    operating results of plants or organizations;

2. Public information on operating results: sharing
    with all employees the financial and productivity
    results for the organization;

3. Economic education: training employees to under-
    stand the operating results which are shared;

4. Egalitarian perquisites: treating all employees
    similarly in such areas as fringe benefits, time
    clocks, parking, rest areas, etc.;

5. Participative structures: elected or represen-
    tative plant committee that makes a wide variety
    of 'management type' decisions;

6. Self managing teams: small groups in which indi-
    viduals know a variety of jobs and which manage
    in a participative way parts or all of an orga-
    nization;

7. Goal setting: the practice of employees having
    specific goals which relate to their performance

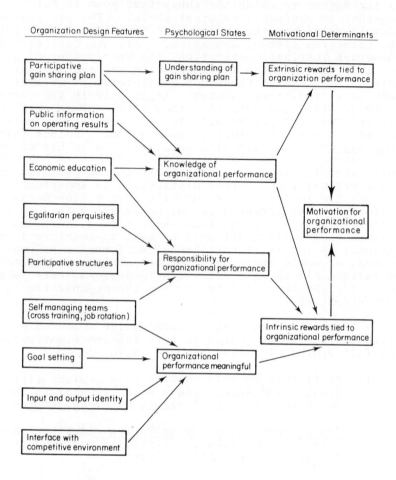

Figure 1.   Model of the determinants of organizational
             motivation.

          and/or that of the organization;

    8.   Input and output identity: organizations having
          a clearly identifiable and measurable set of
          inputs and outputs;

    9.   Interface with competitive environment: employees
          throughout the organization deal with or are aware
          of what the organization has to do to compete
          effectively in the environment in which it
          operates.

As the figure shows, all or most of these design features
need to be present for the necessary psychological states
to exist, since individually and in combination they produce the psychological states.   The four psychological
states in turn are necessary preconditions for motivation
to be present.   For extrinsic motivation to be present,
individuals must understand the pay performance contingencies which are present and they must receive information about the performance of the organization.   For
intrinsic motivation to be present, in addition to knowledge of organizational performance to exist, two other
conditions must exist.   The individual must feel that
he or she has influence on and responsibility for the
performance of the organization.   In addition, the performance of the organization must be meaningful in the
sense that this performance is something that the individual identifies with and values.

        The reader who is familiar with expectancy theory,
the Scanlon plan, and the research on job design, will
recognize that the model draws upon previous work in
these areas.   It goes beyond them, however, in the sense
that it integrates the work in these areas and it attempts
to specify what organization design features are required
in order for an individual to be motivated to contribute
to the performance of the organization.

        At this point a great deal more needs to be
learned and a great deal of developmental work needs to
go on before it will be clear how to create an integrated
sense of the enterprise for people in many work situations.
Nevertheless, the model presented above and the concept
of creating a sense of the enterprise for all employees,
seems to be a promising lead to how motivation theory can
be combined with the problems of administering an organization.   They offer a conceptual way to bring together
the emphases of different writers, and it provides a hope
for integrating the work on job design, pay systems,
information and control systems, and leadership behavior.
It strongly suggests that they must all be looked at as
part of a motivational package which has as its goal providing a meaningful motivational environment for individuals at all levels in the organization.

SUMMARY AND CONCLUSIONS

        The problem of providing a motivating work environ-
ment for individuals is clearly a difficult one to solve,
but it may not be as difficult as it appears to be at
first glance.   First, it is apparent that once the different motivation theories are examined there is a high
level of agreement on some fundamental points.   Admittedly, they have each stressed their own particular
uniqueness and have, therefore, talked about different

kinds of changes that are appropriate in organizations. Many of the changes they have suggested are not competitive with other changes; rather, they are compatible because the theories generally have a common set of points that they agree on.

   In addition, there are some interesting clues around about how various components of a motivating work environment can be put together so that motivating conditions can be created at all levels in an organization. Specifically, a look at the jobs of the top people in an organization shows that they already have many of the conditions present that the work on motivation suggests create a motivating work environment. Their jobs contain the kind of job characteristics that people interested in job design might suggest are desirable. In many cases the pay system at the top is one that is motivating, and the kind of feedback and supervision they get is congruent with what is called for according to the leadership theory that is concerned with motivation. The challenge, therefore, is to create similar conditions at lower levels in the organization. An additional clue comes from the experimentation which has been taking place in new plants. This seems to point to the importance of having an internally consistent approach to such things as pay, decision making, and job design. For purpose of illustration, a model of one set of internally consistent practices was presented.

   Admittedly, there is a paucity of models on how to create highly motivating conditions throughout organizations, but more and more organizations seem to be making some exciting inroads into figuring this out. In some ways the activity in some of the leading organizations seems to be outstripping the available theory and research. The challenge to those interested in motivation theory is to do the kind of research and theory that will lead to practice this is sensitive to the realities of individual differences, and that at the same time can help to close the gap between theory and practice. What kind of theory and research is likely to do this? In my opinion, research which is developmental in nature and theory, which is multiple-systems oriented, and which deals with issues like internal consistency.

REFERENCE

Lawler, E.E. (1978). 'The new plant revolution', Organizational Dynamics, 6 (3), 2-12.

Changes in Working Life
Edited by K.D. Duncan, M.M. Gruneberg, and D. Wallis
© 1980 James C. Naylor, Robert D. Pritchard, and Daniel R. Ilgen

Chapter 30

A Sequential View of Behavior and Motivation

J. C. NAYLOR, R. D. PRITCHARD and D. R. ILGEN

The intent of this paper is to present a very brief summary of a theory of behavior and the motivational process of people at work which has recently been proposed in much greater detail elsewhere (Naylor, Pritchard and Ilgen, 1980). Space here permits only a brief overview of the theory and the motivational process as we view it. We shall present our particular viewpoint, as well as the basic constructs which we have suggested as being most essential for an understanding of the motivational process and for behavior.

The complete theory is not fundamentally different from other theories which view man as a cognitive rational being. What most distinguishes the theory in general - and the motivational process in particular - is the degree of complexity and specificity that we have reached in elaborating the entire behavioral sequence of an individual.

Let us first discuss the theory in general terms. It is basically a theory of cognitive elements. Nearly all of the primary things that are of interest to us are things that are properly considered cognitive states or processes. It is a theory of individual behavior, focusing on the individual organism. As psychologists we are interested in dealing with the behavior of individuals and that certainly is the bias of our orientation throughout the complete theory.

The components constituting the theory may be
classified into three types or groups. The first major
class consists of the entities which represent either
psychological states or observable physical objects or
states. They constitute the essential ingredients which
we feel are necessary for explaining rational behavior.
The second class of elements in the theory are represented by the process stages in the theory. Through these
stages things are transformed or changed from one state
into another state.

The third and final class of elements in the theory
are the relationships among states and processes. These
relationships show the postulated directions of influence
among the different entities and the different processes
explicated in the theory. In this short article we will
not examine all of the states, processes, or interrelationships. We will only concern ourselves with a small
subset of the theory which relates most directly to the
process of motivation. Before we can move to the motivational aspects of the theory, it will, however, be
necessary to examine a number of specific terms which
have rather precise definitions so that we may better
understand what is to follow.

SOME IMPORTANT DEFINITIONS

The terms which we need to define are 'acts',
'products', 'evaluation', 'outcomes', and 'contingencies'.
We will also need to look briefly at what we mean by the
terms 'valence' and 'affect'.

The most fundamental definition for the theory is
the definition of behavior. We are primarily interested in explaining, understanding, and predicting
behavior. In this regard, the basic behavioral unit is
what we call an <u>act</u>. An act is defined as an ongoing
activity, consciously selected, which the individual
expects somehow to influence the amount of positive
effect he or she will experience. We have taken the
position that we are dealing with a hedonistic system in
which behavior is basically determined by the amount of
anticipated pleasure or displeasure likely to result as
a function of that act. Acts are assumed to be discrete and in most cases are not themselves measurable
except in terms of two basic dimensions. An act can be
described in terms of what is commonly referred to as
the direction of behavior, which is the specific act
selected. We can also describe an act in terms of the
amount of commitment that an individual puts into that
activity. It is our contention that the two basic
resources available to individuals to commit to acts are
time and effort. Further, we assume that the process of
understanding behavior is the process of understanding the

allocation strategies of individuals through which they
allocate these precious individual resources of time and
effort to the set of acts at their disposal.   The term
'commitment' therefore refers to an overall measure which
somehow combines the amount of time and the amount of
effort expenditure by an individual into a given act.

In most instances the process of committing time
and energy into a particular kind of activity results in
some observable, tangible entity being created.   That
entity which is created through the process of engaging
in an act is a product of that act.   Thus, the process
of typing tends to create a product consisting of pages
of written typed output, the process of digging tends to
create a product consisting of a hole in the ground, etc.
Not all acts result in products, but most do.

We believe that in everyday behavior people tend to
behave and pay attention much more to products than they
do to acts.   We further believe that rewards and goals
usually are associated with products rather than with
acts and that most techniques for evaluating behavior
are based upon products rather than upon the time and
effort put into the actual act itself.   Since we argue
that the primary resources individuals have available for
the creation of products are time and effort, and since
time and effort lead directly to acts, not products, the
distinction between acts and products is an extremely
important one in the theory.

The term evaluation is very important to the theory.
Products can be observed either directly by the individual or by some external other.   The process of simply
observing these outputs and quantifying them in terms of
size, number, type, quality, etc., may be viewed as a
simple descriptive measurement process involving a fundamental perceptual or judgmental process in the classic
Brunswikian sense.   These observed products at this
point, however, are totally neutral.   What commonly
occurs is that the observed products of individuals are
subsequently evaluated either by the individual or by an
external other.   By the process of evaluation we mean
that according to some set of standards held by the observer the products of the focal person are placed on a
good-bad or favorable-unfavorable continuum resulting in
an evaluative judgment about the products.

Next on our list is the term 'outcome'.   This is a
term that has received considerable attention in expectancy theory and our definition is not substantively different from the traditional.   However, ours is perhaps a
bit broader.   For us, an outcome is any perceivable
characteristic of an individual's environment which is
capable of having motivational properties.   More specifically, it is any attribute or characteristic of an

individual's perceived world which (a) has some degree of
anticipated affect associated with it in the event that
outcome were to be received or (b) which has some actual
degree of affective influence upon an individual when it
is in fact received.   In short, outcomes are simply
things that can happen to people and which, in so doing,
can and do influence the affective state of people.

        The next term which we need to explain is 'contin-
gency'.   We use the term contingency to refer to a
general type of relationship between events.   We use it
to express a type of probabilistic or correlational
relationship between elements of interest in the theory.
These contingencies represent the uncertainty that plays
such an important role in our daily lives.

        Any time that one event is somehow related to
another event in some non-random (i.e. systematic) way,
a contingency relationship exists between these two
events.   This contingency relationship can be viewed in
terms of the two characteristics typically applied to any
kind of contingency relationship, namely the functional
form of that relationship and the degree of fit of that
form to the empirical data.   Thus, contingencies can be
described in terms of the best fitting mathematical
model for describing the function forms, such as linear,
parabolic, etc., and the adequacy with which that
function form truly 'fits' or describes the true contingency between events.   Further, for any given function
form, such as a linear function between X and Y, one can
also talk in terms of the actual magnitude of the con-
stants in that best fitting equation.   We will be using
this notion of function form more extensively in a
moment as we elaborate on the motivational sequence more
explicitly.

        Finally, we need to distinguish between the terms
'affect' and 'valence'.   Our definition of 'affect' is
fairly traditional in that affect is viewed as simply
representing the degree of 'happiness' or 'unhappiness'
of the individual.   Valence also refers to affect but
it is affect which is anticipated to occur as a function
of the receipt of some future outcome.   Thus, valence
simply serves to distinguish between affect for received
outcomes and affect associated with outcomes which have
not yet received but which exist as potential outcomes at
some time in the future.

SOME CRITICAL ISSUES

        As is by now apparent, we are dealing with a theory
of choice in the sense that we view behavior as founded
upon rational choice.   Some have tended to make an artificial distinction between theories which deal in terms of

choice and those which deal in terms of effort; but in
point of fact the effort-oriented theories are themselves best cast in terms of choice, where choice is
simply a choice among various levels of effort.

We have mentioned earlier that we view the motivational process as a process of resource allocation, in
which an individual allocates the resources of time and
effort across a series of acts according to some basic
rational rules or principles. Viewing motivation in
this fashion presents a number of fundamental questions
which need to be at least outlined before proceeding
into a description of the process itself.

The first fundamental issue has to do with the
conceptualization of the basic units of time and effort
that people use in determining behavior.   Theories like
ours which deal with explanations for the way in which
people allocate effort and time to various kinds of activities, have virtually ignored the basic issue involved
in the problem of what sizes of cognitive units people
tend to use in entering into this allocation process.
It is our contention that both of these dimensions
(effort and time) are highly individualistic and that
they form one of the more interesting individual difference parameters of motivation as yet totally unexplored.
To be more explicit, we believe that some people simply
think in terms of larger chunks of effort and larger units
of time than do other people.   Further, we believe that
this individual difference parameter can have a substantial influence upon the way in which resources are allocated to acts.   People who tend to think in terms of
longer time frames, or in terms of larger units of effort,
may tend to allocate their resources in a different pattern across a series of acts than do people who tend to
think in terms of smaller units of time, or smaller units
of effort.   What we are saying is that in order to
explain and to predict behavior on the basis of a motivational sequence such as we are proposing, it is probably necessary that one be able somehow to determine the
size of the overall commitment units which are relevant
to a given individual.

A second fundamental issue which must be recognized
is the issue of the kind of rational rules which an individual uses in the resource allocation process.   If
behavior is assumed to be rational, it must have some
ultimate underlying principle.   Most motivational principles have something to do with need satisfaction and
motivational energy.   For us, the basic cognitive motivational principle is that individuals are assumed to
behave in a way such as to maximize the total amount of
anticipated affect resulting from future behavior.   We
believe that people do tend to behave in a way that is
expected to result in the greatest amount of positive

feeling or the least amount of negative feeling for those
individuals over the amount of time and effort units
being used by the individual.

THE MOTIVATIONAL SEQUENCE

     With this brief background, we are now ready to take
a rapid tour through the motivational sequence which cul-
minates in the final allocation of commitment across
acts.   This process is a process of combining affect,
which is the motivational aspect of the theory, with
uncertainty, which is the rational-cognitive portion of
the theory.

     We begin the process by considering the valence of
outcomes.   Consider a function which shows the perceived
relationship, for a given individual, between the amount
of an anticipated outcome and the degree of affect
(either positive or negative) associated with that particular amount of outcome.   Such a functional relationship
is the valence function for that particular outcome.
In such a function one can further conceptualize the
amount of change occurring in valence for a corresponding
change in amount of the outcome.   This ratio, for any
specified interval change of outcome, is the slope of
the function for that particular interval.   It represents
the amount of 'motivational force' associated with such
an interval change in the magnitude of that outcome.
The greater the slope, the greater the individual's internal incentive for a change in outcomes.

     We believe these 'valence of anticipated outcome'
functions do exist in the cognitions of every individual.
We further believe that they are formed through a complex
process involving (1) perceptions of the possible set of
outcomes which conceivably could occur or accrue to a
given person, (2) the individual's basic needs, (3) the
individual's temporary need state, (4) the individual's
current level of arousal and activity, and (5) the individual's current overall affective state.   These various
elements combine, to form the valence of anticipated
outcome functions.

     For an outcome to have motivational properties,
there must be some type of contingency relationship
relating that outcome to the individual's own behavior.
We see these contingency linkages as existing in three
stages.   Each of these stages plays an important role in
the motivational sequence, each in its proper turn.   The
first stage involves the functional relationship which
exists between the evaluation of an individual's behavior
(in the form of products) and the amount of an outcome
that individual anticipates receiving.   These evaluation-
to-outcome contingencies form the linkage between the way

behavior is evaluated and the way outcomes are allocated
on the basis of that evaluation.   They can be viewed as
a function relating the magnitude of an evaluation to
the magnitude of the outcomes given to the individual.

       To form the evaluation-to-outcome contingencies of
this first stage, several functional relationships must
be utilized.   Given that one has two functional relationships, one describing the valence function of a particular outcome and the other describing the evaluation-to-
outcome function for that same outcome, it is clearly
possible to combine them to obtain a third functional
relationship which relates the magnitude of an evaluation
to the anticipated amount of affect resulting from that
evaluation.   This relationships is referred to as the
utility of evaluation function.   It is computed by
simply summing across all outcomes the amounts of affect
associated with the amounts of outcomes associated with
given levels of evaluations.   This utility of evaluation
function thus incorporates the motivational force
notion, since we can view the slope of this function as
the change in anticipated affect corresponding to a given
change in the magnitude of evaluation.   This slope is
the incentive to achieve or experience that change in
evaluation.   Just as there will be a valence of antici-
-ated outcome function for each outcome, there will be a
utility of evaluation function for each evaluator, which
will be based upon a summation of the valence of anticipated outcome functions for that evaluator.

       The next step in the sequence involves the second
of the three types of contingency functions.   This is
the contingency function relating the size or magnitude
of an observer's evaluation of a focal person's products,
to the amount of the products actually produced by that
focal person's behavior.   We made an important point
earlier in which we said that perceptually, people tend to
deal with behavior in terms of products.   When the
individual evaluates the behavior of others, he or she
will tend to do so in terms of an evaluation of the things
which that individual has actually done or produced.
That is, evaluations are based upon an assessment of
measurable products which are themselves not the direct
behavior of a person, but are simply the results of that
person's behavior.   We can, therefore, conceptualize
that for any evaluator, a functional relationship exists
between the magnitude of the evaluation given by that
evaluator and the quantity of a given product.   There
will be one such function for every combination of product
and evaluator.

       It is now possible to postulate another kind of
utility function known as the utility of products function.
Each product will have a utility function which can be
formed by combining the product-to-evaluation functions

with the utility of evaluation functions previously discussed.   We can take any individual product and, for
each level of that product, sum the amount of anticipated
affect perceived to be associated with the magnitudes of
the evaluations expected to occur from that level of the
product (across all relevant evaluators).   This summation for each level of an individual product will produce
a utility of products function, relating the amount of
the product produced to the anticipated amount of affect
expected given that degree of product output.

There will be a utility function of this nature
for every product.   The slope of this utility function
represents the motivational force associated with a
specified increment in the amount of, or quality of, the
product.   If a specified increase in the amount of a
particular product is associated with a substantial
increase in the amount of anticipated affect, then that
particular product can be said to have strong motivational
force over that particular range.

The third and last of our basic types of contingency relationships is the act-to-product contingency.
An act-to-product contingency relationship is a functional description of an individual's perception of the
degree to which commitment to a particular act will
result in the creation of a particular product.   The act-
to-product contingency functions thus represent the perceived efficacy of a particular act with respect to the
creation of a particular product.   In theory there is an
act-to-product contingency relationship for every possible pair of acts and products.   However, most acts
produce only a small subset of the total set of possible
products;   and it is only those act-to-product contingencies which are of interest.

The act-to-product contingency functions may now be
combined with the utility of products functional relationships to produce the final utility functions of interest
which are the utility of acts functions.   These utility
of acts functions can be formed by the following process.
If we consider a particular act, performed at a particular level of commitment, we can refer to the act-to-
product contingency to see how much of that product is
created for that particular level of commitment.   We can
then examine the utility-of-products function to determine how much anticipated affect is associated with the
amount of product created by that aforesaid amount of
commitment.   If we examine each possible level of commitment to the act in a similar way, and plot the subsequent
amount of anticipated affect associated with the particular amounts of the products produced for those separate
levels of commitment, we can proceed to form a contingency relationship between the amount of commitment to
that act and the amount of anticipated affect anticipated

to result from that commitment, where the process is
mediated by the production of a product.   If the act is
such that it simultaneously produces more than one product, then a summation process would be necessary to com-
pute the utility of acts function.

These utility of acts functions are the key functions within the theory.   In a very real sense they are
composite functions which can be sequentially decomposed
into a series of lower order functions which combine into
this final utility of acts relationship.   It is critical that we point out that this utility of acts function
imbues our concept of motivational force.   For any particular change in commitment, we can conceptualize the
slope associated with a corresponding change in anticipated affect resulting from such a change of commitment.
The larger the change in anticipated affect for a given
change in commitment, the larger the motivational force
associated with such a change.   Another way of stating
this is that the steeper the slope of the function, the
more attractive it is to the individual to commit resources of time and energy to that particular act.

THE RESOURCE ALLOCATION PROCESS

The functional relationships between acts and
anticipated affect will take many different forms.   However, it is safe to say that these functional relationships all share one thing in common.   That is, at
extremely high levels of commitment the functions will
tend to become negatively accelerated and even may flatten
out totally and even decrease.   It is our contention
that the most reasonable theoretical model for resource
allocation is one in which the individual is assumed to
allocate each unit of resource (i.e. commitment unit) to
that act which has the greatest motivational force associated with that additional resource increment.   In
other words, in selecting between two acts, an individual
makes the rational choice to engage in that act which is
likely to result in the greatest increment in anticipated
affect for the size of the commitment unit the person is
willing to invest.   This means that the relative slopes
of the utility of acts functions become of prime importance.   An individual will tend to allocate his initial
resources to those acts having very steep slopes, and
only when those acts begin to level off in terms of their
slope, as one gets into higher levels of commitment, will
commitment be diverted from those activities into other
acts.

We have analytically examined what kinds of resource
allocation patterns might occur on the part of an individual, depending upon what kinds of functions that individual perceived as existing for the several acts available,

as well as examining what influence such things as the
size of the basic unit of commitment might have upon the
overall allocation process.   Some interesting preliminary things are emerging from these analytical exercises.
For example, it seems that within certain ranges of size
for the commitment units, certain acts may totally dominate other acts, even though the motivational force, or
slope, for the dominated act may be higher in certain
ranges than the slope for any range for the dominant
act.   A second and much more fascinating pattern which
seems to arise is that the overall amount of anticipated
affect received on the part of the individual, tends to
be much more robust than one might ordinarily expect
across a wide set of conditions of functional forms and
sizes of the commitment unit.   What these analytical
exercises have shown so far, without attempting to go into
detail, is that it is possible drastically to influence
the patterning of resource allocation across acts as a
function of changing the size of the commitment unit and
the slopes of the functions.   What is most interesting
is that the total amount of return to the individual in
terms of anticipated affect actually seems to fluctuate
far less than one might normally expect as a function of
changes in these other conditions.   In short, the moral
of the story might be that under a model of this sort we
find that the patterning of behavior may be very sensitive
to some of the individual difference parameters of the
model, but the basic total affective payoff is very
robust to such changes in resource allocation strategies.
This means that it may not make a lot of difference in
terms of how people particularly allocate their resources
across the relevant acts.

        This would seem an intuitively appealing and even
appropriate finding since, if such is indeed the case, we
have a very compelling argument in favor of the individual
adopting simplifying and/or heuristic type strategies
which, while they are substantially degraded versions of
the overall theoretical process that we have outlined,
nevertheless result in payoffs to the individual which
are not a great deal less than that individual might
receive by carrying out the entire process in the minutest
cognitive detail.

SUMMARY AND CONCLUSIONS

        In this brief article we have had to present a very
incomplete and rapid tour through the elements of the
basic theory of choice behavior and motivation.   That is
regrettable, since our theoretical view of the behavioral
process is unquestionably extremely detailed and complex.
However, our view is also one that we believe contains all
of the essential ingredients for explaining the process by
which individuals do ultimately assign commitment units to

activities.   Further, we believe that each of these elements that we have discussed is essential to an understanding of the process, even though in practice the individual may bypass or not even use that particular element
of the model in deciding upon a particular act.   Another
way of stating our position is that we believe that, at
one time or another, every individual does perform each
of the processes that we have outlined in this theory.
We would not, however, argue that an individual performs
all of these processes each time that individual behaves.
Rather, we suggest that the individual computes, uses,
and updates only when it becomes dramatically necessary
for the individual to do so.   We do propose, however,
that one can obtain from individuals, estimates of each of
the utilities and each of the contingency relationships
which we have proposed as being important in this theory.
That is, they are all constructs of a cognitive nature
which have relevance to individuals.   Precisely how
relevant remains an empirical question, and is something
to which we will be directing our attention in the near
future.

REFERENCE

Naylor, J.C., Pritchard, R.D. and Ilgen, D.R. (1980).
    A Theory of Behavior in Organizations, Academic
    Press, New York.

Comments on Section IV

D. COPE

In this discussion two sorts of issues will be considered. The first concerns specific points and queries. The second is much broader and is an attempt to tease out major themes.

SPECIFIC ISSUES

The paper by Locke et al. is an interesting review and evaluation of four topics in motivation research, namely studies of money as an incentive, goal setting, participation and job enrichment. It is important to note that their review does not cover a number of techniques such as giving praise, recognition and regular performance reviews, now commonly taught to managers as motivational techniques.

Bringing together such an extensive series of studies is obviously a difficult task. However, before comparisons between different groups of studies can be made, it is necessary to examine the way in which Locke et al. have treated the data. They have treated quantity and quality criteria as equivalent in reaching a median value as an overall measure of performance. This method may, however, obscure a number of important issues. Quantity and quality are very different measures of productivity: it might be much easier to produce a 100% decrease in error rates than to increase the quantity of production by a similar figure. On the other hand, it is typically found that job enrichment produces larger changes in the quality of output and lesser change in quantity. Using median responses, as Locke et al. do, probably obscures the effectiveness of job enrichment studies.

Other criticisms of Locke et al.'s methodology could also be made. Firstly as their tables show, the duration of the different studies varies from 6 minutes to 4 years. Whether to argue from such a range of time intervals is justifiable or not is questionable, especially when, as Walbank notes, individual performance is so variable. Secondly, virtually all the studies which they quote deal exclusively with blue collar workers who, we may suppose, are on poor wages. In such studies it is hardly surprising that money is found to act as a good incentive. It may be that for higher paid groups, e.g. managers, money might not act as such an effective incentive, and certainly it might take on a different significance in terms of perhaps status and recognition instead of security. Such threshold effects, as Gruneberg pointed out, have not been taken into account.

It also appears that a study such as this which takes these factors in isolation may not be a good guide to the practicality or usefulness of motivators. In many situations (especially in European as opposed to North American settings) it is not possible to introduce financial incentives and so we have to rely on other possible satisfiers. Also some techniques may be specifically and intentionally introduced for the spin-offs in other areas that may be produced. For example, when a scheme of worker participation is agreed upon, benefits will be expected not only in employee attitudes, and perhaps direct performance, but also in the application of workers' ideas to changing technology and the organisation of work.

In considering the implications of the Locke et al. paper we need perhaps to tread carefully. Whilst the survey of studies in itself usefully brings together a number of diverse findings, it would appear premature to conclude that financial incentives or still better financial incentives, together with goal setting, are the best method of motivating employees. If organisations only provide financial incentives and workers are motivated to try to obtain these, it does not imply that these are all that workers require. There may well be other, equally important, factors which have not been included in such considerations. It is not yet possible to return from much modern social and industrial psychology to Frederick Winslow Taylor, though the paper rightly reintroduces the importance of pay.

GENERAL ISSUES

A number of interesting common themes emerged from the papers in this section which may point towards the future directions of research.   Firstly there appears to be a change of emphasis away from examining jobs and tasks in detail towards a general analysis of the environment, context and organisation in which jobs or even groups are imbedded.   This was evident in the papers by White, Pen et al., Wallis and Cope, Redfern and Spurgeon, and Hackman.   Secondly, a clear distinction is being made between descriptions or conceptions of what changes could be attempted in tasks, jobs or groups and the process of bringing about such changes.   White, Wallis and Cope and Guest et al. point to the difficulties of bringing about such changes; and Guest et al. and Wallis and Cope emphasise the importance of influence, power and top management support in implementing any change.   The implication for research is that more attention needs to be paid to the process of bringing about change.   This seems to indicate the importance of Action Research or the 'development research' studies described by Lawler. It may well prove not an easy change to implement, because the rewards or pay-offs for researchers do not encourage such time-consuming and long term studies with the attendant risks of failure.

Thirdly, it seems that questions of QWL and job satisfaction are not easily dealt with by objective analyses and can only be clearly understood from the perspective of the individual.   The need for such a phenomenological approach emerges from the papers by Guest et al., Wallis and Cope and Gutek.   Guest et al. point to the need to use subjective criteria; Gutek points to the role of internal processes in assessments of satisfaction; and Wallis and Cope sketch out a possible explanation of such phenomena.

Finally there appeared a move towards a synthesis of ideas in the area of motivation and satisfaction - a move well overdue after the increasing specialisation and individuation of theories in recent years.   This was evident in the paper by Lawler who outlined what he saw as the major themes of present motivational theory, and was also reflected in the papers by White and Wallis and Cope.

Index